Special Edition

USING
VISUAL C++™ 5

Special Edition

USING
VISUAL C++™ 5

Written by Kate Gregory

Special Edition Using Visual C++ 5

Library of Congress Catalog No.: 97-65012

ISBN: 0-7897-1145-1

99 98 97   6   5   4   3   2   1

Interpretation of the printing code: the rightmost double-digit number is the year of the book's printing; the rightmost single-digit number, the number of the book's printing. For example, a printing code of 97-1 shows that the first printing of the book occurred in 1997.

Credits

PRESIDENT
Roland Elgey

PUBLISHER
Stacy Hiquet

PUBLISHING MANAGER
Fred Slone

EDITORIAL SERVICES DIRECTOR
Elizabeth Keaffaber

ACQUISITIONS EDITORS
Kelly Marshall
Tracy Dunkelberger

PRODUCT DEVELOPMENT SPECIALIST
Rob Tidrow

SENIOR EDITOR
Mike La Bonne

EDITORS
Elizabeth Barrett
Sherri Fugit
Lisa Gebken
Kate Givens
Patricia Kinyon
Tonya Maddox
Caroline Roop
Nicholas Zafran

TECHNICAL EDITORS
David Medinets
Mark Robinson
James Snyder

STRATEGIC MARKETING MANAGER
Barry Pruett

PRODUCT MARKETING MANAGER
Kristine Ankney

ASSISTANT PRODUCT MARKETING MANAGERS
Christy M. Miller
Karen Hagen

TECHNICAL SUPPORT SPECIALIST
Nadeem Muhammed

ACQUISITIONS COORDINATOR
Carmen Krikorian

EDITORIAL ASSISTANTS
Andrea Duvall
Chantal Mees Koch

BOOK DESIGNER
Ruth Harvey

COVER DESIGNER
Dan Armstrong

PRODUCTION TEAM
Marcia Brizendine
Amy Gornik
Brian Grossman
Kay Hoskin
Paul Wilson

INDEXER
Craig Small

Composed in *Century Old Style* and *ITC Franklin Gothic* by Que Corporation.

This book is dedicated to Brian, Beth, and Kevin for making it all worthwhile.

About the Author

Kate Gregory is a founding partner of Gregory Consulting Limited (**www.gregcons.com**,), which has been providing consulting and development services throughout North America since 1986. Her experience with C++ stretches back to before Visual C++ existed—she enthusiastically converted upon seeing the first release. Gregory Consulting develops software and Internet sites, and specializes in combining software development with Web site development to create active sites. They build quality custom and off-the-shelf software components for Web pages and other applications. Kate teaches on a variety of related topics including C++, Object Oriented technqiues, using the Internet, HTML, and Java. She speaks at conferences (most recently the Toronto Developer Days for Microsoft) on topics of interest to the Visual C++ community. Kate edits *Visual C++ Developer*, a monthly newsletter for intermediate to advanced developers. Her books for Que include *Using UseNet Newsgroups*, *Building Internet Applications with Visual C++*, and the previous edition of *Special Edition Using Visual C++*. She has also contributed to four other books for Que. Kate welcomes mail at **kate@gregcons.com** and provides updates for this book at the **gregcons** Web site.

Acknowledgments

As always, I must start by thanking my family for accepting the workload that comes during the final stages of a book. Brian, Beth, and Kevin, you make it all worthwhile. Special mention must go to Brian for his support, technical as well as moral, and his cheerful attitude in the face of twenty-three chapters of Author Review. Pamela Campbell chipped in with administrative support that lifted many burdens from my shoulders: thanks Pam.

This is my eighth project for Que, and I'm starting to recognize familiar names among the army of editors, proofers, indexers, illustrators, and general saints who turn my Word documents into the book you hold in your hands. I have been lucky enough to work with a top-notch team once again. Fred Slone provided the vision, and Angela Kozlowski and Tracy Dunkelberger sweated the details to make it happen. While I cheerfully share the credit for the accurate and educational aspects of this book, the mistakes and omissions I have to claim as mine alone. Please bring them to my attention so that they can be corrected in subsequent printings and editions. I am as grateful as ever to readers who have done so in the past and improved this book in the process.

We'd Like to Hear from You!

As part of our continuing effort to produce books of the highest possible quality, Que would like to hear your comments. To stay competitive, we *really* want you to let us know what you like or dislike most about this book or other Que products.

Please send your comments, ideas, and suggestions for improvement to:

The Expert User Team

E-mail: **euteam@que.mcp.com**

CompuServe: 105527,745

Fax: (317) 581-4663

Our mailing address is:

Expert User Team
Que Corporation
201 West 103rd Street
Indianapolis, IN 46290-1097

You can also visit our Team's home page on the World Wide Web at:

http://www.mcp.com/que/developer_expert

Thank you in advance. Your comments will help us to continue publishing the best books available in today's market.

Thank You,

The Expert User Team

Contents at a Glance

Table of Contents

IV | Improving Your User Interface

VII | **Advanced Programming Techniques**

22 **Database Access   529**

8 | Appendixes

Introduction

Visual C++ is a powerful and complex tool for building 32-bit applications for Window 95 and Windows NT. These applications are far larger and more complex than their predecessors for 16-bit Windows, or older programs that did not use a graphical user interface. Yet as program size and complexity has grown, programmer effort has actually decreased, at least for programmers who are using the right tools.

Visual C++ is one of the right tools. With its code-generating Wizards, it can produce the shell of a working Windows application in seconds. The class library included with Visual C++, the Microsoft Foundation Classes, has become the industry standard for Windows software development in a variety of C++ compilers. The visual editing tools make layout of menus and dialog boxes a snap. The time you invest in learning to use this product will pay itself back on your first Windows programming project. ■

Who Should Read This Book?

This book will teach you how to use Visual C++ to build 32-bit Windows applications, including database applications, Internet applications, and applications that tap the power of the ActiveX technology. That's a tall order, and to fit all that in less than a thousand pages, some things had to go. This book will *not* teach you:

- **The C++ programming language:** You should already be familiar with C++. There are occasional mentions of relevent C++ and Object Oriented concepts. The introductory text, *C++ By Example*, is included on the CD.

- **How to use Windows applications:** You should be a proficient Windows user, able to resize and move Windows, double-click, and recognize familiar toolbar buttons, for example.

- **How to use Visual C++ as a C compiler:** If you already work in C, you can use Visual C++ as your compiler, but new developers should take the plunge to C++.

- **Windows programming without MFC:** This too is okay for those who know it, but not something to learn now that MFC exists.

- **The internals of ActiveX programming:** This is referred to in the ActiveX chapters, which tell you only what you need to know to make it work.

You should read this book if you fit one of these categories:

- You know some C++ and some Windows programming techniques, and are new to Visual C++. You will learn the product much more quickly than you would if you just tried writing programs.

- You've been working with previous versions of Visual C++. Many times users learn one way to do things and end up overlooking some of the newer productivity features.

- You've been working with Visual C++ 5.0 for a while and are beginning to suspect you're doing things the hard way. Maybe you are.

- You work in Visual C++ 5.0 regularly, and you need to add a feature to your product. For tasks like Help, printing, and threading, you'll find a "hand up" to get started.

Before You Start Reading

You will need a copy of Visual C++ 5.0 and have it installed. The installation process is simple and easy to follow, so it's not covered in this book.

Before you buy Visual C++ 5.0, you'll need a 32-bit Windows operating system: Windows 95, or Windows NT Server or Workstation. That means your machine will have to be reasonably powerful and modern: say a 486 or better for your processor, at least 16M of RAM and 500M of disk space, and a screen that can do 800×600 pixel displays, or even finer resolutions. The illustrations in this book were all prepared at a resolution of 800×600 and, as you'll see, there are times when things get a little crowded.

Finally, you need to make a promise to yourself that you will follow along in Visual C++ as you read this book, clicking and typing and trying things out. You don't need to type all the code if you don't want to: it's all on the CD for you to look at. But you should be ready to open the files and look at the code as you go.

What This Book Covers

A topic such as Windows programming in Visual C++ covers a lot of ground. This book is split into learning chapters (1 to 28) and appendixes (A to G). Be sure to look over the titles of the appendixes now, and turn to them whenever you aren't quite sure how to do something. They are:

- Appendix A, "Windows Programming Review and a Look Inside *CWnd*," covers the specifics of Windows programming that are now hidden from you by MFC classes like CWnd.

- Appendix B, "The Developer Studio User Interface," explains all the menus, toolbars, editing areas on the screens, shortcuts, and so on that make up the highly complicated and richly powerful interface between you and Developer Studio.

- Appendix C, "Debugging," explains the extra menus, windows, toolbars, and commands involved in debugging a running application.

- Appendix D, "MFC Macros and Globals," summarizes the many preprocessor macros and global variables and functions sprinkled throughout code generated by the Developer Studio Wizards.

- Appendix E, "Useful Classes," describes the classes used throughout the book to manipulate dates, strings, and collections of objects.

- Appendix F, "Visual Basic Script Quick Reference," provides a ready Visual Basic reference for C++ users.

- Appendix G, "What's on the CD?," is self-explanatory.

Depending on your background and your willingness to poke around under menus and in the online help, you may just skim these chapters once and never return, or you may fill them full of bookmarks and yellow post-its. While they don't work you through sample applications, they will teach you a lot.

The mainstream of the book is Chapters 1 through 28. Each chapter teaches you an important programming task, or sometimes two closely related tasks, like building a taskbar, or adding Help to an application. Detailed instructions show you how to build a working application, or several working applications, in each chapter.

The first nine chapters cover concepts that will be in almost every Windows application; after that the tasks become less general. Here's a quick overview of some of the work that is covered.

Dialogs and Controls

What Windows program doesn't have a dialog box? An edit box? A button? Dialog boxes and controls are vital to Windows user interfaces, and all of them, even the simple button or piece of static text, are windows. The common controls allow you to take advantage of the learning time users have put in on other programs, and the programming time developers have put in on the operating system, to use the same File Open dialog box as everybody else, the same hierarchical tree control, and so on. Learn more about all these controls in Chapter 2, "Dialog Boxes and Controls," and Chapter 3, "Windows 95 Common Controls."

Messages and Commands

Messages form the heart of Windows programming. Whenever anything happens on a Windows machine, such as a user clicking the mouse or pressing a key, a message is triggered and sent to one or more windows, which do something about it. Visual C++ makes it easy for you to write code that catches these messages and acts on them. Chapter 4, "Messages and Commands," explains the concept of messages and how MFC and other aspects of Visual C++ lets you deal with them.

The View/Document Paradigm

A *paradigm* is a model, a way of looking at things. The designers of MFC chose to design the framework by using the assumption that every program has something it wants to save in a file. That collection of information is referred to as the *document*. A *view* is one way of looking at a document. There are a lot of advantages to separating the view and the document, and they are explained further in Chapter 5, "Documents and Views." MFC provides classes from which to inherit your document class and your view class, so that common programming tasks like implementing scroll bars are no longer your problem.

Drawing on the Screen

No matter how smart your Windows program is, if you can't tell the user what's going on by putting some words or pictures onto the screen, no one will know what the program has done. A remarkably large amount of the work is done automatically by your view classes (one of the advantages of adopting the document/view paradigm), but there will be times you have to do the drawing yourself. You learn about device contexts, scrolling, and more in Chapter 6, "Drawing on the Screen."

Printing on Paper

Adding printing capabilities to your program is sometimes the simplest thing in the world, because the code you use to draw on the screen can be reused to draw on paper. But if there is more than one page of information involved, things start to get tricky. Chapter 7, "Printing and Print Preview," explains all of this, plus mapping modes, headers and footers, and more.

Persistence and File I/O

Some good things are meant to be only temporary, like the display of a calculator or an online chat window. But most programs can save their documents to a file, and open and load that file to re-create a document that has been stored. MFC makes this remarkably easy by using archives and extending the use of the stream I/O operators >> and <<. You learn all about reading and writing to files in Chapter 8, "Persistence and File I/O."

ActiveX Programming

ActiveX is the successor to OLE, and it is the technology that facilitates communication between applications at the object level, allowing you to embed a Word document in an Excel spreadsheet, or any of hundreds of kinds of objects in any ActiveX application. ActiveX chapters include Chapter 13, "ActiveX Concepts," Chapter 14, "Building an ActiveX Container Application," Chapter 15, "Building an ActiveX Server Application," Chapter 16, "Building an Automation Server," and Chapter 17, "Building an ActiveX Control."

The Internet

Microsoft recognizes that distributed computing, in which work is shared among two or more different computers, is becoming more and more common. Programs need to talk to each other, people need to send messages across a LAN or around the world, and MFC has classes that support these kinds of communication. The four Internet chapters in this book are Chapter 18, "Sockets, MAPI, and the Internet," Chapter 19, "Internet Programming with the WinInet Classes," Chapter 20, "Building an Internet ActiveX Control," and Chapter 21, "The Active Template Library."

Database Access

Database programming just keeps getting easier. ODBC, Microsoft's Open DataBase Connectivity package, allows your code to call API functions that access a huge variety of database files—Oracle, DBase, an Excel spreadsheet, a plain text file, old legacy mainframe systems using SQL, whatever! You call a standard named function and the API provided by the database vendor or a third-party handles the translation. The details are in Chapter 22, "Database Access," and Chapter 23, "Enterprise Edition."

Advanced Material

For developers who have mastered the basics, this book features some advanced chapters to move your programming skills forward. You will learn how to prevent memory leaks, find bottlenecks, and find bugs in your code with the techniques discussed in Chapter 24, "Improving Your Application's Performance."

Reuse is a hugely popular concept in software development at the moment, especially with managers who see a chance to lower their development budget. If you'd like to write reusable code and components, Chapter 25, "Achieving Reuse with the Gallery and Your Own AppWizards," will get you there.

The C++ language is still quite new, and it changes every year. A working ANSI committee is building the C++ standard, and as they work towards a final definition of the language, compiler vendors add entirely new keywords and capabilitities. You will learn in Chapter 26, "Exceptions, Templates, and the Latest Additions to C++," what's new in the language itself.

As user demands for high-performance software continue to rise, developers are having to learn entirely new techniques to produce powerful applications that provide fast response times. For many developers, writing multithreaded applications is a vital technique. Learn about threading in Chapter 27, "Multitasking with Windows Threads."

Chapter 28, "Future Explorations," introduces you to topics that are definitely not for beginners. Learn how to create console applications, use and build your own DLLs, and work with Unicode.

Conventions Used in This Book

One thing this book has plenty of is code. Sometimes you just need to see a line or two, so the code is mixed in with the text like this:

```
int SomeFunction( int x, int y);
{
    return x+y;
}
```

You can tell the difference between code and regular text by the fonts used for each of them. Sometimes, you'll see a piece of code that is too large to mix in with the text: You'll find an example in Listing 1.

Listing 1   Example of a Listing

```
CHostDialog dialog(m_pMainWnd);
    if (dialog.DoModal() == IDOK)
    {
        AppSocket = new CSocket();
        if (AppSocket->Connect(dialog.m_hostname,119))
        {
            while (AppSocket->GetStatus() == CONNECTING)
            {
                YieldControl();
            }
            if (AppSocket->GetStatus() == CONNECTED)
            {
             CString response = AppSocket->GetLine();
                SocketAvailable = TRUE;
            }
        }
    }
     if (!SocketAvailable)
     {
        AfxMessageBox("Can't connect to server. Please
➡ quit.",MB_OK¦MB_ICONSTOP);
     }
```

The character on the second to last line (➡) is called the *code continuation character*. It shows a place where a line of code had to be broken to fit it on the page, but the line is not broken there in reality. If you're typing code in from the book, don't break the line there, just keep going. If you're reading along in the code from the CD, don't get confused when the line doesn't break there.

Remember, the code is in the book so that you can understand what is going on, not for you to type in. All the code is on the CD-ROM as well. Sometimes, you'll work your way through the development of an application and see several versions of a block of code as you go—the final version is on the CD-ROM.

TIP This is a Tip: A shortcut or interesting feature you might want to know about.

N O T E This is a Note: It covers a subtle but important point. Don't skip notes even if you're the kind who skips tips.

CAUTION

This is a caution, and it's serious. It warns you of horrible consequences if you make a false step, so be sure to read all of these that you come across.

TROUBLESHOOTING

What happens if I run into problems while programming? Everyone runs into problems now and then while programming. The Troubleshooting entries anticipated some of them—you learn how to get out of whatever trouble you're in.

When a word is in *italic*, it's usually being defined. (Sometimes the word's just being emphasized.) The names of variables, functions, C++ classes, and things you should type are all in `monospaced` font. Internet URLs are in **bold** type. Remember, an URL never ends with punctuation, so ignore any comma or period after the URL.

Time to Get Started

That just about wraps things up for the introduction. You've learned what you need to get started, including some advanced warning about the notations used throughout the book. Jump right in, learn all about writing Windows applications with MFC, and then get started on some development of your own! Good luck and have fun. ●

Getting Started

Building Your First Application

Visual C++ doesn't just compile code, it generates code. You can create a Windows application in minutes by telling AppWizard to make you a "starter app" with all the Windows boilerplate code you want. AppWizard is a very effective tool. It copies code into your application that almost all Windows applications need. After all, you aren't the first programmer who has needed an application with resizable edges, minimize and maximize buttons, a File menu with Open, Close, Print Setup, Print, and Exit options, are you? ◾

Using AppWizard to make a typical application

When most people think "application," they expect an EXE file. AppWizard makes skeleton, executable Windows programs in less than a minute.

Other applications AppWizard can make

Other application generating wizards can make DLLs, ActiveX controls, console applications, libraries, makefile, Internet Server extensions and filters, and more.

If you change your mind

AppWizard can add a lot of functionality to an application that you are building for the first time. What if you want to add some of the functionality to an application that is already built? This section shows you how.

AppWizard's code

See the code generated for you by AppWizard and understand the different application types.

Other AppWizard decisions

This section directs you to the places in this book where the consequences of AppWizard decisions such as database support, ActiveX technology, and application type are explained in detail.

Creating a Windows Application

AppWizard can make many different kinds of applications, but what most people want, at least at first, is an executable (.exe) program. Most people also want AppWizard to produce boilerplate code—the classes, objects, and functions that have to be in every program. To create a program like this, choose File, New and click the Projects tab in the New dialog box, as shown in Figure 1.1.

FIG. 1.1
The Projects tab of the New dialog box is where you choose the kind of application you want to build.

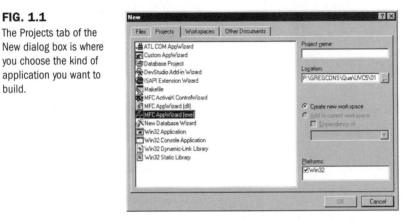

Choose MFC AppWizard (.exe) from the list box on the left, fill in a project name, and click OK. AppWizard then works through a number of steps. At each step, you make a decision about what kind of application you want, and click Next. At any time, you can click Back to return to a previous decision, Cancel to abandon the whole process, Help for more details, or Finish to skip to the end and create the application without answering any more questions (not recommended before the last step). Each step is covered in the following sections.

Deciding How Many Documents the Application Supports

The first decision to communicate to AppWizard, as shown in Figure 1.2, is whether your application should be MDI, SDI, or dialog-based. AppWizard generates different code and classes for each of these application types.

The three application types to choose from are as follows:

■ A Single Document Interface (SDI) application, such as Notepad, has only one document open at a time. When you choose File, Open, the currently open file is closed before the new one is opened.

■ A Multiple Document Interface (MDI) application, such as Excel or Word, can open many documents (typically files) at once. There is a Window menu and a Close item on the File menu. It's a quirk of MFC that if you like multiple views on a single document, you must build an MDI application.

Part
I

Ch
1

■ A dialog-based application, such as the Character Map utility (see Figure 1.3) that comes with Windows, does not have a document at all. There are no menus. (If you'd like to see Character Map in action, it's usually in the Accessories folder reached by clicking Start. You may need to install it using Add/Remove programs under Control Panel.)

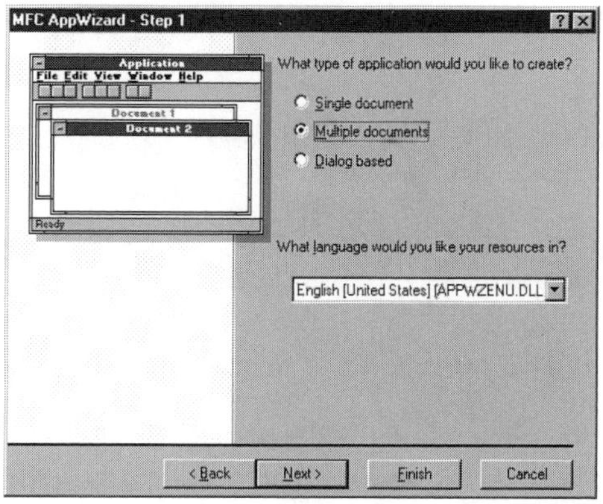

FIG. 1.2
The first step in building a typical application with AppWizard is choosing the interface.

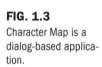

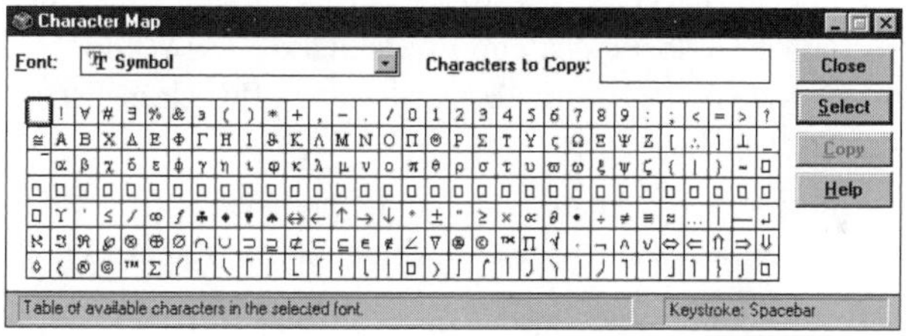

FIG. 1.3
Character Map is a dialog-based application.

As you change the option button selection, the picture on the left of the screen changes to remind you what the application looks like if you choose this type of application.

N O T E   Dialog-based applications are quite different from MDI or SDI applications. The AppWizard dialogs are different when creating a dialog-based application and are presented in the next section entitled "Creating a Dialog-Based Application." ■

Lower on the screen is a drop-down box to select the language for your resources. If you have set your system language to anything other than the default U.S. English, make sure you set your resources to that language too. If you don't, you will encounter unexpected behavior from ClassWizard later. (Of course, if your application is for users who will have their language set to U.S. English, you might not have a choice. In that case, change your system language under Control Panel.) Click Next after you make your choices.

Databases

The second step in creating an executable Windows program with AppWizard is to choose the level of database support, as shown in Figure 1.4.

FIG. 1.4

The second step to
building a typical
application with
AppWizard is to set the
database options you
will use.

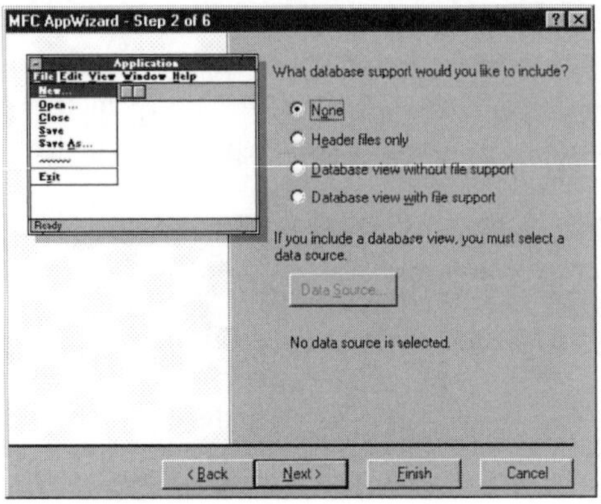

There are four choices for database support, as follows:

- If you are not writing a database application, choose None.

- If you want to have access to a database, but don't want to derive your view from CFormView or have a Record menu, choose Header Files Only.

- If you want to derive your view from CFormView and have a Record menu, but do not need to serialize a document, choose Database View Without File Support. You can update database records with CRecordset, an MFC class discussed in more detail in Chapter 22, "Database Access."

- If you want to support databases as in the previous option, but also need to serialize a document (perhaps some user options), choose Database View With File Support.

Chapter 22, "Database Access," clarifies these choices and demonstrates database programming with MFC. If you choose to have a database view, you must specify a data source now. Click the Data Source button to set this up.

As you select different option buttons, the picture on the left changes to show you the consequences of your choice. Click Next to move to the next step.

Compound Document Support

The third step in running AppWizard to create an executable Windows program is to decide on the amount of compound document support you want to include, as shown in Figure 1.5. OLE (Object Linking and Embedding) has been officially renamed ActiveX to clarify the recent technology shifts, most of which are hidden from you by MFC. ActiveX and OLE technology are jointly referred to as *compound document technology*. Chapter 13, "ActiveX Concepts," covers this technology in detail.

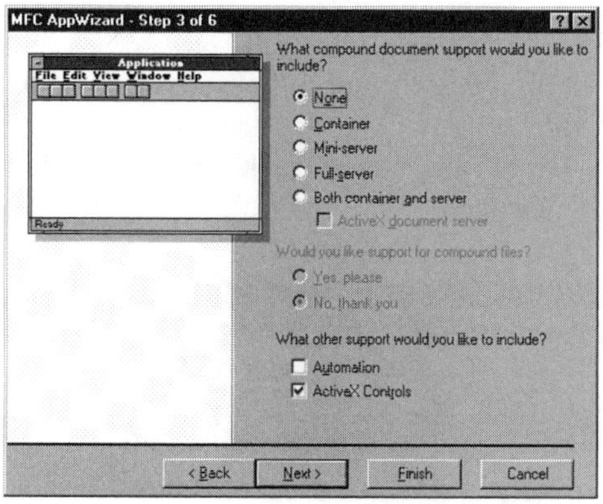

FIG. 1.5

The third step of building a typical application with AppWizard is to set the compound document support you will need.

There are five choices for compound document support, as follows:

- If you are not writing an ActiveX application, choose None.

- If you want your application to be able to contain embedded or linked ActiveX objects, such as Word documents or Excel worksheets, choose Container. You learn to build an ActiveX container in Chapter 14, "Building an ActiveX Container Application."

- If you want your application to serve documents that can be embedded in other applications but that do not need to run as a stand-alone application, choose Mini Server.

- If your application serves documents and also functions as a stand-alone application, choose Full Server. In Chapter 14, "Building an ActiveX Container Application," you learn to build an ActiveX full server.

- If you want your application to have the capability to contain objects from other applications and also to serve its objects to other applications, choose Both Container and Server.

If you choose to support compound documents, you can also support *compound files*. Compound files contain one or more ActiveX objects and are saved in a special way, so that one of the objects can be changed without rewriting the whole file. This can save a great deal of time. Use the option buttons in the middle of this Step 3 dialog box to say Yes, Please or No, or thank you to compound files.

If you want your application to surrender control to other applications through Automation, check the Automation check box. (Automation is the subject of Chapter 16, "Building an Automation Server.") If you want your application to use ActiveX controls, select the ActiveX Controls check box. Click Next to move to the next step.

N O T E If you want your application to be an ActiveX control, you do not create a typical .exe application as described in this section. Creating ActiveX controls with the ActiveX ControlWizard is covered in Chapter 17, "Building an ActiveX Control." ■

Appearance and Other Options

The fourth step in running AppWizard to create an executable Windows program (see Figure 1.6) is to determine some of the interface appearance options for your application. This Step 4 dialog box contains a number of independent check boxes; check them if you want a feature, leave them unchecked if you do not.

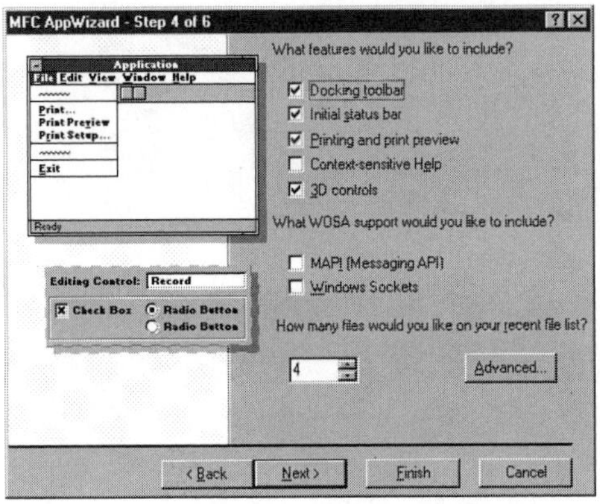

FIG. 1.6

The fourth step of building a typical application with AppWizard is to set some interface options.

Following are the options that affect your interface's appearance:

- *Docking toolbar*—AppWizard sets up a toolbar for you. You can edit it to remove unwanted buttons, or add new ones linked to your own menu items. This is described in Chapter 10, "Status Bars and Toolbars."

- *Initial status bar*—AppWizard creates a status bar to display menu prompts and other messages. Later, you can write code to add indicators and other elements to this bar, as described in Chapter 10, "Status Bars and Toolbars."

- *Printing and print preview*—Your application will have Print and Print Preview options on the File menu, and much of the code you need to implement printing will be generated by AppWizard. Chapter 7, "Printing and Print Preview," discusses the rest.

- *Context sensitive help*—Your Help menu will gain Index and Using Help options, and some of the code needed to implement Help will be provided by AppWizard. This decision is hard to change later since quite a lot of code is added in different places when implementing context-sensitive Help. Chapter 11, "Help," describes Help implementation.

- *3D controls*—Your application will look like a typical Windows 95 application. If you do not select this option, your dialog boxes have a white background and there are no shadows around the edges of edit boxes, check boxes, and other controls.

- *MAPI*—Your application will be able to use the Messaging API to send fax, e-mail, or other messages. Chapter 18, "Sockets, MAPI, and the Internet," discusses the Messaging API.

■ *Sockets*—Your application can access the Internet directly, using protocols like FTP and HTTP (the World Wide Web protocol). Chapter 18, "Sockets, MAPI, and the Internet," discusses Sockets. You can produce Internet programs without enabling socket support if you use the new WinInet classes, discussed in Chapter 19, "Internet Programming with the WinInet Classes."

You can also set how many files you want to appear on the recent file list for this application. Four is the standard number; change it only if you have good reason to do so.

Clicking the Advanced button at the bottom of this Step 4 dialog box brings up the Advanced Options dialog box, which has two tabs. The Document Template Strings tab is shown in Figure 1.7. AppWizard builds many names and prompts from the name of your application, and sometimes it needs to abbreviate your application name. Until you are familiar with the names AppWizard builds, you should check them on this Document Template Strings dialog box and adjust them if necessary. You can also change the main frame caption, which appears in the title bar of your application. The file extension, if you choose one, will be incorporated into file names saved by your application and will restrict the files initially displayed when the user chooses File, Open.

FIG. 1.7

The Document Template Strings tab of the Advanced Options dialog box lets you adjust the way names are abbreviated.

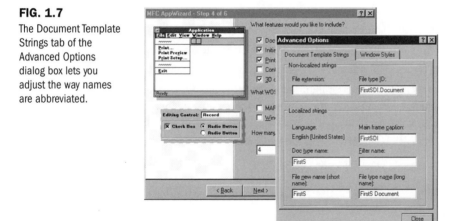

The Window Styles tab is shown in Figure 1.8. Here you can change the appearance of your application quite dramatically. The first check box, Use Split Window, adds all the code needed to implement splitter windows like those in the code editor of Developer Studio. The remainder of the Window Styles dialog box sets the appearance of your *main frame* and, for an MDI application, of your *MDI child frames*. Frames hold windows; the system menu, title bar, minimize and maximize boxes, and window edges are all frame properties. The main frame holds your entire application. An MDI application has a number of MDI child frames—one for each document window, inside the main frame.

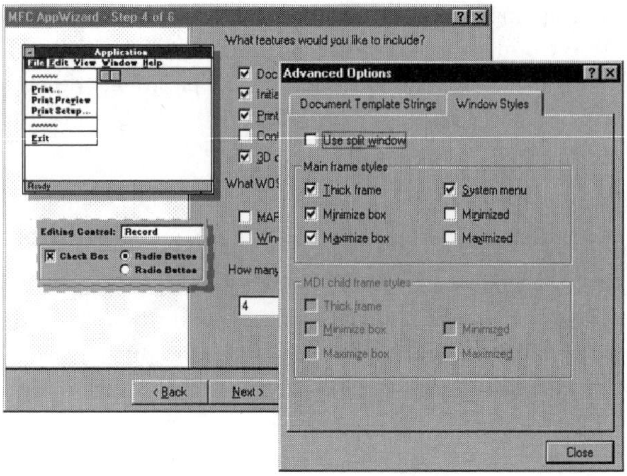

FIG. 1.8

The Window Styles tab of the Advanced Options dialog box lets you adjust the appearance of your windows.

Here are the properties you can set for frames:

- *Thick frame*—The frame has a visibly thick edge and can be resized in the usual Windows way. Uncheck this to prevent resizing.
- *Minimize box*—The frame has a Minimize box in the top-right corner.
- *Maximize box*—The frame has a Maximize box in the top-right corner.
- *System menu*—The frame has a system menu in the top-left corner.
- *Minimized*—The frame is minimized when the application starts. For SDI applications, this option will be ignored when the application is running under Windows 95.
- *Maximized*—The frame is maximized when the application starts. For SDI applications, this option will be ignored when the application is running under Windows 95.

When you have made your selections, click Close to return to Step 4 and Next to move on to the next step.

Other Options

The fifth step in running AppWizard to create an executable Windows program (see Figure 1.9) asks the leftover questions that are not related to menus, OLE, database access, or appearance. Do you want comments inserted in your code? You certainly do. That one is easy.

The next question is not so straightforward. Do you want the MFC library as a shared DLL or statically linked? A *DLL* (Dynamic-Link Library) is a collection of functions used by many different applications. Using a DLL makes your programs smaller, but makes the installation a little more complex. Have you ever moved an executable only to find it won't run any more because it's missing DLLs? If you statically link the MFC library into your application, it is larger, but it is easier to move and copy around.

If your users are likely to be developers themselves and own at least one other application that uses the MFC DLL, or aren't intimidated by needing to install DLLs as well as the program itself, choose the shared DLL option. The smaller executable is convenient for all of you. If your users are not developers, choose the statically linked option. It reduces the technical support issues you have to face with inexperienced users. If you write a good install program, you can feel more confident about using shared DLLs.

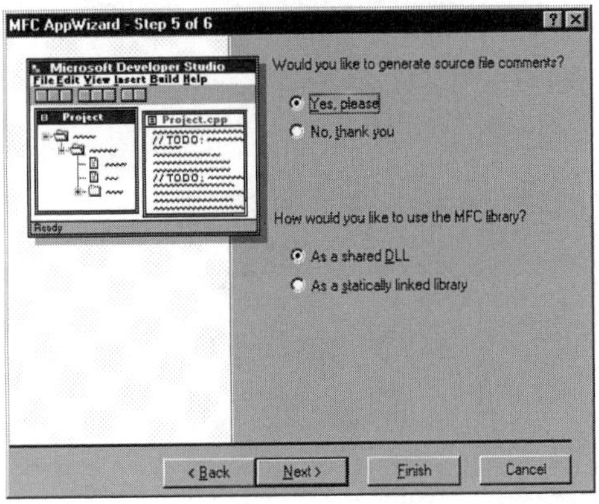

FIG. 1.9
The fifth step of building an application with AppWizard is to decide on comments and the MFC library.

File and Class Names

The final step in running AppWizard to create an executable Windows program is to confirm the class names and the file names that AppWizard creates for you, as shown in Figure 1.10. AppWizard uses the name of the project (FirstSDI in this example) to build the class names and file names. You should not need to change these names. If your application includes a view class, you can change the class from which it inherits; the default is CView but many developers prefer to use another view, such as CScrollView or CEditView. The eight view classes are discussed in Chapter 5, "Documents and Views." Click Finish when this Step 6 dialog box is complete.

FIG. 1.10
The final step of building a typical application with AppWizard is to confirm file names and class names.

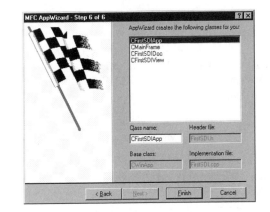

Creating the Application

After you click Finish, AppWizard shows you what is going to be created in a dialog box, like that shown in Figure 1.11. If anything here is wrong, click Cancel and then work your way back through AppWizard with the Back buttons until you reach the dialog box you need to change. Move forward with Next, Finish, review this dialog box again, and then click OK to actually create the application. This takes a few minutes, which is hardly surprising because hundreds of lines of code, menus, dialog boxes, help text, and bitmaps are being generated for you in as many as 20 files. Let it work.

FIG. 1.11

When AppWizard is ready to build your application, you get one more chance to confirm everything.

Try It Yourself

If you haven't started Developer Studio already, do so now. If you've never used it before, you may find the interface a little intimidating. There's a full explanation of all the areas, toolbars, menus, and shortcuts in Appendix B, "The Developer Studio Interface."

Bring up AppWizard by choosing File, New and clicking the Projects tab. On the Projects tab, fill in a folder name where you would like to keep your applications—AppWizard will make a new folder for each project. Fill in **FirstSDI** for the project name, then move through the six AppWizard steps. Choose an SDI application at Step 1, and on all the other steps simply leave the selections as they are and click Next. When AppWizard has created the project, choose Build, Build from the Developer Studio menu to compile and link the code.

When the build is complete, choose Build, Execute. You have a real, working Windows application, shown in Figure 1.12. Play around with it a little: resize it, minimize it, maximize it.

Try out the File menu by choosing File, Open and bring up the familiar Windows File Open dialog (though no matter what file you choose, nothing seems to happen) and then choose File, Exit to close the application. Move the mouse cursor over one of the toolbar buttons and pause; a tool tip will appear reminding you of the purpose of the toolbar button. Click the Open button to confirm that it is connected to the File, Open command you chose earlier. Bring up the View menu and click <u>T</u>oolbar to hide the toolbar, then choose <u>V</u>iew <u>T</u>oolbar again to restore it. Do the same thing with the status bar. Choose Help, About and you'll see it even has an About box with its own name and the current year in the copyright date. (See Figure 1.13.)

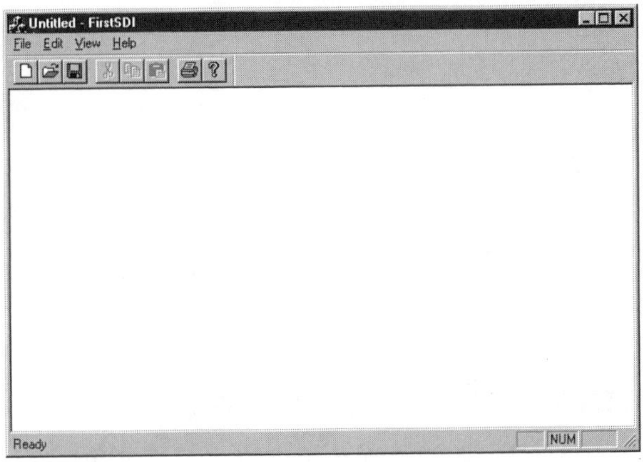

FIG. 1.12

Your first application looks like any full-fledged Windows application.

FIG. 1.13

You even get an About box in this start application.

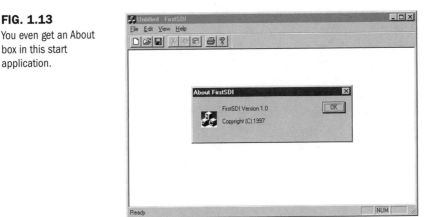

Repeat these steps to create an MDI application called **FirstMDI**. The creation process will only differ on Step 0, where you specify the project name and Step 1, where you choose an MDI application. Accept the defaults on all the other steps, create the application, build it, and execute it. You'll see something like Figure 1.14, an MDI application with a single document open. Try out the same operations you tried with FirstSDI.

Choose <u>F</u>ile, <u>N</u>ew, and a second window, FirstM2, appears. Try minimizing, maximizing, and restoring these windows. Switch among them using the <u>W</u>indow menu. All this functionality is yours from AppWizard, and you don't have to write a single line of code to get it.

FIG. 1.14
An MDI application can display a number of documents at once.

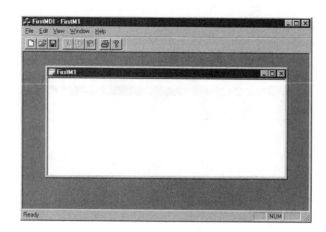

Creating a Dialog-Based Application

A dialog-based application has no menus other than the system menu, and it cannot save or open a file. This makes it good for simple utilities like the Windows Character Map. The AppWizard process is a little different for a dialog-based application, primarily because they cannot have a document, and so cannot support database access or compound documents. To create a dialog-based application, start AppWizard as you did for the SDI or MDI application, but on Step 1 choose a dialog-based application, as shown in Figure 1.15.

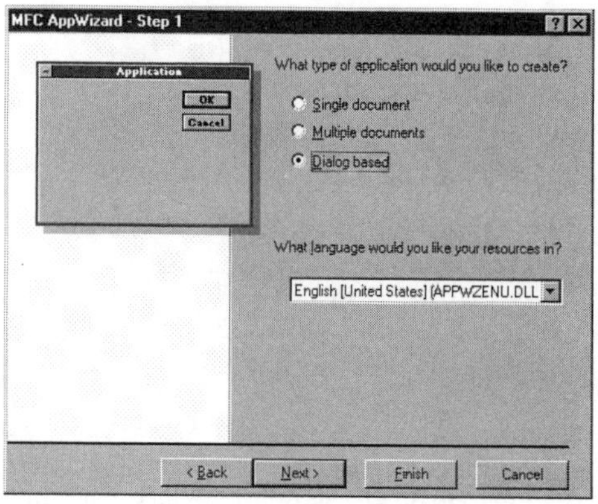

FIG. 1.15
To create a dialog-based application, specify your preference in Step 1 of the AppWizard process.

Choose Dialog Based and click Next to move to Step 2, shown in Figure 1.16.

If you would like an About item on the system menu, select the About Box item. To have AppWizard lay the framework for Help, select the Context Sensitive Help option. The third check box, 3D Controls, should be selected for most Windows 95 and Windows NT applications. If you want your application to surrender control to other applications through Automation, as discussed in Chapter 16, "Building an Automation Server," select the Automation check box. If you want your application to contain ActiveX controls, select the ActiveX Controls check box. If you are planning to have this application work over the Internet with sockets, check the Windows Sockets box. (Dialog-based applications can't use MAPI because they have no document.) Click Next to move to the third step, shown in Figure 1.17.

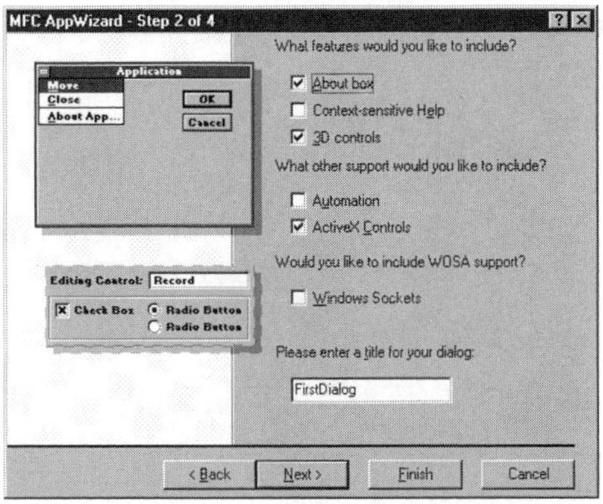

FIG. 1.16
Step 2 of the AppWizard process for a dialog-based application involves choosing Help, Automation, ActiveX, and Sockets settings.

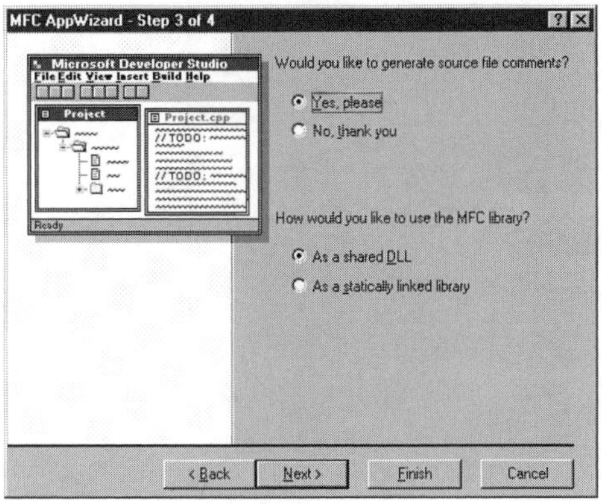

FIG. 1.17
Step 3 of the AppWizard process for a dialog-based application deals with comments and the MFC library.

As with the SDI and MDI applications created earlier, you want comments in your code. The decision between static linking and a shared DLL is also the same as for the SDI and MDI applications. If your users are likely to have the MFC DLLs already (because they are developers or because they have another product that uses the DLL), or if they won't mind installing the DLLs as well as your executable, go with the shared DLL to make a smaller executable file and a faster link. Otherwise choose As A Statically Linked Library. Click Next to move to the final step, shown in Figure 1.18.

In this step you can change the names AppWizard chooses for files and classes. This is rarely a good idea, because it will confuse people who maintain your code if the file names can't be easily determined from the class names, and vice versa. If you realize after looking at this dialog that you made a poor choice of project name, use Back to move all the way back to the New Project Workspace dialog, change the name, click Create, and then use Next to return to this dialog. Click `Finish` to see the summary of the files and classes to be created, like that in Figure 1.19.

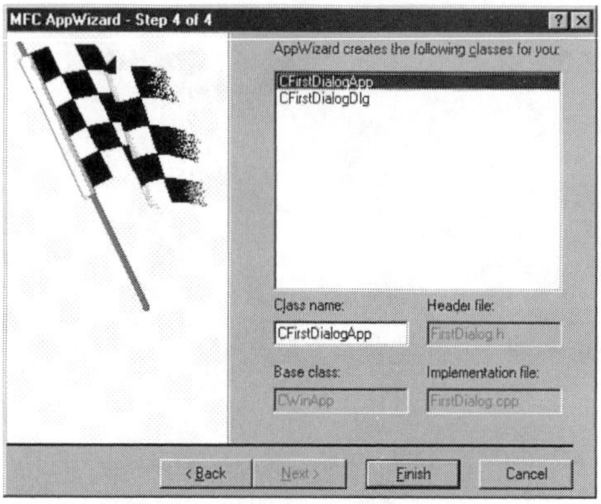

FIG. 1.18
Step 4 of the AppWizard process for a dialog-based application gives you a chance to adjust file and class names.

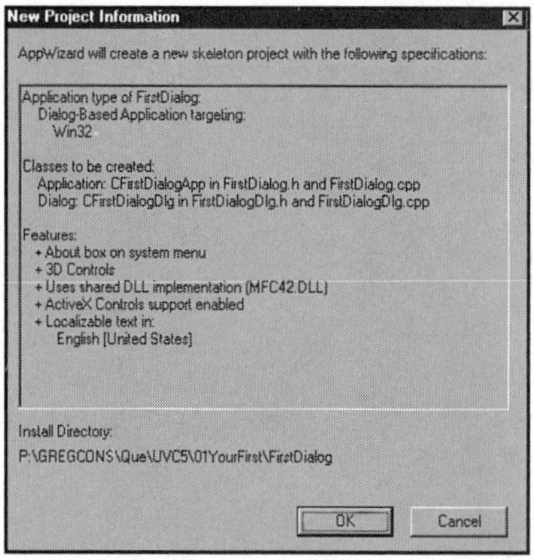

FIG. 1.19
AppWizard confirms the files and classes before creating them.

If any of the information on this dialog is not what you wanted, click `Cancel` and then use `Back` to move to the appropriate step and change your choices. When the information is right, click `OK` and watch as the application is created.

Try It Yourself

Create an empty dialog-based application yourself, call it FirstDialog, and accept the defaults for each step of AppWizard. When it's complete, choose Build, Build to compile and link the application. Choose Build Execute to see it in action. Figure 1.20 shows the empty dialog-based application running.

Clicking the OK or Cancel buttons, or the X in the top-right corner, makes the dialog disappear. Clicking the system menu in the top-left corner gives you a choice of Move, Close, or About. Figure 1.21 shows the About box that was generated for you.

FIG. 1.20
A starter dialog application includes a reminder of the work you have ahead of you.

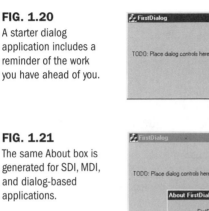

FIG. 1.21
The same About box is generated for SDI, MDI, and dialog-based applications.

Creating DLLs, Console Applications, and More

Although most people use AppWizard to create an executable program, it can make many other kinds of projects. You choose File, New and then the Projects tab as discussed at the start of this chapter, but choose a different wizard from the list on the left of the New dialog box, shown in Figure 1.1. The following are some of the other projects AppWizard can create:

- ATL COM AppWizard
- Custom AppWizard
- Database Project
- DevStudio Add-in Wizard
- ISAPI Extension Wizard
- Makefile
- MFC ActiveX ControlWizard
- MFC AppWizard (DLL)
- New Database Wizard
- Win32 Application
- Win32 Console Application
- Win32 Dynamic-Link Library
- Win32 Static Library

These projects are explained in the following sections.

ATL COM AppWizard

ATL is the Active Template Library, and it's used to write small ActiveX controls. It's generally used by developers who have already mastered writing MFC ActiveX controls. Chapter 17,

"Building an ActiveX Control," introduces important control concepts while demonstrating how to build an MFC control; Chapter 21, "The Active Template Library," teaches you ATL.

Custom AppWizard

Perhaps you work in a large programming shop that builds a lot of applications. Although AppWizard saves a lot of time, your programmers may spend a day or two at the start of each project pasting in your own boilerplate, which is material that is the same in every one of your projects. You may find it well worth your time to build a Custom AppWizard, a wizard of your very own that puts in your boilerplate, as well as the standard MFC material. After you have done this, your application type is added to the list box on the left of the Projects tab of the New dialog box shown in Figure 1.1. Creating and using Custom AppWizards is discussed in Chapter 25, "Achieving Reuse with the Gallery and Your Own AppWizards."

Database Project

If you have installed the Enterprise Edition of Visual C++, you can create a database project. This is discussed in Chapter 23, "Enterprise Edition."

DevStudio Add-in Wizard

Add-ins are like macros that automate Developer Studio, but they are written in C++ or another programming language; macros are written in VBScript. They use Automation to manipulate Developer Studio.

ISAPI Extension Wizard

ISAPI stands for Internet Server API, and refers to functions you can call to interact with a running copy of Microsoft Internet Information Server, a World Wide Web server program that serves out Web pages in response to client requests. You can use this API to write DLLs that can be used by programs that go far beyond browsing the Web to automating information retrieval. This process is discussed in Chapter 18, "Sockets, MAPI, and the Internet."

Makefile

If you want to create a project that is used with a different "make" utility than Developer Studio, choose this wizard from the left-hand list in the New Project Workspace dialog box. No code is generated. If you don't know what a make utility is, don't worry—this wizard is for those who prefer to use a stand-alone tool to replace one portion of Developer Studio.

MFC ActiveX Control Wizard

ActiveX controls are controls you write that can be used on a Visual C++ dialog, a Visual Basic form, even a Web page. These controls are the 32-bit replacement for the VBX controls many developers were using to achieve intuitive interfaces or to save reinventing the wheel on every project. Chapter 17, "Building an ActiveX Control," guides you through building a control with this wizard.

MFC AppWizard (DLL)

If you want to collect a number of functions into a DLL, and these functions use MFC classes, choose this wizard. (If the functions don't use MFC, choose Win32 Dynamic-link Library, discussed a little later in this section.) Building a DLL is covered in Chapter 28, "Future Explorations." AppWizard generates code for you so you can get started.

New Database Wizard

This wizard is for those with Visual InterDev installed. It simplifies connecting a Web page to a SQL database.

Win32 Application

There are times when you want to create an application in Visual C++ that does not use MFC and does not start with the boilerplate code that AppWizard produces for you. To create such an application, choose the Win32 Application wizard from the left-hand list in the Projects tab, fill in the name and folder for your project, and click OK. You are not asked any questions; AppWizard simply creates a project file for you and opens it. You have to create all your code from scratch and insert the files into the project.

Win32 Console Application

A console application looks very much like a DOS application, though it runs in a resizable window. It has a strictly character-based interface with cursor keys rather than mouse movement. You use the Console API and character based I/O functions like printf() and scanf() to interact with the user. No boilerplate code is generated for you, just an empty project. Chapter 28, "Future Explorations," discusses building and using console applications.

Win32 Dynamic-Link Library

If you plan to build a DLL that does not use MFC and does not need a boilerplate, choose the Win32 Dynamic-Link Library option rather than MFC AppWizard (DLL). You get an empty project created right away with no questions.

Win32 Static Library

While most code you reuse is gathered into a DLL, you may prefer to use a static library, because that means you do not have to distribute the DLL with your application. Choose this wizard from the left-hand list in the New Project Workspace dialog box to create a project file into which you can add object files to be linked into a static library, which is then linked into your applications.

Changing Your AppWizard Decisions

Running AppWizard is a one-time task. Assuming you are making a typical application, you choose File, New, click the Projects tab, enter a name and folder, choose MFC Application (exe), go through the six steps, create the application starter files, and then never touch AppWizard again. But what if you choose, for example, not to have online Help, and then later realize you should have included it?

AppWizard, despite the name, is not really magic. It pastes in bits and pieces of code you need, and you can paste in those very same bits yourself. Here's how to find out what you need to paste in.

First, create a project with the same options you used in creating the project whose settings you wish to change, and don't add any code to it. Second, in a different folder create a project with the same name, and all the same settings except the one thing you want to change (context-sensitive Help in this example). Now, compare the files using WinDiff, which comes with Visual C++. Now you know what bits and pieces you need to add to your full-of-code project to implement the feature you forgot to ask AppWizard for.

Some developers, if they discover their mistake soon enough, find it quicker to create a new project with the desired features and then paste their own functions and resources from the partially-built project into the new empty one. It's only a matter of taste, but after you've gone through either process for changing your mind, you probably will move a little more slowly through those AppWizard dialog boxes.

Understanding AppWizard's Code

The code generated by AppWizard may not make sense to you right away, especially if you haven't written a C++ program before. You don't need to understand this code in order to write your own simple applications. But your programs will be better ones if you know what they are doing, and so a quick tour of AppWizard's boilerplate code is a good idea. You'll see the guts of an SDI application, an MDI application, and a dialog-based application.

If you didn't create the starter applications FirstSDI, FirstMDI, and FirstDialog, you can open them from the CD-ROM as you read this chapter. If you did create them, open them from your own hard drive. If you're unfamiliar with the Developer Studio interface, glance through Reference Appendix B, "The Developer Studio Interface," to learn how to edit code and look at classes.

A Single Document Interface Application

An SDI application has menus that the user uses to open one document at a time and work with that document. This section presents the code that is generated when you create an SDI application with no database or compound document support, with a toolbar, a status bar, Help, 3D controls, source file comments, and with the MFC library as a shared DLL. In other words, when you accept all the AppWizard defaults after Step 1.

Five classes have been created for you. For the application called FirstSDI, they are as follows:

- ◼ CAboutDlg, a dialog class for the About dialog box
- ◼ CFirstSDIApp, a CWinApp class for the entire application

■ CFirstSDIDoc, a document class

■ CFirstSDIView, a view class

■ CMainFrame, a frame class

Dialog classes are discussed in Chapter 2, "Dialog Boxes and Controls." Document, view, and frame classes are discussed in Chapter 5, "Documents and Views." The header file for CFirstSDIApp is shown in Listing 1.1.

Listing 1.1   FirstSDI.h—Main Header File for the *FirstSDI* Application

```
// FirstSDI.h : main header file for the FIRSTSDI application
//

#if !defined(AFX_FIRSTSDI_H__CDF38D8A_8718_11D0_B02C_0080C81A3AA2__INCLUDED_)
#define AFX_FIRSTSDI_H__CDF38D8A_8718_11D0_B02C_0080C81A3AA2__INCLUDED_

#if _MSC_VER >= 1000
#pragma once
#endif // _MSC_VER >= 1000

#ifndef __AFXWIN_H__
    #error include 'stdafx.h' before including this file for PCH
#endif

#include "resource.h"        // main symbols

/////////////////////////////////////////////////////////////////////////////
// CFirstSDIApp:
// See FirstSDI.cpp for the implementation of this class
//

class CFirstSDIApp : public CWinApp
{
public:
    CFirstSDIApp();

// Overrides
    // ClassWizard generated virtual function overrides
    //{{AFX_VIRTUAL(CFirstSDIApp)
    public:
    virtual BOOL InitInstance();
    //}}AFX_VIRTUAL

// Implementation

    //{{AFX_MSG(CFirstSDIApp)
    afx_msg void OnAppAbout();
        // NOTE - the ClassWizard will add and remove member functions here.
        //    DO NOT EDIT what you see in these blocks of generated code !
    //}}AFX_MSG
    DECLARE_MESSAGE_MAP()
};
```

continues

Listing 1.1 Continued

```
/////////////////////////////////////////////////////////////////

//{{AFX_INSERT_LOCATION}}
// Microsoft Developer Studio will insert additional declarations immediately
before the previous line.

#endif
// !defined(AFX_FIRSTSDI_H__CDF38D8A_8718_11D0_B02C_0080C81A3AA2__INCLUDED_)
```

This code is confusing at the beginning. The #if(!defined) followed by the very long string (yours will be different) is a clever form of *include guarding*. You may have seen a code snippet like this before:

```
#ifndef test_h
#include "test.h"
#define test_h
#endif
```

This guarantees that the file test.h will never be included more than once. Including the same file more than once is quite likely in C++; imagine you define a class called Employee, and it uses a class called Manager. If the header files for both Employee and Manager include, for example, BigCorp.h, you will get error messages from the compiler about "redefining" the symbols in BigCorp.h the second time it is included.

There is a problem with the approach above: If someone includes test.h but forgets to set test_h, your code will include test.h the second time. The solution is to put the test and the definition in the header file instead, so that test.h looks like this:

```
#ifndef test_h
... the entire header file
#define test_h
#endif
```

All AppWizard did was generate a more complicated variable name than test_h (this wild name prevents problems when you have several files, in different folders and projects, with the same name) and use a slightly different syntax to check the variable. The #pragma once code is also designed to prevent multiple definitions if this file is ever included twice.

The actual "meat" of the file is the definition of the class CFirstSDIApp. This class inherits from CWinApp, an MFC class that provides most of the functionality you need. AppWizard has generated some functions for this class that override the ones inherited from the base class. The section of code that begins //Overrides is for virtual function overrides. AppWizard generated the odd-looking comments that surround the declaration of InitInstance(): they will be used by ClassWizard to simplify the job of adding other overrides later if they are necessary. The next section of code is a message map and declares there is a function called OnAppAbout. You can learn all about message maps in Chapter 4, "Messages and Commands."

AppWizard generated the code for the CFirstSDIApp constructor, InitInstance(), and OnAppAbout() in the file firstsdi.cpp. Here's the constructor, which initializes a CFirstSDIApp object as it is created:

```
CFirstSDIApp::CFirstSDIApp()
{
    // TODO: add construction code here,
    // Place all significant initialization in InitInstance
}
```

This is a typical Microsoft constructor. Because constructors don't return values, there's no easy way to indicate that there has been a problem with the initialization. There are several different ways to deal with this; Microsoft's approach is a two-stage initialization, with a separate initializing function so that construction does no initialization. For an application, that function is called InitInstance(), shown in Listing 1.2.

Listing 1.2 *CFirstSDIApp::InitInstance()*

```
BOOL CFirstSDIApp::InitInstance()
{
    AfxEnableControlContainer();

    // Standard initialization
    // If you are not using these features and wish to reduce the size
    //  of your final executable, you should remove from the following
    //  the specific initialization routines you do not need.

#ifdef _AFXDLL
    Enable3dControls();            // Call this when using MFC in a shared
➡DLL
#else
    Enable3dControlsStatic();      // Call this when linking to MFC statically
#endif

    // Change the registry key under which our settings are stored.
    // You should modify this string to be something appropriate
    // such as the name of your company or organization.
    SetRegistryKey(_T("Local.AppWizard-Generated Applications"));

    LoadStdProfileSettings();  // Load standard INI file options (including
➡MRU)

    // Register the application's document templates. Document templates
    //  serve as the connection between documents, frame windows and views.

    CSingleDocTemplate* pDocTemplate;
    pDocTemplate = new CSingleDocTemplate(
        IDR_MAINFRAME,
        RUNTIME_CLASS(CFirstSDIDoc),
        RUNTIME_CLASS(CMainFrame),       // main SDI frame window
        RUNTIME_CLASS(CFirstSDIView));
    AddDocTemplate(pDocTemplate);
```

continues

Listing 1.2 Continued

```
    // Parse command line for standard shell commands, DDE, file open
    CCommandLineInfo cmdInfo;
    ParseCommandLine(cmdInfo);

    // Dispatch commands specified on the command line
    if (!ProcessShellCommand(cmdInfo))
        return FALSE;

    // The one and only window has been initialized, so show and update it.
    m_pMainWnd->ShowWindow(SW_SHOW);
    m_pMainWnd->UpdateWindow();

    return TRUE;
}
```

InitInstance gets applications ready to go. This one starts by enabling the application to contain ActiveX controls with a call to AfxEnableControlContainer(), then turns on 3D controls. It then sets up the Registry key under which this application will be registered. (The Registry is introduced in Chapter 8, "Persistence and File I/O." If you've never heard of it before, you can ignore it for now.)

InitInstance() goes on to register single document templates, which is what makes this an SDI application. Documents, views, frames, and document templates are all discussed in Chapter 5, "Documents and Views."

Following the comment about parsing the command line, InitInstance() sets up an empty CCommandLineInfo object to hold any parameters that may have been passed to the application when it was run, and calls ParseCommandLine() to fill that. Finally, it calls ProcessShellCommand() to do whatever those parameters requested. This means your application can support command-line parameters to let users save time and effort, without effort on your part. For example, if the user types at the command line FirstSDI fooble, then the application starts and opens the file called fooble. The command-line parameters that ProcessShellCommand() supports are the following:

Parameter	Action
none	Start app and open new file.
Filename	Start app and open file.
/p filename	Start app and print file to default printer.
/pt filename printer driver port	Start app and print file to the specified printer.
/dde	Start app and await DDE command.
/Automation	Start app as an OLE automation server.
/Embedding	Start app to edit an embedded OLE item.

If you would like to implement other behavior, make a class that inherits from CCommandLineInfo to hold the parsed command line, then override CWinApp::ParseCommandLine() and CWinApp::ProcessShellCommand() in your own App class.

 TIP You may have already known that you could invoke many Windows programs from the command line; for example, typing **Notepad blah.txt** at a DOS prompt will open blah.txt in Notepad. Other command line options work too, so typing **Notepad /p blah.txt** will open blah.txt in Notepad and print it.

That's the end of InitInstance(). It returns TRUE to indicate that the rest of the application should now run.

The message map in the header file indicated that the function OnAppAbout() handles a message. Which one? Here's the message map from the source file:

```
BEGIN_MESSAGE_MAP(CFirstSDIApp, CWinApp)
    //{{AFX_MSG_MAP(CFirstSDIApp)
    ON_COMMAND(ID_APP_ABOUT, OnAppAbout)
        // NOTE - the ClassWizard will add and remove mapping macros here.
        //    DO NOT EDIT what you see in these blocks of generated code!
    //}}AFX_MSG_MAP
    // Standard file based document commands
    ON_COMMAND(ID_FILE_NEW, CWinApp::OnFileNew)
    ON_COMMAND(ID_FILE_OPEN, CWinApp::OnFileOpen)
    // Standard print setup command
    ON_COMMAND(ID_FILE_PRINT_SETUP, CWinApp::OnFilePrintSetup)
END_MESSAGE_MAP()
```

This message map catches commands from menus, as discussed in Chapter 4, "Messages and Commands." When the user chooses Help About, CFirstSDIApp::OnAppAbout() will be called. When the user chooses File New, File Open, or File Print Setup, functions from CWinApp will handle that work for you. (You would override those functions if you wanted to do something special for those menu choices.) OnAppAbout() looks like this:

```
void CFirstSDIApp::OnAppAbout()
{
    CAboutDlg aboutDlg;
    aboutDlg.DoModal();
}
```

This code declares an object that is an instance of CAboutDlg and calls its DoModal() function to display the dialog on the screen. (Dialog classes and the DoModal() function are both covered in Chapter 2, "Dialogs and Controls." There's no need to handle OK or Cancel in any special way—this is just an About box.

Other Files

If you selected Context Sensitive Help, AppWizard generates an .HPJ file and a number of .RTF files to give some context-sensitive help. These files are discussed in Chapter 11, "Help," in the "Components of the Help System" section.

AppWizard also generates a README.TXT file that explains what all the other files are and what classes have been created. Read this file if all the similar file names start to get confusing.

Understanding a Multiple Document Interface Application

A Multiple Document Interface application also has menus, and enables the user to have more than one document open at once. This section presents the code that is generated when you choose an MDI application with no database or compound document support, but instead with a toolbar, a status bar, Help, 3-D controls, source file comments, and the MFC library as a shared DLL. As with the SDI application, these are the defaults after Step 1. The focus here is on what is different from the SDI application in the previous section.

Five classes have been created for you; for the application called FirstMDI, they are:

- CAboutDlg, a dialog class for the About dialog box
- CFirstMDIApp, a CWinApp class for the entire application
- CFirstMDIDoc, a document class
- CFirstMDIView, a view class
- CMainFrame, a frame class

The App class header is shown in Listing 1.3.

Listing 1.3   FirstMDI.h—Main Header File for the *FirstMDI* Application

```
// FirstMDI.h : main header file for the FIRSTMDI application
//

#if !defined(AFX_FIRSTMDI_H__CDF38D9E_8718_11D0_B02C_0080C81A3AA2__INCLUDED_)
#define AFX_FIRSTMDI_H__CDF38D9E_8718_11D0_B02C_0080C81A3AA2__INCLUDED_

#if _MSC_VER >= 1000
#pragma once
#endif // _MSC_VER >= 1000

#ifndef __AFXWIN_H__
    #error include 'stdafx.h' before including this file for PCH
#endif

#include "resource.h"        // main symbols

///////////////////////////////////////////////////////////////////////
// CFirstMDIApp:
// See FirstMDI.cpp for the implementation of this class
//

class CFirstMDIApp : public CWinApp
{
public:
    CFirstMDIApp();

// Overrides
    // ClassWizard generated virtual function overrides
```

```
    //{{AFX_VIRTUAL(CFirstMDIApp)
    public:
    virtual BOOL InitInstance();
    //}}AFX_VIRTUAL

// Implementation

    //{{AFX_MSG(CFirstMDIApp)
    afx_msg void OnAppAbout();
        // NOTE - the ClassWizard will add and remove member functions here.
        //    DO NOT EDIT what you see in these blocks of generated code !
    //}}AFX_MSG
    DECLARE_MESSAGE_MAP()
};


/////////////////////////////////////////////////////////////////////////////

//{{AFX_INSERT_LOCATION}}
// Microsoft Developer Studio will insert additional declarations immediately
➡before the previous line.

#endif // !defined(AFX_FIRSTMDI_H__CDF38D9E_8718_11D0_B02C_0080C81A3AA2 __
➡INCLUDED_)
```

How does this differ from FirstSDI.h? Only in the class names. The constructor is also the same as before. And OnAppAbout() is just like the SDI version. How about InitInstance()? It is in Listing 1.4.

Listing 1.4 *CFirstMDIApp::InitInstance()*

```
BOOL CFirstMDIApp::InitInstance()
{
    AfxEnableControlContainer();

    // Standard initialization
    // If you are not using these features and wish to reduce the size
    //   of your final executable, you should remove from the following
    //   the specific initialization routines you do not need.

#ifdef _AFXDLL
    Enable3dControls();             // Call this when using MFC in a shared
➡DLL
#else
    Enable3dControlsStatic();       // Call this when linking to MFC statically
#endif

    // Change the registry key under which our settings are stored.
    // You should modify this string to be something appropriate
    // such as the name of your company or organization.
    SetRegistryKey(_T("Local AppWizard-Generated Applications"));
```

continues

Listing 1.4   Continued

```
    LoadStdProfileSettings();  // Load standard INI file options (including
➡MRU)

    // Register the application's document templates. Document templates
    //  serve as the connection between documents, frame windows and views.

    CMultiDocTemplate* pDocTemplate;
    pDocTemplate = new CMultiDocTemplate(
        IDR_FIRSTMTYPE,
        RUNTIME_CLASS(CFirstMDIDoc),
        RUNTIME_CLASS(CChildFrame), // custom MDI child frame
        RUNTIME_CLASS(CFirstMDIView));
    AddDocTemplate(pDocTemplate);

    // create main MDI Frame window
    CMainFrame* pMainFrame = new CMainFrame;
    if (!pMainFrame->LoadFrame(IDR_MAINFRAME))
        return FALSE;
    m_pMainWnd = pMainFrame;

    // Parse command line for standard shell commands, DDE, file open
    CCommandLineInfo cmdInfo;
    ParseCommandLine(cmdInfo);

    // Dispatch commands specified on the command line
    if (!ProcessShellCommand(cmdInfo))
        return FALSE;

    // The main window has been initialized, so show and update it.
    pMainFrame->ShowWindow(m_nCmdShow);
    pMainFrame->UpdateWindow();

    return TRUE;
}
```

What's different here? Using WinDiff can help. WinDiff is a tool that comes with Visual C++ and is reached from the Tools menu. (If WinDiff is not on your Tools menu, see the "Tools" section of Appendix B, "The Developer Studio Interface." Using WinDiff to compare the FirstSDI and FirstMDI versions of InitInstance() confirms that other than the class names, the differences are:

- The MDI application includes ChildFrm.h; the SDI application does not.
- The MDI application sets up a CMultiDocTemplate and the SDI application sets up a CSingleDocTemplate, as discussed in Chapter 5, "Documents and Views."
- The MDI application sets up a mainframe window and then shows it; the SDI application does not.

This shows a major advantage of the Document/View paradigm: It enables an enormous design decision to affect only a small amount of the code in your project and hides that decision as much as possible.

A Dialog-Based Application

Dialog applications are much simpler than SDI and MDI applications. Create one called FirstDialog, with an About box, no Help, 3D controls, no Automation, ActiveX Control support, no Sockets, source file comments, and MFC as a shared DLL; in other words, accept all the default options.

Three classes have been created for you for the application called FirstMDI, and they are the following:

■ CAboutDlg, a dialog class for the About dialog box

■ CFirstDialogApp, a CWinApp class for the entire application

■ CFirstDialogDlg, a dialog class for the entire application

The dialog classes are the subject of Chapter 2, "Dialogs and Controls." Listing 1.5 shows the header file for CFirstDialogApp.

Listing 1.5   dialog16.h—Main Header File

```
// FirstDialog.h : main header file for the FIRSTDIALOG application
//

#if !defined(AFX_FIRSTDIALOG_H__CDF38DB4_8718_11D0_B02C_0080C81A3AA2__INCLUDED_)
#define AFX_FIRSTDIALOG_H__CDF38DB4_8718_11D0_B02C_0080C81A3AA2__INCLUDED_

#if _MSC_VER >= 1000
#pragma once
#endif // _MSC_VER >= 1000

#ifndef __AFXWIN_H__
     #error include 'stdafx.h' before including this file for PCH
#endif

#include "resource.h"          // main symbols

/////////////////////////////////////////////////////////////////////////////
// CFirstDialogApp:
// See FirstDialog.cpp for the implementation of this class
//

class CFirstDialogApp : public CWinApp
{
public:
     CFirstDialogApp();

// Overrides
     // ClassWizard generated virtual function overrides
     //{{AFX_VIRTUAL(CFirstDialogApp)
     public:
     virtual BOOL InitInstance();
     //}}AFX_VIRTUAL
```

continues

Listing 1.5 Continued

```
// Implementation

    //{{AFX_MSG(CFirstDialogApp)
        // NOTE - the ClassWizard will add and remove member functions here.
        //     DO NOT EDIT what you see in these blocks of generated code !
    //}}AFX_MSG
    DECLARE_MESSAGE_MAP()
};


/////////////////////////////////////////////////////////////////////////////

//{{AFX_INSERT_LOCATION}}
// Microsoft Developer Studio will insert additional declarations immediately
➥before the previous line.

#endif //
!defined(AFX_FIRSTDIALOG_H__CDF38DB4_8718_11D0_B02C_0080C81A3AA2__INCLUDED_)
```

CFirstDialogApp inherits from CWinApp, which provides most of the functionality. CWinApp has a constructor, which does nothing, as did the SDI and MDI constructors earlier in this chapter, and it overrides the virtual function InitInstance(), as shown in Listing 1.6.

Listing 1.6 *CDialog16App::InitInstance()*

```
BOOL CFirstDialogApp::InitInstance()
{
    AfxEnableControlContainer();

    // Standard initialization
    // If you are not using these features and wish to reduce the size
    //  of your final executable, you should remove from the following
    //  the specific initialization routines you do not need.

#ifdef _AFXDLL
    Enable3dControls();            // Call this when using MFC in a shared
➥DLL
#else
    Enable3dControlsStatic();     // Call this when linking to MFC statically
#endif

    CFirstDialogDlg dlg;
    m_pMainWnd = &dlg;
    int nResponse = dlg.DoModal();
    if (nResponse == IDOK)
    {
        // TODO: Place code here to handle when the dialog is
        //  dismissed with OK
    }
    else if (nResponse == IDCANCEL)
    {
```

```
        // TODO: Place code here to handle when the dialog is
        //  dismissed with Cancel
    }

        // Since the dialog has been closed, return FALSE so that we exit the
        //  application, rather than start the application's message pump.
        return FALSE;
    }
```

This enables 3-D controls, because you asked for them, and then puts up the dialog box that is the entire application. To do that, the function declares an instance of CDialog16Dlg, dlg, and then calls the DoModal() function of the dialog, which displays the dialog box on the screen and returns IDOK if the user clicks OK, or IDCANCEL if the user clicks Cancel. (This process is discussed further in Chapter 2, "Dialog Boxes and Controls.") It's up to you to make that dialog box actually do something. Finally, InitInstance() returns FALSE because this is a dialog-based application and when the dialog box is closed, the application is over. As you saw earlier for the SDI and MDI applications, InitInstance() usually returns TRUE to mean "everything is fine, run the rest of the application," or FALSE meaning, "something went wrong while initializing." Because there is no "rest of the application," dialog-based apps always return FALSE from their InitInstance().

Reviewing AppWizard Decisions and This Book

AppWizard asks a lot of questions, and starts you down a lot of roads at once. This chapter explains InitInstance and shows some of the code affected by the very first AppWizard decision: whether to have AppWizard generate a Dialog-based, SDI, or MDI application. Most of the other AppWizard decisions are about topics that take an entire chapter. The following table summarizes those choices and where you can learn more:

Step	Decision	Chapter	Dialog?
0	MFC DLL or non MFC DLL	28, "Future Explorations"	
0	OCX Control	17, "Building an ActiveX Control"	
0	Console Application	28, "Future Explorations"	
0	Custom AppWizard	25, "Achieving Reuse with the Gallery and Your Own AppWizards"	
0	ISAPI Extension Wizard	18, "Sockets, MAPI, and the Internet"	
1	Language support	28, "Future Explorations"	yes
2	Database support	22, "Database Access"	
3	Compound document container	14, "Building an ActiveX Container Application"	

continues

Step	Decision	Chapter	Dialog?
3	Compound document mini-server	15, "Building an ActiveX Server Application"	
3	Compound document full server	15, "Building an ActiveX Server Application"	
3	Compound files	14, "Building an ActiveX Container Application"	
3	Automation	16, "Building an Automation Server"	yes
3	Using ActiveX Controls	17, "Building an ActiveX Control"	yes
4	Docking toolbar	10, "Status Bars and Toolbars"	
4	Status bar	10, "Status Bars and Toolbars"	
4	Printing and print	7, "Printing and Print Preview"	
4	Context sensitive help	11, "Help"	yes
4	3-D Controls	—	yes
4	MAPI	18, "Sockets, MAPI, and the Internet"	
4	Windows Sockets	18, "Sockets, MAPI, and the Internet"	yes
4	Files in MRU list	—	
5	Comments in code	—	yes
5	MFC library	—	yes
6	Base class for View	5, "Documents and Views"	

Because some of these questions are not applicable for dialog-based applications, this table has the Dialog column "yes" that indicates this decision applies to dialog-based applications, too. An entry of—in the Chapter column means that this decision doesn't really warrant discussion. These topics get a sentence or two in passing in this chapter or elsewhere.

From Here...

By now, you know how to create applications that don't do much of anything. To make them do something, you need menus or dialog controls that give commands, and other dialog controls that gather more information. These are the subject of the next chapter, "Dialog Boxes and Controls."

Once you have seen how to get an application to do something, you can move through the rest of the book adding features like these:

- Chapter 7, "Printing and Print Preview," covers the work involved in adding printing capabilities to an application.
- Chapter 10, "Status Bars and Toolbars," discusses toolbars and status bars.
- Chapter 11, "Help," shows you how to implement context sensitive Help.

Part

I

Ch

1

Interacting with Your Application with Dialog Boxes and Controls

Dialog Boxes and Controls

Windows programs have a graphical user interface (GUI). In the days of DOS, the program could simply print a prompt on-screen and direct the user to enter whatever value the program needed. With Windows, however, getting data from the user is not so simple, and most user input is obtained from dialog boxes. For example, a user can give the application details about a request by typing in edit boxes, choosing from list boxes, selecting radio buttons, checking or unchecking check boxes, and more.

This chapter builds several small applications to illustrate the use of dialog boxes in your programs. ■

Create and display a dialog box resource

Creating a resource is the first step. Displaying a dialog box requires only a single function call.

Write a custom dialog box class

You can use MFC's dialog box classes as the starting point for your own custom classes.

Extract information from a dialog box

MFC features automatic data transfer to and from a dialog box.

Validate the contents of a dialog box's controls

Make sure that the user entered the information your application is expecting.

Learn about the different types of Windows controls

Controls enable applications to present and retrieve information to and from the user.

Associate an MFC class with a control

MFC features a special class for every type of control.

Understanding Dialog Boxes

Chances are that your Windows application will have several dialog boxes, each designed to retrieve a different type of information from your user. For each dialog box that appears on-screen, there are two entities you need to develop: a dialog box *resource* and a dialog box *class*.

The dialog box resource is used to draw the dialog box and its controls on the screen. The class holds the values of the dialog box, and it is a member function of the class that causes the dialog box to be drawn on the screen. They work together to achieve the overall effect, making communication with the program easier for your user.

You build a dialog box resource with the resource editor, adding controls to it and arranging them to make the control easy to use. ClassWizard then helps you to create a dialog box class, typically derived from the MFC class CDialog, and to connect the resource to the class. Usually each control on the dialog box resource corresponds to one member variable in the class. To display the dialog box, you call a member function of the class. To set the control values to defaults before displaying the dialog box, or to determine the values of the controls after the user is finished with the box, you use the member variables of the class.

Creating a Dialog Box Resource

The first step in adding a dialog box to your MFC application is creating the dialog box resource, which acts as a sort of template for Windows. When Windows sees the dialog box resource in your program, it uses the commands in the resource to construct the dialog box for you.

In this chapter you learn to work with dialog boxes by adding one to a simple application. You can use the SDI application that you created in Chapter 1 or open it from the CD. You create a dialog box resource and a dialog box class for the application, write code to display the dialog box, and write code to use the values entered by the user.

To create a dialog box resource, first open the application. Choose Insert, Resource from the Developer Studio's menu bar. The Insert Resource dialog box, shown in Figure 2.1, appears. Double-click Dialog in the Resource Type box. The dialog box editor appears, as shown in Figure 2.2.

FIG. 2.1

Double-click Dialog on the Insert Resource dialog box.

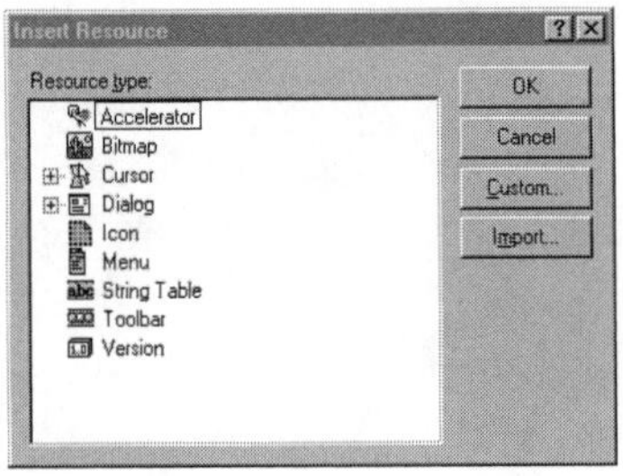

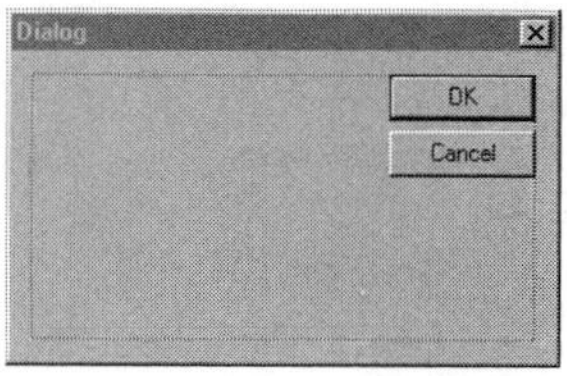

FIG. 2.2
A brand new dialog box resource has a title, an OK button, and a Cancel button.

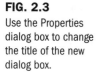

Bring up the Properties dialog box for the new dialog box by choosing View, Properties. Change the caption to **Sample Dialog**, as shown in Figure 2.3. You'll be using the Properties dialog box quite a lot as you work on this dialog box resource, so "pin" it to the screen by clicking the pushpin in the upper-left corner.

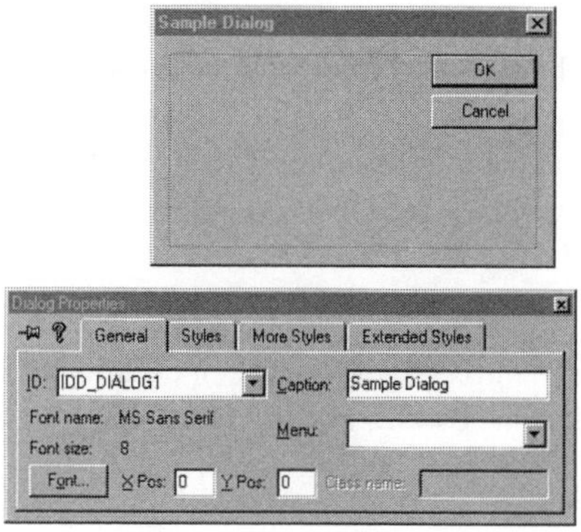

FIG. 2.3
Use the Properties dialog box to change the title of the new dialog box.

The control palette is used to add controls to the dialog box resource. Dialog boxes are built and changed with a very visual WYSIWYG interface. If you need a button on your dialog box, you grab one from the control palette, drop it where you want it, and change the caption from Button1 to Lookup, or Connect, or whatever you want the button to read. All the familiar Windows controls are available for your dialog boxes:

- **Static text.** Not really a control; this is used to label other controls such as edit boxes.
- **Edit boxes.** Single line or multiline; these are places for users to type strings or numbers as input to the program.
- **Buttons.** Every dialog box starts with OK and Cancel buttons, but you can add as many of your own as you want.
- **Check boxes.** Used to set options on or off; each option can be selected or deselected independently.
- **Radio buttons.** These are used to select only one of a number of related options. Selecting one button deselects the rest.
- **List box.** This box type is used to select one item from a list hardcoded into the dialog box or filled in by the program as the dialog box is created. The user cannot type in the selection area.

■ **Combo box.** A combination of an edit box and a list box; this control allows users to select from a list, or type their response if the one they want isn't on the list.

The sample application in this chapter is going to have a dialog box with a selection of controls on it, to demonstrate the way they are used.

Defining Dialog Box and Control IDs

Because dialog boxes are often unique to an application (with the exception of the common dialog boxes), you almost always create your own IDs for both the dialog box and the controls it contains. You can, if you like, accept the default IDs that the dialog box editor creates for you. However, these IDs are generic (for example, IDD_DIALOG1, IDC_EDIT1, IDC_RADIO1, and so on), and so you'll probably want to change them to something more specific. In any case, as you can tell from the default IDs, a dialog box's ID usually begins with the prefix IDD, and control IDs usually begin with the prefix IDC. You change these IDs in the Properties dialog box: Click the control (or the dialog box background to select the entire background), and choose Edit, Properties; then change the resource ID to a descriptive name that starts with IDD for a dialog and IDC for a control.

Creating the Sample Dialog Box

Click the Edit box button on the control palette, and then click in the upper-left corner of the dialog box to place the edit box. If necessary, grab a moving handle and move it until it is in roughly the same place as the edit box in Figure 2.4. Normally, you would change the ID from Edit, but for this sample leave it unchanged.

FIG. 2.4
You can build a simple dialog box quickly in the resource editor.

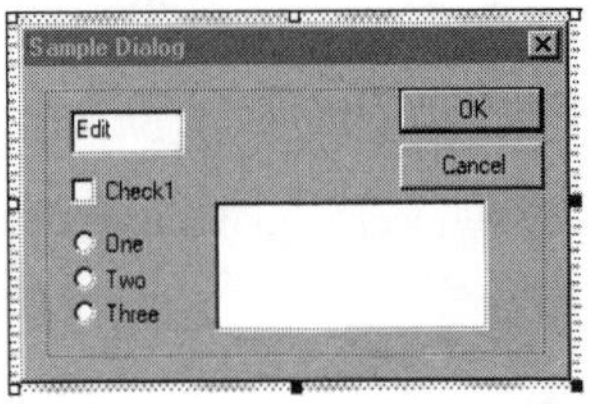

> **TIP** If you aren't sure which control palette button inserts an edit box (or any other type of control), just hold the pointer still over one of the buttons for a short time. A ToolTip will appear reminding you of the name of the control associated with the button. Move the pointer from button to button until you find the one for the edit box.

Add a check box and three radio buttons to the dialog box so that it resembles Figure 2.4. Change the captions on the radio buttons to **One**, **Two**, and **Three**. To align all these controls, click one, and then while holding down the Ctrl key, click each of the rest of them. Choose Layout, Align Controls, Left, and if necessary drag the stack of controls over with the mouse while they are all selected. Then choose Layout, Space Evenly, Down to adjust the vertical spacing.

> **TIP** The commands on the Layout menu are also on the Dialog toolbar, which appears at the bottom of your screen while you are using the resource editor. The toolbar symbols are repeated on the menu to help you learn which button is associated with each menu item.

Click the One radio button again and bring up the Properties dialog box. Select the Group check box. This indicates that this is the first of a group of buttons. When you select a radio button, all the other buttons in the group are deselected.

Add a list box to the dialog box to the right of the radio buttons, and resize it to match Figure 2.4. With the list box highlighted, choose View, Properties to bring up the Properties dialog box. Select the Styles tab and make sure that the Sort box is not selected. When this box is selected, the strings in your list box are automatically presented in alphabetical order. For this application, they should be presented in the order that they are added.

Writing a Dialog Box Class

When the resource is complete, bring up ClassWizard by choosing View, ClassWizard. ClassWizard recognizes that this new dialog box resource does not have a class associated with it and offers to build one for you, as shown in Figure 2.5. Leave the Create a New Class radio button selected, and click OK. The New Class dialog box appears, as shown in Figure 2.6. Fill in the class name as **CSdiDialog** and click OK. ClassWizard creates a new class, prepares the source file (SdiDialog.cpp) and header file (SdiDialog.h), and adds them to your project.

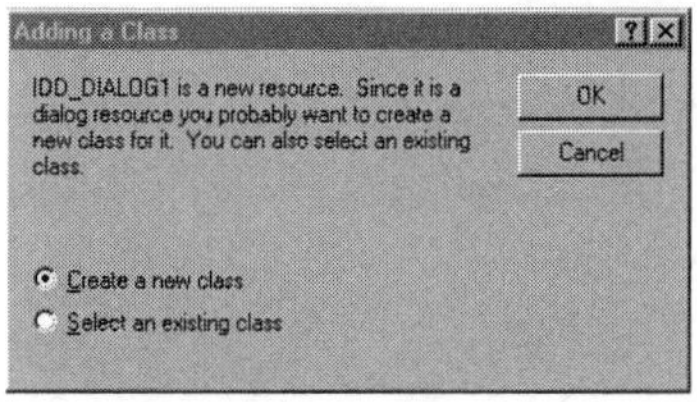

FIG. 2.5
ClassWizard makes sure you don't forget to create a class to go with your new dialog box resource.

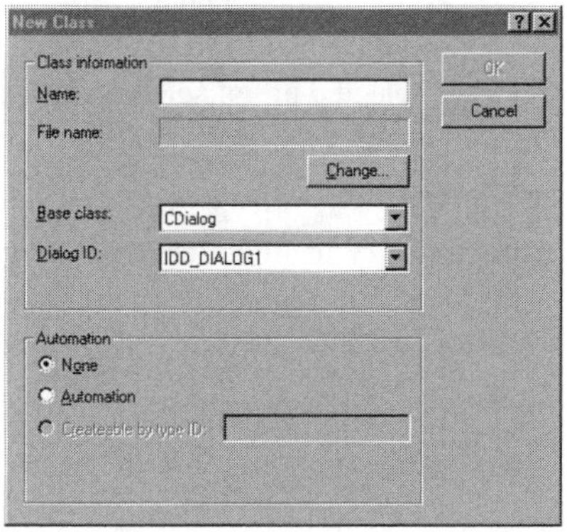

FIG. 2.6
Creating a dialog box class is simple with ClassWizard.

You connect the dialog box resources to your code with the Member Variables tab of ClassWizard, shown in Figure 2.7. Click IDC_CHECK1 and then click the Add Variable button. This brings up the Add Member Variable dialog box, shown in Figure 2.8.

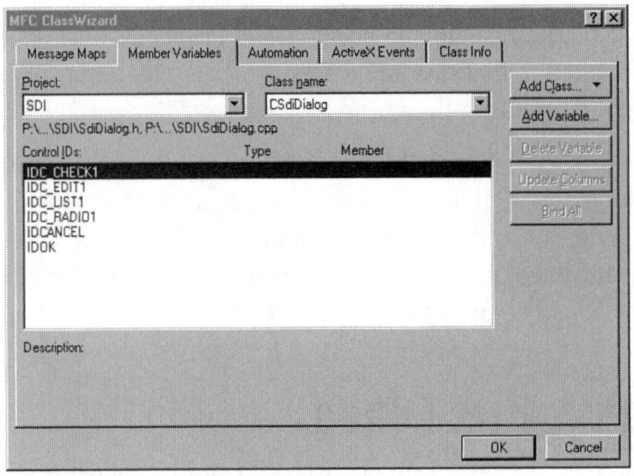

FIG. 2.7

The Member Variables tab of ClassWizard connects dialog box controls to dialog box class member variables.

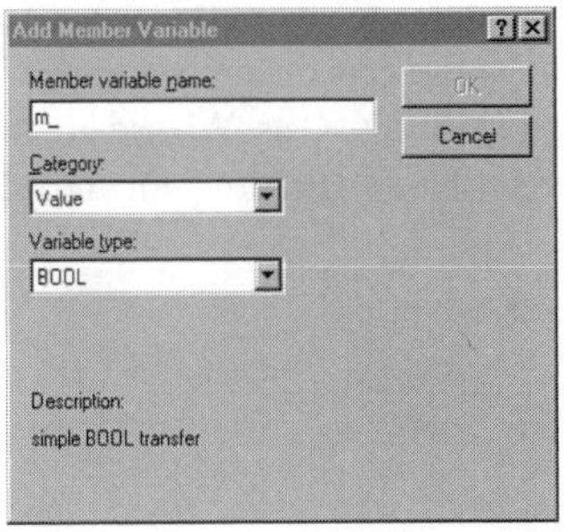

FIG. 2.8

You choose the name for the member variable associated with each control.

A member variable in the new dialog box class can be connected to a control's value, or to the control itself. This sample demonstrates both kinds of connection. For IDC_CHECK1, fill in the variable name as **m_check**, and make sure that the Category drop-down box has Value selected. If you open the Variable Type drop-down box, you will see that the only possible choice is BOOL. Since a check box can be either selected or not selected, it can be connected only to a BOOL variable, which holds the value TRUE or FALSE.

Here are the data types that go with each control type:

- **Edit box.** Usually a string, but also can be other data types including int, float, and long.
- **Check box.** int.
- **Radio button.** int.

- **List box.** String.
- **Combo box.** String.
- **Scroll bar.** int.

Connect IDC_EDIT1 in the same way, to a member variable called m_edit of type CString as a Value. Connect IDC_LIST1 as a Control to a member variable called m_listbox of type CListBox. Connect IDC_RADIO1, the first of the group of radio buttons, as a Value to an int member variable called m_radio.

After you click OK to add the variable, ClassWizard offers, for some kinds of variables, the capability to validate the user's data entry. For example, when an edit control is selected, a field under the list of variables allows you to set the maximum number of characters the user can enter into the edit box (see Figure 2.9). Set it to 10 for m_edit. If the edit box is connected to a number (int or float), this area of ClassWizard is used to specify minimum or maximum values for the number entered by the user. The error messages asking the user to try again are generated automatically by MFC with no work on your part.

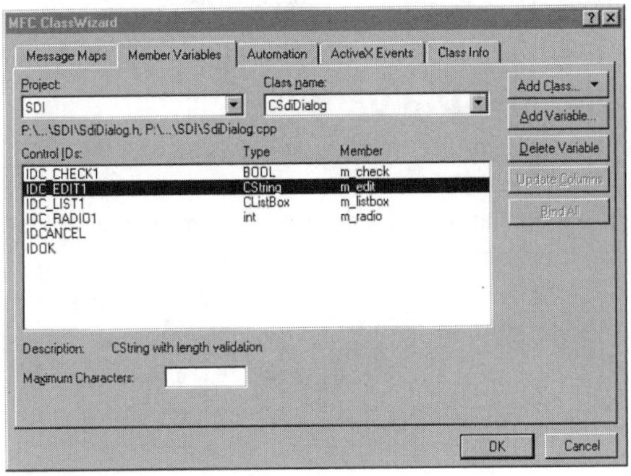

FIG. 2.9
Enter a number in the Maximum Characters field to limit the length of a user's entry.

Using the Dialog Box Class

Now that you have your dialog box resource built and your dialog box class written, you can create objects of that class within your program and display the associated dialog box element. The first step is to decide what will cause the dialog box to display. Typically it is a menu choice, but because adding menu items and connecting them to code are not covered until Chapter 9, "Building a Complete Application: ShowString," you can simply have the dialog box display when the application starts running. To display the dialog box, you call the DoModal() member function of the dialog box class.

Modeless Dialog Boxes

Most of the dialog boxes you will code will be *modal* dialog boxes. A modal dialog box is on top of all the other windows in the application: The user must deal with the dialog box and then close it before going on to other work. An example of this is the dialog box that comes up when the user chooses File, Open in any Windows application.

A *modeless* dialog box allows the user to click the underlying application and do some other work and then return to the dialog box. An example of this is the dialog box that comes up when the user chooses Edit, Find in many Windows applications.

Displaying a modeless dialog box is more difficult than displaying a modal one. The dialog box object—the instance of the dialog box class—must be managed carefully. Typically it is created with new and destroyed with `delete` when the user closes the dialog box with Cancel or OK. You have to override a number of functions within the dialog box class. In short, you should be familiar and comfortable with modal dialog boxes before you attempt to use a modeless dialog box. When you're ready, look at the Visual C++ sample called MODELESS that comes with Developer Studio. The fastest way to open this sample is by searching for **MODELESS** in InfoViewer. Searching in InfoViewer is covered in Appendix B, the "Developer Studio User Interface."

Arranging to Display the Dialog Box

Select the ClassView in the project workspace pane, expand the SDI Classes item, and then expand CSdiApp. Double-click the InitInstance() member function. This function is called whenever the application starts. Scroll down to the very end of the function, and just before the return at the end of the function, add the lines in Listing 2.1.

On the CD

Listing 2.1 SDI.CPP—Lines to Add at the End of *CSdiApp::InitInstance()*

```
CSdiDialog dlg;
dlg.m_check = TRUE;
dlg.m_edit = "hi there";
CString msg;
if (dlg.DoModal() == IDOK)
{
    msg = "You clicked OK. ";
}
else
{
    msg = "You cancelled. ";
}
msg += "Edit box is: ";
msg += dlg.m_edit;
AfxMessageBox (msg);
```

This code first creates an instance of the dialog box class. It sets the check box and edit box to simple default values. (The list box and radio buttons are a little more complex and are added later in this chapter in "Using a List Box Control" and "Using Radio Buttons.") The dialog box displays on-screen by calling its `DoModal()` function, which returns a number represented by `IDOK` if the user clicks OK and `IDCANCEL` if the user clicks Cancel. The code then builds a message and displays it with the `AfxMessageBox` function.

N O T E The `CString` class has a number of useful member functions and operator overloads. As you see here, the `+=` operator tacks characters onto the end of a string. For more about the `CString` class, consult Appendix E, "Useful Classes." ■

At the very beginning of the file, add this directive:

```
#include "sdidialog.h"
```

This makes sure that the compiler knows what a `CSdiDialog` class is when it compiles this file. Build the project by choosing <u>B</u>uild, <u>B</u>uild, or by clicking the Build button on the Build toolbar. Run the application by choosing <u>B</u>uild, <u>E</u>xecute, or by clicking the Execute Program button on the Build toolbar. You will see that the dialog box displays with the default values you just coded, as shown in Figure 2.10. Change them, and click OK. You should get a message box telling you what you did, like the one in Figure 2.11. Now the program sits there, ready to go, but since there is no more for it to do, you can close it by choosing <u>F</u>ile, E<u>x</u>it, or by clicking the X in the top-right corner.

FIG. 2.10

Your application displays the dialog box when it first runs.

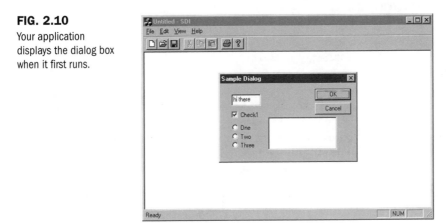

FIG. 2.11

After you click OK, the application echoes the contents of the edit control.

Run it again, change the contents of the edit box, and this time click Cancel on the dialog box. Notice in Figure 2.12 that the edit box is reported as still `hi there`—this is because MFC does not copy the control values into the member variables when the user clicks Cancel. Again, just close the application after the dialog box is gone.

FIG. 2.12
When you click Cancel,
the application ignores
any changes you made.

Be sure to try entering more characters into the edit box than the 10 you specified with ClassWizard. You will find you cannot type more than 10 characters—the system just beeps at you. If you try to paste in something longer than 10 characters, only the first 10 characters appear in the edit box.

Behind the Scenes

You may be wondering what's going on here. When you click OK on the dialog box, MFC arranges for a function called OnOK() to be called. This function is inherited from CDialog, the base class for CSdiDialog. Among other things it calls a function called DoDataExchange(), which ClassWizard wrote for you. Here's how it looks at the moment:

```
void CSdiDialog::DoDataExchange(CDataExchange* pDX)
{
    CDialog::DoDataExchange(pDX);
    //{{AFX_DATA_MAP(CSdiDialog)
    DDX_Control(pDX, IDC_LIST1, m_listbox);
    DDX_Check(pDX, IDC_CHECK1, m_check);
    DDX_Text(pDX, IDC_EDIT1, m_edit);
    DDV_MaxChars(pDX, m_edit, 10);
    DDX_Radio(pDX, IDC_RADIO1, m_radio);
    //}}AFX_DATA_MAP
}
```

The functions with names that start DDX all perform data exchange: their second parameter is the resource ID of a control, and the third parameter is a member variable in this class. This is the way that ClassWizard connected the controls to member variables: by generating this code for you. Remember that ClassWizard also added these variables to the dialog box class by generating code in the header file that declares them.

There are 34 functions whose names start DDX: one for each type of data that might be exchanged between a dialog box and a class. Each has the type in its name. For example, DDX_Check is used to connect a check box to a BOOL member variable. DDX_Text is used to connect an edit box to a CString member variable. ClassWizard chooses the right function name when you make the connection.

N O T E There are some DDX functions that are not generated by ClassWizard. For example, when you connect a list box as a Value, your only choice for type is CString. Choosing that causes ClassWizard to generate a call to DDX_LBString(), which connects the selected string in the list box to a CString member variable. There are cases when the integer index into the list box might be more useful, and there is a DDX_LBIndex() function that performs that exchange. You can add code to DoDataExchange(), outside the special ClassWizard comments, to make this connection. If you do so, remember to add the member variable to the class yourself. You can find the full list of DDX functions in the online documentation. ■

Functions with names that start DDV perform data validation. ClassWizard adds a call to DDV_MaxChars right after the call to DDX_Text that filled m_edit with the contents of IDC_EDIT1. The first parameter of the call is the member variable name and the second is the limit: how many characters can be in the string. If a user ever managed to get extra characters into a length-validated string, the DDV_MaxChars() function contains code that puts up a warning box and gets the user to try again. You can just set the limit and count on its being enforced.

Using a List Box Control

Dealing with the list box is more difficult, because only while the dialog box is on-screen is the list box control a real window. You cannot call a member function of the list box control class unless the dialog box is on-screen. (This is true of any control that you access as a control rather than as a value.) This means that you must initialize the list box (fill it with strings) and use it (determine which string is selected) in functions that are called by MFC while the dialog box is on-screen.

When it is time to initialize the dialog box, just before it displays on-screen, a CDialog function called OnInitDialog() is called. While the full explanation of what you are about to do will have to wait until Chapter 4, "Messages and Commands," follow the steps below to add the function to your class.

In ClassView, right-click CSdiDialog and choose Add Windows Message Handler. The New Windows Message and Event Handlers dialog box shown in Figure 2.13 appears. Choose WM_INITDIALOG from the list and click Add Handler. The message name disappears from the left list and appears in the right list. Click it and then click Edit Existing to see the code.

FIG. 2.13

The New Windows
Message and Event
Handlers dialog box
helps you override
OnInitDialog().

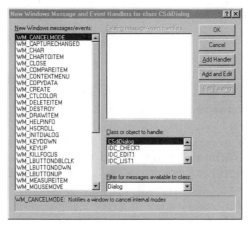

Remove the TODO comment and add calls to the member functions of the list box so that the function is as shown in Listing 2.2.

Listing 2.2 SDIDIALOG.CPP—*CSdiDialog::OnInitDialog()*

```
BOOL CSdiDialog::OnInitDialog()
{
    CDialog::OnInitDialog();

    m_listbox.AddString("First String");
    m_listbox.AddString("Second String");
    m_listbox.AddString("Yet Another String");
    m_listbox.AddString("String Number Four");
    m_listbox.SetCurSel(2);

    return TRUE;   // return TRUE unless you set the focus to a control
                   // EXCEPTION: OCX Property Pages should return FALSE
}
```

This function starts by calling the base class version of OnInitDialog() to do whatever behind-the-scenes work MFC does when dialog boxes are initialized. Then it calls the list box member function AddString() which, as you can probably guess, adds a string to the list box. The strings will be displayed to the user in the order that they were added with AddString(). The final call is to SetCurSel(), which sets the current selection. As you see when you run this program, the index you pass to SetCurSel() is zero-based, which means that item 2 is the third in the list, counting: 0, 1, 2.

N O T E   Typically the strings of a list box are not hardcoded like this. To set them from elsewhere in your program, you have to add a CStringArray member variable to the dialog box class and a function to add strings to that array. The OnInitDialog() would use the array to fill the list box. Alternatively, you can use another one of MFC's collection classes or even fill the list box from a database. For more about CStringArray and other MFC collection classes, consult Appendix E, "Useful Classes." Database programming is covered in Chapter 22, "Database Access." ■

In order to have the message box display some indication of what was selected in the list box, you have to add another member variable to the dialog box class. This member variable will be set as the dialog box closes and can be accessed after it is closed. In ClassView, right-click CSdiDialog and choose Add Member Variable. Fill in the dialog box, as shown in Figure 2.14, and click OK. This adds the declaration of the CString called m_selected to the header file for you. (If the list box allowed multiple selections, you would have to use a CStringArray to hold the list of selected items.) Strictly speaking, the variable should be private, and you should either add a public accessor function or make CSdiApp::InitInstance() a friend function to CSdiDialog in order to be truly object oriented. Here you take an excusable shortcut. The general rule still holds: Member variables should be private.

FIG. 2.14

Add a CString to your class to hold the string that was selected in the list box.

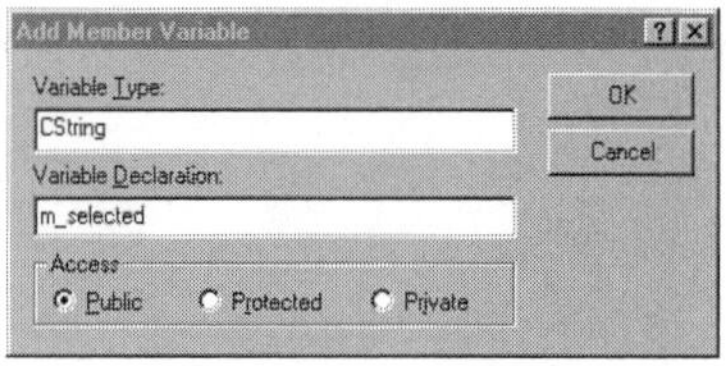

This new member variable is used to hold the string that was selected by the user. It is set when the user clicks OK or Cancel. To add a function that is called when the user clicks OK, follow these steps:

1. Right-click CSdiDialog in the ClassView, and choose Add Windows Message Handler.

2. In the New Windows Message and Event Handlers dialog box, shown in Figure 2.15, highlight ID_OK in the Class or Object to Handle list box.

FIG. 2.15

Add a function to handle the user's clicking OK on your dialog box.

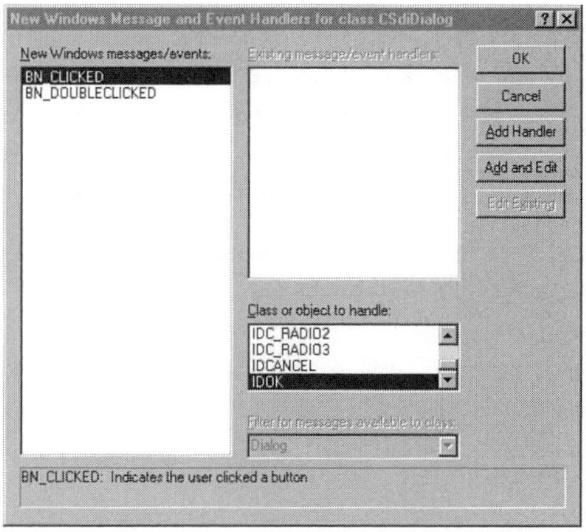

3. In the right-hand list box, select BN_CLICKED. You are adding a function to "handle" the user's clicking the OK button once.

4. Click the Add Handler button. The Add Member Function dialog box shown in Figure 2.16 appears.

FIG. 2.16

ClassWizard suggests a very good name for this event handler: Do not change it.

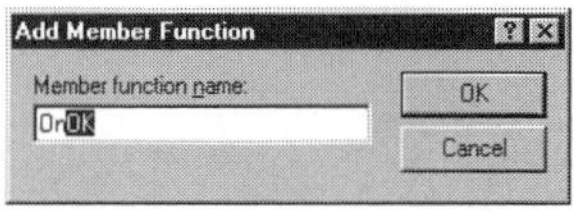

5. Accept the suggested name, OnOK(), by clicking OK.

6. Click the Edit Existing button to edit the code, and add lines so that it is as shown in Listing 2.3.

Part
II
Ch
2

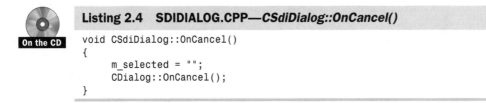

On the CD

Listing 2.3   SDIDIALOG.CPP—*CSdiDialog::OnOK()*

```
void CSdiDialog::OnOK()
{
     int index = m_listbox.GetCurSel();
     if (index != LB_ERR)
     {
          m_listbox.GetText(index, m_selected);
     }
     else
     {
          m_selected = "";
     }


     CDialog::OnOK();
}
```

This code calls the list box member function GetCurSel(), which returns a constant represented by LB_ERR if there is no selection or if more than one string has been selected. Otherwise, it returns the zero-based index of the selected string. The GetText() member function fills m_selected with the string at position index. After filling this member variable, this function calls the base class OnOK() function to do the other processing required.

In a moment, you will add lines to CSdiApp::InitInstance() to mention the selected string in the message box. Those lines will execute whether the user clicks OK or Cancel, so you need to add a function to handle the user's clicking Cancel. Simply follow the numbered steps for adding OnOK, except that you choose ID_CANCEL from the top-right box and agree to call the function OnCancel. The code, as shown in Listing 2.4, resets m_selected since the user canceled the dialog box.

On the CD

Listing 2.4   SDIDIALOG.CPP—*CSdiDialog::OnCancel()*

```
void CSdiDialog::OnCancel()
{
     m_selected = "";
     CDialog::OnCancel();
}
```

Add these lines to CSdiApp::InitInstance() just before the call to AfxMessageBox():

```
msg += ". List Selection: ";
msg += dlg.m_selected;
```

Build the application, run it, and test it. Does it work as you expect? Does it resemble Figure 2.17?

Using Radio buttons

You may have already noticed that when the dialog box first appears on-screen, none of the radio buttons are selected. You can arrange for one of them to be selected by default: Simply add two lines to `CSdiDialog::OnInitDialog()`. These lines set the second radio button and saves the change to the dialog box:

```
m_radio = 1;
UpdateData(FALSE);
```

FIG. 2.17

Your application now displays strings in the list box.

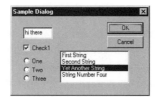

You may recall that `m_radio` is the member variable to which the group of radio buttons is connected. It is a zero-based index into the group of buttons, indicating which one is selected. Button 1 is the second button. The call to `UpdateData()` refreshes the dialog box controls with the member variable values. The parameter indicates the direction of transfer: `UpdateData(TRUE)` would refresh the member variables with the control values, wiping out the setting of `m_radio` you just made.

Unlike list boxes, a group of radio buttons can be accessed after the dialog box is no longer on-screen, so you won't need to add code to `OnOK()` or `OnCancel()`. But you have a problem: how to convert the integer selection into a string to tack on the end of `msg`. There are a lot of approaches, including the `Format()` function of `CString`, but in this case, since there are not many possible selections, a `switch` statement is readable and quick. At the end of `CSdiApp::InitInstance()`, add the lines in Listing 2.5 just before the call to `AfxMessageBox()`.

On the CD

Listing 2.5   SDIDIALOG.CPP—Lines to Add to *CSdiApp::InitInstance()*

```
msg += "\r\n";
msg += "Radio Selection: ";

switch (dlg.m_radio)
{
case 0:
     msg += "0";
     break;
case 1:
     msg += "1";
     break;
case 2:
     msg += "2";
     break;
default:
     msg += "none";
     break;
}
```

The first new line adds two special characters to the message. Return, represented by \r, and new line, represented by \n, combine to form the Windows end-of-line marker. This adds a line break after the part of the message you have built so far. The rest of msg will appear on the second line of the message box. The switch statement is an ordinary piece of C++ code, which was also present in C. It executes one of the case statements, depending on the value of dlg.m_radio.

Once again, build and test the application. Any surprises? It should resemble Figure 2.18. You are going to be building and using dialog boxes throughout this book, so take the time to understand how this application works and what it does. You may want to step through it with the debugger and watch it in action: You can read all about debugging in Appendix C, "Debugging."

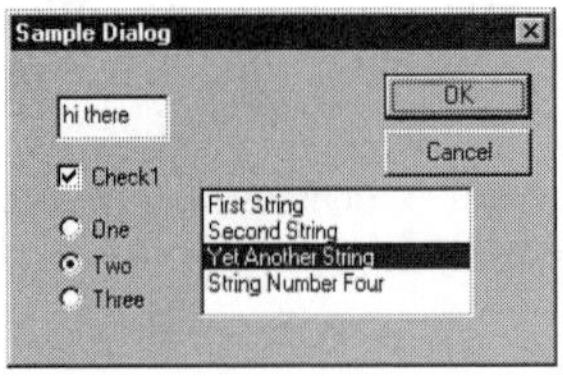

FIG. 2.18
Your application now selects button Two by default.

From Here...

To add a dialog box to your application, you need to build a dialog box resource and a dialog box class and to connect them with ClassWizard. Then your application calls member functions of the dialog box class, or of the individual controls to use the dialog box. You may have to catch messages in order to gain full control of your dialog box.

Almost every sample application in this book features one or more dialog boxes. Some of the chapters that show you the power of dialog boxes include the following:

- Chapter 3, "Windows 95 Common Controls," provides an overview of the many special controls that you can use in Windows 95 applications.

- Chapter 4, "Messages and Commands," covers messages and virtual function overrides in more detail, so you'll know what is was you did with messages in this chapter.

- Chapter 9, "Building a Complete Application: ShowString," shows how to bring up a dialog box when the user chooses a menu item, and how to use the control values in your application.

- Chapter 12, "Property Pages and Sheets and Wizards," shows you how to use property sheets, which are nothing more than a special kind of dialog box, and wizards, which are simply special property sheets.

CHAPTER 3

Windows 95 Common Controls

A s a Windows user, you're accustomed to seeing controls like buttons, list boxes, menus, and edit boxes. As Windows developed, however, Microsoft noticed that developers routinely created other types of controls in their programs. These controls included toolbars, status bars, progress bars, tree views, and others. To make life easier for Windows programmers, Microsoft included these popular controls as part of the Windows 95 operating environment (and the latest version of Windows NT). Now, Windows programmers no longer need to create their own versions of these controls from scratch. This chapter introduces you to many of Windows 95's common controls. The toolbar and status bar controls are covered in Chapter 10, "Status Bars and Toolbars," and property sheets and wizards are covered in Chapter 12, "Property Pages and Sheets and Wizards." ∎

About Progress Bar controls

Progress bars provide feedback to the user about the status of a long operation.

About Slider controls

Slider controls (also known as trackbars) enable users to select values within a given range.

About Up-Down controls

Up-Down controls (or spinners) are another way a user can specify a value from a given range.

About Image List controls

Many Windows 95 controls use a set of images. An Image List holds those images.

About List View controls

List View controls provide a configurable view of items in a data set.

About Tree View controls

Tree View controls display a hierarchical view of data elements.

About Rich Edit controls

Rich Edit controls enable you quickly to add word-processing capabilities to your application.

The Win95 Controls Application

This chapter's sample program is called Win95 Controls App. It demonstrates six of the Windows 95 common controls: the progress bar, the slider, the up-down control, the list view, the tree view, and the rich edit control, all of which are shown in Figure 3.1. In the following sections, you learn the basics of creating and using these controls in your own applications. Because this sample application uses some techniques that have not yet been covered, the sample program is presented as a demonstration rather than as a build-along project. You should open the code in Developer Studio and look through it as you read.

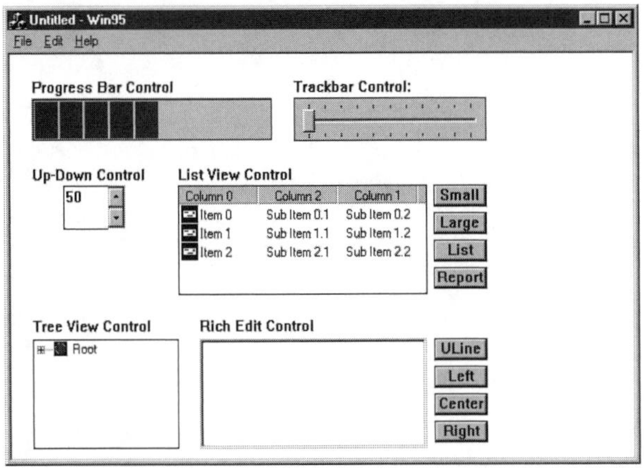

FIG. 3.1
The Win95 sample application demonstrates six Windows 95 common controls.

The controls themselves are declared as data members of the view class, by adding the lines in Listing 3.1 to Win95View.h. As you can see, the progress bar is an object of the CProgressCtrl class. It is discussed in the next section. The other controls will be discussed in later sections of this chapter.

Listing 3.1   Win95View.h—Declaring the Controls

```
protected:
    //Progress Bar
    CProgressCtrl m_progressBar;

    //Trackbar or Slider
    CSliderCtrl m_trackbar;
    BOOL m_timer;

    // Up-Down or Spinner
    CSpinButtonCtrl m_upDown;
    CEdit m_buddyEdit;

    // List View
    CListCtrl m_listView;
    CImageList m_smallImageList;
    CImageList m_largeImageList;
```

```
CButton m_smallButton;
CButton m_largeButton;
CButton m_listButton;
CButton m_reportButton;

  // Tree View
CTreeCtrl m_treeView;
CImageList m_treeImageList;

  // Rich Edit
CRichEditCtrl m_richEdit;
CButton m_boldButton;
CButton m_leftButton;
CButton m_centerButton;
CButton m_rightButton;
```

The Progress Bar Control

Probably the new common control that is easiest to use is the progress bar, which is nothing more than a rectangle that slowly fills in with colored blocks. The more colored blocks filled in, the closer the task is to being complete. When the progress bar is completely filled in, the task associated with the progress bar is also complete. You might use a progress bar to show the status of a sorting operation or to give the user visual feedback about a large file that's being loaded.

To see a progress bar in action, click anywhere in the background of Win95 Controls App's window. When you do, the progress bar begins filling with colored blocks. When the progress bar is completely filled, it starts over again. This continues until you click the window again or exit the program. Of course, in this program, the progress bar isn't tracking a real task in progress. It's simply responding to timer messages. The program does, however, still demonstrate how you might use a progress bar in your own applications.

Creating the Progress Bar

Before you can use a progress bar, you must create it. Often in an MFC program, the controls are created as part of a dialog box. However, Win95 Controls App displays its controls in the application's main window, the *view* of this Single Document Interface (SDI) application. You will learn more about documents and views in Chapter 5, "Documents and Views." All of the controls are created in the view class OnCreate() function, which responds to the WM_CREATE Windows message.

Because creating and initializing each of the six controls requires quite a bit of code, the application delegates the details to separate functions. For example, to create the progress bar control, OnCreate() calls the CreateProgressBar() local member function, shown in Listing 3.2, like this:

```
CreateProgressBar();
```

Listing 3.2   Win95View.cpp—*CWin95View::CreateProgressBar()*

```
void CWin95View::CreateProgressBar()
{
    m_progressBar.Create(WS_CHILD | WS_VISIBLE | WS_BORDER,
        CRect(20, 40, 250, 80), this, IDC_PROGRESSBAR);

    m_progressBar.SetRange(1, 100);
    m_progressBar.SetStep(10);
    m_progressBar.SetPos(50);
    m_timer = FALSE;

}
```

CreateProgressBar() first creates the progress bar control by calling the control's Create() function. This function's four arguments are the control's style flags, the control's size (as a CRect object), a pointer to the control's parent window, and the control's ID. The resource ID, IDC_PROGRESSBAR, is added by hand. To add resource symbols to your own applications, choose View, Resource Symbols and click the New button. Type in a resource ID name, such as IDC_PROGRESSBAR, and use the default number Developer Studio provides.

The style constants are the same constants that you use for creating any type of window (a control is really nothing more than a special kind of window, after all). In this case, you need at least the following:

- ■ WS_CHILD   Indicates that the control is a child window
- ■ WS_VISIBLE   Ensures that the user can see the control

The WS_BORDER is a nice addition because it adds a dark border around the control, setting it off from the rest of the window.

Initializing the Progress Bar

After the progress bar control is created, it must be initialized. The CProgressCtrl class features a number of member functions that enable you to initialize and manipulate the control, as listed in Table 3.1.

Table 3.1   Member Functions of the *CProgressCtrl* Class

Function	Description
Create()	Creates the progress bar control
OffsetPos()	Advances the control the given number of blocks
SetPos()	Sets the control's current value
SetRange()	Sets the control's minimum and maximum values
SetStep()	Sets the value by which the control advances
StepIt()	Advances the control by a one-step unit

To initialize the control, `CWin95View::CreateProgressBar()` calls `SetRange()`, `SetStep()`, and `SetPos()`. Because the range and the step rate are related, a control with a range of 1–10 and a step rate of 1 works almost identically to a control with a range of 1–100 and a step rate of 10.

When this demonstration application starts, the progress bar is already half filled with colored blocks. (This is purely for aesthetic reasons. Usually a progress bar begins its life empty.) It's half full because `CreateProgressBar()` calls `SetPos()` with the value of 50, which is the mid-point of the control's range.

Manipulating the Progress Bar

In Win95 Controls App, the progress bar starts counting forward when you click the window's background. This is because the program responds to the mouse click by starting a timer that sends `WM_TIMER` messages to the program two times per second. In the view class's `OnTimer()` function, the program makes the following function call:

```
m_progressBar.StepIt();
```

The `StepIt()` function increments the progress bar control's value by the step rate, causing new blocks to be displayed in the control as the control's value setting counts upward. When the control reaches its maximum, it automatically starts over.

N O T E Notice that there are no `CProgressCtrl` member functions that control the size or number of blocks that will fit into the control. This attribute is controlled indirectly by the size of the control. ■

The Slider Control

Many times in a program you might need the user to enter a value within a specific range. For this sort of task, you use MFC's `CSliderCtrl` class to create a slider (also called trackbar) control. For example, suppose you need the user to enter a percentage. In this case, you want the user to enter values only in the range from 0 to 100. Other values would be invalid and could cause problems in your program.

By using the slider control, you can force the user to enter a value in the specified range. Although the user can accidentally enter a wrong value (a value that doesn't accomplish what the user wants to do), there is no way to enter an invalid value (one that brings your program crashing down like a stone wall in an earthquake).

For a percentage, you create a slider control with a minimum value of 0 and a maximum value of 100. Moreover, to make the control easier to position, you might want to place tick marks at each setting that's a multiple of 10, providing 11 tick marks in all (including the one at 0). Win95 Controls App creates exactly this type of slider.

To see the slider work, click the slider's slot. When you do, the slider moves forward or back-ward, and the selected value appears to the right of the control's caption, as seen in Figure 3.1. As soon as the slider has the focus, you can also control it with your keyboard's Up and Down arrow keys, as well as with the Page Up and Page Down keys.

Part
II

Ch
3

Creating the Trackbar

In CWin95View, the slider is created in the CreateTrackbar() local member function shown in Listing 3.3. Like CreateProgressBar(), this function is called from CWin95View::OnCreate().

Listing 3.3 Win95View.cpp—*CWin95View::CreateTrackBar()*

```
void CWin95View::CreateTrackbar()
{
    m_trackbar.Create(WS_CHILD | WS_VISIBLE | WS_BORDER |
        TBS_AUTOTICKS | TBS_BOTH | TBS_HORZ,
        CRect(270, 40, 450, 80), this, IDC_TRACKBAR);
    m_trackbar.SetRange(0, 100, TRUE);
    m_trackbar.SetTicFreq(10);
    m_trackbar.SetLineSize(1);
    m_trackbar.SetPageSize(10);
}
```

As with the progress bar, the first step is to create the slider control by calling its Create() member function. This function's four arguments are the control's style flags, the control's size (as a CRect object), a pointer to the control's parent window, and the control's ID. The style constants include the same constants that you would use for creating any type of window, with the addition of special styles used with sliders. Table 3.2 lists these special styles.

Table 3.2 Slider Styles

Style	Description
TBS_AUTOTICKS	Enables the slider to automatically draw its tick marks
TBS_BOTH	Draws tick marks on both sides of the slider
TBS_BOTTOM	Draws tick marks on the bottom of a horizontal slider
TBS_ENABLESELRANGE	Enables a slider to display a sub-range of values
TBS_HORZ	Draws the slider horizontally
TBS_LEFT	Draws tick marks on the left side of a vertical slider
TBS_NOTICKS	Draws a slider with no tick marks
TBS_RIGHT	Draws tick marks on the right side of a vertical slider
TBS_TOP	Draws tick marks on the top of a horizontal slider
TBS_VERT	Draws a vertical slider

Initializing the Trackbar

After the slider control is created, it must be initialized. The `CSliderCtrl` class features many member functions that enable you to initialize and manipulate the control. Those member functions and their descriptions are listed in Table 3.3.

Table 3.3   Member Functions of the *CSliderCtrl* Class

Function	Description
ClearSel()	Clears a selection from the control
ClearTics()	Clears tick marks from the control
Create()	Creates a slider control
GetChannelRect()	Gets the size of the control's slider
GetLineSize()	Gets the control's line size
GetNumTics()	Gets the number of tick marks
GetPageSize()	Gets the control's page size
GetPos()	Gets the control's position
GetRange()	Gets the control's minimum and maximum values
GetRangeMax()	Gets the control's maximum value
GetRangeMin()	Gets the control's minimum value
GetSelection()	Gets the current range selection
GetThumbRect()	Gets the size of the control's thumb
GetTic()	Gets the position of a tick mark
GetTicArray()	Gets all of the control's tick positions
GetTicPos()	Gets the client coordinates of a tick mark
SetLineSize()	Sets the amount to move the value up or down in response to the cursor up or cursor down key
SetPageSize()	Sets the amount to move the value up or down in response to the page up or page down key
SetPos()	Sets the control's position
SetRange()	Sets the control's minimum and maximum values
SetRangeMax()	Sets the control's maximum value
SetRangeMin()	Sets the control's minimum value
SetSelection()	Sets a selected sub-range in the control

Part
II

Ch
3

continues

Table 3.3 Continued

Function	Description
SetTic()	Sets the position of a tick mark
SetTicFreq()	Sets the control's tick frequency
VerifyPos()	Determines whether the control's position is valid

Usually, when you create a slider control, you want to set the control's range and tick frequency. If the user is going to use the control from the keyboard, you also need to set the control's line and page size. In the Win95 Controls App application, the program initializes the trackbar with calls to SetRange(), SetTicFreq(), SetLineSize(), and SetPageSize(), as you saw in Listing 3.3. The call to SetRange() sets the trackbar's minimum and maximum values to 0 and 100. The arguments are the minimum value, the maximum value, and a Boolean value indicating whether the slider should redraw itself after setting the range. Notice the tick frequency and page size are then set to be the same: This isn't absolutely required, but it's a very good idea. Most people assume that the tick marks indicate the size of a page, and you will confuse your users if the tick marks are more or less than a page apart.

Manipulating the Slider

A slider is just a special scrollbar control. When the user moves the slider, the control generates WM_HSCROLL messages, which Win95 Controls App captures in its view class's OnHScroll() member function, as shown in Listing 3.4.

Listing 3.4 Win95View.cpp—*CWin95View::OnHScroll()*

```
void CWin95View::OnHScroll(UINT nSBCode, UINT nPos, CScrollBar* pScrollBar)
{
    CSliderCtrl* slider = (CSliderCtrl*)pScrollBar;
    int position = slider->GetPos();
    char s[10];
    wsprintf(s, "%d    ", position);
    CClientDC clientDC(this);
    clientDC.TextOut(390, 22, s);
    CView::OnHScroll(nSBCode, nPos, pScrollBar);
}
```

Looking at this code, you see that the control itself doesn't display the current position as a number nearby; it's the OnHScroll() function that displays the number. Here's how it works:

1. OnHScroll()'s fourth parameter is a pointer to the scroll object that generated the WM_HSCROLL message.

2. The function first casts this pointer to a CSliderCtrl pointer, then it gets the current position of the trackbar's slider by calling the CSliderCtrl member function GetPos().

3. After the program has the slider's position, it converts the integer to a string and displays that string in the window.

   ▶ **See** "Drawing on the Screen" to learn how to make text appear on the screen, **p. 133**

The Up-Down Control

The trackbar control isn't the only way you can get a value in a predetermined range from the user. If you don't need the trackbar for visual feedback, you can use an up-down control, which is little more than a couple of arrows that the user clicks to increase or decrease the control's setting. Typically an edit control next to the up-down control, called a buddy edit control or just a buddy control, displays the value to the user.

In the Win95 Controls App application, you can change the setting of the up-down control by clicking either of its arrows. When you do, the value in the attached edit box changes, indicating the up-down control's current setting. After the control has the focus, you can also change its value by pressing your keyboard's Up and Down arrow keys.

Creating the Up-Down Control

In the Win95 Controls App application, the up-down control is created in the CreateUpDownCtrl() local member function, which the program calls from the view class's OnCreate() function. In CreateUpDownCtrl(), as shown in Listing 3.5, the program creates the up-down control by first creating the associated *buddy* control to which the up-down control communicates its current value.

Listing 3.5 Win95View.cpp—*CWin95View::CreateUpDownCtrl()*

```
void CWin95View::CreateUpDownCtrl()
{
    m_buddyEdit.Create(WS_CHILD | WS_VISIBLE | WS_BORDER,
        CRect(50, 120, 110, 160), this, IDC_BUDDYEDIT);
    m_upDown.Create(WS_CHILD | WS_VISIBLE | WS_BORDER |
        UDS_ALIGNRIGHT | UDS_SETBUDDYINT | UDS_ARROWKEYS,
        CRect(0, 0, 0, 0), this, IDC_UPDOWN);
    m_upDown.SetBuddy(&m_buddyEdit);
    m_upDown.SetRange(1, 100);
    m_upDown.SetPos(50);
}
```

In most cases, including this one, the buddy control is an edit box, created by calling the CEdit class's Create() member function. This function's four arguments are the control's style flags, the control's size, a pointer to the control's parent window, and the control's ID. If you recall the control declarations, m_buddyEdit is an object of the CEdit class.

Now that the program has created the buddy control, it can create the up-down control in much the same way, by calling the object's Create() member function. As you can probably guess by now, this function's four arguments are the control's style flags, the control's size, a pointer to the control's parent window, and the control's ID. As with most controls, the style constants include the same constants that you use for creating any type of window. The CSpinButtonCtrl class, of which m_upDown is an object, however, defines special styles to be used with up-down controls. Table 3.4 lists these special styles.

Table 3.4 Up-Down Control Styles

Styles	Description
UDS_ALIGNLEFT	Places the up-down control on the left edge of the buddy control
UDS_ALIGNRIGHT	Places the up-down control on the right edge of the buddy control
UDS_ARROWKEYS	Enables the user to change the control's values using the keyboard's Up and Down arrow keys
UDS_AUTOBUDDY	Makes the previous window the buddy control
UDS_HORZ	Creates a horizontal up-down control
UDS_NOTHOUSANDS	Eliminates separators between each set of three digits
UDS_SETBUDDYINT	Displays the control's value in the buddy control
UDS_WRAP	Causes the control's value to wrap around to its minimum when the maximum is reached, and vice versa

After the up-down control is created, it must be initialized. The CSpinButtonCtrl class features member functions that enable you to initialize and manipulate the control, as listed in Table 3.5.

Table 3.5 *CSpinButtonCtrl* Member Functions

Function	Description
Create()	Creates the up-down control
GetAccel()	Gets the control's speed
GetBase()	Gets the control's numerical base
GetBuddy()	Gets a pointer to the control's buddy control
GetPos()	Gets the control's position
GetRange()	Gets the control's minimum and maximum values
SetAccel()	Sets the control's speed
SetBase()	Sets the control's numerical base (10 for decimal, 16 for hex)
SetBuddy()	Sets the control's buddy control
SetPos()	Sets the control's position
SetRange()	Sets the control's minimum and maximum values

This chapter's sample application establishes the up-down control with calls to `SetBuddy()`, `SetRange()`, and `SetPos()`. Thanks to the `UDS_SETBUDDYINT` flag passed to `Create()` and the call to the control's `SetBuddy()` member function, Win95 Controls App does not need to do anything else to have the control's value appear on the screen. The control handles its buddy automatically.

The Image List Control

Often, in programs, you need to use images that are related in some way. For example, your application might have a toolbar with many command buttons, each of which uses a bitmap for its icon. In a case like this, it would be great to have some sort of program object that could not only hold the bitmaps, but also organize them so that they can be accessed easily. That's exactly what an image list control does for you—it stores a list of related images. You can use the images any way that you see fit in your program. Several Windows 95 controls rely on image lists. These controls are:

- List view controls
- Tree view controls
- Property pages
- Toolbars

You will undoubtedly come up with many other uses for image lists. You might, for example, have an animation sequence that you'd like to display in a window. An image list is the perfect storage place for the frames that make up the animation, because you can easily access any frame just by using an index.

If the word *index* makes you think of arrays, you're beginning to understand how an image list stores images. An image list is very similar to an array that holds pictures rather than integers or floating-point numbers. Just as with an array, you initialize each "element" of an image list and thereafter can access any part of the "array" by using an index.

You won't, however, ever see an image list control in your running application in the same way that you can see a status bar or a progress bar control. This is because (again, similar to an array) an image list is only a storage structure for pictures. You can display the images stored in an image list, but you can't display the image list itself. Figure 3.2 shows how an image list is organized.

FIG. 3.2

An image list is much like an array of pictures.

Picture 1   Picture 2   Picture 3   Picture 4   Picture 5

Creating the Image List

In the Win95 Controls App application, image lists are used with the list view and tree view controls, so the image lists for the controls are created in the `CreateListView()` and `CreateTreeView()` local member functions, which the program calls from `CWin95View::OnCreate()`. You'll see those functions shortly, but because they are quite long, this section presents the two function calls that are relevant to the image list. It is created with a call to its `Create()` member function, like this:

```
m_smallImageList.Create(16, 16, FALSE, 1, 0);
```

The `Create()` function's five arguments are:

- The width of the pictures in the control
- The height of the pictures
- A Boolean value indicating whether or not the images contain a mask
- The number of images initially in the list
- The number of images by which the list can dynamically grow

This last value is 0 to indicate that the list is not allowed to grow during runtime. The `Create()` function is overloaded in the `CImageList` class so that you can create image lists in various ways. You can find the other versions of `Create()` in your Visual C++ online documentation.

Initializing the Image List

After you create an image list, you will want to add images to it. After all, an empty image list isn't of much use. The easiest way to add the images is to include the images as part of your application's resource file and load them from there. For example, the following code shows how Win95 Controls App loads an icon into one of its image lists:

```
HICON hIcon = ::LoadIcon (AfxGetResourceHandle(),
    MAKEINTRESOURCE(IDI_ICON1));
m_smallImageList.Add(hIcon);
```

Here, the program first gets a handle to the icon. Then, it adds the icon to the image list by calling the image list's `Add()` member function. You might create these icons by choosing Insert, Resource, double-clicking Icon, and then editing the new blank icon in the Resource Editor.

Table 3.6 lists other member functions you can use to manipulate an object of the `CImageList` class. As you can see, you have a lot of control over an image list if you really want to dig in.

Table 3.6   Member Functions of the *CImageList* Class

Function	Description
Add()	Adds an image to the image list
Attach()	Attaches an existing image list to an object of the CImageList class

Function	Description
BeginDrag()	Starts an image-dragging operation
Create()	Creates an image list control
DeleteImageList()	Deletes an image list
Detach()	Detaches an image list from an object of the CImageList class
DragEnter()	Locks a window for updates and shows the drag image
DragLeave()	Unlocks a window for updates
DragMove()	Moves the drag image
DragShowNolock()	Handles the drag image without locking the window
Draw()	Draws an image that's being dragged
EndDrag()	Ends an image-dragging operation
ExtractIcon()	Creates an icon from an image
GetBkColor()	Gets an image list's background color
GetDragImage()	Gets the image for drag operations
GetImageCount()	Gets the number of images in the control
GetImageInfo()	Gets image information
GetSafeHandle()	Gets an image list's handle
Read()	Gets an image list from the given archive
Remove()	Removes an image from the image list
Replace()	Replaces one image with another
SetBkColor()	Sets an image list's background color
SetDragCursorImage()	Creates an image for drag operations
SetOverlayImage()	Sets the index of an overlay mask
Write()	Writes an image list to the given archive

Part

II

Ch

3

The List View Control

A list view control simplifies the job of building an application that works with lists of objects and organizes those objects in such a way that the program's user can easily determine each object's attributes. For example, consider a group of files on a disk. Each file is a separate object that is associated with a number of attributes including the file's name, size, and the most recent modification date. Windows 95 shows files either as icons in a window or as a table of entries, each entry showing the attributes associated with the files. The user has full control over the way that the file objects are displayed, including which attributes are shown and which are not listed. The Windows 95 common controls include something called a list view control, which enables Windows 95 programmers to organize lists exactly the same way that Windows 95 does with files and other objects.

If you'd like to see an example of a full-fledged list view control, just open the Windows 95 Explorer (see Figure 3.3). The right side of the window shows how the list view control can organize objects in a window. (The left side of the window contains a tree view control, which you learn about later in this chapter, in the section titled "The Tree View Control.") In the figure, the list view is currently set to the report view, in which each object in the list receives its own line showing not only the object's name but also the attributes associated with that object.

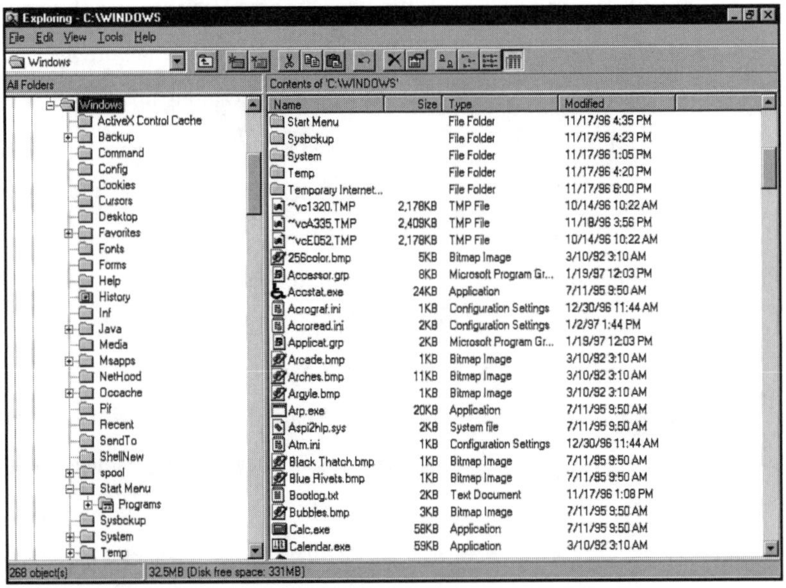

FIG. 3.3
Windows 95 Explorer uses a list view control to organize file information.

The user can change the way objects are organized in a list view control. Figure 3.4, for example, shows the list view portion of the Explorer set to the large-icon setting, whereas Figure 3.5 shows the small-icon setting, which enables the user to see more objects (in this case, files) in the window. With a list view control, the user can edit the names of objects in the list, and in the report view can sort objects based on data displayed in a particular column.

The Win95 Controls App application also sports a list view control, although it's not as fancy as Explorer's. To switch between the small-icon, large-icon, list, and report views, click the appropriate button to the right of the control. Figure 3.1 already showed you the report view for this list view. Figure 3.6 shows the application's list view control displaying small icons, whereas Figure 3.7 shows the large icons.

FIG. 3.4
Here's Explorer's list view control set to large icons.

FIG. 3.5
Here's Explorer's list view control set to small icons.

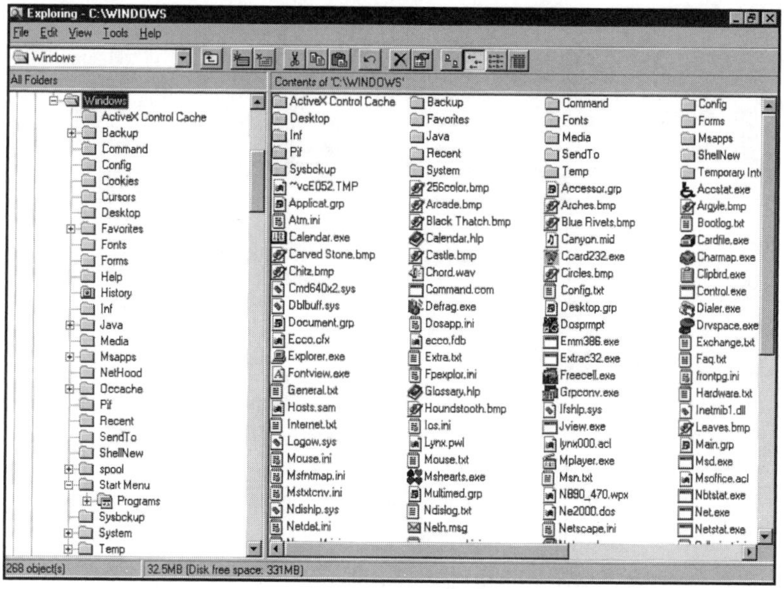

Part

II

Ch

3

FIG. 3.6

Here's the example application's list view control set to small icons.

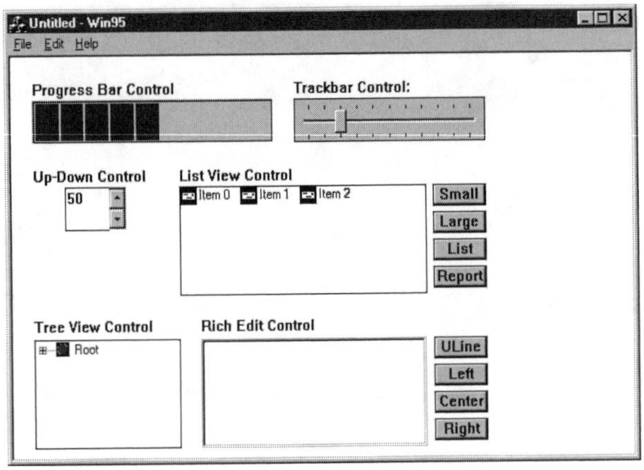

FIG. 3.7

Here's the sample application's list view control set to large icons.

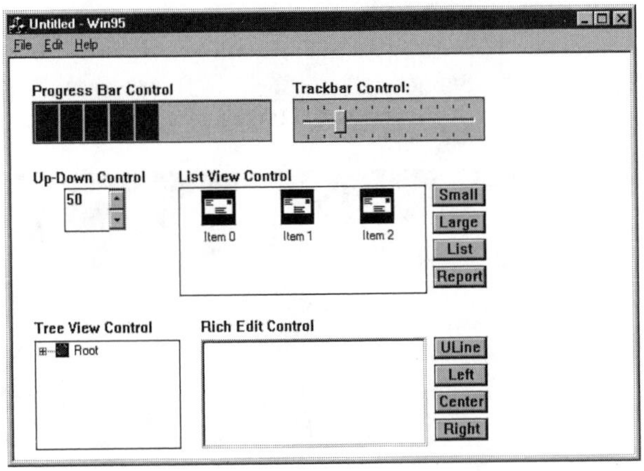

Creating the List View

How does all of this happen? Well, it does require more work than the progress bar, trackbar, or up-down control (it could hardly take less). In the Win95 Controls App application, the list view control is created in the CreateListView() local member function, as shown in Listing 3.6, which the program calls from the view class's OnCreate() function. CreateListView() performs the following tasks:

1. Creates the image list controls

2. Creates the list view control itself

3. Associates the image lists with the list view

4. Creates the columns

5. Sets up the columns

6. Creates the items

7. Sets up the items

8. Creates the buttons

Listing 3.6   Win95View.cpp—*CWin95View::CreateListView()*

```cpp
void CWin95View::CreateListView()
{
    // Create the Image List controls.
    m_smallImageList.Create(16, 16, FALSE, 1, 0);
    m_largeImageList.Create(32, 32, FALSE, 1, 0);
    HICON hIcon = ::LoadIcon (AfxGetResourceHandle(),
        MAKEINTRESOURCE(IDI_ICON1));
    m_smallImageList.Add(hIcon);
    hIcon = ::LoadIcon (AfxGetResourceHandle(),
        MAKEINTRESOURCE(IDI_ICON2));
    m_largeImageList.Add(hIcon);

    // Create the List View control.
    m_listView.Create(WS_VISIBLE | WS_CHILD | WS_BORDER |
        LVS_REPORT | LVS_NOSORTHEADER | LVS_EDITLABELS,
        CRect(160, 120, 394, 220), this, IDC_LISTVIEW);
    m_listView.SetImageList(&m_smallImageList, LVSIL_SMALL);
    m_listView.SetImageList(&m_largeImageList, LVSIL_NORMAL);

    // Create the columns.
    LV_COLUMN lvColumn;
    lvColumn.mask = LVCF_FMT | LVCF_WIDTH | LVCF_TEXT | LVCF_SUBITEM;
    lvColumn.fmt = LVCFMT_CENTER;
    lvColumn.cx = 75;

    lvColumn.iSubItem = 0;
    lvColumn.pszText = "Column 0";
    m_listView.InsertColumn(0, &lvColumn);
    lvColumn.iSubItem = 1;
    lvColumn.pszText = "Column 1";
    m_listView.InsertColumn(1, &lvColumn);
    lvColumn.iSubItem = 2;
    lvColumn.pszText = "Column 2";
    m_listView.InsertColumn(1, &lvColumn);

    // Create the items.
    LV_ITEM lvItem;
    lvItem.mask = LVIF_TEXT | LVIF_IMAGE | LVIF_STATE;
    lvItem.state = 0;
    lvItem.stateMask = 0;
    lvItem.iImage = 0;

    lvItem.iItem = 0;
    lvItem.iSubItem = 0;
    lvItem.pszText = "Item 0";
    m_listView.InsertItem(&lvItem);
    m_listView.SetItemText(0, 1, "Sub Item 0.1");
    m_listView.SetItemText(0, 2, "Sub Item 0.2");
```

continues

Part

II

Ch

3

Listing 3.6 Continued

```
        lvItem.iItem = 1;
        lvItem.iSubItem = 0;
        lvItem.pszText = "Item 1";
        m_listView.InsertItem(&lvItem);
        m_listView.SetItemText(1, 1, "Sub Item 1.1");
        m_listView.SetItemText(1, 2, "Sub Item 1.2");

        lvItem.iItem = 2;
        lvItem.iSubItem = 0;
        lvItem.pszText = "Item 2";
        m_listView.InsertItem(&lvItem);
        m_listView.SetItemText(2, 1, "Sub Item 2.1");
        m_listView.SetItemText(2, 2, "Sub Item 2.2");

        // Create the view-control buttons.
        m_smallButton.Create("Small", WS_VISIBLE | WS_CHILD | WS_BORDER,
            CRect(400, 120, 450, 140), this, IDC_LISTVIEW_SMALL);
        m_largeButton.Create("Large", WS_VISIBLE | WS_CHILD | WS_BORDER,
            CRect(400, 145, 450, 165), this, IDC_LISTVIEW_LARGE);
        m_listButton.Create("List", WS_VISIBLE | WS_CHILD | WS_BORDER,
            CRect(400, 170, 450, 190), this, IDC_LISTVIEW_LIST);
        m_reportButton.Create("Report", WS_VISIBLE | WS_CHILD | WS_BORDER,
            CRect(400, 195, 450, 215), this, IDC_LISTVIEW_REPORT);
}
```

CreateListView() first creates two image lists: one holds the small icon for the list view and the other holds the large icon. (In this case, the list includes only one icon. In other applications, you might have a list of large icons for folders, text files, and so on, plus another list of small icons for the same purposes.)

After creating the image lists, CreateListView() goes on to create the list view control, by calling the class's Create() member function as usual. The CListCtrl class, of which m_listView is an object, defines special styles to be used with list view controls. Table 3.7 lists these special styles and their descriptions.

Table 3.7 List View Styles

Style	Description
LVS_ALIGNLEFT	Left-aligns items in the large-icon and small-icon views
LVS_ALIGNTOP	Top-aligns items in the large-icon and small-icon views
LVS_AUTOARRANGE	Automatically arranges items in the large-icon and small-icon views
LVS_EDITLABELS	Enables the user to edit item labels
LVS_ICON	Sets the control to the large-icon view
LVS_LIST	Sets the control to the list view

Style	Description
LVS_NOCOLUMNHEADER	Shows no column headers in report view
LVS_NOITEMDATA	Stores only the state of each item
LVS_NOLABELWRAP	Disallows multiple-line item labels
LVS_NOSCROLL	Turns off scrolling
LVS_NOSORTHEADER	Turns off the button appearance of column headers
LVS_OWNERDRAWFIXED	Enables owner-drawn items in report view
LVS_REPORT	Sets the control to the report view
LVS_SHAREIMAGELISTS	Prevents the control from destroying its image lists when the control no longer needs them
LVS_SINGLESEL	Disallows multiple selection of items
LVS_SMALLICON	Sets the control to the small-icon view
LVS_SORTASCENDING	Sorts items in ascending order
LVS_SORTDESCENDING	Sorts items in descending order

Part

II

Ch

3

The third task in CreateListView() is to associate the control with its image lists with two calls to SetImageList(). This function takes two parameters: a pointer to the image list and a flag indicating how the list is to be used. There are three constants defined for this flag: LVSIL_SMALL (which indicates that the list contains small icons), LVSIL_NORMAL (large icons), and LVSIL_STATE (state images). The SetImageList() function returns a pointer to the previously set image list, if any.

Creating the List View's Columns

The fourth task is to create the columns for the control's report view. You need one main column for the item itself and one column for each sub-item associated with an item. For example, in Explorer's list view, the main column holds file and folder names. Each additional column holds the sub-items for each item, including the file's size, type, and modification date. To create a column, you must first declare a LV_COLUMN structure. You use this structure to pass information to and from the system. After you add the column to the control with InsertColumn(), you can use the structure to create and insert another column. The LV_COLUMN structure is shown in Listing 3.7.

Listing 3.7 The *LV_COLUMN* Structure, Defined by MFC

```
typedef struct _LV_COLUMN
{
    UINT mask;       // Flags indicating valid fields
    int fmt;         // Column alignment
    int cx;          // Column width
```

continues

Listing 3.7   Continued

```
    LPSTR pszText;      // Address of string buffer
    int cchTextMax;     // Size of the buffer
    int iSubItem;       // Subitem index for this column
} LV_COLUMN;
```

The `mask` member of the structure tells the system which members of the structure to use and which to ignore. The flags you can use are:

- ■ `LVCF_FMT`   `fmt` is valid.
- ■ `LVCF_SUBITEM`   `iSubItem` is valid.
- ■ `LVCF_TEXT`   `pszText` is valid.
- ■ `LVCF_WIDTH`   `cx` is valid.

The `fmt` member denotes the column's alignment and can be `LVCFMT_CENTER`, `LVCFMT_LEFT`, or `LVCFMT_RIGHT`. The alignment determines how the column's label and items are positioned in the column.

> **N O T E**   The first column, which contains the main items, is always aligned to the left. The other columns in the report view can be aligned however you like. ■

The `cx` field specifies the width of each column, whereas `pszText` is the address of a string buffer. When you're using the structure to create a column (you also can use this structure to obtain information about a column), this string buffer contains the column's label. The `cchTextMax` member denotes the size of the string buffer and is valid only when retrieving information about a column.

`CreateListView()` creates a temporary `LV_COLUMN` structure, sets the elements, and then inserts it into the list view as column 0, the main column. This process is repeated for the other two columns.

Creating the List View's Items

The fifth task in `CreateListView()` is to create the items that will be listed in the columns when the control is in its report view. Creating items is not unlike creating columns. As with columns, Visual C++ defines a structure that you must initialize and pass to the function that creates the items. This structure is called `LV_ITEM` and is defined, as shown in Listing 3.8.

Listing 3.8   The *LV_ITEM* Structure, Defined by MFC

```
typedef struct _LV_ITEM
{
    UINT    mask;        // Flags indicating valid fields
    int     iItem;       // Item index
    int     iSubItem;    // Sub-item index
    UINT    state;       // Item's current state
    UINT    stateMask;   // Valid item states.
```

```
    LPSTR   pszText;      // Address of string buffer
    int     cchTextMax;   // Size of string buffer
    int     iImage;       // Image index for this item
    LPARAM  lParam;       // Additional information as a 32-bit value
} LV_ITEM;
```

In the LV_ITEM structure, the mask member specifies the other members of the structure that are valid. The flags you can use are:

- LVIF_IMAGE iImage is valid.
- LVIF_PARAM lParam is valid.
- LVIF_STATE state is valid.
- LVIF_TEXT pszText is valid.

The iItem member is the index of the item, which you can think of as the row number in report view (although the position of the items can change when they're sorted). Each item has a unique index. The iSubItem member is the index of the subitem if this structure is defining a subitem. You can think of this value as the number of the column in which the item will appear. For example, if you're defining the main item (the first column), this value should be 0.

The state and stateMask members hold the item's current state and the item's valid states, which can be one or more of the following:

- LVIS_CUT The item is selected for cut and paste.
- LVIS_DROPHILITED The item is a highlighted drop target.
- LVIS_FOCUSED The item has the focus.
- LVIS_SELECTED The item is selected.

The pszText member is the address of a string buffer. When using the LV_ITEM structure to create an item, the string buffer contains the item's text. When obtaining information about the item, pszText is the buffer where the information will be stored, and cchTextMax is the size of the buffer. If pszText is set to LPSTR_TEXTCALLBACK, the item uses the callback mechanism. Finally, the iImage member is the index of the item's icon in the small icon and large icon image lists. If set to I_IMAGECALLBACK, the iImage member indicates that the item uses the callback mechanism.

CreateListView() creates a temporary LV_ITEM structure, sets the elements, and then inserts it into the list view as item 0. Two calls to SetItemText() add subitems to this item, so that each column has some text in it, and the whole process is repeated for two other items. Now, you have created a list view with three columns and three items. Normally the values would not have been hard-coded as this was, but instead would have been filled in with values calculated by the program.

Manipulating the List View

You can set a list view control to four different types of views: small icon, large icon, list, and report. In Explorer, for example, the toolbar features buttons that you can click to change the view, or you can select the view from the View menu. Although Win95 Controls App doesn't have a snazzy toolbar like Explorer, it does include four buttons (labeled Small, Large, List, and Report) that you can click to change the view. Those buttons are created as the sixth step in CreateListView().

These buttons are associated (by hand-added entries in the view window's message map) with the message-response functions OnSmall(), OnLarge(), OnList(), and OnReport(). As will be explained in Chapter 4, "Messages and Commands," when the user clicks one of these buttons, its matching function is called, and the program changes the list view control to the requested view type. For example, when the user clicks the Small button, OnSmall(), shown in Listing 3.9, changes the view to the small icon view. The other three functions are very similar.

Listing 3.9   Win95View.cpp—*CWin95View::OnSmall()*

```
void CWin95View::OnSmall()
{
    SetWindowLong(m_listView.m_hWnd, GWL_STYLE,
        WS_VISIBLE | WS_CHILD | WS_BORDER |
        LVS_SMALLICON | LVS_EDITLABELS);
}
```

The SetWindowLong() function sets a window's attribute. Its arguments are the window's handle, a flag that specifies the value to be changed, and the new value. In Listing 3.9, the GWL_STYLE flag specifies that the window's style should be changed to the style given in the third argument. Changing the list view control's style (for example, to LVS_SMALLICON) changes the type of view that it displays.

In addition to changing the view, there are a number of other features you can program for your list view controls. When the user does something with the control, Windows sends a WM_NOTIFY message to the parent window. By responding to these notifications, you can give your list view control its various capabilities. The most common notifications sent by a list view control are:

- LVN_COLUMNCLICK   Indicates that the user clicked a column header
- LVN_BEGINLABELEDIT   Indicates that the user is about to edit an item's label
- LVN_ENDLABELEDIT   Indicates that the user is ending the label-editing process

Listing 3.10 shows the OnNotify() function for this sample application.

Listing 3.10   Win95View.cpp—*CWin95View::OnNotify()*

```
BOOL CWin95View::OnNotify(WPARAM wParam, LPARAM lParam, LRESULT* pResult)
{
    LV_DISPINFO* lv_dispInfo = (LV_DISPINFO*) lParam;

    if (lv_dispInfo->hdr.code == LVN_BEGINLABELEDIT)
    {
        CEdit* pEdit = m_listView.GetEditControl();
```

```
        // Manipulate edit control here.
    }
    else if (lv_dispInfo->hdr.code == LVN_ENDLABELEDIT)
    {
        if ((lv_dispInfo->item.pszText != NULL) &&
            (lv_dispInfo->item.iItem != -1))
        {
            m_listView.SetItemText(lv_dispInfo->item.iItem,
                0, lv_dispInfo->item.pszText);
        }
    }

    TV_DISPINFO* tv_dispInfo = (TV_DISPINFO*) lParam;

    if (tv_dispInfo->hdr.code == TVN_BEGINLABELEDIT)
    {
        CEdit* pEdit = m_treeView.GetEditControl();
        // Manipulate edit control here.
    }
    else if (tv_dispInfo->hdr.code == TVN_ENDLABELEDIT)
    {
        if (tv_dispInfo->item.pszText != NULL)
        {
            m_treeView.SetItemText(tv_dispInfo->item.hItem,
                tv_dispInfo->item.pszText);
        }
    }

    return CView::OnNotify(wParam, lParam, pResult);
}
```

The three parameters received by OnNotify() are the message's WPARAM and LPARAM values and a pointer to a result code. In the case of a WM_NOTIFY message coming from a list view control, the WPARAM is the list view control's ID. And, if the WM_NOTIFY message is the LVN_BEGINLABELEDIT or LVN_ENDLABELEDIT notifications, the LPARAM is a pointer to an LV_DISPINFO structure, which itself contains NMHDR and LV_ITEM structures. You use the information in these structures to manipulate the item that the user is trying to edit.

If the notification is LVN_BEGINLABELEDIT, your program can do whatever pre-editing initialization it needs to do, usually by calling GetEditControl() and then working with the pointer returned to you. This sample application only shows you how to get that pointer.

When handling label editing, the other notification to watch out for is LVN_ENDLABELEDIT, which means the user has finished editing the label, either by typing the new label or by canceling the editing process. If the user has canceled the process, the LV_DISPINFO structure's item.pszText member will be NULL or the item.iItem member will be –1. In this case, you need do nothing more than ignore the notification. If, however, the user completed the editing process, the program must copy the new label to the item's text, which OnNotify() does with a call to SetItemText(). The CListCtrl object's SetItemText() member function requires three arguments: the item index, the sub-item index, and the new text.

The second half of this OnNotify() function handles WM_NOTIFY messages coming from the tree view control, to be discussed in the next section.

There are a lot of other things you can do with a list view control. A little time invested in exploring and experimenting can save you a lot of time writing your user interface.

The Tree View Control

In the preceding section, you learned how to use the list view control to organize the display of many items in a window. The list view control enables you to display items both as objects in a window and objects in a report organized into columns. Often, however, the data you'd like to organize for your application's user is best placed in a hierarchical view, where elements of the data are shown as they relate to one other. A good example of such a hierarchical display is the directory tree used by Windows to display directories and the files that they contain.

As is the case with other useful controls, Windows 95 includes the tree view control as one of its common controls. MFC provides access to this control through its CTreeCtrl class. This versatile control enables you to display data in various ways, all the while retaining the hierarchical relationship between the data objects in the view.

If you'd like to see an example of a tree view control, open the Windows 95 Explorer (see Figure 3.8). The left side of the window shows how the tree view control organizes objects in a window. (The right side of the window contains a list view control, which you learned about in the previous section.) In the figure, the tree view displays not only the storage devices on the computer, but also the directories and files stored on those devices. The tree clearly shows the hierarchical relationship between the devices, directories, and files and enables the user to open and close branches on the tree to explore it at different levels.

The Win95 Controls App application also contains a tree view control. You can click the tree's various nodes to expose new levels of the tree. You can even edit the labels of the items in the tree. To do this, select an item and then click it. An edit box appears in which you can type the new label.

Creating the Tree View

In the Win95 Controls App application, the tree view control is created in the CreateTreeView() local member function (see Listing 3.11), called from the view class's OnCreate() function. The steps in CreateTreeView() are as follows:

1. Create an image list
2. Create the tree view itself
3. Associate the image list with the list view
4. Create the root item
5. Create child items

FIG. 3.8

A tree view control displays a hierarchical relationship between items.

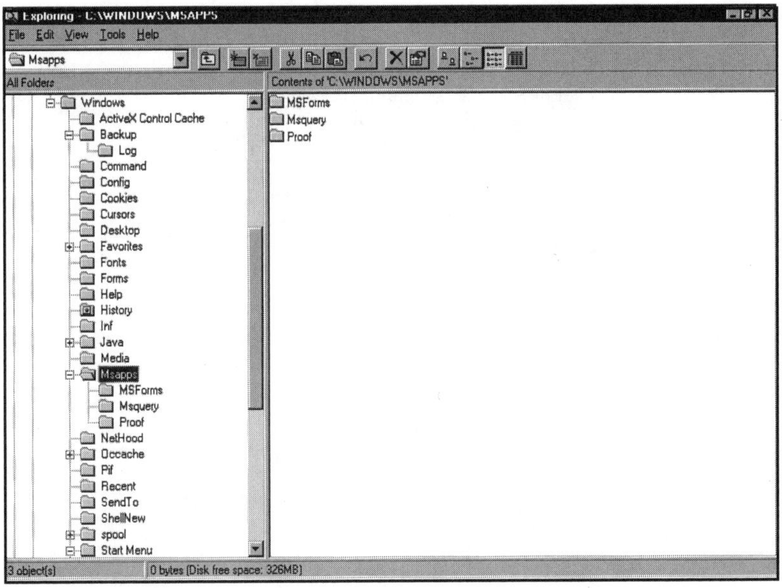

Listing 3.11 Win95View.cpp—_CWin95View:: OnNotify()_

```cpp
void CWin95View::CreateTreeView()
{
    // Create the Image List.
    m_treeImageList.Create(13, 13, FALSE, 3, 0);
    HICON hIcon = ::LoadIcon(AfxGetResourceHandle(),
        MAKEINTRESOURCE(IDI_ICON3));
    m_treeImageList.Add(hIcon);
    hIcon = ::LoadIcon(AfxGetResourceHandle(),
        MAKEINTRESOURCE(IDI_ICON4));
    m_treeImageList.Add(hIcon);
    hIcon = ::LoadIcon(AfxGetResourceHandle(),
        MAKEINTRESOURCE(IDI_ICON5));
    m_treeImageList.Add(hIcon);

    // Create the Tree View control.
    m_treeView.Create(WS_VISIBLE | WS_CHILD | WS_BORDER |
        TVS_HASLINES | TVS_LINESATROOT | TVS_HASBUTTONS |
        TVS_EDITLABELS, CRect(20, 260, 160, 360), this,
        IDC_TREEVIEW);
    m_treeView.SetImageList(&m_treeImageList, TVSIL_NORMAL);

    // Create the root item.
    TV_ITEM tvItem;
    tvItem.mask =
        TVIF_TEXT | TVIF_IMAGE | TVIF_SELECTEDIMAGE;
    tvItem.pszText = "Root";
    tvItem.cchTextMax = 4;
    tvItem.iImage = 0;
```

continues

Listing 3.11 Continued

```
    tvItem.iSelectedImage = 0;
    TV_INSERTSTRUCT tvInsert;
    tvInsert.hParent = TVI_ROOT;
    tvInsert.hInsertAfter = TVI_FIRST;
    tvInsert.item = tvItem;
    HTREEITEM hRoot = m_treeView.InsertItem(&tvInsert);

    // Create the first child item.
    tvItem.pszText = "Child Item 1";
    tvItem.cchTextMax = 12;
    tvItem.iImage = 1;
    tvItem.iSelectedImage = 1;
    tvInsert.hParent = hRoot;
    tvInsert.hInsertAfter = TVI_FIRST;
    tvInsert.item = tvItem;
    HTREEITEM hChildItem = m_treeView.InsertItem(&tvInsert);

    // Create a child of the first child item.
    tvItem.pszText = "Child Item 2";
    tvItem.cchTextMax = 12;
    tvItem.iImage = 2;
    tvItem.iSelectedImage = 2;
    tvInsert.hParent = hChildItem;
    tvInsert.hInsertAfter = TVI_FIRST;
    tvInsert.item = tvItem;
    m_treeView.InsertItem(&tvInsert);

    // Create another child of the root item.
    tvItem.pszText = "Child Item 3";
    tvItem.cchTextMax = 12;
    tvItem.iImage = 1;
    tvItem.iSelectedImage = 1;
    tvInsert.hParent = hRoot;
    tvInsert.hInsertAfter = TVI_LAST;
    tvInsert.item = tvItem;
    m_treeView.InsertItem(&tvInsert);
}
```

Creating the image list, creating the tree control, and associating the control with the image list, are very similar to the steps completed for the image list. The CTreeCtrl class, of which m_treeView is an object, defines special styles to be used with list view controls. Table 3.8 lists these special styles.

Table 3.8 Tree View Control Styles

Style	Description
TVS_DISABLEDRAGDROP	Disables drag-and-drop operations
TVS_EDITLABELS	Enables user to edit labels
TVS_HASBUTTONS	Gives each parent item a button

Style	Description
TVS_HASLINES	Adds lines between items in the tree
TVS_LINESATROOT	Adds a line between the root and child items
TVS_SHOWSELALWAYS	Forces a selected item to stay selected when losing focus

Creating the Tree View's Items

Creating items for a tree view control is much like creating items for a list view control. As with the list view, Visual C++ defines a structure that you must initialize and pass to the function that creates the items. This structure is called TV_ITEM and is defined in Listing 3.12.

On the CD

Listing 3.12   The *TV_ITEM* Structure, Defined by MFC

```
typedef struct _TV_ITEM
{
    UINT        mask;
    HTREEITEM   hItem;
    UINT        state;
    UINT        stateMask;
    LPSTR       pszText;
    int         cchTextMax;
    int         iImage;
    int         iSelectedImage;
    int         cChildren;
    LPARAM      lParam;
} TV_ITEM;
```

In the TV_ITEM structure, the mask member specifies the other members of the structure that are valid. The flags you can use are as follows:

- TVIF_CHILDREN   cChildren is valid.
- TVIF_HANDLE   hItem is valid.
- TVIF_IMAGE   iImage is valid.
- TVIF_PARAM   lParam is valid.
- TVIF_SELECTEDIMAGE   iSelectedImage is valid.
- TVIF_STATE   state and stateMask are valid.
- TVIF_TEXT   pszText and cchTextMax are valid.

The hItem member is the handle of the item, whereas the state and stateMask members hold the item's current state and the item's valid states, which can be one or more of TVIS_BOLD, TVIS_CUT, TVIS_DROPHILITED, TVIS_EXPANDED, TVIS_EXPANDEDONCE, TVIS_FOCUSED, TVIS_OVERLAYMASK, TVIS_SELECTED, TVIS_STATEIMAGEMASK, and TVIS_USERMASK.

The pszText member is the address of a string buffer. When using the LV_ITEM structure to create an item, the string buffer contains the item's text. When obtaining information about the

Part

II

Ch

3

item, pszText is the buffer where the information will be stored, and cchTextMax is the size of the buffer. If pszText is set to LPSTR_TEXTCALLBACK, the item uses the callback mechanism. Finally, the iImage member is the index of the item's icon in the image list. If set to I_IMAGECALLBACK, the iImage member indicates that the item uses the callback mechanism.

The iSelectedImage member is the index of the icon in the image list that represents the item when the item is selected. As with iImage, if this member is set to I_IMAGECALLBACK, the iSelectedImage member indicates that the item uses the callback mechanism. Finally, cChildren specifies whether or not there are child items associated with the item.

In addition to the TV_ITEM structure, you must initialize a TV_INSERTSTRUCT structure that holds information about how to insert the new structure into the tree view control. That structure is declared in Listing 3.13.

Listing 3.13   The *TV_INSERTSTRUCT* Structure, Defined by MFC

```
typedef struct _TV_INSERTSTRUCT
{
    HTREEITEM hParent;
    HTREEITEM hInsertAfter;
    TV_ITEM   item;
} TV_INSERTSTRUCT;
```

In this structure, hParent is the handle to the parent tree-view item. A value of NULL or TVI_ROOT specifies that the item should be placed at the root of the tree. The hInsertAfter member specifies the handle of the item after which this new item should be inserted. It can also be one of the flags TVI_FIRST (beginning of the list), TVI_LAST (end of the list), or TVI_SORT (alphabetical order). Finally, the item member is the TV_ITEM structure containing information about the item to be inserted into the tree.

In Win95 Controls App's CreateTreeView() function, the program initializes the TV_ITEM structure for the root item (the first item in the tree) first. The CTreeCtrl member function InsertItem() actually inserts the item into the tree view control. Its single argument is the address of the TV_INSERTSTRUCT structure.

CreateTreeView() then inserts the remaining items into the tree view control.

Manipulating the Tree View

Just as with the list view control, you can edit the labels of the items in Win95 Controls App's tree view items. Also like the list view control, this process works because the tree view sends WM_NOTIFY messages that trigger a call to the program's OnNotify()function.

As you saw in Listing 3.10, OnNotify() handles the tree view notifications in almost exactly the same way as the list view notifications. The only difference is the names of the structures used.

The tree view control sends a number of other notification messages, including TVN_BEGINDRAG, TVN_BEGINLABELEDIT, TVN_BEGINRDRAG, TVN_DELETEITEM, TVN_ENDLABELEDIT, TVN_GETDISPINFO, TVN_ITEMEXPANDED, TVN_ITEMEXPANDING, TVN_KEYDOWN, TVN_SELCHANGED, TVN_SELCHANGING, and

`TVN_SETDISPINFO`. Check your Visual C++ online documentation for more information about handling these notification messages.

The Rich Edit Control

If you took all the energy that's been expended on writing text-editing software and concentrated that energy on other, less mundane programming problems, computer science would probably be a decade ahead of where it is now. Although that might be an exaggeration, it is true that, when it comes to text editors, a huge amount of effort has been dedicated to reinventing the wheel. Wouldn't it be great to have one piece of text-editing code that all programmers could use as the starting point for their own custom text editors?

With Visual C++'s `CRichEditCtrl` control, which gives programmers access to the Windows 95 rich edit control, you can get a huge jump on any text-editing functionality that you need to install in your applications. The rich edit control is capable of handling fonts, paragraph styles, text color, and other types of tasks that are traditionally found in text editors. In fact, a rich edit control (named for the fact that it handles text in Rich Text Format, RTF) provides a solid starting point for any text-editing tasks that your application must handle. A rich edit control enables the user to perform the following text-editing tasks:

- Type text
- Edit text using cut-and-paste and sophisticated drag-and-drop operations
- Set text attributes such as font, point-size, and color
- Apply underline, bold, italic, strikethrough, superscript, and subscript properties to text
- Format text using various alignments and bulleted lists
- Lock text from further editing
- Save and load files

As you can see, a rich edit control is powerful. It is, in fact, almost a complete word-processor-in-a-box that you can plug into your program and use immediately. Of course, because a rich edit control offers so many features, there's a lot to learn. This section gives you a quick introduction to creating and manipulating a rich edit control.

To get started, try out the rich edit control included in the Win95 Controls App. First, click the text box to give it the focus. Then, just start typing. Want to try out character attributes? Click the ULine button to add underlining to either selected text or the next text you type. To try out paragraph formatting, click either the Left, Center, or Right buttons to specify paragraph alignment. Figure 3.9 shows the rich edit control with some different character and paragraph styles used.

Creating the Rich Edit Control

In the Win95 Controls App application, the rich edit control is created in the `CreateRichEdit()` local member function, as defined in Listing 3.14, called from the view class's `OnCreate()` function.

FIG. 3.9

A rich edit control is almost a complete word processor.

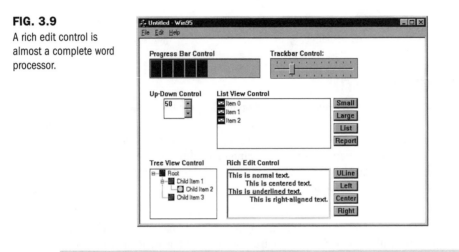

Listing 3.14 Win95View.cpp—CWin95View::CreateRichEdit()

```cpp
void CWin95View::CreateRichEdit()
{
    m_richEdit.Create(WS_CHILD | WS_VISIBLE | WS_BORDER |
        ES_AUTOVSCROLL | ES_MULTILINE,
        CRect(180, 260, 393, 360), this, IDC_RICHEDIT);

    m_boldButton.Create("ULine", WS_VISIBLE | WS_CHILD | WS_BORDER,
        CRect(400, 260, 450, 280), this, IDC_RICHEDIT_ULINE);
    m_leftButton.Create("Left", WS_VISIBLE | WS_CHILD | WS_BORDER,
        CRect(400, 285, 450, 305), this, IDC_RICHEDIT_LEFT);
    m_centerButton.Create("Center", WS_VISIBLE | WS_CHILD | WS_BORDER,
        CRect(400, 310, 450, 330), this, IDC_RICHEDIT_CENTER);
    m_rightButton.Create("Right", WS_VISIBLE | WS_CHILD | WS_BORDER,
        CRect(400, 335, 450, 355), this, IDC_RICHEDIT_RIGHT);
}
```

As usual, things start with a call to the control's `Create()` member function. The style constants include the same constants that you would use for creating any type of window, with the addition of special styles used with rich edit controls. Table 3.9 lists these special styles.

Table 3.9 Rich Edit Styles

Style	Description
ES_AUTOHSCROLL	Automatically scrolls horizontally
ES_AUTOVSCROLL	Automatically scrolls vertically
ES_CENTER	Centers text
ES_LEFT	Left aligns text
ES_LOWERCASE	Lowercases all text

Style	Description
ES_MULTILINE	Enables multiple lines
ES_NOHIDESEL	Doesn't hide selected text when losing the focus
ES_OEMCONVERT	Converts from ANSI characters to OEM characters and back to ANSI
ES_PASSWORD	Displays characters as asterisks
ES_READONLY	Disables editing in the control
ES_RIGHT	Right-aligns text
ES_UPPERCASE	Uppercases all text
ES_WANTRETURN	Inserts return characters into text when enter is pressed

Initializing the Rich Edit Control

After the rich edit control is created, you might want to initialize it in some way. (The Win95 Controls App application doesn't perform additional initialization of the control, and it is perfectly usable as soon as it is created.) The CRichEditCtrl class features a number of member functions that enable you to initialize and manipulate the control. These member functions are described in Table 3.10.

Table 3.10 Member Functions of the CRichEditCtrl Class

Function	Description
CanPaste()	Determines whether or not the Clipboard's contents can be pasted into the control
CanUndo()	Determines whether the last edit can be undone
Clear()	Clears selected text
Copy()	Copies selected text to the Clipboard
Create()	Creates the control
Cut()	Cuts selected text to the Clipboard
DisplayBand()	Displays a portion of the control's text
EmptyUndoBuffer()	Resets the control's undo flag
FindText()	Finds the given text
FormatRange()	Formats text for an output target device
GetCharPos()	Gets the position of a given character
GetDefaultCharFormat()	Gets the default character format

continues

Table 3.10 Continued

Function	Description
GetEventMask()	Gets the control's event mask
GetFirstVisibleLine()	Gets the index of the first visible line
GetIRichEditOle()	Gets the IRichEditOle interface pointer for the control
GetLimitText()	Gets the maximum number of characters that can be entered
GetLine()	Gets the specified text line
GetLineCount()	Gets the number of lines in the control
GetModify()	Determines whether or not the control's contents have changed since the last save
GetParaFormat()	Gets the paragraph format of selected text
GetRect()	Gets the control's formatting rectangle
GetSel()	Gets the position of the currently selected text
GetSelectionCharFormat()	Gets the character format of selected text
GetSelectionType()	Gets the selected text's contents type
GetSelText()	Gets the currently selected text
GetTextLength()	Gets the length of the control's text
HideSelection()	Hides or shows selected text
LimitText()	Sets the maximum number of characters that can be entered
LineFromChar()	Gets the number of the line containing the given character
LineIndex()	Gets the character index of a given line
LineLength()	Gets the length of the given line
LineScroll()	Scrolls the text the given number of lines and characters
Paste()	Pastes the Clipboard's contents into the control
PasteSpecial()	Pastes the Clipboard's contents using the given format
ReplaceSel()	Replaces selected text with the given text
RequestResize()	Forces the control to send EN_REQUESTRESIZE notification messages
SetBackgroundColor()	Sets the control's background color
SetDefaultCharFormat()	Sets the default character format
SetEventMask()	Sets the control's event mask
SetModify()	Toggles the control's modification flag

Function	Description
SetOLECallback()	Sets the control's IRichEditOleCallback COM object
SetOptions()	Sets the control's options
SetParaFormat()	Sets the selection's paragraph format
SetReadOnly()	Disables editing in the control
SetRect()	Sets the control's formatting rectangle
SetSel()	Sets the selected text
SetSelectionCharFormat()	Sets the selected text's character format
SetTargetDevice()	Sets the control's target output device
SetWordCharFormat()	Sets the current word's character format
StreamIn()	Brings text in from an input stream
StreamOut()	Stores text in an output stream
Undo()	Undoes the last edit

Part

II

Ch

3

Manipulating the Rich Edit Control

As you can tell from Table 3.10, you can do a lot more with a rich edit control than can possibly be described in a chapter of this size. This sample application shows you the basics of using the rich edit control, however, by setting character attributes and paragraph formats. When you include a rich edit control in an application, you probably will want to give the user some control over its contents. For this reason, you usually create menu and toolbar commands for selecting the various options that you want to support in the application. Win95 Controls App doesn't have an Options menu or a toolbar. However, it does create four buttons that the user can click to control the rich edit control.

Thanks to MFC's message mapping, these buttons are associated with the functions that respond to them. For example, when the user clicks the ULine button, MFC calls the OnULine() method, as shown in Listing 3.15, which toggles the underline text attribute.

Listing 3.15   Win95View.cpp—CWin95View::OnULine()

```
void CWin95View::OnULine()
{
    CHARFORMAT charFormat;
    charFormat.cbSize = sizeof(CHARFORMAT);
    charFormat.dwMask = CFM_UNDERLINE;
    m_richEdit.GetSelectionCharFormat(charFormat);

    if (charFormat.dwEffects & CFM_UNDERLINE)
        charFormat.dwEffects = 0;
    else
```

continues

Listing 3.15 Continued

```
        charFormat.dwEffects = CFE_UNDERLINE;

    m_richEdit.SetSelectionCharFormat(charFormat);
    m_richEdit.SetFocus();
}
```

`OnULine()` creates and initializes a `CHARFORMAT` structure, which holds information about character formatting and is declared in Listing 3.16.

Listing 3.16 The *CHARFORMAT* Structure, Defined by MFC

```
typedef struct _charformat
{
    UINT     cbSize;
    _WPAD    _wPad1;
    DWORD    dwMask;
    DWORD    dwEffects;
    LONG     yHeight;
    LONG     yOffset;
    COLORREF crTextColor;
    BYTE     bCharSet;
    BYTE     bPitchAndFamily;
    TCHAR    szFaceName[LF_FACESIZE];
    _WPAD    _wPad2;
} CHARFORMAT;
```

In a `CHARFORMAT` structure, `cbSize` is the size of the structure; `dwMask` indicates which members of the structure are valid (can be a combination of `CFM_BOLD`, `CFM_COLOR`, `CFM_FACE`, `CFM_ITALIC`, `CFM_OFFSET`, `CFM_PROTECTED`, `CFM_SIZE`, `CFM_STRIKEOUT`, and `CFM_UNDERLINE`); `dwEffects` is the character effects (can be a combination of `CFE_AUTOCOLOR`, `CFE_BOLD`, `CFE_ITALIC`, `CFE_STRIKEOUT`, `CFE_UNDERLINE`, and `CFE_PROTECTED`); `yHeight` is the character height; `yOffset` is the character baseline offset (for super- and subscript characters); `crTextColor` is the text color; `bCharSet` is the character set value (see the `ifCharSet` member of the `LOGFONT` structure); `bPitchAndFamily` is the font pitch and family; and `szFaceName` is the font name.

After initializing the `CHARFORMAT` structure as needed to toggle underlining, the program calls the control's `GetSelectionCharFormat()` member function. This function, whose single argument is a reference to the `CHARFORMAT` structure, fills the character format structure. `OnULine()` checks the `dwEffects` member of the structure to determine whether to turn underlining on or off. The bitwise and operator, `&`, is used to test a single bit of the variable.

Finally, after setting the character format, the `OnULine()` function returns the focus to the rich edit control. By clicking a button, the user has removed the focus from the rich edit control. You don't want to force the user to keep switching manually back to the control after every button click, so you do it by calling the control's `SetFocus()` member function.

Win95 Controls App also enables the user to switch between the three types of paragraph alignment. This is accomplished similarly to toggling character formats. Listing 3.17 shows the three functions—OnLeft(), OnRight(), and OnCenter()—that handle the alignment commands. As you can see, the main difference is the use of the PARAFORMAT structure instead of CHARFORMAT and the call to SetParaFormat() instead of SetSelectionCharFormat().

Listing 3.17   Win95View.cpp—Changing Paragraph Formats

```cpp
void CWin95View::OnLeft()
{
    PARAFORMAT paraFormat;
    paraFormat.cbSize = sizeof(PARAFORMAT);
    paraFormat.dwMask = PFM_ALIGNMENT;
    paraFormat.wAlignment = PFA_LEFT;
    m_richEdit.SetParaFormat(paraFormat);
    m_richEdit.SetFocus();
}
void CWin95View::OnCenter()
{
    PARAFORMAT paraFormat;
    paraFormat.cbSize = sizeof(PARAFORMAT);
    paraFormat.dwMask = PFM_ALIGNMENT;
    paraFormat.wAlignment = PFA_CENTER;
    m_richEdit.SetParaFormat(paraFormat);
    m_richEdit.SetFocus();
}
void CWin95View::OnRight()
{
    PARAFORMAT paraFormat;
    paraFormat.cbSize = sizeof(PARAFORMAT);
    paraFormat.dwMask = PFM_ALIGNMENT;
    paraFormat.wAlignment = PFA_RIGHT;
    m_richEdit.SetParaFormat(paraFormat);
    m_richEdit.SetFocus();
}
```

Part
II

Ch
3

From Here...

Using the Windows 95 common controls is a huge subject that deserves a book of its own. This chapter has given you an introduction, so that you can explore the controls further. For more information on related topics, try the following chapters in this book:

- Chapter 4, "Messages and Commands," discusses how MFC routes the messages that the various Windows controls and devices generate.

- Chapter 6, "Drawing on the Screen," shows you how to display data and graphics in a window.

- Chapter 10, "Status Bars and Toolbars," describes other ways your application can communicate with its users.

- Chapter 12, "Property Pages and Sheets and Wizards," shows you how to program these special types of dialog boxes.

CHAPTER 4

Messages and Commands

If there is one thing that sets Windows programming apart from other kinds of programming, it is messages. Most DOS programs, for example, relied on watching (sometimes called *polling*) possible sources of input like the keyboard or the mouse to await input from them. A program that wasn't polling the mouse would not react to mouse input. In contrast, everything that happens in a Windows program is mediated by messages. A message is a way for the operating system to tell an application that something has happened—for example, the user has typed, clicked, or moved the mouse, or the printer has become available. A window (and every screen element is a window) can also send a message to another window, and typically most windows react to messages by passing a slightly different message along to another window. MFC has made it much easier to deal with messages, but you must understand what is going on beneath the surface. ■

Message routing

Windows messages direct your program to perform all the things that it does.

Message loops

In Windows C programming, developers write loops to deal with a steady stream of messages.

Message maps

MFC lightens your conceptual load by letting you catch messages without writing a message loop.

How ClassWizard helps you catch messages

Message map entries are easier to add with ClassWizard.

What messages Windows can generate

There are nearly 900 Windows messages.

Messages versus commands

A command can be routed to parts of your function that can't receive messages.

The command update mechanism

You can gray some menu items to reflect the current state of your application.

Message Routing

Messages are all referred to by their names, though the operating system uses integers to refer to them. An enormous list of #define statements connects names to numbers and lets Windows programmers talk about WM_PAINT or WM_SIZE or whatever message they need to talk about. (The WM stands for Window Message.) As well as a name, a message knows what window it is for, and can have up to two parameters. (Often several different values are packed into these parameters, but that's another story.)

Different messages are handled by different parts of the operating system or your application. For example, when the user moves the mouse over a window, the window gets a WM_MOUSEMOVE message, which it almost certainly passes to the operating system to deal with. The operating system redraws the mouse cursor at the new location. When the left button is clicked over a button, the button (which is a window) gets a WM_LBUTTONDOWN message, and handles it, often generating another message to the window that contains the button, saying, in effect, "I was clicked."

MFC has allowed many programmers to completely ignore low-level messages like WM_MOUSEMOVE and WM_LBUTTONDOWN. Instead, programmers deal only with higher-level messages that mean things like "The third item in this list box has been selected" or "The Submit button has been clicked." These kinds of messages move around in your code and the operating system code in the same way as the lower-level messages. The only difference is what piece of code "chooses" to handle them. MFC makes it much simpler to announce, at the individual classes level, which messages each class can handle. The old C way, which you will see in the next section, made those announcements at a higher level and interfered with the object-oriented approach to Windows programming, which involves hiding implementation details as much as possible inside objects.

Message Loops

The heart of any Windows program is the message loop, typically contained in a WinMain() routine. The WinMain() routine is, like the main() in DOS or UNIX, the function called by the operating system when you run the program. You won't write any WinMain() routines because it is now hidden away in the code that AppWizard generates for you. Still, there is a WinMain(), just as there is in Windows C programs. Listing 4.1 shows a typical WinMain().

Listing 4.1   Typical *WinMain()* Routine

```
int APIENTRY WinMain(HINSTANCE hInstance,
                HINSTANCE hPrevInstance,
                LPSTR lpCmdLine,
                int nCmdShow)
    {
```

```
    MSG msg;
    if (! InitApplication (hInstance))
     return (FALSE);

    if (! InitInstance (hInstance, nCmdShow))
     return (FALSE);

    while (GetMessage (&msg, NULL, 0, 0)){
     TranslateMessage (&msg);
     DispatchMessage (&msg);
    }
    return (msg.wParam);
}
```

In a Windows C program like this, InitApplication() typically calls RegisterWindow(), and InitInstance() typically calls CreateWindow(). (More details on this are in Appendix A, "Windows Programming Review and a Look Inside Cwnd.") Then comes the message loop, the while loop that calls GetMessage(). The API function GetMessage() fills msg with a message destined for this application and almost always returns True, so this loop runs over and over until the program is finished. The only thing that makes GetMessage() return False is if the message it gets is WM_QUIT.

TranslateMessage() is an API function that streamlines dealing with keyboard messages. Most of the time, you don't need to know "the A key just went down" or "the A key just went up," and so on. It's enough to know "the user pressed A." TranslateMessage() deals with that. It catches the WM_KEYDOWN and WM_KEYUP messages, and usually sends a WM_CHAR message in their place. Of course, with MFC, most of the time you don't care that the user pressed A. The user types into an edit box or similar control, and you can get the entire string out of it later, when the user has clicked OK. So don't worry too much about TranslateMessage().

The API function DispatchMessage() calls the WndProc for the window that the message is headed for. The WndProc for a Windows C function is a huge switch statement with one case for each message the programmer planned to catch, like the one in Listing 4.2.

Part

II

Ch

4

Listing 4.2 Typical *WndProc()* Routine

```
LONG APIENTRY MainWndProc (HWND hWnd, // window handle
                    UINT message, // type of message
                    UINT wParam, // additional information
                    LONG lParam) // additional information
{
    switch (message) {
     case WM_MOUSEMOVE:
         //handle mouse movement
     break;
```

continues

Listing 4.2   Continued

```
case WM_LBUTTONDOWN:
    //handle left click
break;

case WM_RBUTTONDOWN:
    //handle right click
break;

case WM_PAINT:
    //repaint the window
break;

case WM_DESTROY: // message: window being destroyed
PostQuitMessage (0);
break;

default:
return (DefWindowProc (hWnd, message, wParam, lParam));
}

return (0);
}
```

As you can imagine, these WndProcs get very long in a hurry. Program maintenance can be a nightmare. MFC solves this problem by keeping information about message processing close to the functions that handle the messages, freeing you from maintaining a giant switch statement that is all in one place. Read on to see how it's done.

Message Maps

Message maps are part of the MFC approach to Windows programming. Instead of writing a WinMain() function that sends messages to your WindProc, and then writing a WindProc that checks which kind of message this is and then calls another of your functions, you just write the function that will handle the message, and add a message map to your class that says, in effect, "I will handle this sort of message." The framework handles whatever routing is required to get that message to you.

 TIP If you've worked in Microsoft Visual Basic, you should be familiar with event procedures, which handle specific events like a mouse click. The message-handling functions you will write in C++ are equivalent to event procedures. The message map is the way that events are connected to their handlers.

Message maps come in two parts: one in the .h file for a class and one in the corresponding .cpp. Typically, they are generated by wizards, although in some circumstances you will add entries yourself. Listing 4.3 shows the message map from the header file of one of the classes in a simple application called ShowString, presented in Chapter 9, "Building a Complete Application: ShowString."

Listing 4.3   Message Map from showstring.h

```
//{{AFX_MSG(CShowStringApp)
    afx_msg void OnAppAbout();
        // NOTE - the ClassWizard will add and remove member functions here.
        //    DO NOT EDIT what you see in these blocks of generated code !
    //}}AFX_MSG
    DECLARE_MESSAGE_MAP()
```

This declares a function called OnAppAbout(). The specially formatted comments around the declarations help ClassWizard keep track of which messages are caught by each class. DECLARE_MESSAGE_MAP() is a macro, expanded by the C++ compiler's preprocessor, that declares some variables and functions to set up some of this magic message catching.

The message map in the source file, as shown in Listing 4.4, is quite similar.

Listing 4.4   Message Map from Chapter 10's showstring.cpp

```
BEGIN_MESSAGE_MAP(CShowStringApp, CWinApp)
    //{{AFX_MSG_MAP(CShowStringApp)
    ON_COMMAND(ID_APP_ABOUT, OnAppAbout)
        // NOTE - the ClassWizard will add and remove mapping macros here.
        //    DO NOT EDIT what you see in these blocks of generated code!
    //}}AFX_MSG_MAP
    // Standard file based document commands
    ON_COMMAND(ID_FILE_NEW, CWinApp::OnFileNew)
    ON_COMMAND(ID_FILE_OPEN, CWinApp::OnFileOpen)
    // Standard print setup command
    ON_COMMAND(ID_FILE_PRINT_SETUP, CWinApp::OnFilePrintSetup)
END_MESSAGE_MAP()
```

Part
II

Ch
4

Message Map Macros

BEGIN_MESSAGE_MAP and END_MESSAGE_MAP are macros that, like DECLARE_MESSAGE_MAP in the include file, declare some member variables and functions that the framework can use to navigate the maps of all the objects in the system. There are a number of macros used in message maps, including these:

- DECLARE_MESSAGE_MAP—Used in the include file to declare that there will be a message map in the source file.

- BEGIN MESSAGE MAP—Marks the beginning of a message map in the source file.

- END MESSAGE MAP—Marks the end of a message map in the source file.

- ON_COMMAND—Used to delegate the handling of a specific command to a member function of the class.

- ON_COMMAND_RANGE—Used to delegate the handling of a group of commands, expressed as a range of command IDs, to a single member function of the class.

- ■ ON_CONTROL—Used to delegate the handling of a specific custom-control-notification message to a member function of the class.

- ■ ON_CONTROL_RANGE—Used to delegate the handling of a group of custom-control-notification messages, expressed as a range of control IDs, to a single member function of the class.

- ■ ON_MESSAGE—Used to delegate the handling of a user-defined message to a member function of the class.

- ■ ON_REGISTERED_MESSAGE—Used to delegate the handling of a registered user-defined message to a member function of the class.

- ■ ON_UPDATE_COMMAND_UI—Used to delegate the updating for a specific command to a member function of the class.

- ■ ON_COMMAND_UPDATE_UI_RANGE—Used to delegate the updating for a group of commands, expressed as a range of command IDs, to a single member function of the class.

- ■ ON_NOTIFY—Used to delegate the handling of a specific control-notification message with extra data to a member function of the class.

- ■ ON_NOTIFY_RANGE—Used to delegate the handling of a group of control-notification messages with extra data, expressed as a range of child identifiers, to a single member function of the class. The controls that send these notifications are child windows of the window that catches them.

- ■ ON_NOTIFY_EX—Used to delegate the handling of a specific control-notification message with extra data to a member function of the class that returns TRUE or FALSE to indicate if the notification should be passed on to another object for further reaction.

- ■ ON_NOTIFY_EX_RANGE—Used to delegate the handling of a group of control-notification messages with extra data, expressed as a range of child identifiers, to a single member function of the class that returns TRUE or FALSE to indicate if the notification should be passed on to another object for further reaction. The controls that send these notifications are child windows of the window that catches them.

In addition to these, there are about 100 macros, one for each of the more common messages, that direct a single specific message to a member function. For example, ON_CREATE delegates the WM_CREATE message to a function called OnCreate(). You cannot change the function names in these macros. Typically, these macros are added to your message map by ClassWizard, as demonstrated in Chapter 9, "Building a Complete Application: ShowString."

How Message Maps Work

The message maps presented in Listings 4.3 and 4.4 are for the CShowStringApp class of the ShowString application. This class handles application-level tasks like opening a new file or displaying the About box. The entry added to the header file's message map can be read as "there is a function called OnAppAbout() that takes no parameters." The entry in the source file's map means "when an ID_APP_ABOUT command message arrives, call OnAppAbout()." It shouldn't be a big surprise that the OnAppAbout() member function displays the About box for the application.

But how do message maps really work? Every application has an object that inherits from `CWinApp`, and has a member function called `Run()`. That function calls `CWinThread::Run()`, which is far longer than the simple `WinMain()` presented earlier, but has the same message loop at its heart: call `GetMessage()`, call `TranslateMessage()`, and call `DispatchMessage()`. Almost every window object uses the same old-style windows class, and the same `WindProc`, called `AfxWndProc()`. The `WindProc`, as you've already seen, knows the handle, `hWnd`, of the window the message is for. MFC keeps something called a handle map, a table of window handles and pointers to objects, and the framework uses this to get a pointer to the C++ object, a `CWnd*`. Next, it calls `WindowProc()`, a virtual function of that object. Buttons or views might have different `WindowProc()` implementations, but through the magic of polymorphism, the right function gets called.

Polymorphism

Virtual functions and polymorphism are important C++ concepts for anyone working with MFC. They only arise when you are using pointers to objects, and when the class of objects to which the pointers are pointing is derived from another class. Consider as an example a class called `CDerived` that is derived from a base class called `CBase`, with a member function called `Function()` that is declared in the base class and overridden in the derived class. There are now two functions: one has the full name `CBase::Function()` and the other is `CDerived::Function()`.

If your code has a pointer to a base object, and sets that pointer equal to the address of the derived object, it can then call the function, like this:

```
CDerived derivedobject;
CBase* basepointer;
basepointer = &derivedobject;
basepointer->Function();
```

In this case, `CBase::Function()` will be called. But there are times when that is not what you want, when you have to use a `CBase` pointer but you really want `CDerived::Function()` to be called. To indicate this, in `CBase`, `Function()` is declared to be virtual. Think of it as an instruction to the compiler to override this function if there is any way to do it.

Once `Function()` is declared to be virtual in the base class, `CBase`, the code fragment above would actually call `CDerived::Function()` as desired. That's polymorphism, and that shows up again and again when using MFC classes. You use a pointer to a window, a `CWnd*`, that really points to a `CButton` or a `CView` or some other class derived from `CWnd`, and when a function like `WindowProc()` is called, it will be the derived function, `CButton::WindowProc()` for example, that is called.

`WindowProc()` calls `OnWndMsg()`, the C++ function that really handles messages. First, it checks to see if this is a message, a command, or a notification. Assuming it's a message, it looks in the message map for the class, using the member variables and functions that were set up by

DECLARE_MESSAGE_MAP, BEGIN_MESSAGE_MAP, and END_MESSAGE_MAP. Part of what those macros arrange is to allow access to the message map entries of the base class by the functions that search the message map of the derived class. That means if a class inherits from CView, and doesn't catch a message normally caught by CView, then that message will still be caught by the same CView function as inherited by the derived class. This message map inheritance parallels the C++ inheritance but is independent of it, and saves a lot of trouble carrying virtual functions around.

The bottom line: You add a message map entry and when a message arrives, the functions called by the hidden message loop look in these tables to decide which of your objects, and which member function of the object, should handle the message. That's what's really going on behind the scenes.

Messages Caught by MFC Code

The other great advantage of MFC is that the classes already catch most of the common messages and do the right thing, without any coding on your part at all. For example, you don't need to catch the message that tells you that the user has chosen File, Save As—MFC classes catch it, put up the dialog box to get the new file name, handle all the behind-the-scenes work, and finally call one of your functions, which must be named Serialize(), to actually write out the document. (App Wizard typically makes an empty Serialize() function for you to fill in.) You only need to add message map entries for behavior that is not common to all applications.

ClassWizard Helps You to Catch Messages

Message maps may not be simple to read, but they are simple to create if you use ClassWizard. There are two ways to add an entry to a message map in Visual C++ 5.0: with the main ClassWizard dialog box, or with one of the new dialog boxes that add message handlers or virtual functions.

The ClassWizard Tabbed Dialog Box

The main ClassWizard dialog box is displayed by choosing View, ClassWizard or by pressing Ctrl+W. ClassWizard is a tabbed dialog box, and Figure 4.1 shows the Message Maps tab. At the top of the dialog box are two drop-down list boxes, one that reminds you which project you are working on (ShowString in this case) and the other that reminds you which class owns the message map you are editing. In this case, it is the CShowStringApp class, whose message map you have already seen.

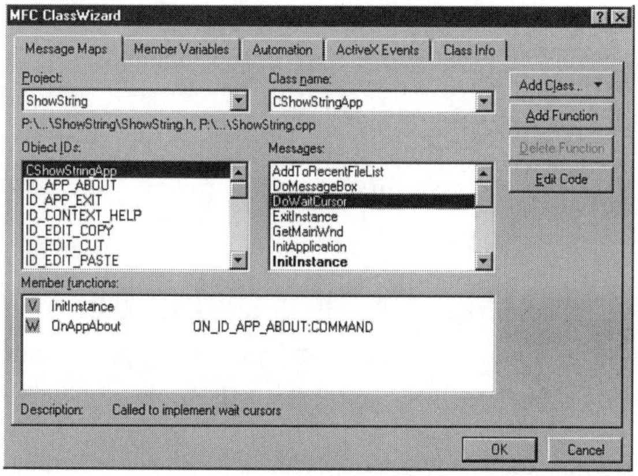

FIG. 4.1

ClassWizard makes catching messages simple.

Below those single line boxes are a pair of multi-line boxes. The one on the left lists the class itself and all the commands that the user interface can generate. Commands are discussed in the "Commands" section later in this chapter. With the class name highlighted, the box on the right lists all the Windows messages this class might catch. It also lists a number of virtual functions that catch common messages.

To the right of those boxes are buttons where you can add a new class to the project, add a function to the class to catch the highlighted message, remove a function that was catching a message, or open the source code for the function that catches the highlighted message. Typically, you select a class, select a message, and click Add Function to catch the message. Here's what the Add Function button sets in motion:

- Adds a skeleton function to the bottom of the source file for the application.
- Adds an entry to the message map in the source file.
- Adds an entry to the message map in the include file.
- Updates the list of messages and member functions in the dialog box.

After you add a function, clicking Edit Code makes it simple to start filling in the behavior of that function. If you prefer, double-click the function name in the Member Functions list box.

Below the Object IDs and Messages boxes is a list of the member functions of this class that are related to messages. This class has two such functions:

- OnAppAbout()—Catches the ID_APP_ABOUT command, and is labeled with a W (for Windows message) in the list.
- InitInstance()—Overrides a virtual function in CWinApp, the base class for CShowStringApp, and is labeled with a V (for virtual function) in the list.

Part
II

Ch
4

The InitInstance function is called whenever an application first starts. You do not need to understand this function to see that ClassWizard reminds you the function has been overridden.

Finally, under the Member Functions box is a reminder of the meaning of the highlighted message. Called to implement wait cursors is a description of the DoWaitCursor virtual function.

The Add Windows Message Handler Dialog Box

In release 5.0 of Visual C++, a new way of catching messages was added. Rather than bringing up ClassWizard and then remembering to set the right class name in a drop-down list box, you right-click the class name in ClassView, and then choose Add Windows Message Handler from the shortcut menu that appears. Figure 4.2 shows the dialog box that comes up when you make this choice.

FIG. 4.2

The New Windows Message and Event Handlers dialog box is another way to catch messages.

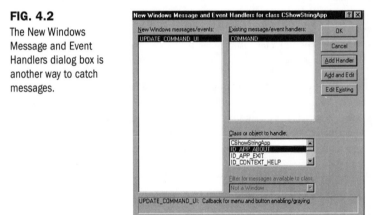

This dialog box does not show any of the virtual functions that were listed in the main ClassView dialog box. It is easy to see that this class catches the command ID_APP_ABOUT but does not catch the command update. (Commands and command updating are discussed in more detail later in this chapter.) To add a new virtual function, you right-click the class in ClassView and choose Add New Virtual Function from the shortcut menu. Figure 4.3 shows this dialog box.

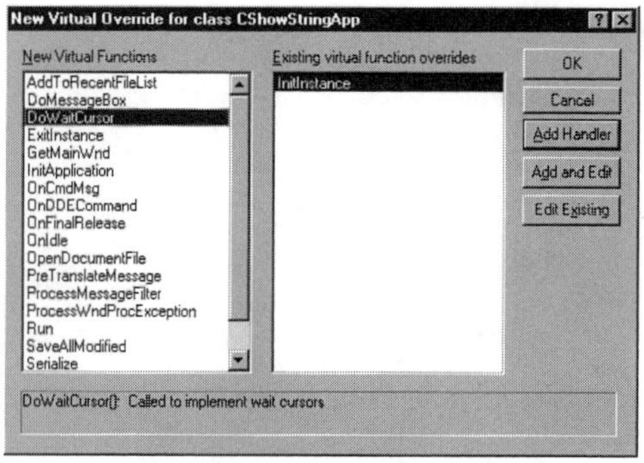

FIG. 4.3
The New Virtual
Override dialog box
simplifies implementing
virtual functions.

You can see in Figure 4.3 that CShowStringApp already overrides the InitInstance() virtual function, and you can see what other functions are available to be overridden. As in the tabbed dialog box, a message area at the bottom of the dialog box reminds you of the purpose of each function: In fact the text—called to implement wait cursors—is identical to that in Figure 4.1.

Which Class Should Catch the Message?

The only tricky part of message maps and message handling is deciding which class should catch the message. That's a decision you can't make until you understand all the different message and command targets that make up a typical application. The choice is usually among the following:

- The active view
- The document associated with the active view
- The frame window that holds the active view
- The application object

Views, documents, and frames are discussed in the next chapter, "Documents and Views."

List of Messages

There are almost 900 Windows messages, so you won't find a list of them all in this chapter. Usually, you arrange to catch messages with ClassWizard, and are presented with a much shorter list that is appropriate for the class you are catching messages with. Not every kind of window can receive every kind of message. For example, only classes that inherit from CListBox receive list box messages like LB_SETSEL, which directs the list box to move the highlight to a specific list item. The first component of a message name indicates the kind of window this message is destined for, or coming from. These window types are listed in Table 4.1.

Part
II

Ch
4

Table 4.1   Windows Message Prefixes and Window Types

Prefix	Window Type
ABM, ABN	Appbar
ACM, ACN	Animation control
BM, BN	Button
CB, CBN	Combo box
CDM, CDN	Common dialog box
CPL	Control Panel application
DBT	Any application (device change message)
DL	Drag list box
DM	Dialog box
EM, EN	Edit box
FM, FMEVENT	File Manager
HDM, HDN	Header control
HKM	HotKey control
IMC, IMN	IME window
LB, LBN	List box
LVM, LVN	List view
NM	Any parent window (notification message)
PBM	Progress bar
PBT	Any application (battery power broadcast)
PSM, PSN	Property sheet
SB	Status bar
SBM	Scroll bar
STM, STN	Static control
TB, TBN	Tool bar
TBM	Track bar
TCM, TCN	Tab control
TTM, TTN	ToolTip
TVM, TVN	Tree view
UDM	Up Down control
WM	Generic window

What's the difference between, say, a BM message and a BN message? A BM message is a message to a button, such as "act as though you were just clicked." A BN message is a notification from a button to the window that owns it, such as "I was clicked." The same pattern holds for all the prefixes that end with M or N in the preceding table.

Sometimes the "message" prefix does not end with M; for example CB is the prefix for a message to a combo box while CBN is the prefix for a notification from a combo box to the window that owns it. For example, CB_SETCURSEL is a message to a combo box directing it to select one of its strings, while CBN_SELCHANGE is a message sent from a combo box notifying its parent that the user has changed which string is selected.

Commands

What is a command? It is a special type of message. Windows generates a command whenever a user chooses a menu item, clicks a button, or otherwise tells the system to do something. In older versions of Windows, both menu choices and button clicks generated a WM_COMMAND message; these days you get a WM_COMMAND for a menu choice and a WM_NOTIFY for a control notification like button clicking or list box selecting. Commands and notifications get passed around by the operating system just like any other message, until they get into the top of OnWndMsg(). At that point, Windows message passing stops and MFC command routing starts.

Command messages all have, as their first parameter, the resource ID of the menu item that was chosen or the button that was clicked. These resource IDs are assigned according to a standard pattern—for example, the menu item File, Save has the resource ID ID_FILE_SAVE.

Command routing is the mechanism OnWndMsg() uses to send the command (or notification) to objects that can't receive messages. Only objects that inherit from CWnd can receive messages, but all objects that inherit from CCmdTarget, including CWnd and CDocument, can receive commands and notifications. That means a class that inherits from CDocument can have a message map. There won't be any entries in it for messages, only for commands and notifications, but it's still called a message map.

How do the commands and notifications get to the class, though? By command routing. (This gets messy, so if you don't want the inner details, skip this paragraph and the next.) OnWndMsg() calls CWnd::OnCommand() or CWnd::OnNotify(). OnCommand() checks all sorts of petty stuff (like whether this menu item was grayed after the user selected it but before this piece of code started to execute) and then calls OnCmdMsg(). OnNotify() checks different conditions and then it, too, calls OnCmdMsg(). OnCmdMsg() is virtual, which means that different command targets have different implementations. The implementation for a frame window sends the command to the views and documents it contains.

This is how something that started out as a message can end up being handled by a member function of an object that is not a window, and therefore can't really catch messages.

Should you care about this? Even if you don't care how it all happens, you should care that you can arrange for the right class to handle whatever happens within your application. If the user resizes the window, a WM_SIZE message is sent, and you may have to rescale an image or do some other work inside your view. If the user chooses a menu item, a command is generated, and that means your document can handle it if that's more appropriate. You see examples of these decisions at work in the next chapter, "Documents and Views."

Command Updates

This under-the-hood tour of just how MFC connects user actions like window resizing or menu choices to your code is almost complete. All that's left is to handle the graying of menus and buttons, a process called *command updating*.

Imagine you are designing an operating system, and you know it's a good idea to have some menu items grayed to show they can't be used right now. There are two ways you can go about implementing this.

One is to have a huge table with one entry for every menu item, and a flag to indicate whether it's available or not. Whenever you have to display the menu, you can quickly check the table. Whenever the program does anything that makes the item available or unavailable, it updates the table. This is called the *continuous-update approach*.

The other way is not to have a table, but to check all the conditions just before your program displays the menu. This is called the *update-on-demand approach* and is the approach taken in Windows. In the old C way of doing things—to check whether each menu option should be grayed or not—the system sent a WM_INITMENUPOPUP message, which means "I'm about to display a menu." The giant switch in the WindProc caught that message and quickly enabled or disabled each menu item. This wasn't very object-oriented though. In an object-oriented program, different pieces of information are stored in different objects and are not generally made available to the entire program.

When it comes to updating menus, different objects "know" whether or not each item should be grayed. For example, the document knows whether it has been modified since it was last saved, so it can decide whether File, Save should be grayed or not; but, only the view knows whether or not some text is currently highlighted; therefore, it can decide if Edit, Cut and Edit, Copy should be grayed. This means that the job of updating these menus should be parcelled out to various objects within the application rather than handled within the WindProc.

The MFC approach is to use a little object called a CCmdUI, a command user interface, and give this object to whomever catches a CN_UPDATE_COMMAND_UI message. You catch those messages by adding (or getting ClassWizard to add) an ON_UPDATE_COMMAND_UI macro in your message map. If you want to know what's going on behind the scenes, it's this: The operating system still sends WM_INITMENUPOPUP, then the MFC base classes like CFrameWnd take over. They make a CCmdUI, set its member variables to correspond to the first menu item, and call one of that object's own member functions, DoUpdate(). Then, DoUpdate() sends out the CN_COMMAND_UPDATE_UI message with a pointer to itself as the CCmdUI object the handlers use. Then the same CCmdUI object is reset to correspond to the second menu item, and so on, until the entire menu is ready to be displayed. The CCmdUI object is also used to gray and ungray buttons and other controls in a slightly different context.

CCmdUI has the following member functions:

- `Enable()`—Takes a True or False (defaults to True). Grays the user interface item if False; makes it available if True.
- `SetCheck()`—Checks or unchecks the item.
- `SetRadio()`—Checks or unchecks the item as part of a group of radio buttons, only one of which can be set at any time.
- `SetText()`—Sets the menu text or button text, if this is a button.
- `DoUpdate()`—Generates the message.

It's usually pretty straightforward to determine which member function you want to use. Here is a shortened version of the message map from an object called `CWhoisView`, a class derived from `CFormView` that is showing information to a user. This form view contains several edit boxes and the user may wish to paste text into one of them. The message map contains an entry to catch the update for the `ID_EDIT_PASTE` command, like this:

```
BEGIN_MESSAGE_MAP(CWhoisView, CFormView)
    ...
    ON_UPDATE_COMMAND_UI(ID_EDIT_PASTE, OnUpdateEditPaste)
    ...
END_MESSAGE_MAP()
```

The function that catches the update, `OnUpdateEditPaste()`, looks like this:

```
void CWhoisView::OnUpdateEditPaste(CCmdUI* pCmdUI)
{
 pCmdUI->Enable(::IsClipboardFormatAvailable(CF_TEXT));
}
```

This calls the API function `::IsClipboardFormatAvailable()` to see if there is text in the Clipboard. Other applications may be able to paste in images or other non-text Clipboard contents, but this application cannot, and grays the menu item if there is no text available to paste. Most command update functions look just like this: They call `Enable()` with a parameter that is a call to a function that returns True or False, or perhaps a simple logical expression. Command update handlers must be fast, because five to ten of them must run from the moment the user clicks to display the menu to before the menu is actually displayed.

ClassWizard Helps You Catch Commands and Command Updates

The ClassWizard dialog box shown in Figure 4.1 has the class name highlighted in the box labeled Object IDs. Below that are resource IDs of every resource (menu, toolbar, dialog box controls, and so on) that can generate a command or message when this object (view, dialog, and so on) is on the screen. If you highlight one of those, the list of messages associated with it is much smaller, as you see in Figure 4.4.

Part

II

Ch

4

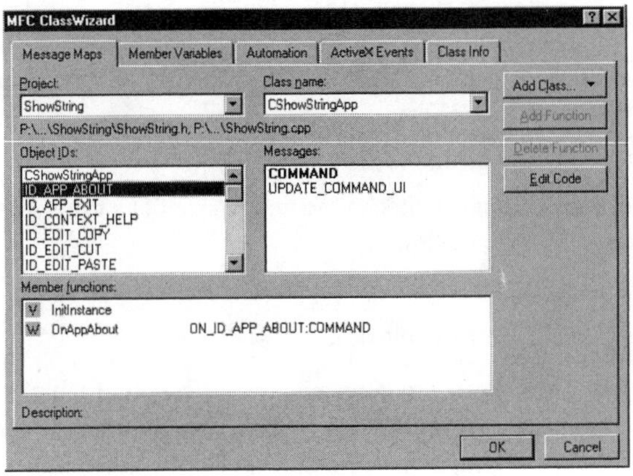

FIG. 4.4

ClassWizard allows you to catch or update commands.

There are only two messages associated with each resource ID: COMMAND and UPDATE_COMMAND_UI. The first allows you to add a function to handle the user selecting the menu option or clicking the button—that is, to catch the command. The second enables you to add a function to set the state of the menu item, button, or other control just as the operating system is about to display it—that is, to update the command. (The COMMAND choice is boldface in Figure 4.4 because this class already catches that command.)

Clicking Add Function to add a function that catches or updates a command involves an extra step. ClassWizard gives you a chance to change the default function name, as shown in Figure 4.5. This is almost never appropriate. There is a regular pattern to the suggested names, and experienced MFC programmers come to count on function names that follow that pattern. Command handler functions, like message handlers, have names that start with On. Typically, the remainder of the function name is formed by removing the ID and the underscores from the resource ID, and capitalizing each word. Command update handlers have names that start with OnUpdate and use the same conventions for the remainder of the function name. For example, the function that catches ID_APP_EXIT should be called OnAppExit(), and the function that updates ID_APP_EXIT should be called OnUpdateAppExit().

Not every command needs an update handler. The framework does some very nice work graying and ungraying for you automatically. Say you have a menu item, Network, Send, whose command is caught by the document. When there is no open document, this menu item is grayed by the framework, without any coding on your part. For many commands, it's enough that an object that can handle them exists, and no special updating is necessary. For others, you may want to check that something is selected or highlighted, or that no errors are present before making certain commands available. That's when you use command updating. If you'd like to see an example of command updating at work, there's one in Chapter 9, "Building a Complete Application: ShowString," in the "Command Updating" section.

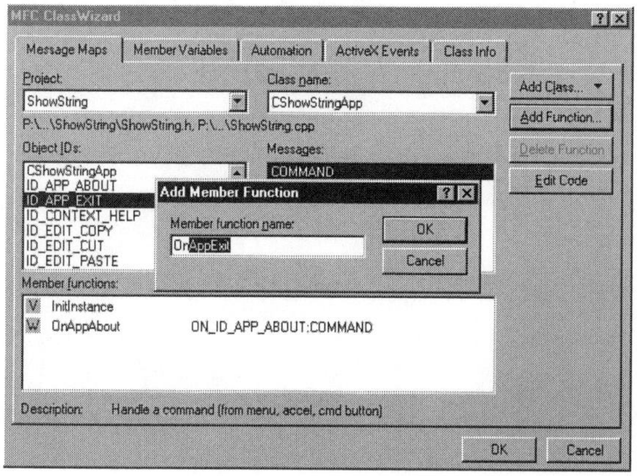

FIG. 4.5

It is possible, but not wise, to change the name for your command handler or command update handler from the name suggested by ClassWizard.

From Here...

This chapter has provided the theory of message handling and command routing, and a behind-the-scenes look at the ways MFC implements these for you. To see this theory in action, check out the following chapters:

- Chapter 5, "Documents and Views," discusses views, documents, and frames, and the way in which they interact. Issues like which class should catch certain messages are explored in more detail here.

- Chapter 6, "Drawing on the Screen," discusses what code, if any, you should write to handle messages like WM_PAINT and WM_SIZE that indicate your window needs to be redrawn.

- Chapter 8, "Persistence and File I/O," discusses the way that documents get saved and loaded in more detail, explains why you need a Serialize() function, and illustrates the sort of code it typically contains.

- Chapter 9, "Building a Complete Application: ShowString," shows how to build your own menus and dialog boxes and assign resource IDs to interface items. You see examples of ClassWizard in action, hooking interface items to code.

- Chapter 10, "Status Bars and Toolbars," draws on what you have learned about menus to explain toolbars.

Part
II

Ch
4

Documents and Views

How document objects declare their data

Any information your application plans to save must be added to the document class.

How view objects access the document's data

It is the view class that shows the data to the user: It asks the document for the data.

Other view classes in MFC

MFC provides 10 different view classes from which your class can inherit.

Document templates

Connections between views and documents are simple to arrange.

When you generate your source code with AppWizard, you get an application featuring all the bells and whistles of a commercial Windows 95 application, including a toolbar, a status bar, ToolTips, menus, and even an About dialog box. However, in spite of all those features, the application really doesn't do anything useful. In order to create an application that does more than look pretty on your desktop, you've got to modify the code that AppWizard generates. This task can be easy or complex, depending upon how you want your application to look and act.

Probably the most important set of modifications are those related to the document—the information the user can save from your application and restore later—and to the view—the way that information is presented to the user. MFC's document/view architecture separates an application's data from the way the user actually views and manipulates that data. Simply, the document object is responsible for storing, loading, and saving the data, whereas the view object (which is just another type of window) enables the user to see the data on-screen and to edit that data in a way that is appropriate to the application. In this chapter, you learn the basics of how MFC's document/view architecture works. ■

Understanding the Document Class

SDI and MDI applications created with AppWizard are document/view applications. That means that AppWizard generates a class for you, derived from CDocument, and delegates certain tasks to this new document class. It also creates a view class, derived from CView, and delegates other tasks to your new view class. Let's look through an AppWizard starter application and see what you get.

Choose File, New, and select the Projects tab. Fill in the project name as **App1** and fill in an appropriate directory for the project files. Make sure that MFC AppWizard (exe) is selected. Click OK.

Move through the AppWizard dialog boxes, changing the settings to match those in the following list, then click Next to continue:

> Step 1: Multiple documents
>
> Step 2: Don't change the defaults presented by AppWizard
>
> Step 3: Don't change the defaults presented by AppWizard
>
> Step 4: Deselect all check boxes except Printing and Print Preview
>
> Step 5: Don't change the defaults presented by AppWizard
>
> Step 6: Don't change the defaults presented by AppWizard

After you click Finish on the last step, the New Project Information box summarizes your work. Click OK to create the project. Expand the App1 classes in ClassView, and you see that six classes have been created: CAboutDlg, CApp1App, CApp1Doc, CApp1View, CChildFrame, and CMainframe.

CApp1Doc represents a document; it holds the application's document data. You add storage for the document by adding data members to the CApp1Doc class. To see how this works, look at Listing 5.1, which shows the header file AppWizard creates for the CApp1Doc class.

On the CD

Listing 5.1   APP1DOC.H—The Header File for the *CApp1Doc* Class

```
// App1Doc.h : interface of the CApp1Doc class
//
/////////////////////////////////////////////////////////////////////////////

#if !defined(AFX_APP1DOC_H__43BB481D_64AE_11D0_9AF3_0080C81A397C__INCLUDED_)
#define AFX_APP1DOC_H__43BB481D_64AE_11D0_9AF3_0080C81A397C__INCLUDED_


class CApp1Doc : public CDocument
{
protected: // create from serialization only
    CApp1Doc();
    DECLARE_DYNCREATE(CApp1Doc)

// Attributes
public:
```

```
// Operations
public:

// Overrides
    // ClassWizard generated virtual function overrides
    //{{AFX_VIRTUAL(CApp1Doc)
    public:
    virtual BOOL OnNewDocument();
    virtual void Serialize(CArchive& ar);
    //}}AFX_VIRTUAL

// Implementation
public:
    virtual ~CApp1Doc();
#ifdef _DEBUG
    virtual void AssertValid() const;
    virtual void Dump(CDumpContext& dc) const;
#endif

protected:

// Generated message map functions
protected:
    //{{AFX_MSG(CApp1Doc)
        // NOTE - the ClassWizard will add and remove member functions here.
        //    DO NOT EDIT what you see in these blocks of generated code !
    //}}AFX_MSG
    DECLARE_MESSAGE_MAP()
};

/////////////////////////////////////////////////////////////////////////////

//{{AFX_INSERT_LOCATION}}
// Microsoft Developer Studio will insert additional declarations immediately
before the previous line.

#endif // !defined(AFX_APP1DOC_H__43BB481D_64AE_11D0_9AF3_ 0080C81A397C__INCLUDED_)
```

Near the top of the listing, you can see the class declaration's Attributes section, which is followed by the public keyword. This is where you declare the data members that will hold your application's data. In the program that you create a little later in this chapter, the application must store an array of CPoint objects as the application's data. That array is declared as a member of the document class, like this:

```
// Attributes
public:
    CPoint points[100];
```

CPoint is an MFC class, that encapsulates the information relevant to a point on the screen, most importantly the x and y coordinates of the point.

Notice also in the class's header file that the CApp1Doc class includes two virtual member functions called OnNewDocument() and Serialize(). MFC calls the OnNewDocument() function whenever the user selects the File, New command (or its toolbar equivalent, if a New button has been implemented in the application). You can use this function to perform whatever initialization must be performed on your document's data. In an SDI application, the open document is closed and a new blank document is loaded into the same object; in an MDI application, a blank document is opened in addition to documents that are already open. The Serialize() member function is where the document class loads and saves its data. This is discussed in Chapter 8, "Persistence and File I/O."

Understanding the View Class

As mentioned previously, the view class displays the data stored in the document object and enables the user to modify this data. The view object keeps a pointer to the document object, which it uses to access the document's member variables in order to display or modify them. Listing 5.2 is the header file for Capp1View, as generated by AppWizard.

TIP

Most MFC programmers add public member variables to their documents to make it easy for the view class to access them. A more object-oriented approach is to add private or protected member variables, and then add public functions to get or change the values of these variables.

On the CD

Listing 5.2   APP1VIEW.H—The Header File for the *CApp1View* Class

```
// App1View.h : interface of the CApp1View class
//
/////////////////////////////////////////////////////////////////////

#if !defined(AFX_APP1VIEW_H__43BB481F_64AE_11D0_9AF3_0080C81A397C__INCLUDED_)
#define AFX_APP1VIEW_H__43BB481F_64AE_11D0_9AF3_0080C81A397C__INCLUDED_

class CApp1View : public CView
{
protected: // create from serialization only
    CApp1View();
    DECLARE_DYNCREATE(CApp1View)

// Attributes
public:
    CApp1Doc* GetDocument();

// Operations
public:

// Overrides
    // ClassWizard generated virtual function overrides
    //{{AFX_VIRTUAL(CApp1View)
    public:
    virtual void OnDraw(CDC* pDC);  // overridden to draw this view
```

```
virtual BOOL PreCreateWindow(CREATESTRUCT& cs);
    protected:
    virtual BOOL OnPreparePrinting(CPrintInfo* pInfo);
    virtual void OnBeginPrinting(CDC* pDC, CPrintInfo* pInfo);
    virtual void OnEndPrinting(CDC* pDC, CPrintInfo* pInfo);
    //}}AFX_VIRTUAL

// Implementation
public:
    virtual ~CApp1View();
#ifdef _DEBUG
    virtual void AssertValid() const;
    virtual void Dump(CDumpContext& dc) const;
#endif

protected:

// Generated message map functions
protected:
    //{{AFX_MSG(CApp1View)
        // NOTE - the ClassWizard will add and remove member functions here.
        //     DO NOT EDIT what you see in these blocks of generated code !
    //}}AFX_MSG
    DECLARE_MESSAGE_MAP()
};

#ifndef _DEBUG  // debug version in App1View.cpp
inline CApp1Doc* CApp1View::GetDocument()
   { return (CApp1Doc*)m_pDocument; }
#endif

/////////////////////////////////////////////////////////////////////////////

//{{AFX_INSERT_LOCATION}}
// Microsoft Developer Studio will insert additional declarations immediately
//before the previous line.

#endif // !defined(AFX_APP1VIEW_H__43BB481F_64AE_11D0_9AF3_0080C81A397C__INCLUDED_)
```

Part

II

Ch

5

Near the top of the listing, you can see the class's public attributes, where it declares the GetDocument() function as returning a pointer to a CApp1Doc object. Anywhere in the view class that you need to access the document's data, you can call GetDocument() to obtain a pointer to the document. For example, to add a CPoint object to the aforementioned array of CPoint objects stored as the document's data, you might use the following line:

```
GetDocument()->m_points[x] = point;
```

You also can do this a little differently, of course, by storing the pointer returned by GetDocument() in a local pointer variable and then using that pointer variable to access the document's data, like this:

```
pDoc = GetDocument();
pDoc->m_points[x] = point;
```

The second version is more convenient when you need to use the document pointer in several places in the function, or if using the less clear GetDocument()->variable version makes the code hard to understand.

> **N O T E** In release versions of your program, the GetDocument() function is inline, which means there is no performance advantage to saving the pointer like this, but it does improve readability. Inline functions are expanded into your code like macros, but offer type checking and other advantages, as discussed in the electronic book, *C++ By Example*, included on the CD with this book. ▨

Notice that the view class, like the document class, overrides a number of virtual functions from its base class. As you'll soon see, the OnDraw() function, which is the most important of these virtual functions, is where you paint your window's display. As for the other functions, MFC calls PreCreateWindow() before the window element (that is, the actual Windows window) is created and attached to the MFC window class, giving you a chance to modify the window's attributes (such as size and position). These two functions are discussed in more detail in Chapter 6, "Drawing on the Screen." OnPreparePrinting() is used to modify the Print dialog box before it displays for the user; the OnBeginPrinting() function gives you a chance to create GDI objects like pens and brushes that you need to handle the print job; and OnEndPrinting() is where you can destroy any objects you may have created in OnBeginPrinting(). These three functions are discussed in Chapter 7, "Printing and Print Preview."

> **N O T E** When you first start using an application framework like MFC, it's easy to get confused about the difference between an object instantiated from an MFC class and the Windows element it represents. For example, when you create an MFC frame-window object, you're actually creating two things: the MFC object that has member functions and member variables, and a Windows window that you can manipulate using the functions of the MFC object. The window element is associated with the MFC class, but is also an entity unto itself. ▨

Creating the Rectangles Application

Now that you've had an introduction to documents and views, a little hands-on experience should help you bettew understand how these classes work. In the steps that follow you build the Rectangles application, which demonstrates the manipulation of documents and views. When you first run this application, it will draw an empty window. Wherever you click in the window, a small rectangle will be drawn. You can resize the window, or minimize and restore it, and the rectangles will be redrawn at all the coordinates where you clicked. This is accomplished by keeping an array of coordinate points in the document and using that array in the view.

> **N O T E** The complete source code and executable file for the Rectangles application can be found in the CHAP06\RECS directory of this book's CD-ROM. ▨

First, use AppWizard to create the basic files for the Rectangles program by selecting the options listed in the following table. (AppWizard is first discussed in Chapter 1, "Building Your First Application.") When you're finished, the New Project Information dialog box appears; it should look like Figure 5.1. Click the OK button to create the project files.

Dialog Box Name	Options to Select
New Project	Name the project **recs**, and set the project path to the directory into which you want to store the project's files. Leave the other options set to their defaults.
Step 1 of 6	Select Single Document.
Step 2 of 6	Leave set to defaults.
Step 3 of 6	Leave set to defaults.
Step 4 of 6	Turn off all application features except Printing and Print Preview.
Step 5 of 6	Leave set to defaults.
Step 6 of 6	Leave set to defaults.

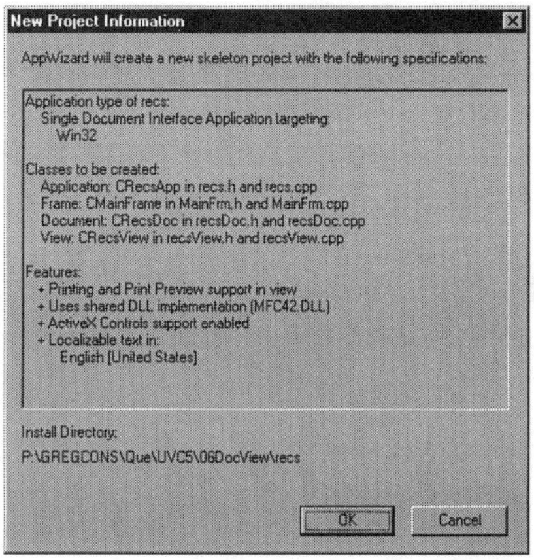

FIG. 5.1

When you create an SDI application with AppWizard, the project information summary confirms your settings.

Part
II

Ch
5

Now that you have a starter application, it's time to add code to the document and view classes in order to create an application that actually does something. This application will draw many rectangles in the view and save the coordinates of the rectangles in the document.

Follow these steps to add the code that modifies the document class to handle the application's data, which is an array of CPoint objects that determine where rectangles should be drawn in the view window:

1. Click the ClassView tab to display the ClassView in the project workspace window at the left of the screen.

2. Expand the Recs classes by clicking the + sign before them.

3. Right-click the CRecsDoc class, and choose Add Member Variable from the shortcut menu that appears.

4. Fill in the Add Member Variable dialog box. For Variable Type, enter **CPoint**. For Variable Declaration, enter **m_points[100]**. Make sure the Public radio button is selected. Click OK.

5. Again, right-click the CRecsDoc class, and choose Add Member Variable.

6. For Variable Type, enter **UINT**. For Variable Declaration, enter **m_pointIndex**. Make sure the Public radio button is selected. Click OK.

7. Click the + next to CRecsDoc in ClassView to see the member variables and functions. The two member variables you added are now listed.

The m_points[] array holds the locations of rectangles displayed in the view window. The m_pointIndex data member holds the index of the next empty element of the array.

TIP If you've programmed in C++ before and are not used to the ClassView, you can open RecsDoc.h from the FileView and add (after a public: specifier) the two lines of code that declare these variables:

```
UINT m_pointIndex;
CPoint m_points[100];
```

Now you need to get these variables initialized to appropriate values and then use them to draw the view. MFC applications that use the document/view paradigm initialize document data in a function called OnNewDocument(), which is called automatically when the application first runs and whenever the user chooses File, New.

The list of member variables and functions of CRecsDoc should still be displayed in ClassView. Double-click OnNewDocument() in that list to edit the code. Using Listing 5.3 as a guide, remove the comments left by AppWizard and initialize m_pointIndex to zero.

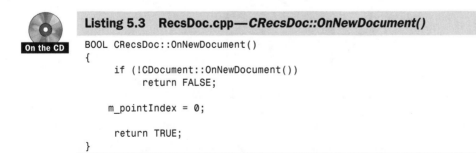

Listing 5.3   RecsDoc.cpp—*CRecsDoc::OnNewDocument()*

```
BOOL CRecsDoc::OnNewDocument()
{
    if (!CDocument::OnNewDocument())
        return FALSE;

    m_pointIndex = 0;

    return TRUE;
}
```

There is no need to initialize the array of points, since the index into the array will be used to ensure no code tries to use an uninitialized element of the array. At this point, your modifications to the document class are complete. As you'll see in Chapter 8, "Persistence and

File I/O," there are a few simple changes to make if you want this information actually saved in the document. In order to focus on the way documents and views work together, you will not be making those changes to the Recs application.

Now turn your attention to the view class. It will use the document data to draw rectangles on-screen. A full discussion of the way that drawing works must wait for Chapter 6, "Drawing on the Screen." For now it is enough to know that the `OnDraw()` function of your view class does the drawing. Expand the `CRecsView` class in ClassView and double-click `OnDraw()`. Using Listing 5.4 as a guide, remove the comments left by AppWizard and add code to draw a rectangle at each point in the array.

On the CD

Listing 5.4   RECSVIEW.CPP—*CRecsView::OnDraw()*

```
void CRecsView::OnDraw(CDC* pDC)
{
    CRecsDoc* pDoc = GetDocument();
    ASSERT_VALID(pDoc);

    UINT pointIndex = pDoc->m_pointIndex;

    for (UINT i=0; i<pointIndex; ++i)
    {
        UINT x = pDoc->m_points[i].x;
        UINT y = pDoc->m_points[i].y;
        pDC->Rectangle(x, y, x+20, y+20);
    }
}
```

Your modifications to the starter application generated by AppWizard are almost complete. You have added member variables to the document, initialized those variables in the document's `OnNewDocument()` function, and used those variables in the view's `OnDraw()` function. All that remains is to enable the user to add points to the array. You catch the mouse message with ClassWizard and then add code to the message handler. Follow these steps:

Part

II

Ch

5

1. Choose View, ClassWizard. The ClassWizard dialog box appears.

2. Make sure that `CRecsView` is selected in the Class Name and Object IDs boxes. Then, double-click `WM_LBUTTONDOWN` in the Messages box to add the `OnLButtonDown()` message-response function to the class. Whenever the application receives a `WM_LBUTTONDOWN` message, it will call `OnLButtonDown()`.

3. Click the Edit Code button to jump to the `OnLButtonDown()` function in your code. Then, add the code shown in Listing 5.5 to the function.

Listing 5.5   RECSVIEW.CPP—*CRecsView::OnLButtonDown()*

```
void CRecsView::OnLButtonDown(UINT nFlags, CPoint point)
{
    CRecsDoc *pDoc = GetDocument();

    // don't go past the end of the 100 points allocated
    if (pDoc->m_pointIndex == 100)
        return;

    //store the click location
    pDoc->m_points[pDoc->m_pointIndex] = point;
    pDoc->m_pointIndex++;

    pDoc->SetModifiedFlag();
    Invalidate();

    CView::OnLButtonDown(nFlags, point);
}
```

The new OnLButtonDown() adds a point to the document's point array each time the user clicks the left mouse button over the view window. It increments m_pointIndex so that the next click goes into the point on the array after this one.

The call to SetModifiedFlag() marks this document as modified, or "dirty." MFC automatically prompts the user to save any dirty files on exit. (The details are in Chapter 8, "Persistence and File I/O.") Any code you write that changes any document variables should call SetModifiedFlag().

N O T E   Earlier in this chapter you were reminded that public access functions in the document had some advantages. One such advantage: Any document member function that changed a variable also could call SetModifiedFlag(), thus guaranteeing no programmer could forget it. ■

Finally, the call to Invalidate() causes MFC to call the OnDraw() function, where the window's display is redrawn with the new data. Invalidate() takes a single parameter (with the default value TRUE) that determines if the background is erased before calling OnDraw(). On rare occasions you may choose to call Invalidate(FALSE), so that OnDraw() draws over whatever was already on the screen.

Finally, a call to the base class OnLButtonDown() takes care of the rest of the work involved in handling a mouse click.

You've now finished the complete application. Click the toolbar's Build button, or choose Build, Build to compile and link the application. After you have the Rectangles application compiled and linked, run it by choosing Build, Execute. When you do, you see the application's main window. Place your mouse pointer over the window's client area and click. A rectangle appears. Go ahead and keep clicking. You can place up to 100 rectangles in the window (see Figure 5.2).

FIG. 5.2
The Rectangles application draws rectangles wherever you click.

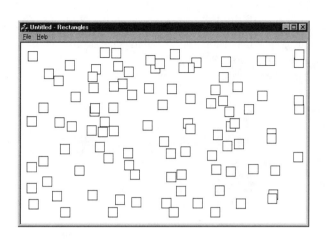

Other View Classes

The view classes generated by AppWizard in this chapter's sample applications have been derived from MFC's CView class. There are cases, however, when it is to your advantage to derive your view class from one of the other MFC view classes that are themselves derived from CView. These additional classes provide your view window with special capabilities, such as scrolling and text editing. Table 5.1 lists the various view classes along with their descriptions.

Table 5.1   View Classes

Class	Description
CView	The base view class from which the specialized view classes are derived.
CScrollView	A view class that provides scrolling capabilities.
CCtrlView	A base class from which view classes that implement new Windows 95 common controls (such as the ListView, TreeView, and RichEdit controls) are derived.
CEditView	A view class that provides basic text-editing features.
CRichEditView	A view class that provides more sophisticated text-editing capabilities by using the Windows 95 RichEdit control.
CListView	A view class that displays a Windows 95 ListView control in its window.
CTreeView	A view class that displays a Windows 95 TreeView control in its window.
CFormView	A view class that implements a form-like window using a dialog box resource.
CRecordView	A view class that can display database records along with controls for navigating the database.
CDaoRecordView	Same as CRecordView, except used with the new DAO database classes.

Part
II
Ch
5

To use one of these classes, you just substitute the desired class for the CView class in the application's project. When using AppWizard to generate your project, you can specify the view class you want in the wizard's Step 6 of 6 dialog box, as shown in Figure 5.3. Once you have the desired class installed as the project's view class, you can use the specific class's member functions to control the view window. Chapter 6, "Drawing on the Screen," demonstrates using the CScrollView class to implement a scrolling view.

FIG. 5.3

You can use AppWizard to select your application's base view class.

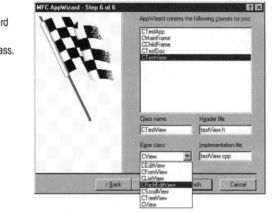

A CEditView object, on the other hand, gives you all the features of a Windows edit control in your view window. Using this class, you can handle various editing and printing tasks, including find-and-replace. You can retrieve or set the current printer font by calling the GetPrinterFont() or SetPrinterFont() member function or get the currently selected text by calling GetSelectedText(). Moreover, the FindText() member function locates a given test string, and OnReplaceAll() replaces all occurrences of a given text string with another string.

The CRichEditView class adds many features to an edit view, including paragraph formatting (such as centered, right-aligned, and bulleted text), character attributes (including underlined, bold, and italic), and the capability to set margins, fonts, and paper size. As you may have guessed, the CRichEditView class features a rich set of methods you can use to control your application's view object.

Figure 5.4 shows how the view classes fit into MFC's class hierarchy. Describing these various view classes fully is beyond the scope of this chapter. However, you can find plenty of information about them in your Visual C++ online documentation.

FIG. 5.4
The view classes all trace their ancestry back to CView.

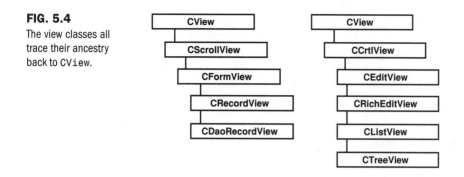

Document Templates, Views, and Frame Windows

Because you've been working with AppWizard-generated applications in this chapter, you've taken for granted a lot of what goes on in the background of an MFC document/view program. That is, much of the code that enables the frame window (your application's main window), the document, and the view window to work together is automatically generated by AppWizard and manipulated by MFC.

For example, if you look at the InitInstance() method of the Rectangles application's CRecsApp class, you see (among other things) the lines shown in Listing 5.6.

On the CD

Listing 5.6   RECS.CPP—Initializing an Application's Document

```
CSingleDocTemplate* pDocTemplate;
pDocTemplate = new CSingleDocTemplate(
     IDR_MAINFRAME,
     RUNTIME_CLASS(CRecsDoc),
     RUNTIME_CLASS(CMainFrame),
     RUNTIME_CLASS(CRecsView));
AddDocTemplate(pDocTemplate);
```

Part

II

Ch

5

In Listing 5.6, you discover one of the secrets that makes the document/view system work. In that code, the program creates a document-template object. These document templates have nothing to do with C++ templates. They pull together the following objects:

- **A resource ID identifying a menu resource:** IDR_MAINFRAME in this case.
- **A document class:** CRecsDoc in this case.
- **A frame window class:** always CMainFrame.
- **A view class:** CRecsView in this case.

Notice that you are not passing an object or a pointer to an object. You are passing the *name* of the class to a macro called RUNTIME_CLASS. It enables the framework to create instances of a class at runtime, which the application object must be able to do in a program that uses the document/view architecture. In order for this macro to work, the classes that will be created dynamically must be declared and implemented as such. To do this, the class must have the DECLARE_DYNCREATE macro in its declaration (in the header file) and the IMPLEMENT_DYNCREATE macro in its implementation. AppWizard takes care of this for you.

For example, if you look at the header file for the Rectangles application's CMainFrame class, you see the following line near the top of the class's declaration:

```
DECLARE_DYNCREATE(CMainFrame)
```

As you can see, the DECLARE_DYNCREATE macro requires the class's name as its single argument.

Now, if you look near the top of CMainFrame's implementation file (MAINFRM.CPP), you see this line:

```
IMPLEMENT_DYNCREATE(CMainFrame, CFrameWnd)
```

The IMPLEMENT_DYNCREATE macro requires as arguments the name of the class and the name of the base class.

If you explore the application's source code further, you find that the document and view classes also contain the DECLARE_DYNCREATE and IMPLEMENT_DYNCREATE macros.

If you haven't heard of frame windows before, you should know that they contain all the windows involved in the applications—this means control bars as well as views. They also route messages and commands to views and documents, as discussed in Chapter 4, "Messages and Commands."

The last line of Listing 5.6 calls AddDocTemplate() in order to pass the object on to the application object, CRecsApp, which keeps a list of documents. AddDocTemplate() adds this document to this list and uses the document template to create the document object, the frame, and the view window.

Since this is a Single Document Interface, a single document template (CSingleDocTemplate) is created. Multiple Document Interface applications use one CMultiDocTemplate object for each kind of document they support. For example, a spreadsheet program might have two kinds of documents: tables and graphs. Each would have its own view and its own set of menus. Two instances of CMultiDocTemplate would be created in InitInstance(), each pulling together the menu, document, and view that belong together. If you've ever seen the menus in a program change as you switched from one view or document to another, now you know how you can achieve the same effect: Simply associate them with different menu resource IDs as you build the document templates.

From Here...

In this chapter, you examined how an AppWizard-generated application uses MFC to coordinate an application's document and view objects. There is, of course, a great deal more to learn about MFC before you can create your own sophisticated Windows 95 applications. If you would like to learn more about some topics presented in this chapter, refer to the following:

- Chapter 6, "Drawing on the Screen," demonstrates how to display data in an application's window.

- Chapter 7, "Printing and Print Preview," shows how to include these powerful features in your application.

- Chapter 8, "Persistence and File I/O," provides the details of how to use MFC's file-handling classes.

- Appendix B, "The Developer Studio User Interface," explains how to control your programming projects with Developer Studio.

Part

II

Ch

5

Getting Information from Your Application

CHAPTER 6

Drawing on the Screen

Most applications need to display some type of data in their windows. One would think that, because Windows is a device-independent operating system, creating window displays would be easier than luring a kitten with a saucer of milk. However, it is exactly Windows' device independence that places a little extra burden on the programmer's shoulders. Because you can never know in advance exactly what type of devices may be connected to a user's system, you can't make many assumptions about display capabilities. Functions that draw to the screen must do so indirectly through something called a *device context* (DC).

Visual C++'s MFC includes many classes that make dealing with DCs easier. These classes encapsulate graphical objects: not only the DC itself, but also pens, brushes, fonts, and more. ∎

How device contexts control your displays

You have to know how to manage device contexts before you can display anything on the screen.

Respond to window-painting requests from Windows

When Windows knows that your application's display needs updating, it sends a message to the application.

Create and use fonts, pens, and brushes

The basic elements that determine how your display looks are the fonts, pens, and brushes that you've created for the device context.

How to use scrolling windows

Often, your application will need to display more information than will fit in a window. Scrolling is the answer to this problem, and the MFC CScrollView class makes it simple.

Understanding Device Contexts

As you know, every Windows application (in fact, every computer application) must manipulate data in some way. Most applications must also display data. Unfortunately, because of Windows' device independence, this task is not as straightforward in Windows as it is in a nongraphical operating system like DOS.

Although device independence forces you, the programmer, to deal with data displays indirectly, it helps you by ensuring that your programs run on all popular devices. In most cases, Windows handles devices for you through the device drivers that the user has installed on the system. These device drivers intercept the data that the application needs to display and then translates the data appropriately for the device on which it will appear, whether that is a screen, a printer, or some other output device.

To understand how all of this device independence works, imagine an art teacher trying to design a course of study appropriate for all types of artists. The teacher creates a course outline that stipulates the subject of a project, the suggested colors to be used, the dimensions of the finished project, and so on. What the teacher doesn't stipulate is the surface on which the project will be painted or the materials needed to paint on that surface. In other words, the teacher stipulates only general characteristics. The details of how these characteristics are applied to the finished project are left up to each specific artist.

For example, an artist using oil paints will choose canvas as his drawing surface and oil paints, in the colors suggested by the instructor, as the paint. On the other hand, an artist using watercolors will select watercolor paper on which to create her work, and she will, of course, use watercolors rather than oils for paint. Finally, the charcoal artist will select the appropriate drawing surface for charcoal and will use a single color.

The instructor in the preceding scenario is much like a Windows programmer. The programmer has no idea who may eventually use the program and what kind of system that user may have. The programmer can recommend the colors in which data should be displayed and the coordinates at which the data should appear, for example, but it is the device driver—the Windows artist—that ultimately decides how the data appears.

A system with a VGA monitor may display data with fewer colors than a system with a Super VGA monitor. Likewise, a system with a monochrome monitor displays the data in only a single color. Monitors with high resolutions can display more data than lower-resolution monitors. The device drivers, much like the artists in the imaginary art school, must take the display requirements and fine-tune them to the device on which the data will actually appear. And it is a data structure called a *device context* that links the application to the device's driver.

A device context (DC) is little more than a data structure that keeps track of the attributes of a window's drawing surface. These attributes include the currently selected pen, brush, and font that will be used to draw on the screen. Unlike an artist, who can have many brushes and pens with which to work, a DC can use only a single pen, brush, or font at a time. If you want to use a pen that draws wider lines, for example, you need to create the new pen and then replace the DC's old pen with the new one. Similarly, if you want to fill shapes with a red brush, you must create the brush and "select it into the DC," which is how Windows programmers describe replacing a tool in a DC.

A window's client area is a versatile surface that can display anything a Windows program can draw. The client area can display any type of data because everything displayed in a window, whether it be text, spreadsheet data, a bitmap, or any other type of data, is displayed graphically. MFC helps you display data by encapsulating Windows' GDI functions and objects into its DC classes.

Introducing the Paint1 Application

In this chapter, you will build the Paint1 application, which demonstrates fonts, pens, and brushes. Paint1 will use the document/view paradigm discussed in Chapter 5, "Documents and Views," and the view will handle displaying the data. When run, the application will display text in several different fonts. When the user clicks the application, it displays lines drawn with several different pens. After another click it displays boxes filled with a variety of brushes.

The first step in creating Paint1 is to build an empty shell with AppWizard, as first discussed in Chapter 1, "Building Your First Application." Choose File, New, and select the Projects tab. As shown in Figure 6.1, fill in the project name as Paint1 and fill in an appropriate directory for the project files. Make sure that MFC AppWizard (exe) is selected. Click OK.

FIG. 6.1
Start an AppWizard project workspace called Paint1.

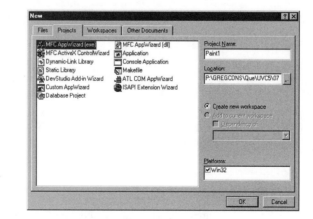

Move through the AppWizard dialog boxes, change the settings to match those in the list that follows, and then click Next to move to the next step:

Step 1: Single document

Step 2: Default settings

Step 3: Default settings

Step 4: Uncheck all check boxes

Step 5: Default settings

Step 6: Default settings

Part
III

Ch
6

After you click Finish on the last step, the New Project Information box should resemble Figure 6.2. Click OK to create the project.

FIG. 6.2

The starter application for Paint1 is very simple.

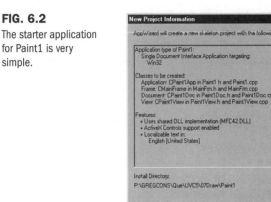

Now that you have a starter application, it's time to add code to make it demonstrate some of the ways an MFC program can display data on the screen. By the time you get to the end of this chapter, the words *display context* won't make you scratch your head in perplexity.

NOTE Your starter application has menus, but you are going to ignore them completely. It would be quite a bit of work to remove them; just pretend they aren't there. ▩

Building the Paint1 Application

In order to build the Paint1 application, you first need to understand how painting and drawing work in an MFC program. Then you can set up the skeleton code to handle the clicks from the user and the three different kinds of display. Finally, you will fill in the code for each kind of display in turn.

Painting in an MFC Program

In Chapter 4, "Messages and Commands," you learned about message maps and how you can tell MFC which functions to call when it receives messages from Windows. One important message that every Windows program with a window must handle is WM_PAINT. Windows sends the WM_PAINT message to an application's window when the window needs to be redrawn. There are several events that cause Windows to send a WM_PAINT message. The first event occurs when the user simply runs the program. In a properly written Windows application, the application's window gets a WM_PAINT message almost immediately after being run, in order to ensure that the appropriate data is displayed from the very start.

Another time a window might receive the WM_PAINT message is when the window has been resized or has recently been uncovered—either fully or partially—by another window. In either case, part of the window that wasn't visible before is now on the screen, and must be updated.

Finally, a program can indirectly send itself a WM_PAINT message by invalidating its client area. Having this ability ensures that an application can change its window's contents almost any time it wishes. For example, a word processor might invalidate its window after the user pastes some text from the Clipboard.

When you studied message maps, you learned to convert a message name to a message-map macro and function name. You now know, for example, that the message-map macro for a WM_PAINT message is ON_WM_PAINT(). You also know that the matching message-map function should be called OnPaint(). This is another case where MFC has already done most of the work of matching a Windows message with its message-response function. (If all this message-map stuff doesn't sound familiar, you might want to review Chapter 4, "Messages and Commands.")

You might guess that the next step for you is to catch the WM_PAINT message, or to override the OnPaint() function that your view class inherited from CView, but you are not going to do that. The code for CView::OnPaint() is in Listing 6.1. As you can see, WM_PAINT is already caught and handled for you.

Listing 6.1   *CView::OnPaint()*

```
void CView::OnPaint()
{
    // standard paint routine
    CPaintDC dc(this);
    OnPrepareDC(&dc);
    OnDraw(&dc);
}
```

CPaintDC is a special class for managing *paint DCs,* which are device contexts that are used only when responding to WM_PAINT messages. An object of the CPaintDC class does more than just create a DC; it also calls the BeginPaint() Windows API function in the class's constructor and calls EndPaint() in its destructor. When a program responds to WM_PAINT messages, calls to BeginPaint() and EndPaint() are required. The CPaintDC class handles this requirement without your having to get involved in all the messy details. As you can see, the CPaintDC constructor takes a single argument, which is a pointer to the window for which you're creating the DC. The this pointer points to the current view, so it is passed to the constructor to make a DC for the current view.

OnPrepareDC() is a CView function that prepares a DC for use. You'll learn more about it in Chapter 7, "Printing and Print Preview."

Part

III

Ch

6

Switching the Display

The design for Paint1 states that when you click the application's window, the window's display changes. This seemingly magical feat is actually easy to accomplish. You add a member variable to the view to store what kind of display is being done, and change it when the user clicks the window. In other words, the program routes WM_LBUTTONDOWN messages to the OnLButtonDown() message-response function, which sets the m_display flag as appropriate.

First, add the member variable. You must add it by hand rather than through the shortcut menu because the type includes an enum declaration. Open CPaint1View.h from the File, View and add these lines after the //Attributes comment:

```
protected:
    enum {Fonts, Pens, Brushes} m_Display;
```

TIP This is an *anonymous* or unnamed enum. You can learn more about enum types in the electronic book *C++ by Example* included on this book's CD.

Choose ClassView in the Project Workspace pane, expand the classes, expand CPaint1View, and then double-click the constructor, CPaint1View(). Add this line of code in place of the TODO comment:

```
m_Display = Fonts;
```

This initializes the display selector to the font demonstration. You use the display selector in the OnDraw() function called by CView::OnPaint(). AppWizard has created CPaint1View::OnDraw(), but it doesn't do anything at the moment. Double-click the function name in ClassView, and add the code shown in Listing 6.2 to the function, removing the TODO comment left by AppWizard.

Listing 6.2 *Cpainr1View::OnDraw()*

```
void CPaint1View::OnDraw(CDC* pDC)
{
    CPaint1Doc* pDoc = GetDocument();
    ASSERT_VALID(pDoc);

    switch (m_Display)
    {
        case Fonts:
            ShowFonts(pDC);
            break;
        case Pens:
            ShowPens(pDC);
            break;
        case Brushes:
            ShowBrushes(pDC);
            break;
    }
}
```

You will write the three functions ShowFonts(), ShowPens(), and ShowBrushes() in upcoming sections of this chapter. Each of these functions uses the same DC pointer that was passed to OnDraw() by OnPaint(). Add them to the class now, by following these steps:

1. Right-click the CPaint1View class in ClassView and select Add Member Function.

2. Enter void for the Function Type.

3. Enter ShowFonts(CDC* pDC) for the Function Declaration.

4. Change the access to protected. Click OK.

5. Repeat steps 1 to 4 for ShowPens(CDC* pDC) and ShowBrushes(CDC* pDC).

The last step in arranging for the display to switch is to catch left mouse clicks and write code in the message-handler to change m_display.

Right-click CPaint1View in the ClassView and select Add Windows Message Handler from the shortcut menu that appears. Double-click WM_LBUTTONDOWN in the New Windows Message and Event Handlers listbox. ClassWizard adds a function called OnLButtonDown() to the view and adds entries to the message map so that this function will be called whenever the user clicks the left mouse button over this view.

Click Edit Existing to edit the empty OnLButtonDown() you just created, and add the code shown in Listing 6.3.

Listing 6.3 *CPaint1View::OnLButtonDown()*

```
void CPaint1View::OnLButtonDown(UINT nFlags, CPoint point)
{
    if (m_Display == Fonts)
        m_Display = Pens;
    else if (m_Display == Pens)
        m_Display = Brushes;
    else
        m_Display = Fonts;

    Invalidate();

    CView::OnLButtonDown(nFlags, point);
}
```

Part
III

Ch

6

As you can see, depending on its current value, m_display gets set to the next display type in the series. Of course, just changing the value of m_display doesn't accomplish much. The program still needs to redraw the contents of its window. The call to Invalidate() tells Windows that all of the window needs to be repainted. This causes Windows to generate a WM_PAINT message for the window, which means that eventually OnDraw() will be called, and the view will be redrawn as a font, pen, or brush demonstration.

Using Fonts

Changing the font used in a view is a technique you will want to use in a variety of situations. It's not as simple as you might think, because you can never be sure that any given font is actually installed on the user's machine. You set up a structure that holds information about the font you want, attempt to create it, and then work with the font you actually got, which might not be quite the font you asked for.

A Windows font is described in the LOGFONT structure, which is outlined in Table 6.1. The LOGFONT structure uses 14 fields to hold a complete description of the font. Many of the fields can be set to 0 or the default values, depending on the program's needs.

Table 6.1 *LOGFONT* **Fields and Their Descriptions**

Field	Description
lfHeight	Height of font in logical units.
lfWidth	Width of font in logical units.
lfEscapement	Angle at which to draw the text.
lfOrientation	Character tilt in tenths of a degree.
lfWeight	Font weight.
lfItalic	A nonzero value indicates italics.
lfUnderline	A nonzero value indicates an underlined font.
lfStrikeOut	A nonzero value indicates a strikethrough font.
lfCharSet	Font character set.
lfOutPrecision	How to match requested font to actual font.
lfClipPrecision	How to clip characters that run over clip area.
lfQuality	Print quality of the font.
lfPitchAndFamily	Pitch and font family.
lfFaceName	Typeface name.

Some of the terms in Table 6.1 need a little explanation. The first is *logical units*. How high is a font that has a height of 8 logical units, for example? The meaning of a logical unit depends on the *mapping mode* you are using, as shown in Table 6.2. The default mapping mode is MM_TEXT, which means that one logical unit is equal to one pixel. Mapping modes are discussed in more detail in Chapter 7, "Printing and Print Preview."

Table 6.2   Mapping Modes

Mode	Unit
MM_HIENGLISH	0.001 inch
MM_HIMETRIC	0.01 millimeter
MM_ISOTROPIC	arbitrary
MM_LOENGLISH	0.01 inch
MM_LOMETRIC	0.1 millimeter
MM_TEXT	Device pixel
MM_TWIPS	1/1440 inch

Escapement refers to writing text along an angled line; *orientation* refers to writing angled text along a flat line. The font weight refers to the thickness of the letters. A number of constants have been defined for use in this field: They are FW_DONTCARE, FW_THIN, FW_EXTRALIGHT, FW_ULTRALIGHT, FW_LIGHT, FW_NORMAL, FW_REGULAR, FW_MEDIUM, FW_SEMIBOLD, FW_DEMIBOLD, FW_BOLD, FW_EXTRABOLD, FW_ULTRABOLD, FW_BLACK, and FW_HEAVY. Not all fonts are available in all weights. There are four character sets available (ANSI_CHARSET, OEM_CHARSET, SYMBOL_CHARSET, and UNICODE_CHARSET) but for writing English text you will almost always use ANSI_CHARSET. (Unicode is discussed in Chapter 28, "Future Explorations.") The last field in the LOGFONT structure is the face name, such as Courier or Helvetica.

Listing 6.4 shows the code you need to add to the empty ShowFonts() function you created earlier.

Listing 6.4   *CPaint1View::ShowFonts()*

```
void CPaint1View::ShowFonts(CDC * pDC)
{
    // Initialize a LOGFONT structure for the fonts.
    LOGFONT logFont;
    logFont.lfHeight = 8;
    logFont.lfWidth = 0;
    logFont.lfEscapement = 0;
    logFont.lfOrientation = 0;
    logFont.lfWeight = FW_NORMAL;
    logFont.lfItalic = 0;
    logFont.lfUnderline = 0;
    logFont.lfStrikeOut = 0;
    logFont.lfCharSet = ANSI_CHARSET;
    logFont.lfOutPrecision = OUT_DEFAULT_PRECIS;
    logFont.lfClipPrecision = CLIP_DEFAULT_PRECIS;
    logFont.lfQuality = PROOF_QUALITY;
    logFont.lfPitchAndFamily = VARIABLE_PITCH | FF_ROMAN;
    strcpy(logFont.lfFaceName, "Times New Roman");
```

Part
III

Ch

6

continues

Listing 6.4 Continued

```
    // Initialize the position of text in the window.
    UINT position = 0;

    // Create and display eight example fonts.
    for (UINT x=0; x<8; ++x)
    {
        // Set the new font's height.
        logFont.lfHeight = 16 + (x * 8);

        // Create a new font and select it into the DC.
        CFont font;
        font.CreateFontIndirect(&logFont);
        CFont* oldFont = pDC->SelectObject(&font);

        // Print text with the new font.
        position += logFont.lfHeight;
        pDC->TextOut(20, position, "A sample font.");

        // Restore the old font to the DC.
        pDC->SelectObject(oldFont);
    }
}
```

ShowFonts() starts by setting up a Times Roman font eight pixels high, with a width that best matches the height, and all other attributes set to normal defaults.

In order to show the many fonts that are displayed in its window, the Paint1 application creates its fonts in a for loop, modifying the value of the LOGFONT structure's lfHeight member each time through the loop, using the loop variable, x, to calculate the new font height, like this:

```
logFont.lfHeight = 16 + (x * 8);
```

Because x starts at 0, the first font created in the loop will be 16 pixels high. Each time through the loop, the new font will be eight pixels higher than the previous one.

After setting the font's height, the program creates a CFont object and calls its CreateFontIndirect() function, which attempts to create a CFont object corresponding to the LOGFONT you created. It will change the LOGFONT to describe the CFont that was actually created, given the fonts that are installed on the user's machine.

After ShowFonts() calls CreateFontIndirect(), the CFont object has been associated with a Windows font. Now you can select it into the DC. Selecting objects into device contexts is a crucial concept in Windows output programming. You cannot use any graphical object, such as a font, directly; instead you select it into the DC and then use the DC. You always save a pointer to the old object that was in the DC (the pointer is returned from the SelectObject() call) and use it to restore the device context by selecting the old object again when you are finished. The same function, SelectObject() is used to select a variety of objects into a device context: The font you are using in this section, a pen, a brush, or a number of other drawing objects.

After selecting the new font into the DC, you can use the font to draw text on the screen. The local variable position holds the vertical position in the window at which the next line of text should be printed. This position depends upon the height of the current font. After all, if there's not enough space between the lines, the larger fonts will overlap the smaller ones. When Windows created the new font, it stored the font's height (which is most likely the height that you requested, but might not be) in the LOGFONT structure's lfHeight member. By adding the value stored in lfHeight, the program can determine the next position at which to display the line of text. To make the text appear on the screen, ShowFonts() calls TextOut().

TextOut()'s first two arguments are the X and Y coordinates at which to print the text. The third argument is the text to print. Having printed the text, you restore the old font to the DC in case this is the last time through the loop.

Build the application and run it. It should look something like Figure 6.3. If you click the window it will go blank, because the ShowPens() routine doesn't draw anything. Click again and it is still blank, this time because the ShowBrushes() routine doesn't draw anything. Click a third time and you are back to the fonts screen.

FIG. 6.3
The font display shows how you can create different types of text output.

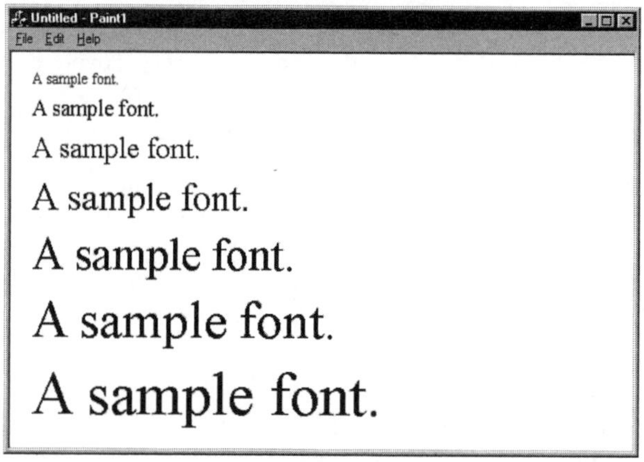

Sizing and Positioning the Window

As you can see in Figure 6.3, Paint1 does not display eight different fonts: Only seven can fit in the window. To correct this, you need to set the size of the window a little larger than the Windows default. In an MFC program, you do this in the mainframe class PreCreateWindow() function. This is called for you just before the mainframe window is created. The mainframe window surrounds the entire application and governs the size of the view.

PreCreateWindow() takes one parameter, a reference to a CREATESTRUCT structure. The CREATESTRUCT structure contains essential information about the window that is about to be created, as shown in Listing 6.5.

Listing 6.5 The *CREATESTRUCT* Structure

```
typedef struct tagCREATESTRUCT {
    LPVOID    lpCreateParams;
    HANDLE    hInstance;
    HMENU     hMenu;
    HWND      hwndParent;
    int       cy;
    int       cx;
    int       y;
    int       x;
    LONG      style;
    LPCSTR    lpszName;
    LPCSTR    lpszClass;
    DWORD     dwExStyle;
} CREATESTRUCT;
```

If you've programmed Windows without application frameworks like MFC, you'll recognize the information stored in the CREATESTRUCT structure. You used to supply much of this information when calling the Windows API function CreateWindow() to create your application's window. Of special interest to MFC programmers are the cx, cy, x, and y members of this structure. By changing cx and cy, you can set the width and height, respectively, of the window. Similarly, modifying x and y changes the window's position. By overriding PreCreateWindow(), you get a chance to fiddle with the CREATESTRUCT structure before Windows uses it to create the window.

AppWizard created a CMainFrame::PreCreateWindow() function. Expand CMainFrame in ClassView, double-click PreCreateWindow() to edit it, and add the code shown in Listing 6.6. This sets the height and width of the application. It also prevents the user from resizing the application, by using the bitwise and operator, &, to turn off the WS_SIZEBOX style bit. Now the user cannot resize the application.

Listing 6.6 *CMainFrame::PreCreateWindow()*

```
BOOL CMainFrame::PreCreateWindow(CREATESTRUCT& cs)
{
    cs.cx = 440;
    cs.cy = 480;

    cs.style &= ~WS_SIZEBOX;

    return CFrameWnd::PreCreateWindow(cs);
}
```

It's important that, after your own code in PreCreateWindow(), you call the base class's PreCreateWindow(). Failure to do this will leave you without a valid window, because MFC never gets a chance to pass the CREATESTRUCT structure on to Windows, and so Windows never creates your window. When overriding class member functions, you usually need to call the base class's version.

Build and run Paint1 to confirm that all eight fonts fit in the application's window. Now you are ready to demonstrate pens.

Using Pens

You'll be pleased to know that pens are much easier to deal with than fonts, mostly because you don't have to fool around with complicated data structures like LOGFONT. In fact, to create a pen, you need only supply the pen's line style, thickness, and color. The Paint1 application's ShowPens() function displays in its window lines drawn using different pens created within a for loop. The code is shown in Listing 6.7.

Listing 6.7   CPaint1View::ShowPens()

```
void CPaint1View::ShowPens(CDC * pDC)
{
    // Initialize the line position.
    UINT position = 10;

    // Draw sixteen lines in the window.
    for (UINT x=0; x<16; ++x)
    {
        // Create a new pen and select it into the DC.
CPen pen(PS_SOLID, x*2+1, RGB(0, 0, 255));
        CPen* oldPen = pDC->SelectObject(&pen);

        // Draw a line with the new pen.
        position +=  x * 2 + 10;
        pDC->MoveTo(20, position);
        pDC->LineTo(400, position);

        // Restore the old pen to the DC.
        pDC->SelectObject(oldPen);
    }
}
```

Within the loop, ShowPens() first creates a custom pen. The constructor takes three parameters. The first is the line's style, one of the styles listed in Table 6.3. (Only solid lines can be drawn with different thicknesses. Patterned lines always have a thickness of 1.) The second argument is the line thickness, which increases each time through the loop. The third argument is the line's color. The RGB macro takes three values for the red, green, and blue color components and converts them into a valid Windows color reference. The values for the red, green, and blue color components can be anything from 0 to 255—the higher the value, the brighter that color component. This code creates a bright blue pen. If all the color values were 0, the pen would be black; if the color values were all 255, the pen would be white.

Part III
Ch 6

Table 6.3 Pen Styles

Style	Description
PS_DASH	Specifies a pen that draws dashed lines
PS_DASHDOT	Specifies a pen that draws dash-dot patterned lines
PS_DASHDOTDOT	Specifies a pen that draws dash-dot-dot patterned lines
PS_DOT	Specifies a pen that draws dotted lines
PS_INSIDEFRAME	Specifies a pen that's used with shapes, where the line's thickness must not extend outside of the shape's frame
PS_NULL	Specifies a pen that draws invisible lines
PS_SOLID	Specifies a pen that draws solid lines

N O T E If you want to control the style of a line's end points or want to create your own custom patterns for pens, you can use the alternate CPen constructor, which requires a few more arguments than the CPen constructor described in this section. To learn how to use this alternate constructor, look up CPen in your Visual C++ online documentation. ■

After creating the new pen, ShowPens() selects it into the DC, saving the pointer to the old pen. The MoveTo() function moves the pen to an X,Y co-ordinate without drawing as it moves; the LineTo() function moves the pen while drawing. The style, thickness, and color of the pen are used. Finally, you select the old pen into the DC.

T I P There are a number of line drawing functions other than LineTo(), including Arc(), ArcTo(), AngleArc(), PolyDraw(), and more.

Build and run Paint1 again. When the font display appears, click the window. You should see a pen display like Figure 6.4.

Using Brushes

A pen draws a line of a specified thickness on the screen. A brush fills a shape on the screen. You can create both solid and patterned brushes, and even create brushes from bitmaps that contain your own custom fill patterns. Paint1 will display both patterned and solid rectangles in the ShowBrushes() function, shown in Listing 6.8.

Listing 6.8 *CPaint1View::ShowBrushes()*

```
void CPaint1View::ShowBrushes(CDC * pDC)
    // Initialize the rectangle position.
    UINT position = 0;
```

```
// Select pen to use for rectangle borders
CPen pen(PS_SOLID, 5, RGB(255, 0, 0));
CPen* oldPen = pDC->SelectObject(&pen);

// Draw seven rectangles.
for (UINT x=0; x<7; ++x)
{
    CBrush* brush;

    // Create a solid or hatched brush.
    if (x == 6)
        brush = new CBrush(RGB(0,255,0));
    else
        brush = new CBrush(x, RGB(0,160,0));

    // Select the new brush into the DC.
    CBrush* oldBrush = pDC->SelectObject(brush);

    // Draw the rectangle.
    position += 50;
    pDC->Rectangle(20, position, 400, position + 40);

    // Restore the DC and delete the brush.
    pDC->SelectObject(oldBrush);
    delete brush;
}

// Restore the old pen to the DC.
pDC->SelectObject(oldPen);
}
```

FIG. 6.4

The Pen display shows the effect of setting line thickness.

The rectangles painted with the various brushes in this routine will all be drawn with a border. To arrange this, just create a pen (this one is solid, 5 pixels thick, and bright red) and select it into the DC. It will be used to border the rectangles without any further work on your part. Like ShowFonts() and ShowPens(), this routine creates its graphical objects within a for loop. Unlike those two functions, ShowBrushes() creates a graphical object (in this routine, a brush) with a call to new. This allows you to call either the one-argument constructor, which creates a solid brush, or the two argument constructor, which creates a hatched brush.

In Listing 6.8, the first argument to the two argument constructor is just the loop variable, x. Usually you do not want to show all the hatch patterns, but want to select a specific one. Use one of these constants for the hatch style:

- HS_HORIZONTAL   Horizontal
- HS_VERTICAL   Vertical
- HS_CROSS   Horizontal and vertical
- HS_FDIAGONAL   Forwards diagonal
- HS_BDIAGONAL   Backwards diagonal
- HS_DIAGCROSS   Diagonal in both directions

In a pattern that should be familiar by now, ShowBrushes() selects the brush into the DC, determines the position at which to work, uses the brush by calling Rectangle(), and then restores the old brush. When the loop is complete, the old pen is restored as well.

Rectangle() is just one of the shape-drawing functions that you can call. Rectangle() takes as arguments the coordinates of the rectangle's upper-left and lower-right corners. Some others of interest are Chord(), DrawFocusRect(), Ellipse(), Pie(), Polygon(), PolyPolygon(), Polyline(), and RoundRect(), which draws a rectangle with rounded corners.

Once again, build and run Paint1. Click twice, and you should see the demonstration of brushes, as shown in Figure 6.5.

FIG. 6.5

The Brushes display shows a number of different patterns inside thick-bordered rectangles.

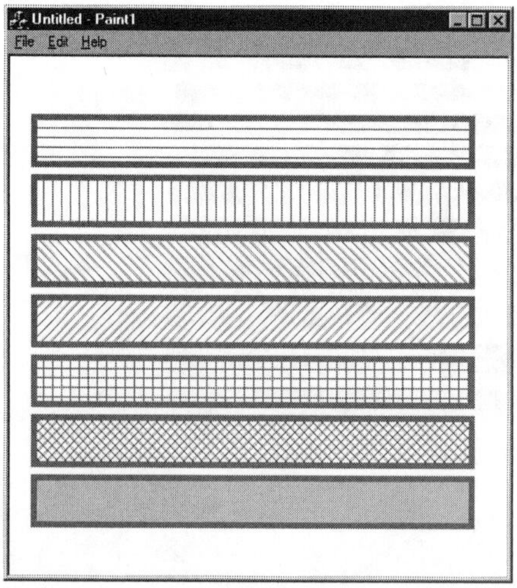

NOTE Remember the call to `Invalidate()` in `CPaint1View::OnLButtonDown()`? `Invalidate()` actually takes an argument, with a default value of `TRUE`. This Boolean argument tells Windows whether to erase the window's background. If you use `FALSE` for this argument, the background is not erased. In Figure 6.6, you can see what happens to the Paint1 application if `Invalidate()` gets called with an argument of `FALSE`.

FIG. 6.6
Without erasing the background, the Paint1 application's windows get a bit messy.

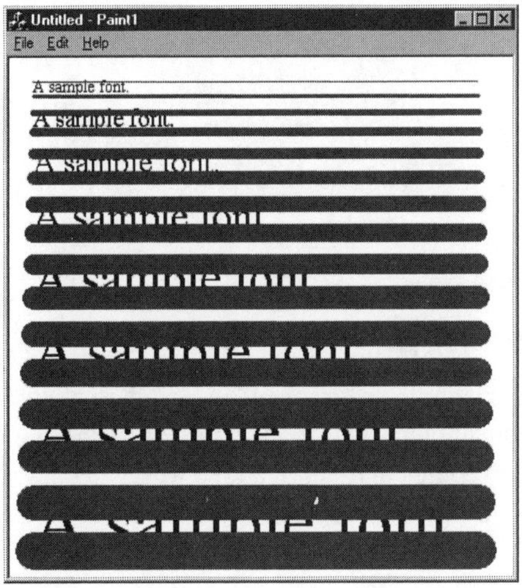

Scrolling Windows

Those famous screen rectangles called *windows* were developed for two reasons. The first reason is to partition screen space between various applications and documents. The second reason is to enable the user to view portions of a document when the document is too large to completely fit into the window. The Windows operating system and MFC pretty much take care of the partitioning of screen space. However, if you want to enable the user to view portions of a large document, you must create scrolling windows.

Adding scroll bars to an application from scratch is a complicated task. Luckily for Visual C++ programmers, MFC handles many of the details involved in scrolling windows over documents. If you use the document/view architecture and derive your view window from MFC's `CScrollView` class, you get scrolling capabilities almost for free. I say "almost" because there are still a few details that you must handle. You'll learn those details in the following sections.

NOTE If you create your application using AppWizard, you can specify that you want to use `CScrollView` as the base class for your view class. To do this, in the Step 6 Of 6 dialog box displayed by AppWizard, select your view window in the class list and then select `CScrollView` in the Base Class dialog box, as shown in Figure 6.7.

FIG. 6.7
You can create a
scrolling window from
within AppWizard.

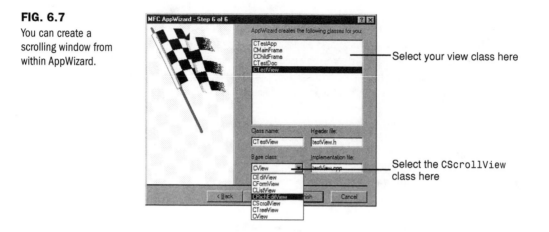

Select your view class here

Select the CScrollView
class here

Building the Scroll Application

In this section, you will build a sample program called Scroll, to experiment with a scrolling window. When Scroll first runs, it displays five lines of text. Each time you click the window with your left mouse button, five lines of text are added to the display. When you get more lines of text than fit in the window, a vertical scroll bar appears enabling you to scroll to the parts of the documents that you can't see.

As usual, building the application starts with AppWizard. Choose File, New, and select the Projects tab. Fill in the project name as Scroll and fill in an appropriate directory for the project files. Make sure that MFC AppWizard (exe) is selected. Click OK.

Complete the AppWizard steps, selecting the following options:

     Step 1: Single document

     Step 2: Default settings

     Step 3: Default settings

     Step 4: Unselect all check boxes

     Step 5: Default settings

     Step 6: Select CScrollView from the Base Class drop-down box as in Figure 6.7.

The New Project Information dialog box should resemble Figure 6.8. Click OK to create the project.

This application generates very simple lines of text. You only need to keep track of the number of lines that are in the scrolling view at the moment. To do this, add a variable to the document class by following these steps:

    1. In ClassView, expand the classes, and then right-click CScrollDoc.

    2. Choose Add Member Variable from the shortcut menu

3. Fill in `int` as the variable type

4. Fill in `m_NumLines` as the variable declaration

FIG. 6.8

Create a scroll application with AppWizard.

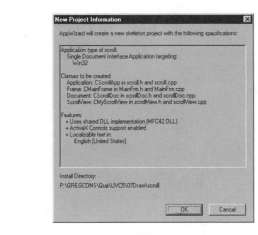

Variables associated with a document are initialized in `OnNewDocument()`. In ClassView, expand CScrollDoc, then double-click `OnNewDocument()` to expand it. Replace the `TODO` comments with this line of code:

```
m_NumLines = 5;
```

To arrange for this variable to be saved with the document and restored when the document is loaded, you must serialize it. Edit `CScrollDoc::Serialize()`, as shown in Listing 6.9.

Listing 6.9 *CScrollDoc::Serialize()*

```
void CScrollDoc::Serialize(CArchive& ar)
{
    if (ar.IsStoring())
    {
        ar << m_NumLines;
    }
    else
    {
        ar >> m_NumLines;
    }
}
```

Part
III

Ch
6

Now all you need to do is use `m_NumLines` to draw the appropriate number of lines. Expand the view class, `CMyScrollView`, in ClassView, and then double-click `OnDraw()`. Edit it until it is the same as Listing 6.10. This is very similar to the `ShowFonts()` code from the Paint1 application earlier in this chapter.

Listing 6.10   *CMyScrollView::OnDraw()*

```
void CMyScrollView::OnDraw(CDC* pDC)
{
    CScrollDoc* pDoc = GetDocument();
    ASSERT_VALID(pDoc);

    // get the number of lines from the document
    int numLines = pDoc->m_NumLines;

    // Initialize a LOGFONT structure for the fonts.
    LOGFONT logFont;
    logFont.lfHeight = 24;
    logFont.lfWidth = 0;
    logFont.lfEscapement = 0;
    logFont.lfOrientation = 0;
    logFont.lfWeight = FW_NORMAL;
    logFont.lfItalic = 0;
    logFont.lfUnderline = 0;
    logFont.lfStrikeOut = 0;
    logFont.lfCharSet = ANSI_CHARSET;
    logFont.lfOutPrecision = OUT_DEFAULT_PRECIS;
    logFont.lfClipPrecision = CLIP_DEFAULT_PRECIS;
    logFont.lfQuality = PROOF_QUALITY;
    logFont.lfPitchAndFamily = VARIABLE_PITCH | FF_ROMAN;
    strcpy(logFont.lfFaceName, "Times New Roman");

    // Create a new font and select it into the DC.
    CFont* font = new CFont();
    font->CreateFontIndirect(&logFont);
    CFont* oldFont = pDC->SelectObject(font);

    // Initialize the position of text in the window.
    UINT position = 0;

    // Create and display eight example lines.
    for (int x=0; x<numLines; ++x)
    {
        // Create the string to display.
        char s[25];
        wsprintf(s, "This is line #%d", x+1);

        // Print text with the new font.
        pDC->TextOut(20, position, s);
        position += logFont.lfHeight;
    }

    // Restore the old font to the DC, and
    // delete the font the program created.
    pDC->SelectObject(oldFont);
    delete font;
}
```

Build and run the Scroll application, and you should see a display like Figure 6.9. There are no scroll bars, because all the lines fit in the window.

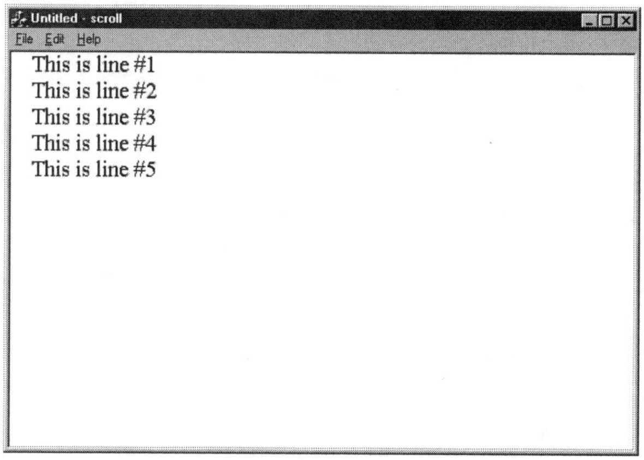

FIG. 6.9
At first, the Scroll
application displays five
lines of text and no
scroll bars.

```
Untitled - scroll
File  Edit  Help
    This is line #1
    This is line #2
    This is line #3
    This is line #4
    This is line #5
```

To increase the number of lines whenever the user clicks the window, you need to add a message handler to handle left mouse clicks, then write the code for the handler. Right-click CMyScrollView in ClassView, and choose Add Windows Message Handler. Double-click WM_LBUTTONDOWN to add a handler, and then click the Edit Existing button to change the code. Listing 6.11 shows the completed handler: It simply increases the number of lines, and then calls Invalidate() to force a redraw. Like so many message handlers, it finishes by passing the work on to the base class version of this function.

Listing 6.11 *CMyScrollView::OnLButtonDown()*

```cpp
void CMyScrollView::OnLButtonDown(UINT nFlags, CPoint point)
{
    CScrollDoc* pDoc = GetDocument();
    ASSERT_VALID(pDoc);

    // Increase number of lines to display.
    pDoc->m_NumLines += 5;

    // Redraw the window.
    Invalidate();

    CScrollView::OnLButtonDown(nFlags, point);
}
```

Part

III

Ch

6

So that you can watch scroll bars disappear as well as appear, why not implement a way for the user to decrease the number of lines in the window? If left-clicking increases the number of lines, it makes sense that right-clicking would decrease it. Add a handler for WM_RBUTTONDOWN just as you did for WM_LBUTTONDOWN, and edit it until it is just like Listing 6.12. This function is a little more complicated, because it ensures that the number of lines is never negative.

Listing 6.12   *CMyScrollView::OnRButtonDown()*

```
void CMyScrollView::OnRButtonDown(UINT nFlags, CPoint point)
{
    CScrollDoc* pDoc = GetDocument();
    ASSERT_VALID(pDoc);

    // Decrease number of lines to display.
    pDoc->m_NumLines -= 5;

    if (pDoc->m_NumLines < 0)
    {
        pDoc->m_NumLines = 0;
    }

    // Redraw the window.
    Invalidate();

    CScrollView::OnRButtonDown(nFlags, point);
}
```

If you build and run Scroll now, and click the window, you can increase the number of lines, but scroll bars do not appear. You need to add some lines to OnDraw() to make that happen. Before you do, it would be a good idea to review the way that scroll bars work. There are three places that you can click on a vertical scroll bar: the *thumb* (some people call it the elevator), above the thumb, or below it. Clicking the thumb does nothing, but you can click and hold to drag it up or down. Clicking above it moves you one page (screenful) up within the data. Clicking below it moves you one page down. What's more, the size of the thumb is a visual representation of the size of a page in proportion to the entire document. Clicking the up arrow at the top of the scroll bar moves you up one line in the document, and clicking the down arrow at the bottom moves you down one line.

What all this means is that the code that draws the scroll bar and handles the clicks needs to know the size of the entire document, the size of a page, and the size of a line. You don't have to write code to draw scroll bars, or code to handle clicks on the scroll bar, but you do have to pass along some information about the size of the document and the current view. The lines of code you need to add to OnDraw() are in Listing 6.13; add them after the for loop and before the old font is selected back into the DC.

Listing 6.13   **Lines to Add to *OnDraw()***

```
    // Calculate the document size.
    CSize docSize(100, numLines*logFont.lfHeight);

    // Calculate the page size.
       CRect rect;
    GetClientRect(&rect);
    CSize pageSize(rect.right, rect.bottom);
```

```
// Calculate the line size.
CSize lineSize(0, logFont.lfHeight);

// Adjust the scrollers.
SetScrollSizes(MM_TEXT, docSize, pageSize, lineSize);
```

This new code must determine the document, page, and line sizes. The document size is the width and height of the screen area that could hold the entire document. This is calculated by using the number of lines in the entire document, and the height of a line. (CSize is an MFC class that was created especially for storing the widths and heights of objects.) The page size is simply the size of the client rectangle of this view, and the line size is the height of the font. By setting the horizontal component of the line size to zero, you prevent horizontal scrolling.

These three sizes must be passed along in order to implement scrolling. Simply call SetScrollSizes(), which takes the mapping mode, document size, page size, and line size. MFC will set the scroll bars properly for any document, and handle the user's interaction with the scroll bars.

Build and run Scroll again, and generate some more lines. You should see a scroll bar like the one in Figure 6.10. Add even more lines and you should see the thumb shrink as the document size grows. Finally, resize the application horizontally so that the text will not all fit, and notice how no horizontal scroll bars appear, because you set the horizontal line size to zero.

FIG. 6.10
After displaying more lines than fit in the window, the vertical scroll bar appears.

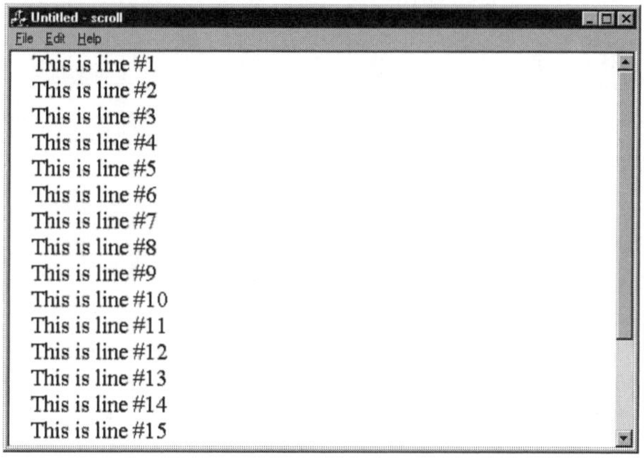

From Here...

You're really starting to master Visual C++ now. Take some time at this point to look over the CDC class, and the several classes derived from CDC, in your Visual C++ online documentation. You'll discover a wealth of member functions that you can use to create displays for your views. To learn more about related topics, check out the following chapters:

Part

III

Ch

6

■ Chapter 4, "Messages and Commands," describes MFC's message-mapping system, which enables you to respond to Windows messages.

■ Chapter 17, "Building an ActiveX Control," uses many of these drawing techniques to build the user interface of an ActiveX control.

■ Appendix B, "Working with Developer Studio," tells you what you need to know to create your own projects using Visual C++'s development tools.

Printing and Print Preview

If you brought together 10 Windows programmers and asked them what part of creating Windows applications they thought was the hardest, probably at least half of them would choose printing documents. Although Windows' device-independent nature makes it easier for the user to get peripherals working properly, the programmer must take up some of the slack by programming all devices in a general way. There was a time when printing from a Windows application was a nightmare that only the most experienced programmers could handle. Now, however, thanks to application frameworks like MFC, the job of printing documents from a Windows application is much simpler. ■

How to create an application with basic printing capabilities

MFC does almost all the work required to get document printing and print preview incorporated into your AppWizard-generated application.

How to use graphics mapping modes to scale printer output

The different Windows mapping modes use different units of measure when interpreting output coordinates.

How to print a multiple-page document

Although MFC can handle basic printing tasks almost automatically, it needs a little help when it comes to multiple-page documents.

How MFC class member functions control the printing process

Knowing which member functions to override is the key to controlling the printing and print preview process in your applications.

Understanding Basic Printing and Print Preview with MFC

MFC handles so much of the printing task for you that, when it comes to simple one-page documents, there's little you have to do on your own. To see what I mean, follow these steps to create a basic MFC application that supports printing and print preview:

1. Choose File, New; then select the Projects tab and start a new AppWizard project workspace called Print1, as shown in Figure 7.1.

FIG. 7.1

Start an AppWizard project workspace called Print1.

2. Give the new project the following settings in the AppWizard dialog boxes. The New Project Information dialog box should then look like Figure 7.2.

   Step 1: Single document

   Step 2: Don't change the defaults presented by AppWizard

   Step 3: Don't change the defaults presented by AppWizard

   Step 4: Turn off all features except Printing and Print Preview

   Step 5: Don't change the defaults presented by AppWizard

   Step 6: Don't change the defaults presented by AppWizard

3. Expand the classes in ClassView, expand CPrint1View, double-click the OnDraw() function, and add the following line of code to it, right after the comment that says TODO: add draw code for native data here:

   ```
   pDC->Rectangle(20, 20, 220, 220);
   ```

   You've seen the Rectangle() function twice already: in the Recs app of Chapter 5, "Documents and Views" and the Paint1 app of Chapter 6, "Drawing on the Screen." Adding this function to the OnDraw() function of an MFC program's view class causes the program to draw a rectangle. This one is 200 pixels by 200 pixels, located 20 pixels down from the top of the view and 20 pixels over from the left edge.

FIG. 7.2
The New Project
Information dialog box.

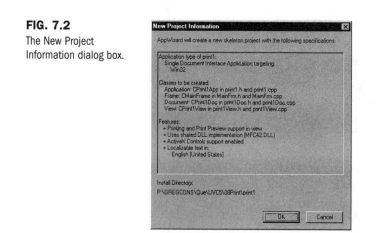

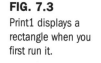 If you haven't read Chapter 6, "Drawing on the Screen," and are not comfortable with device contexts, go back and read it now. Also, if you didn't read Chapter 5, "Documents and Views," and aren't comfortable with the document/view paradigm, you should read it, too. In this chapter, you override a number of virtual functions in your view class and work extensively with device contexts.

Believe it or not, you've just created a fully print-capable application that can display its data (a rectangle) not only in its main window, but also in a print preview window and on the printer. To run the Print1 application, first compile and link the source code by choosing Build, Build, or by pressing F7 on your keyboard. Then, choose Build, Execute to run the program. When you do, you should see the window shown in Figure 7.3. This window contains the application's output data, which is simply a rectangle. Next, choose File, Print Preview. You see the print preview window shown in Figure 7.4. This window displays the document as it will appear if you print it. Go ahead and print the document (choose File, Print). These commands have been implemented for you, because you chose support for printing and print preview when you created this application with AppWizard.

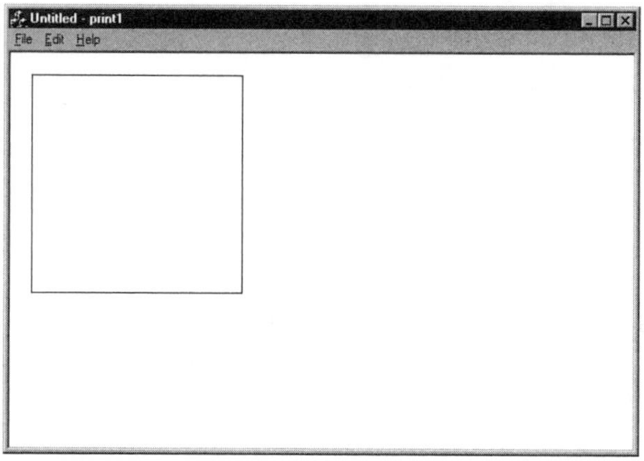

FIG. 7.3
Print1 displays a
rectangle when you
first run it.

Part
III

Ch
7

FIG. 7.4
The Print1 application automatically handles print previewing thanks to the MFC AppWizard.

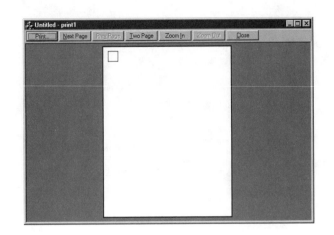

Scaling

One thing you may notice about the printed document and the one displayed on-screen is that, although the screen version of the rectangle takes up a fairly large portion of the application's window, the printed version is pretty tiny. That's because the pixels on your screen and the dots on your printer are different sizes. Although the rectangle is 200 dots square in both cases, the smaller printer dots yield a rectangle that appears smaller. This is how Windows' MM_TEXT graphics mapping mode, which is the default, works. If you want to scale the printed image to a specific size, you might want to choose a different mapping mode. Table 7.1 lists the mapping modes from which you can choose.

Table 7.1   Mapping Modes

Mode	Unit	X	Y
MM_HIENGLISH	0.001 inch	Increases right	Increases up
MM_HIMETRIC	0.01 millimeter	Increases right	Increases up
MM_ISOTROPIC	User defined	User defined	User defined
MM_LOENGLISH	0.01 inch	Increases right	Increases up
MM_LOMETRIC	0.1 millimeter	Increases right	Increases up
MM_TEXT	Device pixel	Increases right	Increases down
MM_TWIPS	1/1440 inch	Increases right	Increases up

Working with graphics in MM_TEXT mode causes problems when printers and screens can accommodate a different number of pixels per page. A better mapping mode for working with graphics is MM_LOENGLISH, which uses a hundredth of an inch, rather than a dot or pixel, as a unit of measure. To change the Print1 application so that it uses the MM_LOENGLISH mapping mode, replace the line you added to the OnDraw() function with the following two lines:

```
pDC->SetMapMode(MM_LOENGLISH);
pDC->Rectangle(20, -20, 220, -220);
```

The first line sets the mapping mode for the device context. The second line draws the rectangle using the new coordinate system. Why the negative values? If you look at MM_LOENGLISH in Table 7.1, you see that although X coordinates increase to the right as you expect, Y coordinates increase upward rather than downward. Moreover, the default coordinates for the window are located in the lower-right quadrant of the Cartesian coordinate system, as shown in Figure 7.5. Figure 7.6 shows the print preview window when the application uses the MM_LOENGLISH mapping mode. When you print the document, the rectangle is exactly two inches square. This is because a unit is now 1/100 of an inch and the rectangle is 200 units square.

FIG. 7.5

The MM_LOENGLISH mapping mode's default coordinates are derived from the Cartesian coordinate system.

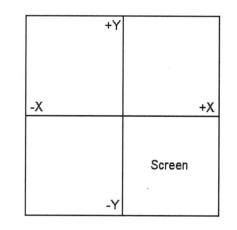

FIG. 7.6

The rectangle to be printed matches the rectangle on the screen when you use MM_LOENGLISH as your mapping mode.

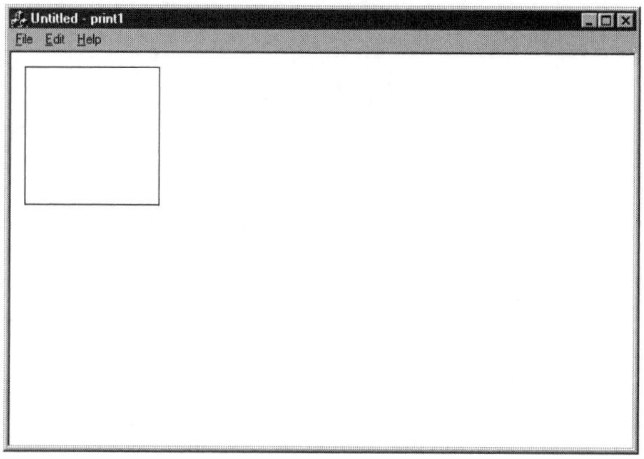

Part
III

Ch
7

Printing Multiple Pages

When your application's document is as simple as Print1's, adding printing and print previewing capabilities to the application is virtually automatic. This is because the document is only a single page and requires no pagination. No matter what you draw in the document's window (except bitmaps), MFC handles all the printing tasks for you. Your view's OnDraw() function is used for drawing on-screen, for printing to the printer, and for drawing the print preview screen. Things get more complex, however, when you have larger documents that require pagination or some other special handling, like the printing of headers and footers.

To get an idea of the problems with which you're faced with a more complex document, you are going to modify Print1 so that it prints lots of rectangles—so many that they can't fit on a single page. This will give you an opportunity to deal with pagination. Just to make things more interesting, you will add a member variable to the document class to hold the number of rectangles to be drawn, and then allow the user to increase or decrease the number of rectangles by left- or right-clicking. Follow these steps:

1. Expand CPrint1Doc in ClassView, right-click it, and choose Add Member Variable from the shortcut menu. The variable type is int, the declaration is m_numRects, and the access should be public. This variable will hold the number of rectangles to display.

2. Double-click the CPrint1Doc constructor, and add this line to it:

    ```
    m_numRects = 5;
    ```

    This line arranges to display five rectangles in a brand-new document.

3. Use ClassWizard to catch mouse clicks (WM_LBUTTONDOWN messages) with the OnLButtonDown() function of the view class, as shown in Figure 7.7.

FIG. 7.7
Use ClassWizard to add the OnLButtonDown() function.

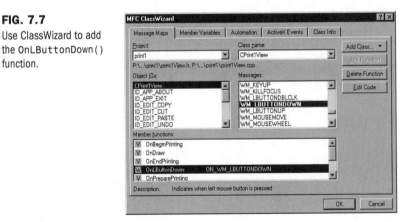

4. Click the Edit Code button to edit the new OnLButtonDown() function. It should resemble Listing 7.1. Now the number of rectangles to be displayed increases each time the user clicks the left mouse button.

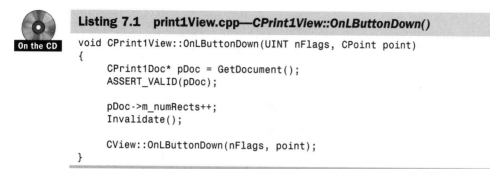

Listing 7.1 print1View.cpp—*CPrint1View::OnLButtonDown()*

```
void CPrint1View::OnLButtonDown(UINT nFlags, CPoint point)
{
    CPrint1Doc* pDoc = GetDocument();
    ASSERT_VALID(pDoc);

    pDoc->m_numRects++;
    Invalidate();

    CView::OnLButtonDown(nFlags, point);
}
```

5. Use ClassWizard to add the OnRButtonDown() function to the view class, as shown in Figure 7.8.

FIG. 7.8
Use ClassWizard to add the OnRButtonDown() function.

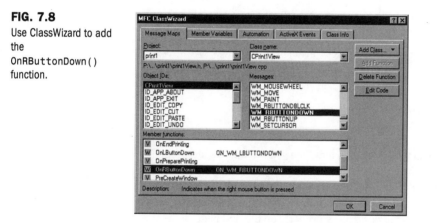

6. Click the Edit Code button to edit the new OnRButtonDown() function. It should resemble Listing 7.2. Now the number of rectangles to be displayed decreases each time the user clicks the right mouse button.

Listing 7.2 print1View.cpp—*CPrint1View::OnRButtonDown()*

```
void CPrint1View::OnRButtonDown(UINT nFlags, CPoint point)
{
    CPrint1Doc* pDoc = GetDocument();
    ASSERT_VALID(pDoc);

    if (pDoc->m_numRects > 0)
    {
        pDoc->m_numRects—;
        Invalidate();
    }

    CView::OnRButtonDown(nFlags, point);
}
```

Part
III

Ch

7

7. Rewrite the view's OnDraw() to draw many rectangles. The code is in Listing 7.3. Print1 now draws the selected number of rectangles one below the other, which may cause the document to span multiple pages. It also displays the number of rectangles that have been added to the document.

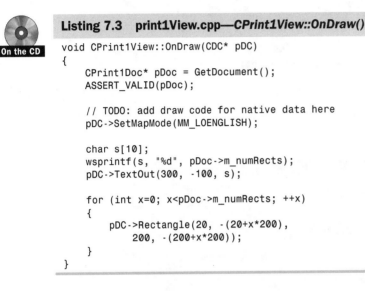

On the CD

Listing 7.3 print1View.cpp—*CPrint1View::OnDraw()*

```
void CPrint1View::OnDraw(CDC* pDC)
{
    CPrint1Doc* pDoc = GetDocument();
    ASSERT_VALID(pDoc);

    // TODO: add draw code for native data here
    pDC->SetMapMode(MM_LOENGLISH);

    char s[10];
    wsprintf(s, "%d", pDoc->m_numRects);
    pDC->TextOut(300, -100, s);

    for (int x=0; x<pDoc->m_numRects; ++x)
    {
        pDC->Rectangle(20, -(20+x*200),
            200, -(200+x*200));
    }
}
```

When you run the application now, you see the window shown in Figure 7.9. The window not only displays the rectangles, but also displays the rectangle count so you can see how many rectangles you've requested. When you choose the File, Print Preview command, you see the print preview window. Click the Two Page button, and you see the window shown in Figure 7.10. The five rectangles display properly on the first page, with the second page blank.

FIG. 7.9

Print1 now displays multiple rectangles.

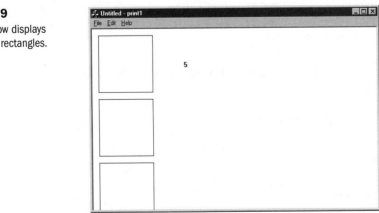

FIG. 7.10

Five rectangles are previewed properly: They will print on a single page.

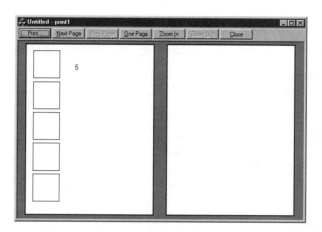

Now, go back to the application's main window and click inside the window three times to add three more rectangles. Right-click to remove one. (The rectangle count displayed in the window should be seven.) After you add the additional rectangles, choose File, Print Preview again to see the two-page print preview window. Figure 7.11 shows what you see. The program hasn't a clue as to how to print or preview the additional page. The sixth rectangle runs off the bottom of the first page, but nothing appears on the second page.

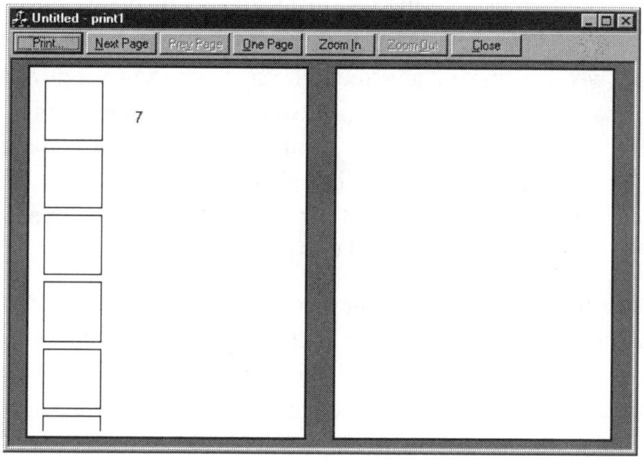

FIG. 7.11

Seven rectangles do not yet appear correctly on multiple pages.

The first step is to tell MFC how many pages to print (or preview), by calling the SetMaxPage() function in the view class's OnBeginPrinting() function. AppWizard gave you a skeleton OnBeginPrinting() that does nothing. You are going to modify it so that it resembles Listing 7.4.

Part III

Ch 7

Listing 7.4   print1View.cpp—*CPrint1View::OnBeginPrinting()*

```
void CPrint1View::OnBeginPrinting(CDC* pDC, CPrintInfo* pInfo)
{
    CPrint1Doc* pDoc = GetDocument();
    ASSERT_VALID(pDoc);

    int pageHeight = pDC->GetDeviceCaps(VERTRES);
    int logPixelsY = pDC->GetDeviceCaps(LOGPIXELSY);
    int rectHeight = (int)(2.2 * logPixelsY);
    int numPages = pDoc->m_numRects * rectHeight / pageHeight + 1;
    pInfo->SetMaxPage(numPages);
}
```

OnBeginPrinting() takes two parameters: a pointer to the printer device context and a pointer
to a CPrintInfo object. Because the default version of OnBeginPrinting() doesn't refer to
these two pointers, the parameter names are commented out to avoid compilation warnings,
like this:

```
void CPrint1View::OnBeginPrinting(CDC* /*pDC*/ , CPrintInfo* /*pInfo*/)
```

However, to set the page count, you need to access both the CDC and CPrintInfo objects, so
your first task is to uncomment the function's parameters.

Now, you need to get some information about the device context (which, in this case, is a
printer device context). Specifically, you need to know the height of a page (in single dots) and
the number of dots per inch. You obtain the height of a page with a call to GetDeviceCaps().
This function gives you information about the capabilities of the device context. You ask for
the vertical resolution (the number of printable dots from the top of the page to the bottom)
by passing the constant VERTRES as the argument. Passing HORZRES gets you the horizontal
resolution. There are 29 constants you can pass to GetDeviceCaps(), such as NUMFONTS for the
number of fonts that are supported and DRIVERVERSION for the driver version number. For a
complete list, consult the online Visual C++ documentation.

Print1 uses the MM_LOENGLISH mapping mode for the device context, which means that the
printer output uses units of 1/100 of an inch. To know how many rectangles are going to fit on
a page, you have to know the height of a rectangle in dots so that you can divide "dots per
page" by "dots per rectangle" to get "rectangles per page." (You can see now why your application must know all about your document to calculate the page count.) You know that each
rectangle is two inches high with 20/100 of an inch of space between each rectangle. The total
distance from the start of one rectangle and the start of the next, then, is 2.2 inches. The call
to GetDeviceCaps() with an argument of LOGPIXELSY gives the dots per inch of this printer:
Multiplying by 2.2 gives the dots per rectangle.

You now have all the information to calculate the number of pages needed to fit the requested number of rectangles. You pass that number to SetMaxPage(), and the new OnBeginPrinting() is complete.

Once again, build and run the program. Increase the number of rectangles to seven by clicking twice in the main window. The displayed rectangle count should then be seven. Now, choose File, Print Preview and take a look at the two-page, print preview window (see Figure 7.12). Whoops! You've obviously still got a problem somewhere. Although the application is previewing two pages, as it should with seven rectangles, it's printing exactly the same thing on both pages. Obviously, page two should take up where page one left off, rather than redisplay the same data from the beginning. There's still some work to do.

FIG. 7.12
The Print1 application still doesn't display multiple pages correctly.

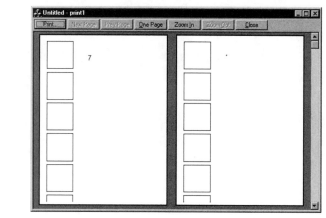

Setting the Origin

To get the second and subsequent pages to print properly, you have to change where MFC believes the top of the page to be. Currently, MFC just draws the pages exactly as you told it to do in CPrint1View::OnDraw(), which displays all seven rectangles from the top of the page to the bottom. To tell MFC where the new top of the page should be, you first need to override the view class's OnPrepareDC() function.

Bring up ClassWizard, and choose the Message Maps tab. Ensure that CPrintView is selected in the class name box, as shown in Figure 7.13. Click CPrintView in the Object IDs box and OnPrepareDC in the Messages box, and then click Add Function. Click the Edit Code button to edit the newly added function. Add the code shown in Listing 7.5.

Part
III

Ch
7

FIG. 7.13

Use ClassWizard to override the OnPrepareDC() function.

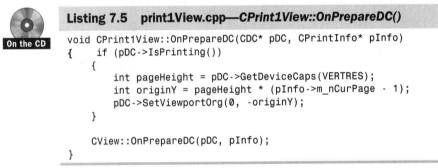

Listing 7.5   print1View.cpp—CPrint1View::OnPrepareDC()

```cpp
void CPrint1View::OnPrepareDC(CDC* pDC, CPrintInfo* pInfo)
{    if (pDC->IsPrinting())
     {
         int pageHeight = pDC->GetDeviceCaps(VERTRES);
         int originY = pageHeight * (pInfo->m_nCurPage - 1);
         pDC->SetViewportOrg(0, -originY);
     }

     CView::OnPrepareDC(pDC, pInfo);
}
```

The MFC framework calls OnPrepareDC() right before it displays data on-screen or before it prints the data to the printer. (One of the strengths of the device context approach to screen display is that the same code can often be used for on-screen display and printing.) If the application is about to display data on-screen, you (probably) don't want to change the default processing performed by OnPrepareDC(). So, you must check whether the application is printing data by calling IsPrinting(), a member function of the device context class.

If the application is printing, you will determine which part of the data belongs on the current page. You will need the height in dots of a printed page, so you call GetDeviceCaps() again.

Next, you must determine a new viewport origin (the position of the coordinates 0,0) for the display. Changing the origin tells MFC where to begin displaying data. For page one, the origin is zero. For page two, it is moved down by the number of dots on a page. In general, the vertical component is the size of a page times the current page minus one. The page number is a member variable of the CPrintInfo class.

After you calculate the new origin, you need only give it to the device context by calling SetViewportOrg(). Your changes to OnPrepareDC() are complete.

To see your changes in action, build and run your new version of Print1. When the program's main window appears, click twice in the window to add two additional rectangles to the display.

(The displayed rectangle count should be seven.) Once again, choose File, Print Preview and look at the two-page print preview window (see Figure 7.14). Now the program previews the document correctly. If you print the document, it will look the same in hard copy as it does in the preview.

FIG. 7.14
Print1 finally previews
and prints properly.

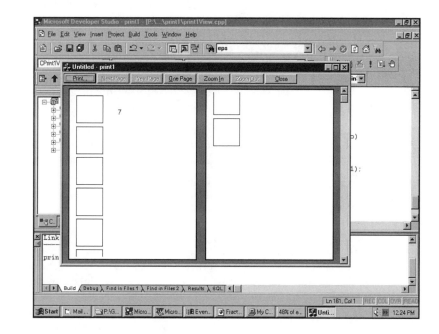

MFC and Printing

Now you've had a chance to see MFC's printing and print preview support in action. As you added more functionality to the Print1 application, you modified several member functions that were overridden in the view class, including OnDraw(), OnBeginPrinting(), and OnPrepareDC(). These functions are important to the printing and print preview process. However, there are also other functions that enable you to add even more printing power to your applications. The functions important to the printing process are listed in Table 7.2 along with their descriptions.

Table 7.2 Printing Functions of a View Class

Function	Description
OnBeginPrinting()	Override this function to create resources, such as fonts, that you need for printing the document. You also set the maximum page count here.

continues

Table 7.2 Continued

Function	Description
OnDraw()	This function serves triple duty, displaying data in a frame window, a print preview window, or on the printer, depending on the device context sent as the function's parameter.
OnEndPrinting()	Override this function to release resources created in OnBeginPrinting().
OnPrepareDC()	Override this function to modify the device context that is used to display or print the document. You can, for example, handle pagination here.
OnPreparePrinting()	Override this function to provide a maximum page count for the document. If you don't set the page count here, you should set it in OnBeginPrinting().
OnPrint()	Override this function to provide additional printing services, such as printing headers and footers, not provided in OnDraw().

To print a document, MFC calls the functions listed in Table 7.2 in a specific order. First it calls OnPreparePrinting(), which simply calls DoPreparePrinting(), as shown in Listing 7.6. DoPreparePrinting() is responsible for displaying the Print dialog box and creating the printer DC.

Listing 7.6 print1View.cpp—*CPrint1View::OnPreparePrinting()* as generated by AppWizard

```
BOOL CPrint1View::OnPreparePrinting(CPrintInfo* pInfo)
{
    // default preparation
    return DoPreparePrinting(pInfo);
}
```

As you can see, OnPreparePrinting() receives as a parameter a pointer to a CPrintInfo object. Using this object, you can obtain information about the print job, as well as initialize attributes such as the maximum page number. Table 7.3 lists the most useful data and function members of the CPrintInfo class, along with their descriptions.

Table 7.3 Members of the *CPrintInfo* Class

Member	Description
SetMaxPage()	Sets the document's maximum page number.
SetMinPage()	Sets the document's minimum page number.

Member	Description
GetFromPage()	Gets the number of the first page that the user selected for printing.
GetMaxPage()	Gets the document's maximum page number, which may be changed in OnBeginPrinting().
GetMinPage()	Gets the document's minimum page number, which may be changed in OnBeginPrinting().
GetToPage()	Gets the number of the last page the user selected for printing.
m_bContinuePrinting	Controls the printing process. Setting the flag to FALSE ends the print job.
m_bDirect	Indicates whether the document is being directly printed.
m_bPreview	Indicates whether the document is in print preview.
m_nCurPage	Holds the current number of the page being printed.
m_nNumPreviewPages	Holds the number of pages (1 or 2) that are being displayed in print preview.
m_pPD	Holds a pointer to the print job's CPrintDialog object.
m_rectDraw	Holds a rectangle that defines the usable area for the current page.
m_strPageDesc	Holds a page-number format string.

When the DoPreparePrinting() function displays the Print dialog box, the user can set the value of many of the data members of the CPrintInfo class. Your program then can use or set any of these values. Usually, you'll at least call SetMaxPage(), which sets the document's maximum page number, before DoPreparePrinting(), so that the maximum page number displays in the Print dialog box. If you cannot determine the number of pages until you calculate a page length based on the selected printer, you have to wait until you have a printer DC for the printer.

After OnPreparePrinting(), MFC calls OnBeginPrinting(), which is not only another place to set the maximum page count, but also the place to create resources, such as fonts, that you need to complete the print job. OnPreparePrinting() receives, as parameters, a pointer to the printer DC and a pointer to the associated CPrintInfo object.

Next, MFC calls OnPrepareDC() for the first page in the document. This is the beginning of a print loop that is executed once for each page in the document. OnPrepareDC() is the place to control what part of the whole document prints on the current page. As you saw previously, you handle this task by setting the document's viewport origin.

After OnPrepareDC(), MFC calls OnPrint() to print the actual page. Normally, OnPrint() calls OnDraw() with the printer DC, which automatically directs OnDraw()'s output to the printer rather than to the screen. You can override OnPrint() to control how the document is printed.

You can print headers and footers in OnPrint() and then call the base class's version (which in turn calls OnDraw()) to print the body of the document, as demonstrated in Listing 7.7. To prevent the base class version from overwriting your header and footer area, restrict the printable area by setting the m_rectDraw member of the CPrintInfo object to a rectangle that does not overlap the header or footer.

Listing 7.7 Possible *OnPrint()* with Headers and Footers

On the CD

```
void CPrint1View::OnPrint(CDC* pDC, CPrintInfo* pInfo)
{
    // TODO: Add your specialized code here and/or call the base class

    // Call local functions to print a header and footer.
    PrintHeader();
    PrintFooter();

    CView::OnPrint(pDC, pInfo);
}
```

Or you can remove OnDraw() from the print loop entirely by doing your own printing in OnPrint() and not calling OnDraw() at all (see Listing 7.8).

Listing 7.8 Possible *OnPrint()* Without *OnDraw()*

```
void CPrint1View::OnPrint(CDC* pDC, CPrintInfo* pInfo)
{
    // TODO: Add your specialized code here and/or call the base class

    // Call local functions to print a header and footer.
    PrintHeader();
    PrintFooter();

    // Call a local function to print the body of the document.
    PrintDocument();
}
```

As long as there are more pages to print, MFC continues to call OnPrepareDC() and OnPrint() for each page in the document. After the last page is printed, MFC calls OnEndPrinting(), where you can destroy any resources you created in OnBeginPrinting(). The entire printing process is summarized in Figure 7.15.

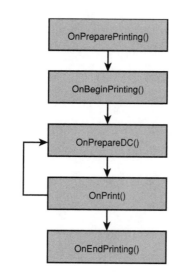

FIG. 7.15
MFC calls various member functions during the printing process.

From Here...

Under MFC, printing and print preview can be as simple or complex as you want or need them to be. For example, MFC can print simple one-page documents almost automatically. All you have to do is supply code for the OnDraw() function, which is responsible for displaying data both in a window and on the printer. If you need to, however, you can override other member functions of the view class to gain more control over the printing process. You have to do this, for example, when printing multiple-page documents or when you want to separate the display duties of OnDraw() from the printing and print preview process.

Please refer to the following for more information on the topics covered in this chapter:

- Chapter 5, "Documents and Views," explains how to coordinate your document and view classes in an MFC application.
- Chapter 6, "Drawing on the Screen," describes how to display graphics and text in a window.

Part
III

Ch
7

Persistence and File I/O

One of the most important things a program must do is save a user's data after that data has been changed in some way. Without the capability to save edited data, the work the user performs with an application exists only as long as the application is running, vanishing the instant the user exits from the application. Not a good way to get work done! In many cases, especially when using AppWizard to create an application, Visual C++ provides much of the code you need to save and load data. However, in some cases—most notably when you create your own object types—you have to do a little extra work to keep your user's files up-to-date. ■

How persistent objects help you keep documents up-to-date

Because persistent objects know how to save and load their own data, they're perfect for dealing with documents that contain custom data types.

How a standard document/view application deals with persistence

When you create an application with AppWizard, you get a default version of a persistent object in the form of the document class.

How to create your own persistent class

Creating a custom persistent class requires completing several programming steps, but it's easy when you know the tricks.

How to use MFC's *CFile* class to read and write files directly

You don't need persistent objects to deal with file I/O. You can handle files the old-fashioned way if you like.

How to create your own archive objects

Objects of the CArchive class are the heart of persistent objects. Once you understand the CFile class, you're ready to create CArchive objects, too.

Objects and Persistence

When you're writing an application, you deal with a lot of different types of objects. Some of your data objects might be simple types like integers and characters. Other objects might be instances of classes, like strings from the CString class or even objects created from your own custom classes. When using objects in applications that must create, save, and load documents, you need a way to save and load the state of those objects so that you can recreate them exactly as the user left them at the end of the last session.

An object's capability to save and load its state is called *persistence*. Almost all of the MFC classes are persistent because they are derived either directly or indirectly from MFC's CObject class, which provides the basic functionality for saving and loading an object's state. In the following section you get a review of how MFC makes a document object persistent.

The File Demo Application

When you create a program by using Visual C++'s AppWizard, you get an application that uses document and view classes to organize, edit, and display its data. As discussed in Chapter 5, "Documents and Views," the document object, which is derived from the CDocument class, is responsible for holding the application's data during a session and for saving and loading the data so that the document persists from one session to another.

In the CHAP9\FILE folder of this book's CD-ROM, you'll find the File Demo application, which demonstrates the basic techniques behind saving and loading data of an object derived from CDocument. When you run the application, you see the window shown in Figure 8.1. This window displays the contents of the current document. In this case, a document is a single string containing a short message.

FIG. 8.1
The File Demo application demonstrates basic document persistence.

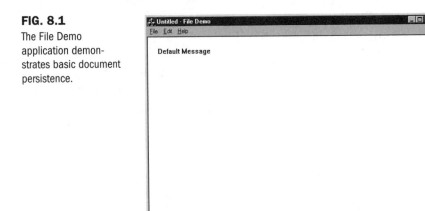

When the program first begins, the message is automatically set to the string "Default Message." However, you can change this message to anything you like. To do this, select the Edit,

Change Message command. You then see the dialog box shown in Figure 8.2. Type a new message in the edit box and click the OK button. The new message appears in the window.

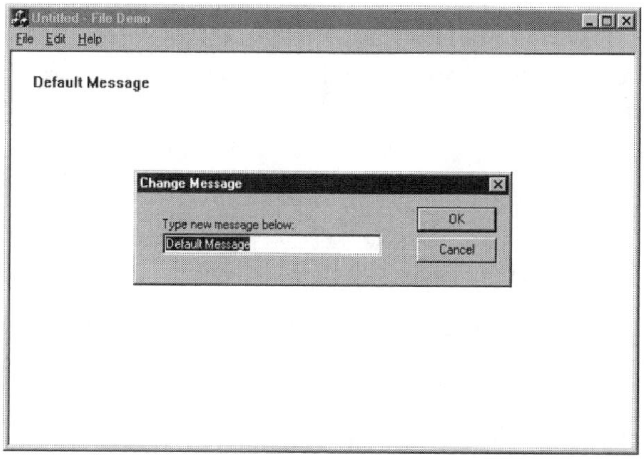

FIG. 8.2
You can use the Change Message dialog box to edit the application's message string.

If you choose to exit the program, the document's current state is lost. The next time you run the program, you again have to change the message string. To avoid this complication, you can save the document before exiting from the program. Choose the File, Save command to do this (see Figure 8.3). After saving the document, you can reload it at any time by choosing File, Open.

FIG. 8.3
Use the File menu to save and load documents.

A Review of Document Classes

What you've just experienced, saving and opening files, is object persistence from the user's point of view. The programmer, of course, needs to know much more about how persistence works. Although you had some experience with document classes in Chapter 5, "Documents and Views," you'll now review the basic concepts with an eye toward extending those concepts to your own custom classes.

When working with an application created by AppWizard, you must complete several steps to enable your document to save and load its state. Those steps, as they apply to an SDI (Single Document Interface) application, will be discussed in this section. The steps are as follows:

1. Define the member variables that will hold the document's data.
2. Initialize the member variables in the document class's OnNewDocument() member function.
3. Display the current document in the view class's OnDraw() member function.
4. Provide member functions in the view class that enable the user to edit the document.
5. Add, to the document class's Serialize() member function, the code needed to save and load the data that comprises the document.

You will see these new member variables, and the way that OnDraw() and Serialize use them, in the samples in this chapter.

A Quick Look at File Demo's Source Code

In the File Demo application, the document class declares its document storage in its header file (FILEDOC.H), like this:

```
// Attributes
public:
    CString m_message;
```

In this case, the document's storage is nothing more than a single string object. Usually, your document's storage needs are much more complex. This single string, however, is enough to demonstrate the basics of a persistent document.

The document class also must initialize the document's data, which it does in the OnNewDocument() member function, as shown in Listing 8.1.

On the CD

Listing 8.1   FILEDOC.CPP—Initializing the Document's Data

```
BOOL CFileDoc::OnNewDocument()
{
    if (!CDocument::OnNewDocument())
        return FALSE;

    // TODO: add reinitialization code here
    // (SDI documents will reuse this document)

    m_message = "Default Message";

    return TRUE;
}
```

With the document class's m_message data member initialized, the application can display the data in the view window, which it does in the view class's OnDraw() function, as shown in Listing 8.2.

On the CD

Listing 8.2 FILEVIEW.CPP—Displaying the Document's Data

```
void CFileView::OnDraw(CDC* pDC)
{
    CFileDoc* pDoc = GetDocument();
    ASSERT_VALID(pDoc);

    // TODO: add draw code for native data here

    pDC->TextOut(20, 20, pDoc->m_message);
}
```

As long as the user is happy with the contents of the document, the program doesn't need to do anything else. But, of course, an application that doesn't allow the user to edit the application's documents is mostly useless. The File Demo application displays a dialog box the user can use to edit the contents of the document, as shown in Listing 8.3.

On the CD

Listing 8.3 FILEVIEW.CPP—Changing the Document's Data

```
void CFileView::OnEditChangemessage()
{
    // TODO: Add your command handler code here

    CChangeDlg dialog(this);
    CFileDoc* pDoc = GetDocument();
    dialog.m_message = pDoc->m_message;

    int result = dialog.DoModal();

    if (result == IDOK)
    {
        pDoc->m_message = dialog.m_message;
        pDoc->SetModifiedFlag();
        Invalidate();
    }
}
```

This function, which responds to the application's Edit, Change Message command, displays the dialog box and, if the user exits from the dialog box by clicking the OK button, transfers the string from the dialog box to the document's data member. The call to the document class's SetModifiedFlag() function notifies the class that its contents have been changed. After the user has changed the document's contents, they must save the data before exiting the application (unless, that is, the user doesn't want to save the changes). The document class's Serialize() function, handles the saving and loading of the document's data. Listing 8.4 shows the empty shell of Serialize() generated by AppWizard.

On the CD

Listing 8.4   FILEVIEW.CPP—The Document Class's *Serialize()* Function

```
void CFileDoc::Serialize(CArchive& ar)
{
    if (ar.IsStoring())
    {
        // TODO: add storing code here

    }
    else
    {
        // TODO: add loading code here

    }
}
```

Because the CString class (of which m_message is an object) defines the >> and << operators for transferring strings to and from an archive, it's a simple task to save and load the document class's data. Simply add this line where the comment reminds you to add storing code:

```
ar << m_message;
```

Add this similar line where the loading code belongs:

```
ar >> m_message;
```

The << operator sends the CString m_message to the archive; the >> operator fills m_message from the archive. As long as all the document's member variables are simple data types like integers or characters, or MFC classes like CString with these operators already defined, it is easy to save and load the data. The operators are defined for these simple data types:

- BYTE
- WORD
- int
- LONG
- DWORD
- float
- double

Creating a Persistent Class

But what if you've created your own custom class for holding the elements of a document? How can you make an object of this class persistent? You find the answers to these questions in this section.

Suppose that you now want to enhance the File Demo application so that it contains its data in a custom class called CMessages. The member variable is now called m_messages and is an instance of CMessages. This class holds three CString objects, each of which must be saved and loaded if the application is going to work correctly. One way to arrange this is to save and load each individual string, as shown in Listing 8.5.

On the CD

Listing 8.5   One Possible Way to Save the New Class's Strings

```
void CFileDoc::Serialize(CArchive& ar)
{
    if (ar.IsStoring())
    {
        ar << m_messages.m_message1;
        ar << m_messages.m_message2;
        ar << m_messages.m_message3;
    }
    else
    {
        ar >> m_messages.m_message1;
        ar >> m_messages.m_message2;
        ar >> m_messages.m_message3;
    }
}
```

You can write the code in Listing 8.5 only if the three member variables of the CMessages class are public and if you know the implementation of the class itself. Later, if the class is changed in any way, this code also has to be changed. It's more object-oriented to delegate the work of storing and loading to the CMessages class itself. This requires some preparation. The basic steps to create a class that can serialize its member variables are the following:

1. Derive the class from CObject.
2. Place the DECLARE_SERIAL() macro in the class's declaration.
3. Place the IMPLEMENT_SERIAL() macro in the class's implementation.
4. Override the Serialize() function in the class.
5. Provide an empty, default constructor for the class.

In the following section, you explore an application that creates persistent objects exactly as described in the preceding steps.

The File Demo 2 Application

The next sample application, File Demo 2, demonstrates the steps you take to create a class from which you can create persistent objects. When you run the application, you see the window shown in Figure 8.4. The program's window displays the three strings that make up the document's data. These three strings are contained in a custom class.

FIG. 8.4

The three strings displayed in the window are data members of a custom class.

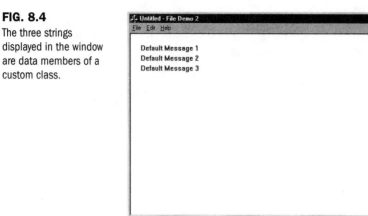

You can edit any of the three strings by choosing the Edit, Change Messages command. When you do, the dialog box shown in Figure 8.5 appears. Type the new string or strings that you want to display in the window, and then click the OK button. The program displays the edited strings, and stores the new string values in the document object.

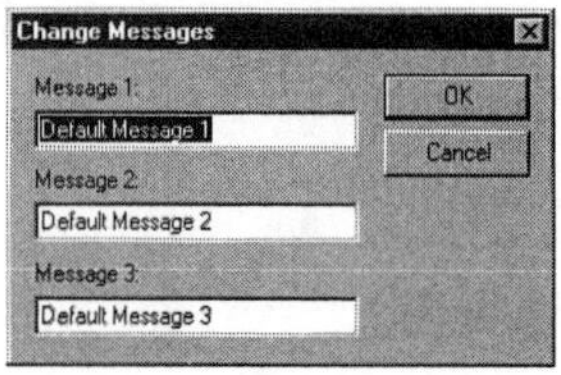

FIG. 8.5

Use the Change Messages dialog box to edit the application's data.

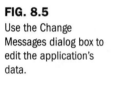

The application's File menu contains the commands you need to save or load the contents of a document. If you save the changes you make before exiting the application, you can reload the document when you restart the application. In this case, unlike the first version of the program, the document class is using a persistent object—an object that knows how to save and load its own state—as the document's data.

Looking at the *CMessages* Class

Before you can understand how the document class manages to save and load its contents successfully, you have to understand how the CMessages class, of which the document class's m_messages data member is an object, works. As you examine this class, you see how the aforementioned five steps for creating a persistent class have been implemented. Listing 8.6 shows the class's header file.

On the CD

Listing 8.6   MESSAGES.H—The *CMessages* Class's Header File

```
// messages.h
class CMessages : public CObject
{
    DECLARE_SERIAL(CMessages)
    CMessages(){};

protected:
    CString m_message1;
    CString m_message2;
    CString m_message3;

public:
    void SetMessage(UINT msgNum, CString msg);
    CString GetMessage(UINT msgNum);
    void Serialize(CArchive& ar);
};
```

First, notice that the CMessages class is derived from MFC's CObject class. Also, notice the
DECLARE_SERIAL() macro near the top of the class's declaration. This macro's single argument
is the name of the class you're declaring. MFC uses this macro to provide the additional function and member variable declarations needed to implement object persistence.

Next, the class declares a default constructor that requires no arguments. This constructor is
necessary because MFC needs to be able to create objects of the class when loading data from
disk. If your class had no default constructor, MFC cannot create a blank object to fill from an
archive.

After the default constructor comes the class's data members, which are three objects of the
CString class. Notice that they are protected member variables now. The public member functions are next. SetMessage(), whose arguments are the index of the string to set and the
string's new value, enables a program to change a data member. GetMessage() is the comple-
mentary function, enabling a program to retrieve the current value of any of the strings. Its
single argument is the number of the string to retrieve.

Finally, the class overrides the Serialize() function, where all the data saving and loading
takes place. The Serialize() function is the heart of a persistent object, with each persistent
class implementing it in a different way. Listing 8.7 is the class's implementation file, which
defines the various member functions.

On the CD

Listing 8.7   MESSAGES.CPP—The *CMessages* Class's Implementation File

```
// messages.cpp

#include "stdafx.h"
#include "messages.h"

IMPLEMENT_SERIAL(CMessages, CObject, 0)
```

continues

Listing 8.7   Continued

```
void CMessages::SetMessage(UINT msgNum, CString msg)
{
    switch (msgNum)
    {
    case 1:
        m_message1 = msg;
        break;

    case 2:
        m_message2 = msg;
        break;

    case 3:
        m_message3 = msg;
        break;
    }
}

CString CMessages::GetMessage(UINT msgNum)
{
    switch (msgNum)
    {
      case 1:
        return m_message1;
      case 2:
        return m_message2;
      case 3:
        return m_message3;
      default
        return "";
    }
}

void CMessages::Serialize(CArchive& ar)
{
    CObject::Serialize(ar);

    if (ar.IsStoring())
    {
        ar << m_message1 << m_message2 << m_message3;
    }
    else
    {
        ar >> m_message1 >> m_message2 >> m_message3;
    }
}
```

The IMPLEMENT_SERIAL() macro is partner to the DECLARE_SERIAL() macro, providing implementation for the functions that give the class its persistent capabilities. The macro's three arguments are the name of the class, the name of the immediate base class, and a schema number, which is like a version number. In most cases, you use 0 or 1 for the schema number.

There's nothing tricky about the SetMessage() and GetMessage() functions, which perform their assigned tasks straightforwardly. The Serialize() function, however, may inspire a couple of questions. First, note that the first line of the body of the function calls the base class's Serialize() function. This is a standard practice for many functions that override functions of a base class. In this case, the call to CObject::Serialize() doesn't do much, since the CObject class's Serialize() function is empty. Still, calling the base class's Serialize() function is a good habit to get into, because you may not always be working with classes derived directly from CObject.

After calling the base class's version of the function, Serialize() saves and loads its data in much the same way a document object does. Because the data members that must be serialized are CString objects, the program can use the >> and << operators to write the strings to the disk.

Using the *CMessages* Class in the Program

Now that you know how the CMessages class works, you can examine how it's used in the File Demo 2 application's document class. As you look over the document class, you see that the class uses the same steps to handle its data as the original File Demo application. The main difference is that it's now dealing with a custom class, rather than simple data types or classes defined by MFC. First, the object is declared in the document class's declaration, like this:

```
// Attributes
public:
    CMessages m_messages;
```

Next, the program initializes the data object in the document class's OnNewDocument() class, as seen in Listing 8.8.

On the CD

Listing 8.8 FILE2DOC.CPP—Initializing the Data Object

```
BOOL CFile2Doc::OnNewDocument()
{
    if (!CDocument::OnNewDocument())
        return FALSE;

    // TODO: add reinitialization code here
    // (SDI documents will reuse this document)

    m_messages.SetMessage(1, "Default Message 1");
    m_messages.SetMessage(2, "Default Message 2");
    m_messages.SetMessage(3, "Default Message 3");

    return TRUE;
}
```

Because the document class cannot directly access the data object's data members, it must initialize each string by calling the CMessages class's SetMessage() member function. The view class must edit the data the same way, by calling the CMessages object's member functions, as shown in Listing 8.9. The view class's OnDraw() function also calls the GetMessage() member function in order to access the CMessages class's strings.

On the CD

Listing 8.9   FILE2VIEW.CPP—Editing the Data Strings

```
void CFile2View::OnEditChangemessages()
{
    // TODO: Add your command handler code here

    CFile2Doc* pDoc = GetDocument();

    CChangeDialog dialog(this);
    dialog.m_message1 = pDoc->m_messages.GetMessage(1);
    dialog.m_message2 = pDoc->m_messages.GetMessage(2);
    dialog.m_message3 = pDoc->m_messages.GetMessage(3);

    int result = dialog.DoModal();

    if (result == IDOK)
    {
        pDoc->m_messages.SetMessage(1, dialog.m_message1);
        pDoc->m_messages.SetMessage(2, dialog.m_message2);
        pDoc->m_messages.SetMessage(3, dialog.m_message3);
        pDoc->SetModifiedFlag();
        Invalidate();
    }
}
```

The real action, however, happens in the document class's Serialize() function, where the m_messages data object is serialized out to disk. This is accomplished by calling the data object's own Serialize() function inside the document's Serialize(), as shown in Listing 8.10.

On the CD

Listing 8.10   FILE2DOC.CPP—Serializing the Data Object

```
void CFile2Doc::Serialize(CArchive& ar)
{
    m_messages.Serialize(ar);

    if (ar.IsStoring())
    {
        // TODO: add storing code here

    }
    else
    {
        // TODO: add loading code here

    }
}
```

As you can see, after serializing the `m_messages` data object, there's not much left to do in the document class's `Serialize()` function. Notice that the call to `m_messages.Serialize()` passes the archive object as its single parameter.

Reading and Writing Files Directly

Although using MFC's built-in serialization capabilities is a handy way to save and load data, sometimes you need more control over the file-handling process. For example, you might need to deal with your files non-sequentially, something the `Serialize()` function and its associated `CArchive` object can't handle because they do stream I/O. In this case, you can handle files almost exactly as they are handled by non-Windows programmers: creating, reading, and writing files directly. Even when you need to dig down to this level of file handling, though, MFC offers help. Specifically, you can use the `CFile` class and its derived classes to handle files directly.

The File Demo 3 Application: Working with *CFile*

This book's CD-ROM contains an example program that shows how the `CFile` class works. You can find this program in the `CHAP9\FILE3` folder. When you run the program, you see the window shown in Figure 8.6. By choosing Edit, Change Message, you can edit the string that's displayed in the window (see Figure 8.7). Finally, you can save and load the displayed text string by choosing the File, Save, and File, Open commands, respectively (see Figure 8.8). (File Demo 3 uses one hardcoded file name, as you'll see shortly.)

FIG. 8.6

The File Demo 3 application uses the `CFile` class for direct file handling.

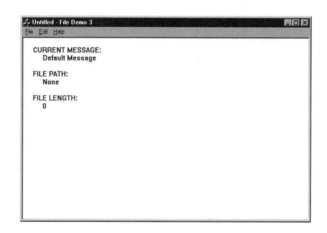

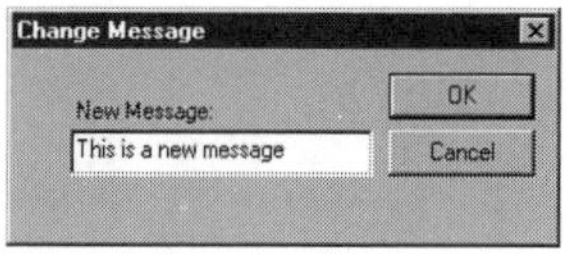

FIG. 8.7

Use the Change Message dialog box to edit the application's display string.

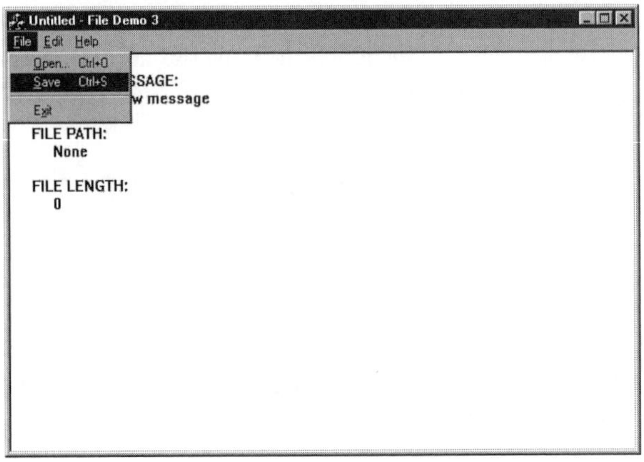

FIG. 8.8
The File menu enables you to save and load the application's display string.

The *CFile* Class

MFC's CFile class encapsulates all the functions you need to handle any type of file. Whether you want to perform common sequential data saving and loading or want to construct a random-access file, the CFile class gets you there. Using the CFile class is a lot like handling files the old-fashioned C-style way, except the class hides some of the busy-work details from you so that you can get the job done quickly and easily. For example, you can create a file for reading with only a single line of code. Table 8.1 shows the CFile class's member functions and their descriptions.

Table 8.1 Member Functions of the *CFile* Class

Function	Description
Constructor	Creates the CFile object. If passed a file name, it opens the file.
Destructor	Cleans up a CFile object that is going out of scope. If the file is open, it closes that file.
Abort()	Immediately closes the file with no regard for errors.
Close()	Closes the file.
Duplicate()	Creates a duplicate file object.
Flush()	Flushes data from the stream.
GetFileName()	Gets the file's filename.

Function	Description
GetFilePath()	Gets the file's full path.
GetFileTitle()	Gets the file's title (the filename without the extension).
GetLength()	Gets the file's length.
GetPosition()	Gets the current position within the file.
GetStatus()	Gets the file's status.
LockRange()	Locks a portion of the file.
Open()	Opens the file.
Read()	Reads data from the file.
Remove()	Deletes a file.
Rename()	Renames the file.
Seek()	Sets the position within the file.
SeekToBegin()	Sets the position to the beginning of the file.
SeekToEnd()	Sets the position to the end of the file.
SetFilePath()	Sets the file's path.
SetLength()	Sets the file's length.
SetStatus()	Sets the file's status.
UnlockRange()	Unlocks a portion of the file.
Write()	Writes data to the file.

Part

III

Ch

8

As you can see from the table, the CFile class offers up plenty of file-handling power. The File Demo 3 application demonstrates how to call a few of the CFile class's member functions. However, most of the other functions are just as easy to use.

Exploring the File Demo 3 Application

When the File Demo 3 application starts up, the program sets its display string to "Default Message," sets the file path to "None," and sets the file's length to 0. Whenever the user saves a document to a file, or opens a file, the view is updated with new file information. (For the sake of simplicity, all of the file handling is done in the view class.) When the user chooses the Edit, Change Message command, the program displays the Change Message dialog box, which happens in the view class's OnEditChangemessage() member function, shown in Listing 8.11.

Listing 8.11 FILE3VIEW.CPP—Changing the Display String

```
void CFile3View::OnEditChangemessage()
{
    // TODO: Add your command handler code here

    CChangeDlg dialog(this);
    dialog.m_message = m_message;

    int result = dialog.DoModal();

    if (result == IDOK)
    {
        m_message = dialog.m_message;
        Invalidate();
    }
}
```

In this function, the program displays the dialog box, and if the user exits the dialog box by clicking the OK button, the program sets the view class's m_message data member to the string entered in the dialog box. A call to Invalidate() ensures that the new string displays in the window. The process of displaying dialog boxes and extracting data from them was first covered in Chapter 2, "Dialog Boxes and Controls."

When the user chooses the File, Save command, MFC calls the view class's OnFileSave() member function, which is shown in Listing 8.12.

Listing 8.12 FILE3VIEW.CPP—The Application's *OnFileSave()* Function

```
void CFile3View::OnFileSave()
{
    // TODO: Add your command handler code here

    // Create the file.
    CFile file("TESTFILE.TXT",
        CFile::modeCreate | CFile::modeWrite);

    // Write data to the file.
    int length = m_message.GetLength();
    file.Write((LPCTSTR)m_message, length);

    // Obtain information about the file.
    m_filePath = file.GetFilePath();
    m_fileLength = file.GetLength();

    // Repaint the window.
Invalidate();
}
```

In OnFileSave(), the program first creates the file, as well as sets the file's access mode, by calling the CFile class's constructor. Notice that you do not have to explicitly open the file when you pass a file name to the constructor. Its arguments are the name of the file and the file access mode flags. You can use several flags at a time simply by ORing their values together, as you can see in the previous listing. These flags, which describe how to open the file and which specify the types of valid operations, are defined as part of the CFile class. They are listed in Table 8.2 along with their descriptions.

Table 8.2   The File Mode Flags

Flag	Description
CFile::modeCreate	Creates a new file or truncates an existing file to length 0
CFile::modeNoInherit	Disallows inheritance by a child process
CFile::modeNoTruncate	When creating the file, does not truncate the file if it already exists
CFile::modeRead	Allows read operations only
CFile::modeReadWrite	Allows both read and write operations
CFile::modeWrite	Allows write operations only
CFile::shareCompat	Allows other processes to open the file
CFile::shareDenyNone	Allows other processes read or write operations on the file
CFile::shareDenyRead	Disallows read operations by other processes
CFile::shareDenyWrite	Disallows write operations by other processes
CFile::shareExclusive	Denies all access to other processes
CFile::typeBinary	Sets binary mode for the file
CFile::typeText	Sets text mode for the file

If you continue to examine the code in Listing 8.12, you will see that after creating the file, OnFileSave() gets the length of the current message and writes it out to the file by calling the CFile object's Write() member function. This function requires, as arguments, a pointer to the buffer containing the data to write and the number of bytes to write. Notice the LPCTSTR casting operator in the call to Write(). This operator is defined by the CString class and extracts the string from the class.

Finally, the program calls the CFile object's GetFilePath() and GetLength() member functions to get the file's complete path and length so that they can be displayed by OnDraw(), not shown here. Finally, a call to the view class's Invalidate() function causes the window to display the new information. Notice that there is no call to Close()—the CFile destructor will close the file automatically.

Reading from a file is not much different from writing to one, as you can see in Listing 8.13, which shows the view class's OnFileOpen() member function.

On the CD

Listing 8.13 FILE3VIEW.CPP—Reading from the File

```
void CFile3View::OnFileOpen()
{
    // TODO: Add your command handler code here

    // Open the file.
    CFile file("TESTFILE.TXT", CFile::modeRead);

    // Read data from the file.
    char s[81];
    int bytesRead = file.Read(s, 80);
    s[bytesRead] = 0;
    m_message = s;

    // Get information about the file.
    m_filePath = file.GetFilePath();
    m_fileLength = file.GetLength();

    // Repaint the window.
Invalidate();
}
```

This time the file is opened by the `CFile::modeRead` flag, which opens the file for read operations only, after which the program creates a character buffer and calls the file object's `read()` member function to read data into the buffer. The `read()` function's two arguments are the address of the buffer and the number of bytes to read. The function returns the number of bytes actually read, which in this case is almost always less than the 80 requested. Using the number of bytes read, the program can add a 0 to the end of the character data, thus creating a standard C-style string that can be used to set the `m_message` data member. As you can see, the `OnFileOpen()` function calls the file object's `GetFilePath()`, `GetLength()`, and `Close()` member functions exactly as `OnFileSave()` did.

Creating Your Own *CArchive* Objects

Although you can handle files using `CFile` objects, you can go a step further and create your own `CArchive` object that you can use exactly as you use the `CArchive` object in the `Serialize()` function. This lets you take advantage of `Serialize` functions already written for other objects, passing them a reference to your own archive object.

To create an archive, you create a `CFile` object and pass that object to the `CArchive` constructor. For example, if you plan to write out objects to a file through an archive, create the archive like this:

```
CFile file("FILENAME.EXT", CFile::modeWrite);
CArchive ar(&file, CArchive::store);
```

After creating the archive object, you can use it just like the archive objects that MFC creates for you. Since you've created it with the `CArchive::store` flag, any calls to `IsStoring()` return `TRUE`, and the code that dumps objects to the archive executes. When you're through with the archive object, you can close both the archive and the file like this:

```
ar.Close();
file.Close();
```

If the objects go out of scope soon after you're finished with them, you can safely omit the calls to `Close()` since both `CArchive` and `CFile` have `Close()` calls in the destructor.

The Registry

In the early days of Windows programming, applications saved settings and options in initialization files, typically with the INI extension. The days of huge `WIN.INI` files or myriad private INI files are now gone—when an application wants to store information about itself, it does so using a centralized system registry. And, although the Registry makes sharing information between processes easier, it can make things more confusing for the programmer. In this section, you uncover some of the mysteries of the Registry and learn how to manage it in your applications.

How the Registry Is Set Up

Unlike INI files, which are plain text files that can be edited with any text editor, the Registry contains binary and ASCII information that can be edited only using the Registry Editor or special API function calls specially created for managing the Registry. If you've ever used the Registry Editor to browse your system's Registry, you know that it contains a huge amount of information that's organized into a tree structure. Figure 8.9 shows how the Registry appears when you first run the Registry Editor. (You can find the Registry Editor, called `REGEDIT.EXE`, in your main Windows folder, or you can run it with the Start menu's Run command by choosing Run, typing **regedit**, and then clicking OK.)

FIG. 8.9

The Registry Editor displays the Registry.

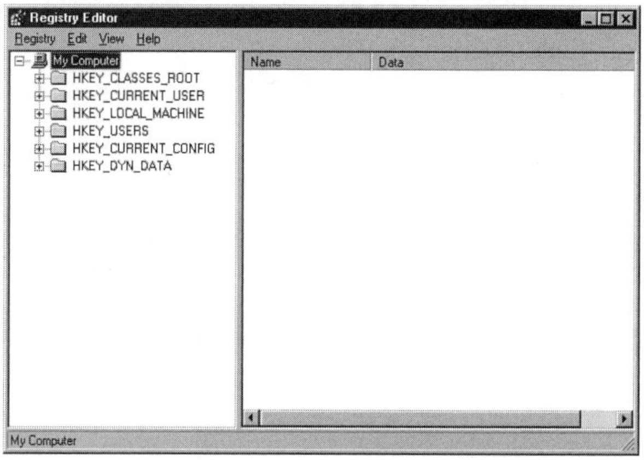

The left-hand window lists the Registry's predefined keys. The plus marks next to the keys in the tree indicate that you can "open" the keys and view more detailed information associated with them. Keys can have subkeys, and subkeys can themselves have subkeys. Any key or subkey may or may not have a value associated with it. If you explore deep enough in the hierarchy, you see a list of values in the right-hand window. In Figure 8.10, you can see the values associated with the current user's screen appearance. To see these values yourself, browse from HKEY_CURRENT_USER to Control Panel to Appearance to Schemes, and you will see the desktop schemes that are installed on your system.

FIG. 8.10
The Registry is structured as a tree containing a huge amount of information.

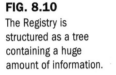

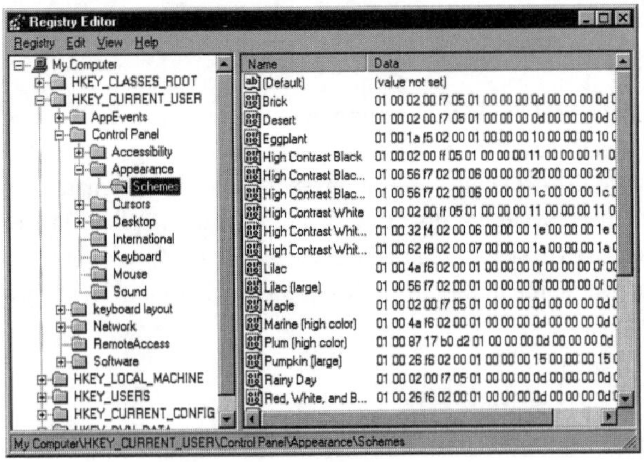

The Predefined Keys

In order to know where things are stored in the Registry, you need to know about the predefined keys and what they mean. From Figure 8.9, you can see that the six predefined keys are:

- HKEY_CLASSES_ROOT
- HKEY_CURRENT_USER
- HKEY_LOCAL_MACHINE
- HKEY_USERS
- HKEY_CURRENT_CONFIG
- HKEY_DYN_DATA

The HKEY_CLASSES_ROOT key holds document types and properties, as well as class information about the various applications installed on the machine. For example, if you explored this key on your system, you'd probably find an entry for the DOC file extension, under which you'd find entries for the applications that can handle this type of document (see Figure 8.11).

FIG. 8.11
HKEY_CLASSES_ROOT key holds document information.

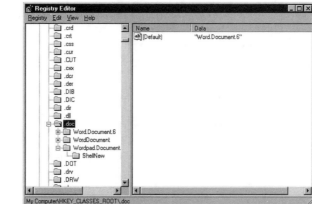

The HKEY_CURRENT_USER key contains all the system settings the current user has established, including color schemes, printers, and program groups. The HKEY_LOCAL_MACHINE key, on the other hand, contains status information about the computer, and the HKEY_USERS key organizes information about each user of the system, as well as the default configuration. Finally, the HKEY_CURRENT_CONFIG key holds information about the hardware configuration, and the HKEY_DYN_DATA key contains information about dynamic registry data, which is data that changes frequently.

Using the Registry in an MFC Application

Now that you know a little about the Registry, let me say that it would take an entire book to explain how to fully access and use the Registry. As you may imagine, the Win32 API features many functions for manipulating the Registry. And, if you're going to use those functions, you sure better know what you're doing! However, you can easily use the Registry with your MFC applications to store information that the application needs from one session to another. To make this task as easy as possible, MFC provides the CWinApp class with the SetRegistryKey() member function, which creates (or opens) a key entry in the Registry for your application. All you have to do is supply a key name (usually a company name) for the function to use, like this:

```
SetRegistryKey("MyCoolCompany");
```

You should call SetRegistryKey() in the application class's InitInstance() member function, which is called once at program startup.

After you've called SetRegistryKey(), your application can create the subkeys and values it needs by calling one of two functions. The WriteProfileString() function adds string values to the Registry, and the WriteProfileInt() function adds integer values to the Registry. To get values from the Registry, you can use the GetProfileString() and GetProfileInt() functions. (You also can use RegSetValueEx() and RegQueryValueEx() to set and retrieve Registry values.)

N O T E When they were first written, the `WriteProfileString()`, `WriteProfileInt()`, `GetProfileString()`, and `GetProfileInt()` functions transferred information to and from an INI file. Used alone, they still do. But when you call `SetRegistryKey()` first, MFC reroutes these profile functions to the Registry, making using the Registry an almost painless process. ▩

The File Demo 2 Application Revisited

In this chapter, you have already built an application that used the Registry. Listing 8.14 is an excerpt from `CFile2App::InitInstance()`—this code was generated by AppWizard.

Listing 8.14   FILE3VIEW.CPP—Reading from the File

```
// Change the registry key under which our settings are stored.
// You should modify this string to be something appropriate
// such as the name of your company or organization.
SetRegistryKey(_T("Local AppWizard-Generated Applications"));

LoadStdProfileSettings();  // Load standard INI file options
(including MRU)
```

MRU stands for *Most Recently Used* and refers to the list of files that appears on the File menu after you have opened files with an application. Figure 8.12 shows the Registry Editor displaying the key that stores this information, `HKEY_CURRENT_USER\Software\Local AppWizard-Generated Applications\File2\Recent File List`. In the foreground, File2's File menu shows the single entry in the MRU list.

FIG. 8.12

The most recently used files list is stored in the Registry automatically.

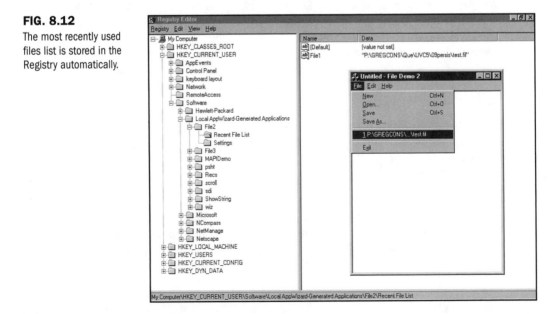

From Here...

When it comes to file handling, Visual C++ and MFC give you a number of options. The easiest way to save and load (serialize) data is to take advantage of the CArchive object created for you by MFC and passed to the document class's Serialize() function. Sometimes, however, you need to create your own persistent objects, by deriving the object's class from MFC's CObject class and then adding a default constructor, as well as the DECLARE_SERIAL() and IMPLEMENT_SERIAL() macros. You can then override the Serialize() function in your new class. If necessary, you can control file handling more directly by creating a CFile object and using that object's member functions to save and load data.

Although not a visible component of an application, the Registry is the place where you should store data that your application needs from session to session. Using the Registry can be tricky when relying solely on the Win32 Registry functions. However, MFC makes dealing with the Registry as easy as writing values to the old-fashioned INI files.

For more information on related topics, please refer to the following chapters:

- Chapter 2, " Dialog Boxes and Controls," explains how to use dialog boxes in your applications.
- Chapter 4, "Messages and Commands," describes MFC's message-mapping system, which enables you to respond to Windows messages.
- Chapter 5, "Documents and Views," discusses how data is handled in an application's document and view classes.
- Chapter 22, "Database Access," describes how Visual C++ programs can interact with information stored in database files.

CHAPTER 9

Building a Complete Application: ShowString

In this chapter, you pull together the concepts demonstrated in previous chapters to create an application that really does something. You add a menu, a menu item, a dialog box, and persistence to an application that draws output based on user settings. In subsequent chapters, this application serves as a base for more advanced work. ■

The ShowString application

A variation on the traditional C "Hello, world!" program, ShowString displays a string and allows the user to control the display.

Adding menu items

You use the ResourceView of Developer Studio to add a menu of items to an application, or to add an item to a menu.

Adding a dialog box

Building dialog boxes in Developer Studio is what earned Visual C++ its name. Drag, drop, and click your way to a custom interface.

Connecting menus to code

ClassWizard simplifies message handling and makes menus intuitive.

Connecting the dialog box to code

ClassWizard handles dialog boxes almost as easily as it does menus.

Changing the appearance of the view

The control over the display is added in this section. Users can set the color and centering of the text after you change the dialog box and drawing code.

Building an Application that Displays a String

In this chapter, you see how to develop an application very much like the traditional "Hello, world!" of C programming. The application simply displays a text string in the main window. The *document* (what you save in a file) contains the string and a few settings. There is a new menu item to bring up a dialog box to change the string and the settings, which control the appearance of the string. This is a deliberately simple application so that the concepts of adding menu items and dialogs are not obscured by trying to understand the actual brains of the application. So bring up Developer Studio and follow along.

Creating an Empty Shell with AppWizard

First, use AppWizard to create the starter application. (Chapter 1, "Building Your First Application," covers AppWizard and creating starter applications.) Choose File, New and the Project tab. Name the project ShowString so that your class names will match those shown throughout this chapter. Click OK.

In Step 1 of AppWizard, it doesn't matter much whether you choose Single Document Interface (SDI) or Multiple Document Interface (MDI), but MDI will allow you to see for yourself how little effort is required to have multiple documents open at once, so choose MDI. Choose US English, and then click Next.

The ShowString application needs no database support and no compound document support, so click Next on Step 2 and Step 3 without changing anything. In AppWizard's Step 4 dialog box, select a docking toolbar, status bar, printing and print preview, context-sensitive help, and 3-D controls, and then click Next. Choose source-file comments and shared DLL, and then click Next. The class names and file names are all fine, so click Finish. Figure 9.1 shows the final confirmation dialog box. Click OK.

FIG. 9.1

AppWizard summarizes the design choices for ShowString.

Displaying a String

The ShowString application displays a string that will be kept in the document. You need to add a member variable to the document class, CShowStringDoc, and add loading and saving code to the Serialize() function. You can initialize the string by adding code to OnNewDocument() for the document and, in order to actually display it, override OnDraw() for the view. Documents and views were introduced in Chapter 5, "Documents and Views."

Member Variable and Serialization   Add a private variable to the document and a public function to get the value by adding these lines to ShowStringDoc.h:

```
private:
    CString string;
public:
    CString GetString() {return string;}
```

The inline function gives other parts of your application a copy of the string to use whenever necessary but makes it impossible for other parts to change the string.

Next, change the skeleton CShowStringDoc::Serialize() function provided by AppWizard to look like Listing 9.1. (Expand CShowStringDoc in ClassView and double-click Serialize() to edit the code.) Since you used the MFC CString class, the archive has operators << and >> already defined, so this is a simple function to write. It fills the archive from the string when you are saving the document and fills the string from the archive when you are loading the document from a file. Chapter 8, "Persistence and File I/O," introduces serialization.

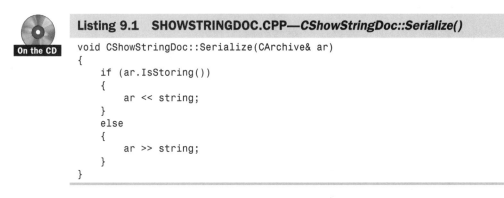

Listing 9.1   SHOWSTRINGDOC.CPP—*CShowStringDoc::Serialize()*

```cpp
void CShowStringDoc::Serialize(CArchive& ar)
{
    if (ar.IsStoring())
    {
        ar << string;
    }
    else
    {
        ar >> string;
    }
}
```

Initializing the String   Whenever a new document is created, you want your application to initialize string to "Hello, world!" A new document is created when the user chooses File, New. This message is caught by CShowStringApp (the message map is shown in Listing 9.2) and handled by CWinApp::OnFileNew(). (Message maps and message handlers are discussed in Chapter 4, "Messages and Commands.") Starter applications generated by AppWizard call OnFileNew() to create a blank document when they run. OnFileNew() calls the document's OnNewDocument(), which actually initializes the member variables of the document.

Part

III

Ch

9

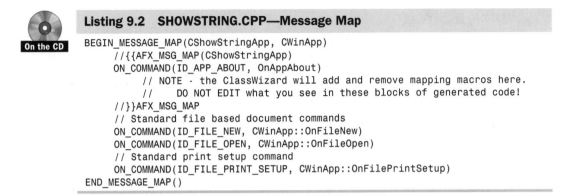

Listing 9.2 SHOWSTRING.CPP—Message Map

```
BEGIN_MESSAGE_MAP(CShowStringApp, CWinApp)
    //{{AFX_MSG_MAP(CShowStringApp)
    ON_COMMAND(ID_APP_ABOUT, OnAppAbout)
        // NOTE - the ClassWizard will add and remove mapping macros here.
        //    DO NOT EDIT what you see in these blocks of generated code!
    //}}AFX_MSG_MAP
    // Standard file based document commands
    ON_COMMAND(ID_FILE_NEW, CWinApp::OnFileNew)
    ON_COMMAND(ID_FILE_OPEN, CWinApp::OnFileOpen)
    // Standard print setup command
    ON_COMMAND(ID_FILE_PRINT_SETUP, CWinApp::OnFilePrintSetup)
END_MESSAGE_MAP()
```

AppWizard gives you the simple `OnNewDocument()` shown in Listing 9.3.

Listing 9.3 SHOWSTRINGDOC.CPP—*CShowStringDoc::OnNewDocument()*

```
BOOL CShowStringDoc::OnNewDocument()
{
    if (!CDocument::OnNewDocument())
        return FALSE;

    // TODO: add reinitialization code here
    // (SDI documents will reuse this document)

    return TRUE;
}
```

Take away the comments and add this line in their place:

```
string = "Hello, world!";
```

(What else could it say, after all?) Leave the call to `CDocument::OnNewDocument()` because that will handle all the other work involved in making a new document.

Getting the String on the Screen   As you learned in Chapter 6, "Drawing on the Screen," a view's `OnDraw()` function is called whenever that view needs to be drawn, such as when your application is first started, resized, or restored, or when a window that had been covering it is taken away. AppWizard has provided a skeleton, shown in Listing 9.4. To edit this function, expand `CShowStringView` in ClassView and then double-click `OnDraw()`.

Listing 9.4 SHOWSTRINGVIEW.CPP—*CShowStringView::OnDraw()*

```
void CShowStringView::OnDraw(CDC* pDC)
{
    CShowStringDoc* pDoc = GetDocument();
    ASSERT_VALID(pDoc);

    // TODO: add draw code for native data here
}
```

OnDraw() takes a pointer to a device context, as discussed in Chapter 6, "Drawing on the Screen." The device context class, CDC, has a member function called DrawText() that draws text on the screen. It is declared like this:

```
int DrawText( const CString& str, LPRECT lpRect, UINT nFormat )
```

▶ **See** "Understanding Device Contexts," **p. 134**

The CString to be passed to this function is going to be the string from the document class, which can be accessed as pDoc->GetString(). The *lpRect* is the client rectangle of the view, returned by GetClientRect(). Finally, nFormat is the way the string should display; for example, DT_CENTER means that the text should be centered from left to right within the view. DT_VCENTER means that the text should be centered up and down, but this works only for single lines of text that are identified with DT_SINGLELINE. Multiple format flags can be combined with |, so DT_CENTER|DT_VCENTER|DT_SINGLELINE is the *nFormat* that you want. The drawing code to be added to CShowStringView::OnDraw() looks like this:

```
CRect rect;
GetClientRect(&rect);
pDC->DrawText(pDoc->GetString(), &rect, DT_CENTER|DT_VCENTER|DT_SINGLELINE);
```

This sets up a CRect and passes its address to GetClientRect(), which sets the CRect to the client area of the view. DrawText() draws the document's string in the rectangle, centered vertically and horizontally.

At this point, the application should display the string properly. Build and execute it, and you should see something like Figure 9.2. You have quite a lot of functionality: menus, toolbars, status bar, and so on, but nothing that any other Windows application doesn't have, yet. Starting with the next section, that changes.

FIG. 9.2
ShowString starts simply, with the usual greeting.

Building the ShowString Menus

AppWizard creates two menus for you, shown in the ResourceView window in Figure 9.3. IDR_MAINFRAME is the menu shown when no file is open; IDR_SHOWSTTYPE is the menu shown when a ShowString document is open. Notice that IDR_MAINFRAME has no Edit or Window menus and that the File menu is much shorter than the one on the IDR_SHOWSTTYPE menu, with only New, Open, Print Setup, recent files, and Exit items.

FIG. 9.3

AppWizard creates two menus for ShowString.

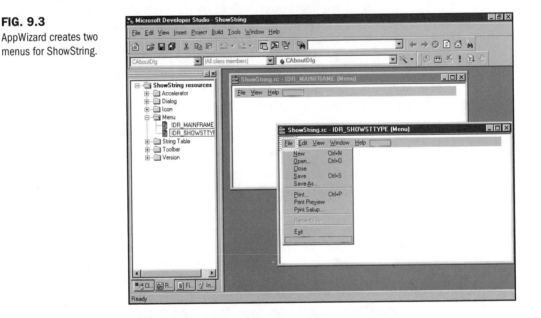

You are going to add a menu item to ShowString, so the first decision is where to add it. The user will be able to edit the string that displays and sets the format of the string. You could add a Value item to the Edit menu that brings up a small dialog box for only the string and then create a Format menu with one item, Appearance, that brings up the dialog box to set the appearance. But the option you are going to see here is to combine everything into one dialog box and then put it on a new Tools menu under the Options item.

N O T E   You may have noticed already that more and more Windows applications are standardizing on Tools, Options as the place for miscellaneous settings. ▓

Do you need to add the item to both menus? No. When there is no document open, there is nowhere to save the changes made with this dialog box. So only IDR_SHOWSTTYPE needs to have a menu added. Bring up the menu by double-clicking it in the ResourceView window. At the far right of the menu, after Help, is an empty menu. Click it and type **&Tools**. The Properties dialog box appears; pin it to the background by clicking the pushpin. The Caption box contains &Tools. The menu at the end becomes the Tools menu, with an empty item underneath it; another empty menu then appears to the right of the Tools menu, as shown in Figure 9.4.

FIG. 9.4
Adding the Tools menu is easy in the ResourceView window.

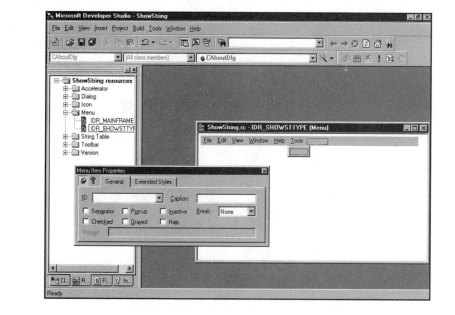

> **T I P** The & in the Caption edit box precedes the letter that serves as the mnemonic key for selecting that menu with the keyboard (for example, Alt + T in the case of Tools). This letter appears underlined in the menu. There is no further work required on your part. You can opt to select a different mnemonic key by moving the & so it precedes a different letter in the menu or menu item name (for example, T&ools changes the key from 'T' to 'o').

Click the new Tools menu and drag it between the View and Window menus, corresponding to the position of Tools in products like Developer Studio and Microsoft Word. Next, click the empty sub-item. The Properties dialog box changes to show the blank properties of this item; change the caption to **&Options** and enter a sensible prompt, as shown in Figure 9.5.

All menu items have a resource ID, and this resource ID is the way the menu items are connected to your code. Developer Studio will choose a good one for you, but it doesn't appear in the Properties dialog box right away. Click some other menu item, and then click Options again; you see that the resource ID is ID_TOOLS_OPTIONS. Alternatively, press Enter when you are finished and the highlight moves down to the empty menu item below Options. Press the up-arrow cursor key to return the highlight to the Options item.

Part
III

Ch
9

FIG. 9.5

The menu command Tools, Options will control everything that ShowString does.

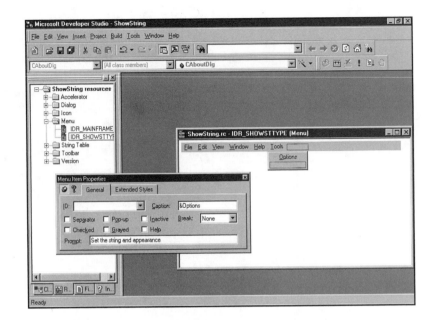

If you'd like to provide an accelerator, such as Ctrl+C for Edit, Copy, this is a good time to do it. Click the + next to Accelerator in the ResourceView window and then double-click IDR_MAINFRAME, the only Accelerator table in this application. At a glance, you can see what key combinations are already in use. Ctrl+O is already taken, but Ctrl+T is available. To connect Ctrl+T to Tools, Options, follow these steps:

1. Click the empty line at the bottom of the Accelerator table. If you have closed the Properties dialog box, bring it back by choosing View, Properties, and then pin it in place. (Alternatively, double-click the empty line to bring up the Properties dialog box.)

2. Click the drop-down list box labeled ID and choose ID_TOOLS_OPTIONS from the list, which is in alphabetical order. (There are a lot of entries before ID_TOOLS_OPTIONS; drag the elevator down almost to the bottom of the list or start typing the resource ID—by the time you enter ID_TO, the highlight will be in the right place.)

3. Enter **T** in the Key box; then make sure that the Ctrl check box is selected and that the Alt and Shift boxes are deselected. Alternatively, click the Next Key Typed button and then type **Ctrl+T**, and the dialog box will be filled in properly.

4. Click another line in the Accelerator table to commit the changes.

Figure 9.6 shows the Properties dialog box for this accelerator after clicking the newly entered line again.

FIG. 9.6
Keyboard accelerators
are connected to
resource IDs.

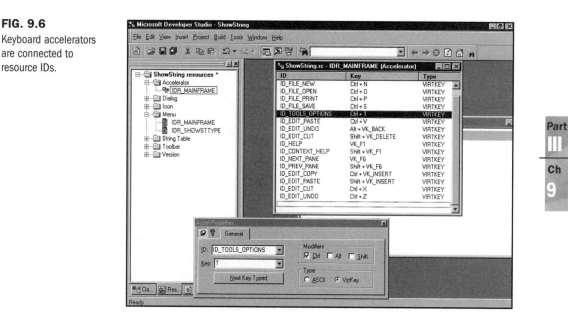

What happens when the user chooses this new menu item, Tools, Options? A dialog box displays. So, tempting as it may be to start connecting this menu to code, it makes more sense to build the dialog box first.

Building the ShowString Dialog Boxes

Chapter 2, "Dialog Boxes and Controls," introduced dialog boxes. This section builds on that background. ShowString is actually going to have two custom dialog boxes: one brought up by Tools, Options, and also an About dialog box. An About dialog box has been provided by AppWizard, but it needs to be changed a little; you build the Options dialog box from scratch.

ShowString's About Dialog Box

Figure 9.7 shows the About dialog box that AppWizard makes for you; it contains the name of the application and the current year. To view the About dialog box for ShowString, click the ResourceView tab in the project workspace window, expand the Dialogs list by clicking the + icon next to the word Dialogs, and then double-click IDD_ABOUTBOX to bring up the About dialog box resource.

FIG. 9.7

AppWizard makes an About dialog box for you.

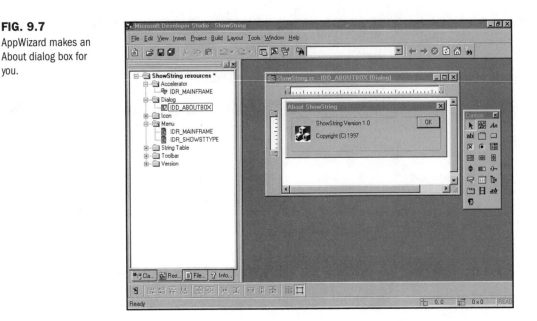

You might want to add a company name to your About dialog box. Here's how to add "Que Books," as an example. Click the line of text that reads Copyright©1997, and it will be surrounded by a selection box. Bring up the Properties dialog box, if it is not up. Edit the caption to add Que Books at the end; the changes are reflected immediately in the dialog box.

> **TIP** If the rulers you see in Figure 9.7 don't appear when you open IDD_ABOUTBOX in Developer Studio, you can turn them on by choosing Layout, Guide Settings and then selecting the Rulers and Guides option button in the top half of the Guide Settings dialog box.

I decided to add a text string reminding users what book this application is from. Here's how to do that:

1. Size the dialog box a little taller by clicking the whole dialog box to select it, then clicking the sizing square in the middle of the bottom border, and dragging the bottom border down a little. (This visual editing is what gave Visual C++ its name when it first came out.)

2. In the floating toolbar called Controls, click the button labeled Aa to get a *static control,* which means a piece of text that the user cannot change, perfect for labels like this. Click within the dialog box under the other text to insert the static text there.

3. In the Properties dialog box, change the caption from Static to Using Visual C++ 5. The box automatically resizes to fit the text.

4. Hold down the Ctrl key and click the other two static text lines in the dialog box. Choose Layout, Align Controls, Left, which aligns the edges of the three selected controls. The one you select last stays still, and the others move to align with it.

5. Choose Layout, Space Evenly, Down. These menu options can save you a great deal of dragging, squinting at the screen, and then dragging again.

The About dialog box should look like Figure 9.8.

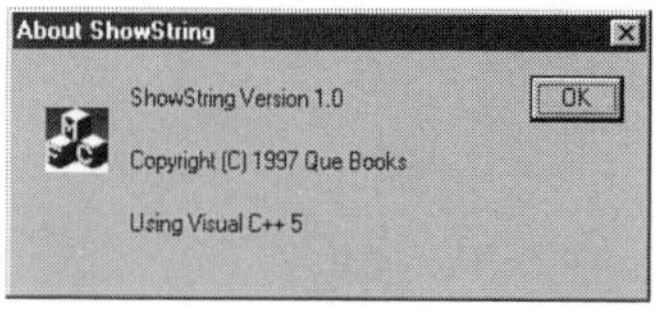

FIG. 9.8

In a matter of minutes, you can customize your About dialog box.

Part

III

Ch

9

T I P All the Layout menu items are on the Dialog toolbar.

ShowString's Options Dialog Box

The Options dialog box is pretty simple to build. First, make a new dialog box by choosing Insert, Resource, and then double-clicking Dialog. An empty dialog box called Dialog1 appears, with an OK and a Cancel button, as shown in Figure 9.9.

FIG. 9.9

A new dialog box always has OK and Cancel buttons.

Next, follow these steps to convert the empty dialog box into the Options dialog box:

1. Change the ID to IDD_OPTIONS and the caption to **Options**.
2. In the floating toolbar called Controls, click the button labeled ab¦ to get an edit box in which the user can enter the new value for the string. Click inside the dialog box to place the control and then change the ID to IDC_OPTIONS_STRING. (Control IDs should all start with "IDC" and then mention the name of their dialog box and an identifier that is unique to that dialog box.)
3. Drag the sizing squares to resize the edit box as wide as possible.
4. Add a static label above the edit box and change that caption to **String:**.

You will revisit this dialog box later when adding the appearance capabilities, but for now it's ready to be connected. It should look like Figure 9.10.

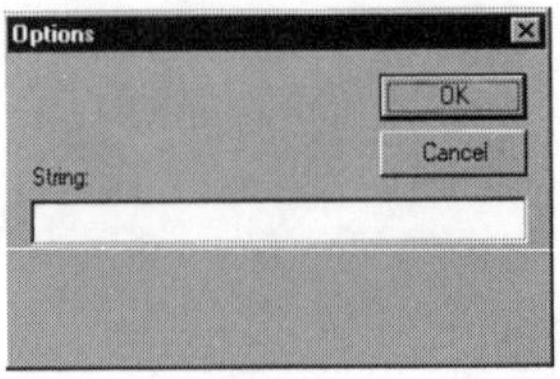

FIG. 9.10

The Options dialog box is the place to change the string.

Making the Menu Work

When the user chooses Tools, Options, the Options dialog box should display. You use ClassWizard to arrange for one of your functions to be called when the item is chosen, and then you write the function, which creates an object of your dialog box class and then displays it.

The Dialog Box Class

ClassWizard makes the dialog box class for you. While the window displaying the IDD_OPTIONS dialog box has focus, choose View, ClassWizard. ClassWizard realizes there is not yet a class that corresponds to this dialog box and offers to create one, as shown in Figure 9.11.

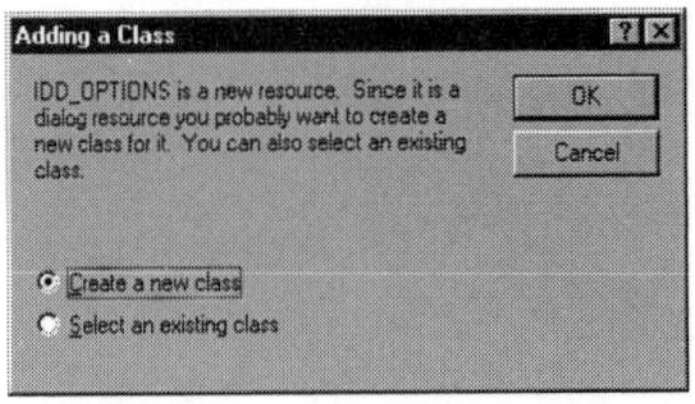

FIG. 9.11

Create a C++ class to go with the new dialog box.

Leave Create a New Class selected and then click OK. The Create New Class dialog box, shown in Figure 9.12, appears.

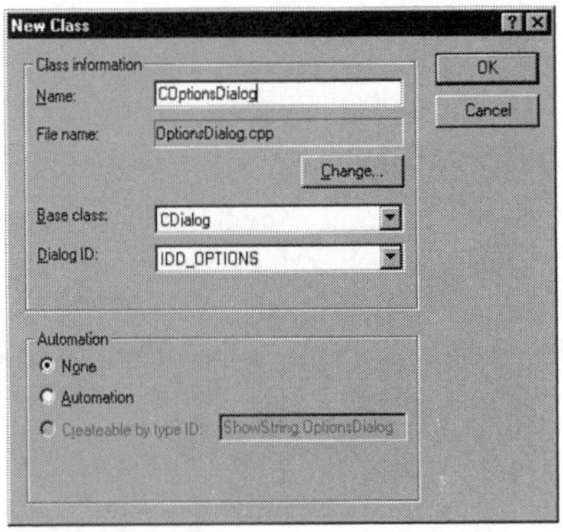

FIG. 9.12

The dialog box class inherits from CDialog.

Fill in the dialog box as follows:

1. Choose a sensible name for the class, one that starts with C and contains the word Dialog; this example uses COptionsDialog.

2. The base class defaults to CDialog, which is perfect for this case.

3. Click OK to create the class.

The ClassWizard dialog box has been waiting behind these other dialog boxes, and now you use it. Click the Member Variables tab and connect IDC_OPTIONS_STRING to a CString called m_string, just as you connected controls to member variables of the dialog box class in Chapter 2, "Dialog Boxes and Controls." Click OK to close ClassWizard.

Perhaps you're curious about what code was created for you when ClassWizard made the class. The header file is shown in Listing 9.5.

Part III
Ch 9

On the CD

Listing 9.5   OPTIONSDIALOG.H—Header File for *COptionsDialog*

```cpp
// OptionsDialog.h : header file
//
/////////////////////////////////////////////////////////////////////////////
// COptionsDialog dialog

class COptionsDialog : public CDialog
{
// Construction
public:
    COptionsDialog(CWnd* pParent = NULL);   // standard constructor

// Dialog Data
    //{{AFX_DATA(COptionsDialog)
    enum { IDD = IDD_OPTIONS };
    CString     m_string;
    //}}AFX_DATA
// Overrides
    // ClassWizard generated virtual function overrides
    //{{AFX_VIRTUAL(COptionsDialog)
    protected:
    virtual void DoDataExchange(CDataExchange* pDX);   // DDX/DDV support
    //}}AFX_VIRTUAL
// Implementation
protected:
    // Generated message map functions
    //{{AFX_MSG(COptionsDialog)
        // NOTE: the ClassWizard will add member functions here
    //}}AFX_MSG
    DECLARE_MESSAGE_MAP()
};
```

There are an awful lot of comments here to help ClassWizard find its way around in the file when the time comes to add more functionality, but there is only one member variable, m_string; one constructor; and one member function, DoDataExchange(), which gets the control value into the member variable, or vice versa. The source file is not much longer; it's shown in Listing 9.6.

Listing 9.6 OPTIONSDIALOG.CPP—Implementation File for *COptionsDialog*

```
// OptionsDialog.cpp : implementation file
//

#include "stdafx.h"
#include "ShowString.h"
#include "OptionsDialog.h"

#ifdef _DEBUG
#define new DEBUG_NEW
#undef THIS_FILE
static char THIS_FILE[] = __FILE__;
#endif
/////////////////////////////////////////////////////////////////////////////
// COptionsDialog dialog
COptionsDialog::COptionsDialog(CWnd* pParent /*=NULL*/)
    : CDialog(COptionsDialog::IDD, pParent)
{
    //{{AFX_DATA_INIT(COptionsDialog)
    m_string = _T("");
    //}}AFX_DATA_INIT
}
void COptionsDialog::DoDataExchange(CDataExchange* pDX)
{
    CDialog::DoDataExchange(pDX);
    //{{AFX_DATA_MAP(COptionsDialog)
    DDX_Text(pDX, IDC_OPTIONS_STRING, m_string);
    //}}AFX_DATA_MAP
}
BEGIN_MESSAGE_MAP(COptionsDialog, CDialog)
    //{{AFX_MSG_MAP(COptionsDialog)
        // NOTE: the ClassWizard will add message map macros here
    //}}AFX_MSG_MAP
END_MESSAGE_MAP()
```

The constructor sets the string to an empty string; this code is surrounded by special ClassWizard comments that enable it to add other variables later. The DoDataExchange() function calls DDX_Text() to transfer data from the control with the resource ID IDC_OPTIONS_STRING to the member variable m_string, or vice versa. This code, too, is surrounded by ClassWizard comments. Finally, there is an empty message map, because COptionsDialog doesn't catch any messages.

Catching the Message

The next step in building ShowString is to catch the command message sent when the user chooses Tools, Options. There are seven classes in ShowString: CAboutDlg, CChildFrame, CMainFrame, COptionsDialog, CShowStringApp, CShowStringDoc, and CShowStringView. Which one should catch the command? The string and the options will be saved in the document and displayed in the view, so one of those two classes should handle the changing of the string. The document owns the private variable and will not let the view change the string unless you implement a public function to set the string. So it makes the most sense to have the document catch the message.

To catch the message, follow these steps:

1. Bring up ClassWizard (if it is not already up).

2. Click the Message Maps tab.

3. Select CShowStringDoc from the Class Name drop-down list box.

4. Select ID_TOOLS_OPTIONS from the Object IDs list box on the left, and select COMMAND from the Messages list box on the right.

5. Click Add Function to add a function to handle this command.

6. The Add Member Function dialog box, shown in Figure 9.13, appears, giving you an opportunity to change the function name from the usual one. Do not change it; just click OK.

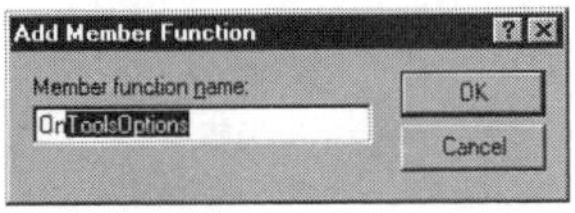

FIG. 9.13
ClassWizard suggests a good name for the message-catching function.

TIP You should almost never change the names that ClassWizard suggests for message catchers. If you find that you have to (perhaps because the suggested name is too long or conflicts with another function name in the same object), be sure to choose a name that starts with On.

Click Edit Code to close ClassWizard and edit the newly added function. What happened to CShowStringDoc when you arranged for the ID_TOOLS_OPTIONS message to be caught? The new message map in the header file is shown in Listing 9.7.

Listing 9.7 SHOWSTRINGDOC.H—Message Map for *CShowStringDoc*

```
// Generated message map functions
protected:
    //{{AFX_MSG(CShowStringDoc)
    afx_msg void OnToolsOptions();
    //}}AFX_MSG
    DECLARE_MESSAGE_MAP()
```

This is just declaring the function. In the source file, ClassWizard changed the message maps shown in Listing 9.8.

On the CD

Listing 9.8   SHOWSTRINGDOC.CPP—Message Map for *CShowStringDoc*

```
BEGIN_MESSAGE_MAP(CShowStringDoc, CDocument)
    //{{AFX_MSG_MAP(CShowStringDoc)
    ON_COMMAND(ID_TOOLS_OPTIONS, OnToolsOptions)
    //}}AFX_MSG_MAP
END_MESSAGE_MAP()
```

This arranges for OnToolsOptions() to be called when the command ID_TOOLS_OPTIONS is sent. ClassWizard also added a skeleton for OnToolsOptions():

```
void CShowStringDoc::OnToolsOptions()
{
    // TODO: Add your command handler code here

}
```

Making the Dialog Box Work

OnToolsOptions() should initialize and display the dialog box and then do something with the value that the user provided. (This process was first discussed in Chapter 2, "Dialog Boxes and Controls.") You have already connected the edit box to a member variable, m_string, of the dialog box class. You initialize this member variable before displaying the dialog box and use it afterwards.

OnToolsOptions(), shown in Listing 9.9, displays the dialog box. Add this code to the empty function ClassWizard generated for you when you arranged to catch the message.

Listing 9.9   SHOWSTRINGDOC.CPP—*OnToolsOptions()*

```
void CShowStringDoc::OnToolsOptions()
{
    COptionsDialog dlg;
    dlg.m_string = string;
    if (dlg.DoModal() == IDOK)
    {
        string = dlg.m_string;
        SetModifiedFlag();
        UpdateAllViews(NULL);
    }

}
```

This code fills the member variable of the dialog box with the member variable of the document (ClassWizard added m_string as a public member variable of COptionsDialog, so the document can change it) and then brings up the dialog box by calling DoModal(). If the user clicks OK, the member variable of the document changes, the modified flag is set (so that the user is prompted to save the document on exit), and the view is asked to redraw itself with a call to `UpdateAllViews()`. In order for this to compile, of course, the compiler must know what a `COptionsDialog` is, so add this line at the beginning of `ShowStringDoc.cpp`:

```
#include "OptionsDialog.h"
```

At this point, you can build the application and run it. Choose Tools, Options, and change the string. Click OK and you see the new string in the view. Exit the application; you are asked whether to save the file. Save it, restart the application, and open the file again. The default "Hello, world!" document remains open, and the changed document is open with a different string. The application works, as you can see in Figure 9.14 (the windows are resized to let them both fit in the figure).

FIG. 9.14
ShowString can change the string, save it to a file, and reload it.

Adding Appearance Options to the Options Dialog Box

ShowString doesn't have much to do; it just demonstrates menus and dialog boxes. But the only dialog box control that ShowString uses is an edit box. In this section, you add a set of option buttons and check boxes to change the way the string is drawn in the view.

Changing the Options Dialog Box

It is quite simple to incorporate a full-fledged Font dialog box into an application, but the example in this section is going to do something much simpler. A group of option buttons will let the user choose among several colors. One check box will allow the user to specify that the text should be centered horizontally, and another that the text be centered vertically. Because these are check boxes, the text can be either, neither, or both.

Open the IDD_OPTIONS dialog box by double-clicking it in the ResourceView window, and then add the option buttons by following these steps:

1. Stretch the dialog box taller to make room for the new controls.

2. Click the radio button in the Controls floating toolbar, and then click the Options dialog box to drop the control.

3. Choose View, Properties, and then pin the Properties dialog box in place.

4. Change the resource ID of the first radio button to IDC_OPTIONS_BLACK, and change the caption to **&Black**.

5. Select the Group box to indicate that this is the first of a group of option buttons.

6. Add another option button with resource ID IDC_OPTIONS_RED and **&Red** as the caption. Do not select the Group box since the Red option button does not start a new group but is part of the group that started with the Black option button.

7. Add a third option button with resource ID IDC_OPTIONS_GREEN and **&Green** as the caption. Again, do not select Group.

8. Drag the three option buttons into a horizontal arrangement, and select all three.

9. Choose Layout, Align Controls, Bottom (to even them up).

10. Choose Layout, Space Evenly, Across to space the controls across the dialog box.

Next, add the check boxes by following these steps:

1. Click the check box in the Controls floating toolbar and then click the Options dialog box, dropping a check box onto it.

2. Change the resource ID of this check box to IDC_OPTIONS_HORIZCENTER and the caption to **Center &Horizontally**.

3. Select the Group box to indicate the start of a new group after the option buttons.

4. Drop another check box onto the dialog box as in step 1 and give it the resource ID IDC_OPTIONS_VERTCENTER and the caption **Center &Vertically**.

5. Arrange the check boxes under the option buttons.

6. Click the Group box on the Controls floating toolbar, and then click and drag a group box around the option buttons. Change the caption to **Text Color**.

7. Move the OK and Cancel buttons down to the bottom of the dialog box.

8. Select each horizontal group of controls, and use Layout, Center in Dialog, Horizontal to make things neater.

9. Choose Edit, Select All, and then drag all the controls up toward the top of the dialog box. Shrink the dialog box to fit around the new controls. It should now resemble Figure 9.15.

FIG. 9.15

The options dialog box for ShowString has been expanded.

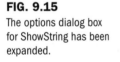 If you don't recognize the icons on the Controls toolbar, use the ToolTips. If you hold the cursor over any of the toolbar buttons, a tip pops up after a few seconds, telling you what control the button represents.

Finally, set the tab order by choosing Layout, Tab Order, and then clicking the controls, in this order:

1. IDC_OPTIONS_STRING
2. IDC_OPTIONS_BLACK
3. IDC_OPTIONS_RED
4. IDC_OPTIONS_GREEN
5. IDC_OPTIONS_HORIZCENTER
6. IDC_OPTIONS_VERTCENTER
7. IDOK
8. IDCANCEL

Then click away from the dialog box to leave the two static text controls as positions 9 and 10.

Adding Member Variables to the Dialog Box Class

Having added controls to the dialog box, you need to add corresponding member variables to the COptionsDialog class. Bring up ClassWizard, select the Member Variable tab, and add member variables for each control. Figure 9.16 shows the summary of the member variables created. The check boxes are connected to BOOL variables; these member variables are TRUE if the box is selected and FALSE if it is not. The option buttons are handled differently. Only the first—the one with the Group box selected in its Properties dialog box—is connected to a member variable. That integer is a zero-based index that indicates which button is selected. In other words, when the Black button is selected, m_color is 0; when Red is selected, m_color is 1; and when Green is selected, m_color is 2.

FIG. 9.16

Member variables in the dialog box class are connected to individual controls or the group of option buttons.

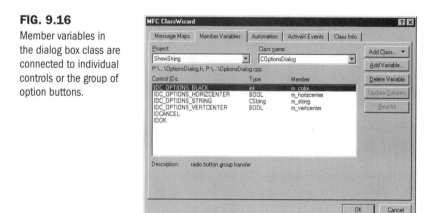

Adding Member Variables to the Document

The variables to be added to the document are the same ones that were added to the dialog box. You add them to the CShowStringDoc class definition in the header file, to `OnNewDocument()`, and to `Serialize()`. Add the lines in Listing 9.10 at the top of the `CShowStringDoc` definition in `ShowStringDoc.h`, replacing the previous definition of `string` and `GetString()`.

Listing 9.10   SHOWSTRINGDOC.H—*CShowStringDoc* Member Variables

```
private:
    CString string;
    int     color;
    BOOL horizcenter;
    BOOL vertcenter;
public:
    CString GetString() {return string;}
    int     GetColor() {return color;}
    BOOL GetHorizcenter() {return horizcenter;}
    BOOL GetVertcenter() {return vertcenter;}
```

As with `string`, these are private variables with public `get` functions but no set functions. All these options should be serialized; the new `Serialize()` is shown in Listing 9.11. Change your copy by double-clicking the function name in ClassView and adding the new code.

Listing 9.11   SHOWSTRINGDOC.CPP—*Serialize()*

```
void CShowStringDoc::Serialize(CArchive& ar)
{
    if (ar.IsStoring())
    {
        ar << string;
        ar << color;
        ar << horizcenter;
        ar << vertcenter;
    }
    else
    {
        ar >> string;
        ar >> color;
        ar >> horizcenter;
        ar >> vertcenter;
    }
}
```

Finally, you need to initialize these variables in `OnNewDocument()`. What are good defaults for these new member variables? Black text, centered in both directions, was the old behavior, and it makes sense to use it as the default. The new `OnNewDocument()` is shown in Listing 9.12.

Listing 9.12   SHOWSTRINGDOC.CPP—*OnNewDocument()*

```
BOOL CShowStringDoc::OnNewDocument()
{
    if (!CDocument::OnNewDocument())
        return FALSE;
```

```
string = "Hello, world!";
color = 0;      //black
horizcenter = TRUE;
vertcenter = TRUE;

return TRUE;
}
```

Of course, at the moment, users cannot change these member variables from the defaults. To allow the user to change the variables, you have to change the function that handles the dialog box.

Changing *OnToolsOptions()*

The OnToolsOptions() function sets the values of the dialog box member variables from the document member variables and then displays the dialog box. If the user clicks OK, the document member variables are set from the dialog box member variables, and the view is redrawn. Having just added three member variables to the dialog box and the document, you have three lines to add before the dialog box displays and then three more to add in the block that's called after OK is clicked. The new OnToolsOptions() is shown in Listing 9.13.

On the CD

Listing 9.13   SHOWSTRINGDOC.CPP—*OnToolsOptions()*

```
void CShowStringDoc::OnToolsOptions()
{
    COptionsDialog dlg;
    dlg.m_string = string;
    dlg.m_color = color;
    dlg.m_horizcenter = horizcenter;
    dlg.m_vertcenter = vertcenter;

    if (dlg.DoModal() == IDOK)
    {
        string = dlg.m_string;
        color = dlg.m_color;
        horizcenter = dlg.m_horizcenter;
        vertcenter = dlg.m_vertcenter;
        SetModifiedFlag();
        UpdateAllViews(NULL);
    }

}
```

So what happens when the user brings up the dialog box and changes the value of a control, say, by deselecting Center Horizontally? The framework—through Dialog Data Exchange (DDX), as set up by ClassWizard—changes the value of COptionsDialog::m_horizcenter to FALSE. This code in OnToolsOptions() changes the value of CShowStringDoc::horizcenter to FALSE. When the user saves the document, Serialize() saves horizcenter. This is all good, but none of this code actually changes the way the view is drawn. That involves OnDraw().

Changing *OnDraw()*

The single call to DrawText() in OnDraw() gets a little more complex now. The document member variables are used to set the appearance of the view. Edit OnDraw() by expanding CShowStringView in the ClassView, and double-clicking OnDraw().

The color is set with CDC::SetTextColor() before the call to DrawText(). You should always save the old text color and restore it when you are finished. The parameter to SetTextColor() is a COLORREF, and you can directly specify combinations of red, green, and blue as hex numbers in the form 0x00bbggrr, so that, for example, 0x000000FF is bright red. Most people prefer to use the RGB macro, which takes hex numbers from 0x0 to 0xFF, specifying the amount of each color; bright red is RGB(FF,0,0), for instance. Add the lines shown in Listing 9.14 before the call to DrawText() to set up everything.

Listing 9.14 SHOWSTRINGDOC.CPP—*OnDraw()* Additions Before *DrawText()* Call

```
COLORREF oldcolor;
switch (pDoc->GetColor())
{
case 0:
    oldcolor = pDC->SetTextColor(RGB(0,0,0)); //black
    break;
case 1:
    oldcolor = pDC->SetTextColor(RGB(0xFF,0,0)); //red
    break;
case 2:
    oldcolor = pDC->SetTextColor(RGB(0,0xFF,0)); //green
    break;
}
```

Add this line after the call to DrawText():

```
pDC->SetTextColor(oldcolor);
```

There are two approaches to setting the centering flags. The brute-force way is to list the four possibilities (neither, horizontal, vertical, and both) and have a different DrawText() statement for each. If you were to add other settings, this would quickly become unworkable. It's better to set up an integer to hold the DrawText() flags and "or in" each flag, if appropriate. Add the lines shown in Listing 9.15 before the call to DrawText().

Listing 9.15 SHOWSTRINGDOC.CPP—*OnDraw()* Additions After *DrawText()* Call

```
int DTflags = 0;
if (pDoc->GetHorizcenter())
{
    DTflags |= DT_CENTER;
}
```

```
if (pDoc->GetVertcenter())
    {
        DTflags |= (DT_VCENTER|DT_SINGLELINE);
}
```

The call to DrawText() now uses the DTflags variable:

```
pDC->DrawText(pDoc->GetString(), &rect, DTflags);
```

Now the settings from the dialog box have made their way to the dialog-box class, to the document, and finally to the view, to actually affect the appearance of the text string. Build and execute ShowString and then try it out. Any surprises? Be sure to change the text, experiment with various combinations of the centering options, and try all three colors.

Part

III

Ch

9

From Here...

This is not the last you will see of ShowString; it reappears in Chapter 11, "Help," and throughout Part V, "ActiveX Applications and ActiveX Controls" (Chapters 13–17). But there's a lot of other material to cover between here and there. The rest of this part of the book presents sample applications and how-to instructions for everyday tasks all developers face:

- Printing is covered in Chapter 7, "Printing and Print Preview."
- Adding buttons to toolbars and implementing status bars are covered in Chapter 10, "Status Bars and Toolbars."
- Implementing property sheets is covered in Chapter 12, "Property Pages and Sheets and Wizards."

Improving Your User Interface

CHAPTER 10

Status Bars and Toolbars

Add or delete toolbar buttons

The buttons on a toolbar must reflect your application's specific command set.

Specify ToolTips and descriptions for your toolbar buttons

When a user places the mouse pointer over a button, your application can display useful information about the command associated with that particular button.

Respond to toolbar buttons

Just like menu commands, toolbar buttons must be associated with message-response functions.

Adding panes to a status bar

You're not stuck with MFC's default status bar. Your application's status bar can display whatever information you'd like it to display.

Building a good user interface is half the battle of programming a Windows application. Luckily, Visual C++ and its AppWizard supply an amazing amount of help in creating an application that supports all the expected user-interface elements, including menus, dialog boxes, toolbars, and status bars. The subjects of menus and dialog boxes are covered elsewhere in this book. In this chapter, you learn how to get the most out of toolbars and status bars. ■

Working with Toolbars

The buttons on a toolbar correspond to commands, just as the items on a menu do. Although you can add a toolbar to your application with AppWizard, you still need to use a little programming polish to get things just right. This is because every application is different, and AppWizard can create only the most generally useful toolbar for most applications. When you create your own toolbars, you'll probably want to add or delete buttons to support your application's unique command set.

For example, when you create a standard AppWizard application with a toolbar, AppWizard creates the toolbar shown in Figure 10.1. This toolbar provides buttons for the commonly used commands in the File and Edit menus, as well as a button for displaying the About dialog box. But what if your application doesn't support these commands? It's up to you to modify the default toolbar to fit your application.

FIG. 10.1
The default toolbar provides buttons for commonly used commands.

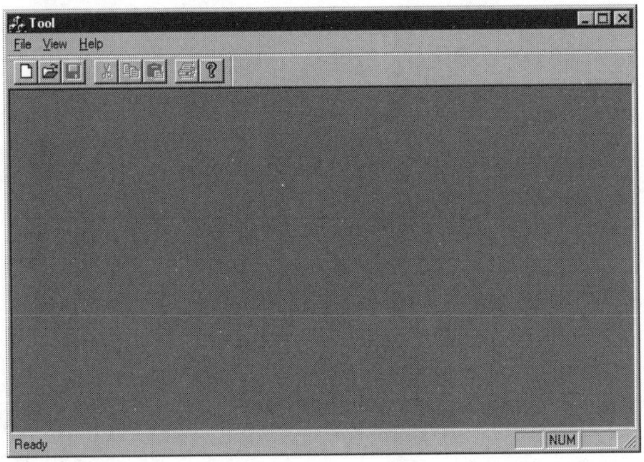

Deleting Toolbar Buttons

Create a multiple document interface application with a toolbar by choosing File, New, selecting the Project tab, naming the application **Tool**, and accepting the defaults in every dialog box. If you like, you can click the Finish button in step 1 to speed up the process. AppWizard provides a docking toolbar by default. Build and run the application, and you should see a toolbar of your own, just like Figure 10.1.

Before moving on, play with this toolbar a little. On the View menu, you can toggle whether the toolbar is displayed or not. Turn it off, then on again. Now click and hold the toolbar between buttons, and pull it down into the working area of your application. Let it go, and it's a floating palette. Drag it around and drop it at the bottom of the application, or one of the sides—it will dock against any side of the main window. Watch the tracking rectangle change shape to show you it will dock if you drop it. Drag it back off again so that it's floating, and close it by clicking the small x in the upper-right corner. Bring it back with the View menu, and notice that it comes back right where you left it. All this functionality is yours free from AppWizard and MFC.

The first step in modifying the toolbar is to delete buttons you no longer need. To do this, first select the ResourceView tab to display your application's resources. Click the + next to Toolbar, and double-click the IDR_MAINFRAME toolbar resource to edit it, as shown in Figure 10.2.

FIG. 10.2
Use the toolbar editor to customize your application's toolbar.

Toolbar being edited

Toolbar editor

ResourceView window

ResourceView tab

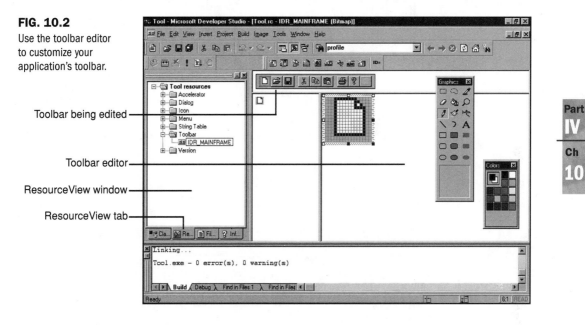

After you have the toolbar editor on the screen, deleting buttons is as easy as dragging the unwanted buttons from the toolbar. Just place your mouse pointer on the button, hold down the left mouse button, and drag the unwanted button away from the toolbar. When you release the mouse button, the toolbar button disappears. In the Tool application, delete all the buttons except the Help button with a yellow question mark. Figure 10.3 shows the edited toolbar with only the Help button remaining. The single blank button template is only a starting point for the next button you may want to create. If you leave it blank, it doesn't appear in the final toolbar.

Adding Buttons to a Toolbar

Adding buttons to a toolbar is a two step process: First, you draw the button's icon, and then you match the button with its command. To draw a new button, first click the blank button template in the toolbar. The blank button appears, enlarged, in the edit window, as shown in Figure 10.4.

FIG. 10.3
This edited toolbar has only a single button left (not counting the blank button template).

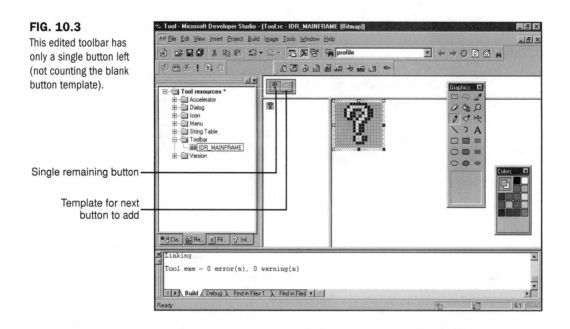

Single remaining button ———

Template for next button to add ———

FIG. 10.4
Click the button template to bring it up in the button editor.

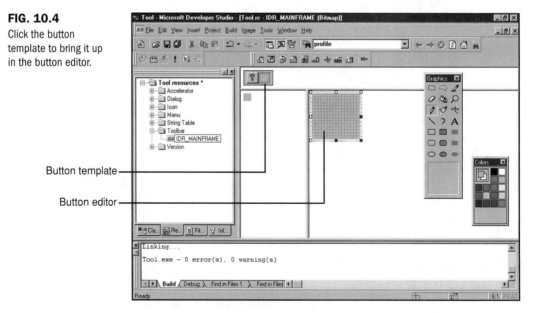

Button template ———

Button editor ———

Suppose you want to create a toolbar button that draws a red circle in the application's window. Draw a red circle on the blank button (via the Ellipse tool), which takes care of creating the button's icon. Bring up the properties box and give the button an appropriate ID, which in this case might be something like **ID_CIRCLE**.

Now you need to define the button's ToolTip and description. The ToolTip appears whenever the user leaves the mouse pointer over the button for a second or two and acts as a reminder of the button's purpose. A ToolTip of "Circle" would be appropriate for the circle button. The description appears in the application's status bar. In this case, a description of "Draws a red circle in the window" might be good. Type these two text strings into the Prompt box. The description comes first, followed by the newline character (\n) and the ToolTip, as shown in Figure 10.5.

FIG. 10.5

After drawing the button, specify its properties.

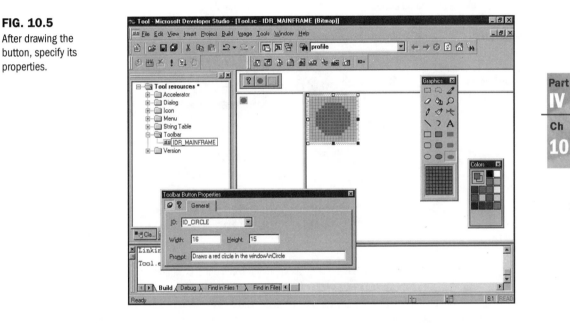

You've now defined a command ID for your new toolbar button. Usually, you use the command ID of an existing menu item that is already connected to some code. In those cases, simply choose the existing command ID from the drop-down box and your work is done. The prompt is taken from the properties of the menu item, and the message handler has already been arranged for the menu item. In this application, the toolbar button does not mirror a menu item, so you associate the ID with a message-handler function which MFC automatically calls when the user clicks the button.

To do this, follow these steps:

1. Make sure the button for which you want to create a message hander is selected in the custom toolbar, and then bring up ClassWizard.

2. The MFC ClassWizard property sheet appears, with the button's ID already selected (see Figure 10.6). To add the message-response function, select in the Class Name box the class to which you want to add the function (the sample application uses the view class).

3. Double-click the COMMAND selection in the Messages box.

4. Accept the function name that MFC suggests in the next message box, and you're all set. Click the OK button to finalize your changes.

N O T E If you haven't defined a message-response function for a toolbar button, or if there is no instance of the class that catches the message, MFC disables the button when you run the application. For example, if the message is caught by the document or view in an MDI application and there is no open document, the button is disabled. The same is true for menu commands—in fact, for all intents and purposes, toolbar buttons *are* menu commands. ▪

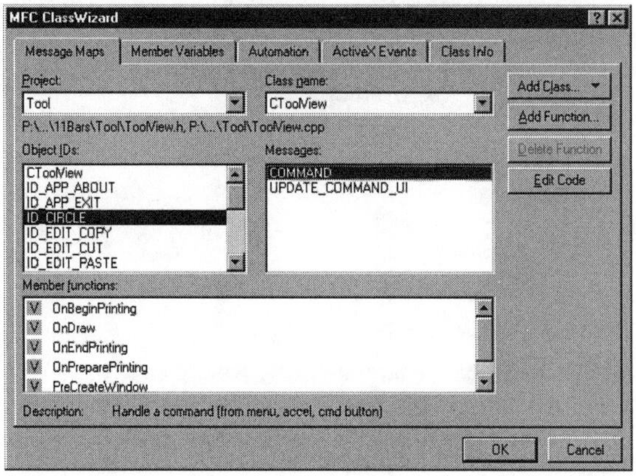

FIG. 10.6

You can use ClassWizard to catch messages from your toolbar buttons.

N O T E Ordinarily, toolbar buttons duplicate menu commands, providing a quicker way for the user to select commonly used commands in the menus. In this case, the menu item and the toolbar button both represent the exact same command and you give both the same ID. Then, the same message-response function gets called whether the user selects the command from the menu bar or from the toolbar. ▪

If you compile and run the application now, you'll see the window shown in Figure 10.7. In the figure, you can see the new toolbar button, as well as its ToolTip and description line. The toolbar looks a little sparse in this example, but you can add as many buttons as you like.

You can create as many buttons as you need; just follow the aforementioned procedures for each. After you have the buttons created, you're through with the toolbar resources and are ready to write the code that responds to the buttons. For example, in the previous example, a circle button was added to the toolbar and a message-response function, called `OnCircle()`, was added to the program. MFC calls that message-response function whenever the user clicks the associated button. However, right now, that function doesn't do anything, as shown in Listing 10.1.

FIG. 10.7

The new toolbar button shows its ToolTip and description.

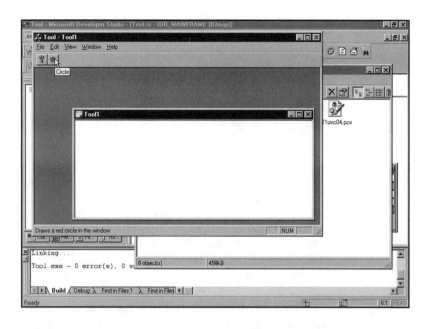

On the CD

Listing 10.1 An Empty Message-Response Function

```
void CToolView::OnCircle()
{
    // TODO: Add your command handler code here

}
```

Although the circle button is supposed to draw a red circle in the window, you can see that the `OnCircle()` function is going to need a little help accomplishing that task. Add the lines shown in Listing 10.2 to the function so that the circle button will actually do what it's supposed to do, as shown in Figure 10.8.

On the CD

Listing 10.2 *CToolView::OnCircle()*

```
void CToolView::OnCircle()
{
    CClientDC clientDC(this);
    CBrush newBrush(RGB(255,0,0));
    CBrush* oldBrush = clientDC.SelectObject(&newBrush);
    clientDC.Ellipse(20, 20, 200, 200);
    clientDC.SelectObject(oldBrush);
}
```

N O T E You can find the circle-drawing application in the CHAP11\TOOL directory of this book's CD-ROM. ■

FIG. 10.8
After adding code to *OnCircle()*, the new toolbar button actually does something.

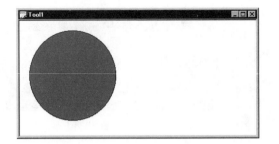

The *CToolBar* Class's Member Functions

In most cases, after you have created your toolbar resource and associated its buttons with the appropriate command IDs, you don't need to bother any more with the toolbar. The code generated by AppWizard creates the toolbar for you, and MFC takes care of calling the buttons' response functions for you. However, there may be times when you want to change the toolbar's default behavior or appearance in some way. In those cases, you can call upon the CToolBar class's member functions, which are listed in Table 10.1 along with their descriptions. The toolbar is accessible from the CMainFrame class as the m_wndToolBar member variable. Usually, you change the toolbar behavior in CMainFrame::OnCreate().

Table 10.1 Member Functions of the *CToolBar* Class

Function	Description
CommandToIndex()	Gets the index of a button given its ID.
Create()	Creates the toolbar.
GetButtonInfo()	Gets information about a button.
GetButtonStyle()	Gets a button's style.
GetButtonText()	Gets a button's text label.
GetItemID()	Gets the ID of a button given its index.
GetItemRect()	Gets an item's display rectangle given its index.
GetToolBarCtrl()	Gets a reference to the CToolBarCtrl object represented by the CToolBar object.
LoadBitmap()	Loads the toolbar's button images.
LoadToolBar()	Loads a toolbar resource.
SetBitmap()	Sets a new toolbar button bitmap.
SetButtonInfo()	Sets a button's ID, style, and image number.
SetButtons()	Sets the IDs for the toolbar buttons.
SetButtonStyle()	Sets a button's style.

Function	Description
SetButtonText()	Sets a button's text label.
SetHeight()	Sets the toolbar's height.
SetSizes()	Sets the buttons' sizes.

Normally, you don't need to call the toolbar's methods, but you can get some unusual results when you do, such as the extra high toolbar shown in Figure 10.9. (The buttons are the same size, but the toolbar window is bigger.) This toolbar resulted from a call to the toolbar object's SetHeight() member function. The CToolBar class's member functions enable you to perform this sort of toolbar trickery, but use them with great caution.

FIG. 10.9
You can use a toolbar object's member functions to change how the toolbar looks and acts.

Part
IV

Ch
10

Working with Status Bars

Status bars are mostly benign objects that sit at the bottom of your application's window, doing whatever MFC instructs them to do. This consists of displaying command descriptions and the status of various keys on the keyboard, including the Caps Lock and Scroll Lock keys. In fact, status bars are so mundane from the programmer's point of view (at least they are in an AppWizard application) that they aren't even represented by a resource that you can edit like a toolbar. When you tell AppWizard to incorporate a status bar into your application, there's not much left for you to do.

Or is there? A status bar, just like a toolbar, must reflect the interface needs of your specific application. For that reason, the CStatusBar class features a set of methods with which you can customize the status bar's appearance and operation. Table 10.2 lists the methods along with brief descriptions.

Table 10.2   Methods of the *CStatusBar* Class

Method	Description
CommandToIndex()	Gets an indicator's index given its ID.
Create()	Creates the status bar.
GetItemID()	Gets an indicator's ID given its index.
GetItemRect()	Gets an item's display rectangle given its index.

continues

Table 10.2   Continued

Method	Description
GetPaneInfo()	Gets information about an indicator.
GetPaneStyle()	Gets an indicator's style.
GetPaneText()	Gets an indicator's text.
GetStatusBarCtrl()	Gets a reference to the CStatusBarCtrl object represented by the CStatusBar object.
SetIndicators()	Sets the indicators' IDs.
SetPaneInfo()	Sets the indicators' IDs, widths, and styles.
SetPaneStyle()	Sets an indicator's style.
SetPaneText()	Sets an indicator's text.

When you create a status bar as part of an AppWizard application, you get a window similar to that shown in Figure 10.10. (To make your own, create a project called **Status** and accept all the defaults, as you did for the Tool application.) The status bar has several parts, called *panes*, that display certain information about the status of the application and the system. These panes, which are marked in Figure 10.10, include indicators for the Caps Lock, Num Lock, and Scroll Lock keys, as well as a message area for showing status text and command descriptions. To see a command description, place your mouse pointer over a button on the toolbar (see Figure 10.11).

FIG. 10.10
The default MFC status bar contains a number of informative panes.

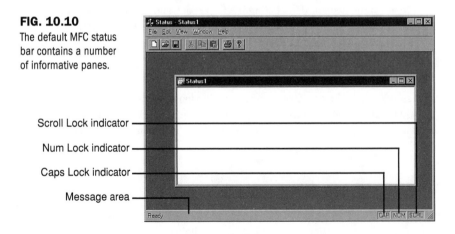

Scroll Lock indicator

Num Lock indicator

Caps Lock indicator

Message area

The most common way to customize a status bar is to add new panes. To add a pane to a status bar, complete these steps:

1. Create a command ID for the new pane.
2. Create a default string for the pane.

3. Add the pane's command ID to the status bar's indicators array.

4. Create a command-update handler for the pane.

FIG. 10.11

The message area is used mainly for command descriptions.

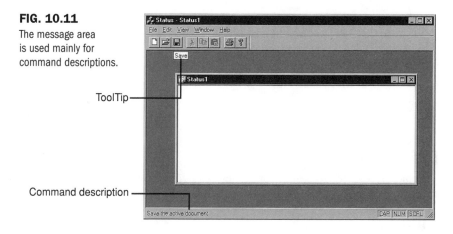

The following sections cover these steps in detail.

Creating a New Command ID

This step is easy, thanks to Visual C++'s symbol browser. To add the command ID, start by choosing View, Resource Symbols. When you do, you see the Resource Symbols dialog box (see Figure 10.12), which displays the currently defined symbols for your application's resources. Click the New button, and the New Symbol dialog box appears. Type the new ID, **ID_MYNEWPANE**, into the Name box (see Figure 10.13). Usually, you can just accept the value that MFC suggests for the ID.

FIG. 10.12

Use the Resource Symbols dialog box to add new command IDs to your application.

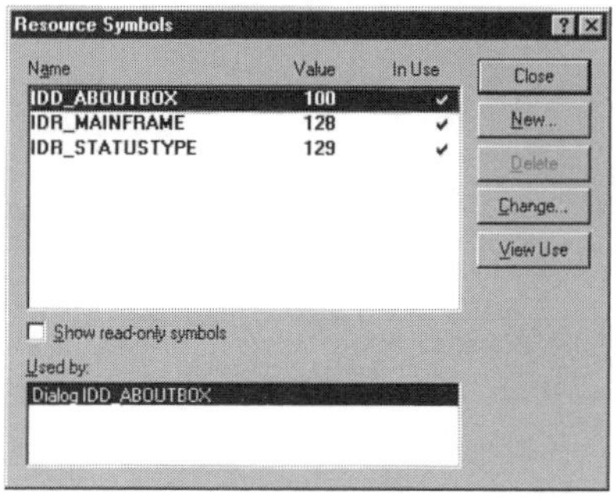

Click the OK and Close buttons to finalize your selections, and your new command ID is defined.

FIG. 10.13

Type the new ID's name and value into the New Symbol dialog box.

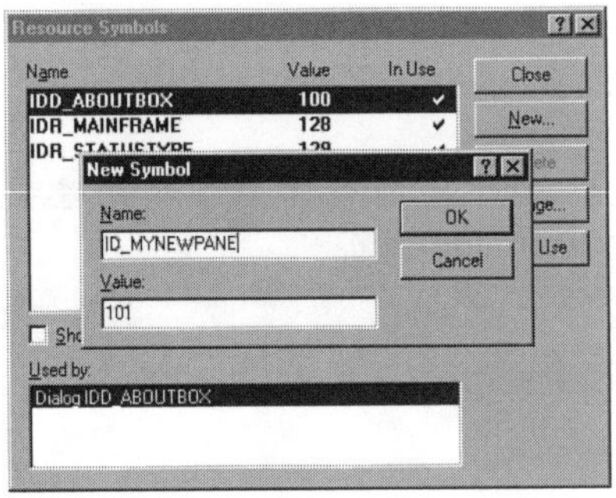

Creating the Default String

You have now defined a resource ID, but it is not being used. To represent a status bar pane, the ID must have a default string defined for it. To define the string, first go to the ResourceView window (by clicking the ResourceView tab) and double-click the String Table resource to open it in the string table editor, as shown in Figure 10.14.

FIG. 10.14

Define the new pane's default string in the string table.

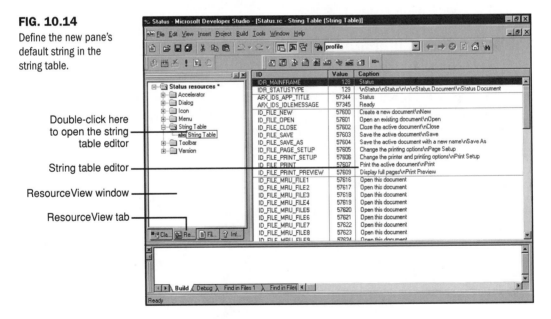

Now, choose Insert, New String to bring up the String Properties dialog box. Type the new pane's command ID into the ID box (or choose it from the drop-down list) and the default string (**Default string** in this case) into the Caption box (see Figure 10.15).

FIG. 10.15
Use the String
Properties dialog box to
define the new pane's
default string.

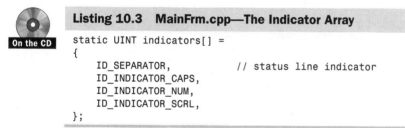

Adding the ID to the Indicators Array

When MFC constructs your status bar, it uses an array of IDs to determine which panes to display and where to display them. This array of IDs is passed as an argument to the status bar's SetIndicators() member function, which is called in the CMainFrame class's OnCreate() function. You find this array of IDs, shown in Listing 10.3, near the top of the MainFrm.cpp file. One way to reach these lines in the source code editor is to switch to ClassView, expand CMainFrame, double-click OnCreate(), and scroll up one page. Alternatively, you could use FileView to open MainFrm.cpp and scroll down to this code.

Listing 10.3   MainFrm.cpp—The Indicator Array

```
static UINT indicators[] =
{
    ID_SEPARATOR,              // status line indicator
    ID_INDICATOR_CAPS,
    ID_INDICATOR_NUM,
    ID_INDICATOR_SCRL,
};
```

To add your new pane to the array, type the pane's ID into the array at the position in which you want it to appear in the status bar, followed by a comma. (The first pane, ID_SEPARATOR, should always remain in the first position.) Listing 10.4 shows the indicator array with the new pane added.

Listing 10.4   MainFrm.cpp—The Expanded Indicator Array

```
static UINT indicators[] =
{
    ID_SEPARATOR,              // status line indicator
    ID_MYNEWPANE,
    ID_INDICATOR_CAPS,
    ID_INDICATOR_NUM,
    ID_INDICATOR_SCRL,
};
```

Creating the Pane's Command-Update Handler

MFC does not automatically enable new panes when it creates the status bar. Instead, you must create a command-update handler for the new pane and enable the pane yourself. (You first learned about command-update handlers in Chapter 4, "Messages and Commands.") Also, for most applications, the string displayed in the pane is calculated on-the-fly—the default string you defined in an earlier step is only a placeholder.

Normally you use ClassWizard to arrange for the message to be caught, but ClassWizard does not help you catch status bar messages. You must add the handler entries to the message map yourself, and then add the code for the handler. You add entries to the message map in the header file and the map in the source file, and you add them outside the special AFX_MSG_MAP comments used by ClassWizard.

Double-click CMainFrame to open the header file, and scroll to the bottom. Edit the message map so that it resembles Listing 10.5. When you write your own applications, you will use a variety of function names to update status bar panes, but the rest of the delcaration will always be the same.

Listing 10.5   MainFrm.h—Message Map

```
// Generated message map functions
protected:
    //{{AFX_MSG(CMainFrame)
    afx_msg int OnCreate(LPCREATESTRUCT lpCreateStruct);
        // NOTE - the ClassWizard will add and remove member functions here.
        //    DO NOT EDIT what you see in these blocks of generated code!
    //}}AFX_MSG
    afx_msg void OnUpdateMyNewPane(CCmdUI *pCmdUI);
    DECLARE_MESSAGE_MAP()
```

Next, you add the handler to the source message map to actually associate the command ID with the handler. Open any CMainFrame function and scroll upwards until you find the message map, then edit it so that it looks like Listing 10.6.

Listing 10.6   MainFrm.cpp—Message Map

```
BEGIN_MESSAGE_MAP(CMainFrame, CFrameWnd)
    //{{AFX_MSG_MAP(CMainFrame)
        // NOTE - the ClassWizard will add and remove mapping macros here.
        //    DO NOT EDIT what you see in these blocks of generated code !
    ON_WM_CREATE()
    //}}AFX_MSG_MAP
    ON_UPDATE_COMMAND_UI(ID_MYNEWPANE, OnUpdateMyNewPane)
END_MESSAGE_MAP()
```

You have now arranged that whenever the status bar pane ID_MYNEWPANE needs to be updated, the CMainFrame member function OnUpdateMyNewPane() will be called.

Now you're ready to write the new command-update handler. In the handler, you will enable the new pane and set its contents. Listing 10.7 shows the command-update handler for the new pane. As you can see, it uses a member variable called m_paneString. Update handlers should be very quick—the job of making sure that m_paneString holds the right string should be tackled in a function that is called less often.

On the CD

> **Listing 10.7**   *CMainFrame::OnUpdateMyNewPane()*

```
void CMainFrame::OnUpdateMyNewPane(CCmdUI *pCmdUI)
{
    pCmdUI->Enable();
    pCmdUI->SetText(m_paneString);
}
```

Setting the Status Bar's Appearance

To add the last touch to your status bar demonstration application, you will want a way to set m_paneString. To initialize it, add this line to the CMainFrame constructor:

```
m_paneString = "Default string";
```

The value you entered in the string table is only to keep Developer Studio sure that the resource ID you created is in use. Right-click CMainFrame in ClassView and choose Add Member Variable to add m_paneString as a private member variable. The type should be CString.

To set up the status bar for the first time, add these lines to CMainFrame::OnCreate(), just before the return statement:

```
CClientDC dc(this);
SIZE size = dc.GetTextExtent(m_paneString);
int index = m_wndStatusBar.CommandToIndex(ID_MYNEWPANE);
m_wndStatusBar.SetPaneInfo(index,ID_MYNEWPANE, SBPS_POPOUT, size.cx);
```

These lines set the text string and the size of the pane. You set the size of the pane with a call to SetPaneInfo(), which needs the index of the pane and the new size. CommandToIndex() gets you the index of the pane, and GetTextExtent() gets you the size. As a nice touch, the call to SetPaneInfo() uses the SBPS_POPOUT style to create a pane that seems to stick out from the status bar, rather than being indented.

The user will change the string by making a menu selection. Open the IDR_STATUSTYPE menu in the resource editor and add a Change String item to the File menu. (Working with menus is discussed for the first time in Chapter 9, "Building a Complete Application: ShowString.") Let Developer Studio assign it the resource ID ID_FILE_CHANGESTRING.

Bring up ClassWizard and add a handler for this command; it should be caught by CMainFrame, because that's where the m_paneString variable is kept. ClassWizard offers to call the handler OnFileChangestring() and you should accept this name. Click OK to close ClassWizard.

Insert a new dialog box into the application and call it IDD_PANEDLG. The title should be Change Pane String. Add a single edit box, stretched the full width of the dialog box, and leave the ID as IDC_EDIT1. Add a static text item just above the edit box with the caption **New String:**. With the dialog box open in the resource editor, bring up ClassWizard. Create a new class for the dialog box called CPaneDlg, and associate the edit control, IDC_EDIT1, with a CString member variable of the dialog class called m_paneString.

N O T E Adding dialog boxes to applications and associating them with classes is discussed in more depth in several earlier chapters, including Chapter 2, "Dialog Boxes and Controls," and Chapter 9, "Building a Complete Application: ShowString." ■

Switch to ClassView, expand CMainFrame, and double-click OnFileChangeString() to edit it. Add the code shown in Listing 10.8.

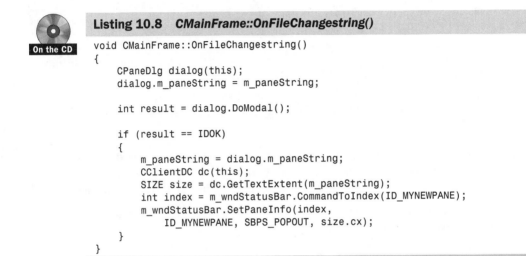

Listing 10.8   CMainFrame::OnFileChangestring()

```
void CMainFrame::OnFileChangestring()
{
    CPaneDlg dialog(this);
    dialog.m_paneString = m_paneString;

    int result = dialog.DoModal();

    if (result == IDOK)
    {
        m_paneString = dialog.m_paneString;
        CClientDC dc(this);
        SIZE size = dc.GetTextExtent(m_paneString);
        int index = m_wndStatusBar.CommandToIndex(ID_MYNEWPANE);
        m_wndStatusBar.SetPaneInfo(index,
            ID_MYNEWPANE, SBPS_POPOUT, size.cx);
    }
}
```

This code displays the dialog box, and, if the user exits the dialog box by clicking the OK button, changes the text string and resets the size of the pane. The code is very similar to the lines you added to OnCreate(). Scroll up to the top of MainFrm.cpp and add this line:

```
#include "panedlg.h"
```

This tells the compiler what the CPaneDlg class is. Build and run the Status application, and you should see the window shown in Figure 10.16. As you can see, the status bar contains an extra panel displaying the text Default string. If you choose File, Change String, a dialog box appears into which you can type a new string for the panel. When you exit the dialog box via the OK button, the text appears in the new panel and the panel resizes itself to accommodate the new string (see Figure 10.17).

FIG. 10.16
The Status Bar Demo application shows how to add and manage a status bar panel.

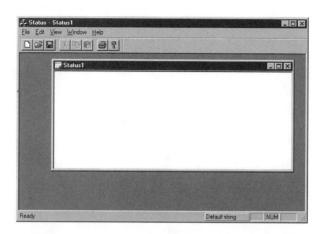

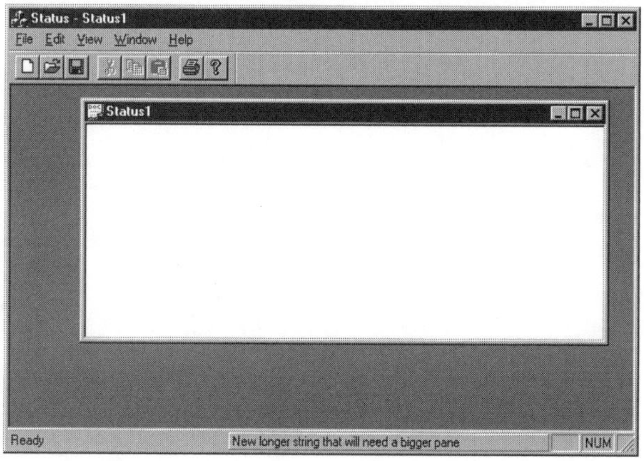

FIG. 10.17
The panel resizes itself to fit the new string.

From Here...

Users of Windows applications expect to find certain user-interface elements in place when they run a new application. Two of the most visible of these interface elements are the toolbar and the status bar, which have become standard parts of just about every Windows application. The toolbar provides the user with shortcut buttons for selecting menu commands, whereas the status bar keeps the user apprised of the application's state, as well as displays messages such as command descriptions.

AppWizard and MFC provide a terrific starting point for implementing these useful interface elements, and with a little effort you can make your application truly user-friendly.

For more information, refer to the following chapters:

- Chapter 2, "Dialog Boxes and Controls," explains how to use dialog boxes in your applications.

■ Chapter 4, "Messages and Commands," describes MFC's message-mapping system, which enables you to respond to menu commands, as well as enable and disable those commands.

■ Chapter 9, "Building a Complete Application: ShowString," provides the information you need to build menus, dialog boxes, and other user interface elements.

CHAPTER 11

Help

Too many programmers neglect Help entirely. Even those who add Help to an application tend to leave it to the end of a project, and when the inevitable time squeeze comes, guess what? There's no time to write the Help text or make the software adjustments that arrange for that text to display when the user requests Help. One of the reasons people do this is because they believe implementing Help is really hard. But with Visual C++, it's a lot easier than you might anticipate. Visual C++ even writes some of your Help text for you! This chapter is going to add Help after the fact to the ShowString application built in Chapter 9, "Building a Complete Application: ShowString." ∎

Types of Help

There are a number of different kinds of Help. Users, developers, and technical writers all divide Help along different lines.

The file types that make up Help

AppWizard and the Help compiler between them generate over 10 files related to Help. This section explains them.

What AppWizard provides

Code is added to your program and files are added to your project when you ask for context-sensitive Help.

Designing your Help

Good Help, like a good program, is designed before it is implemented. There are many tasks involved in the implementation, and there's a risk of getting lost if you're not sure where you're going.

Connecting command Help to your application

Dealing with Windows messages associated with menu items or buttons that request Help is quite simple.

Connecting context Help to your application

Dealing with Windows messages requesting context-sensitive Help is more difficult, but can be done. This section works you through it.

Different Kinds of Help

There are a variety of ways of characterizing Help. This section presents four different questions you might ask about Help:

- How does the user invoke it?
- How does it look on-screen?
- What sort of answers does the user want?
- How does the developer implement it in code?

None of these questions has a single answer. There are at least nine different ways for a user to invoke Help, three standard Help appearances, and three different programming tasks you must implement in order to display Help. These different ways of looking at Help can help you understand why the implementation has a number of different techniques, which can be confusing at first.

Getting Help

The first way of characterizing Help is to ask "How does the user bring it up?" There are a number of ways to bring up Help:

- By choosing an item from the Help menu, such as Help, Topics (Choosing What's This? or About does not bring up Help immediately.)
- By pressing F1
- By clicking the Help button on a dialog box
- By clicking a What's This? button on a toolbar and then clicking something else
- By choosing What's This? from the Help menu (the System menu for dialog box-based applications) and then clicking something
- By clicking a Question button on a dialog box and then clicking part of the dialog box
- By right-clicking something and choosing What's This? from the pop-up menu
- In some older applications, by pressing Shift+F1 and then clicking something
- Outside the application completely, by double-clicking the HLP file

For the first three actions in this list, the user does one thing (chooses a menu item, presses F1, or clicks a button) and Help appears immediately. For the next five actions there are two steps: typically one click to get into "Help mode" (more formally called "What's This?" mode) and another to indicate what Help is required. Users generally divide Help into single-step Help and two-step Help accordingly.

NOTE You will get confused if you try to use Developer Studio itself to understand Help, in general. Much of the information is presented in HTML by InfoViewer, though there are some circumstances under which more traditional Help appears. Use simple utilities and accessories that come with your operating system, or use your operating system itself, to follow along. If you have old versions of software like Word or Excel, they probably don't follow the Windows 95 guidelines for Help either, because these are quite different than the old Help guidelines. ■

Presenting Help

The second way of characterizing Help is to ask "How does it look?" There are a number of different-looking ways of showing Help:

- **Help Topics dialog box.** As shown in Figure 11.1, this dialog box allows users to scroll through an index, look at a table of contents, or find a word within the Help text.

- **Ordinary Help window.** As shown in Figure 11.2, this window has buttons like Help Topics, Back, and Options. It can be resized, minimized, maximized, or closed, and in many cases is always on top, like the system clock and other popular utilities.

- **Pop-up windows.** As shown in Figure 11.3, pop-up windows are relatively small and do not have buttons or menus. They disappear when you click outside them, cannot be resized or moved, and are perfect for a definition or quick explanation.

Part
IV

Ch
11

FIG. 11.1
The Help Topics dialog box allows users to go through the contents or index, or search the Help text with Find.

FIG. 11.2

An ordinary Help window has buttons and may have menus. It can be treated like any other window.

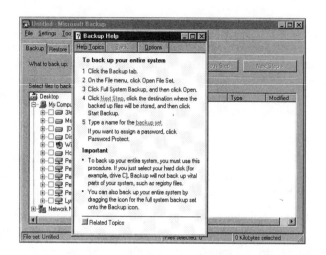

FIG. 11.3

A pop-up Help topic window gives the user far less control and should be used only for short explanations.

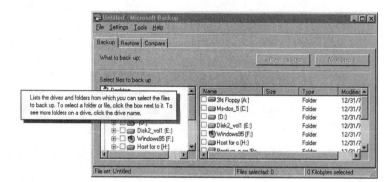

Using Help

A third way of characterizing Help, is according to the user's reasons for invoking it. Microsoft categorizes Help in this way and lists these kinds of Help:

- **Contextual user assistance.** Answers questions like "What does this button do?" or "What does this setting mean?"

- **Task-oriented Help.** Explains how to accomplish a certain task such as printing a document (it often contains numbered steps).

- **Reference Help.** Look up function parameters or font names, or other material that expert users need to refer to from time to time.

These describe the content of the material presented to the user. While these content descriptions are important to a Help designer and writer, they are not very useful from a programming point of view.

Programming Help

The final way of characterizing Help, and perhaps the most important to a developer, is by examining the code behind the scenes. There are three Windows messages that are sent when the user invokes Help in any of these ways:

- WM_COMMAND
- WM_HELP
- WM_CONTEXTMENU

N O T E Windows messages are discussed in Chapter 4, "Messages and Commands."

When the user chooses a Help item from a menu, or clicks the Help button on a dialog box, the system sends a WM_COMMAND message as always. To display the associated Help, you catch these messages and call the WinHelp system.

When the user right-clicks an element of your application, a WM_CONTEXTMENU message is sent. You catch the message and build a shortcut menu on the spot. Because in most cases you will want a shortcut menu with only one item on it, What's This?, you can use a pre-built menu with just that item, and delegate the display of that menu to the Help system. More on this later, in the "Programming for Context Help" section.

When the user brings up Help in any other way, the framework handles most of it. You do not catch the message that puts the application into What's This? mode, you do not change the cursor, and you do not deal with clicks while in that mode. You catch a WM_HELP message that identifies the control, dialog box, or menu for which Help is required, and you provide that Help. Whether the user pressed F1, or went into What's This? mode and clicked the item does not matter. In fact, you cannot tell from within your application.

The WM_HELP and WM_CONTEXTMENU messages are handled almost identically, so from the point of view of the developer, there are two kinds of help. We'll call these *command help* and *context help*. Each are discussed later in this chapter, in the "Programming for Command Help" and "Programming for Context Help" sections, but keep in mind that there is no relationship between this split (between command and context help) and the split between one-step and two-step Help that users think of.

Components of the Help System

As you might expect, a large number of files interact to make online Help work. The final product, which you deliver to your user, is the Help file, with the .HLP extension. It is built

Part
IV

Ch
11

from component files. In the list that follows, appname refers to the name of your application's .EXE file. If no name appears, there may be more than one file with a variety of names. The component files produced by AppWizard are as follows:

.h	These *Header* files define resource IDs and Help topic IDs for use within your C++ code.
.hm	These *Help Mapping* files define Help topic IDs. appname.hm is generated every time you build your application—do not change it yourself.
.rtf	These *Rich Text Format* files contain the Help text for each Help topic.
appname.cnt	You use this table of contents file to create the Contents tab of the Help Topics dialog box. (You should distribute this contents file with your application in addition to the Help file.)
appname.hpj	This *Help ProJect* file pulls together .hm and .rtf files to produce, when compiled, an .hlp file.

While being used, the Help system generates other files. When you uninstall your application be sure to look for and remove the following files, in addition to the .hlp file:

- **appname.gid** is a configuration file, typically hidden.
- **appname.fts** is a full text search file, generated when your user does a Find through your Help text.
- **appname.ftg** is a full text search group list, also generated when your user does a Find.

Help Topic IDs are the connection between your Help text and the Help system. Your program eventually directs the Help system to display a Help topic, using a name like HID_FILE_OPEN, and the system looks for this Help topic ID in the Help file, compiled from the .rtf files, including the .rtf file that contains your Help text for that Help topic ID. (This process is illustrated in Figure 11.4.) These topic IDs have to be defined twice—once for use by the Help system and once for use by your program. When the Help system is displaying a topic or the Help Topics dialog box, it takes over displaying other Help topics as the user requests them, with no work on your part.

FIG. 11.4
Your program, the Help system, and your Help files all work together to display a topic.

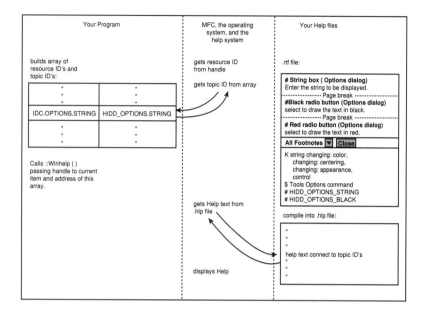

Help Support from AppWizard

When you build an MDI application (no database or OLE support) with AppWizard and choose the Context Sensitive Help option, here's what you get:

- Message map entries are added to catch the commands ID_HELP_FINDER, ID_HELP, ID_CONTEXT_HELP, and ID_DEFAULT_HELP. No code is added to handle these; they are passed to CMDIFrameWnd member functions.

- A What's This? button is added to the toolbar.

- A Help Topics item is added to the Help menu for both menus provided by AppWizard: the one used when a file is open and the smaller one used when no files are open.

- Accelerators for F1 (ID_HELP) and Shift+F1 (ID_CONTEXT_HELP) are added.

- The default message in the status bar is changed from Ready to For Help, press F1.

- A status bar prompt is added, to be displayed while in What's This? mode: Select an object on which to get Help.

- Status bar prompts are added for the Help menu and its items.

■ `afxcore.rtf`, a Help text file for standard menu items like File, Open, is copied into the project.

■ `afxprint.rtf`, a Help text file for printing and print previewing, is copied into the project. (These files are added separately because not all projects include printing and print previewing. If this project has database- or OLE-related features, more help is provided.)

■ Twenty-two .bmp files, included as illustrations in the Help for topics like File, Open, are copied into the project.

With this solid foundation, the task of implementing Help for this application breaks down into three steps:

1. You must plan your Help. Do you intend to provide reference material only, task-oriented instructions only, or both? To what extent will you supplement these with context pop-ups?

2. You must provide the programming "hooks" that will result in the display of the Help topics you have designed. This is done differently for command and context Help, as you see in the sections that follow.

3. You must build the .rtf files with the Help topic IDs and text to explain your application. If you have designed the Help system well and truly understand your application, this should be simple, though time-consuming.

N O T E   On large projects, the Help text is often written by a technical writer rather than a program-mer. This requires careful coordination: for example, you have to provide Topic IDs to the Help writer, and you may have to explain some functions so that they can be described in the Help. You have to work closely together throughout a project like this and respect each other's area of expertise. ■

Planning Your Help Approach

Developing Help is like developing your software. You shouldn't do it without a plan. And, strictly speaking, you shouldn't do it last. A famous experiment decades ago split a programming class into two groups. One group was required to hand in a completed user manual for a program before writing the program, the other to finish the program before writing the manual. The group who wrote the manual first produced better programs: They noticed design errors early, before they were carved in code, and they found the program much easier to write, as well.

If your application is of any size, the work involved in developing a Help system for it would fill a book. If you need further information on how to do this, consider the book *Designing Windows 95 Help: A Guide to Creating Online Documents*, by Mary Deaton and Cheryl Lockett Zubak, published by Que. In this section, there is only room for a few basic guidelines.

The result of this planning process is a list of Help topics and the primary way they will be reached. The topics you plan are likely to include:

- A page or so of Help on each menu item, reached by getting into What's This? mode and clicking the item.
- A page, reachable from the Contents, that lists all the menus and their menu items, with links to the pages for those items.
- A page, reachable from the Contents, for each major task that a user might perform with the application. This includes examples or tutorials.
- Context Help for the controls on all dialog boxes.

While that may seem like a lot of work, remember that all the boilerplate resources have been documented already in the material provided by AppWizard. That includes menu items, common dialog boxes, and more.

After you have a complete list of material and the primary way each page is reached, think about links between pages (for example, the AppWizard-supplied Help for File, Open mentions using File, New, and vice versa) and pop-up definitions for jargon and keywords.

In this section you plan Help for ShowString, the application introduced in Chapter 9, "Building a Complete Application: ShowString." This simple application displays a string that the user can set. The string may be centered vertically or horizontally, and it can be black, green, or red. There is a new menu (Tools) with one item (Options) that brings up a dialog box on which the user can set all these options at once. The Help tasks you need to tackle include:

- Changing AppWizard's placeholder strings to ShowString or other strings specific to this application
- Adding a topic about the Tools menu and the Options item
- Adding a topic about each control on the Options dialog box
- Adding a Question button to the Options dialog box
- Changing the text supplied by AppWizard and displayed when the user requests context Help about the view
- Adding an Understanding Centering topic to the Help menu and writing it
- Adjusting the Contents to point to the new pages

The remainder of this chapter tackles this list of tasks.

Programming for Command Help

Command Help is actually quite simple from a developer's point of view. (Of course, you probably still have to write the explanations, so don't get too relaxed.) As you've seen, AppWizard added the Help Topics menu item and the message map entries to catch it, and the MFC class `CMDIChildFrame` has the member function to process it, so you have no work to do for that. But if you choose to add another menu item to your Help menu, you do so just like any other menu, using the Resource View. Then have your application class, `CShowStringApp`, catch the message. Say, for example, that ShowString deserves an item on the Help menu called Understanding Centering. Add this item to both menus and let Developer Studio assign it the resource ID `ID_HELP_UNDERSTANDINGCENTERING`. Actually, this is one occasion where a slightly shorter resource ID wouldn't hurt, but this chapter presents it with the longer ID.

Use ClassWizard to arrange for `CShowStringApp` to catch this message, as discussed in Chapter 9, "Building a Complete Application: ShowString." (You may want to open the Help version of this project now from the CODE\CHAP11 directory on the C and follow along, or make a copy of the ShowString you built in Chapter 9 and make these changes as you read.) The new function looks like this:

```
void CShowStringApp::OnHelpUnderstandingcentering()
{
    WinHelp(HID_CENTERING);
}
```

This single line of code fires up the Help system, passing it the Help topic ID `HID_CENTERING`. For this to compile, that Help topic ID has to be known to the compiler, so in `ShowString.h`, add this line:

```
#define HID_CENTERING 0x01
```

The Help topic IDs in the range `0x0000` to `0xFFFF` are reserved for user-defined Help topics, so `0x01` is a fine choice. Now the C++ compiler is happy, but when this runs, the call to `WinHelp()` is not going to find the topic that explains centering. You need to add a *help mapping entry*. This should be done in a new file, named `ShowStringx.hm` (the x is for extra, because extra help mapping entries are added here.) Choose File, New, select the Files tab, highlight Text File, fill in the file name as ShowStringx.hm, and click OK. In the new file, type in this line:

```
HID_CENTERING       0x01
```

Save the file. Next you need to edit the Help project file, `ShowString.hpj`. If you double-click this from a folder such as Windows 95 Explorer, the Help Compiler opens it. In this case you actually want to edit it as text, so you should open it with Developer Studio. In Developer Studio's Project Workspace Window, click the FileView tab and then open `ShowString.hpj` by double-clicking it in the File View (and you wondered what the File View was good for) and add this line at the very bottom:

```
#include <ShowStringX.hm>
```

Now both the Help system and the compiler know about this new Help topic ID. Later in this chapter, when you write the Help text, you add a section that explains centering and connect it to this Help topic ID.

The other common use of command Help is to add a Help button to a dialog box that gives an overview of the dialog box. This used to be standard behavior but is now recommended only for large dialog boxes, especially those with complex interactions between the various controls. Simply follow the steps you followed to add the menu item Help, Understanding Centering, but add a button rather than a menu item. Do not create a new .hm file; add the button's Help topic ID to `ShowStringX.hm`, which continues to grow in the next section.

Programming for Context Help

Your first task in arranging for context Help is to get a Question button onto the Options dialog box, since AppWizard already added one to the toolbar. Open the Options dialog box by double-clicking it in the Resource View, and then choose View, Properties. Click the Extended Styles tab, and then make sure that the Context Help check box is selected, as shown in Figure 11.5.

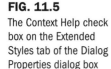

FIG. 11.5

The Context Help check box on the Extended Styles tab of the Dialog Properties dialog box arranges for the Question box on the Options dialog box of ShowString.

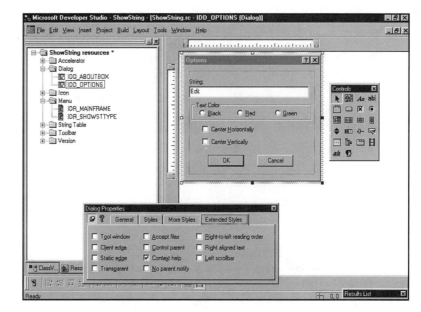

As mentioned earlier, there are two messages sent in context Help: WM_HELP when a user clicks something while in What's This? mode, and WM_CONTEXTMENU when a user right-clicks something. You need to arrange for your dialog box class, COptionsDialog, to catch these messages. You do so by adding entries outside the special ClassWizard comments. The message map in OptionsDialog.h should look like this:

```
// Generated message map functions
    //{{AFX_MSG(COptionsDialog)
        // NOTE: the ClassWizard will add member functions here
    //}}AFX_MSG
    afx_msg BOOL OnHelpInfo(HELPINFO* lpHelpInfo);
    afx_msg void OnContextMenu(CWnd* pWnd, CPoint point);
    DECLARE_MESSAGE_MAP()
```

The message map in OptionsDialog.cpp should look like this:

```
BEGIN_MESSAGE_MAP(COptionsDialog, CDialog)
    //{{AFX_MSG_MAP(COptionsDialog)
        // NOTE: the ClassWizard will add message map macros here
    //}}AFX_MSG_MAP
```

Part

IV

Ch

11

```
    ON_WM_HELPINFO()
    ON_WM_CONTEXTMENU()
END_MESSAGE_MAP()
```

These macros arrange for WM_HELP to be caught by OnHelpInfo(), and for WM_CONTEXTMENU to be caught by OnContextMenu(). The next step is to write those functions. They both need to use a table to connect resource IDs to Help topic IDs. Add these lines at the beginning of OptionsDialog.cpp, after the comment block that reads // COptionsDialog dialog:

```
static DWORD aHelpIDs[] =
{
    IDC_OPTIONS_STRING, HIDD_OPTIONS_STRING,
    IDC_OPTIONS_BLACK, HIDD_OPTIONS_BLACK,
    IDC_OPTIONS_RED, HIDD_OPTIONS_RED,
    IDC_OPTIONS_GREEN, HIDD_OPTIONS_GREEN,
    IDC_OPTIONS_HORIZCENTER, HIDD_OPTIONS_HORIZCENTER,
    IDC_OPTIONS_VERTCENTER, HIDD_OPTIONS_VERTCENTER,
    IDOK, HIDD_OPTIONS_OK,
    IDCANCEL, HIDD_OPTIONS_CANCEL,
    0, 0
};
```

The Help system uses this array (you pass the address to the WinHelp() function) to connect resource IDs and Help topic IDs. The compiler, however, has never heard of HIDD_OPTIONS_STRING, so add these lines to OptionsDialog.h, before the definition of the COptionsDialog class:

```
#define HIDD_OPTIONS_STRING 2
#define HIDD_OPTIONS_BLACK 3
#define HIDD_OPTIONS_RED 4
#define HIDD_OPTIONS_GREEN 5
#define HIDD_OPTIONS_HORIZCENTER 6
#define HIDD_OPTIONS_VERTCENTER 7
#define HIDD_OPTIONS_OK 8
#define HIDD_OPTIONS_CANCEL 9
```

The numbers are chosen arbitrarily. Now, as before, the compiler is happy, since all these constants are defined, but the Help system doesn't know what's going on because these topics are not in the Help mapping file yet. So, add these lines to ShowStringX.hm:

```
HIDD_OPTIONS_STRING      0x02
HIDD_OPTIONS_BLACK       0x03
HIDD_OPTIONS_RED      0x04
HIDD_OPTIONS_GREEN       0x05
HIDD_OPTIONS_HORIZCENTER      0x06
HIDD_OPTIONS_VERTCENTER      0x07
HIDD_OPTIONS_OK      0x08
HIDD_OPTIONS_CANCEL      0x09
```

Be sure to use the same numbers as in the #define statements in OptionsDialog.h. The stage is set; all that remains is to write the functions. Here's what OnHelpInfo() looks like:

```
BOOL COptionsDialog::OnHelpInfo(HELPINFO *lpHelpInfo)
{
```

```
    if (lpHelpInfo->iContextType == HELPINFO_WINDOW) // must be for a control
    {
        // have to call SDK WinHelp not CWinApp::WinHelp
        // because CWinApp::WinHelp doesn't take a
        // handle as a parameter.
        ::WinHelp((HWND)lpHelpInfo->hItemHandle,
            AfxGetApp()->m_pszHelpFilePath,
            HELP_WM_HELP, (DWORD)aHelpIDs);
    }
    return TRUE;
}
```

This function just calls the SDK WinHelp function and passes the handle to the control, the path to the Help file, the command HELP_WM_HELP to request a context-sensitive pop-up Help topic, and the table of resource IDs and Help topic IDs built earlier. There's no other work for your function to do after kicking WinHelp() into action.

> **T I P** If you've never seen the :: scope resolution operator used without a class name before it, it means call the function that is not in any class, and in Windows programming that generally means the SDK function.

> **N O T E** The third parameter of this call to WinHelp directs the Help system to put up a certain style of Help window. HELP_WM_HELP gets you a pop-up menu, as does HELP_WM_CONTEXTMENU. HELP_CONTEXT gets an ordinary Help window, which can be resized and moved, and allows Help navigation. HELP_FINDER brings up the Help Topics dialog box. HELP_CONTENTS and HELP_INDEX are obsolete and should be replaced with HELP_FINDER if you maintain code that uses them. ■

OnContextMenu() is even simpler:

```
void COptionsDialog::OnContextMenu(CWnd *pWnd, CPoint /*point*/)
{
    ::WinHelp((HWND)*pWnd, AfxGetApp()->m_pszHelpFilePath,
        HELP_CONTEXTMENU, (DWORD)aHelpIDs);
}
```

This function doesn't need to check that the right-click is on a control as OnHelpInfo() did, so it just calls the SDK WinHelp. WinHelp() takes care of displaying the shortcut menu with only a What's This item and then displays Help when that item is chosen.

To check your typing, build the project by choosing Build, Build, and then compile the Help file by giving focus to ShowString.hpj and choosing Build, Compile. (You also can right-click ShowString.hpj in the File View of the Project Workspace Window and choose Compile from the shortcut menu.) There's not much point in testing it, though; the AppWizard stuff is sure to work, and without Help content connected to those topics, none of the code you just added can succeed in displaying content.

Writing Help Text

You write Help text in an .RTF file, using special formatting codes, which mean something rather different than they usually do. The traditional way to do this was in Word, but a large crop of Help authoring tools have sprung up that are far easier to use than Word. Rather than teach you yet another tool, this section presents instructions for writing Help text in Word. However, do keep in mind that there are easier ways, and on a project of a decent size you easily save the time and money you invest in a Help authoring tool. There is an entire chapter in *Designing Windows 95 Help* on choosing an authoring tool.

> **TIP**
>
> You can open Word documents from within Developer Studio. Choose File, Open, and select the file. The Word menus and toolbars will appear. This works because Word documents are ActiveX Document Objects, discussed in Chapter 15, "Building an ActiveX Server Application." Most developers prefer to switch from Word to Developer Studio with the taskbar than to have a number of files open in Developer Studio and to switch among them with the Window menu, so the explanations in this section assume you are running Word separately. If you would rather work entirely within Developer Studio, feel free to so do.

Figure 11.6 shows `afxcore.rtf` open in Word. Choose View, Footnotes to display the footnotes across the bottom of the screen—they are vital. This is how the text connects to the Help topic IDs. Choose Tools, Options, select the View tab, and make sure the hidden text check box is selected. This is how links between topics are entered. The topics are separated by page breaks.

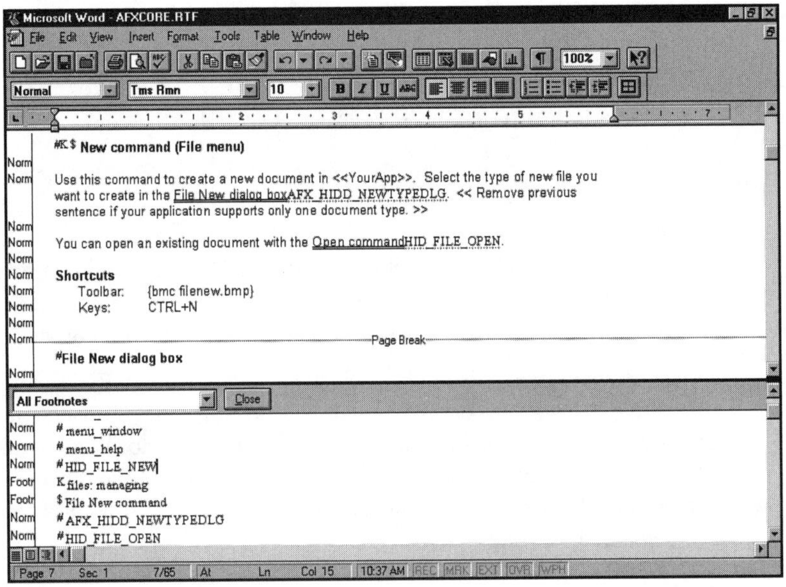

FIG. 11.6

Help text, like this boilerplate provided by AppWizard, can be edited in Word for Windows.

There are eight kinds of footnotes and each has a different meaning. Only the first three foot-note types in the following list are in general use:

- **#, the Help topic ID.** The SDK WinHelp function looks for this topic ID when display-ing Help.
- **$, the topic title.** This title displays in search results.
- **K, keywords.** These appear in the Index tab of the Help Topics dialog box.
- **A, A-keyword.** These keywords can be jumped to but do not appear in the Index tab of the Help Topics dialog box.
- **+, browse code.** This marks the topic's place in a sequence of topics.
- **!, macro entry.** This makes the topic a macro to be run when the user requests the topic.
- ***, build tag.** You use this to include certain tags only in certain builds of the Help file.
- **>, window type.** This overrides the type of window for this topic.

The double-underlined text, followed by hidden text, identifies a jump to another Help topic. If a user clicks to follow the link, this Help topic leaves the screen. If the text before the hidden text was single-underlined, following the link opens a pop-up over this Help topic, perfect for definitions and notes. (You also may see Help text files in which strikethrough text is used; this is exactly the same as double-underlined—a jump to another topic.) In all three cases, the hidden text is the topic ID of the material to be jumped to or popped up.

Figure 11.7 shows how the File, New Help material appears from within ShowString. To display it yourself, run ShowString by choosing Build, Execute from within Developer Studio, and then choose Help, Help topics in ShowString. Open the menus book, double-click the File menu topic, and click New.

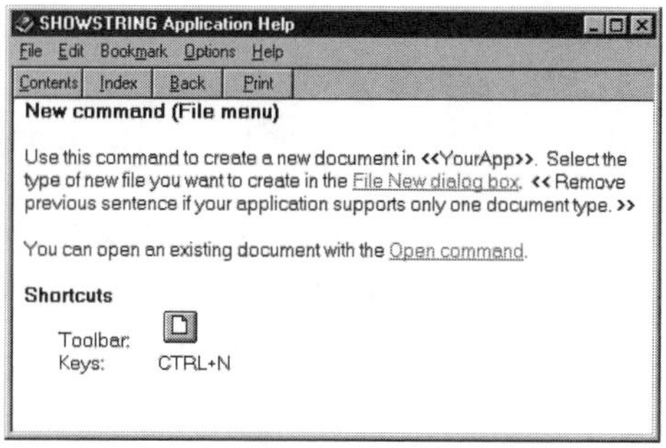

Part

IV

Ch

11

FIG. 11.7

ShowString displays the boilerplate Help generated by AppWizard.

With the programming out of the way, it's time to tackle the list of Help tasks for ShowString from the "Planning Your Help Approach" section earlier in this chapter. These instructions assume you are using Word.

Changing Placeholder Strings

To change the placeholder strings left behind by AppWizard in the boilerplate Help files, open `afxcore.rtf` in Word. (It's in the hlp folder of the ShowString project folder.) Then follow these steps:

1. Position the cursor at the very beginning of the document and choose <u>E</u>dit, <u>R</u>eplace.
2. Enter **<<YourApp>>** in the Fi<u>n</u>d What box and **ShowString** in the Re<u>p</u>lace With box.
3. Click Replace All.

Open `afxprint.rtf` and repeat these steps.

Switch back to `afxcore.rtf`, and look through the text for << characters (use <u>E</u>dit, <u>F</u>ind, and remember that Shift+F4 is the shortcut to repeat your previous Find). These identify places where you must make a change or a decision. For ShowString, the changes in `afxcore.rtf` are these:

1. The first section in the file is the ShowString Help Index. Remove the How To section and the reminder to add some How To topics. In a real application, you add topics here.
2. The next section, after the page break, is a table describing the items on the <u>F</u>ile menu. Since there is no Send item on ShowString's <u>F</u>ile menu, remove the Send row of the File menu table.
3. The third section is a table listing the items on the <u>E</u>dit menu. Remove the Paste Link, Insert New Object, and Links rows.
4. The fourth section is for the <u>V</u>iew menu and does not need any changes.
5. The fifth section is for the <u>W</u>indow menu. Remove the Split row from the Window menu table.
6. The sixth section is for the <u>H</u>elp menu and does not need any changes.
7. The seventh section is for the New command (<u>F</u>ile menu). Remove the sentence about choosing a file type and the reminder to remove it.
8. Delete the eighth section, the File New dialog box topic, entirely, including the page break before or after it, but not both. Whenever you remove a section, remove one of the breaks so that the file does not contain two consecutive page breaks.
9. The next topic is for the File Open command and does not need any changes.
10. Moving on to the File Open dialog box topic, edit the text to mention that the List Files of Type list box contains only `All Files`.
11. Continue down the file until you find the File Send topic and remove it entirely, including the page break before or after it.
12. In the File Save As topic, remove the suggestion to describe other options since there are none.

13. When you reach the Edit Undo topic, you start to see why programs written after their manuals are better programs. The way ShowString was written in Chapter 9, "Building a Complete Application: ShowString," the Undo item will never be enabled, nor will Cut, Copy, or Paste. You could remove the Help topics about these unsupported menu items, but it's probably better to plan to add support for the menu items to a later version of ShowString. Add some text to all these topics explaining that they are not implemented in this version of the product. Leave the shortcuts sections there so that users can find out why Ctrl+Z does nothing.

14. Continue down through the file to the Toolbar topic, where you find this reminder: `<< Add or remove toolbar buttons from the list below according to which ones your application offers. >>` Remove the reminder and delete the references to the Undo, First Record, Previous Record, Next Record, and Last Record buttons.

15. About halfway down the file is a topic for `#Split` Command (Window menu). Remove the entire topic.

16. Move down to the `#Index` command (Help menu) topic and remove it. Also remove the Using Help command (Help menu) and `#About` command (Help menu) topics.

17. In the Title Bar topic, remove the directive to insert a graphic. If you would rather follow the directive, create a bitmap in a .bmp file of the title bar with screen shot software, cropping the shot down to just the title bar, and insert the graphic with the `bmc` directive, just as the `bullet.bmp` graphic is inserted a few lines lower in the file.

18. Because the ShowString view does not inherit from `CScrollView`, it doesn't scroll. Remove the Scrollbars Help topic and its page break.

19. In the Close command topic (not the File Close topic, which was much earlier in the file,) the shortcut for Alt+F4 should be described like this: `closes ShowString`.

20. Remove the Ruler, Choose Font, Choose Color, Edit Find, Find Dialog, Edit Replace, Replace dialog box, Edit Repeat, Edit Clear, Edit Clear All, Next Pane, and Previous Pane topics.

21. Skip the How To Modify Text topic for now and leave it unchanged.

22. Remove the final directive about tailoring the No Help Available messages to each message box.

That completes the extensive changes required to the boilerplate `afxcore.rtf` file generated by AppWizard. In the other boilerplate file, `afxprint.rtf`, simply scroll to the bottom and remove the Page Setup topic.

Would you like to test all this work? Save `afxcore.rtf` and `afxprint.rtf` within Word. Switch to Developer Studio and choose Build, Build to bring the project up to date. Then open `ShowString.hpj` and choose Build, Compile. This pulls all the .rtf files together into `ShowString.hlp`. Choose Build, Execute to run ShowString, and choose Help, Help Topics from the ShowString menus. As you can see in Figure 11.8, the Window menu topic is now substantially shorter. You can check that your other changes have been made, as well.

Part
IV

Ch
11

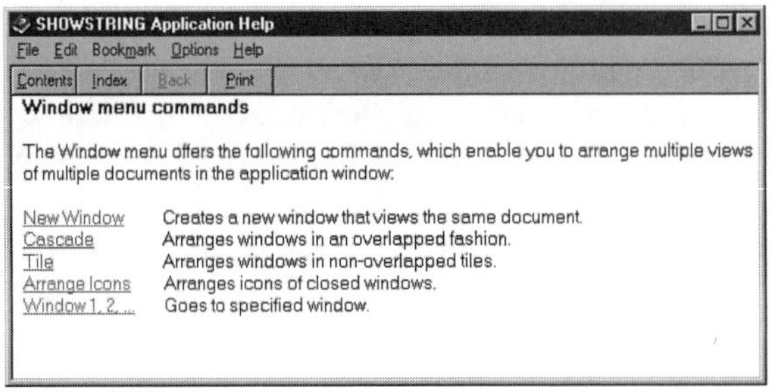

FIG. 11.8

After saving the .rtf files and compiling the Help project, you can test to see that your changes have been made successfully.

Adding Topics

When you are adding new topics, you don't add new topics to the boilerplate files that were provided. Those files should stay untouched unless you want to change the description of File Open or other boilerplate topics. Instead, create a new file by choosing File, New in Word and saving it in the hlp folder of the ShowString project folder as ShowString.rtf. (Make sure to change the Save File As Type list box selection to Rich Text Format.) If this was a large project, you could divide it up into several .RTF files, but one will suffice for ShowString. In Developer Studio, open ShowString.hpj by double-clicking it in the FileView tab, and find the section headed [FILES]. Add this line at the end of that section:

```
showstring.rtf
```

The Tools Menu   Back in Word, switch to afxcore.rtf and copy the topic for the File menu into the Clipboard; then switch back to ShowString.rtf and paste it in. (Don't forget to include the page break after the topic in the selection when you copy.) Choose View, Footnotes to display the footnotes, and Tools, Options, View tab, Hidden Text to display the hidden text. Now you are going to edit the copied File topic to make it the Tools topic. Change the footnotes first. They are as follows:

- The # footnote is the topic ID. The Help system uses this to find this topic from the Contents page. Change it to **menu_tools**.

- The K footnote is the keyword entry. Although the Options dialog box probably deserves several keywords, this menu doesn't, so remove that footnote by selecting the letter K in the Help topic and pressing Delete. You must select the letter; it is not enough to click just before it. The footnote is deleted at the same time.

- The $ footnote is the topic title. Change it to **Tools menu commands**.

In the topic, change File to **Tools** on the first two lines, and delete all the rows of the table but one. Change the underlined text of that row to Options, the hidden text immediately following to HID_TOOLS_OPTIONS, and the right column of that row to Changes string, color, and centering. Figure 11.9 shows the way ShowString.rtf looks in Word after these changes.

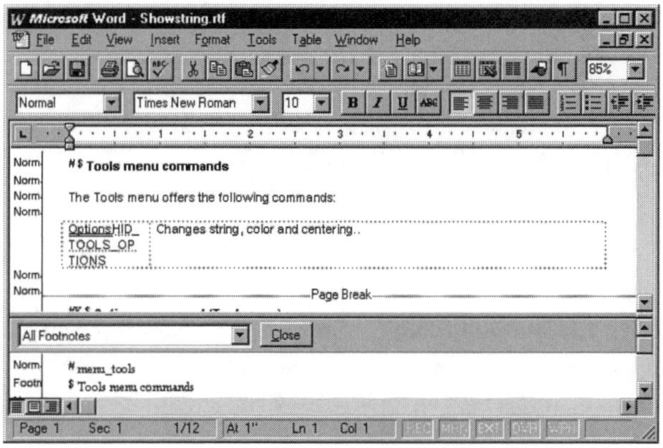

FIG. 11.9
Change the `ShowString.rtf` file to explain the new menu item.

TIP If you can't remember the Help topic IDs your project is using, check your .hm files. The ones added by Developer Studio, such as `HID_TOOLS_OPTIONS` for the menu item with resource ID `ID_TOOLS_OPTIONS`, are in `ShowString.hm`, whereas `ShowStringx.hm` contains the Help topic IDs added by hand for context Help.

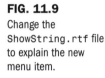

The Tools, Options menu item Switch back to `afxcore`, copy the File New topic, and paste it into `ShowString.rtf` as before. The topic and its footnotes are copied together. Watch carefully to be sure you are working with the footnotes for the Tools Options topic and not the ones for the Tools menu. Follow these steps:

1. Change the # footnote to **`HID_TOOLS_OPTIONS`**.
2. Change the K keyword. There are several keywords that should lead here, and each needs to be separated from the next by a semicolon (;). Some need to be two-level keywords with the levels separated by commas. A good first start is **`string, changing;color, changing;centering, changing;appearance, controlling`**.
3. Change the $ keyword to **`Tools Options command`**.
4. Change the first line of the topic to **`Options command (Tools menu)`**.
5. Delete the rest of the topic and replace it with a short description of this menu item. The following text is OK:

```
Use this command to change the appearance of the ShowString
display with the Options dialog box. The string being displayed,
color of the text, and vertical and horizontal centering are
all controlled from this dialog.
```

If you want to test this, too, save the files in Word, compile the Help project, run ShowString, and choose Tools. Highlight the Options item by moving the highlight with the cursor keys, but do not click Options to select it; press `F1` instead. Figure 11.10 shows the Help window that displays.

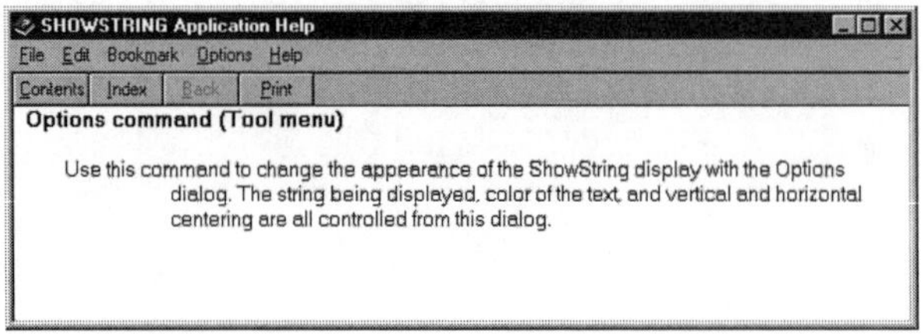

FIG. 11.10

The new Tools Options Help is reached by pressing F1 while the item is highlighted on the menu.

Each Control on the Options Dialog   Copy the File New topic into ShowString.rtf again and cut it down drastically. To do this, follow these steps:

1. Remove the K and $ footnotes.
2. Change the # footnote to **HIDD_OPTIONS**.
3. Change the first line to **(Options dialog)**.
4. Delete the other text in the topic.

Copy this block into the Clipboard and paste it in seven more times, so that you have a skeleton for each control on the dialog box. Remember to copy the page break before or after the topic, too. Then edit each skeleton to document the following topic IDs:

- HIDD_OPTIONS_STRING
- HIDD_OPTIONS_BLACK
- HIDD_OPTIONS_RED
- HIDD_OPTIONS_GREEN
- HIDD_OPTIONS_HORIZCENTER
- HIDD_OPTIONS_VERTCENTER
- HIDD_OPTIONS_OK
- HIDD_OPTIONS_CANCEL

Change the topic ID and add a sentence or two of text. Be consistent. The samples included with this chapter are all a single sentence that starts with an imperative verb like "Click" or "Select" and ends with a period (.). If you would rather choose a different style for your pop-up boxes, use the same style for all of them. It confuses the user if pop-up boxes are inconsistent and tends to make them believe your coding is sloppy, too.

To test your work, compile ShowString.hpj again, run ShowString, and choose Tools, Options. Click the question mark button and then click somewhere on the dialog box. Explore each of the controls to be sure you have entered the correct text. Figure 11.11 shows the context Help for the String edit box.

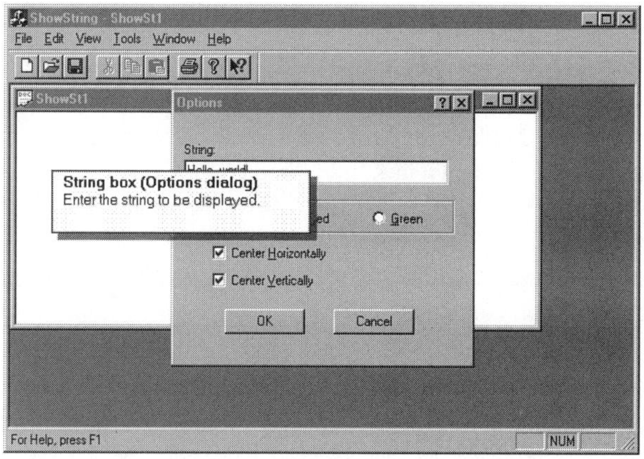

FIG. 11.11

Display Help for a dialog box control by clicking the Question button in the upper-right corner and then clicking a control.

Understanding Centering In ShowString.rtf, paste in another copy of the File New topic. Make the following changes:

1. Change the # footnote to **HID_CENTERING** (the topic ID you added to ShowStringx.hm and called in CShowStringApp::OnHelpUnderstandingcentering()).

2. Change the K footnote to **centering**.

3. Change the $ footnote to **Understanding Centering**.

4. Change the title on the first line to **Understanding Centering**.

5. Replace the text with a short explanation of centering, like this:

    ```
    ShowString can center the displayed string within the view. The two
    options, "center horizontally" and "center vertically", can be set
    independently on the Options dialog box, reached by choosing the Options
    item on the Tools menu. Text that is not centered horizontally is
    displayed at the left edge of the window. Text that is not centered
    vertically is displayed at the top of the window.
    ```

6. Add links from the word Tools to the menu_tools topic and from the word Options to HID_TOOLS_OPTIONS, as before. Remember to watch for extra spaces.

Test this change in the usual way, and when you choose Help, Understanding Centering from the ShowString menus, you should see something like Figure 11.12. Try following the links; you can use the Back button to return to the centering topic.

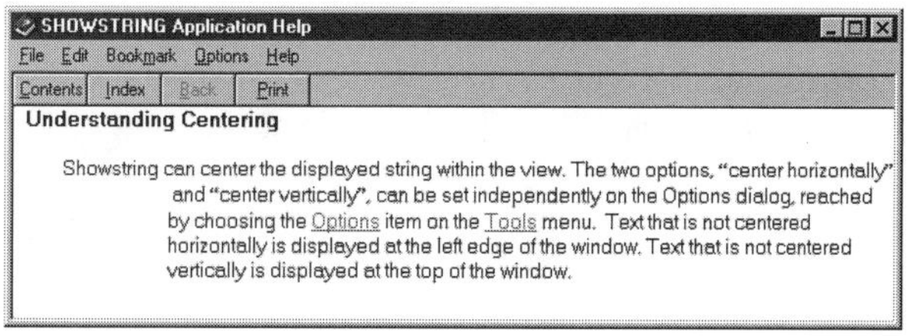

FIG. 11.12

Display a teaching Help topic by choosing it from the Help menu.

Part

IV

Ch

11

Changing the "How to Modify Text" Topic

App Wizard already provided a How to Modify Text topic at the bottom of `afxcore.rtf` that needs to be edited to explain how ShowString works. It displays when the user selects the view area for context Help. Replace the text with a much shorter explanation that tells the user to choose Tools, Options. To add a link to that topic (short though it is), type **HID_TOOLS_OPTIONS** immediately after the word `Options` in the Help topic. While you're at it, type **menu_tools** immediately after the word `Tools`. Select the word `Options` and press Ctrl+Shift+D to double-underline it; then do the same for `Tools`. Select `HID_TOOLS_OPTIONS` and press Ctrl+Shift+H to hide it; then do the same for `menu_tools`.

> **TIP**
> If you've reassigned these keys, you can do the formatting the long way. To double-underline text, select it and choose Format, Font. Drop down the Underline box and choose Double, then click OK. To hide text, select it and choose Format, Font, then select the Hidden box and click OK.

> **TIP**
> There cannot be any spaces between the double-underlined text and the hidden text, or at the end of the hidden text. Word can give you some trouble about this, because the Smart Cut and Paste feature that works so nicely with words can insert extra spaces where you don't want them, or make it impossible to select only half a word. You can turn the feature off in Word by choosing Tools, Options, the Edit tab, and by deselecting the Automatic Word Selection and Use Smart Cut and Paste check boxes.

Ready to test again? Save the files in Word, compile the Help project file, and execute ShowString; then click the What's This? button on the toolbar, and click in the main view. Your new "How to Modify Text" entry should appear.

Adjustments to the Contents

This tiny little application is almost entirely documented now. You need to add the Tools menu and Understanding Centering to the Contents and check the index. The easiest way to tackle the Contents is with Help Workshop. Close all the Help-related files that are open in Developer Studio and Word, and bring up Help Workshop (it's in the Developer Studio folder). Open `ShowString.cnt` by choosing File, Open and working your way through the Open dialog box. This is the Contents file for ShowString.

In the first open book, click the View Menu item and then click the Add Below button. (Alternatively, click the Window Menu item and then the Add Above button.) The Edit Contents Tab Entry dialog box, shown in Figure 11.13, appears. Fill it in as shown; by leaving the last two entries blank, the default Help File and Window Type are used. Click OK.

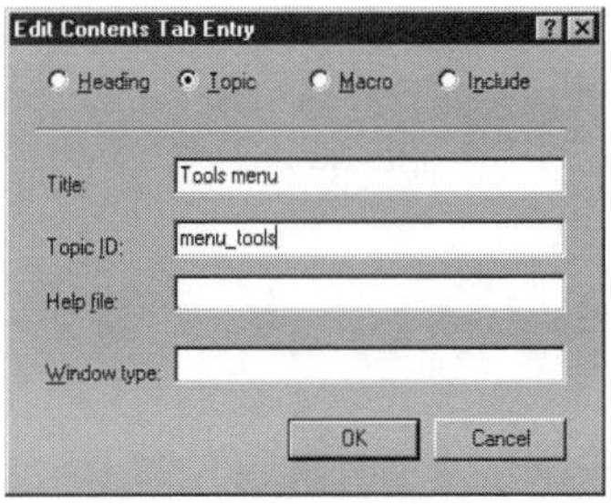

FIG. 11.13

Add entries to the Contents tab with Help Workshop's Edit Contents Tab Entry dialog box.

Click the placeholder book, and click Add Above again. When the Edit Contents Tab Entry dialog box appears, select the Heading radio button from the list across the top. As shown in Figure 11.14, you can change only the title here. Do not use Understanding Centering, since that is the title of the only topic under this heading. Click OK.

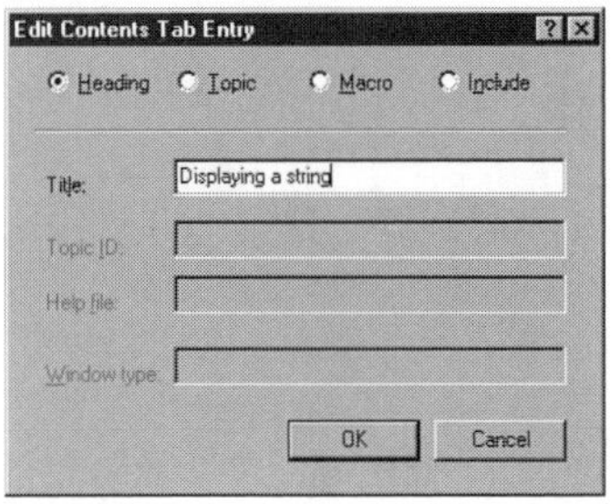

FIG. 11.14

Add headings to the Contents tab with Help Workshop's Edit Contents Tab Entry dialog box by selecting the Heading radio button.

Part
IV
Ch
11

Add a topic below the new heading for Understanding Centering, whose ID is HID_CENTERING, and remove the placeholder heading and topic. Save your changes, close Help Workshop, compile ShowString.hpj in Developer Studio again, and test your Help. Choose Help, Help Topics, and you should see something like Figure 11.15.

FIG. 11.15

After saving the .cnt file and compiling the .hpj file, display the new table of contents by choosing Help, Help Topics.

While you have the Help Topics dialog box open, click the Index tab. Figure 11.16 shows how the K footnotes you entered throughout this section have all been added to the index. If it looks a little sparse, you can always go to the .rtf files and add more keywords, remembering to separate them with semicolons.

FIG. 11.16
The index has been built from the K footnotes in the .rtf files.

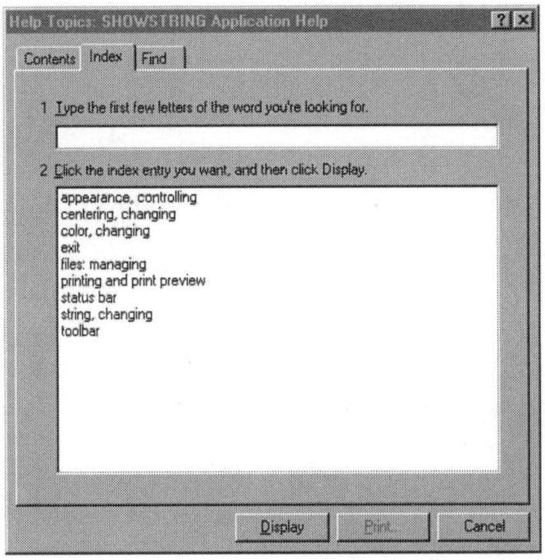

Help Topics: SHOWSTRING Application Help

Contents | Index | Find

1 Type the first few letters of the word you're looking for.

2 Click the index entry you want, and then click Display.

appearance, controlling
centering, changing
color, changing
exit
files: managing
printing and print preview
status bar
string, changing
toolbar

Display   Print...   Cancel

From Here...

This chapter has shown you all of the types of Help, the different ways the user invokes it, and the behind-the-scenes code that brings it up on the screen. You have also seen how to edit and write Help topics and Help contents files. Of course, there is much more to cover. If you have a large system to document, you need a book just on Help to give you a good perspective on designing and writing your Help content. Other parts of this book that might interest you include:

- Chapter 4, "Messages and Commands," gives more details on catching the messages generated when a user chooses a menu item or clicks a button.

- Chapter 9, "Building a Complete Application: ShowString," introduces you to the sample application that was documented in this chapter.

- Chapter 10, "Status Bars and Toolbars," shows you some other ways to help your user understand your application.

- Part V, "ActiveX Applications and ActiveX Controls," continues to expand ShowString by adding various kinds of ActiveX functionality. (Part V consists of Chapters 13–17.)

CHAPTER 12

Property Pages and Sheets and Wizards

One of the newest types of graphical objects is the tabbed dialog box, also known as a *property sheet*. A property sheet is a dialog box with two or more pages. Windows 95 is loaded with property sheets, which organize the many options that can be modified by the user. You flip the pages by clicking labeled tabs located at the top of the dialog box. By using such dialog boxes to organize complex groups of options, Windows 95 enables users to more easily find the information and settings that they need. As you've probably guessed, Visual C++ 5.0 supports the Windows 95 property sheets, with the classes CPropertySheet and CPropertyPage.

Similar to property sheets are *wizards,* which use buttons to move from one page to another (rather than using tabs). You've seen a lot of wizards, too. These special types of dialog boxes guide the user step-by-step through complicated processes. For example, when you use AppWizard to generate source code for a new project, the wizard guides you through the entire process. To control the wizard, you click buttons labeled Back, Next, and Finish. ■

How to create property page resources

Property sheets contain property pages, which are much like dialog boxes.

How to associate property sheets and pages with their MFC classes

MFC provides classes that enable you to easily manipulate property pages and property sheets.

How to initialize and display property sheets

Creating a property sheet is only half the battle. You also have to get the sheet up on the screen for the user.

How to convert a property sheet to a wizard

Wizards are a special type of property sheet. They guide users through complex tasks.

How to respond to wizard buttons

Every wizard contains buttons that enable the user to navigate through the wizard.

Introducing Property Sheets

Finding a sample property sheet in Windows 95 is as easy as finding sand at the beach. Just click virtually any Properties command or double-click an icon in the Control Panel. For example, Figure 12.1 shows the dialog box that you see when you double-click the Control Panel's Add/Remove Programs icon. This is a property sheet that contains three pages labeled Install/Uninstall, Windows Setup, and Startup Disk. Each page contains commands and options related to the page's title topic.

FIG. 12.1

The Add/Remove Programs Properties sheet contains three tabbed pages.

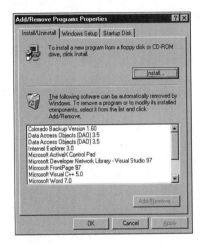

N O T E Many people forget the difference between a property sheet and a property page. A *property sheet* is a window that contains property pages. *Property pages* are windows that hold controls. They appear on the property sheet's pages. ▪

In Figure 12.1, you can see programs installed on your computer that Windows can automatically uninstall. There's also an Install button that leads to other dialog boxes that help you install new programs from floppy disk or CD-ROM. On the other hand, the Windows Setup page (Figure 12.2) helps you add or remove files from the Windows system. To get to this page, you need only click the Windows Setup tab. The Startup Disk page, of course, houses yet another set of options.

As you can see, property sheets are a great way to organize many types of related options. Gone are the days of dialog boxes so jam-packed with options that you needed a college-level course just to figure them out. In the sections that follow, you will learn to program your own tabbed property sheets using MFC's `CPropertySheet` and `CPropertyPage` classes.

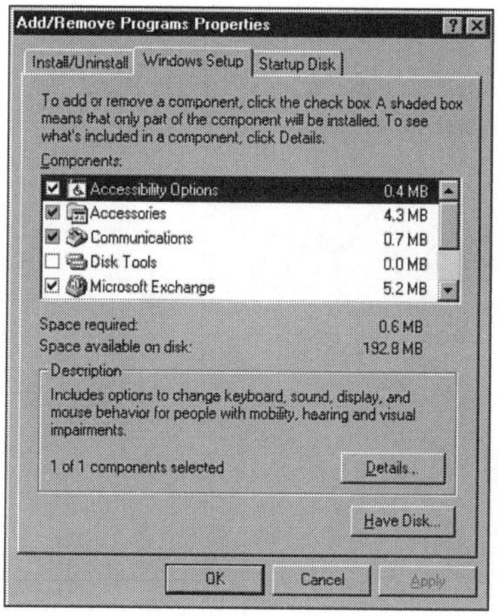

FIG. 12.2

Click the Windows
Setup tab to move to
the Windows Setup
page.

Creating the Property Sheet Demo Application

Now that you've had an introduction to property sheets, it's time to learn how to build an application that uses these handy specialized dialog boxes. You are about to build the Property Sheet Demo application, which demonstrates the creation and manipulation of property sheets. Follow these steps to create the basic application and modify its resources.

First, use AppWizard to create the basic files for the Property Sheet Demo program, selecting the options listed in the following table. When you're done, the New Project Information dialog box appears; it should look like Figure 12.3. Click the OK button to create the project files.

Dialog Box Name	Options to Select
New, Project tab	Name the project Propsheet and then set the project path to the directory into which you want to store the project's files. Make sure MFC AppWizard (exe) is highlighted. Leave the other options set to their defaults.
Step 1	Select Single Document.
Step 2 of 6	Leave set to defaults.
Step 3 of 6	Leave set to defaults.
Step 4 of 6	Turn off all application features.
Step 5 of 6	Leave set to defaults.
Step 6 of 6	Leave set to defaults.

Now you are going to edit the resources in the application generated for you by AppWizard, removing unwanted menus and accelerators, editing the About box, and most importantly adding a menu item that will bring up a property sheet. Follow these steps:

1. Select the ResourceView tab in the project workspace window. Developer Studio displays the ResourceView window, as shown in Figure 12.4.

Part
IV

Ch

12

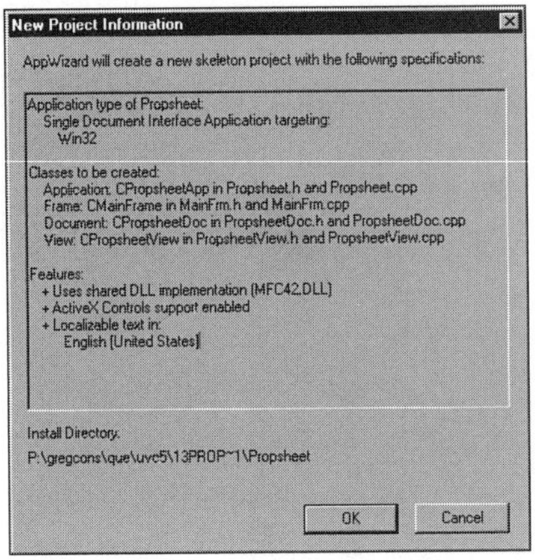

FIG. 12.3

Your New Project
Information dialog box
should look like this.

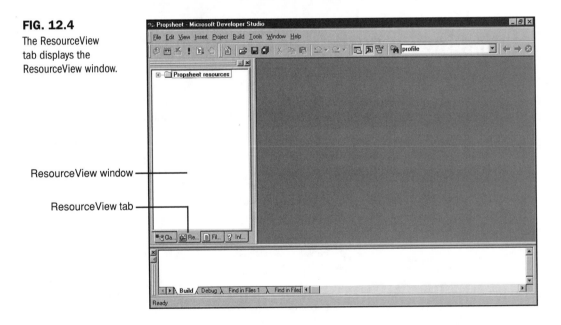

FIG. 12.4

The ResourceView
tab displays the
ResourceView window.

ResourceView window ——————

ResourceView tab ——————

2. In the ResourceView window, click the plus sign next to `Propsheet resources` to display the application's resources. Click the plus sign next to Menu and then double-click the `IDR_MAINFRAME` menu ID. Visual C++'s menu editor appears, displaying the IDR_MAINFRAME menu generated by AppWizard.

3. Click the Property Sheet Demo application's Edit menu (not Visual C++'s Edit menu), and then press your keyboard's Delete key to delete the Edit menu. When you do, a dialog box asks for verification of the delete command. Click OK.

4. Double-click the About Propsheet... item in the Help menu to bring up its properties dialog box. Change the caption to &About Property Sheet Demo. Pin the properties dialog box in place by clicking the pushpin in the upper left corner.

5. On the application's File menu, delete all menu items except Exit.

6. Select the blank menu item at the end of the File menu, and change the caption to &Property Sheet... and the command ID to ID_PROPSHEET, as shown in Figure 12.5. Then use your mouse to drag the new command above the Exit command, so that it's the first command in the File menu.

FIG. 12.5
Add a Property Sheet command to the File menu.

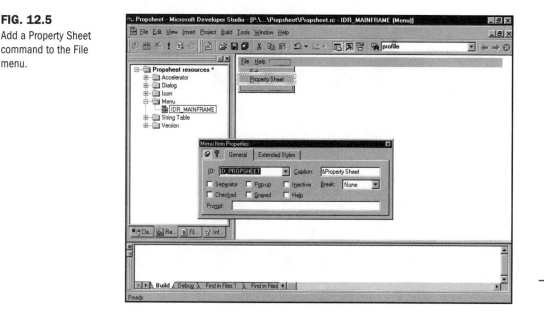

Part
IV

Ch
12

7. Click the + next to Accelerator in the ResourceView window and highlight the IDR_MAINFRAME accelerator ID. Press your Delete key to delete all accelerators from the application.

8. Click the + next to Dialog Resource in the ResourceView window. Double-click the IDD_ABOUTBOX dialog box ID to bring up the dialog box editor.

9. Modify the dialog box by clicking the title so that the properties box refers to the whole dialog box. Change the caption to "About Property Sheet Demo."

10. Click the first static text string and change the caption to "Property Sheet Demo, Version 1.0." Click the second and add "Que books" to the end of the copyright string.

11. Add a third static string with the text "Special Edition Using Visual C++ 5" so that your About box resembles the one in Figure 12.6. Close the dialog box editor.

FIG. 12.6

The About box should look like this.

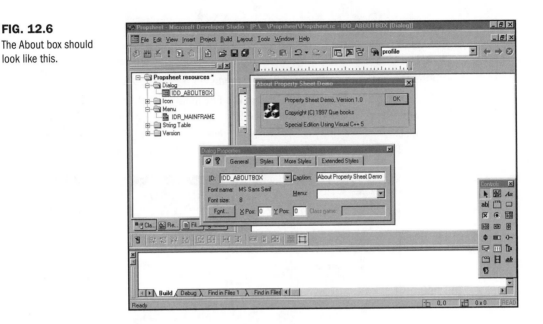

12. Click the + next to String Table in the ResourceView window. Double-click the String Table ID to bring up the string table editor.

13. Double-click the `IDR_MAINFRAME` string and then change the first segment of the string to "Property Sheet Demo," as shown in Figure 12.7. The meanings of these strings are discussed in Chapter 16, "Building an Automation Server," in the "Shortcomings of this Server" section. The one you just changed is the Window Title, used in the title bar of the application.

Now that you have the application's basic resources the way you want them, it's time to add the resources that define the application's property sheet. This means creating dialog box resources for each page in the property sheet. Follow these steps:

1. Click the New Dialog button on the Resource toolbar, or press Ctrl+1 on your keyboard, to create a new dialog box resource. The new dialog box, called `IDD_DIALOG1`, appears in the dialog box editor.

   This dialog box, when it is set up properly, will represent the first page of the property sheet.

2. Delete the OK and Cancel buttons by selecting each with your mouse and then pressing your keyboard's Delete key.

3. If the Properties box is not still up, bring it up by choosing View, Properties. Change the ID of the dialog box to `IDD_PAGE1DLG` and the caption to `Page 1`, as shown in Figure 12.8.

4. Click the Styles tab of the dialog box's property sheet. In the Style drop-down box, select Child, and in the Border drop-down box, select Thin. Turn off the System Menu check box. Your properties dialog box should resemble Figure 12.9.

FIG. 12.7

The first segment of the IDR_MAINFRAME string appears in your main window's title bar.

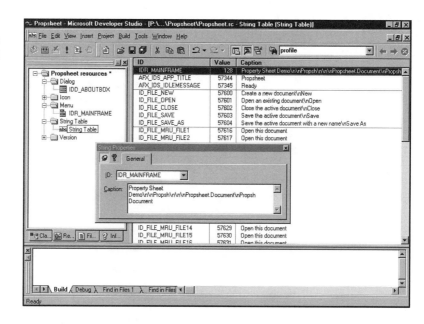

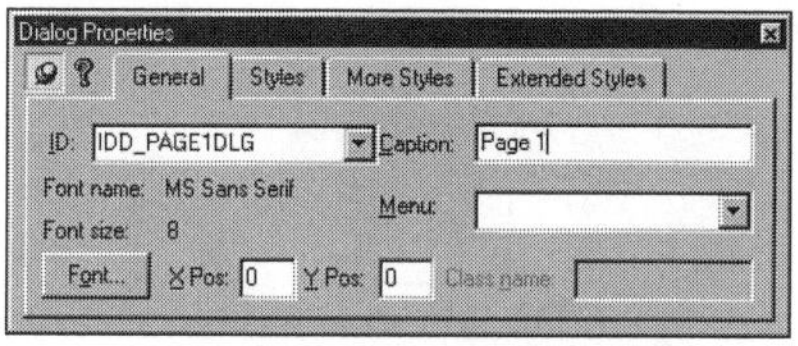

FIG. 12.8

Change the caption and resource ID of the new dialog box.

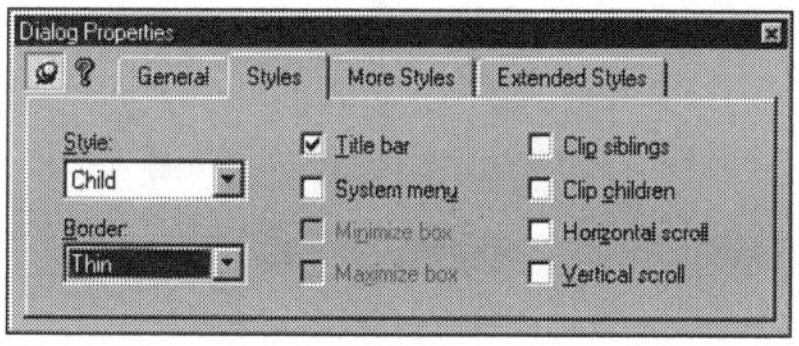

FIG. 12.9

A property page uses styles different from those used in regular dialog boxes.

Part
IV

Ch
12

The Child style is necessary because the property page will be a child window of the property sheet. The property sheet itself will provide the container for the property pages.

5. Add an edit box to the property page, as shown in Figure 12.10. In most applications you would change the resource ID from IDC_EDIT1, but for this demonstration application, leave it unchanged.

6. Create a second property page by following steps 1 through 5 again. For this property page, use the ID IDD_PAGE2DLG, a caption of Page 2, and add a check box rather than an edit control, as shown in Figure 12.11.

FIG. 12.10
A property page can hold whatever controls you like.

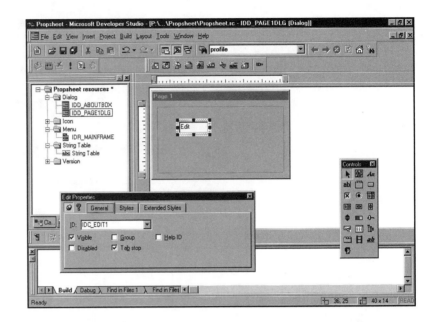

FIG. 12.11
The second property page should look like this.

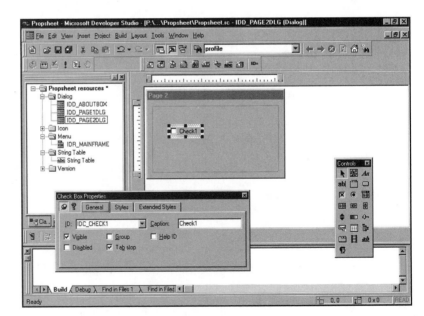

You now have all your resources created. Next, associate your two new property-page resources with C++ classes so that you can control them in your program. You also need a class for your property sheet, which will hold the property pages that you've created. Follow these steps to create the new classes:

1. Make sure that the Page 1 property page is visible in the dialog box edit area, and then double-click it. If you prefer, choose View, ClassWizard from the menu bar. The MFC ClassWizard property sheet appears, displaying the Adding A Class dialog box first discussed in Chapter 2, "Dialog Boxes and Controls."

2. Select the Create New Class option and then click OK. The New Class dialog box appears.

3. In the Name box, type CPage1, and in the Base Class box, select CPropertyPage. (Don't accidentally select CPropertySheet.) Then click the OK button to create the class.

   You've now associated the property page with an object of the CPropertyPage class, which means that you can use the object to manipulate the property page as needed. The CPropertyPage class will be especially important when you learn about wizards.

4. Select the Member Variables tab of the MFC ClassWizard property sheet. With IDC_EDIT1 highlighted, click the Add Variable button. The Add Member Variable dialog box appears.

5. Name the new member variable m_edit, as shown in Figure 12.12, and then click the OK button. ClassWizard adds the member variable, which will hold the value of the property page's control, to the new CPage1 class.

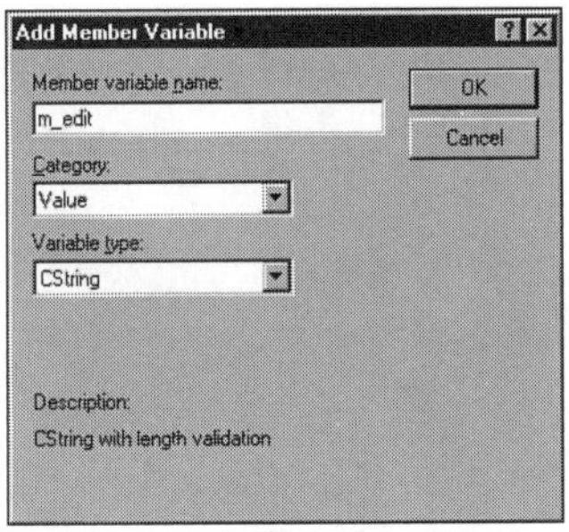

FIG. 12.12

ClassWizard makes it easy to connect controls on a dialog box to member variables of the class representing the dialog box.

Part IV

Ch 12

6. Click OK on the MFC ClassWizard Properties sheet to finalize the creation of the CPage1 class.

7. Follow steps 1 through 7 for the second property sheet. Name the class CPage2 and add a Boolean member variable called m_check for the IDC_CHECK1 control, as shown in Figure 12.13.

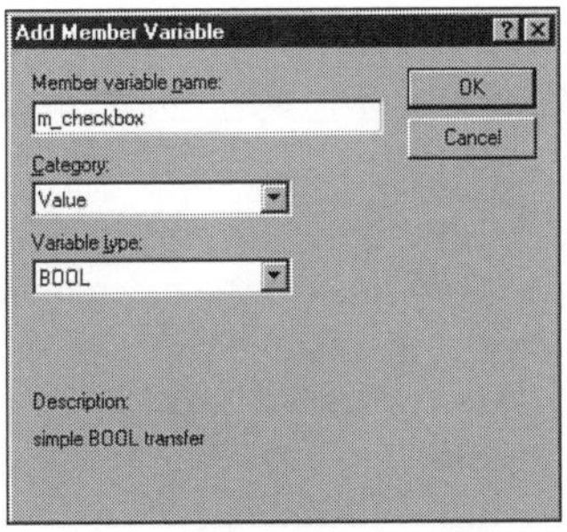

FIG. 12.13

The second property page needs a Boolean member variable called m_checkbox.

At this point you have done all the resource editing, and there is no need to have so many windows open. Choose <u>W</u>indow, Close Al<u>l</u> from the menu bar and close the properties box. You will now create a property sheet class that displays the property pages already created. Follow these steps:

1. Bring up ClassWizard and click the Add Class button. A tiny menu appears below the button—choose New. The New Class dialog box appears.

2. In the <u>N</u>ame box, type CPropSheet, select CPropertySheet in the <u>B</u>ase Class box, and then click OK.

3. ClassWizard creates the CPropSheet class. Click the MFC ClassWizard Properties sheet's OK button to finalize the class.

At this point, you have three new classes—CPage1, CPage2, and CPropSheet—in your program. The first two classes are derived from MFC's CPropertyPage class, and the third is derived from CPropertySheet. Although ClassWizard has created the basic source-code files for these new classes, you still have to add code to the classes to make them work the way you want. Follow these steps to complete the Property Sheet Demo application:

1. Click the ClassView tab to display the ClassView window. Expand the Propsheet classes, as shown Figure 12.14.

FIG. 12.14

The ClassView window lists the classes that make up your project.

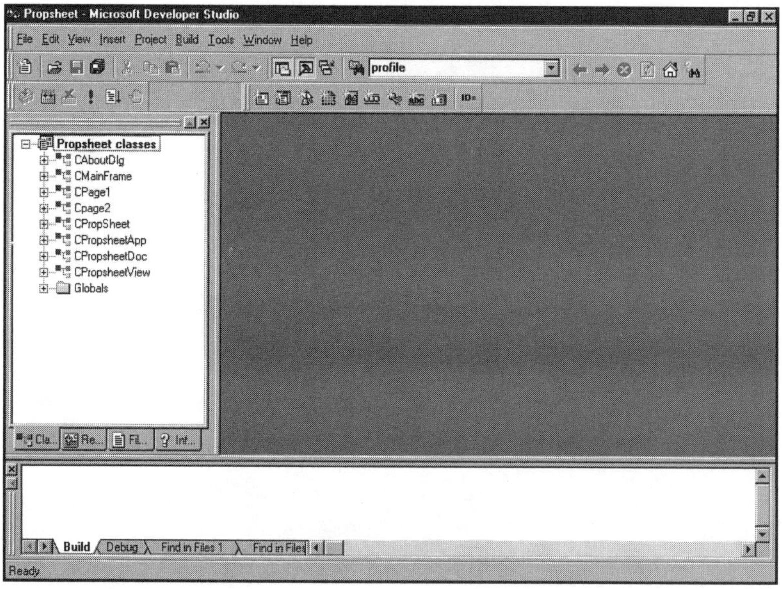

2. Double-click CPropSheet to open the header file for your property sheet class. Because the name of this class (CPropSheet) is so close to the name of the application as a whole (PropSheet), you will find two classes in this file: CPropSheetApp, generated by AppWizard, and CPropSheet, generated by ClassWizard when you created the new class.

N O T E If the new class for the property sheet was in a file of its own, you would have to add #include statements to any file that used the CPropSheet class. Keep this in mind when you create your own property sheets. ▪

3. Add the following lines near the middle of the file, right before the CPropSheet class declaration:

```
#include "page1.h"
#include "page2.h"
```

These lines give the CPropSheet class access to the CPage1 and CPage2 classes, so that the property sheet can declare member variables of these property page classes.

4. Add the following lines to the CPropSheet class's // Attributes section, right after the public keyword:

```
CPage1 m_page1;
CPage2 m_page2;
```

These lines declare the class's data members, which are the property pages that will be displayed in the property sheet.

5. Expand the CPropSheet class the ClassView pane, and double-click the first constructor. Add these lines to it:

```
AddPage(&m_page1);
AddPage(&m_page2);
```

This will add the two property pages to the property sheet whenever the sheet is constructed. The second constructor is right below the first; add the same lines there.

6. Double-click CPropsheetView in ClassView to edit the header file, and add the following lines to the //Attributes section, right after the line CPropsheetDoc* GetDocument();

```
protected:
CString m_edit;
BOOL m_check;
```

These lines declare two data members of the view class to hold the selections made in the property sheet by the user.

7. Add the following lines to the CPropsheetView constructor:

```
m_edit = "Default";
m_check = FALSE;
```

These lines initialize the class's data members so that, when the property sheet appears, these default values can be copied into the property sheet's controls. After the user changes the contents of the property sheet, these data members will always hold the last values from the property sheet, so those values can be restored to the sheet when needed.

8. Edit CPropsheetView::OnDraw() so that it resembles Listing 12.1. The new code displays the current selections from the property sheet. At the start of the program, the default values are displayed.

Part IV

Ch 12

Listing 12.1 *CPropsheetView::OnDraw()*

```
void CPropsheetView::OnDraw(CDC* pDC)
{
    CPropsheetDoc* pDoc = GetDocument();
    ASSERT_VALID(pDoc);

    pDC->TextOut(20, 20, m_edit);
    if (m_check)
        pDC->TextOut(20, 50, "TRUE");
    else
        pDC->TextOut(20, 50, "FALSE");
}
```

9. Bring up ClassWizard, click the Message Maps tab, and make sure that CPropsheetView is selected in the Class Name box. Select IDD_PROPSHEET in the Object IDs box. This is the ID of the new item you added to the File menu. Click Add Function to add a function that will handle the command message generated when a user chooses this menu item. Name the function OnPropsheet(), as shown in Figure 12.15.

The OnPropsheet() function is now associated with the Property Sheet command that you previously added to the File menu. That is, when the user selects the Property Sheet command, MFC calls OnPropsheet(), where you can respond to the command.

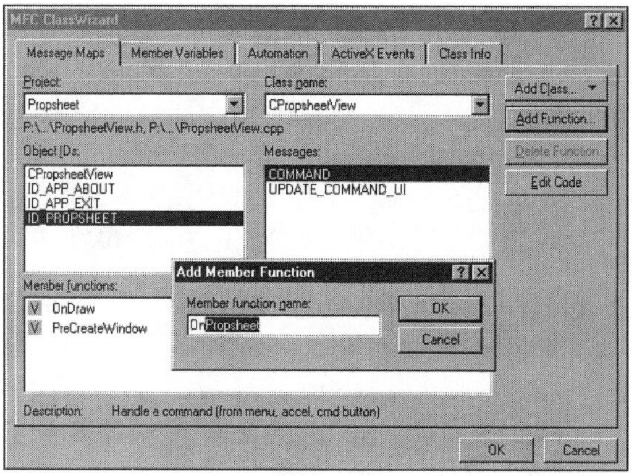

FIG. 12.15

Use ClassWizard to add the OnPropsheet() member function.

10. Click the Edit Code button to jump to the OnPropsheet() function, and then add the lines shown in Listing 12.2.

Listing 12.2 *CPropsheetView::OnPropsheet()*

```
void CPropsheetView::OnPropsheet()
{
    CPropSheet propSheet("Property Sheet", this, 0);
    propSheet.m_page1.m_edit = m_edit;
    propSheet.m_page2.m_checkbox = m_check;
```

```
int result = propSheet.DoModal();
if (result == IDOK)
{
    m_edit = propSheet.m_page1.m_edit;
    m_check = propSheet.m_page2.m_checkbox;
    Invalidate();
}

}
```

The code segment in Listing 12.2, which is discussed in more detail a little later in this chapter, creates an instance of the CPropSheet class, and sets the member variables of each of its pages. It displays the sheet using the familiar DoModal function first discussed in Chapter 2, "Dialog Boxes and Controls." If the user clicks OK, it updates the view member variables to reflect the changes made on each page, and forces a redraw with a call to Invalidate.

Running the Property Sheet Demo Application

You've now finished the complete application. Click the Build button on the Build mini-bar (or choose Build, Build) to compile and link the application. Run it by choosing Build, Execute or clicking the Execute button on the Build mini-bar. When you do, you see the window shown in Figure 12.16. As you can see, the window displays two values, which are the default values for the controls in the application's property sheet. You can change these values using the property sheet. Choose File, Property Sheet—the property sheet appears on the screen (Figure 12.17). The property sheet contains two pages, each of which holds a single control. When you change the settings of these controls and click the property sheet's OK button, the application's window displays the new values. Try it!

Part
IV
Ch
12

FIG. 12.16

When it first starts, the Property Sheet Demo application displays default values for the property sheet's controls.

FIG. 12.17

The application's property sheet contains two pages.

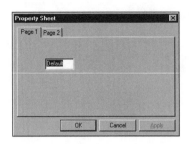

Adding Property Sheets to Your Applications

In order to add a property sheet to one of your own applications, you will follow steps very similar to those you followed in the previous section to create the demo application. Those steps are:

1. Create a dialog box resource for each page in the property sheet. These resources should have the Child and Thin styles and should have no system menu.

2. Associate each property page resource with an object of the CPropertyPage class. You can do this easily with ClassWizard. Connect controls on the property page to members of the class you create.

3. Create a class for the property sheet, deriving the class from MFC's CPropertySheet class. You can generate this class using ClassWizard.

4. In the property sheet class, add member variables for each page you'll be adding to the property sheet. These member variables must be instances of the property page classes that you created in step 2.

5. In the property sheet's constructor, call AddPage() for each page in the property sheet.

6. To display the property sheet, call the property sheet's constructor, and then call the property sheet's DoModal() member function, just as you would with a dialog box.

After you have written your application and have defined the resources and classes that represent the property sheet (or sheets; you can have more than one), you need a way to enable the user to display the property sheet when it's needed. In Property Sheet Demo, this is done by associating a menu item with a message-response function. However you handle the command to display the property sheet, though, the process of creating the property sheet is the same. First, you must call the property sheet class's constructor, which Property Sheet Demo does like this:

```
CPropSheet propSheet("Property Sheet", this, 0);
```

Here, the program is creating an instance of the CPropSheet class. This instance (or object) is called propSheet. The three arguments are the property sheet's title string, a pointer to the parent window (which, in this case, is the view window), and the zero-based index of the first page to display. Because the property pages are created in the property sheet's constructor, creating the property sheet also creates the property pages.

After you have the property sheet object created, you can initialize the data members that hold the values of the property page's controls, which Property Sheet Demo does like this:

```
propSheet.m_page1.m_edit = m_edit;
propSheet.m_page2.m_checkbox = m_check;
```

Now it's time to display the property sheet on the screen, which you do just as if it were a dialog box, by calling the property sheet's `DoModal()` member function:

```
int result = propSheet.DoModal();
```

`DoModal()` doesn't take any arguments, but it does return a value indicating which button the user clicked to exit the property sheet. In the case of a property sheet or dialog box, you'll usually want to process the information entered into the controls only if the user clicked the OK button, which is indicated by a return value of `IDOK`. If the user exits the property sheet by clicking the Cancel button, the changes are ignored and the view or document member variables are not updated.

Changing Property Sheets to Wizards

Here's a piece of information that surprises most people: A wizard is just a special property sheet. Instead of tabs on each sheet that allow the user to fill in the information in any order, or to skip certain pages entirely, a wizard has Back, Next, and Finish buttons to move the user through a process in a certain order. This forced sequence makes wizards terrific for guiding your application's users through the steps needed to complete a complex task. You've already seen how AppWizard in Visual C++ makes it easy to start a new project. You can create your own wizards that are suited to whatever application you want to build. In the following sections, you'll see how easy it is to convert a property sheet to a wizard.

Running the Wizard Demo Application

On the CD

In the CHAP13\WIZ folder of this book's CD-ROM, you'll find the Wizard Demo application. This application was built in much the same way as the Property Sheet Demo application that you created earlier in this chapter. This chapter will not present step-by-step instructions to build Wizard Demo. You should be able to build it yourself if you wish, using the general steps presented earlier and the code snippets shown here.

When you run the Wizard Demo application, the main window appears, looking very much like the Property Sheet Demo main window. The File menu now includes a Wizard item—choosing File, Wizard brings up the wizard shown in Figure 12.18.

The wizard isn't too fancy, but it does demonstrate what you need to know in order to program more complex wizards. As you can see, this wizard has three pages. On the first page is an edit control and three buttons called Back, Next, and Cancel. The Back button is disabled, because there is no previous page to go back to. The Cancel button enables the user to dismiss the wizard at any time, canceling whatever process the wizard was guiding the user through. The Next button causes the next page in the wizard to be displayed.

Part
IV

Ch
12

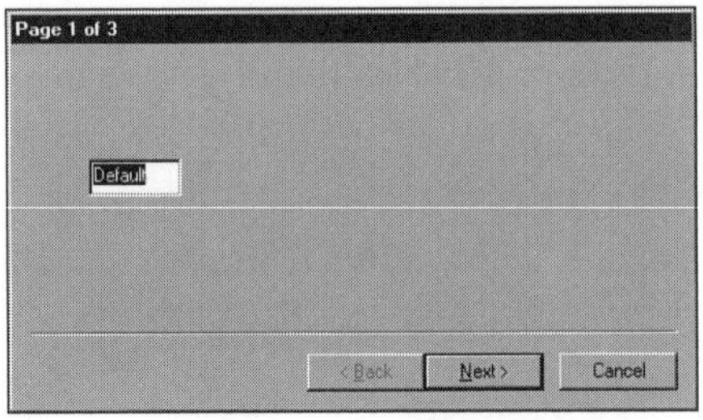

FIG. 12.18

The Wizard Demo application displays a wizard rather than a property sheet.

You can change whatever is displayed in the edit control if you like. However, the magic really starts when you click the Next button, which displays Page 2 of the wizard, as shown in Figure 12.19. Page 2 contains a check box and the Back, Next, and Cancel buttons. Now, the Back button is enabled, so that you can return to Page 1 if you want to. Go ahead and click the Back button. The wizard tells you that the check box must be checked, as shown in Figure 12.20. As you'll soon see, this feature of a wizard enables you to verify the contents of a specific page before allowing the user to advance to another step.

FIG. 12.19

In Page 2 of the wizard, the Back button is enabled.

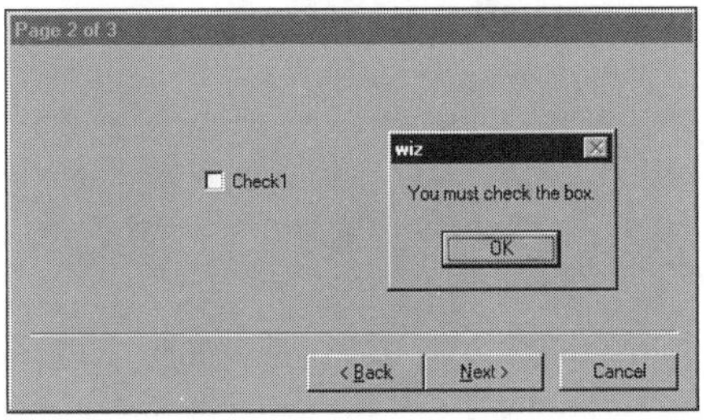

FIG. 12.20

You must select the check box before the wizard will let you leave Page 2.

After checking the check box, you can click the Back button to move back to Page 1 or click the Next button to advance to Page 3. Assuming you advance to Page 3, you see the display shown in Figure 12.21. Here, the Next button has changed to the Finish button, because you are on the wizard's last page. If you click the Finish button, the wizard disappears.

FIG. 12.21

This is the last page of the Wizard Demo Application's wizard.

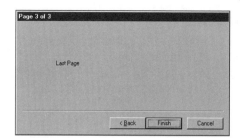

Creating Wizard Pages

As far as your application's resources go, you create wizard pages exactly as you create property sheet pages: by creating dialog boxes and changing the dialog box styles. (The dialog titles—Page 1 of 3, Page 2 of 3, and Page 3 of 3—are hardcoded onto each dialog box. You associate each dialog box resource with an object of the CPropertyPage class. Then, in order to take control of the pages in your wizard and keep track of what the user is doing with the wizard, you override the OnSetActive(), OnWizardBack(), OnWizardNext(), and OnWizardFinish() functions of your property page classes. Read on to see how to do this.

Displaying a Wizard

The File, Wizard command is caught by CWizView's OnFileWizard() function. It is very similar to the OnPropSheet function in the Property Sheet demo, as you can see from Listing 12.3. The first difference is the call to SetWizardMode() before the call to DoModal(). This function call tells MFC that it should display the property sheet as a wizard rather than as a conventional property sheet. The only other difference is that the user arranges for property sheet changes to be accepted by clicking Finish, not OK, so this code checks for ID_WIZFINISH rather than IDOK as a return from DoModal().

Part

IV

Ch

12

Listing 12.3 *CWizView::OnFileWizard()*

```
void CWizView::OnFileWizard()
{
    CWizSheet wizSheet("Sample Wizard", this, 0);
    wizSheet.m_page1.m_edit = m_edit;
    wizSheet.m_page2.m_check = m_check;
    wizSheet.SetWizardMode();
    int result = wizSheet.DoModal();
    if (result == ID_WIZFINISH)
    {
        m_edit = wizSheet.m_page1.m_edit;
        m_check = wizSheet.m_page2.m_check;
        Invalidate();
    }
}
```

Setting the Wizard's Buttons

MFC automatically calls the OnSetActive() member function immediately upon displaying a specific page of the wizard. So, when the program displays Page 1 of the wizard, the CPage1 class's OnSetActive() function gets called. You add code to this function that makes the wizard behave as you wish. CPage1::OnSetActive() looks like Listing 12.5.

Listing 12.5   *CPage1::OnSetActive()*

```
BOOL CPage1::OnSetActive()
{
    CPropertySheet* parent = (CPropertySheet*)GetParent();
    parent->SetWizardButtons(PSWIZB_NEXT);
    return CPropertyPage::OnSetActive();
}
```

OnSetActive() first gets a pointer to the wizard's property sheet window, which is the page's parent window. Then the program calls the wizard's SetWizardButtons() function, which determines the state of the wizard's buttons. SetWizardButtons() takes a single argument, which is a set of flags indicating how the page should display its buttons. These flags are PSWIZB_BACK, PSWIZB_NEXT, PSWIZB_FINISH, and PSWIZB_DISABLEDFINISH. Because the call to SetWizardButtons() in Listing 12.4 includes only the PSWIZB_NEXT flag, only the Next button in the page will be enabled.

Because the CPage2 class represents Page 2 of the wizard, its call to SetWizardButtons() enables both the Back and Next buttons, by combining the appropriate flags with the bitwise *or* operator (¦), like this:

```
parent->SetWizardButtons(PSWIZB_BACK ¦ PSWIZB_NEXT);
```

Because Page 3 of the wizard is the last page, the CPage3 class calls SetWizardButtons() like this:

```
parent->SetWizardButtons(PSWIZB_BACK ¦ PSWIZB_FINISH);
```

This set of flags enables the Back button and provides a Finish button instead of a Next button.

Responding to the Wizard's Buttons

In the simplest case, MFC takes care of everything that needs to be done in order to flip from one wizard page to the next. That is, when the user clicks a button, MFC springs into action and performs the Back, Next, Finish, or Cancel command. However, you'll often want to perform some action of your own when the user clicks a button. For example, you may want to verify that the information that the user entered into the currently displayed page is correct. If there's a problem with the data, you can force the user to fix it before moving on.

To respond to the wizard's buttons, you override the OnWizardBack(), OnWizardNext(), and OnWizardFinish() member functions. Use the Message Maps tab of ClassWizard to do this; you will find the names of these functions in the Messages window when a property page class is selected in the Class name box. When the user clicks a wizard button, MFC calls the matching function in which you can do whatever is needed to process that page. An example is the way the wizard in the Wizard Demo application won't let you leave Page 2 until you've checked the check box. This is accomplished by overriding the functions shown in Listing 12.6.

Listing 12.6   Responding to Wizard Buttons

```
LRESULT CPage2::OnWizardBack()
{
    CButton *checkBox = (CButton*)GetDlgItem(IDC_CHECK1);
    if (!checkBox->GetCheck())
    {
        MessageBox("You must check the box.");
        return -1;
    }
    return CPropertyPage::OnWizardBack();
}

LRESULT CPage2::OnWizardNext()
{
    UpdateData();
    if (!m_check)
    {
        MessageBox("You must check the box.");
        return -1;
    }
    return CPropertyPage::OnWizardNext();
}
```

These functions demonstrate two ways to examine the check box on Page 2. OnWizardBack() gets a pointer to the page's check box by calling the GetDlgItem() function. With the pointer in hand, the program can call the check box class's GetCheck() function, which returns a 1 if the check box is checked. OnWizardNext() calls UpdateData() to fill all the CPage2 member variables with values from the dialog box controls, then looks at m_check. In both functions, if the box is not checked, the program displays a message box and returns –1 from the function. Returning –1 tells MFC to ignore the button click and not change pages. As you can see, it is simple to arrange for different conditions to leave the page in the Back or Next directions.

Part IV
Ch 12

From Here...

Whether you're creating property sheets or wizards, Visual C++'s many classes enable you to get the job done easily. Property sheets are great for organizing many options and controls, whereas wizards (which are a special type of property sheet) are best used for guiding the user step-by-step through a complex task. To learn more about related topics, check out the following chapters:

- Chapter 1, "Building Your First Application," tells you what you need to know to create your own projects using Visual C++'s development tools.
- Chapter 2, "Dialog Boxes and Controls," gives you background in programming dialog boxes and the controls they can contain.

■ Chapter 4, "Messages and Commands," describes MFC's message-mapping system, which enables you to respond to Windows messages.

■ Chapter 6, "Drawing on the Screen," describes how to display information in a window.

ActiveX Applications and ActiveX Controls

CHAPTER 13

ActiveX Concepts

This chapter covers the theory and concepts of ActiveX, which is built on the Component Object Model (COM). Until recently, the technology built on COM was called OLE, and OLE still exists, but the emphasis now is on ActiveX. Most new programmers have found OLE intimidating, and the switch to ActiveX is unlikely to lessen that. However, if you think of ActiveX technology as a way to use code already written and tested by someone else, and to save yourself the trouble of reinventing the wheel, you'll see why it's worth learning. Developer Studio and MFC make ActiveX much easier to understand and implement by doing much of the groundwork for you. There are five chapters in Part V, "ActiveX Applications and ActiveX Controls," and together they demonstrate what ActiveX has become. ∎

What ActiveX is for

ActiveX represents the future of Windows and the future of software development according to Microsoft.

Object linking

ActiveX is a document-focused technology. Linking connects one document to another and enables a user to build a document from parts that were created with a variety of applications.

Object embedding

Embedding one document within another creates a compound document. Each portion of the document is accessed with its own application.

Containers, servers, and why you would write one

ActiveX containers can contain embedded objects. ActiveX servers handle the editing of an object that is linked or embedded within another document.

Drag-and-drop

One of the features many users find so intuitive about Windows today is the ability to click an object, and then, holding the mouse button down, drag the object to another folder or application. Adding this feature to your application will dramatically increase its usability.

The Purpose of ActiveX

Windows has always been a way to have several applications running at once, and right from the beginning programmers wanted to have a way for those applications to exchange information while running. The Clipboard was a marvelous innovation, though the user had to do a lot of the work. DDE (Dynamic Data Exchange) allowed applications to "talk" to each other but had some major limitations. Then came OLE 1 (Object Linking and Embedding). Later there was OLE 2, then Microsoft just called it OLE, until it moved so far beyond its original roots that it was renamed ActiveX.

N O T E   Experienced Windows users will probably be familiar with the examples presented in the early part of this chapter. If you know what ActiveX can do for users, and are interested in why it works, jump ahead to the "Component Object Model" section, which looks under the hood a little. ■

ActiveX lets users and applications be document-centered, and this is probably the most important thing about it. If a user wants to create an annual report by choosing ActiveX-enabled applications, the user stays focused on that annual report. Perhaps parts of it are being done with Word and parts with Excel, but to the user, these applications are not really the point. This shift in focus is happening on many fronts, and corresponds to a more object-oriented way of thinking among many programmers. It seems more natural now to share work among several different applications and arrange for them to communicate, than to write one huge application that can do everything.

Here's a simple test to see whether you are document-centered or application-centered: How is your hard drive organized?

The directory structure in Figure 13.1 is application-centered: the directories are named for the applications that were used to create the documents they hold. All Word documents are together, even though they may be for very different clients or projects.

The directory structure in Figure 13.2 is document-centered: the directories are named for the client or project involved. All the sales files are together, even though they can be accessed with a variety of different applications.

If you've been using desktop computers long enough, you remember when using a program involved a program disk and a data disk. Perhaps you remember installing software that demanded to know the data directory where you would keep all the files created with that product. That was application-centered thinking, and it's fast being supplanted by document-centered thinking.

FIG. 13.1

An application-centered directory structure arranges documents by type.

```
Microsoft Office
    Word
        Building Internet Apps
        Using Visual C++
        Acme Corp
            Training
            Web Pages
    Excel
        Journal
        Sales estimates
        Invoices
    ABC Inc
        Payroll System
        Inventory System
Microsoft Developer Studio
    ABC Inc Payroll System
    ABC Inc Inventory System
```

FIG. 13.2

A document-centered directory structure arranges documents by meaning or content.

```
Clients
    Acme Corp
        Training
        Web Pages
        Invoices
    ABC Inc
        Payroll System
        Inventory System
        Invoices
Books
    Building Internet Apps
    Using Visual C++
        ...
Overhead
    Accounting
    Sales
```

Why? What's wrong with application-centered thinking? Well, where do you put the documents that are used with two applications equally often? There was a time when each product could read its own file formats and no others. But these days, the lines between applications are blurring; a document created in one word processor can easily be read into another, a spreadsheet file can be used as a database, and so on. If a client sends you a WordPerfect document, and you don't have WordPerfect, do you make a \WORDPERFECT\DOCS directory to put it in, or add it to your \MSOFFICE\WORD\DOCS directory, or what? If you have your hard drive arranged in a more document-centered manner, you can just put it in the directory for that client.

The Windows 95 interface, now incorporated into Windows NT as well, encourages document-centered thinking by having users double-click documents to automatically launch the applications that created them. This isn't new; File Manager has had that capability for years, but it feels very different to double-click an icon that's just sitting on the desktop than it does to start an application and then double-click an entry in a list box. More and more it doesn't matter just what application or applications were involved in creating this document; you just want to see and change your data, and you want to do that quickly and simply.

After you begin being document-centered, you begin to see the appeal of compound documents—files created with more than one application. If your report needs an illustration, you create it in some graphic program and then insert it into your text when it's done. If your annual report needs a table, and you already have the numbers in a spreadsheet, you don't retype them into the table feature of your word processor, or even import them. You incorporate them as a spreadsheet excerpt, right in the middle of your text. This isn't earth-shatteringly new, of course. Early desktop publishing programs, such as Ventura, pulled together text and graphics from a variety of sources into one complex compound document. What's new is being able to do it simply, intuitively, and with so many different applications.

Object Linking

Figure 13.3 shows a Word document with an Excel spreadsheet linked to it.

Follow these steps to create a similar document yourself:

1. Start Word and enter your text.
2. Click where you want the table to go.
3. Choose Insert, Object.
4. Select the Create From File tab.
5. Enter or select the file name as though this was a File Open dialog box.
6. Be sure to check the Link to File box.
7. Click OK.

FIG. 13.3
A Microsoft Word
document can contain
a link to an Excel file.

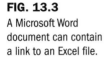

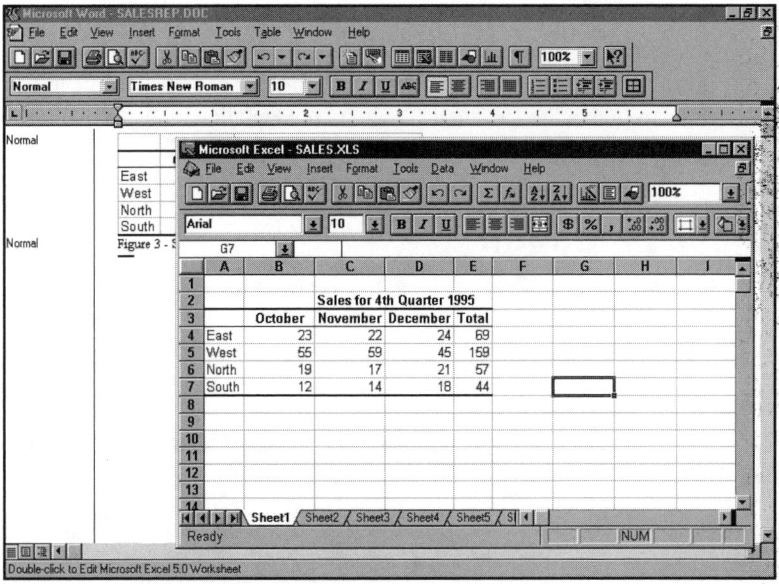

The entire file appears in your document. If you make a change in the file on disk, the change
is reflected in your document. You can edit the file in its own application by double-clicking it
within Word. The other application is launched to edit it, as shown in Figure 13.4. If you delete
the file from disk, your Word document still displays what the file last looked like, but you are
not able to edit it.

FIG. 13.4
Double-clicking a
linked object launches
the application that
created it.

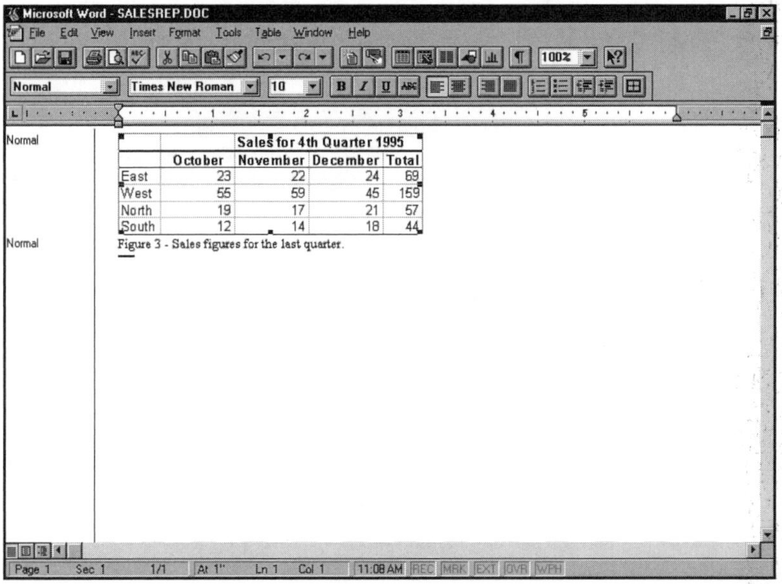

You link files into your documents if you plan to use the same file in many documents and contexts, because your changes to that file are automatically reflected everywhere that you have linked it. Linking doesn't increase the size of your document files dramatically, since only the location of the file and a little bit of presentation information needs to be kept in your document.

Object Embedding

Embedding is similar to linking, but a copy of the object is made and placed into your document. If you change the original, the changes are not reflected in your document. You can't tell by looking whether the Excel chart you see in your Word document is linked or embedded. Figure 13.5 shows a spreadsheet embedded within a Word document.

FIG. 13.5

A file embedded within another file looks just like a linked file.

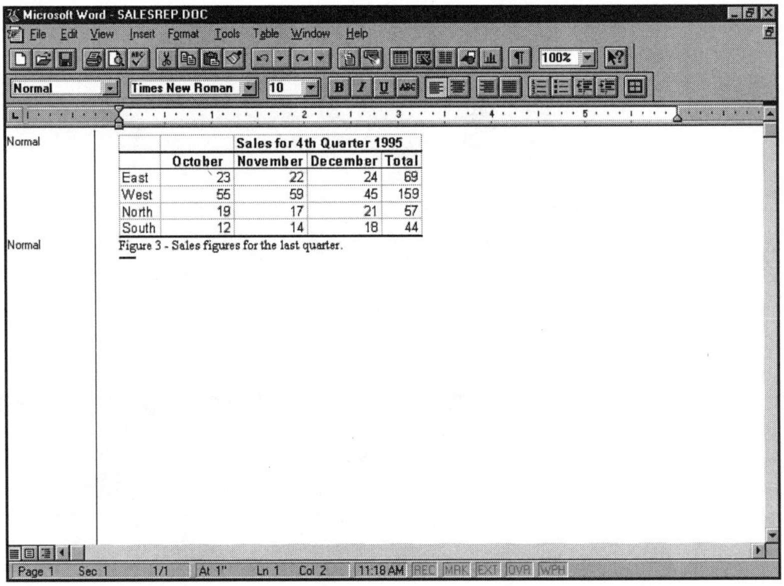

Follow these steps to create a similar document yourself:

1. Start Word and enter your text.
2. Click where you want the table to go.
3. Choose Insert, Object.
4. Select the Create From File tab.
5. Enter or select the file name as though this was a File Open dialog box.
6. Do not check the Link to File box.
7. Click OK.

What's the difference? You'll see when you double-click the object to edit it. The menus and toolbars of Word disappear and are replaced with their Excel equivalents, as shown in Figure 13.6. Changes you make here are not made in the file you originally embedded. They are made in the copy of that file that has become part of your Word document.

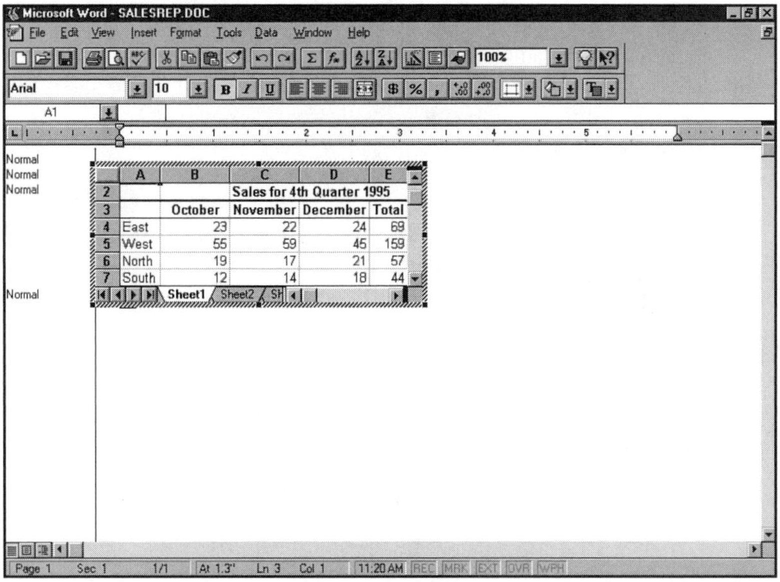

FIG. 13.6

Editing in place is the magic of OLE embedding.

You embed files into your documents if you plan to build a compound document and then use it as a self-contained whole, without using the individual parts again. Any changes you make do not affect any other files on your disk, not even the one you copied from in the first place. Embedding makes your document much larger than it was, but you can delete the original if space is a problem.

Containers and Servers

To embed or link one object into another, you need a *container* and a *server*. The container is the application into which the object is linked or embedded—Word in these examples. The server is the application that made them, and that can be launched (perhaps in place) when the object is double-clicked—Excel in these examples.

Why would you develop a container application? To save yourself work. Imagine you have a product already developed and in the hands of your users. It does a specific task like gets a sales team organized, or schedules games in a league sport, or calculates life insurance rates. Then your users tell you that they wish it had a spreadsheet capability, so they could do small calculations on-the-fly. How long will it take you to add that functionality? Do you really have time to learn how spreadsheet programs parse the functions that users type?

Part

V

Ch

13

If your application is a container app, it doesn't take any time at all. Tell users to link or embed in an Excel sheet, and let Excel do the work. If they don't own a copy of Excel, they need some spreadsheet application that can be an ActiveX server. You get to piggyback on the effort of other developers.

It's not just spreadsheets, either. What if users want a scratch pad, a place to scribble a few notes? Let them embed a Word document. And for bitmaps and other illustrations? Microsoft Paint, or a more powerful graphics package if they have one and it can act as an ActiveX server. You don't have to concern yourself with adding functionality like this to your programs because you can just make your application a container and your users can embed whatever they want without any more work on your part.

Why would you develop a server application, then? Look back over the reasons for writing a container application. A lot of users are going to contact developers asking for a feature to be added, and be told they can have that feature immediately—they just need an application that does spreadsheets, text, pictures, or whatever, and can act as an ActiveX server. If your application is an ActiveX server, people will buy it so that they can add its functionality to their container apps.

Together, container and server apps allow users to build the documents they want. They represent a move toward building-block software and a document-centered approach to work. And if you want your application to carry the Windows 95 logo, it must be a server, a container, or both. But there is much more to ActiveX than just linking and embedding.

Toward a More Intuitive User Interface

What if the object you want to embed is not in a file, but is part of a document you have open at the moment? You may have already discovered that you can use the Clipboard to transfer ActiveX objects. For example, to embed part of a Word document into an Excel spreadsheet, you can follow these steps:

1. Open Excel.
2. Open Word.
3. In Excel, select the portion you want to copy.
4. Choose Edit, Copy to copy the block onto the Clipboard.
5. Switch to Word and choose Edit, Paste Special.
6. Select the Paste radio button.
7. Select Microsoft Excel Worksheet from the list box.
8. Make sure that Display as Icon is not selected.
9. The dialog box should look like Figure 13.7. Click OK.

FIG. 13.7

The Paste Special dialog box is used to link or embed selected portions of a document.

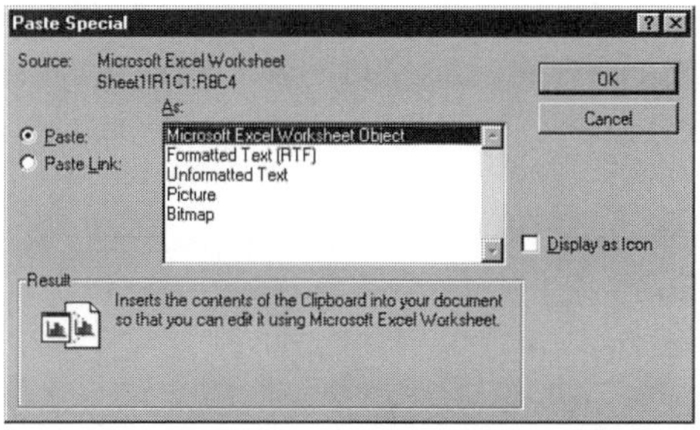

Paste Special	? X
Source: Microsoft Excel Worksheet Sheet1!R1C1:R8C4	OK
As:	Cancel
⦿ Paste: Microsoft Excel Worksheet Object	
○ Paste Link: Formatted Text (RTF) Unformatted Text Picture Bitmap	☐ Display as Icon
Result	
Inserts the contents of the Clipboard into your document so that you can edit it using Microsoft Excel Worksheet.	

A copy of the block is now embedded into the spreadsheet. If you choose Paste Link, changes in the spreadsheet are reflected immediately in the Word document, not just when you save them. (You may have to click the selection in Word to get it updated.) This is true even if the spreadsheet document has no name and has never been saved. Try it yourself! This is certainly better than saving dummy files just to embed them into compound documents, then deleting them, isn't it?

Another way to embed part of a document into another is drag and drop. This is a user-interface paradigm that works in a variety of contexts. You click on something (an icon, a highlighted block of text, a selection in a list box) and hold the mouse button down while moving it. The thing you clicked moves with the mouse, and when you let go of the mouse button, it is dropped to the new location. That's very intuitive for things like moving or resizing windows, but now you can use it to do much, much more. For example, here's how that Excel-in-Word example would be done with drag and drop:

1. Open Word and size it to less than full screen.
2. Open Excel and size it to less than full screen. If you can arrange the Word and Excel windows so they don't overlap, that's great.
3. In Excel, select the portion you want to copy by highlighting it with the mouse or cursor keys.
4. Click the border of the selected area (the thick black line) and hold.
5. Drag the block into the Word window and let go.

The selected block is embedded into the Word document. If you double-click it, you are editing in place with Excel. Dragging and dropping also works within a document to move or copy a selection.

TIP The block is moved by default, which means it is deleted from the Excel sheet. If you want a copy, hold down the Ctrl key while dragging, and release the mouse button before the Ctrl key.

You can also use drag and drop with icons. On your desktop, if you drag a file to a folder, it is moved there. (Hold down Ctrl while dragging to copy it.) If you drag it to a program icon, it is opened with that program. This is very useful when you have a document you use with two applications. For example, pages on the World Wide Web are HTML documents, often created

Part
V

Ch
13

with an HTML editor, but viewed with a World Wide Web browser like Netscape Navigator. If you double-click an HTML document icon, your browser is launched to view it. If you drag that icon onto the icon for your HTML editor, the editor is launched and opens the file you dragged. After you realize you can do this, you will find your work speeds up dramatically.

All of this is ActiveX, and all of this requires a little bit of work from programmers to make it happen. So what's going on?

The Component Object Model

The heart of modern ActiveX is the Component Object Model. This is an incredibly complex topic that deserves a book of its own. Luckily, the Microsoft Foundation Classes and the Visual C++ AppWizard do much of the behind-the-scenes work for you, and so the discussion in these chapters is just what you need to know to use OLE as a developer.

The Component Object Model (COM) is a binary standard for Windows objects. That means that the executable code (in a .DLL or .EXE) that describes an object can be executed by other objects. Even if two objects were written in different languages, they are able to interact using the COM standard.

N O T E   Because the code in a DLL executes in the same process as the calling code, it's the fastest way for applications to communicate. When two separate applications communicate through COM, function calls from one application to another must be *marshaled*: COM gathers up all the parameters and invokes the function itself. A stand-alone server (.EXE) is therefore slower than an in-process server (.DLL). ▪

How do they interact? Through an *interface*. An ActiveX interface is a collection of functions, or really just function names. It's a C++ class with no data, only pure virtual functions. Your objects inherit from this class and provide code for the functions. (Remember, as discussed in Reference A, "C++ Review and (O O Concepts)," a class that inherits a pure virtual function does not inherit code for that function.) Other programs get to your code by calling these functions. All ActiveX objects must have an interface called IUnknown (and usually have many more, all with names that start with I, the prefix for interfaces).

The IUnknown interface has only one purpose: finding other interfaces. It has a function called QueryInterface() that takes an interface ID and returns a pointer to that interface for this object. All the other interfaces inherit from IUnknown, so they have a QueryInterface() too, and you have to write the code, or you would if there was no MFC. MFC implements a number of macros that simplify the job of writing interfaces and their functions, as you will shortly see. The full declaration of IUnknown is in Listing 14.1. The macros take care of some of the work of declaring an interface and won't be discussed here. There are three functions declared: QueryInterface(), AddRef(), and Release(). These latter two functions are used to keep track of which applications are using an interface. All three of these functions are inherited by all interfaces and must be implemented by the developer of the interface.

Listing 13.1 IUnknown, Defined in \DevStudio\vc\include\unknwn.h

```
interface IUnknown
    {
    public:
        BEGIN_INTERFACE
        virtual HRESULT STDMETHODCALLTYPE QueryInterface(
            /* [in] */ REFIID riid,
            /* [iid_is][out] */ void __RPC_FAR *__RPC_FAR *ppvObject) = 0;

        virtual ULONG STDMETHODCALLTYPE AddRef( void) = 0;

        virtual ULONG STDMETHODCALLTYPE Release( void) = 0;

        END_INTERFACE
    };
```

ActiveX Automation

An ActiveX Automation application lets other applications tell it what to do. It *exposes* functions and data, called *methods* and *properties*. For example, Microsoft Excel is an ActiveX Automation object, and programs written in Visual C++ or Visual Basic can call Excel functions and set properties like column widths. That means you don't need to write a scripting language for your application any more. If you expose all the functions and properties of your application, any programming language that can use an ActiveX Automation application can be a scripting language for your application. Your users, your customers, may already know your scripting language. They essentially will have no learning curve for writing macros to automate your application (though they will need to learn the names of the methods and properties you expose).

The important thing to know about interacting with ActiveX Automation is that one program is always in control, calling the methods or changing the properties of the other running application. The application in control is called an ActiveX Automation controller. The application that exposes methods and functions is called an ActiveX Automation server. Excel, Word, and other members of the Microsoft Office suite are ActiveX Automation servers, and your programs can use the functions of these applications to really save you coding time.

For example, imagine being able to use the function called by the Word menu item Format, Change Case to convert the blocks of text your application uses to all uppercase, all lowercase, sentence case (the first letter of the first word in each sentence is uppercase, the rest are not), or title case (the first letter of every word is uppercase, the rest are not).

The description of how ActiveX Automation really works is far longer and more complex than the interface summary of the previous section. It involves a special interface called IDispatch, a simplified interface that works from a number of different languages, including those like Visual Basic that can't use pointers. The declaration of IDispatch is in Listing 13.2.

Part
V

Ch
13

Listing 13.2   *IDispatch*, Defined in \DevStudio\vc\include\oaidl.h

```
interface IDispatch : public IUnknown
    {
    public:
        virtual HRESULT STDMETHODCALLTYPE GetTypeInfoCount(
            /* [out] */ UINT __RPC_FAR *pctinfo) = 0;

        virtual HRESULT STDMETHODCALLTYPE GetTypeInfo(
            /* [in] */ UINT iTInfo,
            /* [in] */ LCID lcid,
            /* [out] */ ITypeInfo __RPC_FAR *__RPC_FAR *ppTInfo) = 0;

        virtual HRESULT STDMETHODCALLTYPE GetIDsOfNames(
            /* [in] */ REFIID riid,
            /* [size_is][in] */ LPOLESTR __RPC_FAR *rgszNames,
            /* [in] */ UINT cNames,
            /* [in] */ LCID lcid,
            /* [size_is][out] */ DISPID __RPC_FAR *rgDispId) = 0;

        virtual /* [local] */ HRESULT STDMETHODCALLTYPE Invoke(
            /* [in] */ DISPID dispIdMember,
            /* [in] */ REFIID riid,
            /* [in] */ LCID lcid,
            /* [in] */ WORD wFlags,
            /* [out][in] */ DISPPARAMS __RPC_FAR *pDispParams,
            /* [out] */ VARIANT __RPC_FAR *pVarResult,
            /* [out] */ EXCEPINFO __RPC_FAR *pExcepInfo,
            /* [out] */ UINT __RPC_FAR *puArgErr) = 0;

    };
```

Although IDispatch seems more complex than IUnknown, it declares only a few more functions: GetTypeInfoCount(), GetTypeInfo(), GetIDsOfNames(), and Invoke(). Since it inherits from Iunknown, it has also inherited QueryInterface(), AddRef(), and Release(). They are all pure virtual functions, so any COM class that inherits from IDispatch must implement these functions. The most important of these is Invoke(), used to call functions of the Automation server and to access its properties.

ActiveX Controls

ActiveX controls are tiny little ActiveX Automation servers that load *in process*. That means they are remarkably fast. They were originally called OLE Custom Controls and were designed to replace VBX controls, 16-bit controls written for use in Visual Basic and Visual C++. (There are a number of good technical reasons why the VBX technology could not be extended to the 32-bit world.) Since OLE Custom Controls were traditionally kept in files with the extension .OCX, many people referred to an OLE Custom Control as an OCX control or just an OCX. Although the OLE has been supplanted by ActiveX, ActiveX controls produced by Visual C++ 4.2 are still kept in files with the .OCX extension.

The original purpose of VBX controls was to allow programmers to provide unusual interface controls to their users. Controls that looked like gas gauges or volume knobs became easy to develop. But almost immediately, VBX programmers moved beyond simple controls to modules that involved significant amounts of calculation and processing. In the same way, many ActiveX controls are far more than just controls; they are *components* that can be used to build powerful applications quickly and easily.

N O T E If you have built an OCX in earlier versions of Visual C++, you might think it is a difficult thing to do. The Control Developer Kit, now integrated into Visual C++, takes care of the ActiveX aspects of the job and allows you to concentrate on the calculations, display, or whatever else it is that makes your control worth using. The ActiveX Control Wizard makes getting started with an empty ActiveX control simple. ■

Because controls are little ActiveX Automation servers, they need to be used by an ActiveX Automation controller, but the terminology is too confusing if there are controls and controllers, so we say that ActiveX controls are used by *container* applications. Visual C++ and Visual Basic are both container applications, as are many members of the Office suite and many non-Microsoft products.

In addition to properties and methods, ActiveX Controls have *events*. To be specific, a control is said to *fire* an event, and it does so when there is something that the container needs to be aware of. For example, when the user clicks a portion of the control, the control deals with it, perhaps changing its appearance or making a calculation, but it may also need to pass on word of that click to the container application so that a file can be opened or some other container action can be performed.

From Here...

This chapter has given you a brief tour through the concepts and terminology used in ActiveX technology, and a glimpse of the power you can add to your applications by incorporating ActiveX into them. The remainder of the chapters in this part work you through the creation of ActiveX applications using MFC and the wizards in Visual C++. Check out the following:

- Chapter 14, "Building an ActiveX Container Application," demonstrates a simple ActiveX container, a program that can contain embedded or linked objects.

- Chapter 15, "Building an ActiveX Server Application," demonstrates a simple ActiveX server. This application can create objects that can be embedded or linked into ActiveX container applications.

- Chapter 16, "Building an Automation Server," builds an ActiveX Automation object that can use Visual Basic as its scripting language.

- Chapter 17, "Building an ActiveX Control," builds an ActiveX control that can be embedded into a Visual C++ or Visual Basic program.

Part
V

Ch
13

■ Chapter 20, "Building an Internet ActiveX Control," modifies the control built in Chapter 17 to work over the Internet.

■ Chapter 21, "The Active Template Library," demonstrates another way to build ActiveX controls.

CHAPTER 14

Building an ActiveX Container Application

You can get a rudimentary ActiveX container by asking AppWizard to make you one, but it will have a lot of short-comings. A far harder task is to understand how an ActiveX container works and what you have to do to really use it. In this chapter, by turning the ShowString application of earlier chapters into an ActiveX container and then making it a truly functional container, you get a backstage view of ActiveX in action. Adding drag-and-drop support brings your application into the modern age of intuitive, document-centered user interface design. If you have not yet read Chapter 13, "ActiveX Concepts," it would be a good idea to read it before this one. ∎

Transforming ShowString into a container

An ActiveX container can contain documents that were created in another application. This section shows you how to build one, and how they work.

Moving, resizing, and tracking the contained object

The container code generated for you does not handle some of the user interface tasks well. This section shows you how to handle those tasks yourself.

Handling multiple objects and object selection

Improving your container so that it can contain more than one object and letting the user click an object to select it is another enhancement to your user interface.

Implementing drag and drop

Users love drag and drop. This section shows you how to implement drag and drop in your ActiveX container.

Deleting a contained object

A final improvement to your user interface is enabling the user to delete an object that has been embedded or linked into the container.

Changing ShowString

ShowString was built originally in Chapter 9, "Building a Complete Application: ShowString," and has no ActiveX support. You could make the changes by hand to implement ActiveX container support, but there would be more than 30 changes. It's quicker to build a new ShowString application—this time asking for ActiveX container support—and then make changes to that code to get the ShowString functionality again.

AppWizard-Generated ActiveX Container Code

Build the new ShowString in a different directory, making almost exactly the same AppWizard choices when you built ShowString in the "Creating an Empty Shell with AppWizard" section of Chapter 9. Name the project ShowString, choose an MDI application, no database support, compound document support: container, a docking toolbar, status bar, printing and print preview, context-sensitive Help, and 3-D controls. Finally, select source file comments and a shared DLL.

> **N O T E** Even though the technology is now called ActiveX, the AppWizard dialogs refer to compound document support. Also, many of the class names that are used throughout this chapter have Ole in their names, and comments refer to OLE. While Microsoft has changed the name of the technology, it has not propagated that change throughout Visual C++ yet. You have to live with these contradictions until the next release of Visual C++. ■

There are a lot of differences between the application you have just built and a do-nothing application without ActiveX container support. The remainder of this section describes and explains these differences and their effects.

Menus There's another menu, called IDR_SHOWSTTYPE_CNTR_IP, shown in Figure 14.1. The name refers to a container whose *contained* object is being edited *in place*. During in-place editing, the menu bar is built from the container's in-place menu and the server's in-place menu. The pair of vertical bars in the middle of IDR_SHOWSTTYPE_CNTR_IP are separators; the server menu items will be put between them. This is discussed in more detail in Chapter 15, "Building an ActiveX Server Application."

The Edit menu, shown in Figure 14.2, has four new items:

- **Paste Special.** The user chooses this item to insert an item into the container from the Clipboard.
- **Insert New Object.** Choosing this item brings up the Insert Object dialog box, shown in Figures 14.3 and 14.4, so the user can insert an item into the container.

FIG. 14.1

AppWizard adds
another menu for
editing in place.

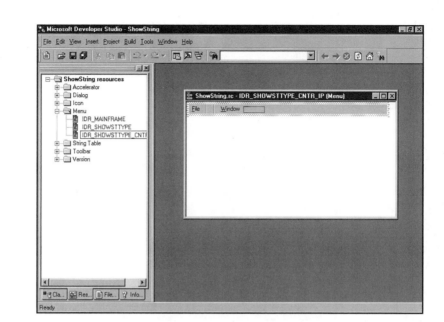

FIG. 14.1

AppWizard adds
another menu for
editing in place.

FIG. 14.2

AppWizard adds items
to the Edit menu of the
IDR_SHOWSTTYPE
resource.

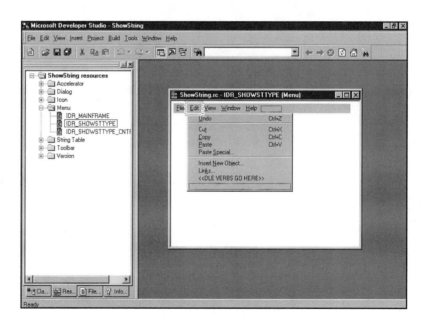

FIG. 14.3

The Insert Object dialog box can be used to embed new objects.

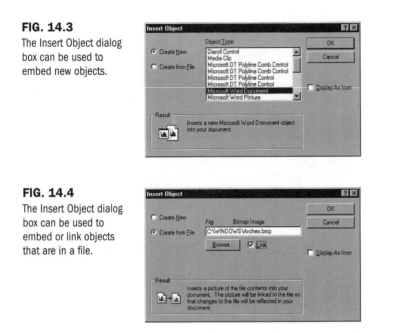

FIG. 14.4

The Insert Object dialog box can be used to embed or link objects that are in a file.

■ **Links.** When an object has been linked into the container, choosing this item brings up the Links dialog box, shown in Figure 14.5, to allow control of the way that the copy of the object is updated after a change is saved to the file.

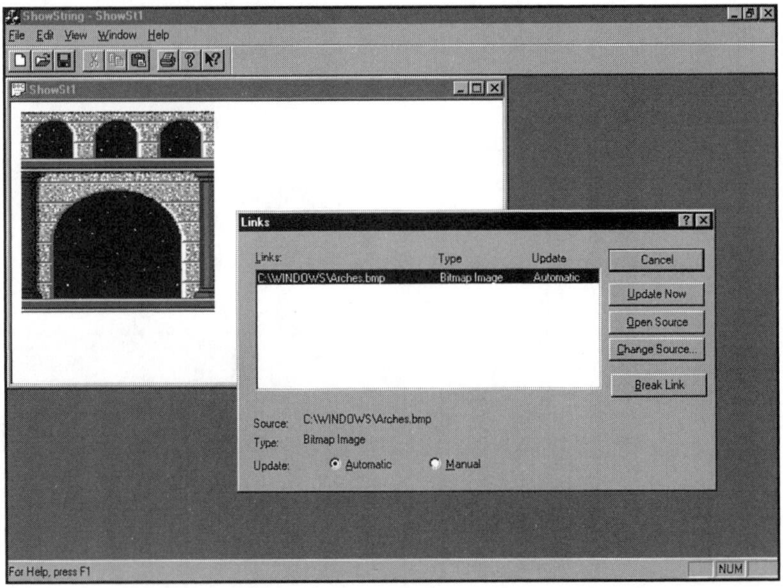

FIG. 14.5

The Links dialog box controls the way linked objects are updated.

- **<<OLE VERBS GO HERE>>.** Each kind of item has different verbs associated with it, like Edit, Open, or Play. When a contained item has focus, this spot on the menu is replaced by an object type like those in the Insert Object dialog box, with a menu cascading from it that lists the verbs for this type, such as the one shown in Figure 14.6.

FIG. 14.6

Each object type adds a cascading menu item to the Edit menu when it has focus.

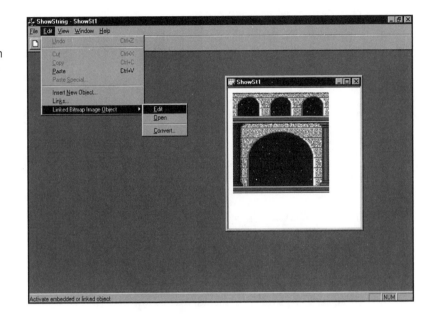

CShowStringApp   CShowStringApp::InitInstance() has several changes from the InitInstance() method provided by AppWizard for applications that are not ActiveX containers. The lines in Listing 14.1 initialize the ActiveX (OLE) libraries.

Listing 14.1   Excerpt from ShowString.cpp—Library Initialization

```
// Initialize OLE libraries
if (!AfxOleInit())
{
    AfxMessageBox(IDP_OLE_INIT_FAILED);
    return FALSE;
}
```

Still in CShowStringApp::InitInstance(), after the MultiDocTemplate is initialized, but before the call to AddDocTemplate(), this line is added to register the menu used for in-place editing:

```
pDocTemplate->SetContainerInfo(IDR_SHOWSTTYPE_CNTR_IP);
```

CShowStringDoc   The document class, CShowStringDoc, now inherits from COleDocument rather than CDocument. This line is also added at the top of ShowStringDoc.cpp:

```
#include "CntrItem.h"
```

CntrItem.h describes the container item class, CShowStringCntrItem, discussed later. Still in ShowStringDoc.cpp, the macros in Listing 14.2 have been added to the message map.

Listing 14.2   Excerpt from ShowString.cpp—Message Map Additions

```
ON_UPDATE_COMMAND_UI(ID_EDIT_PASTE,
➡COleDocument::OnUpdatePasteMenu)
ON_UPDATE_COMMAND_UI(ID_EDIT_PASTE_LINK,
➡COleDocument::OnUpdatePasteLinkMenu)
ON_UPDATE_COMMAND_UI(ID_OLE_EDIT_CONVERT,
➡COleDocument::OnUpdateObjectVerbMenu)
ON_COMMAND(ID_OLE_EDIT_CONVERT,
➡COleDocument::OnEditConvert)
ON_UPDATE_COMMAND_UI(ID_OLE_EDIT_LINKS,
➡COleDocument::OnUpdateEditLinksMenu)
ON_COMMAND(ID_OLE_EDIT_LINKS,
➡COleDocument::OnEditLinks)
ON_UPDATE_COMMAND_UI(ID_OLE_VERB_FIRST,
➡COleDocument::OnUpdateObjectVerbMenu)
```

These commands enable and disable the following menu items:

- Edit, Paste
- Edit, Paste Link
- Edit, Links
- The OLE verbs section, including the Convert verb

The new macros also handle Convert and Edit, Links. Notice that the messages are handled by functions of COleDocument and don't have to be written by you.

The constructor, CShowStringDoc::CShowStringDoc(), has a line added:

```
EnableCompoundFile();
```

This turns on the use of compound files. CShowStringDoc::Serialize() has a line added as well:

```
COleDocument::Serialize(ar);
```

This call to the base class Serialize() takes care of serializing all the contained objects, with no further work for you.

CShowStringView   The view class, CShowStringView, includes CntrItem.h just as the document does. The view class has these new entries in the message map:

```
ON_WM_SETFOCUS()
ON_WM_SIZE()
ON_COMMAND(ID_OLE_INSERT_NEW, OnInsertObject)
ON_COMMAND(ID_CANCEL_EDIT_CNTR, OnCancelEditCntr)
```

These are in addition to the messages caught by the view before it was a container. These catch WM_SETFOCUS, WM_SIZE, the menu item Edit, Insert New Object, and the cancellation of editing in place. An accelerator has already been added to connect this message to Esc.

In `ShowStringView.h`, a new member variable has been added, as shown in Listing 14.3.

Listing 14.3   Excerpt from ShowStringView.h—*m_pSelection*

```
// m_pSelection holds the selection to the current
// CShowStringCntrItem. For many applications, such
// a member variable isn't adequate to represent a
// selection, such as a multiple selection or a selection
// of objects that are not CShowStringCntrItem objects.
// This selection mechanism is provided just to help you
// get started.

// TODO: replace this selection mechanism with one appropriate to your app.
CShowStringCntrItem* m_pSelection;
```

This new member variable shows up again in the view constructor, Listing 14.4, and the revised `OnDraw()`, in Listing 14.5.

Listing 14.4   ShowStringView.cpp—Constructor

```
CShowStringView::CShowStringView()
{
    m_pSelection = NULL;
    // TODO: add construction code here
}
```

Listing 14.5   ShowStringView.cpp—*CShowStringView::OnDraw()*

```
void CShowStringView::OnDraw(CDC* pDC)
{
    CShowStringDoc* pDoc = GetDocument();
    ASSERT_VALID(pDoc);

    // TODO: add draw code for native data here
    // TODO: also draw all OLE items in the document

    // Draw the selection at an arbitrary position.  This code should be
    //   removed once your real drawing code is implemented.  This position
    //   corresponds exactly to the rectangle returned by CShowStringCntrItem,
    //   to give the effect of in-place editing.

    // TODO: remove this code when final draw code is complete.

    if (m_pSelection == NULL)
    {
        POSITION pos = pDoc->GetStartPosition();
        m_pSelection = (CShowStringCntrItem*)pDoc->GetNextClientItem(pos);
    }
    if (m_pSelection != NULL)
        m_pSelection->Draw(pDC, CRect(10, 10, 210, 210));
}
```

The code supplied for OnDraw() draws only a single contained item. It doesn't draw any native data—in other words, elements of ShowString that are not contained items. At the moment there is no native data, but after the string is added to the application, OnDraw() is going to have to draw it. What's more, this code only draws one contained item, and it does so in an arbitrary rectangle. OnDraw() is going to see a lot of changes as you work through this chapter.

The view class has gained a lot of new functions. They are as follows:

- OnInitialUpdate()
- IsSelected()
- OnInsertObject()
- OnSetFocus()
- OnSize()
- OnCancelEditCntr()

Each of these new functions is discussed in the subsections that follow.

OnInitialUpdate()   OnInitialUpdate() is called just before the very first time the view is to be displayed. The boilerplate code (Listing 14.6) is pretty dull.

Listing 14.6   ShowStringView.cpp—*CShowStringView::OnInitialUpdate()*

```
void CShowStringView::OnInitialUpdate()
{
    CView::OnInitialUpdate();

    // TODO: remove this code when final selection
    // model code is written
    m_pSelection = NULL;    // initialize selection

}
```

The base class OnInitialUpdate() calls the base class OnUpdate(), which calls Invalidate(), requiring a full repaint of the client area.

IsSelected()   IsSelected() currently isn't working, because the selection mechanism is so rudimentary. Listing 14.7 shows the code that was generated for you. Later, when you have implemented a proper selection method, you will improve how this code works.

Listing 14.7   ShowStringView.cpp—*CShowStringView::IsSelected()*

```
BOOL CShowStringView::IsSelected(const CObject* pDocItem) const
{
    // The implementation below is adequate if your selection consists of
    //  only CShowStringCntrItem objects.  To handle different selection
    //  mechanisms, the implementation here should be replaced.

    // TODO: implement this function that tests for a selected OLE client item
```

```
        return pDocItem == m_pSelection;
}
```

This function is passed a pointer to a container item. If that pointer is the same as the current selection, it returns TRUE.

OnInsertObject() OnInsertObject() is called when the user chooses Edit, Insert New Object. It's quite a long function, so it is presented in parts. The overall structure is presented in Listing 14.8.

Listing 14.8 ShowStringView.cpp—*CShowStringView::OnInsertObject()*

```
void CShowStringView::OnInsertObject()
{
    //display the Insert Object dialog box

    CShowStringCntrItem* pItem = NULL;
    TRY
    {
        // Create new item connected to this document.
        // Initialize the item
        // set selection and update all views
    }
    CATCH(CException, e)
    {
        // handle failed create
    }
    END_CATCH

    // tidy up
}
```

Each comment here is replaced with a small block of code, discussed in the remainder of this section. The TRY and CATCH statements, by the way, are an old-fashioned form of exception handling, discussed in Chapter 26, "Exceptions, Templates, and the Latest Additions to C++."

First, this function displays the Insert Object dialog box, as shown in Listing 14.9.

Listing 14.9 ShowStringView.cpp—Display the Insert Object Dialog Box

```
// Invoke the standard Insert Object dialog box to obtain information
//   for new CShowStringCntrItem object.
COleInsertDialog dlg;
if (dlg.DoModal() != IDOK)
    return;
BeginWaitCursor();
```

Part
V

Ch

14

If the user clicks Cancel, this function returns and nothing is inserted. If the user clicks OK, the cursor is set to an hourglass while the rest of the processing occurs.

To create a new item, the code in Listing 14.10 is inserted.

Listing 14.10   ShowStringView.cpp—Create a New Item

```
// Create new item connected to this document.
CShowStringDoc* pDoc = GetDocument();
ASSERT_VALID(pDoc);
pItem = new CShowStringCntrItem(pDoc);
ASSERT_VALID(pItem);
```

This code makes sure there is a document, even though the menu item is only enabled if there is one, and then creates a new container item, passing it the pointer to the document. As you see in the CShowStringCntrItem section, container items hold a pointer to the document that contains them.

The code in Listing 14.11 initializes that item.

Listing 14.11   ShowStringView.cpp—Initializing the Inserted Item

```
// Initialize the item from the dialog data.
if (!dlg.CreateItem(pItem))
    AfxThrowMemoryException();  // any exception will do
ASSERT_VALID(pItem);
// If item created from class list (not from file) then launch
//  the server to edit the item.
if (dlg.GetSelectionType() == COleInsertDialog::createNewItem)
    pItem->DoVerb(OLEIVERB_SHOW, this);

ASSERT_VALID(pItem);
```

The code in Listing 14.11 calls the CreateItem() function of the dialog class, ColeInsertDialog. That may seem a strange place to keep such a function, but the function needs to know all the answers that were given on the dialog box. So, if it were a member of another class, it would have to interrogate the dialog box for the type and file name, find out whether it was a link or embedded, and so on. It calls member functions of the container item like CreateLinkFromFile(), CreateFromFile(), CreateNewItem(), and so on. So it's not that the code to actually fill the object from the file is in the dialog box, but rather that the work is partitioned between the objects instead of passing information back and forth between them.

Then, one question is asked of the dialog box: Was this a new item? If so, the server is called to edit it. Objects created from a file can just be displayed.

Finally, the selection is updated and so are the views, as shown in Listing 14.12.

Listing 14.12   ShowStringView.cpp—Update Selection and Views

```
// As an arbitrary user interface design, this sets the selection
//  to the last item inserted.
```

```
    // TODO: reimplement selection as appropriate for your application

    m_pSelection = pItem;    // set selection to last inserted item
    pDoc->UpdateAllViews(NULL);
```

If the creation of the object failed, execution ends up in the CATCH block, shown in Listing 14.13.

Listing 14.13 ShowStringView.cpp—*CATCH* Block

```
CATCH(CException, e)
{
    if (pItem != NULL)
    {
        ASSERT_VALID(pItem);
        pItem->Delete();
    }
    AfxMessageBox(IDP_FAILED_TO_CREATE);
}
END_CATCH
```

This deletes the item that was created and gives the user a message box.

Finally, that hourglass cursor can go away:

```
EndWaitCursor();
```

OnSetFocus() OnSetFocus(), shown in Listing 14.14, is called whenever this view gets focus.

Listing 14.14 ShowStringView.cpp—*CShowStringView::OnSetFocus()*

```
void CShowStringView::OnSetFocus(CWnd* pOldWnd)
{
    COleClientItem* pActiveItem = GetDocument()->GetInPlaceActiveItem(this);
    if (pActiveItem != NULL &&
        pActiveItem->GetItemState() == COleClientItem::activeUIState)
    {
        // need to set focus to this item if it is in the same view
        CWnd* pWnd = pActiveItem->GetInPlaceWindow();
        if (pWnd != NULL)
        {
            pWnd->SetFocus();    // don't call the base class
            return;
        }
    }

    CView::OnSetFocus(pOldWnd);
}
```

Part
V

Ch
14

If there is an active item and its server is loaded, then that active item gets focus. If not, focus remains with the old window, and to the user, it appears that the click was ignored.

OnSize() OnSize(), shown in Listing 14.15, is called when the application is resized by the user.

Listing 14.15 ShowStringView.cpp—*CShowStringView::OnSize()*

```
void CShowStringView::OnSize(UINT nType, int cx, int cy)
{
    CView::OnSize(nType, cx, cy);
    COleClientItem* pActiveItem = GetDocument()->GetInPlaceActiveItem(this);
    if (pActiveItem != NULL)
        pActiveItem->SetItemRects();
}
```

This resizes the view by using the base class function, and then, if there is an active item, tells it to adjust to the resized view.

OnCancelEditCntr() OnCancelEditCntr() is called when a user who has been editing in place presses Esc. The server must be closed, and the object stops being active. The code is shown in Listing 14.16.

Listing 14.16 ShowStringView.cpp—*CShowStringView::OnCancelEditCntr()*

```
void CShowStringView::OnCancelEditCntr()
{
    // Close any in-place active item on this view.
    COleClientItem* pActiveItem =
        GetDocument()->GetInPlaceActiveItem(this);
    if (pActiveItem != NULL)
    {
        pActiveItem->Close();
    }
    ASSERT(GetDocument()->GetInPlaceActiveItem(this) == NULL);
}
```

CShowStringCntrItem The container item class is a completely new addition to ShowString. It describes an item that is contained in the document. As you've already seen, the document and the view use this object quite a lot, primarily through the m_pSelection member variable of CShowStringView. It has no member variables other than those inherited from the base class, COleClientItem. It has overrides for a lot of functions, though. They are as follows:

- A constructor
- A destructor
- GetDocument()
- GetActiveView()
- OnChange()
- OnActivate()

- OnGetItemPosition()
- OnDeactivateUI()
- OnChangeItemPosition()
- AssertValid()
- Dump()
- Serialize()

The constructor simply passes the document pointer along to the base class. The destructor does nothing. `GetDocument()` and `GetActiveView()` are inline functions that return member variables inherited from the base class by calling the base class function with the same name and casting the result.

`OnChange()` is the first of these functions that has more than one line of code (see Listing 14.17).

Listing 14.17 Cntrltem.cpp—CShowStringCntrltem::OnChange()

```
void CShowStringCntrItem::OnChange(OLE_NOTIFICATION nCode,
    DWORD dwParam)
{
    ASSERT_VALID(this);

    COleClientItem::OnChange(nCode, dwParam);

    // When an item is being edited (either in-place or fully open)
    //  it sends OnChange notifications for changes in the state of the
    //  item or visual appearance of its content.

    // TODO: invalidate the item by calling UpdateAllViews
    //  (with hints appropriate to your application)

    GetDocument()->UpdateAllViews(NULL);
        // for now just update ALL views/no hints
}
```

Actually, there are three lines of code. The comments are actually more useful than the code. When the user changes the contained item, the server notifies the container. Calling `UpdateAllViews()` is a rather drastic way of refreshing the screen, but it gets the job done.

`OnActivate()` (shown in Listing 14.18) is called when a user double-clicks an item to activate it and edit it in place. ActiveX objects are usually *outside-in*, which means that a single click of the item selects it but does not activate it. Activating an outside-in object requires a double-click, or a single click followed by choosing the appropriate OLE verb from the Edit menu.

Listing 14.18 Cntrltem.cpp—CShowStringCntrltem::OnActivate()

```
void CShowStringCntrItem::OnActivate()
{
    // Allow only one inplace activate item per frame
    CShowStringView* pView = GetActiveView();
    ASSERT_VALID(pView);
    COleClientItem* pItem = GetDocument()->GetInPlaceActiveItem(pView);
    if (pItem != NULL && pItem != this)
        pItem->Close();

    COleClientItem::OnActivate();
}
```

Part
V

Ch
14

This code makes sure that the current view is valid, closes the active item, if any, and then activates this item.

OnGetItemPosition() (shown in Listing 14.19) is called as part of the in-place activation process.

Listing 14.19 CntrItem.cpp—*CShowStringCntrItem::OnGetItemPosition()*

```
void CShowStringCntrItem::OnGetItemPosition(CRect& rPosition)
{
    ASSERT_VALID(this);

    // During in-place activation,
    // CShowStringCntrItem::OnGetItemPosition
    // will be called to determine the location of this item.
    // The default implementation created from AppWizard simply
    // returns a hard-coded rectangle.  Usually, this rectangle
    // would reflect the current position of the item relative
    // to the view used for activation. You can obtain the view
    // by calling CShowStringCntrItem::GetActiveView.

    // TODO: return correct rectangle (in pixels) in rPosition

    rPosition.SetRect(10, 10, 210, 210);
}
```

Like OnChange(), the comments are more useful than the actual code. At the moment, the View's OnDraw() function draws the contained object in a hard-coded rectangle, so this function returns that same rectangle. You are instructed to write code that asks the active view where the object is.

OnDeactivateUI() (see Listing 14.20) is called when the object goes from being active to inactive.

Listing 14.20 CntrItem.cpp—*CShowStringCntrItem::OnDeactivateUI()*

```
void CShowStringCntrItem::OnDeactivateUI(BOOL bUndoable)
{
    COleClientItem::OnDeactivateUI(bUndoable);

    // Hide the object if it is not an outside-in object
    DWORD dwMisc = 0;
    m_lpObject->GetMiscStatus(GetDrawAspect(), &dwMisc);
    if (dwMisc & OLEMISC_INSIDEOUT)
        DoVerb(OLEIVERB_HIDE, NULL);
}
```

While the default behavior for contained objects is outside-in, as discussed earlier, you can write *inside-out objects*. These are activated simply by moving the mouse pointer over them; clicking the object has the same effect that clicking that region has while editing the object.

For example, if the contained item is a spreadsheet, clicking might select the cell that was clicked. This can be really nice for the user, who can completely ignore the borders between the container and the contained item, but it is harder to write.

`OnChangeItemPosition()` is called when the item is moved during in-place editing. It, too, contains mostly comments, as shown in Listing 14.21.

Listing 14.21   Cntrltem.cpp—*CShowStringCntrItem::OnChangeItemPosition()*

```
BOOL CShowStringCntrItem::OnChangeItemPosition(const CRect& rectPos)
{
    ASSERT_VALID(this);

    // During in-place activation
    // CShowStringCntrItem::OnChangeItemPosition
    // is called by the server to change the position
    // of the in-place window.  Usually, this is a result
    // of the data in the server document changing such that
    // the extent has changed or as a result of in-place resizing.
    //
    // The default here is to call the base class, which will call
    //   COleClientItem::SetItemRects to move the item
    //   to the new position.

    if (!COleClientItem::OnChangeItemPosition(rectPos))
        return FALSE;

    // TODO: update any cache you may have of the item's rectangle/extent

    return TRUE;
}
```

This code is supposed to handle moving the object, but it doesn't really. That's because `OnDraw()` always draws the contained item in the same place.

`AssertValid()` and `Dump()` are debug functions that simply call the base class functions. The last function in `CShowStringCntrItem` is `Serialize()`, which is called by `COleDocument::Serialize()`, which in turn is called by the document's `Serialize()`, as you've already seen. It is shown in Listing 14.22.

Listing 14.22   Cntrltem.cpp—*CShowStringCntrItem::Serialize()*

```
void CShowStringCntrItem::Serialize(CArchive& ar)
{
    ASSERT_VALID(this);

    // Call base class first to read in COleClientItem data.
    // Because this sets up the m_pDocument pointer returned from
//  CShowStringCntrItem::GetDocument, it is a good idea to call
    //  the base class Serialize first.
    COleClientItem::Serialize(ar);
```

Part

V

Ch

14

continues

Listing 14.22 Continued

```
    // now store/retrieve data specific to CShowStringCntrItem
    if (ar.IsStoring())
    {
        // TODO: add storing code here
    }
    else
    {
        // TODO: add loading code here
    }
}
```

All this code does at the moment is call the base class function. `COleDocument::Serialize()` stores or loads a number of counters and numbers to keep track of several different contained items, then calls helper functions such as `WriteItem()` or `ReadItem()` to actually deal with the item. These functions and the helper functions they call are a bit too "behind-the-scenes" for most people, but if you'd like to take a look at them, they are in the MFC source folder (C:\MSDEV\MFC\SRC on many installations) in the file `olecli1.cpp`. They do their job, which is to serialize the contained item for you.

Shortcomings of This Container   This container application isn't ShowString yet, of course, but it has more important things wrong with it. It isn't a very good container, and that's a direct result of all those TODO tasks that haven't been accomplished. Still, the fact that it is a functioning container is a good measure of the power of the MFC classes `COleDocument` and `COleClientItem`. So why not build the application now and run it? After it's running, choose Edit, Insert New Object and insert a bitmap image. Now that you've seen the code, it shouldn't be a surprise that Paint is immediately launched to edit the item in place, as you see in Figure 14.7.

FIG. 14.7

The boilerplate container can contain items and activate them for in-place editing, like this bitmap image being edited in Paint.

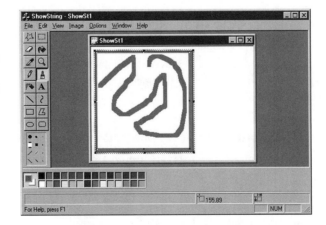

Click outside the bitmap to unselect the item and return control to the container; you see that nothing happens. Click outside the document, and again nothing happens. You're probably asking yourself, "Am I still in ShowString?" Choose File, New, and you see that you are. The Paint menus and toolbars go away, and a new ShowString document is created. Click the bitmap item again, and you are still editing it in Paint. How can you insert another object into the first document when the menus are those of Paint? Press Esc to cancel in-place editing so the menus become ShowString menus again. Insert an Excel chart into the container, and the bitmap disappears as the new Excel chart is inserted, as shown in Figure 14.8. Obviously, this container leaves a lot to be desired.

FIG. 14.8

Inserting an Excel chart gets you a default chart, but it completely covers the old bitmap.

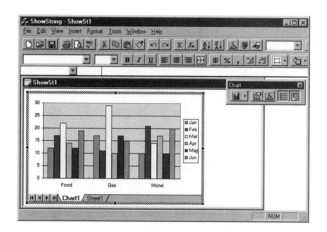

Press Esc to cancel the in-place editing, and notice that the view changes a little, as shown in Figure 14.9. That's because `CShowStringView::OnDraw()` draws the contained item in a 200×200 pixel rectangle, so the chart has to be squeezed a little to fit into that space. It is the server—Excel, in this case—that decides how to fit the item into the space given to it by the container.

FIG. 14.9

Items can look quite different when they are not active.

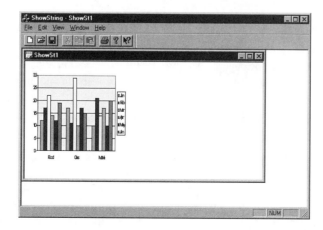

Part

V

Ch

14

As you can see, there's a lot to be done to make this feel like a real container. But first, you have to turn it back into ShowString.

Returning the ShowString Functionality

This section provides a quick summary of the steps presented in Chapter 9, "Building a Complete Application: ShowString." Open the files from the old ShowString as you go so that you can copy code and resources wherever possible. Follow these steps:

1. In ShowStringDoc.h, add the private member variables and public Get functions to the class.

2. In CShowStringDoc::Serialize(), paste the code that saves or restores these member variables. Leave the call to COleDocument::Serialize() in place.

3. In CShowStringDoc::OnNewDocument(), paste the code that initializes the member variables.

4. In CShowStringView::OnDraw(), add the code that draws the string before the code that handles the contained items. Remove the TODO task about drawing native data.

5. Copy the Tools menu from the old ShowString to the new container ShowString. Choose File, Open to open the old ShowString.rc, open the IDR_SHOWSTTYPE menu, click the Tools menu, and choose Edit, Copy. Open the new ShowString's IDR_SHOWSTTYPE menu, click the Window menu, and choose Edit, Paste. Do not paste it into the IDR_SHOWSTTYPE_CNTR_IP menu.

6. Add the accelerator Ctrl+T for ID_TOOLS_OPTIONS. Add it to the IDR_MAINFRAME accelerator only.

7. Delete the IDD_ABOUTBOX dialog box from the new ShowString. Copy IDD_ABOUTBOX and IDD_OPTIONS from the old ShowString to the new.

8. While IDD_OPTIONS has focus, choose View, Class Wizard. Create the COptionsDialog class as in the original ShowString.

9. Use the Class Wizard to connect the dialog controls to COptionsDialog member variables.

10. Use the Class Wizard to arrange for CShowStringDoc to catch the ID_TOOLS_OPTIONS command.

11. In ShowStringDoc.cpp, replace the Class Wizard version of CShowStringDoc::OnToolsOptions() with the OnToolsOptions() from the old ShowString, which puts up the dialog box.

12. In ShowStringDoc.cpp, add **#include "OptionsDialog.h"** after the #include statements already present.

Build the application, fix any typos or other simple errors, then execute it. It should run as before, saying Hello, world! in the center of the view. Convince yourself that the Options dialog box still works and that you have restored all the old functionality. Then resize the application and the view as large as possible, so that when you insert an object it does not land on the string. Insert an Excel chart as before, and press Esc to stop editing in place. There you have it: a version of ShowString that is also an ActiveX container. Now it's time to get to work making it a *good* container.

Moving, Resizing, and Tracking

The first task you want to do, even when there is only one item contained in ShowString, is to allow the user to move and resize that item. It makes life simpler for the user if you also provide a *tracker rectangle*, a hashed line around the contained item. This is easy to do with the MFC class CRectTracker.

The first step is to add a member variable to the container item (CShowStringCntrItem) definition in CntrItem.h, to hold the rectangle occupied by this container item. Right-click CShowStringCntrItem in ClassView and choose Add Member Variable. The variable type is CRect, the declaration is m_rect; leave the access public.

m_rect needs to be initialized in a function that is called when the container item is first used and then never again. While view classes have OnInitialUpdate() and document classes have OnNewDocument(), container item classes have no such called-only-once function except the constructor. So, initialize the rectangle in the constructor, as shown in Listing 14.23.

Listing 14.23 CntrItem.cpp—*Constructor*

```
CShowStringCntrItem::CShowStringCntrItem(CShowStringDoc* pContainer)
    : COleClientItem(pContainer)
{
    m_rect = CRect(10,10,210,210);
}
```

The numerical values used here are those in the boilerplate OnDraw() provided by AppWizard. Now, you need to start using the m rect member variable and setting it. The functions affected are presented in the same order as in the earlier section, CShowStringView.

First, CShowStringView::OnDraw(). Find this line:

m_pSelection->Draw(pDC, CRect(10, 10, 210, 210));

Replace it with this:

m_pSelection->Draw(pDC, m_pSelection->m_rect);

Next, change CShowStringCntrItem::OnGetItemPosition(), which needs to return this rectangle. Take away all the comments and the old hard-coded rectangle (leave the ASSERT_VALID macro call), and add this line:

rPosition = m_rect;

The partner function

CShowStringCntrItem::OnChangeItemPosition()

is called when the user moves the item. Here is where m_rect is changed from the initial value. Remove the comments and add code immediately after the the call to the base class function,

Part
V

Ch
14

`COleClientItem::OnChangeItemPosition()`. The code to add is:

```
m_rect = rectPos;
GetDocument()->SetModifiedFlag();
GetDocument()->UpdateAllViews(NULL);
```

Finally, the new member variable needs to be incorporated into
`CShowStringCntrItem::Serialize()`. Remove the comments and add lines in the storing and
saving blocks so that the function looks like Listing 14.24.

Listing 14.24 Cntrltem.cpp—*CShowStringCntrltem::Serialize()*

```
void CShowStringCntrItem::Serialize(CArchive& ar)
{
    ASSERT_VALID(this);

    // Call base class first to read in COleClientItem data.
    // Because this sets up the m_pDocument pointer returned from
 //   CShowStringCntrItem::GetDocument, it is a good idea to call
    //   the base class Serialize first.
    COleClientItem::Serialize(ar);

    // now store/retrieve data specific to CShowStringCntrItem
    if (ar.IsStoring())
    {
        ar << m_rect;
    }
    else
    {
        ar >> m_rect;
    }
}
```

Build and execute the application, insert a bitmap, and scribble something in it. Press Esc
to cancel editing in place, and your scribble shows up in the top-right corner, next to
`Hello, world!`. Choose Edit, Bitmap Image Object and then Edit. (Choosing Open allows you
to edit it in a different window.) Use the resizing handles that appear to drag the image over to
the left, then press Esc to cancel in-place editing. The image is drawn at the new position, as
expected.

Now for the tracker rectangle. The Microsoft tutorials recommend writing a helper function,
`SetupTracker()`, to handle this. Add these lines to `CShowStringView::OnDraw()`, just after the
call to `m_pSelection->Draw()`:

```
CRectTracker trackrect;
SetupTracker(m_pSelection,&trackrect);
trackrect.Draw(pDC);
```

CAUTION

The one-line statement after the `if` was not in brace brackets before; don't forget to add them. The entire if statement should look like this:

```
if (m_pSelection != NULL)
{
    m_pSelection->Draw(pDC, m_pSelection->m_rect);
    CRectTracker trackrect;
    SetupTracker(m_pSelection,&trackrect);
    trackrect.Draw(pDC);
}
```

Add the following public function to ShowStringView.h (inside the class definition):

```
void SetupTracker(CShowStringCntrItem* item,
        CRectTracker* track);
```

Add the code in Listing 14.25 to ShowStringView.cpp immediately after the destructor.

Listing 14.25 ShowStringView.cpp—*CShowStringView::SetupTracker()*

```
void CShowStringView::SetupTracker(CShowStringCntrItem* item,
    CRectTracker* track)
{
    track->m_rect = item->m_rect;

    if (item == m_pSelection)
    {
        track->m_nStyle |= CRectTracker::resizeInside;
    }

    if (item->GetType() == OT_LINK)
    {
        track->m_nStyle |= CRectTracker::dottedLine;
    }
    else
    {
        track->m_nStyle |= CRectTracker::solidLine;
    }
    if (item->GetItemState() == COleClientItem::openState ||
        item->GetItemState() == COleClientItem::activeUIState)
    {
        track->m_nStyle |= CRectTracker::hatchInside;
    }
}
```

Part

V

Ch

14

This code first sets the tracker rectangle to the container item rectangle. Then it adds styles to the tracker. The styles available are as follows:

- `solidLine`. Used for an embedded item.
- `dottedLine`. Used for a linked item.
- `hatchedBorder`. Used for an in-place active item.
- `resizeInside`. Used for a selected item.
- `resizeOutside`. Used for a selected item.
- `hatchInside`. Used for an item whose server is open.

This code first compares the pointers to this item and the current selection. If they are the same, this item is selected and it gets resize handles. It's up to you whether these handles go on the inside or the outside. Then this code asks the item whether it is linked (dotted line) or not (solid line). Finally, it adds hatching to active items.

Build and execute the application, and try it out. You still cannot edit the contained item by double-clicking it: choose Edit from the cascading menu added at the bottom of the Edit menu. You can't move and resize an inactive object, but if you activate it, you can resize it while active. Also, when you press Esc, the inactive object is drawn at its new position.

Handling Multiple Objects and Object Selection

The next step is to catch mouse clicks and double clicks so that the item can be resized, moved, and activated more easily. This involves testing to see if a click is on a contained item or not.

Hit Testing

You need to write a helper function that returns a pointer to the contained item that the user clicked, or NULL if the user clicked an area of the view that has no contained item. This function runs through all the items contained in the document. Add the code in Listing 14.26 to ShowStringView.cpp immediately after the destructor.

Listing 14.26 ShowStringView.cpp—*CShowStringView::SetupTracker()*

```
CShowStringCntrItem* CShowStringView::HitTest(CPoint point)
{
    CShowStringDoc* pDoc = GetDocument();
    CShowStringCntrItem* pHitItem = NULL;

    POSITION pos = pDoc->GetStartPosition();
    while (pos)
    {
        CShowStringCntrItem* pCurrentItem =
            (CShowStringCntrItem*) pDoc->GetNextClientItem(pos);
        if ( pCurrentItem->m_rect.PtInRect(point) )
        {
```

```
                    pHitItem = pCurrentItem;
            }
        }

        return pHitItem;
}
```

T I P Don't forget to add the declaration of this `public` function to the header file.

This function is given a `CPoint` that describes the point on the screen where the user clicked. Each container item has a rectangle, `m_rect`, as you've seen earlier, and the `CRect` class has a member function called `PtInRect()` that takes a `CPoint` and returns `TRUE` if the point is in the rectangle or `FALSE` if it is not. This code simply loops through the items in this document, using the OLE document member function `GetNextClientItem()`, and calls `PtInRect()` for each.

What happens if there are several items in the container, and the user clicks at a point where two or more overlap? The one on top is selected. That's because `GetStartPosition()` returns a pointer to the bottom item, and `GetNextClientItem()` works its way up through the items. If two items cover the spot where the user clicked, `pHitItem` is set to the lower one first, and then on a later iteration of the `while` loop, it is set to the higher one. The pointer to the higher item is returned.

Drawing Multiple Items

While that code to loop through all the items is still fresh in your mind, why not fix `CShowStringView::OnDraw()` so it draws all the items? Leave all the code that draws the string, and replace the code in Listing 14.27 with that in Listing 14.28.

Listing 14.27 ShowStringView.cpp—Lines in *OnDraw()* to Replace

```
// Draw the selection at an arbitrary position.  This code should
// be removed once your real drawing code is implemented.  This
// position corresponds exactly to the rectangle returned by
// CShowStringCntrItem, to give the effect of in-place editing.

// TODO: remove this code when final draw code is complete.

if (m_pSelection == NULL)
{
    POSITION pos = pDoc->GetStartPosition();
    m_pSelection = (CShowStringCntrItem*)pDoc->GetNextClientItem(pos);
}
if (m_pSelection != NULL)
{
    m_pSelection->Draw(pDC, m_pSelection->m_rect);
    CRectTracker trackrect;
    SetupTracker(m_pSelection,&trackrect);
    trackrect.Draw(pDC);
}
```

Listing 14.28 ShowStringView.cpp—New Lines in *OnDraw()*

```
POSITION pos = pDoc->GetStartPosition();
while (pos)
{
    CShowStringCntrItem* pCurrentItem =
        (CShowStringCntrItem*) pDoc->GetNextClientItem(pos);
    pCurrentItem->Draw(pDC, pCurrentItem->m_rect);

    if (pCurrentItem == m_pSelection )
    {
        CRectTracker trackrect;
        SetupTracker(pCurrentItem,&trackrect);
        trackrect.Draw(pDC);
    }
}
```

Now each item is drawn, starting from the bottom and working up, and if it is selected, it gets a tracker rectangle.

Handling Single Clicks

When the user clicks the client area of the application, a WM_LBUTTONDOWN message is sent. This message should be caught by the view. Right-click CShowStringView in ClassView, and choose Add Windows Message Handler from the shortcut menu. Click WM_LBUTTONDOWN in the New Windows Messages/Events box on the left (see Figure 14.10), then click Add and Edit to add a handler function and edit the code immediately.

FIG. 14.10

Add a function to handle left mouse button clicks.

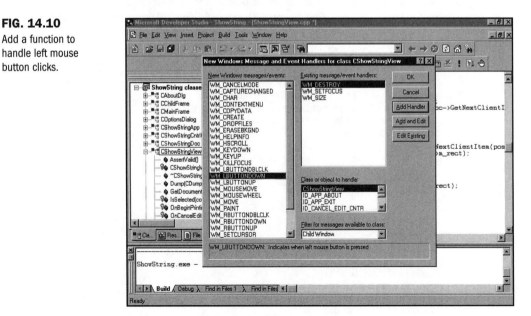

Add the code in Listing 14.29 to the empty OnLButtonDown() that Add Windows Message Handler generated.

Listing 14.29 ShowStringView.cpp—*CShowStringView::OnLButtonDown()*

```
void CShowStringView::OnLButtonDown(UINT nFlags, CPoint point)
{
    CShowStringCntrItem* pHitItem = HitTest(point);
    SetSelection(pHitItem);
    if (pHitItem == NULL)
        return;

    CRectTracker track;
    SetupTracker(pHitItem, &track);
    UpdateWindow();
        if (track.Track(this,point))
            {
                Invalidate();
                pHitItem->m_rect = track.m_rect;
                GetDocument()->SetModifiedFlag();
            }
        }
}
```

This code determines which item has been selected and sets it. (SetSelection() isn't written yet.) Then, if something has been selected, it draws a tracker rectangle around it and calls CRectTracker::Track(), which allows the user to resize the rectangle. After the resizing, the item is sized to match the tracker rectangle and is redrawn.

SetSelection() is pretty straightforward. Add the definition of this public member function to the header file, ShowStringView.h, and the code in Listing 14.30 to ShowStringView.cpp.

Listing 14.30 ShowStringView.cpp—*CShowStringView::SetSelection()*

```
void CShowStringView::SetSelection(CShowStringCntrItem* item)
{
    // if an item is being edited in place, close it
    if ( item == NULL || item != m_pSelection)
    {
        COleClientItem* pActive =
            GetDocument()->GetInPlaceActiveItem(this);
        if (pActive != NULL && pActive != item)
        {
            pActive->Close();
        }
    }
    Invalidate();
    m_pSelection = item;
}
```

Part

V

Ch

14

When the selection is changed, any item that is being edited in place should be closed. `SetSelection()` checks that the item passed in represents a change, then gets the active object from the document and closes that object. Then it calls for a redraw, and sets m_pSelection. Build and execute ShowString, insert an object, and press Esc to stop in-place editing. Click and drag to move the inactive object, and insert another—you should see something like Figure 14.11. Notice the resizing handles around the bitmap, indicating that it is selected.

FIG. 14.11

ShowString can now hold multiple items, and the user can move and resize them intuitively.

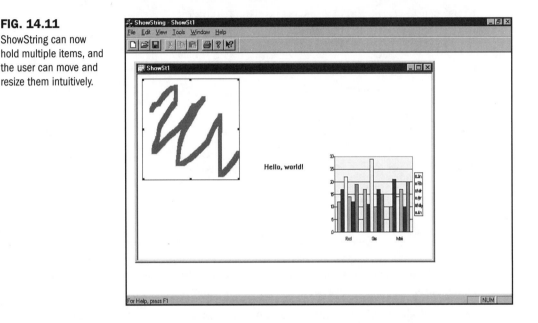

You may have noticed that the cursor doesn't change as you move or resize. That's because you didn't tell it to. Luckily, it's easy to tell it to: CRectTracker has a SetCursor() member function, and all you need to do is call it when a WM_SETCURSOR message is sent. Again, it should be the view that catches this message; right-click CShowStringView in ClassView, and choose Add Windows Message Handler from the shortcut menu. Click WM_SETCURSOR in the New Windows Messages/Events box on the left, then click Add and Edit to add a handler function and edit the code immediately. Add the code in Listing 14.31 to the empty function that was generated for you.

Listing 14.31   ShowStringView.cpp—*CShowStringView::OnSetCursor()*

```
BOOL CShowStringView::OnSetCursor(CWnd* pWnd, UINT nHitTest,
    UINT message)
{
    if (pWnd == this && m_pSelection != NULL)
    {
        CRectTracker track;
        SetupTracker(m_pSelection, &track);
```

```
        if (track.SetCursor(this, nHitTest))
        {
            return TRUE;
        }
    }

    return CView::OnSetCursor(pWnd, nHitTest, message);
}
```

This code does nothing unless the cursor change involves this view and there is a selection. It gives the tracking rectangle's SetCursor() function a chance to change the cursor, because the tracking object knows where the rectangle is and whether the cursor is over a boundary or sizing handle. If SetCursor() didn't change the cursor, this code lets the base class handle it. Build and execute ShowString, and you should see cursors that give you feedback as you move and resize.

Handling Double Clicks

When a user double-clicks a contained item, the *primary verb* should be called. For most objects, the primary verb is to Edit in place, but for some, such as sound files, it is Play. Arrange as before for CShowStringView to catch the WM_LBUTTONDBLCLK message, and add the code in Listing 14.32 to the new function.

Listing 14.32   ShowStringView.cpp—*CShowStringView::OnLButtonDblClk()*

```
void CShowStringView::OnLButtonDblClk(UINT nFlags, CPoint point)
{
    OnLButtonDown(nFlags, point);

    if( m_pSelection)
    {
        if (GetKeyState(VK_CONTROL) < 0)
        {
            m_pSelection->DoVerb(OLEIVERB_OPEN, this);
        }
        else
        {
            m_pSelection->DoVerb(OLEIVERB_PRIMARY, this);
        }
    }

    CView::OnLButtonDblClk(nFlags, point);
}
```

First, this function handles the fact that this item has been clicked; calling OnLButtonDown() draws the tracker rectangle, sets m_pSelection, and so on. Then, if the user holds down Ctrl while double-clicking, the item is opened; otherwise, the primary verb is called. Finally, the base class function is called. Build and execute ShowString and try double-clicking. Insert an object, press Esc to stop editing it, move it, resize it, and double-click it to edit in place.

Part
V

Ch
14

Implementing Drag and Drop

The last step to make ShowString a completely up-to-date ActiveX container application is to implement drag and drop. The user should be able to grab a contained item and drag it out of the container, or hold down Ctrl while dragging to drag out a copy and leave the original behind. The user should also be able to drag items from elsewhere and drop them into this container just as though they had been inserted through the Clipboard. In other words, the container should operate as a *drag source* and a *drop target*.

Implementing a Drag Source

Because CShowStringCntrItem inherits from COleClientItem, implementing a drag source is really easy. By clicking a contained object, Edit these lines at the end of CShowStringView::OnLButtonDown() so that it resembles Listing 14.33. The new lines are in bold type.

Listing 14.33 *CShowStringView::OnLButtonDown()* **Implementing a Drag Source**

```
void CShowStringView::OnLButtonDown(UINT nFlags, CPoint point)
{
        CShowStringCntrItem* pHitItem = HitTest(point);
        SetSelection(pHitItem);
        if (pHitItem == NULL)
                return;

        CRectTracker track;
        SetupTracker(pHitItem, &track);
        UpdateWindow();

        if (track.HitTest(point) == CRectTracker::hitMiddle)
        {
                CRect rect =  pHitItem->m_rect;
                CClientDC dc(this);
                OnPrepareDC(&dc);
                dc.LPtoDP(&rect); // convert logical rect to device rect
                rect.NormalizeRect();
                CPoint newpoint = point - rect.TopLeft();

                DROPEFFECT dropEffect = pHitItem->DoDragDrop(rect, newpoint);
                if (dropEffect == DROPEFFECT_MOVE)
                {
                        Invalidate();
                        if (pHitItem == m_pSelection)
                        {
                                m_pSelection = NULL;
                        }
                        pHitItem->Delete();
                }
        }
        else
        {
```

```
        if (track.Track(this,point))
        {
                Invalidate();
                pHitItem->m_rect = track.m_rect;
                GetDocument()->SetModifiedFlag();
        }
    }
}
```

This code first confirms that the mouse click was inside the tracking rectangle, rather than on the sizing border. It sets up a temporary CRect object that will be passed to DoDragDrop() after some coordinate scheme conversions are complete. The first conversion is from logical to device units, and is accomplished with a call to CDC::LPtoDP(). In order to call this function, the new code must create a temporary device context, based on the CShowStringView for which OnLButtonDown() is being called. Having converted CRect to device units, the new code normalizes it and calculates the point within the rectangle where the user clicked.

Then the new code calls the DoDragDrop() member function of CShowStringCntrItem, inherited from COleClientItem and not overridden. It passes in the converted CRect and the offset of the click. If DoDragDrop() returns DROPEFFECT_MOVE, the item was moved and needs to be deleted. The code to handle a drop, which is not yet written, will create a new container item and set it as the current selection. This means that if the object was dropped elsewhere in the container, the current selection will no longer be equal to the hit item. If these two pointers are still equal, the object must have been dragged away. If it was dragged away, this code sets m_pSelection to NULL. In either case, pHitItem should be deleted.

Build and execute ShowString, insert a new object, press Esc to stop editing in place, then drag the inactive object to an ActiveX container application such as Microsoft Excel. You can also try dragging to the desktop. Be sure to try dragging an object down to the taskbar and pausing over the icon of a minimized container application, then waiting while the application is restored so that you can drop the object.

Implementing a Drop Target

It is harder to make ShowString a drop target (it could hardly be easier). If you dragged a contained item out of ShowString and dropped it into another container, try dragging that item back into ShowString. The cursor changes to a circle with a slash through it, meaning "you can't drop that here." In this section, you make the necessary code changes that allow you to drop it there after all.

You need to register your view as a place where items can be dropped. Next, you need to handle the following four events that can occur:

- An item might be dragged across the boundaries of your view. This action will require a cursor change or other indication you will take the item.

- In the view, the item will be dragged around within your boundaries, and you should give the user feedback about that process.

Part
V

Ch
14

- That item might be dragged out of the window again, having just passed over your view on the way to its final destination.
- The user may drop the item in your view.

Registering the View as a Drop Target

To register the view as a drop target, add a COleDropTarget member variable to the view. In ShowStringView.h, add this line to the class definition:

```
COleDropTarget m_droptarget;
```

To handle registration, override OnCreate() for the view, which is called when the view is created. Arrange for CShowStringView to catch the WM_CREATE message. Add the code in Listing 14.34 to the empty function generated for you.

Listing 14.34   ShowStringView.cpp—CShowStringView::OnCreate()

```cpp
int CShowStringView::OnCreate(LPCREATESTRUCT lpCreateStruct)
{
    if (CView::OnCreate(lpCreateStruct) == -1)
        return -1;

    if (m_droptarget.Register(this))
    {
        return 0;
    }
    else
    {
        return -1;
    }
}
```

OnCreate() returns zero if everything is going well, and -1 if the window should be destroyed. This code calls the base class function, then uses COleDropTarget::Register() to register this view as a place to drop items.

Setting Up Function Skeletons and Adding Member Variables

The four events that happen in your view correspond to four virtual functions you must override: OnDragEnter(), OnDragOver(), OnDragLeave(), and OnDrop(). Right-click CShowStringView in ClassView and choose Add Virtual Function to add overrides of these functions. Highlight OnDragEnter in the New Virtual Functions list, click Add Handler, and repeat for the other three functions.

OnDragEnter() sets up a *focus rectangle* that shows the user where the item would go if it were dropped here. This is maintained and drawn by OnDragOver(). But first, a number of member variables related to the focus rectangle must be added to CShowStringView. Add these lines to ShowStringView.h, in the public section:

```
CPoint m_dragpoint;
CSize m_dragsize;
CSize m_dragoffset;
```

A data object contains a great deal of information about itself, in various formats. There is, of course, the actual data as text, *device independent bitmap (DIB)*, or whatever other format is appropriate. But there is also information about the object itself. If you request data in the Object Descriptor format, you can find out the size of the item and where on the item the user originally clicked, and the offset from the mouse to the upper-left corner of the item. These formats are generally referred to as *Clipboard formats* because they were originally used for cut and paste via the Clipboard.

To ask for this information, you call the data object's `GetGlobalData()` member function, passing it a parameter that means "Object Descriptor, please." Rather than building this parameter from a string every time, you build it once and store it in a static member of the class. When a class has a static member variable, every instance of the class looks at the same memory location to see that variable. It is initialized (and memory is allocated for it) once, outside the class.

Add this line to showstringview.h:

```
static CLIPFORMAT m_cfObjectDescriptorFormat;
```

In showstringview.cpp, just before the first function, add these lines:

```
CLIPFORMAT CShowStringView::m_cfObjectDescriptorFormat =
    (CLIPFORMAT) ::RegisterClipboardFormat("Object Descriptor");
```

This makes a `CLIPFORMAT` from the string `"Object Descriptor"` and saves it in the static member variable for all instances of this class to use. Using a static member variable speeds up dragging over your view.

Your view does not accept any and all items that are dropped on it. Add a `BOOL` member variable to the view that indicates whether it accepts the item that is now being dragged over it:

```
BOOL m_OKtodrop;
```

There is one last member variable to add to `CShowStringView`. As the item is dragged across the view, a focus rectangle is repeatedly drawn and erased. Add another `BOOL` member variable that tracks the status of the focus rectangle:

```
BOOL m_FocusRectangleDrawn;
```

Initialize m_FocusRectangleDrawn, in the view constructor, to `FALSE`:

```
CShowStringView::CShowStringView()
{
    m_pSelection = NULL;
    m_FocusRectangleDrawn = FALSE;
}
```

Part
V

Ch
14

OnDragEnter

OnDragEnter() is called when the user first drags an item over the boundary of the view. It sets up the focus rectangle and then calls OnDragOver(). As the item continues to move, OnDragOver() is called repeatedly until the user drags the item out of the view or drops it in the view. The overall structure of OnDragEnter() is shown in Listing 14.35.

Listing 14.35   ShowStringView.cpp—*CShowStringView::OnDragEnter()*

```
DROPEFFECT CShowStringView::OnDragEnter(COleDataObject* pDataObject,
    DWORD dwKeyState, CPoint point)
{
    ASSERT(!m_FocusRectangleDrawn);

    // check that the data object can be dropped in this view
    // set dragsize and dragoffset with call to GetGlobalData
    // convert sizes with a scratch dc
    // hand off to OnDragOver
    return OnDragOver(pDataObject, dwKeyState, point);
}
```

First, check that whatever pDataObject carries is something from which you can make a COleClientItem (and therefore a CShowsStringCntrItem). If not, the object cannot be dropped here, and you return DROPEFFECT_NONE, as shown in Listing 14.36.

Listing 14.36   ShowStringView.cpp—Can the Object Be Dropped?

```
// check that the data object can be dropped in this view
m_OKtodrop = FALSE;
if (!COleClientItem::CanCreateFromData(pDataObject))
    return DROPEFFECT_NONE;

m_OKtodrop = TRUE;
```

Now the weird stuff starts. The GetGlobalData() member function of the data item that is being dragged into this view is called to get the object descriptor information mentioned earlier. It returns a handle of a global memory block. Then the SDK function GlobalLock() is called to convert the handle into a pointer to the first byte of the block and to prevent any other object from allocating the block. This is cast to a pointer to an object descriptor structure (the curious can check about 2,000 lines into oleidl.h, in the C:\MSDEV\include folder for most installations, to see the members of this structure) so that the sizel and pointl elements can be used to fill the m_dragsize and m_dragoffset member variables.

TIP There is not a number 1 at the end of those structure elements, but a lowercase letter L. And the elements of the sizel structure are cx and cy, but the elements of the pointl structure are x and y. Don't get carried away cutting and pasting.

Finally, `GlobalUnlock()` reverses the effects of `GlobalLock()`, making the block accessible to others, and `GlobalFree()` frees the memory. It ends up looking like Listing 14.37.

Listing 14.37 ShowStringView.cpp—Set *dragsize* and *dragoffset*

```
// set dragsize and dragoffset with call to GetGlobalData
HGLOBAL hObjectDescriptor = pDataObject->GetGlobalData(
    m_cfObjectDescriptorFormat);
if (hObjectDescriptor)
{
    LPOBJECTDESCRIPTOR pObjectDescriptor =
        (LPOBJECTDESCRIPTOR) GlobalLock(hObjectDescriptor);
    ASSERT(pObjectDescriptor);
    m_dragsize.cx = (int) pObjectDescriptor->sizel.cx;
    m_dragsize.cy = (int) pObjectDescriptor->sizel.cy;
    m_dragoffset.cx = (int) pObjectDescriptor->pointl.x;
    m_dragoffset.cy = (int) pObjectDescriptor->pointl.y;
    GlobalUnlock(hObjectDescriptor);
    GlobalFree(hObjectDescriptor);
}
else
{
    m_dragsize = CSize(0,0);
    m_dragoffset = CSize(0,0);
}
```

N O T E Global memory, also called *shared application memory*, is allocated from a different place than the memory available from your process space. It is the memory to use when two different processes need to read and write the same memory, and so it comes into play when using ActiveX.

For some ActiveX operations, global memory is too small—imagine trying to transfer a 40M file through global memory! There is a more general function than `GetGlobalData`, called (not surprisingly) `GetData`, which can transfer the data through a variety of storage medium choices. Because the object descriptors are small, asking for them in global memory is a sensible approach. ∎

If the call to `GetGlobalData()` didn't work, set both member variables to zero by zero rectangles. Next, convert those rectangles from OLE coordinates (which are device-independent) to pixels:

```
// convert sizes with a scratch dc
    CClientDC dc(NULL);
    dc.HIMETRICtoDP(&m_dragsize);
    dc.HIMETRICtoDP(&m_dragoffset);
```

`HIMETRICtoDP()` is a very useful function that happens to be a member of `CClientDC`, which inherits from the familiar `CDC` of Chapter 6, "Drawing on the Screen." You create an instance of `CClientDC` just so you can call the function.

`OnDragEnter()` closes with a call to `OnDragOver()`, so that's the next function to write.

Part V
Ch 14

OnDragOver

This function returns a DROPEFFECT. As you saw earlier in the "Implementing a Drag Source" section, if you return DROPEFFECT_MOVE, the source deletes the item from itself. Returning DROPEFFECT_NONE rejects the copy. It is OnDragOver() that deals with preparing to accept or reject a drop. The overall structure of the function looks like this:

```
DROPEFFECT CShowStringView::OnDragOver(COleDataObject* pDataObject,
    DWORD dwKeyState, CPoint point)
{
    // return if dropping is already rejected
    // determine drop effect according to keys depressed
    // adjust focus rectangle
}
```

First, check to see if OnDragEnter() or an earlier call to OnDragOver() already rejected this possible drop:

```
// return if dropping is already rejected
if (!m_OKtodrop)
{
return DROPEFFECT_NONE;
}
```

Next, look at the keys that the user is holding down now, available in the parameter passed to this function, dwKeyState. The code you need to add (see Listing 14.38) is pretty straight-forward.

Listing 14.38 ShowStringView.cpp—Determine the Drop Effect

```
// determine drop effect according to keys depressed
DROPEFFECT dropeffect = DROPEFFECT_NONE;

if ((dwKeyState & (MK_CONTROL|MK_SHIFT) )
    == (MK_CONTROL|MK_SHIFT))
{
    // Ctrl+Shift force a link
    dropeffect = DROPEFFECT_LINK;
}

else if ((dwKeyState & MK_CONTROL)     == MK_CONTROL)
{
    // Ctrl forces a copy
    dropeffect = DROPEFFECT_COPY;
}
else if ((dwKeyState & MK_ALT) == MK_ALT)
{
    // Alt forces a move
    dropeffect = DROPEFFECT_MOVE;
}
else
{
    // default is to move
    dropeffect = DROPEFFECT_MOVE;
}
```

N O T E This code has to be a lot more complex if the document might be smaller than the view, as can happen when you are editing a bitmap in Paint, and especially if the view can scroll. The Microsoft ActiveX container sample, DRAWCLI, (included on the Visual C++ CD) handles these contingencies. Look in the CD folder \DevStudio\Vc\Samples\Mcl\Mfc\Ole\DrawCli for the file drawvw.cpp and compare that code for `OnDragOver` to this code. ■

If the item has moved since the last time `OnDragOver()` was called, the focus rectangle has to be erased and redrawn at the new location. Because the focus rectangle is a simple XOR of the colors, drawing it a second time in the same place removes it. The code to adjust the focus rectangle is in Listing 14.39.

Listing 14.39 ShowStringView.cpp—Adjust the Focus Rectangle

```
// adjust focus rectangle

point -= m_dragoffset;
if (point == m_dragpoint)
{
    return dropeffect;
}

CClientDC dc(this);

if (m_FocusRectangleDrawn)
{
    dc.DrawFocusRect(CRect(m_dragpoint, m_dragsize));
    m_FocusRectangleDrawn = FALSE;
}

if (dropeffect != DROPEFFECT_NONE)
{
    dc.DrawFocusRect(CRect(point, m_dragsize));
    m_dragpoint = point;
    m_FocusRectangleDrawn = TRUE;
}
```

To test if the focus rectangle should be redrawn, this code adjusts the point where the user clicked by the offset into the item to determine the top-left corner of the item. It can then compare that location to the top-left corner of the focus rectangle. If they are the same, there is no need to redraw it. If they are different, the focus rectangle might need to be erased.

N O T E The first time `OnDragOver()` is called, `m_dragpoint` is uninitialized. That doesn't matter, because `m_FocusRectangleDrawn` is FALSE, and an ASSERT in `OnDragEnter()` guarantees it. When `m_FocusRectangleDrawn` is set to TRUE, `m_dragpoint` gets a value at the same time. ■

Finally, replace the return statement that was generated for you with one that returns the calculated DROPEFFECT:

```
return dropeffect;
```

OnDragLeave

Sometimes a user drags an item right over your view and out the other side. OnDragLeave() just tidies up a little by removing the focus rectangle, as shown in Listing 14.40.

Listing 14.40   ShowStringView.cpp—*ShowStringView::OnDragLeave()*

```
void CShowStringView::OnDragLeave()
{
    CClientDC dc(this);
    if (m_FocusRectangleDrawn)
    {
        dc.DrawFocusRect(CRect(m_dragpoint, m_dragsize));
        m_FocusRectangleDrawn = FALSE;
    }
}
```

OnDragDrop

If the user lets go of an item that is being dragged over ShowString, the item lands in the container and OnDragDrop() is called. The overall structure is in Listing 14.41.

Listing 14.41   ShowStringView.cpp—Structure of *OnDrop()*

```
BOOL CShowStringView::OnDrop(COleDataObject* pDataObject,
    DROPEFFECT dropEffect, CPoint point)
{
    ASSERT_VALID(this);
    // remove focus rectangle
    // paste in the data object
    // adjust the item dimensions, and make it the current selection
    // update views and set modified flag
    return TRUE;
}
```

Removing the focus rectangle is simple, as shown in Listing 14.42.

Listing 14.42   ShowStringView.cpp—Removing the Focus Rectangle

```
// remove focus rectangle
CClientDC dc(this);
if (m_FocusRectangleDrawn)
{
    dc.DrawFocusRect(CRect(m_dragpoint, m_dragsize));
    m_FocusRectangleDrawn = FALSE;
}
```

Next, create a new item to hold the data object, as shown in Listing 14.43. Note the use of the bitwise and (&) to test for a link.

Listing 14.43   ShowStringView.cpp—Paste the Data Object

```
// paste the data object
CShowStringDoc* pDoc = GetDocument();
CShowStringCntrItem* pNewItem = new CShowStringCntrItem(pDoc);
ASSERT_VALID(pNewItem);
if (dropEffect & DROPEFFECT_LINK)
{
    pNewItem->CreateLinkFromData(pDataObject);
}
else
{
    pNewItem->CreateFromData(pDataObject);
}
ASSERT_VALID(pNewItem);
```

The size of the container item needs to be set, as shown in Listing 14.44.

Listing 14.44   ShowStringView.cpp—Adjust Item Dimensions

```
// adjust the item dimensions, and make it the current selection
CSize size;
pNewItem->GetExtent(&size, pNewItem->GetDrawAspect());
dc.HIMETRICtoDP(&size);
point -= m_dragoffset;
pNewItem->m_rect = CRect(point,size);
m_pSelection = pNewItem;
```

Notice that this code adjusts the place where the user drops the item (point) by m_dragoffset, the coordinates into the item where the user clicked originally.

Part
V

Ch
14

Finally, make sure the document gets saved on exit, because pasting in a new container item changes it, and redraw the view:

```
// update views and set modified flag
pDoc->SetModifiedFlag();
pDoc->UpdateAllViews(NULL);
return TRUE;
```

This function always returns TRUE because there is no error checking at the moment that might require a return of FALSE. Notice, however, that most problems have been prevented; for example, if the data object cannot be used to create a container item, then the DROPEFFECT would have been set to DROPEFFECT_NONE in OnDragEnter() and this code would never have been called. You can be confident this code works.

Testing the Drag Target

All the confidence in the world is no substitute for testing. Build and execute ShowString, and try dragging something into it. To test both the drag source and drop target aspects at once, drag something out and then drag it back in. Now this is starting to become a really useful container. There's only one task left to do.

Deleting an Object

You can remove an object from your container by dragging it away somewhere, but it makes sense to implement deleting in a more obvious and direct way. The menu item generally used for this is Edit, Delete, so you start by adding this item to the IDR_SHOWSTTYPE menu before the Insert New Object item. Don't let Developer Studio set the ID to ID_EDIT_DELETE; instead, change it to ID_EDIT_CLEAR, the traditional resource ID for the command that deletes a contained object. Move to another menu item and then return to Edit, Delete, and you see that the prompt has been filled in for you as Erase the selection\nErase automatically.

It is the view that needs to handle this command, so add a message handler as you have done throughout this chapter. Follow these steps:

1. Bring up Class Wizard.
2. Choose ID_EDIT_CLEAR from the Class or Object to Handle drop-down box at the lower right.
3. Choose COMMAND from the New Windows Messages/Events box that appears when you click ID_EDIT_CLEAR box.
4. Click Add Handler.
5. Click OK to accept the suggested name.
6. Choose UPDATE_COMMAND_UI from the New Windows Messages/Events box and click Add Handler again.
7. Accept the suggested name.
8. Click OK on the large dialog box to complete the process.

The code for these two handlers is very simple. Because the update handler is simpler, add code to it first:

```
void CShowStringView::OnUpdateEditClear(CCmdUI* pCmdUI)
{
    pCmdUI->Enable(m_pSelection != NULL);
}
```

If there is a current selection, it can be deleted. If there is not a current selection, the menu item is disabled (grayed). The code to handle the command isn't much longer: it's in Listing 14.45.

Listing 14.45 ShowStringView.cpp—*CShowStringView::OnEditClear()*

```
void CShowStringView::OnEditClear()
{
    if (m_pSelection)
    {
        m_pSelection->Delete();
        m_pSelection = NULL;
        GetDocument()->SetModifiedFlag();
        GetDocument()->UpdateAllViews(NULL);
    }
}
```

This code checks that there is a selection (even though the menu item is grayed when there is no selection), and then deletes it, sets it to NULL so there is no longer a selection, makes sure the document is marked as modified so the user is prompted to save it when exiting, and gets the view redrawn without the deleted object.

Build and execute ShowString, insert something, and delete it by choosing Edit, Delete. Now it's an intuitive container that does what you expect a container to do.

From Here...

This chapter developed a powerful container. The boilerplate code generated by AppWizard produced a container that has a number of shortcomings, but the steps presented in this chapter corrected them and built an intuitive interface for the ActiveX container version of ShowString. To learn more about related topics, check these chapters:

- Chapter 13, "ActiveX Concepts," is a roadmap to Part V of this book and defines many of the concepts used in this and related chapters.
- Chapter 15, "Building an ActiveX Server Application," builds the third version of ShowString, which acts as an ActiveX server.
- Chapter 16, "Building an Automation Server," builds the fourth version of ShowString— an ActiveX Automation server that can be controlled from Visual Basic.
- Chapter 17, "Building an ActiveX Control," leaves ShowString behind and builds a control you can include in any Visual C++ or Visual Basic program.

Part
V

Ch
14

CHAPTER 15

Building an ActiveX Server Application

Just as AppWizard builds ActiveX containers, it also builds ActiveX servers. However, unlike containers, the AppWizard code is complete, so there isn't much work to do for improving the AppWizard code. This chapter builds a version of ShowString that is only a server and discusses how to build another version that is both a container and a server. You also learn about ActiveX documents and how they can be used in other applications. ■

Transforming ShowString into a server

An ActiveX server can supply its documents to ActiveX container applications like the one in the previous chapter. This section shows you how to build one and how they work.

Container and server applications

An application can be both a container and a server at the same time. This section discusses the implications of nested objects.

ActiveX documents

ActiveX document objects take being an ActiveX server one step further. This section explains what an ActiveX document object is, how to make one, and gives you a peek at what Windows will become.

Adding Server Capabilities to ShowString

Like Chapter 14, "Building an ActiveX Container Application," this chapter starts by building an ordinary server application with AppWizard and then adds the functionality that makes it ShowString. This is far quicker than adding ActiveX functionality to ShowString, because ShowString doesn't have much code and can be written quickly.

AppWizard's Server Boilerplate

Build the new ShowString in a different directory, making almost exactly the same AppWizard choices as when you built versions of ShowString in Chapter 9, "Building a Complete Application: ShowString," and Chapter 14, "Building an ActiveX Container Application." Call it ShowString, and choose an MDI application with no database support. In AppWizard's Step 3, select full server as your compound document support. This enables the check box for ActiveX document support. Leave this deselected for now. Later in this chapter, you see the consequences of selecting this option. Continue the AppWizard process, selecting a docking toolbar, status bar, printing and print preview, context-sensitive Help, and 3-D controls. Finally, select source file comments and a shared DLL.

> **N O T E** Even though the technology is now called ActiveX, the AppWizard dialog boxes refer to compound document support. Many of the class names that are used throughout this chapter have Ole in their names as well. While Microsoft has changed the name of the technology, it has not propagated that change throughout Visual C++ yet. You will have to live with these contradictions until the next release of Visual C++. ■

There are many differences between the application you have just generated and a do-nothing application without ActiveX server support. These differences are explained in the next few sections.

Menus   There are two new menus in an ActiveX server application. The first, called IDR_SHOWSTTYPE_SRVR_IP, is shown in Figure 15.1. When an item is being edited in place, the container in-place menu (called IDR_SHOWSTTYPE_CNTR_IP in the container version of ShowString) is combined with the server in-place menu, IDR_SHOWSTTYPE_SRVR_IP, to build the in-place menu as shown in Figure 15.2. The double separators in each partial menu show where the menus are joined.

The second new menu is IDR_SHOWSTTYPE_SRVR_EMB, used when an embedded item is being edited in a separate window. Figure 15.3 shows this new menu next to the more familiar IDR_SHOWSTTYPE menu, which is used when ShowString is acting not as a server but as an ordinary application. The File menus have different items: IDR_SHOWSTTYPE_SRVR_EMB has Update in place of Save, and Save Copy As in place of Save As. This is because the item the user is working on in the separate window is not a document of its own, but is embedded in another document. File, Update updates the embedded item; File, Save Copy As does not save the whole document, just a copy of this embedded portion.

FIG. 15.1

AppWizard adds another menu for editing in place.

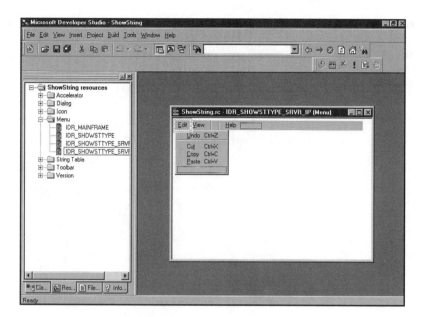

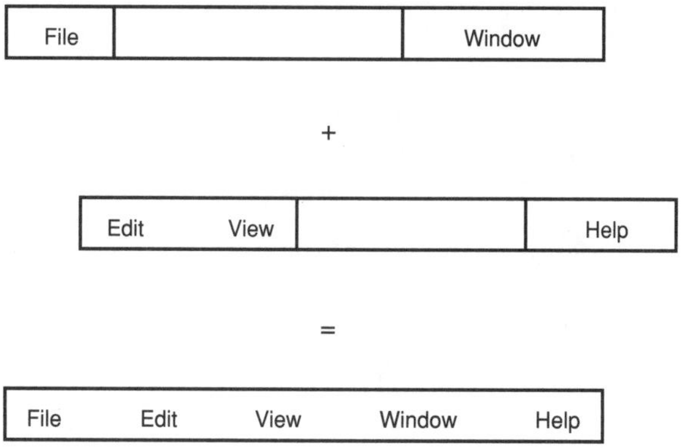

FIG. 15.2

The container and server in-place menus are interlaced during in- place editing.

File		Window

+

Edit	View		Help

=

File	Edit	View	Window	Help

CShowStringApp Another member variable has been added to this class. It is declared in showstring.h as:

```
COleTemplateServer m_server;
```

`COleTemplateServer` handles the majority of the work involved in connecting documents to code, as you will see.

FIG. 15.3

The embedded menu has different items under <u>F</u>ile than the usual menu.

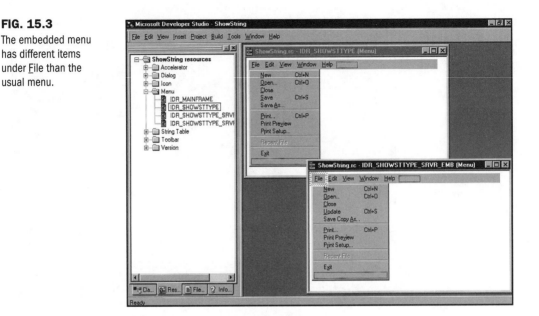

On the CD

The following line is added at the top of showstring.cpp:

```
#include "IpFrame.h"
```

This sets up the class `CInPlaceFrame`, discussed later in this chapter. Just before `InitInstance()`, the lines shown in Listing 15.1 are added:

Listing 15.1 Excerpt from ShowString.cpp—*CLSID*

```
// This identifier was generated to be statistically unique for
// your app. You may change it if you prefer to choose a specific
// identifier.

// {0B1DEE40-C373-11CF-870C-00201801DDD6}
static const CLSID clsid =
{ 0xb1dee40, 0xc373, 0x11cf,
    { 0x87, 0xc, 0x0, 0x20, 0x18, 0x1, 0xdd, 0xd6 } };
```

The numbers will be different in your code. This Class ID identifies your server application and document type. Applications that support several kinds of documents (for example, text and graphics) use a different CLSID for each type of document.

As it did for the OLE container version of ShowString, `CShowStringApp::InitInstance()` has several changes from the non-ActiveX ShowString you developed in Chapter 9, "Building a Complete Application: ShowString." The code in Listing 15.2 initializes the ActiveX (OLE) libraries:

On the CD

Listing 15.2   Excerpt from ShowString.cpp—Initializing Libraries

```
// Initialize OLE libraries
if (!AfxOleInit())
{
    AfxMessageBox(IDP_OLE_INIT_FAILED);
    return FALSE;
}
```

Part
V

Ch
15

While still in `CShowStringApp::InitInstance()`, after the `MultiDocTemplate` is initialized, but before the call to `AddDocTemplate()`, the following line is added to register the menu used for in-place editing and for separate-window editing:

```
pDocTemplate->SetServerInfo(
        IDR_SHOWSTTYPE_SRVR_EMB, IDR_SHOWSTTYPE_SRVR_IP,
        RUNTIME_CLASS(CInPlaceFrame));
```

A change that was not in the container version is connecting the template for the document to the class ID, like this:

```
// Connect the COleTemplateServer to the document template.
    //  The COleTemplateServer creates new documents on behalf
    //  of requesting OLE containers by using information
    //  specified in the document template.
    m_server.ConnectTemplate(clsid, pDocTemplate, FALSE);
```

Now when a user chooses Create New when inserting an object, the document used for that creation will be available.

When a server application is launched to edit an item in place or in a separate window, the system DLLs add /Embedded to the invoking command line. But if the application is already running, and it is an MDI application, a new copy is not launched. Instead, a new MDI window is opened in that application. That particular piece of magic is accomplished with one function call, as shown in Listing 15.3.

On the CD

Listing 15.3   Excerpt from ShowString.cpp—Registering Running MDI Apps

```
// Register all OLE server factories as running.  This enables the
//  OLE libraries to create objects from other applications.
COleTemplateServer::RegisterAll();
// Note: MDI applications register all server objects without regard
//  to the /Embedding or /Automation on the command line.
```

After parsing the command line, the AppWizard boilerplate code checks to see if this application is being launched as an embedded (or automation) application. If so, there is no need to continue with the initialization, so this function returns, as shown in Listing 15.4.

On the CD

Listing 15.4   Excerpt from ShowString.cpp—Checking How the App Was Launched

```
// Check to see if launched as OLE server
if (cmdInfo.m_bRunEmbedded ¦¦ cmdInfo.m_bRunAutomated)
{
    // Application was run with /Embedding or /Automation.
    // Don't show the main window in this case.
    return TRUE;
}
```

If the application is being run stand-alone, execution continues with a registration update:

```
// When a server application is launched stand-alone, it is a good idea
    //  to update the system registry in case it has been damaged.
    m_server.UpdateRegistry(OAT_INPLACE_SERVER);
```

ActiveX information is stored in the Registry. (The Registry is discussed in Chapter 8, "Persistence and File I/O.") When a user chooses Insert, Object or Edit, Insert Object, the Registry provides the list of object types that can be inserted. So, before ShowString can appear in such a list, it must be registered. Many developers add code to their install programs to register their server applications, and MFC takes this one step further, registering the application every time it is run. If the application files are moved or changed, the registration is automatically updated the next time the application is run stand-alone.

CShowStringDoc   The document class, `CShowStringDoc`, now inherits from `COleServerDoc` rather than `CDocument`. As well, the following line is added at the top of showstringdoc.cpp:

```
#include "SrvrItem.h"
```

This header file describes the server item class, `CShowStringSrvrItem`, discussed in the `CShowStringSrvrItem` subsection of this section. The constructor, `CShowStringDoc::CShowStringDoc()`, has the following line added:

```
EnableCompoundFile();
```

This turns on the use of compound files.

There is a new public function, inlined in the header file, so that other functions can access the server item:

```
CShowStringSrvrItem* GetEmbeddedItem()
        { return (CShowStringSrvrItem*)COleServerDoc::GetEmbeddedItem(); }
```

This calls the base class `GetEmbeddedItem()`, which in turn calls the virtual function `OnGetEmbedded Item()`. That function must be overridden in the ShowString document class as shown in Listing 15.5.

Listing 15.5   ShowStringDoc.cpp—*CShowStringDoc::OnGetEmbeddedItem()*

```
COleServerItem* CShowStringDoc::OnGetEmbeddedItem()
{
    // OnGetEmbeddedItem is called by the framework to get the COleServerItem
    //  that is associated with the document.  It is only called when
    ➥necessary.

    CShowStringSrvrItem* pItem = new CShowStringSrvrItem(this);
    ASSERT_VALID(pItem);
    return pItem;
}
```

This makes a new server item from this document and returns a pointer to it.

CShowStringView   The view class has a new entry in the message map:

```
ON_COMMAND(ID_CANCEL_EDIT_SRVR, OnCancelEditSrvr)
```

This catches ID_CANCEL_EDIT_SRVR, and the cancellation of editing is in place. An accelerator has already been added to connect this message to Esc. The function that catches it looks like this:

```
void CShowStringView::OnCancelEditSrvr()
{
    GetDocument()->OnDeactivateUI(FALSE);
}
```

This function simply deactivates the item. There are no other view changes—server views are so much simpler than container views.

CShowStringSrvrItem   The server item class is a completely new addition to ShowString. It provides an interface between the container application that causes ShowString to launch and a ShowString document. It describes an entire ShowString document that is embedded into another document, or a portion of a ShowString document that is linked to part of a container document. It has no member variables other than those inherited from the base class, COleServerItem. It has overrides for eight functions. They are as follows:

- A constructor
- A destructor
- GetDocument()
- AssertValid()
- Dump()
- Serialize()
- OnDraw()
- OnGetExtent()

The constructor simply passes the document pointer along to the base class. The destructor does nothing. GetDocument() is an inline function that calls the base class function with the same name and casts the result. AssertValid() and Dump() are debug functions that simply call the base class functions. Serialize() actually does some work, as shown in Listing 15.6.

Listing 15.6 SrvrItem.cpp—*CShowStringSrvrItem::Serialize()*

```
void CShowStringSrvrItem::Serialize(CArchive& ar)
{
    // CShowStringSrvrItem::Serialize will be called by the framework if
    //  the item is copied to the clipboard.  This can happen automatically
    //  through the OLE callback OnGetClipboardData.  A good default for
    //  the embedded item is simply to delegate to the document's Serialize
    //  function.  If you support links, then you will want to serialize
    //  just a portion of the document.

    if (!IsLinkedItem())
    {
        CShowStringDoc* pDoc = GetDocument();
        ASSERT_VALID(pDoc);
        pDoc->Serialize(ar);
    }
}
```

There is no need to duplicate effort here. If the item is embedded, then it is an entire document, and that document has a perfectly good Serialize() that can handle the work. AppWizard doesn't provide boilerplate to handle serializing a linked item, because it is application-specific. You would save just enough information to describe what part of the document has been linked in, for example, cells A3 to D27 in a spreadsheet. This doesn't make sense for ShowString, so don't add any code to Serialize().

You may feel that OnDraw() is out of place here. It is normally thought of as a view function. But this OnDraw() draws a depiction of the server item when it is inactive. It should look very much like the view when it is active, and it makes sense to share the work between CShowStringView::OnDraw() and CShowStringSrvrItem::OnDraw(). The boilerplate that AppWizard provides is in Listing 15.7.

Listing 15.7 SrvrItem.cpp—*CShowStringSrvrItem::OnDraw()*

```
BOOL CShowStringSrvrItem::OnDraw(CDC* pDC, CSize& rSize)
{
    CShowStringDoc* pDoc = GetDocument();
    ASSERT_VALID(pDoc);

    // TODO: set mapping mode and extent
    //  (The extent is usually the same as the size returned from OnGetExtent)
    pDC->SetMapMode(MM_ANISOTROPIC);
    pDC->SetWindowOrg(0,0);
    pDC->SetWindowExt(3000, 3000);

    // TODO: add drawing code here.  Optionally, fill in the HIMETRIC extent.
    //  All drawing takes place in the metafile device context (pDC).

    return TRUE;
```

This will change a great deal, but it's worth noting now that unlike `CShowStringView::OnDraw()`, this function takes two parameters. The second is the size in which the inactive depiction is to be drawn. The extent, as mentioned in the boilerplate comments, typically comes from `OnGetExtent()`, which is shown in Listing 15.8.

On the CD

Listing 15.8   Srvrltem.cpp—*CShowStringSrvrltem:: OnGetExtent()*

```
BOOL CShowStringSrvrItem::OnGetExtent(DVASPECT dwDrawAspect, CSize& rSize)
{
    // Most applications, like this one, only handle drawing the content
    //  aspect of the item.  If you wish to support other aspects, such
    //  as DVASPECT_THUMBNAIL (by overriding OnDrawEx), then this
    //  implementation of OnGetExtent should be modified to handle the
    //  additional aspect(s).

    if (dwDrawAspect != DVASPECT_CONTENT)
        return COleServerItem::OnGetExtent(dwDrawAspect, rSize);

    // CShowStringSrvrItem::OnGetExtent is called to get the extent in
    //  HIMETRIC units of the entire item.  The default implementation
    //  here simply returns a hard-coded number of units.

    CShowStringDoc* pDoc = GetDocument();
    ASSERT_VALID(pDoc);

    // TODO: replace this arbitrary size

    rSize = CSize(3000, 3000);   // 3000 x 3000 HIMETRIC units

    return TRUE;
}
```

You will replace this with real code very shortly.

CInPlaceFrame   The in-place frame class, which inherits from `COleIPFrameWnd`, handles the frame around the server item and the toolbars, status bars, and dialog-box bars, collectively known as *control bars*, that it displays. It has the following three protected member variables:

```
CToolBar      m_wndToolBar;
COleResizeBar   m_wndResizeBar;
COleDropTarget m_dropTarget;
```

The `CToolBar` class is discussed in Chapter 10, "Status Bars and Toolbars." `COleDropTarget` is discussed in the drag-and-drop section of Chapter 14, "Building an ActiveX Container Application." `COleResizeBar` looks just like a `CRectTracker`, which was used extensively in Chapter 14, but allows the resizing of a server item rather than a container item.

The following are the seven member functions of `CInPlaceFrame`:

- A constructor
- A destructor

■ AssertValid()

■ Dump()

■ OnCreate()

■ OnCreateControlBars()

■ PreCreateWindow()

The constructor and destructor do nothing. AssertValid() and Dump() are debug functions that simply call the base class functions. OnCreate() actually has code, shown in Listing 15.9.

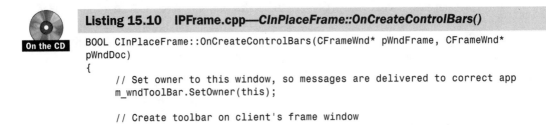

Listing 15.9   IPFrame.cpp—*CInPlaceFrame::OnCreate()*

```
int CInPlaceFrame::OnCreate(LPCREATESTRUCT lpCreateStruct)
{
    if (COleIPFrameWnd::OnCreate(lpCreateStruct) == -1)
        return -1;

    // CResizeBar implements in-place resizing.
    if (!m_wndResizeBar.Create(this))
    {
        TRACE0("Failed to create resize bar\n");
        return -1;       // fail to create
    }

    // By default, it is a good idea to register a drop-target that does
    //   nothing with your frame window.  This prevents drops from
    //   "falling through" to a container that supports drag-drop.
    m_dropTarget.Register(this);

    return 0;
}
```

This function catches the WM_CREATE message that is sent when an in-place frame is created and drawn on the screen. It calls the base class function, then creates the resize bar. Finally, it registers a drop target, so that if anything is dropped over this in-place frame, it is dropped on this server rather than the underlying container.

When a server document is activated in place, COleServerDoc::ActivateInPlace() calls CInPlaceFrame::OnCreateControlBars(), which is shown in Listing 15.10.

Listing 15.10   IPFrame.cpp—*CInPlaceFrame::OnCreateControlBars()*

```
BOOL CInPlaceFrame::OnCreateControlBars(CFrameWnd* pWndFrame, CFrameWnd*
pWndDoc)
{
    // Set owner to this window, so messages are delivered to correct app
    m_wndToolBar.SetOwner(this);

    // Create toolbar on client's frame window
```

```
if (!m_wndToolBar.Create(pWndFrame) ||
    !m_wndToolBar.LoadToolBar(IDR_SHOWSTTYPE_SRVR_IP))
{
    TRACE0("Failed to create toolbar\n");
    return FALSE;
}

// TODO: Remove this if you don't want tool tips or a resizeable toolbar
m_wndToolBar.SetBarStyle(m_wndToolBar.GetBarStyle() |
    CBRS_TOOLTIPS | CBRS_FLYBY | CBRS_SIZE_DYNAMIC);

// TODO: Delete these three lines if you don't want the toolbar to
//   be dockable
m_wndToolBar.EnableDocking(CBRS_ALIGN_ANY);
pWndFrame->EnableDocking(CBRS_ALIGN_ANY);
pWndFrame->DockControlBar(&m_wndToolBar);

    return TRUE;
}
```

This function creates a docking, resizable toolbar with tool tips, docked against the edge of the main frame window for the application.

TIP
If you are developing an MDI application and prefer the toolbar against the document frame, use pWndDoc instead of PWndFrame in the call to m_wndToolBar.Create() but be sure to check that it is not NULL.

The last function in CInPlaceFrame is PreCreateWindow(). At the moment, it just calls the base class, as shown in Listing 15.11.

Listing 15.11   IPFrame.cpp—*CInPlaceFrame::PreCreateWindow()*

```
BOOL CInPlaceFrame::PreCreateWindow(CREATESTRUCT& cs)
{
    // TODO: Modify the Window class or styles here by modifying
    //   the CREATESTRUCT cs

    return COleIPFrameWnd::PreCreateWindow(cs);
}
```

This function is called before OnCreate() and sets up the styles for the frame window through a CREATESTRUCT.

CAUTION
Modifying these styles is not for the faint of heart. The Microsoft documentation recommends reading the source code for all the classes in the hierarchy of your CInPlaceFrame (Cwnd, CFrameWnd, COleIPFrameWnd) to see what CREATESTRUCT elements are already set before making any changes. For this sample application, don't change the CREATESTRUCT.

Shortcomings of This Server   Apart from the fact that the starter application from AppWizard doesn't show a string, what's missing from this server? The OnDraw() and GetExtent() TODOs are the only significant tasks left for you by AppWizard. Try building ShowString, then run it once stand-alone just to register it.

Figure 15.4 shows the Object dialog box in Microsoft Word, reached by choosing Insert, Object. ShowString appears in this list as ShowSt Document—not surprising considering the menu name was IDR_SHOWSTTYPE. Developer Studio calls this document a ShowSt document. This setting could have been overridden in AppWizard by choosing the Advanced button in Step 4 of AppWizard. Figure 15.5 shows this dialog box and the long and short names of the file type.

FIG. 15.4

The ShowString document type, called ShowSt Document, now appears in the Object dialog box when inserting a new object into a Word document.

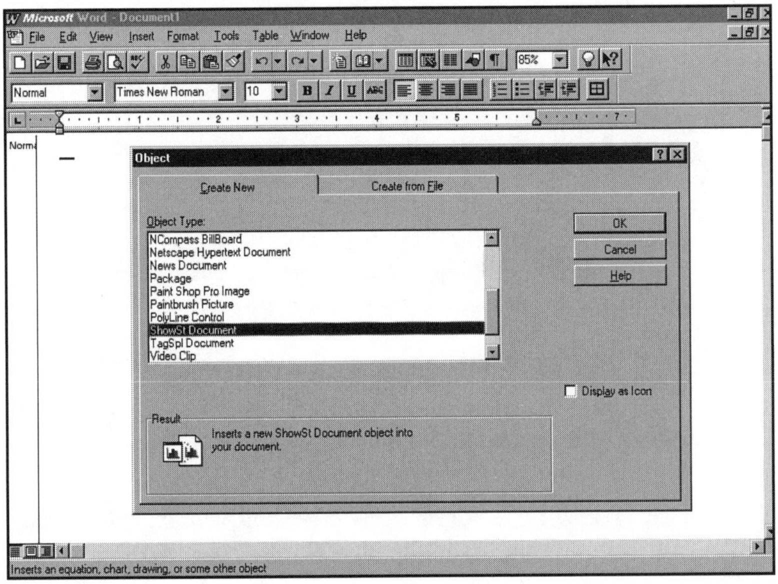

So, the file type names used by the Registry have been set incorrectly for this project. The next few pages take you on a tour of the way file type names are stored and show you how difficult they are to change.

The file type name has been stored in the string table. It is the caption of the IDR_SHOWSTTYPE resource, and AppWizard has set it to:

`\nShowSt\nShowSt\n\n\nShowString.Document\nShowSt Document`

To look at this string, choose String Table from the Resource View, open the only string table there, click IDR_SHOWSTTYPE once to highlight it, and choose View, Properties. This string is saved in the document template when a new one is constructed in CShowStringApp:: InitInstance(), like this:

FIG. 15.5

The Advanced Options dialog box of Step 4 in AppWizard provides an opportunity to change the name of the file type.

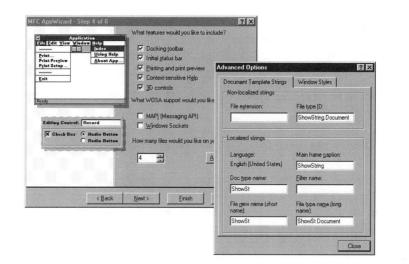

Listing 15.12   ShowString.cpp—Excerpt from *ShowStringApp::InitInstance()*

```
pDocTemplate = new CMultiDocTemplate(
    IDR_SHOWSTTYPE,
    RUNTIME_CLASS(CShowStringDoc),
    RUNTIME_CLASS(CChildFrame), // custom MDI child frame
    RUNTIME_CLASS(CShowStringView));
```

The caption of the menu resource holds seven strings, and each is used by a different part of the framework. They are separated by the newline character, \n. The seven strings, their purposes, and the values provided by AppWizard for ShowString are as follows:

- **Window Title**—Used by SDI applications in the title bar. For ShowString: not provided.

- **Document Name**—Used as the root for default document names. For ShowString: ShowSt, so that new documents will be ShowSt1, ShowSt2, and so on.

- **File New Name**—Prompt in the File New dialog box for file type. (For example, in Developer Studio there are eight file types, including Text File and Project Workspace.) For ShowString: ShowSt.

- **Filter Name**—An entry for the drop-down box List File of Type in the File Open dialog box. For ShowString: not provided.

- **Filter Extension**—The extension that matches the filter name. For ShowString: not provided.

- **Registry File Type ID**—A short string to be stored in the Registry. For ShowString: ShowString.Document.

- **Registry File Type Name**—A longer string that shows in dialog boxes involving the Registry. For Showstring: ShowSt Document.

(Look again at Figure 15.5 and you can see where these values came from.) Try changing the last entry. In the Properties dialog box, change the caption so that the last element of the string is ShowString Document. Build the project. Run it once and exit. In the output section of Developer Studio, you see these messages:

```
Warning: Leaving value 'ShowSt Document' for key 'ShowString.Document'
 in registry
 intended value was 'ShowString Document'.
Warning: Leaving value 'ShowSt Document' for key
 'CLSID\{0B1DEE40-C373-11CF-870C-00201801DDD6}' in registry
 intended value was 'ShowString Document'.
```

This means that the call to UpdateRegistry() did not change these two keys. There is a way to provide parameters to UpdateRegistry() to insist that the keys be updated, but it's even more complicated than the route you will follow. Because no code has been changed from that provided by AppWizard, it's much quicker just to delete the ShowString directory and create it again, this time setting the long file type to ShowString Document.

> **CAUTION**
>
> Always test AppWizard-generated code before you add changes of your own. Until you are familiar with every default you are accepting, it is worth a few moments to see what you have before moving on. Rerunning AppWizard is easy, but if you've made several hours' worth of changes and then decide to rerun it, it's not such a simple thing.

Delete the ShowString folder entirely and generate a new application with AppWizard as before. This time, in Step 4, click the Advanced button and change the file type names as shown in Figure 15.6. After you click Finish, AppWizard asks whether you wish to reuse the existing CLSID, as shown in Figure 15.7. Click Yes and then OK to create the project. This makes a new showstring.reg file for you with the correct Registry values.

FIG. 15.6
The Advanced Options dialog box of Step 4 of AppWizard is the place to improve the file type names.

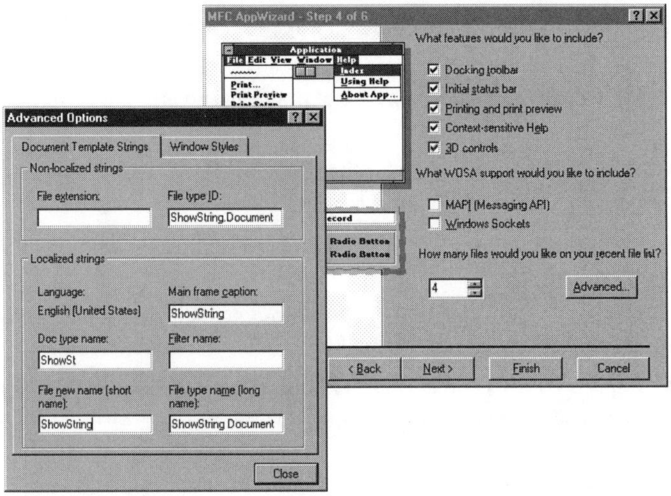

FIG. 15.7
AppWizard makes
sure that you don't
accidentally reuse a
CLSID.

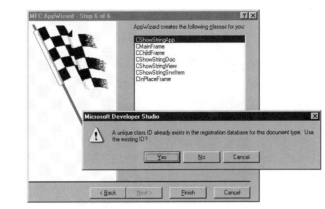

This changes the string table as well as the showstring.reg file, so you might be tempted to build and run the application to make this fix complete. And it's true, when you run the application, it will update the Registry for you, using the values from the new string table. Alas, the registration update will fail yet again. If you were to try it, these messages would appear in the output window:

```
Warning: Leaving value 'ShowSt Document' for key
 'ShowString.Document' in registry
 intended value was 'ShowString Document'.
Warning: Leaving value 'ShowSt Document' for key
 'CLSID\{0B1DEE40-C373-11CF-870C-00201801DDD6}' in registry
 intended value was 'ShowString Document'.
Warning: Leaving value 'ShowSt' for key
 'CLSID\{0B1DEE40-C373-11CF-870C-00201801DDD6}\AuxUserType\2'
 in registry
 intended value was 'ShowString'.
```

So, how do you get out of this mess? You have to edit the Registry. If that sounds intimidating, it should be. Messing with the Registry can leave your system unusable. But you are not going to go in by hand and change keys; instead, you are going to use the registry file that AppWizard generated for you. Here's what to do:

1. Choose Start, Run
2. Type **regedit** and press Enter.
3. Choose Registry, Import Registry File from the Registry Editor menu.
4. Using the Import Registry File dialog box, move through your folders until you reach the one where the replacement ShowString server was just generated by AppWizard, as shown in Figure 15.8. Click Open.
5. A success message is shown. Click OK.
6. Close the Registry Editor.

FIG. 15.8

Registry files generated by AppWizard have the extension .reg.

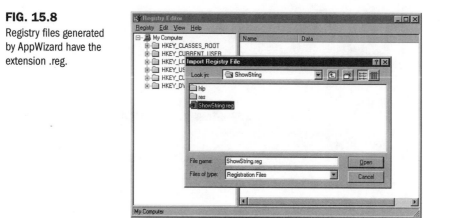

Now if you run ShowString again, those error messages do not appear. Run Word again, and choose Insert Object. The Object dialog box now has a more meaningful ShowString entry, as shown in Figure 15.9.

FIG. 15.9

The updated long file type name appears in the Object dialog box of other applications.

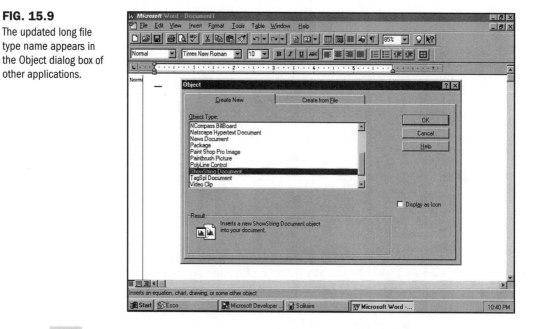

NOTE There are three morals to this side trip. The first is that you should think really carefully before clicking Finish on the AppWizard dialog box. The second is that you cannot ignore the Registry if you are an ActiveX programmer. The third is that anything can be changed if you have the nerve for it. ■

Click OK on the Object dialog box to insert a ShowString object into the Word document. You can immediately edit it in place, as shown in Figure 15.10. You can see that the combined server and container in-place menus are being used. There's not much you can do to the embedded object at this point, because the ShowString code that actually shows a string has not been added. Press Esc to finish editing in place and the menus return to the usual Word menus, as shown in Figure 15.11.

FIG. 15.10
While editing in place, the in-place menus replace the Word menus.

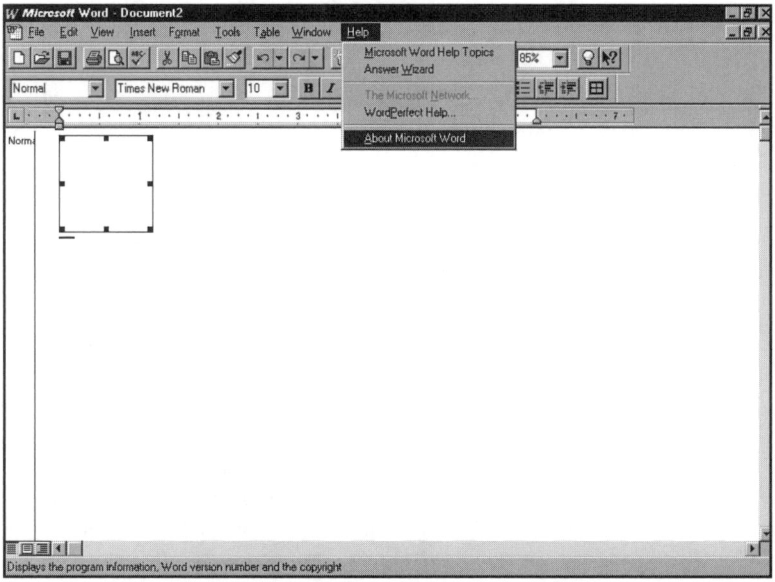

FIG. 15.11
When the object is inactive, Word reminds the user of the object type.

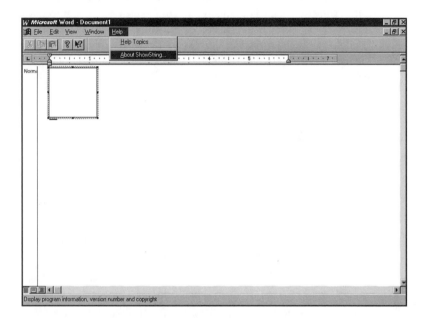

Although this server doesn't do anything, it is a perfectly good server. You can resize and move the embedded item while it is active or inactive, and everything operates exactly as you expect. All that remains is to restore the ShowString functionality.

Showing a String Again

As you did in Chapter 14, "Building an ActiveX Container Application," it is time to add the ShowString functionality to this version of the program. If you went through this process before, it will be even quicker this time. Remember to open the ShowString files from Chapter 9, "Building a Complete Application: ShowString," so that you can copy code and resources from the functional ShowString to the do-nothing ActiveX server you have just created and explored. Here's what to do:

1. In ShowStringDoc.h, add the private member variables and public Get functions to the class.

2. In CShowStringDoc::Serialize(), paste in the code that saves or restores these member variables.

3. In CShowStringDoc::OnNewDocument(), paste in the code that initializes the member variables.

4. Copy the entire Tools menu from the old ShowString to the new server ShowString: choose File, Open to open the old ShowString.rc, open the IDR_SHOWSTTYPE menu, click the Tools menu, and choose Edit, Copy. Open the new ShowString's IDR_SHOWSTTYPE menu, click the Window menu, and choose Edit, Paste.

5. Paste the Tools menu into the IDR_SHOWSTTYPE_SRVR_IP (before the separator bars) and IDR_SHOWSTTYPE_SRVR_EMB menus in the same way.

6. Add the accelerator Ctrl+T for ID_TOOLS_OPTIONS as described in Chapter 9, "Building a Complete Application: ShowString." Add it to all three accelerators.

7. Delete the IDD_ABOUTBOX dialog box from the new ShowString. Copy IDD_ABOUTBOX and IDD_OPTIONS from the old ShowString to the new.

8. While IDD_OPTIONS has focus, choose View, ClassWizard. Create the COptionsDialog class as in the original ShowString.

9. Use ClassWizard to arrange for CShowStringDoc to catch the ID_TOOLS_OPTIONS command.

10. In ShowStringDoc.cpp, replace the ClassWizard version of CShowStringDoc::OnToolsOptions() with the one that puts up the dialog box.

11. In ShowStringDoc.cpp, add **#include "OptionsDialog.h"** after the #include statements already present.

12. Use ClassWizard to connect the dialog box controls to COptionsDialog member variables as before.

You haven't restored CShowStringView::OnDraw() yet, because there are actually going to be two OnDraw() functions. The first is in the view class, shown in Listing 15.13. It draws the string when ShowString is running stand-alone and when the user is editing in place, and it's the same as in the old version of ShowString. Just copy it into the new one.

Listing 15.13   ShowStringView.cpp—*CShowStringView::OnDraw()*

```
void CShowStringView::OnDraw(CDC* pDC)
{
    CShowStringDoc* pDoc = GetDocument();
    ASSERT_VALID(pDoc);

    COLORREF oldcolor;
    switch (pDoc->GetColor())
    {
    case 0:
        oldcolor = pDC->SetTextColor(RGB(0,0,0)); //black
        break;
    case 1:
        oldcolor = pDC->SetTextColor(RGB(0xFF,0,0)); //red
        break;
    case 2:
        oldcolor = pDC->SetTextColor(RGB(0,0xFF,0)); //green
        break;
    }

    int DTflags = 0;
    if (pDoc->GetHorizcenter())
    {
        DTflags |= DT_CENTER;
    }
    if (pDoc->GetVertcenter())
    {
        DTflags |= (DT_VCENTER|DT_SINGLELINE);
    }

    CRect rect;
    GetClientRect(&rect);
    pDC->DrawText(pDoc->GetString(), &rect, DTflags);
    pDC->SetTextColor(oldcolor);
}
```

When the embedded ShowString item is inactive, `CShowStringSrvrItem::OnDraw()` draws it. The code in here should be very like the view's `OnDraw`, but because it is a member of `CShowStringSrvrItem` rather than `CShowStringView`, it doesn't have access to the same member variables. So although there is still a `GetDocument()` function you can call, `GetClientRect` doesn't work. It's a member of the view class but not of the server item class. You use a few CDC member functions instead. It's a nice touch to draw the item slightly differently, to help remind the user that it is not active, as shown in Listing 15.14.

Listing 15.14   Srvrltem.cpp—*CShowStringSrvrltem::OnDraw()*

```
BOOL CShowStringSrvrItem::OnDraw(CDC* pDC, CSize& rSize)
{
    CShowStringDoc* pDoc = GetDocument();
    ASSERT_VALID(pDoc);
```

continues

Listing 15.14 Continued

```
// TODO: set mapping mode and extent
//  (The extent is usually the same as the size returned from OnGetExtent)
pDC->SetMapMode(MM_ANISOTROPIC);
pDC->SetWindowOrg(0,0);
pDC->SetWindowExt(3000, 3000);

COLORREF oldcolor;
switch (pDoc->GetColor())
{
case 0:
    oldcolor = pDC->SetTextColor(RGB(0x80,0x80,0x80)); //gray
    break;
case 1:
    oldcolor = pDC->SetTextColor(RGB(0xB0,0,0)); // dull red
    break;
case 2:
    oldcolor = pDC->SetTextColor(RGB(0,0xB0,0)); // dull green
    break;
}

int DTflags = 0;
if (pDoc->GetHorizcenter())
{
    DTflags |= DT_CENTER;
}
if (pDoc->GetVertcenter())
{
    DTflags |= (DT_VCENTER|DT_SINGLELINE);
}

CRect rect;
rect.TopLeft() = pDC->GetWindowOrg();
rect.BottomRight() = rect.TopLeft() + pDC->GetWindowExt();
pDC->DrawText(pDoc->GetString(), &rect, DTflags);
pDC->SetTextColor(oldcolor);

return TRUE;
}
```

The function starts with the boilerplate from AppWizard. With an application that doesn't just draw itself in whatever space is provided, you would want to add code to determine the extent rather than just using (3000,3000). (You'd want to add the code to OnGetExtent(), too.) But hardcoding the numbers works for this simple example. Next, paste in the drawing code from the view's OnDraw(), but change the colors slightly to give the user a reminder.

Build the application, fix any typos or other simple errors, and then start Excel and insert a ShowString document into your worksheet. ShowString should run as before, with Hello, world! in the center of the view. Convince yourself that the Options dialog box still works and that you have restored all the old functionality. Be sure to change at least one thing: the string, the color, or the centering. Then, press Esc to finish editing in place. Oops! It still draws the old Hello, world! in gray in the center of the server area. Why?

Remember that in CShowStringDoc::OnToolsOptions(), after the user clicks OK, you tell the document that it has been changed and arrange to have the view redrawn:

```
SetModifiedFlag();
UpdateAllViews(NULL);
```

You need to add another line there to make sure that any containers that are containing this document are also notified:

```
NotifyChanged();
```

Now, build it again, and insert a different ShowString object into a Word document. This time the changes are reflected in the inactive server display as well. Figure 15.12 shows a ShowString item being edited in place, and Figure 15.13 shows the same item inactive.

FIG. 15.12

This ShowString item is being edited in place.

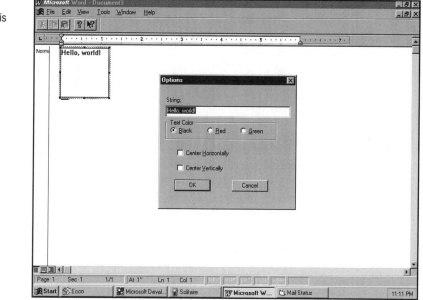

N O T E There is one oddity you may notice as you edit. If you choose to have the string centered horizontally when it is inactive, the first character of the string is centered, but when it is active the entire string is centered. Because the code is identical for these cases, this behavior has to be blamed on MFC. ▓

Good old ShowString has been through a lot. It's time for one more transformation.

FIG. 15.13

This ShowString item is inactive.

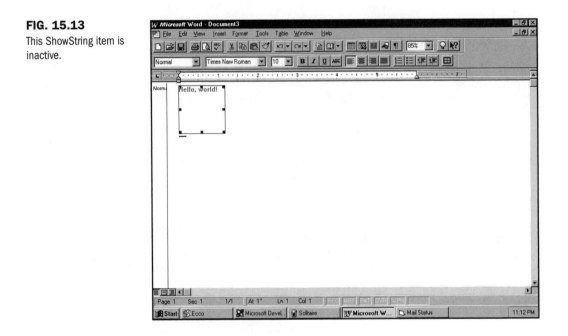

Applications that Are Both Container and Server

As you might expect, adding container features to this version of ShowString is as difficult as adding them to the ordinary ShowString of the previous chapter. If you add these features, you gain an application that can tap the full power of ActiveX to bring extraordinary power to your work and your documents.

Building Another Version of ShowString

The way to get a ShowString that is both a container and a server is to follow these steps:

1. Build a new ShowString with AppWizard that is a container and a full server. Run AppWizard as usual, but in a different directory than the one where you created the server-only ShowString. Be sure to select the Both Container And Server radio button in Step 3. In Step 4, be sure to click the Advanced button and change the file name types as you did earlier in this chapter. And finally, when asked whether you want to use the same CLSID, say No. This is a different application.

2. Make the container changes from the previous chapter. When adding the Tools Options menu item and accelerator, add it to the main menu, the server in-place menu, and the server-embedded menu.

3. Make the server changes from this chapter.

4. Add the ShowString functionality.

This section does not present the process of building a container and server application in detail; that is covered in the "Adding Server Capabilities to ShowString" section of this chapter and all of the previous chapters. Rather, the focus here is on the consequences of building such an application.

Nesting and Recursion Issues

After an application is both a server (meaning its documents can be embedded in other applications) and a container, it is possible to create nested documents. For example, an Excel spreadsheet might contain a Word document, which, in turn, contains a bitmap, as shown in Figure 15.14.

FIG. 15.14

This Excel spreadsheet contains a Word document that contains a bitmap.

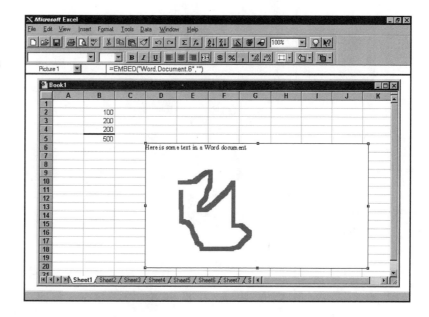

Within Excel, you can double-click the Word document to edit it in place, as shown in Figure 15.15, but you cannot go on to double-click the bitmap and edit it in place, too. You can edit it in a window of its own, as shown in Figure 15.16. It is a limitation of ActiveX that you cannot nest in-place editing sessions indefinitely.

FIG. 15.15
This Word document is being edited in place.

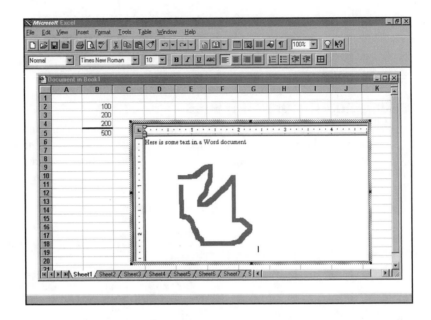

FIG. 15.16
This bitmap is nested within a Word document within an Excel spreadsheet, and so cannot be edited in place. Instead, it is edited in a separate window.

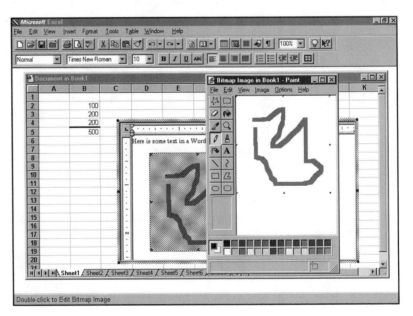

ActiveX Documents

The final, important recent addition to ActiveX is ActiveX documents, also known as ActiveX Document Objects. An ordinary ActiveX server takes over the menus and interface of a container application when the document is being edited in place, but does so in cooperation with the container application. An ActiveX Document server takes over far more dramatically.

What ActiveX Documents Do

The first application to demonstrate the use of ActiveX Documents is the Microsoft Office Binder, shown in Figure 15.17. To the user, it appears that this application can open any Office document. In reality, the documents are opened with their own server applications while the frame around them and the list of other documents remain intact. Microsoft Internet Explorer 3.0 is also an ActiveX Document container—Figure 15.18 shows a Word document open in Explorer. Notice the menus are Word menus, but the Explorer toolbar can still be used. For example, clicking the Back button closes this Word document and opens the document that was loaded previously.

FIG. 15.17

The Microsoft Office Binder makes it simple to pull Office documents together.

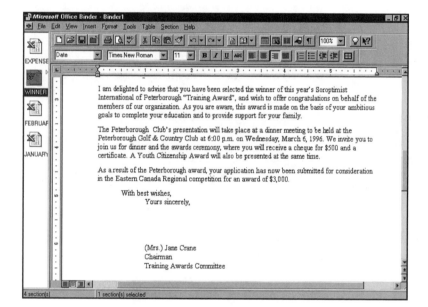

What this means to users is a complete transition to a document-centered approach. No matter what application the user is working with, any kind of document can be opened and edited, using the code written to work with that document but the interface that the user has learned for his or her own application.

Making ShowString an ActiveX Document Server

Making yet another version of ShowString, this one as an ActiveX document server, is pretty simple. Follow the instructions from the "AppWizard's Server Boilerplate" subsection at the beginning of this chapter, with two exceptions: In AppWizard's Step 3, select ActiveX document support, and in AppWizard's Step 4, click the Advanced button. Fix the file type names, and fill in the file extension as .sst, as shown in Figure 15.19. This helps ActiveX document containers determine what application to launch when you open a ShowString file.

FIG. 15.18

Microsoft Internet
Explorer is also a
container for ActiveX
documents.

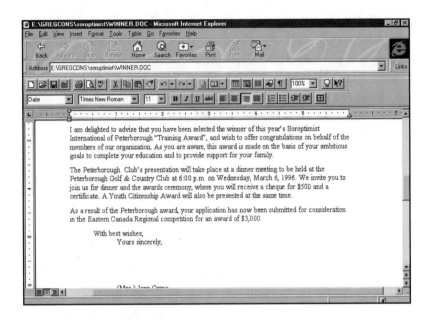

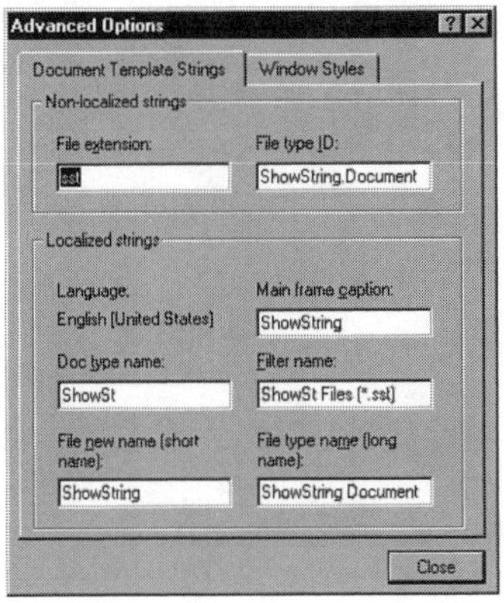

FIG. 15.19

The Advanced Options
dialog box of App
Wizard's Step 4 is
where you specify the
extension for ShowString
files.

Document Extension Boilerplate   Any one of the versions of ShowString built up to
this point could have had a document extension specified. AppWizard adds these lines to
`CShowStringApp::InitInstance()` when you specify a document extension for an ActiveX
document server application:

```
// Enable drag/drop open
m_pMainWnd->DragAcceptFiles();

// Enable DDE Execute open
EnableShellOpen();
RegisterShellFileTypes(TRUE);
```

It is the call to `RegisterShellFileTypes` that matters here, though the drag and drop is a nice touch. You're able to drag files from your desktop or a folder onto the ShowString icon or an open copy of ShowString, and the file opens in ShowString.

ActiveX Document Server Boilerplate   Selecting ActiveX document support makes remarkably little difference to the code generated by AppWizard. In `CShowStringApp::InitInstance()`, the versions of ShowString that were not ActiveX document servers had this call to update the Registry:

```
m_server.UpdateRegistry(OAT_INPLACE_SERVER);
```

The ActiveX document version of Showstring has this line:

```
m_server.UpdateRegistry(OAT_DOC_OBJECT_SERVER);
```

In both cases, `m_server` is a `CShowStringSrvrItem`, but now the ActiveX document server version has a server item that inherits from `CDocObjectServerItem`. This causes a number of little changes throughout the source and includes files for `CShowStringSrvrItem`, where base class functions are called. Similarly, the in-place frame object, `CInPlaceFrame`, now inherits from `COleDocIPFrameWnd`.

Showing Off the Newest ShowString   Restore the ShowString functionality once again as described in the section "Showing a String Again," earlier in this chapter. Build the application, run it once to register it, and then run the Microsoft Binder (if you have Office installed). Choose Section Add to bring up the Add Section dialog box shown in Figure 15.20. Highlight ShowString Document and click OK.

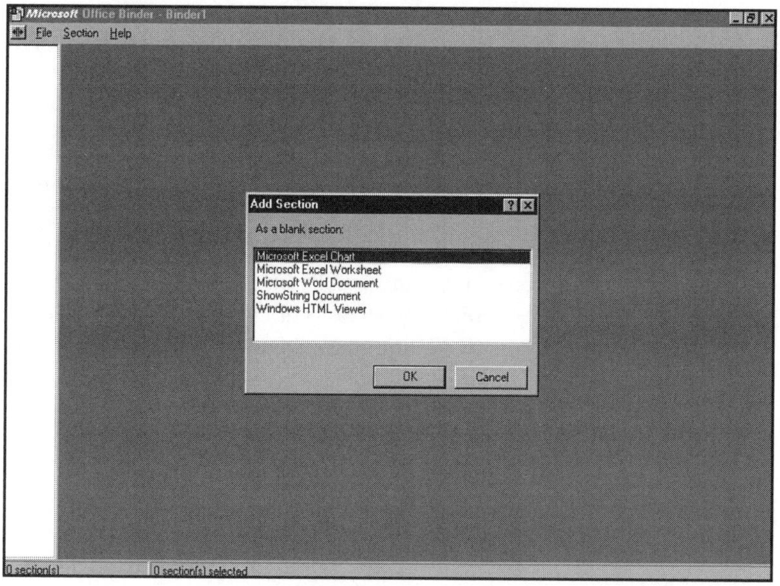

FIG. 15.20
Not many applications on the market are ActiveX document servers, but you can write one in minutes.

The menus include ShowString's Tools menu, as before. Choose Tools Options and change something—for example, in Figure 15.21, the string has been changed to "Hello from the Binder" and the vertical centering has been turned off. You have access to all of ShowString's functionality, although it doesn't look as though you are running ShowString.

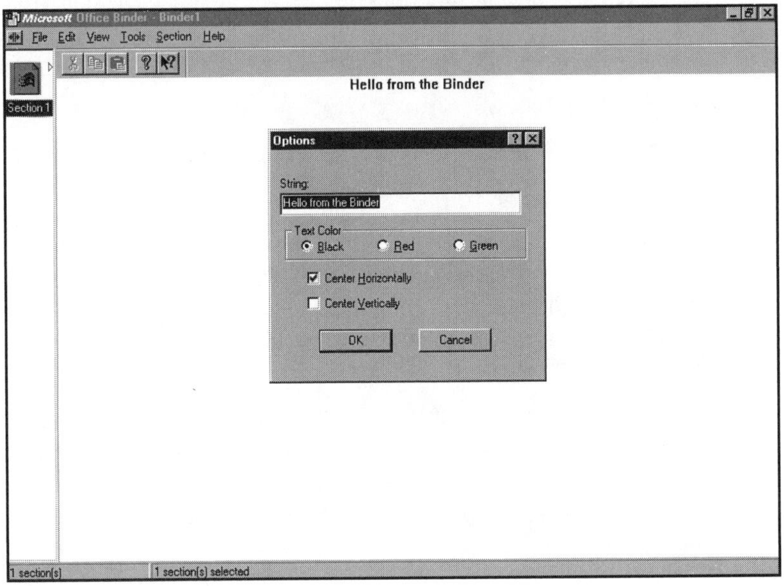

FIG. 15.21

All of ShowString's functionality is available from within the Binder.

Now run ShowString alone and save a document by choosing File, Save. You do not need to enter an extension: The extension .sst is used automatically. Open Internet Explorer 3.0 and choose File, Open. On the Open dialog box, shown in Figure 15.22, click Browse and explore until you reach the file you saved, then click Open.

Your ShowString document opens in Explorer, as you can see in Figure 15.23. The toolbar is clearly the Explorer toolbar, but the menu has the Tools item, and you can change the string, centering, and color as before. If you use the Back button on the Explorer toolbar, you reload the previous document you had open. If you change the ShowString document before clicking Back, you'll even be prompted to save your changes! Microsoft plans to integrate the desktop in the next generation of Windows with the Internet Explorer interface. What you see here is a sneak preview of how that will work.

FIG. 15.22
The Internet Explorer
Open dialog box is
used to open files on
your hard drive or the
Internet.

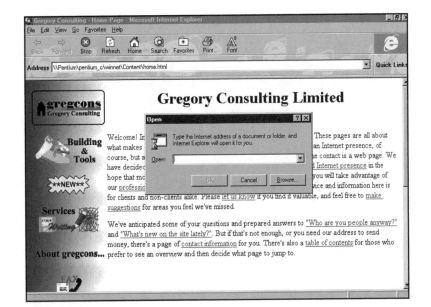

FIG. 15.23
Internet Explorer
appears to be able
to read and write
ShowString files now.

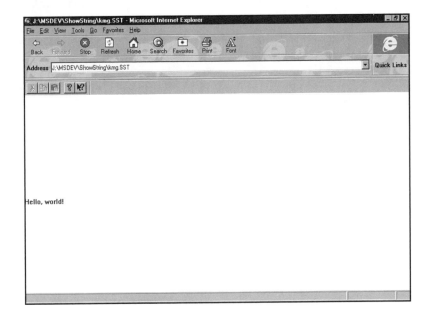

From Here...

This chapter built a third version of ShowString that can act as an ActiveX server. The AppWizard boilerplate did not need to be modified much, and now you can embed a ShowString document in any ActiveX container. You also saw how to construct a ShowString that is both a server and a container. Your glimpse into the future of Windows came with the ActiveX Document Objects, the Microsoft Office Binder, and the idea of opening a Word document in another application like Microsoft Internet Explorer. Eventually Windows will look very much like Internet Explorer, and it's ActiveX Document Objects that will make that possible.

To explore some related material, try these chapters:

- Chapter 9, "Building a Complete Application: ShowString," introduced the ShowString application.

- Chapter 13, "ActiveX Concepts," is a road map to Part V of this book and defines many of the concepts used in this and related chapters.

- Chapter 14, "Building an ActiveX Container Application," builds the second version of ShowString, which acts as an ActiveX container.

- Chapter 16, "Building an Automation Server," builds a fourth version of ShowString; this time it's an ActiveX Automation server that can be controlled from Visual Basic.

- Chapter 17, "Building an ActiveX Control," leaves ShowString behind and builds a control you can include in any Visual C++ or Visual Basic program.

Building an Automation Server

Automation, formerly called OLE Automation and then ActiveX Automation, is about writing code that other programs can call. Other programs call your code, not in the insulated manner of a DLL, but directly. The jargon is that your code *exposes* both *methods* (functions) and *properties* (variables) to other applications. The good part is that if your application is an automation server, you don't have to create a macro language for your application; you only have to make hooks for a more universal macro language, Visual Basic for Applications, to grab onto. ■

Designing ShowString Again

If you've been building the sample applications throughout this book, you can probably design ShowString in your sleep by now, but it's time to do it once again. This time, ShowString is not going to have a Tools, Options menu—instead, other programs will directly set the string and other display options. The member variables in the document will be the same, and the code in OnDraw() will be the same as in all the other implementations of ShowString.

AppWizard's Automation Boilerplate

To build the version of ShowString that is an automation server, first use AppWizard to create an empty shell. Run AppWizard as usual, but in a different directory from your other versions of ShowString. Make almost exactly the same AppWizard choices as before: call it ShowString and then choose an MDI application and no database support. In AppWizard's Step 4, choose No Compound Document Support (the radio buttons at the top of the dialog box), but turn on support for Automation. Continue through the AppWizard process, selecting a docking toolbar, status bar, printing and print preview, context-sensitive Help, and 3-D controls. Finally, select source file comments and a shared DLL.

> **N O T E**   Even though the technology is now called ActiveX, and ActiveX Automation is starting to be known simply as Automation, the AppWizard dialog boxes refer to Compound Document Support. As well, many of the class names that are used throughout this chapter have Ole in their names, and comments refer to OLE. While Microsoft has changed the name of the technology, it has not propagated that change throughout Visual C++, yet. You will have to live with these contradictions until the next release of Visual C++. ▓

There are just a few differences in this application from the do-nothing application without Automation support, primarily in the application object and the document.

CShowStringApp   The application object, CShowStringApp, has a number of changes. In the source file, just before InitInstance(), the code shown in Listing 16.1 has been added:

Listing 16.1   ShowString.cpp—*CLSID*

```
// This identifier was generated to be statistically unique for your app.
// You may change it if you prefer to choose a specific identifier.

// {61C76C05-70EA-11D0-9AFF-0080C81A397C}
static const CLSID clsid =
{ 0x61c76c05, 0x70ea, 0x11d0, { 0x9a, 0xff, 0x0, 0x80, 0xc8,
    0x1a, 0x39, 0x7c } };
```

The numbers will be different in your code. This class ID identifies your automation application.

CShowStringApp::InitInstance() has several changes. The lines of code in Listing 16.2 initialize the ActiveX (OLE) libraries.

Listing 16.2   ShowString.cpp—Initializing Libraries

```
// Initialize OLE libraries
if (!AfxOleInit())
{
    AfxMessageBox(IDP_OLE_INIT_FAILED);
    return FALSE;
}
```

As with the server application, `InitInstance()` goes on to connect the document template to the `COleTemplateServer`, after the document template has been initialized:

```
m_server.ConnectTemplate(clsid, pDocTemplate, FALSE);
```

Then `InitInstance()` checks to see if the server is being launched to edit an embedded object or as an automation server; if so, there is no need to display the main window, so the function returns early, as shown in Listing 16.3.

Listing 16.3   ShowString.cpp—How the App Was Launched

```
// Check to see if launched as OLE server
if (cmdInfo.m_bRunEmbedded ¦¦ cmdInfo.m_bRunAutomated)
{
    // Application was run with /Embedding or /Automation.  Don't show the
    //   main window in this case.
    return TRUE;
}

// When a server application is launched stand-alone, it is a good idea
//   to update the system registry in case it has been damaged.
m_server.UpdateRegistry(OAT_DISPATCH_OBJECT);
COleObjectFactory::UpdateRegistryAll();
```

If ShowString is being run as a stand-alone application, the code in Listing 16.3 updates the Registry as discussed in Chapter 15, "Building an ActiveX Server Application."

CShowStringDoc   The document class, `CShowStringDoc`, still inherits from `CDocument` rather than from any OLE document class, but that's where the similarities to the old non-OLE `CShowStringDoc` end. The first block of new code in ShowStringDoc.cpp is right after the message map and is shown in Listing 16.4

Listing 16.4   ShowStringDoc.cpp—Dispatch Map

```
BEGIN_DISPATCH_MAP(CShowStringDoc, CDocument)
    //{{AFX_DISPATCH_MAP(CShowStringDoc)
        // NOTE - the ClassWizard will add and remove mapping macros here.
        //        DO NOT EDIT what you see in these blocks of generated code!
    //}}AFX_DISPATCH_MAP
END_DISPATCH_MAP()
```

This is an empty *dispatch map*. A dispatch map is like a message map, in that it maps events in the real world into function calls within this C++ class. When you expose methods and properties of this document with ClassWizard, the dispatch map will be updated.

After the dispatch map is another unique identifier, the IID (interface identifier). As Listing 16.5 shows, the IID is added as a static member, like the CLSID.

Listing 16.5 ShowStringDoc.cpp—*IID*

```
// Note: we add support for IID_IShowString to support typesafe binding
//   from VBA.  This IID must match the GUID that is attached to the
//   dispinterface in the .ODL file.

// {61C76C07-70EA-11D0-9AFF-0080C81A397C}
static const IID IID_IShowString =
{ 0x61c76c07, 0x70ea, 0x11d0, { 0x9a, 0xff, 0x0, 0x80,
    0xc8, 0x1a, 0x39, 0x7c } };
```

Then the *interface map* looks like this:

```
BEGIN_INTERFACE_MAP(CShowStringDoc, CDocument)
    INTERFACE_PART(CShowStringDoc, IID_IShowSt, Dispatch)
END_INTERFACE_MAP()
```

An interface map hides ActiveX functions like QueryInterface() from you, the programmer, and, like a message map, allows you to think at a more abstract level. ShowString will not have multiple entries in the interface map, but many applications do. Entries in the interface map are managed for you by ClassWizard.

The document constructor has some setting up to do. The AppWizard code is in Listing 16.6.

Listing 16.6 ShowStringDoc.cpp—Constructor

```
CShowStringDoc::CShowStringDoc()
{
    // TODO: add one-time construction code here
    EnableAutomation();
    AfxOleLockApp();
}
```

EnableAutomation() does just what its name suggests: It enables automation for this document. AfxOleLockApp() is used to ensure that an application is not closed while one of its documents is still in use elsewhere. Imagine that a user has two applications open that use ShowString objects. When the first application is closed, ShowString should not be closed, because it is needed by the other application. ActiveX technology implements this by keeping a count, within the framework, of the number of active objects. AfxOleLockApp() increases this count. If it is nonzero when the user tries to close an application, the application is hidden but not actually closed.

It shouldn't be surprising, then, to see the destructor for ShowString's document:

```
CShowStringDoc::~CShowStringDoc()
{
     AfxOleUnlockApp();
}
```

`AfxOleUnlockApp()` decreases the count of active objects so that eventually, the application can be closed.

Properties to Expose

At this point, you have an automation server that does not expose any methods or properties. Also, the four member variables of the document that have been in all the previous versions of ShowString have not been added to this version. These member variables are the following:

- `string`. The string to be shown
- `color`. 0 for black, 1 for red, and 2 for green
- `horizcenter`. TRUE if the string should be centered horizontally
- `vertcenter`. TRUE if the string should be centered vertically

These variables will be added as automation properties, so you will not type their names into the class definition for `CShowStringDoc`. Bring up ClassWizard by clicking its toolbar button or choosing View, ClassWizard. Click the Automation tab, shown in Figure 16.1, to add properties and methods. Make sure that `CShowStringDoc` is selected in the Class name box.

FIG. 16.1
ClassWizard's Automation tab handles most of the work of building an Automation server.

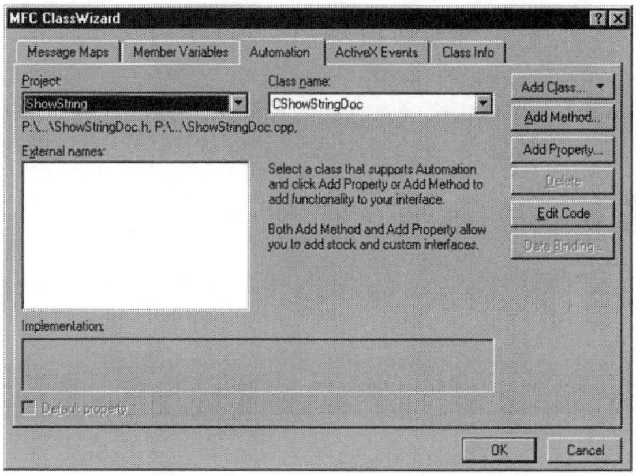

The first step in restoring the old ShowString functionality is to add member variables to the document class that will be exposed as properties of the automation server. There are two ways to expose properties: as a variable, and with functions. Exposing a property as a variable is rather like declaring a public member variable of a C++ class; other applications can look at the value of the property and change it directly. A notification function within your server is called when the variable is changed from the outside. Exposing with `Get` and `Set` functions is like implementing a private member variable with public access functions. Other applications appear to access the variable directly, but the framework arranges for a call to your functions to Get and Set the property. Your Get may make sure that the object is in a valid state (for example, that a sorted list is currently sorted or that a total has been calculated) before returning the property value. Your Set function may do error checking (validation) or may calculate other variables that depend on the property that the outside application is changing. To make a property read-only, you add it as a Get/Set function property and then do not implement a Set function.

For the purposes of this chapter, you will add the two centering flags to the CShowStringDoc class with Get and Set functions, and the string and color properties as direct-access properties. To do so, follow these steps:

1. Make sure that CShowStringDoc is the selected class, then click the Add Property button to bring up the Add Property dialog box.

2. Type **String** in the External name box, and ClassWizard types along with you, filling in the Variable name and Notification function boxes for you.

3. Choose CString from the drop-down list box for Type, and then the dialog box should resemble Figure 16.2.

FIG. 16.2

Add String as a direct-access property.

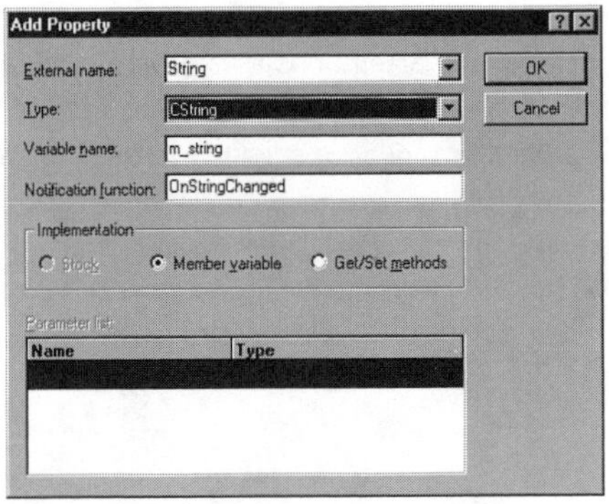

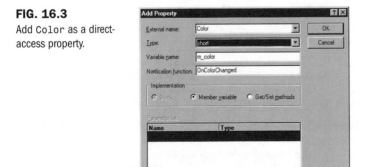

4. Click OK, click Add Property again, and then add Color as a direct-access property, as shown in Figure 16.3. Use short as the data type.

FIG. 16.3

Add Color as a direct-access property.

5. Click OK, click Add Property again, and then add HorizCenter.

6. Choose BOOL for the type and then select the Get/Set methods radio button. The Variable name and Notification function boxes are replaced by Get function and Set function, already filled in, as shown in Figure 16.4. (If the type changes from BOOL, choose BOOL again.) Click OK.

7. Add VertCenter in the same way that you added HorizCenter.

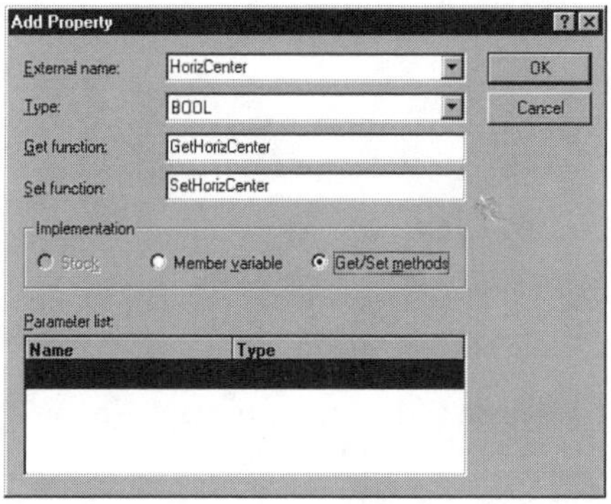

FIG. 16.4

Add HorizCenter as a Get/Set method property.

CAUTION

Once you have clicked OK to add a property, you cannot change the type, external name, or other properties of the property. You will have to delete it and then add one that has the new type or external name, or whatever. Always look over the Add Property dialog box before clicking OK.

Figure 16.5 shows the ClassWizard summary of exposed properties and methods. The details of each property are shown in the Implementation box below the list of properties. In Figure 16.5, VertCenter is highlighted, and the Implementation box reminds you that VertCenter has a Get function and a Set function, showing their declarations. Click OK to close ClassWizard.

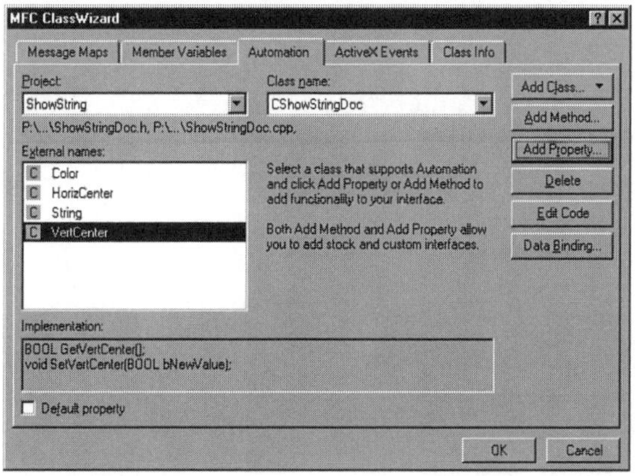

FIG. 16.5

ClassWizard provides a summary of the properties you have added.

Part

V

Ch

16

It should come as no surprise that as a result of these additions, ClassWizard has made changes to the header and source files for `CShowStringDoc`. The new dispatch map in the header file is in Listing 16.7.

Listing 16.7 ShowStringDoc.h—Dispatch Map

```
//{{AFX_DISPATCH(CShowStringDoc)
CString m_string;
afx_msg void OnStringChanged();
short m_color;
afx_msg void OnColorChanged();
afx_msg BOOL GetHorizCenter();
afx_msg void SetHorizCenter(BOOL bNewValue);
afx_msg BOOL GetVertCenter();
afx_msg void SetVertCenter(BOOL bNewValue);
//}}AFX_DISPATCH
DECLARE_DISPATCH_MAP()
```

Two new member variables have been added: `m_string` and `m_color`.

N O T E It's natural to wonder if these are actually public member variables; they are not. Just above this dispatch map is this line:

```
DECLARE_MESSAGE_MAP()
```

And that macro, when it expands, declares a number of protected variables. Since these declarations are immediately afterward, they are protected member variables and protected functions. They are accessed in just the same way that protected message-catching functions are: They are called by a member function hidden in the class that directs traffic using these maps. ■

A block of code has been added in the source file, but it's pretty boring, as you can see by looking at Listing 16.8.

Listing 16.8 ShowStringDoc.cpp—Notification, *Get*, and *Set* functions

```
/////////////////////////////////////////////////////////
// CShowStringDoc commands


void CShowStringDoc::OnColorChanged()
{
    // TODO: Add notification handler code

}

void CShowStringDoc::OnStringChanged()
{
    // TODO: Add notification handler code

}
```

```
BOOL CShowStringDoc::GetHorizCenter()
{
     // TODO: Add your property handler here

     return TRUE;
}

void CShowStringDoc::SetHorizCenter(BOOL bNewValue)
{
     // TODO: Add your property handler here

}

BOOL CShowStringDoc::GetVertCenter()
{
     // TODO: Add your property handler here

     return TRUE;
}

void CShowStringDoc::SetVertCenter(BOOL bNewValue)
{
     // TODO: Add your property handler here

}
```

Part

V

Ch

16

The class still does not have member variables for the centering flags. Add them by hand to the header file, as private member variables:

```
// Attributes
private:
     BOOL m_horizcenter;
     BOOL m_vertcenter;
```

Now you can write their Get and Set functions; Listing 16.9 shows the code.

Listing 16.9   ShowStringDoc.cpp—*Get* and *Set* Functions for the Centering Flags

```
BOOL CShowStringDoc::GetHorizCenter()
{
     return m_horizcenter;
}

void CShowStringDoc::SetHorizCenter(BOOL bNewValue)
{
     m_horizcenter = bNewValue;
}

BOOL CShowStringDoc::GetVertCenter()
{
     return m_vertcenter;
}
```

continues

Listing 16.9   Continued

```
void CShowStringDoc::SetVertCenter(BOOL bNewValue)
{
    m_vertcenter = bNewValue;
}
```

The *OnDraw()* function

Restoring the member variables takes you halfway to the old functionality of ShowString. Changing the view's OnDraw() function will take you most of the rest of the way.

To write a version of OnDraw() that shows a string properly, open an old version of ShowString—either from your own work in Chapter 9, "Building a Complete Application: ShowString," or from the CD that comes with this book—and then paste in the following bits of code. (If any of this code is unfamiliar to you, Chapter 9 explains it fully.) First, CShowStringDoc::OnNewDocument() (Listing 16.10) should initialize the member variables.

Listing 16.10   ShowStringDoc.cpp—CShowStringDoc::OnNewDocument()

```
BOOL CShowStringDoc::OnNewDocument()
{
    if (!CDocument::OnNewDocument())
        return FALSE;

    m_string = "Hello, world!";
    m_color = 0;      //black
    m_horizcenter = TRUE;
    m_vertcenter = TRUE;

    return TRUE;
}
```

Next, edit the document's Serialize function; the new code is shown in Listing 16.11.

Listing 16.11   ShowStringDoc.cpp—CShowStringDoc::Serialize()

```
void CShowStringDoc::Serialize(CArchive& ar)
{
    if (ar.IsStoring())
    {
        ar << m_string;
        ar << m_color;
        ar << m_horizcenter;
        ar << m_vertcenter;
    }
    else
    {
        ar >> m_string;
        ar >> m_color;
```

```
            ar >> m_horizcenter;
            ar >> m_vertcenter;
        }
    }
```

Finally, the view's OnDraw() function (Listing 16.12) actually shows the string.

Listing 16.12   ShowStringView.cpp—*CShowStringView::OnDraw()*

```
void CShowStringView::OnDraw(CDC* pDC)
{

    CShowStringDoc* pDoc = GetDocument();
    ASSERT_VALID(pDoc);

    COLORREF oldcolor;
    switch (pDoc->GetColor())
    {
    case 0:
        oldcolor = pDC->SetTextColor(RGB(0,0,0)); //black
        break;
    case 1:
        oldcolor = pDC->SetTextColor(RGB(0xFF,0,0)); //red
        break;
    case 2:
        oldcolor = pDC->SetTextColor(RGB(0,0xFF,0)); //green
        break;
    }

    int DTflags = 0;
    if (pDoc->GetHorizcenter())
    {
        DTflags |= DT_CENTER;
    }
    if (pDoc->GetVertcenter())
    {
        DTflags |= (DT_VCENTER|DT_SINGLELINE);
    }

    CRect rect;
    GetClientRect(&rect);
    pDC->DrawText(pDoc->GetString(), &rect, DTflags);
    pDC->SetTextColor(oldcolor);

}
```

When you added m_string, m_color, m_horizcenter, and m_vertcenter to the document with ClassWizard, they were added as protected member variables. This view code needs access to them. As you can see, the view calls public functions to get to these member variables of the document.

N O T E You could have chosen instead to make the view a friend to the document so that it could access the member variables directly, but that would give view functions the ability to use and change all the private and protected member variables of the document. This more limited access is more appropriate, and better preserves encapsulation. ■

There are already several functions in the document class that access these variables, but they are protected functions for use by ActiveX. The four public functions you will add have not-so-good names. Add them inline, as shown in Listing 16.13, to ShowStringDoc.h.

Listing 16.13   ShowStringDoc.h—Public Access Functions

```
public:
    CString GetDocString() {return m_string;}
    int     GetDocColor() {return m_color;}
    BOOL GetHorizcenter() {return m_horizcenter;}
    BOOL GetVertcenter() {return m_vertcenter;}
```

In `CShowStringView::OnDraw()`, change the call to `GetColor()` to a call to `GetDocColor()`, and change the call to `GetString()` to a call to `GetDocString()`. Build the project to check for any typing mistakes or forgotten changes. While it may be tempting to run ShowString now, it's not going to do what you expect until you make a few more changes.

Showing the Window

By default, automation servers do not have a main window. Remember the little snippet from `CShowStringApp::InitInstance()` shown in Listing 16.14.

Listing 16.14   ShowString.cpp—How the App Was Launched

```
// Check to see if launched as OLE server
if (cmdInfo.m_bRunEmbedded || cmdInfo.m_bRunAutomated)
{
    // Application was run with /Embedding or /Automation.  Don't show the
    //  main window in this case.
    return TRUE;
}
```

This code returns before showing the main window. While you could remove this test so that ShowString always shows its window, it's more common to add a `ShowWindow()` method for the controller application to call. You'll also need to add a `RefreshWindow()` method that updates the view after a variable is changed; ClassWizard makes it simple to add these functions. Bring up ClassWizard, click the Automation tab, make sure that `CShowStringDoc` is still the selected class, and then click Add Method. Fill in the external name as `ShowWindow`. ClassWizard fills in the internal name for you, and there's no need to change it. Choose `void` from the Return type drop-down list box. Figure 16.6 shows the dialog box after it has been filled in.

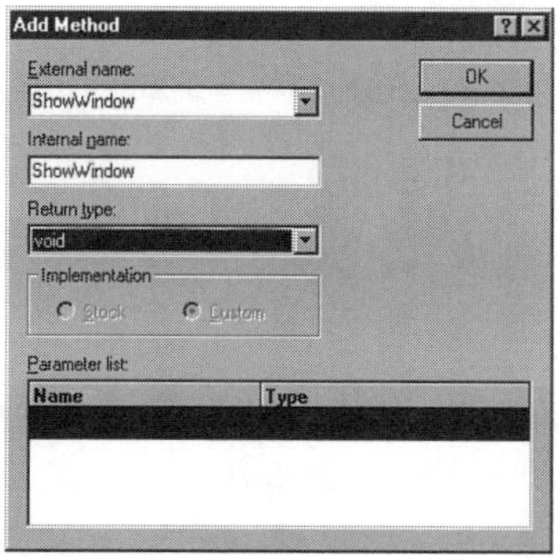

FIG. 16.6

ClassWizard makes it simple to add a `ShowWindow()` method.

Click OK, and `ShowWindow()` appears in the middle of the list of properties, which turns out to be a list of properties and methods in alphabetical order. The *C* next to the properties reminds you that these properties are custom properties (other types of properties are discussed in the "Displaying the Current Value" section of the next chapter, "Building an ActiveX Control"). The *M* next to the methods reminds you that these are methods. With `ShowWindow()` highlighted, click Edit Code and then type in the function, as shown in Listing 16.15

Listing 16.15 ShowStringDoc.cpp—*CShowStringDoc::ShowWindow()*

```
void CShowStringDoc::ShowWindow()
{
    POSITION pos = GetFirstViewPosition();
    CView* pView = GetNextView(pos);
    if (pView != NULL)
    {
        CFrameWnd* pFrameWnd = pView->GetParentFrame();
        pFrameWnd->ActivateFrame(SW_SHOW);
        pFrameWnd = pFrameWnd->GetParentFrame();
        if (pFrameWnd != NULL)
            pFrameWnd->ActivateFrame(SW_SHOW);
    }
}
```

This code activates the view and asks for it to be shown. Bring up ClassWizard again, click Add Method, and add `RefreshWindow()`, returning `void`. Click OK and then Edit Code. The code for `RefreshWindow()`, shown in Listing 16.16, is even simpler.

Listing 16.16 ShowStringDoc.cpp—*CShowStringDoc::RefreshWindow()*

```
void CShowStringDoc::RefreshWindow()
{
    UpdateAllViews(NULL);
    SetModifiedFlag();
}
```

Part

V

Ch

16

This arranges for the view (now that it's active) and its parent frame to be redrawn. And, because a change to the document is almost certainly the reason for the redraw, this is a handy place to put the call to `SetModifiedFlag()`, though if you prefer, you can put it in each `Set` function and the notification functions for the direct-access properties. You will add a call to `RefreshWindow()` to each of those functions now. For example, `SetHorizCenter()` is shown in Listing 16.17.

Listing 16.17 ShowStringDoc.cpp—*CShowStringDoc::SetHorizCenter()*

```
void CShowStringDoc::SetHorizCenter(BOOL bNewValue)
{
    m_horizcenter = bNewValue;
    RefreshWindow();
}
```

And `OnColorChanged()` looks like this:

```
void CShowStringDoc::OnColorChanged()
{
    RefreshWindow();
}
```

Add the same `RefreshWindow()` call to `SetVertCenter()` and `OnStringChanged()`. Now you are ready to build and test. Build the project and correct any typing errors. Run ShowString as a stand-alone application, both to register it and to test your drawing code. You cannot change the string, color, or centering as you could with older versions of ShowString, because this version does not implement the Tools, Options menu item and its dialog box. The controller application is going to do that for this version.

Visual Basic

This chapter has mentioned a controller application several times, and you may have wondered where it's going to come from. You are going to put it together in Visual Basic. Figure 16.7 shows the Visual Basic interface.

T I P If you don't have Visual Basic, but you do have an earlier release of Visual C++, you can use DispTest, a watered-down version of Visual Basic that once came with Visual C++. It was never added to the Start menu, but you can run DISPTEST.EXE from the C:\MSDEV\BIN folder or from your old Visual C++ CD-ROM's \MSDEV\BIN folder. If you've written VBA macros in Excel and have a copy of Excel, you can use that, too. For testing OLE Automation servers, it doesn't matter which you choose.

To build a controller application for the ShowString Automation server, start by running Visual Basic. In the window at the upper-right labeled Project1, click the View Code button. Choose Form from the left-hand drop-down list box in the new window that appears, and the `Form_Load()` subroutine is displayed. Enter the code in Listing 16.18 into that subroutine.

FIG. 16.7
Visual Basic makes
Automation controller
applications very
quickly.

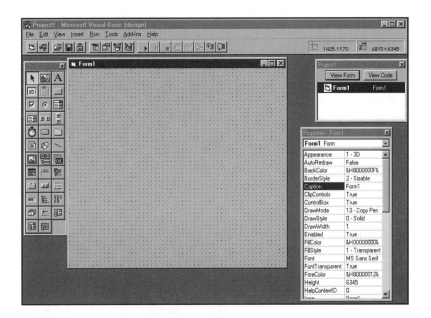

Part
V

Ch
16

Listing 16.18   Form1.frm—Visual Basic Code

```
Private Sub Form_Load ()
    Set ShowTest = CreateObject("ShowString.Document")
    ShowTest.ShowWindow
    ShowTest.HorizCenter = False
    ShowTest.Color = 1
    ShowTest.String = "Hello from VB"
    Set ShowTest = Nothing
End Sub
```

Choose (General) from the left-hand drop-down list box and then enter this line of code:

```
Dim ShowTest As Object
```

For those of you who don't read Visual Basic, this code will be easier to understand if you execute it one line at a time. Choose Run, Step Into to execute the first line of code. Then repeatedly press F8 to move through the routine. (Wait after each press until the cursor is back to normal.) The line in the general code sets up an object called ShowTest. When the form is loaded (which is whenever you run this little program), an instance of the ShowString object is created. The next line calls the ShowWindow method to display the main window on the screen. Whenever the debugger pauses, the dashed box is around the line of code that will run next. You should see something like Figure 16.8 with the default ShowString behavior.

Press F8 again to run the line that turns off horizontal centering. Notice that you do not call the function SetHorizCenter. You exposed HorizCenter as a property of the OLE Automation server, and from Visual Basic, you access it as a property. The difference is that the C++ framework code calls SetHorizCenter to make the change, rather than just making the change and then calling a notification function to tell you that it was changed. After this line has executed, your screen will resemble Figure 16.9, because the `SetHorizCenter` method calls `RefreshWindow()` to immediately redraw the screen.

FIG. 16.8

The `ShowWindow` method displays the main ShowString window.

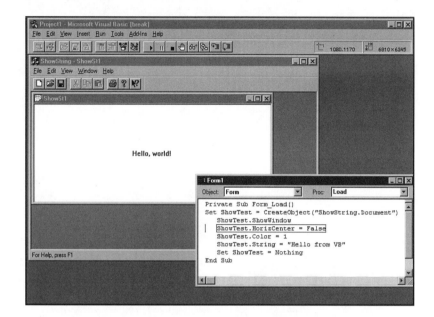

FIG. 16.9

The Visual Basic program has turned off centering.

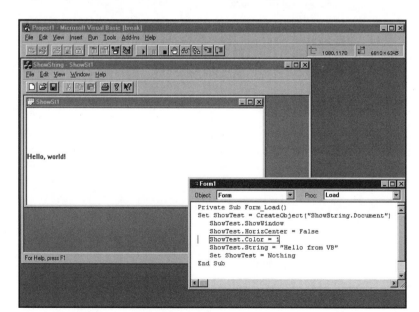

As you continue through this program, pressing F8 to move a step at a time, the string will turn red and then change to `Hello from VB`. Notice that the change to these directly exposed properties looks no different than the change to the `Get/Set` method property, `HorizCenter`. When the program finishes, the window goes away. You have successfully controlled your Automation server from Visual Basic.

Type Libraries and ActiveX Internals

Part
V

Ch
16

Many programmers are intimidated by ActiveX, and the last thing they want is to know what's happening under the hood. There's nothing wrong with that attitude at all. It's quite object-oriented, really, to trust the already-written ActiveX framework to handle the black magic of translating `ShowTest.HorizCenter = False` into a call to `CShowStringDoc::SetHorizCenter()`. But if you want to know how that "magic" happens, or what to do if it doesn't, you need to add one more piece to the puzzle. You have already seen the dispatch map for ShowString, but you haven't seen the *type library*. It is not meant for humans to read, but it's for ActiveX and the Registry. It is generated for you as part of a normal build from your Object Definition Language (ODL) file. This file was generated by AppWizard and is maintained by ClassWizard.

Perhaps you've noticed, as you built this application, a new entry in the ClassView pane. Figure 16.10 shows this entry expanded: It contains all the properties and methods exposed in the `IShowString` interface of your Automation Server. If you right-click `IShowString` in this list, you can use the shortcut menu to add methods or properties. If you double-click any of the properties or methods, the old file is opened for you to view. Listing 16.19 shows ShowString.odl.

FIG. 16.10
Automation servers have an entry in the ClassView for each of their interfaces

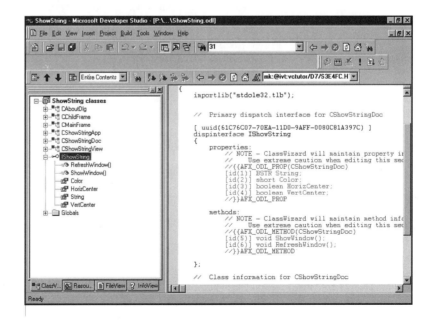

Listing 16.19 ShowString.odl—*ShowString* Type Library

```
// ShowString.odl : type library source for ShowString.exe

// This file will be processed by the MIDL compiler to produce the
// type library (ShowString.tlb).

[ uuid(61C76C06-70EA-11D0-9AFF-0080C81A397C), version(1.0) ]
library ShowString
{
    importlib("stdole32.tlb");


    //  Primary dispatch interface for CShowStringDoc

    [ uuid(61C76C07-70EA-11D0-9AFF-0080C81A397C) ]
    dispinterface IShowString
    {
        properties:
            // NOTE - ClassWizard will maintain property information here.
            //    Use extreme caution when editing this section.
            //{{AFX_ODL_PROP(CShowStringDoc)
            [id(1)] BSTR String;
            [id(2)] short Color;
            [id(3)] boolean HorizCenter;
            [id(4)] boolean VertCenter;
            //}}AFX_ODL_PROP

        methods:
            // NOTE - ClassWizard will maintain method information here.
            //    Use extreme caution when editing this section.
            //{{AFX_ODL_METHOD(CShowStringDoc)
            [id(5)] void ShowWindow();
            [id(6)] void RefreshWindow();
            //}}AFX_ODL_METHOD

    };

    //  Class information for CShowStringDoc

    [ uuid(61C76C05-70EA-11D0-9AFF-0080C81A397C) ]
    coclass Document
    {
        [default] dispinterface IShowString;
    };

    //{{AFX_APPEND_ODL}}
    //}}AFX_APPEND_ODL}}
};
```

This explains why Visual Basic just thought of all four properties as properties; that's how they are listed in this ODL file. The two methods are here, too, in the methods section. The reason you passed "ShowString.Document" to CreateObject() is that there is a coclass Document section here. It points to a dispatch interface (dispinterface) called IShowString. Here's the interface map from ShowStringDoc.cpp:

```
BEGIN_INTERFACE_MAP(CShowStringDoc, CDocument)
    INTERFACE_PART(CShowStringDoc, IID_IShowString, Dispatch)
END_INTERFACE_MAP()
```

So a call to CreateObject("ShowString.Document") leads to the coclass section of the odl file, which points to IShowString. The interface map points from IShowString to CShowStringDoc, which has a dispatch map that connects the properties and methods in the outside world to C++ code. You can see that editing any of these sections by hand could have disastrous results. Trust the wizards to do this for you.

From Here...

In this chapter, you built an Automation server and controlled it from Visual Basic. Automation servers are far more powerful than older ways of application interaction, but your server doesn't have any user interaction. If the Visual Basic program wanted to allow the user to choose the color, that would have to be built into the Visual Basic program. The next logical step is to allow the little embedded object to react to user events like clicks and drags, and to report to the controller program what has happened. That's what ActiveX controls do, as you'll see in the next chapter. Some chapters you may want to read include:

- Chapter 9, "Building a Complete Application: ShowString," introduced the ShowString application.
- Chapter 13, "ActiveX Concepts," is a roadmap to Part IV of this book and defines many of the concepts used in this and related chapters.
- Chapter 14, "Building an ActiveX Container Application," built the second version of ShowString, which acts as an ActiveX container.
- Chapter 15, "Building an ActiveX Server Application," built the third version of ShowString, which acts as an ActiveX server.
- Chapter 17, "Building an ActiveX Control," leaves ShowString behind and builds a control you can include in any Visual C++ or Visual Basic program.

Building an ActiveX Control

ActiveX controls replace OLE controls, though the change affects more the name than anything else. (Much of the Microsoft documentation still refers to OLE controls.) The exciting behavior of these controls is powered by ActiveX, formerly known as OLE. This chapter draws, in part, on the ActiveX work of the previous chapters. An ActiveX control is similar to an ActiveX Automation server, but an ActiveX control also exposes *events*, and those enable the control to direct the container's behavior.

ActiveX controls take the place that VBX controls held in 16-bit Windows programming, allowing programmers to extend the control set provided by the compiler. The original purpose of VBX controls was to allow programmers to provide their users with unusual interface controls. Controls that looked like gas gauges or volume knobs became easy to develop. Almost immediately, however, VBX programmers moved beyond simple controls to modules that involved significant amounts of calculation and processing. In the same way, many ActiveX controls are far more than just controls—they are *components* that can be used to build powerful applications quickly and easily. ■

Designing a die-roll control

The sample application for this chapter rolls a die. This section describes the control and starts the building process.

Displaying the die

Drawing a control and adding a property to a control are explained in this section.

Reacting to clicks: rolling the die

ActiveX controls notify their containers of user activities with events. This section explains events and works you through the process of getting your control to roll a new number whenever a user clicks the control.

Improving the user interface

Adding more properties gives the user more flexibility. This section shows you how.

Implementing property sheets

Adding property sheets to a control is quite simple, with much of the work already done for you. This section demonstrates the process.

A Rolling-Die Control

The sample application for this chapter is a *die,* one of a pair of dice. Imagine a picture of a cubic die with the familiar pattern of dots indicating the current value, between 1 and 6. When the user clicks the picture, a new, randomly-chosen number is shown. You might implement one or more dice into any game program.

Building the Control Shell

The process of building this die control starts, as always, with AppWizard. Start Developer Studio and then choose File, New. Click the Project tab, then click MFC ActiveX ControlWizard, which is in the list at the left of the dialog box; fill in a project name at the top, choose an appropriate folder for the project files, and then click OK. Figure 17.1 shows the completed dialog box, with the project name `Dieroll`.

> **NOTE** Even though the technology is now called ActiveX, many of the class names that are used throughout this chapter have `Ole` in their names, and comments refer to OLE. Though Microsoft has changed the name of the technology, it has not yet propagated that change throughout Visual C++. You will have to live with these contradictions until the next release of Visual C++. ∎

FIG. 17.1

AppWizard makes creating an ActiveX control simple.

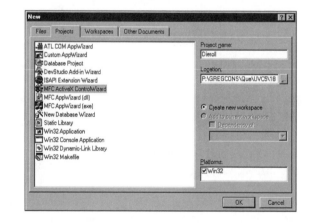

There are two steps in the ActiveX control wizard. Fill out the first dialog box as shown in Figure 17.2: you want one control, no runtime licensing, source-file comments, and no help files. After you have completed the dialog box, click Next.

FIG. 17.2

AppWizard's first step sets your control's basic parameters.

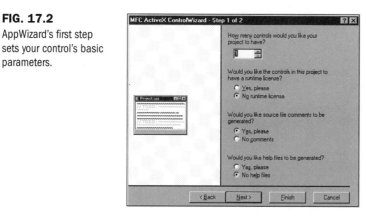

Part

V

Ch

17

Runtime Licensing

Many developers produce controls as a product that they sell. Other programmers buy the rights to use such a control in their programs. Imagine that a developer, Alice, produces a fantastic die control and sells it to Bob, who incorporates it into the best backgammon game ever. Carol buys the backgammon game and loves the die control, and she decides that it would be perfect for a children's board game she is planning. Since the DIEROLL.OCX file is in the backgammon package, there is nothing (other than ethics) to stop her from doing this.

Runtime licensing is simple: There is a second file—DIEROLL.LIC—that contains the licensing information. Without that file, a control cannot be embedded into a form or program, though a program into which the control is already embedded will work perfectly. Alice ships both DIEROLL.OCX and DIEROLL.LIC to Bob, but their licensing agreement states that only DIEROLL.OCX goes out with the backgammon game. Now Carol can admire DIEROLL.OCX, and it will work perfectly in the backgammon game, but if she wants to include it in the game she builds, she'll have to buy a license from Alice.

You arrange for runtime licensing with AppWizard when you first build the control. If you decide, after the control is already built, that you should have asked for runtime licensing after all, build a new control with licensing and copy your changes into that control.

The second and final AppWizard step allows you to set the new control's features. Make sure that Activates when visible, Available in "Insert Object" dialog, and Has an "About" box are selected, as shown in Figure 17.3, and then click Finish. AppWizard summarizes your settings in a final dialog box. Click OK, and AppWizard creates 19 files for you and adds them to a project to make them easy to work with. These files are ready to compile, but they don't do anything at the moment. You have an empty shell; it is up to you to fill it.

FIG. 17.3

AppWizard's second step governs the appearance and behavior of your control.

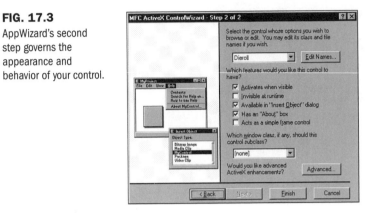

AppWizard's Code

Nineteen files sounds like a lot, but it isn't. There are only three classes: CDierollApp, CDierollCtrl, and CDierollPropPage. They take up six files; the other 13 are the project file, make file, resource file, ClassWizard database, ODL file, and so on.

CDierollApp   CDierollApp is a very small class. It inherits from COleControlModule and provides overrides of InitInstance() and ExitInstance() that do nothing but call the base-class versions of these functions. This is where you find _tlid, the external globally unique ID for your control, and some version numbers that make delivering upgrades of your control simpler. The lines in Dieroll.cpp that set up these identifiers are the following:

```
const GUID CDECL BASED_CODE _tlid =
    { 0x914b21a5, 0x7946, 0x11d0, { 0x9b, 0x1, 0, 0x80, 0xc8, 0x1a, 0x39, 0x7c }
};const WORD _wVerMajor = 1;
const WORD _wVerMinor = 0;
```

CDierollCtrl   The CDierollCtrl class inherits from COleControl, and it overrides the constructor and destructor, plus these four functions:

- OnDraw() draws the control.
- DoPropExchange() implements persistence and initialization.
- OnResetState() causes the control to be reinitialized.
- AboutBox() displays the About box for the control.

None of the code for these functions is particularly interesting. However, some of the maps that have been added to this class are interesting. There is an empty message map, which is ready to accept new entries, and an empty dispatch map, which is ready for the properties and methods that you choose to expose.

TIP   Message maps were explained in the "Message Maps" section of Chapter 4, "Messages and Commands." Dispatch maps are discussed the "AppWizard's Automation Boilerplate" section in Chapter 16, "Building an Automation Server."

Below the empty message and dispatch maps comes a new map: the *event map*. The event map in the header file is shown in Listing 17.1, and the source file event map is shown in Listing 17.2.

Listing 17.1   Excerpt from DierollCtl.h—Event map

```
// Event maps
    //{{AFX_EVENT(CDierollCtrl)
        // NOTE - ClassWizard will add and remove member functions here.
        //    DO NOT EDIT what you see in these blocks of generated code !
    //}}AFX_EVENT
    DECLARE_EVENT_MAP()
```

Listing 17.2   Excerpt from DierollCtl.cpp—Event map

```
BEGIN_EVENT_MAP(CDierollCtrl, COleControl)
    //{{AFX_EVENT_MAP(CDierollCtrl)
    // NOTE - ClassWizard will add and remove event map entries
    //    DO NOT EDIT what you see in these blocks of generated code !
    //}}AFX_EVENT_MAP
END_EVENT_MAP()
```

Event maps, like message maps and dispatch maps, link real-world happenings to your code. Message maps catch things the user does, such as choosing a menu item or clicking a button. They also catch messages sent from one part of an application to another. Dispatch maps direct requests to access properties or invoke methods of an Automation server or ActiveX control. Event maps direct notifications from an ActiveX control to the application that contains the control (and are discussed in more detail later in this chapter).

There's one more piece of code worth noting in DierollCtl.cpp. It is shown in Listing 17.3.

Listing 17.3   Excerpt from DierollCtl.cpp—Property pages

```
/////////////////////////////////////////////////////////////////////////
// Property pages

// TODO: Add more property pages as needed.   Remember to increase the count!
BEGIN_PROPPAGEIDS(CDierollCtrl, 1)
    PROPPAGEID(CDierollPropPage::guid)
END_PROPPAGEIDS(CDierollCtrl)
```

The code in Listing 17.3 is part of the mechanism that implements powerful and intuitive property pages in your controls. That mechanism is discussed later in this chapter.

CDierollPropPage   The entire CDierollPropPage class is the property of ClassWizard. Like any class with a dialog box in it, it has significant data exchange components. The constructor will initialize the dialog box fields by using code added by ClassWizard. This code is shown in Listing 17.4.

Listing 17.4 DierollPpg.cpp—*CDierollPropPage::CDierollPropPage()*

```
CDierollPropPage::CDierollPropPage() :
    COlePropertyPage(IDD, IDS_DIEROLL_PPG_CAPTION)
{
    //{{AFX_DATA_INIT(CDierollPropPage)
    // NOTE: ClassWizard will add member initialization here
    //    DO NOT EDIT what you see in these blocks of generated code !
    //}}AFX_DATA_INIT
}
```

The DoDataExchange() function moderates the exchange of data between CDierollPropPage, which represents the dialog box that is the property page, and the actual boxes on the user's screen. It, too, is written by ClassWizard—see Listing 17.5.

Listing 17.5 DierollPpg.cpp—*CDierollPropPage::DoDataExchange()*

```
void CDierollPropPage::DoDataExchange(CDataExchange* pDX)
{
    //{{AFX_DATA_MAP(CDierollPropPage)
    // NOTE: ClassWizard will add DDP, DDX, and DDV calls here
    //    DO NOT EDIT what you see in these blocks of generated code !
    //}}AFX_DATA_MAP
    DDP_PostProcessing(pDX);
}
```

There is, not surprisingly, a message map for CDierollPropPage, and some registration code (shown in Listing 17.6), that will enable the ActiveX framework to call this code when a user edits the control's properties.

Listing 17.6 DierollPpg.cpp—*CDierollPropPage::UpdateRegistry()*

```
/////////////////////////////////////////////////////////////////////
// Initialize class factory and guid

IMPLEMENT_OLECREATE_EX(CDierollPropPage, "DIEROLL.DierollPropPage.1",
    0x914b21a8, 0x7946, 0x11d0, 0x9b, 0x1, 0, 0x80, 0xc8, 0x1a, 0x39, 0x7c)


/////////////////////////////////////////////////////////////////////
// CDierollPropPage::CDierollPropPageFactory::UpdateRegistry -
// Adds or removes system registry entries for CDierollPropPage

BOOL CDierollPropPage::CDierollPropPageFactory::UpdateRegistry(BOOL bRegister)
{
    if (bRegister)
        return AfxOleRegisterPropertyPageClass(AfxGetInstanceHandle(),
            m_clsid, IDS_DIEROLL_PPG);
    else
        return AfxOleUnregisterClass(m_clsid, NULL);
}
```

Designing the Control

Typically, a control has *internal data* (properties) and shows them in some way to the user. The user provides input to the control to change its internal data and perhaps the way the control looks. Some controls present data to the user from other sources, such as databases or remote files. The only internal data that makes sense for the die-roll control, other than some appearance settings that is covered later, is a single integer between one and six that represents the current number showing in the die. Eventually, the control will show a dot pattern like a real-world die, but the first implementation of `OnDraw()` will simply display the digit. Another simplification is to hard code the digit to a single value while coding the basic structure; add the code to roll the die later, while dealing with input from the user.

Displaying the Current Value

Before the value can be displayed, the control must have a value to display. That involves adding a property to the control and then writing the drawing code.

Part
V

Ch
17

Adding a Property

ActiveX controls have four types of properties:

- ▓ `Stock`: These are standard properties supplied to every control, such as font or color. The developer must activate stock properties, but there is little or no coding involved.

- ▓ `Ambient`: These are properties of the environment that surrounds the control—of the container into which it has been placed. These cannot be changed, but the control can use them to adjust its own properties. For example, it can set the control's background color to match the container's background color.

- ▓ `Extended`: These are properties that will be handled by the container, typically involving size and placement on the screen.

- ▓ `Custom`: These are properties added by the control developer.

To add the value to the die-roll control, use ClassWizard to add a custom property called `Number`. Follow these steps:

1. Choose <u>V</u>iew, Class<u>W</u>izard, and then click the Automation tab.
2. Make sure that the drop-down list box at the upper-left of the dialog box is set to `Dieroll` (unless you chose a different name when building the control with AppWizard) and that the right-hand box has the class name `CDieRollCtrl`.
3. Click the Add <u>P</u>roperty button and fill in the dialog box as shown in Figure 17.4.
4. Type **Number** into the External Name combo box and notice how ClassWizard fills in suggested values for the Variable name and Notification function boxes.
5. Select `short` for the type.
6. Click OK to close the Add Property dialog box and OK to close ClassWizard.

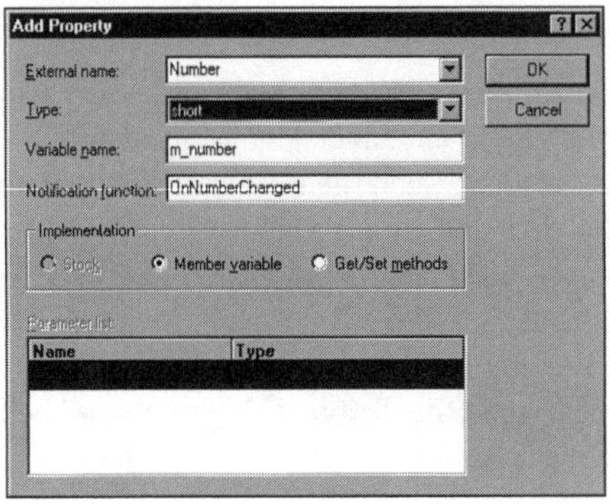

FIG. 17.4
ClassWizard simplifies the process of adding a custom property to your die-rolling control.

Before you can write code to display the value of the Number property, the property must have a value to display. Control properties are initialized in DoPropExchange(). This method actually implements *persistence*; that is, it allows the control to be saved as part of a document and read back in when the document is opened. Whenever a new control is created, the properties cannot be read from a file, so they are set to the default values provided in this method. Controls do not have a Serialize() method.

AppWizard generated a skeleton DoPropExchange() method whose code is in Listing 17.7.

Listing 17.7   DierollCtl.cpp—*CDierollCtrl::DoPropExchange()*

```
void CDierollCtrl::DoPropExchange(CPropExchange* pPX)
{
    ExchangeVersion(pPX, MAKELONG(_wVerMinor, _wVerMajor));
    COleControl::DoPropExchange(pPX);

    // TODO: Call PX_ functions for each persistent custom property.

}
```

Notice the use of the version numbers to be sure that a file holding the values was saved by the same version of the control. Take away the TODO comment that AppWizard left for you, and add this line:

```
PX_Short( pPX, "Number",  m_number, (short)3 );
```

PX_Short() is one of many property-exchange functions that you can call—one for each property type that is supported. The parameters you supply are as follows:

- ■ The pointer that was passed to DoPropExchange()
- ■ The external name of the property as you typed it on the ClassWizard Add Property dialog box
- ■ The member variable name of the property as you typed it on the ClassWizard Add Property dialog box

- The default value for the property (later, you can replace this hard-coded 3 with a random value)

The following are the PX functions:

```
PX_Blob()  (for binary large object [BLOB] types)
PX_Bool()
PX_Color()  (OLE_COLOR)
PX_Currency()
PX_DATAPATH  (CDataPathProperty)
PX_Double()
PX_Float()
PX_Font()
PX_IUnknown()  (for LPUNKNOWN types, COM interface pointer)
PX_Long()
PX_Picture()
PX_Short()
PX_String()
PX_ULong()
PX_UShort()
```

Filling in the property's default value is simple for some properties, but not so simple for others. For example, you set colors with the RGB() macro, which takes values for red, green, and blue from 0 to 255 and returns a COLORREF. Say that you had a property with the external name EdgeColor and the internal name m_edgecolor, and you wanted the property to default to gray. You would code that like the following:

```
PX_Short( pPX, "EdgeColor", m_edgecolor, RGB(128,128,128) );
```

Controls with font properties should, by default, set the font to whatever the container is using. To get this font, call the COleControl method AmbientFont().

Writing the Drawing Code

The code to display the number belongs in the OnDraw() method of the control class, CDierollCtrl. (Controls do not have documents or views.) This function is called automatically whenever Windows needs to repaint the part of the screen that includes the control. AppWizard generated a skeleton of this method too, shown in Listing 17.8.

Listing 17.8 DierollCtl.cpp—*CDierollCtrl::OnDraw()*

```
void CDierollCtrl::OnDraw(CDC* pdc, const CRect& rcBounds,
    const CRect& rcInvalid)
{
    // TODO: Replace the following code with your own drawing code.
    pdc->FillRect(rcBounds,
    CBrush::FromHandle((HBRUSH)GetStockObject(WHITE_BRUSH)));
    pdc->Ellipse(rcBounds);
}
```

As discussed in the "Scrolling Windows" section of Chapter 6, "Drawing On the Screen," the framework passes the function a device context to draw in, a CRect describing the space occupied by your control, and another CRect describing the space that has been invalidated. The code in Listing 17.8 draws a white rectangle throughout rcBounds and then draws an ellipse inside that rectangle, using the default foreground color. Although you can keep the white rectangle for now, rather than draw an ellipse on it, draw a character that corresponds to the value in Number. To do that, replace the last line in the skeletal OnDraw() with these lines:

```
CString val; //character representation of the short value
val.Format("%i",m_number);
pdc->ExtTextOut( 0, 0, ETO_OPAQUE, rcBounds, val, NULL );
```

These lines of code convert the short value in m_number (which you associated with the Number property on the Add Property dialog box) to a CString variable called val, using the new CString::Format() function (which eliminates one of the last uses of sprintf() in C++ programming). The ExtTextOut() function draws a piece of text—the character in val—within the rcBounds rectangle. As the die-roll control is written now, that number will always be 3.

You can build and test the control right now if you would like to see how little effort it takes to make a control that does something. Unlike the other ActiveX applications, a control is not run as a stand-alone application in order to register it. Build the project and fix any typing mistakes that you may have made. Choose Tools, ActiveX Control Test Container to bring up the control test container, shown in Figure 17.5.

FIG. 17.5

The ActiveX control test container is the ideal place to test your control.

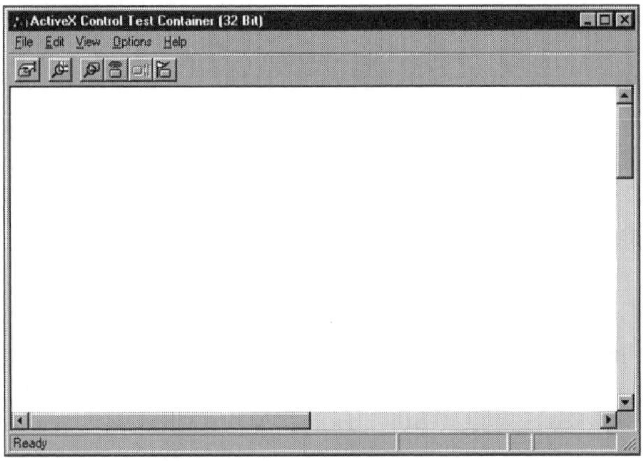

N O T E If the Tools menu in Developer Studio does not include an ActiveX Control Test Container item, you can add it to the menu by following these steps:

1. Choose Tools, Customize.

2. Click the Tools tab.

3. Look over the list of tools and make sure that ActiveX Control Test Container isn't there.

4. Go to the bottom of the list and double-click the empty entry.

5. Type **ActiveX Control Test Container** in the entry and press Enter.

6. Click the ... button to the right of the Command box and browse to your CD, or to the hard drive on which you installed Visual C++, and to the BIN folder beneath the Developer Studio folder. Highlight tstcon32.exe and click OK to finish browsing. On many systems the full path will be `C:\Program Files\DevStudio\VC\BIN\TSTCON32.EXE`. Your system may be different.

7. Click the rightward-pointing arrow beside the Initial Directory box and choose Target Directory from the list that appears.

8. Make sure that the three check boxes across the bottom of the directory are not selected.

9. Click the Close button.

If you have not built a release version, and your target is a release version, or if you have not built a debug version and your target is a release version, you will get an error message when you choose Tools, ActiveX Control Test Container. Simply build the control and you will be able to choose the menu item.

After you have installed the test container once, you will not need to do so again. By bringing up the test container from within Developer Studio like this, you make it simpler to load your die-roll control into the test container. ■

Part
V

Ch
17

Within the test container, choose Edit, Insert OLE Control, and then choose Dieroll Control from the displayed list. As Figure 17.6 shows, the control appears as a white rectangle displaying a small number 3. You can move and resize this control within the container, but that little 3 stays doggedly in the upper-left corner. The next step is to make that number change when a user clicks the die.

FIG. 17.6
By adding one property and changing two functions, you have transformed the empty shell into a control that displays a 3.

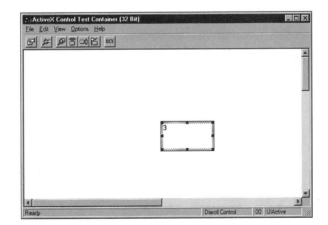

Reacting to a Mouse Click and Rolling the Die

There are actually two things that you want your control to do when the user clicks the mouse on the control: inform the container that the control has been clicked and roll the die and display the new internal value.

Notifying the Container

Let's first tackle using an *event* to notify a container. Events are how controls notify the container of a user action. Just as there are stock properties, there are stock events. These events are already coded for you:

- Click is coded to indicate to the container that the user clicked.
- DblClick is coded to indicate to the container that the user double-clicked.
- Error is coded to indicate an error that can't be handled by firing any other event.
- KeyDown is coded to indicate to the container that a key has gone down.
- KeyPress is coded to indicate to the container that a complete keypress (down and then up) has occurred.
- KeyUp is coded to indicate to the container that a key has gone up.
- MouseDown is coded to indicate to the container that the mouse button has gone down.
- MouseMove is coded to indicate to the container that the mouse has moved over the control.
- MouseUp is coded to indicate to the container that the mouse button has gone up.

The best way to tell the container that the user has clicked over the control is to fire a Click stock event. The first thing to do is to add it to the control with ClassWizard. Follow these steps:

1. Bring up ClassWizard by choosing View, ClassWizard, and click the ActiveX Events tab. Make sure that the selected class is CDierollCtrl.
2. Click the Add Event button and fill in the Add Event dialog box, as shown in Figure 17.7.

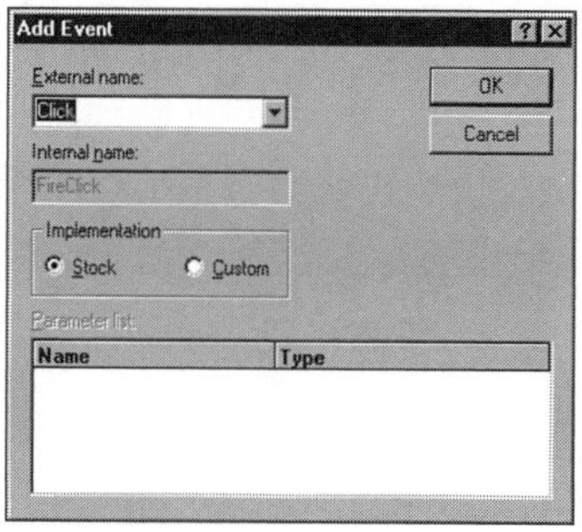

FIG. 17.7
ClassWizard helps you add events to your control.

3. The external name is Click; choose it from the drop-down list box and notice how the internal name is filled in as FireClick.
4. Click OK to add the event, and your work is done.

You may notice the ClassView pane has a new addition: two icons resembling handles. Click the + next to DDierollEvents to see that Click is now listed as an event for this application, as shown in Figure 17.8.

FIG. 17.8
ClassView displays
events as well as
classes.

Now when the user clicks the control, the container class will be notified. So if you are writing a backgammon game, for example, the container can respond to the click by using the new value on the die to evaluate possible moves or do some other backgammon-specific task.

The second part of reacting to clicks involves actually rolling the die and redisplaying it. Not surprisingly, ClassWizard helps implement this. When the user clicks over your control, you catch it with a message map entry, just as with an ordinary application. ClassWizard should still be up; if it is not, bring it up and follow these steps:

1. Select the Message Maps tab this time and make sure that your control class, CDierollCtrl, is selected in the Class Name combo box.

2. Scroll through the Messages list box until you find the WM_LBUTTONDOWN message, which is generated by Windows whenever the left mouse button is clicked over your control.

3. Click Add Function to add a function that will be called automatically whenever this message is generated—in other words, whenever the user clicks your control. This function must always be named OnLButtonDown(), so ClassWizard doesn't give you a dialog box asking you to confirm the name.

4. ClassWizard has made a skeleton version of OnLButtonDown() for you; click the Edit Code button to close ClassWizard and look at the new OnLButtonDown() code. Here's the skeleton:

```
void CDierollCtrl::OnLButtonDown(UINT nFlags, CPoint point)
{
    // TODO: Add your message handler code here and/or call default

    COleControl::OnLButtonDown(nFlags, point);
}
```

5. Replace the TODO comment with a call to a new function, Roll(), that you will write in the next section. This function will return a random number between 1 and 6.

```
m_number = Roll();
```

6. To force a redraw, next add this line:

```
InvalidateControl();
```

7. Leave the call to `COleControl::OnLButtonDown()` at the end of the function; it handles the rest of the work involved in processing the mouse click.

Rolling the Die

To add `Roll()` to `CDierollCtrl`, right-click `CDierollCtrl` in the ClassView pane, and then choose Add Member Function from the shortcut menu that appears. As shown in Figure 17.9, `Roll()` should be a public function that takes no parameters and returns a `short`.

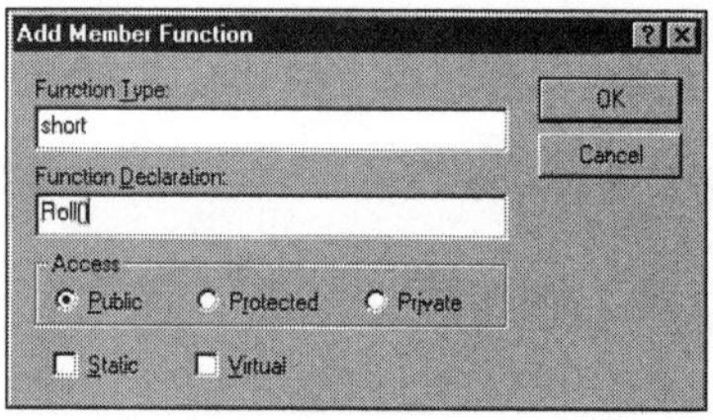

FIG. 17.9
Use the Add Member Function dialog box to speed routine tasks.

What should `Roll()` do? It should calculate a random value between 1 and 6. The C++ function that returns a random number is `rand()`, which returns an integer between 0 and `RAND_MAX`. Dividing by `RAND_MAX + 1` gives a positive number that will always be less than 1, and multiplying by 6 gives a positive number that is less than 6. The integer part of the number will be between 0 and 5, in other words. Adding 1 produces the result that you want: a number between 1 and 6. The code is shown in Listing 17.9.

Listing 17.9   DierollCtl.cpp—*CDierollCtrl::Roll()*

```
short CDierollCtrl::Roll(void)
{
    double number = rand();
    number /= RAND_MAX + 1;
    number *= 6;
    return (short)number + 1;
}
```

N O T E If `RAND_MAX + 1` isn't a multiple of 6, this code will roll low numbers slightly more often than high ones. A typical value for `RAND_MAX` is 32,767, which means that 1 and 2 will, on the average, come up 5,462 times in 32,767 rolls. However, 3 through 6 will, on the average, come up 5,461 times. You're neglecting this inaccuracy.

Some die-rolling programs use the modulo function instead of this approach, but it is far less accurate. The lowest digits in the random number are least likely to be accurate. The algorithm used here produces a much more random die roll. ■

The random number generator must be seeded before it is used, and it's traditional (and practical) to use the current time as a seed value. In `DoPropExchange()`, add the following line before the call to `PX_Short()`:

```
srand( (unsigned)time( NULL ) );
```

Instead of hard-coding the start value to 3, call `Roll()` to determine a random value. Change the call to `PX_Short()` so that it reads as follows:

```
PX_Short( pPX, "Number", m_number, Roll());
```

Build and test the control again in the test container. As you click the control, the displayed number should change with each click. Play around with it a little: Do you ever see a number less than 1 or more than 6? Any surprises at all?

A Better User Interface

Part

V

Ch

17

Now that the basic functionality of the die-roll control is in place, it's time to neaten it a little. It needs an icon, and it needs to display dots instead of a single digit.

A Bitmap Icon

Because some die-roll control users might want to add this control to the Control Palette in Visual Basic or Visual C++, you should have an icon to represent it. Actually, AppWizard has already created one, but it is simply an MFC logo that doesn't represent your control in particular. You can create a more specialized one with Developer Studio. Click the ResourceView tab of the Project Workspace window, click the + next to Bitmap, and double-click IDB_DIEROLL. You can now edit the bitmap one pixel at a time. Figure 17.10 shows an icon appropriate for a die. From now on, when you load the die-roll control into the test container, you will see your icon on the toolbar.

FIG. 17.10

The ResourceView of Visual C++ allows you to build your own icon to be added to the Control Palette in Visual Basic.

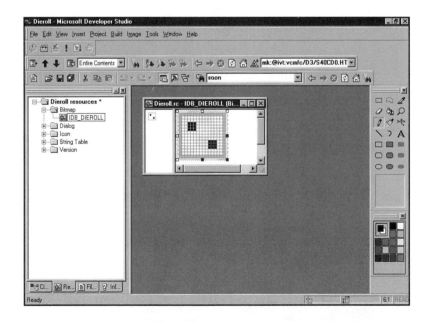

Displaying Dots

The next step in building this die-roll control is to make the control look like a die. A nice, three-dimensional effect with parts of some of the other sides showing is beyond the reach of an illustrative chapter like this one, but you can at least display a dot pattern.

The first step is to set up a switch statement in OnDraw(). Comment out the three drawing lines and then add the switch statement so that OnDraw() looks like Listing 17.10.

Listing 17.10   DierollCtl.cpp—*CDierollCtrl::OnDraw()*

```
void CDierollCtrl::OnDraw(
                CDC* pdc, const CRect& rcBounds, const CRect& rcInvalid)
{
    pdc->FillRect(rcBounds,
        CBrush::FromHandle((HBRUSH)GetStockObject(WHITE_BRUSH)));
//  CString val; //character representation of the short value
//  val.Format("%i",m_number);
//  pdc->ExtTextOut( 0, 0, ETO_OPAQUE, rcBounds, val, NULL );

    switch(m_number)
    {
    case 1:
        break;
    case 2:
        break;
    case 3:
        break;
    case 4:
        break;
    case 5:
        break;
    case 6:
        break;
    }
}
```

Now all that remains is adding code to the case 1: block that draws one dot, to the case 2: block that draws two dots, and so on. If you happen to have a real die available to you, take a close look at it. The width of each dot is about one quarter of the width of the whole die's face. Dots near the edge are about one-sixteenth of the die's width from the edge. All the other rolls except 6 are contained within the layout for 5, anyway; for example, the single dot for 1 is in the same place as the central dot for 5.

The second parameter of OnDraw(), rcBounds, is a CRect that describes the rectangle occupied by the control. It has member variables and functions that return the upper-left coordinates, width, and height of the control. The default code that AppWizard generated called CDC::Ellipse() to draw an ellipse within that rectangle. Your code will call Ellipse() too, passing a small rectangle within the larger rectangle of the control. Your code will be easier to read—and will execute slightly faster—if you work in units that are one-sixteenth of the total width or height. Each dot will be four units wide or high. Add the following code before the switch statement:

```
int Xunit = rcBounds.Width()/16;
    int Yunit = rcBounds.Height()/16;

    int Top = rcBounds.top;
    int Left = rcBounds.left;
```

Before drawing a shape by calling `Ellipse()`, you need to select a tool with which to draw. Because your circles should be filled in, they should be drawn with a brush. This code creates a brush and tells the device context `pdc` to use it, while saving a pointer to the old brush so that it can be restored later:

```
CBrush Black;
Black.CreateSolidBrush(RGB(0x00,0x00,0x00)); //solid black brush
CBrush* savebrush = pdc->SelectObject(&Black);
```

After the switch statement, add this line to restore the old brush:

```
pdc->SelectObject(savebrush);
```

Now you're ready to add lines to those `case` blocks to draw some dots. For example, rolls of 2, 3, 4, 5, or 6 all need a dot in the upper-left corner. This dot will be in a rectangular box that starts one unit to the right and down from the upper-left corner and extends five units right and down. The call to `Ellipse` looks like this:

```
pdc->Ellipse(Left+Xunit, Top+Yunit,
                Left+5*Xunit, Top + 5*Yunit);
```

The coordinates for the other dots are determined similarly. The switch statement ends up as show in in Listing 17.11.

Part
V

Ch
17

Listing 17.11   DierollCtl.cpp—CDierollCtrl::OnDraw()

```
switch(m_number)
    {
    case 1:
        pdc->Ellipse(Left+6*Xunit, Top+6*Yunit,
                        Left+10*Xunit, Top + 10*Yunit); //center
        break;
    case 2:
        pdc->Ellipse(Left+Xunit, Top+Yunit,
                        Left+5*Xunit, Top + 5*Yunit);    //upper left
        pdc->Ellipse(Left+11*Xunit, Top+11*Yunit,
                        Left+15*Xunit, Top + 15*Yunit); //lower right
        break;
    case 3:
        pdc->Ellipse(Left+Xunit, Top+Yunit,
                        Left+5*Xunit, Top + 5*Yunit);    //upper left
        pdc->Ellipse(Left+6*Xunit, Top+6*Yunit,
                        Left+10*Xunit, Top + 10*Yunit); //center
```

continues

Listing 17.11   Continued

```
            pdc->Ellipse(Left+11*Xunit, Top+11*Yunit,
                         Left+15*Xunit, Top + 15*Yunit); //lower right
            break;
        case 4:
            pdc->Ellipse(Left+Xunit, Top+Yunit,
                         Left+5*Xunit, Top + 5*Yunit);    //upper left
            pdc->Ellipse(Left+11*Xunit, Top+Yunit,
                         Left+15*Xunit, Top + 5*Yunit);   //upper right
            pdc->Ellipse(Left+Xunit, Top+11*Yunit,
                         Left+5*Xunit, Top + 15*Yunit);   //lower left
            pdc->Ellipse(Left+11*Xunit, Top+11*Yunit,
                         Left+15*Xunit, Top + 15*Yunit);  //lower right
            break;
        case 5:
            pdc->Ellipse(Left+Xunit, Top+Yunit,
                         Left+5*Xunit, Top + 5*Yunit);    //upper left
            pdc->Ellipse(Left+11*Xunit, Top+Yunit,
                         Left+15*Xunit, Top + 5*Yunit);   //upper right
            pdc->Ellipse(Left+6*Xunit, Top+6*Yunit,
                         Left+10*Xunit, Top + 10*Yunit);  //center
            pdc->Ellipse(Left+Xunit, Top+11*Yunit,
                         Left+5*Xunit, Top + 15*Yunit);   //lower left
            pdc->Ellipse(Left+11*Xunit, Top+11*Yunit,
                         Left+15*Xunit, Top + 15*Yunit);  //lower right
            break;
        case 6:
            pdc->Ellipse(Left+Xunit, Top+Yunit,
              Left+5*Xunit, Top + 5*Yunit);    //upper left
            pdc->Ellipse(Left+11*Xunit, Top+Yunit,
              Left+15*Xunit, Top + 5*Yunit);   //upper right
            pdc->Ellipse(Left+Xunit, Top+6*Yunit,
              Left+5*Xunit, Top + 10*Yunit);   //center left
            pdc->Ellipse(Left+11*Xunit, Top+6*Yunit,
                Left+15*Xunit, Top + 10*Yunit); //center right
            pdc->Ellipse(Left+Xunit, Top+11*Yunit,
              Left+5*Xunit, Top + 15*Yunit);   //lower left
            pdc->Ellipse(Left+11*Xunit, Top+11*Yunit,
              Left+15*Xunit, Top + 15*Yunit);  //lower right
            break;
    }
```

Build the OCX again and try it out in the test container. You should see something similar to Figure 17.11, which actually looks like a die!

If you're sharp-eyed or if you stretch the die very small, you might notice that the pattern of dots is just slightly off-center. That's because the control's height and width are not always an exact multiple of 16. For example, if Width() returned 31, Xunit would be 1, and all the dots would be arranged between positions 0 and 16—leaving a wide blank band at the far right of the control. Luckily, the width is typically far more than 31 pixels, and so the asymmetry is less noticeable.

FIG. 17.11

Your rolling-die control now looks like a die.

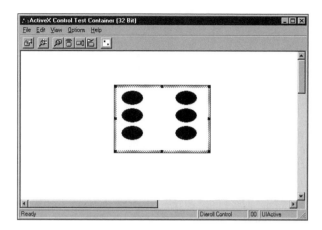

To fix this, center the dots in the control. Find the lines that calculate Xunit and Yunit, then add the new lines from the code fragment in Listing 17.12.

Listing 17.12   DierollCtl.cpp—Adjusting *Xunit* and *Yunit*

```
//dots are 4 units wide and high, one unit from the edge
int Xunit = rcBounds.Width()/16;
int Yunit = rcBounds.Height()/16;
int Xleft = rcBounds.Width()%16;
int Yleft = rcBounds.Height()%16;

// adjust top left by amount left over
int Top = rcBounds.top + Yleft/2;
int Left = rcBounds.left + Xleft/2;
```

Xleft and Yleft are the "leftovers" in the X and Y direction. By moving Top and Left over by half the leftover, we center the dots in the control without having to change any other code.

Property Sheets

ActiveX controls have property sheets that enable the user to set properties without any change to the container application. (Property sheets and pages are discussed in Chapter 12, "Property Pages and Sheets and Wizards.") You set these up as dialog boxes, taking advantage of prewritten pages for font, color, and other common properties. For this control, the obvious properties to add are the following:

- A flag to indicate whether the value should be displayed as a digit or a dot pattern
- Foreground color
- Background color

Part
V

Ch
17

N O T E It's easy to get confused about what, exactly, a property page is: Is each one of the tabs on a dialog box a separate page, or is the whole collection of tabs a page? Each tab is called a *page* and the collection of tabs is called a *sheet*. You set up each page as a dialog box and use ClassWizard to connect the values on that dialog box to member variables. ■

Digits versus Dots

It's a simple enough matter to allow the user to choose whether to display the current value as a digit or a dot pattern. Simply add a property that indicates this preference and then use the property in OnDraw(). The user can set the property using the property page.

First, add the property by using ClassWizard. Here's how: Bring up ClassWizard and select the Automation tab. Make sure that the CDierollCtrl class is selected and then click Add Property. On the Add Property dialog box, provide the external name Dots and the internal name m_dots. The type should be BOOL, because Dots can be either TRUE or FALSE. Implement this new property as a member variable (direct-access) property. Click OK to complete the Add Property dialog box and click OK to close ClassWizard. The member variable is added to the class, the dispatch map is updated, and a stub is added for the notification function, OnDotsChanged().

To initialize Dots and arrange for it to be saved with a document, add the following line to DoPropExchange() after the call to PX_Short():

```
PX_Bool( pPX, "Dots", m_dots, TRUE);
```

Initializing the Dots property to TRUE ensures that the default behavior of the control is to display the dot pattern.

In OnDraw(), uncomment those lines that displayed the digit. Wrap an if around them so the digit is displayed if m_dots is FALSE, and dots are displayed if it is TRUE. The code looks like Listing 17.13.

Listing 17.13   DierollCtl.cpp—*CDierollCtrl::OnDraw()*

```
void CDierollCtrl::OnDraw(
            CDC* pdc, const CRect& rcBounds, const CRect& rcInvalid)
{
    pdc->FillRect(rcBounds,
        CBrush::FromHandle((HBRUSH)GetStockObject(WHITE_BRUSH)));

    if (!m_dots)
    {
        CString val; //character representation of the short value
        val.Format("%i",m_number);
        pdc->ExtTextOut( 0, 0, ETO_OPAQUE, rcBounds, val, NULL );
    }
    else
    {
        //dots are 4 units wide and high, one unit from the edge
            int Xunit = rcBounds.Width()/16;
```

```
        int Yunit = rcBounds.Height()/16;
        int Xleft = rcBounds.Width()%16;
        int Yleft = rcBounds.Height()%16;

        // adjust top left by amount left over
        int Top = rcBounds.top + Yleft/2;
        int Left = rcBounds.left + Xleft/2;

        CBrush Black;
        Black.CreateSolidBrush(RGB(0x00,0x00,0x00)); //solid black brush

        CBrush* savebrush = pdc->SelectObject(&Black);

        switch(m_number)
        {
        case 1:
                ...
        }
        pdc->SelectObject(savebrush);
    }
}
```

To give the user a way to set Dots, you build a property page by following these steps:

1. Click the ResourceView tab in the Project Workspace window and then click the + next to Dialog.

2. The OCX has two dialog boxes: one for the About box and one for the property page. Double-click IDD_PROPPAGE_DIEROLL to open it. The boilerplate property page generated by AppWizard is shown in Figure 17.12.

FIG. 17.12

AppWizard generates an empty property page.

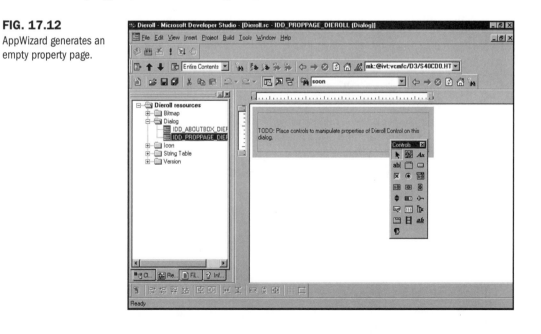

3. Remove the static control with the TODO reminder by highlighting it and pressing Delete.

4. Drag a check box from the Control Palette onto the dialog box; choose View, Properties; and then pin the Property dialog box in place.

5. Change the caption to Display Dot Pattern and change the resource ID to IDC_DOTS, as shown in Figure 17.13.

FIG. 17.13
You build the property page for the die-roll control like any other dialog box.

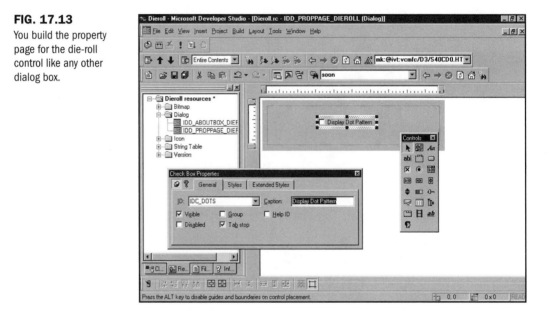

When the user brings up the property page and clicks to set or unset the check box, that does not directly affect the value of m_dots or the Dots property. To connect the dialog box to member variables, use ClassWizard and follow these steps:

1. Bring up Class Wizard while the dialog box is still open and on top and then select the Member Variables tab.

2. Make sure that CDierollPropPage is the selected class and that the IDC_DOTS resource ID is highlighted, and then click the Add Variable button.

3. Fill in m_dots as the name and BOOL as the type, and fill in the Optional Property Name combo box with Dots, as shown in Figure 17.14.

4. Click OK, and ClassWizard generates code to connect the property page with the member variables in CDierollPropPage::DoDataExchange().

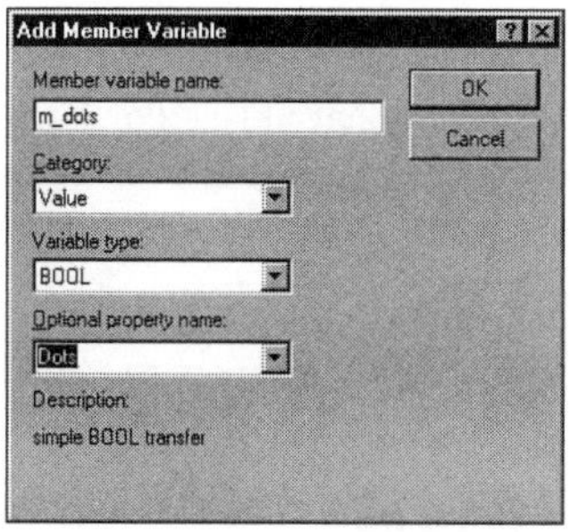

FIG. 17.14

You connect the property page to the properties of the control with ClassWizard.

The path that data follows can be a little twisty. When the user brings up the property sheet, the value of TRUE or FALSE is in a temporary variable. Clicking the check box toggles the value of that temporary variable. When the user clicks OK, that value goes into CDierollPropPage::m_dots and also to the Automation property Dots. That property has already been connected to CDierollCtrl:: m_dots, so the dispatch map in CDierollCtrl will make sure that the other m_dots gets changed. Since the OnDraw() function uses CDierollCtrl:: m_dots, the appearance of the control changes in response to the change made by the user on the property page. Having the same name for the two member variables makes things more confusing to first-time control builders, but makes it less confusing in the long run.

This works now. Build the control and insert it into the test container. To change the properties, choose Edit, Dieroll Control Object, and Properties; your own property page should appear, as shown in Figure 17.15. Prove to yourself that the control displays dots or a digit, depending on the page's setting, by changing the setting, clicking OK, and then watching the control redraw.

FIG. 17.15

Your own property page is displayed by the control test container.

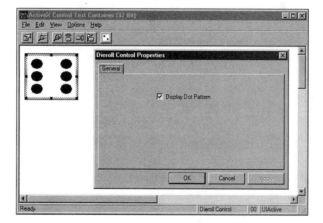

When the control is displaying the value as a number, you might want to display that number in a font that's more in proportion with the control's current width and height and centered within the control. That's a relatively simple modification to OnDraw(), which you can investigate on your own.

Part

V

Ch

17

User-Selected Colors

The die you've created up to this point will always have black dots on a white background, but giving the user control to change this is remarkably simple. You will need a property for the foreground color and another for the background color. These have already been implemented as stock properties: BackColor and ForeColor.

Stock Properties   Here is the complete list of stock properties available to a control that you write:

- Appearance, which specifies the control's general look
- BackColor, which specifies the control's background color
- BorderStyle, which specifies either the standard border or no border
- Caption, which specifies the control's caption or text
- Enabled, which specifies whether the control can be used
- Font, which specifies the control's default font
- ForeColor, which specifies the control's foreground color
- Text, which also specifies the control's caption or text
- hWnd, which specifies the control's window handle

Ambient Properties   Controls can also access *ambient properties,* which are properties of the environment that surrounds the control—that is, properties of the *container* into which you place the control. You cannot change ambient properties, but the control can use them to adjust its own properties; for example, the control can set its background color to match that of the container.

The container provides all support for ambient properties. Any of your code that uses an ambient property should be prepared to use a default value if the container does not support that property. Here's how to use an ambient property called UserMode:

```
BOOL bUserMode;
    if( !GetAmbientProperty( DISPID_AMBIENT_USERMODE,
        VT_BOOL, &bUserMode ) )
    {
        bUserMode = TRUE;
    }
```

This code calls GetAmbientProperty() with the display ID (dispid) and variable type (vartype) required. It also provides a pointer to a variable into which the value is placed. This variable's type must match the vartype. If GetAmbientProperty() returns FALSE, bUserMode is set to a default value.

The following dispids are displayed in olectl.h. :

```
DISPID_AMBIENT_BACKCOLOR
DISPID_AMBIENT_DISPLAYNAME
DISPID_AMBIENT_FONT
DISPID_AMBIENT_FORECOLOR
DISPID_AMBIENT_LOCALEID
```

```
DISPID_AMBIENT_MESSAGEREFLECT
DISPID_AMBIENT_SCALEUNITS
DISPID_AMBIENT_TEXTALIGN
DISPID_AMBIENT_USERMODE
DISPID_AMBIENT_UIDEAD
DISPID_AMBIENT_SHOWGRABHANDLES
DISPID_AMBIENT_SHOWHATCHING
DISPID_AMBIENT_DISPLAYASDEFAULT
DISPID_AMBIENT_SUPPORTSMNEMONICS
DISPID_AMBIENT_AUTOCLIP
DISPID_AMBIENT_APPEARANCE
```

Remember that not all containers support all of these properties; some might not support any, and still others might support properties not included in the preceding list.

The vartypes include those shown in Table 17.1.

Part

V

Ch

17

Table 17.1   Variable Types for Ambient Properties

Vartype	Description
VT_BOOL	BOOL
VT_BSTR	CString
VT_I2	short
VT_I4	long
VT_R4	float
VT_R8	double
VT_CY	CY
VT_COLOR	OLE_COLOR
VT_DISPATCH	LPDISPATCH
VT_FONT	LPFONTDISP

Remembering which vartype goes with which dispid and checking the return from GetAmbientProperty() is a bothersome process, so the framework provides member functions of COleControl, to get the most popular ambient properties:

- OLE_COLOR AmbientBackColor()
- CString AmbientDisplayName()
- LPFONTDISP AmbientFont() (Don't forget to release the font by using Release().)
- OLE_COLOR AmbientForeColor()
- LCID AmbientLocaleID()
- CString AmbientScaleUnits()
- short AmbientTextAlign() (0 means general—numbers right, text left—1 means left-justify, 2 means center, and 3 means right-justify.)

■ BOOL AmbientUserMode() (TRUE means user mode; FALSE means design mode.)

■ BOOL AmbientUIDead()

■ BOOL AmbientShowHatching()

■ BOOL AmbientShowGrabHandles()

All these functions assign reasonable defaults if the container does not support the requested property.

Implementing *BackColor* and *ForeColor*   To add BackColor and ForeColor to the control, follow these steps:

1. Bring up ClassWizard, and select the Automation tab.

2. Make sure that CDierollCtrl is the selected class, and click Add Property.

3. Choose BackColor from the top combo box, and the rest of the dialog box is filled out for you; it is grayed out to remind you that you cannot set any of these fields for a stock property. Figure 17.16 shows the values that are provided for you.

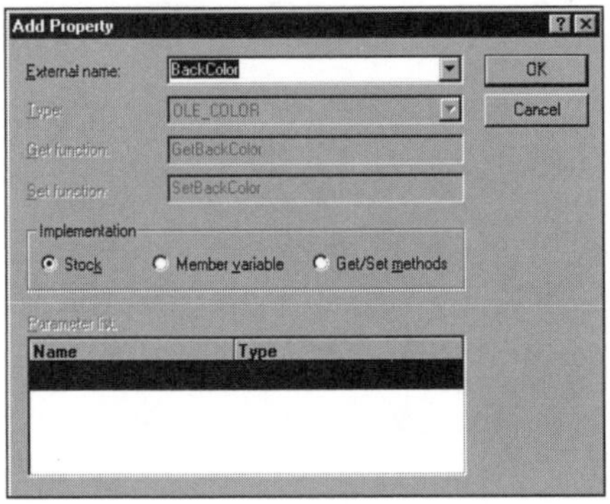

FIG. 17.16

Stock properties are described for you by Class Wizard.

4. Click OK and then add ForeColor in the same way. After you click OK, ClassWizard's Automation tab should resemble Figure 17.17. The *S* next to these new properties reminds you that they are stock properties.

5. Click OK to close ClassWizard.

Setting up the property pages for these colors is almost as simple, because there is a prewritten page that you can use. Look through DierollCtl.cpp for a block of code like Listing 17.14.

Listing 17.14   DierollCtl.cpp—Property pages

```
/////////////////////////////////////////////////////////////
// Property pages

// TODO: Add more property pages as needed.  Remember to increase the
count!BEGIN_PROPPAGEIDS(CDierollCtrl, 1)
    PROPPAGEID(CDierollPropPage::guid)
END_PROPPAGEIDS(CDierollCtrl)
```

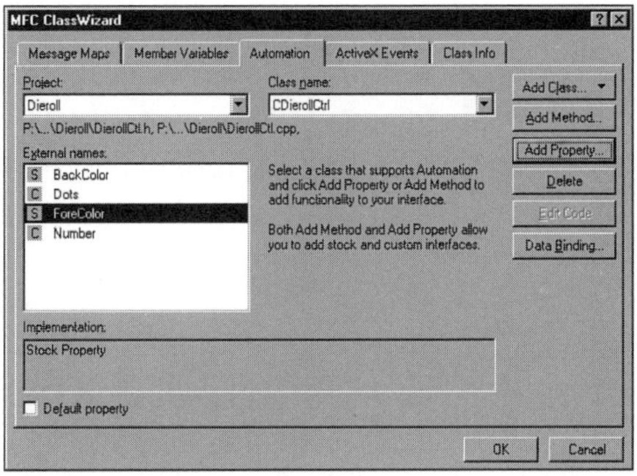

FIG. 17.17
Stock properties are highlighted with an *S* in the OLE Automation list of properties and methods.

Remove the TODO reminder, change the count to 2, and add another PROPPAGEID, so that the block looks like Listing 17.15.

Listing 17.15 DierollCtl.cpp—Property pages

```
//////////////////////////////////////////////////////////////////////////////
// Property pages

BEGIN_PROPPAGEIDS(CDierollCtrl, 2)
    PROPPAGEID(CDierollPropPage::guid)
    PROPPAGEID(CLSID_CColorPropPage)
END_PROPPAGEIDS(CDierollCtrl)
```

CLSID_CColorPropPage is a class ID for a property page that is used to set colors. Now when the user brings up the property sheet, there will be two property pages: one to set colors and the general page that you already created. Both ForeColor and BackColor will be available on this page, so all that remains to be done is using the values that are set by the user. You get a chance to see that very soon, but first, your code needs to use these colors.

Changes to *OnDraw()*   In OnDraw(), your code can access the background color with GetBackColor(). Though you can't see it, this function was added by ClassWizard when you added the stock property. The dispatch map for CDierollCtrl now looks like Listing 17.16.

Listing 17.16 DierollCtl.cpp—Dispatch Map

```
BEGIN_DISPATCH_MAP(CDierollCtrl, COleControl)
    //{{AFX_DISPATCH_MAP(CDierollCtrl)
    DISP_PROPERTY_NOTIFY(CDierollCtrl, "Number", m_number, OnNumberChanged,
➥VT_I2)
    DISP_PROPERTY_NOTIFY(CDierollCtrl, "Dots", m_dots, OnDotsChanged, VT_BOOL)
    DISP_STOCKPROP_BACKCOLOR()
```

continues

Listing 17.16 Continued

```
      DISP_STOCKPROP_FORECOLOR()
      //}}AFX_DISPATCH_MAP
      DISP_FUNCTION_ID(CDierollCtrl, "AboutBox", DISPID_ABOUTBOX, AboutBox,
      ➥VT_EMPTY, VTS_NONE)
  END_DISPATCH_MAP()
```

The macro DISP_STOCKPROP_BACKCOLOR() expands to these lines:

```
#define DISP_STOCKPROP_BACKCOLOR() \
    DISP_PROPERTY_STOCK(COleControl, "BackColor", \
    DISPID_BACKCOLOR,        COleControl::GetBackColor, \
    COleControl::SetBackColor, VT_COLOR)
```

This code is calling another macro, DISP_PROPERTY_STOCK, which ends up declaring the GetBackColor() function as a member of CDierollCtrl, which inherits from COleControl. So although you can't see it, this function is available to you. It returns an OLE_COLOR, which you translate to a COLORREF with TranslateColor(). You can pass this COLORREF to CreateSolidBrush() and use that brush to paint the background. Access the foreground color with GetForeColor() and give it the same treatment. (Use SetTextColor() in the digit part of the code.) Listing 17.17 shows the completed OnDraw (with most of the switch statement cropped out).

Listing 17.17   DierollCtl.cpp—*CDierollCtrl::OnDraw()*

```
void CDierollCtrl::OnDraw(CDC* pdc, const CRect& rcBounds,
                          const CRect& rcInvalid)
{
    COLORREF back = TranslateColor(GetBackColor());
    CBrush backbrush;
    backbrush.CreateSolidBrush(back);
    pdc->FillRect(rcBounds, &backbrush);

    if (!m_dots)
    {
        CString val; //character representation of the short value
        val.Format("%i",m_number);
        pdc->SetTextColor(TranslateColor(GetForeColor()));
        pdc->ExtTextOut( 0, 0, ETO_OPAQUE, rcBounds, val, NULL );
    }
    else
    {
        //dots are 4 units wide and high, one unit from the edge
        int Xunit = rcBounds.Width()/16;
        int Yunit = rcBounds.Height()/16;

        int Top = rcBounds.top;
        int Left = rcBounds.left;

        COLORREF fore = TranslateColor(GetForeColor());
        CBrush forebrush;
        forebrush.CreateSolidBrush(fore);
```

```
        CBrush* savebrush = pdc->SelectObject(&forebrush);

        switch(m_number)
                ...
    }
}
```

Build the control once again, insert it into the test container, and again bring up the property sheet by choosing Edit, Dieroll Control Object, Properties. As Figure 17.18 shows, the new property page is just fine for setting colors. Change the foreground and background colors a few times and experiment with both dots and digit display to exercise all your new code.

FIG. 17.18
Stock property pages make short work of letting the user set colors.

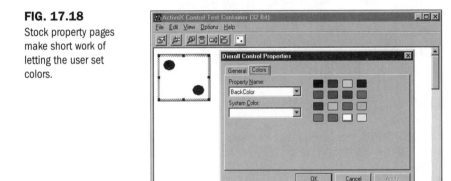

Rolling on Demand

ActiveX controls expose methods (functions) just as Automation servers do. This control rolls when the user clicks it, but you might want the container application to request a roll without the user's intervention. To do this, you add a function called DoRoll() and expose it.

Bring up ClassWizard, click the Automation tab, then click Add Method. Name the new function DoRoll, select Return type of void, then when it is added, click Edit Code and fill it in like this:

```
void CDierollCtrl::DoRoll()
{
    m_number = Roll();
    InvalidateControl();
}
```

This simple code just rolls the die and requests a redraw. Not everything about ActiveX controls needs to be difficult!

Future Improvements

The die-rolling control may seem complete, but it could be made even better.

Enable and Disable Rolling

In many dice games, you can roll the die only when it is your turn. At the moment, this control rolls whenever it is clicked, no matter what. By adding a custom property called RollAllowed, you can allow the container to control the rolling. When RollAllowed is FALSE, CDieCtrl::OnLButtonDown should just return without rolling and redrawing. Perhaps OnDraw should draw a slightly different die (gray dots?) when RollAllowed is FALSE. You decide; it's your control. The container would set this property like any Automation property, according to the rules of the game in which the control is embedded.

Dice with Unusual Numbers of Sides

Why restrict yourself to six-sided dice? There are dice that have four, eight, 12, 20, and even 30 sides; wouldn't they make an interesting addition to a dice game? You'll need to get one pair of these odd dice so that you can see what they look like and change the drawing code in CDierollCtrl::OnDraw( ). You then need to change the hard-coded 6 in Roll( ) to a custom property: an integer with the external name Sides and a member variable m_sides. Don't forget to change the property page to allow the user to set Sides, and add a line to CDieCtrl::DoPropExchange( ) to make Sides persistent and initialize it to 6.

 There is such a thing as a two-sided die; it's commonly called a *coin*.

Arrays of Dice

If you were writing a backgammon game, you would need two dice. One approach would be to embed two individual die controls. But how would you synchronize them so that they both rolled at once with a single click? Why not expand the control to be an *array* of dice? The number of dice would be another custom property, and the control would roll the dice all at once. The RollAllowed flag would apply to all of the dice, as would Sides, so that you could have two six-sided dice or three 12-sided dice, but not two four-sided dice and a 20-sider. Number would become an array.

 In Chapter 20, "Building an Internet ActiveX Control," you discover one way to synchronize two or more separate dice within one control container, and some of the difficulties involved.

From Here...

The die-roll control presented in this chapter is not significantly different from the OLE controls of earlier versions of Visual C++. Even in the documentation there has not been a decision as to whether they should be called OLE controls or ActiveX controls. No matter what they are called, you will want to incorporate ActiveX controls into your programming repertoire so that you can build a user interface that is just what you want. To learn more about some related topics, check these chapters:

- Chapter 12, "Property Pages and Sheets and Wizards," explains how to add property pages to applications that are not ActiveX controls. You might want to compare that process to the one presented in this chapter.

- Chapter 13, "ActiveX Concepts," is a roadmap to Part IV of this book and defines many of the concepts used in this and related chapters.

- Chapter 14, "Building an ActiveX Container Application," shows you how to build the second version of ShowString, which acts as an ActiveX container.

- Chapter 15, "Building an ActiveX Server Application," builds the third version of ShowString, which acts as an ActiveX server.

- Chapter 16, "Building an Automation Server," shows you how to build a fourth version of ShowString—an Automation server that can be controlled from Visual Basic.

- Chapter 20, "Building an Internet ActiveX Control," discusses small, efficient controls designed to run quickly and smoothly in an Internet Web page and makes some eye-opening changes to your die-roll control.

Part
V

Ch
17

Internet Programming

CHAPTER 18

Sockets, MAPI, and the Internet

There are a number of ways for your applications to communicate with other applications through a network like the Internet. This chapter introduces you to the concepts involved with these programming techniques. Subsequent chapters will cover some of these concepts in more detail.

Before the Windows operating system even existed, the Internet existed. As it grew, it became the largest TCP/IP network in the world. The early sites were UNIX machines, and a set of conventions called Berkeley sockets became the standard for TCP/IP communication between UNIX machines on the Internet. Other operating systems implemented TCP/IP communications, too, which contributed immensely to the growth of the Internet. On those operating systems, things were starting to get messy, with a wide variety of proprietary implementations of TCP/IP, when a group of over 20 vendors banded together to create the Winsock specification. ■

Using Windows Sockets (Winsock)

Describes the role that Winsock.dll plays in developing communications applications.

Messaging API (MAPI)

The capability to send messages is a must to receive a Windows 95 stamp of approval from Microsoft. This section shows you how to use this powerful API.

New Internet classes in Visual C++ 4.2

These powerful classes make Internet development fast and easy.

Internet Server API (ISAPI) classes

An Application Programmer Interface is a collection of utility functions collected for a similar purpose. The Internet Server API puts your World Wide Web server under your control.

Using Windows Sockets

The Winsock specification defines the interface to a DLL, typically called WINSOCK.DLL or WSOCK32.DLL. Vendors write the code for the functions themselves. Applications can call the functions, confident that the name, parameter meaning, and final behavior of the function is the same no matter which DLL is installed on the machine. For example, the DLLs included with Windows 95 and Windows NT are not the same at all, but a 32-bit Winsock application can run unchanged on a Windows 95 or Windows NT machine, calling the Winsock functions in the appropriate DLL.

> **N O T E**   Winsock is not confined to TCP/IP communication. IPX/SPX support is the second protocol supported, and there will be others. For more information, check the Winsock specification itself. The Stardust Labs Winsock Resource Page at **http://www.stardust.com/wsresource/** is a great starting point. ■

An important concept in sockets programming is a socket's *port*. Every site on the Internet has a numeric address called an *IP address,* typically written as four numbers separated by dots: **198.53.145.3**, for example. Programs running on that machine are all willing to talk, using sockets, to other machines. If a request arrives at **198.53.145.3**, which program should handle it?

Requests arrive at the machine carrying a *port number,* a number from 1,024 and up that indicates for which program the request is intended. Some port numbers are reserved for standard use; for example, port 80 is traditionally used by Web servers to listen for Web document requests from client programs like Netscape Navigator.

Most socket work is *connection-based*: the two programs form a connection with a socket at each end and then send and receive data along the connection. Some applications prefer to send the data without a connection, but there is no guarantee that this data arrives. The classic example is a time server that regularly sends out the current time to every machine near it, without waiting until it is asked. The delay in establishing a connection might make the time sent through the connection outdated, so it makes sense in this case to use a connectionless approach.

Winsock in MFC

At first, sockets programming in Visual C++ meant making API calls into the DLL. Many developers built socket classes to encapsulate these calls. Visual C++ 2.1 introduced two new classes: CAsyncSocket and CSocket, which inherits from CAsyncSocket. These classes handle the API calls for you, including the startup and cleanup calls that would otherwise be easy to forget.

Windows programming is *asynchronous*: There are lots of different things going on at the same time. In older versions of Windows, if one part of an application got stuck in a loop or otherwise hung up, the entire application—and sometimes the entire operating system—would stick or hang with it. This was obviously something to be avoided at all costs. Yet a socket call, perhaps a call to read some information through a TCP/IP connection to another site on the Internet, might take a long time to complete. (A function that is waiting to send or receive information on a socket is said to be *blocking*.) There are three ways around this problem:

1. Put the function that might block in a thread of its own. The thread will block, but the rest of the application will carry on.

2. Have the function return immediately after making the request, and have another function check regularly (*poll* the socket) to see if the request has completed.

3. Have the function return immediately, and send a Windows message when the request has been completed.

Option 1 was not available until recently, and Option 2 is inefficient under Windows. So most Winsock programming adopts Option 3. The class CAsyncSocket implements this approach. For example, to send a string across a connected socket to another site on the Internet, you call that socket's Send() function. Send() doesn't necessarily send any data at all; it tries to, but if the socket isn't ready and waiting, Send() just returns. When the socket is ready, a message is sent to the socket window, which catches it and sends the data across. This is called *asynchronous Winsock programming*.

N O T E Winsock programming is not a simple topic; entire books have been written on it. One you might like to look at is Que's *Developing Internet Applications in Visual C++*. If you decide that this low-level sockets programming is the way to go, building standard programs is a good way to learn the process. ▪

Part
VI
App
18

CAsyncSocket The CAsyncSocket class is a wrapper class for the asynchronous Winsock calls. It has a number of useful functions, which facilitate using the Winsock API. Table 18.1 lists the CAsyncSocket member funtions and responsibilities.

Table 18.1 *CAsyncSocket* Member Functions

Method Name	Description
Accept	Handles an incoming connection on a listening socket, filling a new socket with the address information.
AsyncSelect	Requests that a Windows message be sent when a socket is ready.
Attach	Attaches a socket handle to a CAsyncSocket instance, so that it can form a connection to another machine.
Bind	Associates an address with a socket.
Close	Closes the socket.
Connect	Connects the socket to a remote address and port.
Create	Completes the initialization process begun by the constructor.
Detach	Detaches a previously attached socket handle.
FromHandle	Returns a pointer to the CAsyncSocket attached to the handle it was passed.

continues

Table 18.1   Continued

Method Name	Description
GetLastError	Returns the error code of the socket. Call `GetLastError` after an operation fails, to find out why.
GetPeerName	Finds the IP address and port number of the remote socket that the calling object socket is connected to, or fills a socket address structure with that information.
GetSockName	Returns the IP address and port number of `this` socket, or fills a socket address structure with that information.
GetSockOpt	Returns the socket options that are currently set.
IOCtl	Sets the mode of the socket; most commonly, to blocking or non-blocking.
Listen	Instructs a socket to watch for incoming connections.
OnAccept	Handles the Windows message generated when a socket has an incoming connection to accept. Often overridden by derived classes.
OnClose	Handles the Windows message generated when a socket closes. Often overridden by derived classes.
OnConnect	Handles the Windows message generated when a socket becomes connected or a connection attempt ends in failure. Often overridden by derived classes.
OnOutOfBandData	Handles the Windows message generated when a socket has urgent, out-of-band data ready to read.
OnReceive	Handles the Windows message generated when a socket has data that could be read with `Receive()`. Often overridden by derived classes.
OnSend	Handles the Windows message generated when a socket is ready to accept data that could be sent with `Send()`. Often overridden by derived classes.
Receive	Reads data from the remote socket to which this socket is connected.
ReceiveFrom	Reads a datagram from a connectionless remote socket.
Send	Sends data to the remote socket to which this socket is connected.
SendTo	Sends a datagram without a connection.
SetSockOpt	Sets socket options.
ShutDown	Keeps the socket open but prevents any further `Send()` or `Receive()` calls.

If you use the CAsyncSocket class, you will have to fill the socket address structures yourself, and many developers would rather delegate a lot of this work. In that case, CSocket is a better socket class.

CSocket CSocket inherits from CAsyncSocket and so has all the functions listed for CAsyncSocket. Table 13.2 describes the new methods added and the virtual methods that are overridden in the derived CSocket class.

Table 18.2 *CSocket* Methods

Method Name	Description
Attach	Attaches a socket handle to a CAsyncSocket instance, so that it can form a connection to another machine.
Create	Completes the initialization after the constructor constructs a blank socket.
FromHandle	Returns a pointer to the CSocket attached to the handle it was passed.
IsBlocking	Returns TRUE if the socket is blocking at the moment, waiting for something to happen.
CancelBlockingCall	Cancels whatever request had left the socket blocking.
OnMessagePending	Handles the Windows messages generated for other parts of your application while the socket is blocking. Often overridden by derived classes.

Part
VI

App
18

In many cases, socket programming is no longer necessary because the WinInet classes, ISAPI programming, and ActiveX controls for Web pages are bringing more and more power to Internet programmers. If you would like to explore a sample socket program, try Chatter and ChatSrvr, provided with Visual C++. Search on either name in the online help, or open the files, located on the CD in the \DevStudio\VC\Samples\MFC\Advanced\Chatter and \DevStudio \VC\Samples\MFC\Advanced\Chatsrvr folders.

Each session of Chatter emulates a user server. The ChatSrvr program is the server, acting as traffic manager among several clients. Each Chatter can send messages to the ChatSrvr—by typing in some text—and the ChatSrvr sends the message to everyone logged into the session. Several channels of traffic are managed at once.

If you've worked with sockets before, this short overview may be all you need to get started. If not, you may not need to learn them. If you plan to write a client/server application that runs over the Internet and does not use the existing standard applications like mail or the Web, then learning sockets is probably in your future. But, if you want to use e-mail, the Web, ftp, and other popular Internet information sources, you don't have to do it by writing socket programs at all. You may be able to use MAPI, the WinInet classes, or ISAPI to achieve the results you are looking for.

Messaging API (MAPI)

The most popular networking feature in most offices is electronic mail. You could add code to your application to generate the right commands over a socket to transmit a mail message, but it's simpler to build on the work of others.

What Is MAPI?

MAPI is a way of pulling together applications that need to send and receive messages (*messaging applications*) with applications that know how to send and receive messages (*messaging services* and *service providers*) in order to lower the work load of all the developers involved. Figure 18.1 shows the scope of MAPI. Note that the word *messaging* actually covers far more than just electronic mail: A MAPI service could send a fax or voice-mail message rather than an electronic mail message. If your application uses MAPI, the messaging services, such as e-mail clients, that the user has installed will carry out the work of sending the messages your application generates.

FIG. 18.1

The Messaging API covers applications that need messaging and those that provide it.

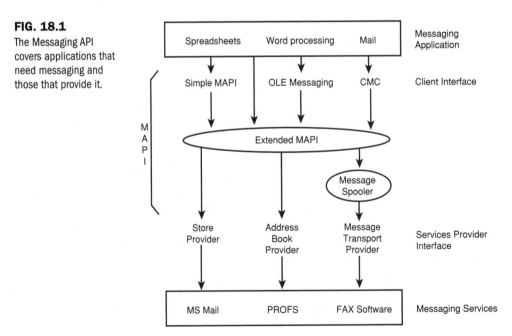

The extent to which an application uses messaging varies widely:

- Some applications can send a message, but sending messages is not really what the application is about. For example, a word processor is fundamentally about entering and formatting text and then printing or saving that text. If the word processor can also send the text in a message, fine, but that's incidental. Applications like this are said to be *messaging aware* and typically use just the tip of the MAPI functionality.

■ Some applications are useful without being able to send messages, but they are far more useful in an environment where messages can be sent. For example, a personal scheduler program can manage one person's To Do list whether messaging is enabled or not, but if it is enabled, a number of workgroup and client-contact features—such as sending e-mail to confirm an appointment—become available. Applications like this are said to be *messaging enabled* and use some, but not all, of the MAPI features.

■ Finally, some applications are all about messaging. Without messaging, these applications are useless. They are said to be *messaging based,* and they use all of MAPI's functionality.

Win95 Logo Requirements

The number-one reason for a developer to make an application messaging aware is to meet the requirements of the Windows 95 Logo program. To qualify for the logo, an application must have a Send item on the File menu that uses MAPI to send the document. (Exceptions are granted to applications without documents.)

To add this feature to your applications, it's best to think of it before you create the empty shell with AppWizard. If you are planning ahead, here is a list of all the work you have to do to meet this part of the logo requirement:

1. In Step 4 of AppWizard, select the MAPI (Messaging API) check box.

That's it! The menu item is added, and message maps and functions are generated to catch the menu item and call functions that use your `Serialize()` function to send the document through MAPI. Figure 18.2 shows an application called MAPIDemo, included on the book's CD-ROM, that is just an AppWizard empty shell.

Part
VI

App
18

FIG. 18.2
AppWizard adds the Send item to the File menu, as well as the code that handles the item.

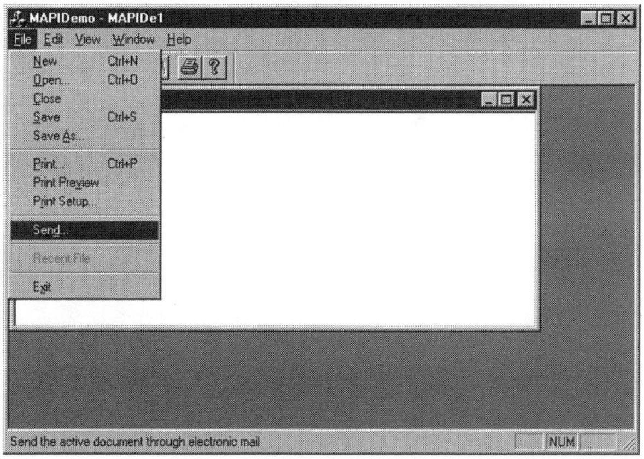

No additional code was added, beyond the code generated by the AppWizard, to this application, and the Send item is on the File menu, as you can see. If you choose this menu item, your MAPI mail client is launched to send the message. Figures 18.2 and 18.3 were captured on a machine with Microsoft Exchange installed as an Internet mail client, and so it is Microsoft

Exchange that is launched, as shown in Figure 18.3. The message contains the current document, and it is up to you to fill in the recipient, the subject, and any text you wish to send with the document.

FIG. 18.3

Microsoft Mail is launched so the user can fill in the rest of the e-mail message around the document that is being sent.

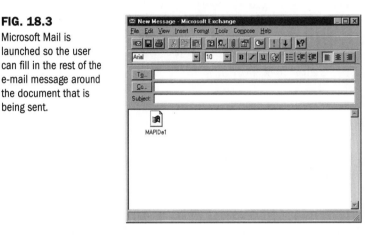

 TIP If the Send item does not appear on your menu, make sure that you have a MAPI client installed. Microsoft Exchange is an easy-to-get MAPI client. The OnUpdateFileSendMail() function removes the menu item Send from the menu if no MAPI client is registered on your computer.

If you didn't request MAPI support from AppWizard when you built your application, here are the steps to follow which will manually add the Send item:

1. Add the Send item to the File menu. Use a resource ID of ID_FILE_SEND_MAIL. The prompt will be supplied for you.

2. Add these two lines to the document's message map, outside the //AFX comments:

```
ON_COMMAND(ID_FILE_SEND_MAIL, OnFileSendMail)
ON_UPDATE_COMMAND_UI(ID_FILE_SEND_MAIL, OnUpdateFileSendMail)
```

Adding the mail support to your application manually is not much harder than asking AppWizard to do it.

Advanced Use of MAPI

If you want more from MAPI than just meeting the logo requirements, things do get harder. There are actually four kinds of MAPI client interfaces:

- Simple MAPI, an older API not recommended for use in new applications
- Common Messaging Calls (CMC), a simple API for messaging-aware and messaging-enabled applications
- Extended MAPI, a full-featured API for messaging-based applications

- OLE Messaging, an API with somewhat fewer features than Extended MAPI but ideal for use with Visual C++

Common Messaging Calls There are only ten functions in the CMC API. That makes it easy to learn, yet packs enough punch to get the job done. They are the following:

- `cmc_logon()` connects to a mail server and identifies the user.
- `cmc_logoff()` disconnects from a mail server.
- `cmc_send()` sends a message.
- `cmc_send_documents()` sends one or more files.
- `cmc_list()` lists the messages in the user's mailbox.
- `cmc_read()` reads a message from the user's mailbox.
- `cmc_act_on()` saves or deletes a message.
- `cmc_look_up()` resolves names and addresses.
- `cmc_query_configuration()` reports what mail server is being used.
- `cmc_free()` frees any memory allocated by other functions.

The header file XCMC.H declares a number of structures used to hold the information that is passed to these functions. For example, recipient information is kept in this structure:

```
/*RECIPIENT*/
typedef struct {
    CMC_string          name;
    CMC_enum            name_type;
    CMC_string          address;
    CMC_enum            role;
    CMC_flags           recip_flags;
    CMC_extension FAR   *recip_extensions;
} CMC_recipient;
```

You could fill this structure with the name and address of the recipient of a mail message by using a standard dialog box or by hard-coding the entries, like this:

```
CMC_recipient recipient = {
    "Kate Gregory",
    CMC_TYPE_INDIVIDUAL,
    "SMTP:kate@gregcons.com",
    CMC_ROLE_TO,
    CMC_RECIP_LAST_ELEMENT,
    NULL };
```

The type, role, and flags use one of these predefined values:

Listing 18.1   (Excerpt from \MSDev\Include\XCMC.H) Command Definitions/

```
* NAME TYPES */
#define CMC_TYPE_UNKNOWN           ((CMC_enum) 0)
#define CMC_TYPE_INDIVIDUAL        ((CMC_enum) 1)
#define CMC_TYPE_GROUP             ((CMC_enum) 2)
```

continues

Part
VI

App
18

Listing 18.1   Continued
```
/* ROLES */
#define CMC_ROLE_TO                    ((CMC_enum) 0)
#define CMC_ROLE_CC                    ((CMC_enum) 1)
#define CMC_ROLE_BCC                   ((CMC_enum) 2)
#define CMC_ROLE_ORIGINATOR            ((CMC_enum) 3)
#define CMC_ROLE_AUTHORIZING_USER      ((CMC_enum) 4)

/* RECIPIENT FLAGS */
#define CMC_RECIP_IGNORE               ((CMC_flags) 1)
#define CMC_RECIP_LIST_TRUNCATED       ((CMC_flags) 2)
#define CMC_RECIP_LAST_ELEMENT         ((CMC_flags) 0x80000000)
```

There is a message structure you could fill in the same way, or by presenting the user with a dialog box to enter the message details. This structure includes a pointer to the recipient structure you have already filled. Your program then calls `cmc_logon()`, `cmc_send()`, and `cmc_logoff()` to complete the process.

Extended MAPI   Extended MAPI is based on COM, the OLE Component Object Model. Messages, recipients, and many other entities are defined as objects rather than as C structures. There are far more object types in Extended MAPI than there are structure types in CMC. Access to these objects is through OLE (ActiveX) interfaces. The objects expose properties, methods, and events. These concepts are discussed in Part V, Chapter 14, "ActiveX Concepts."

OLE Messaging   If you understand Automation (described in Chapter 16, "Building an Automation Server"), then you will easily understand OLE Messaging. Your application must be an Automation client, however, and building such a client is beyond the scope of this chapter. Some ways to use OLE Messaging are in Visual Basic programming and VBA scripts for programs like Excel. Your program would set up objects and then set their exposed properties (for example, the subject line of a message object) and invoke their exposed methods (for example, the `Send()` method of a message object).

The objects used in OLE Messaging include the following:

- Session
- Message
- Recipient
- Attachment

A detailed reference of these objects, as well as their properties and methods, can be found in Visual C++ Books Online (the help files) from within Developer Studio. Follow the Books Online hierarchy: SDKs, Win32 SDK, Win32 Messaging (MAPI), and OLE Messaging Library.

Using New Internet Classes in Visual C++ 4.2

MFC 4.2 introduced a number of new classes that eliminated the need to learn socket programming when your applications need to access standard Internet client services. Figure 18.4 shows the way these classes relate to each other. Collectively known as the WinInet classes, they are the following:

- CInternetSession
- CInternetConnection
- CInternetFile
- HttpConnection
- CHttpFile
- CGopherFile
- CFtpConnection

- CGopherConnection
- CFileFind
- CFtpFileFind
- CGopherFileFind
- CGopherLocator
- CInternetException

FIG. 18.4

The WinInet classes make writing Internet client programs easier.

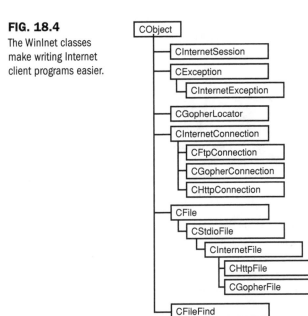

Part

VI

App

18

T I P These classes help you write Internet *client* applications with which users interact directly. If you want to write *server* applications, which interact with client applications, you'll be interested in ISAPI, discussed in the next section.

First, your program establishes a session by creating a CInternetSession. Then, if you have a Uniform Resource Locator (URL) to a Gopher, FTP, or Web (HTTP) resource, you can call that session's OpenURL() function to retrieve the resource as a read-only CInternetFile. Your application can read the file using CStdioFile functions and manipulate that data in whatever way you need.

If you do not have an URL or do not want to retrieve a read-only file, you proceed differently after establishing the session. You make a connection with a specific protocol by calling the session's GetFtpConnection(), GetGopherConnection(), or GetHttpConnection() functions, which return the appropriate connection object. You then call the connection's OpenFile() function. CFtpConnection::OpenFile() returns a CInternetFile; CGopherConnection:: OpenFile() returns a CGopherFile; and CHttpConnection::OpenFile() returns a CHttpFile. The CFileFind class and its derived classes help you find the file you want to open.

Chapter 19, "Internet Programming with the WinInet Classes," works through an example client program using WinInet classes to establish an Internet session and retrieve information.

N O T E   Though e-mail is a standard Internet application, you'll notice that the WinInet classes do not have any e-mail functionality. That's because e-mail is handled by MAPI. There is no support for Usenet news either, in the WinInet classes or elsewhere. ■

Using Internet Server API (ISAPI) Classes

ISAPI is used to enhance and extend the capabilities of your HTTP (World Wide Web) server. ISAPI developers produce *extensions* and *filters*. Extensions are DLLs that are invoked by a user from a Web page in much the same way as CGI applications are invoked from a Web page. Filters are DLLs that run with the server and look at or change the data going to and from the server. For example, a filter might redirect requests for one file to a new location.

N O T E   In order for the ISAPI extensions and filters that you write to be useful, your Web pages must be kept on a server that is running as an ISAPI-compliant server like the Microsoft IIS Server. You must have permission to install DLLs onto the server, and for an ISAPI filter, you must be able to change the Registry on the server. If your Web pages are kept on a machine administered by your Internet Service Provider (ISP), you will probably not be able to use ISAPI to bring more power to your Web pages. You may choose to move your pages to a dedicated server (a powerful Intel machine running Windows NT Server 4.0 and Microsoft IIS is a good combination) so that you can use ISAPI, but this will involve considerable expense. Make sure you understand the constraints of your current Web server before embarking on a project with ISAPI.

One of the major advantages of ActiveX controls for the Internet (discussed in Chapter 21, "The Active Template Library," is that you do not need access to the server in order to implement them. ■

The five MFC ISAPI classes form a wrapper for the API to make it easier to use. They are:

■ CHttpServer

■ CHttpFilter

- CHttpServerContext

- CHttpFilterContext

- CHtmlStream

Your application will have a server or a filter class (or both) that inherit from CHttpServer or CHttpFilter. These are rather like the classes in a normal application that inherit from CWinApp. There is only one instance of the class in each DLL, and each interaction of the server with a client is done through its own instance of the appropriate context class. (A DLL may contain both a server and a filter, but at most one of each.) CHtmlStream is a helper class that describes a stream of HTML to be sent by a server to a client.

The ISAPI Extension Wizard is an AppWizard that simplifies creating extensions and filters. To use this wizard, choose File, New, as always, and then the Project tab. Scroll down the list on the left and select ISAPI Extension Wizard (as shown in Figure 18.5) and then fill in the project name and folder, and click OK.

Creating a server extension is a one-step process. That step, which is also the first step for a filter, is shown in Figure 18.6. The names and descriptions for the filter and extension are based on the project name that you chose.

FIG. 18.5

The ISAPI Extension Wizard is another kind of AppWizard.

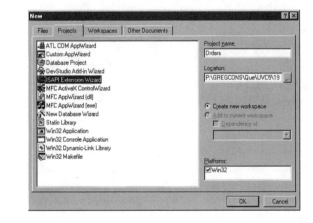

If you choose to create a filter, the Next button is enabled and you can move to the second step for filters, shown in Figure 18.7. This list of parameters gives you an idea of the power of an ISAPI filter. You can monitor all incoming and outgoing requests and raw data, authenticate users, log traffic, and more.

AppWizard shows you a final confirmation screen before creating the files. When you create a server and a filter at the same time, 11 files are created for you, including source and headers for the class that inherits from CHttpServer and the class that inherits from CHttpFilter.

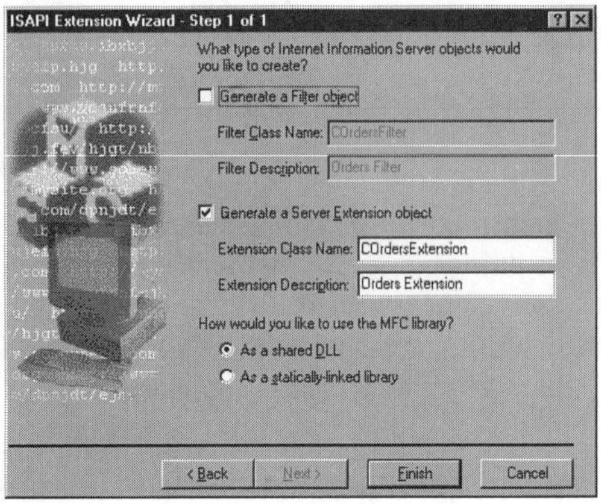

FIG. 18.6

The first step in the
ISAPI Extension Wizard
process is to name the
components of the DLL
that you are creating.

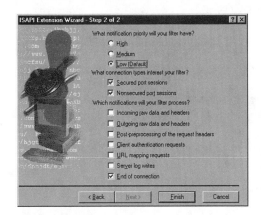

FIG. 18.7

The second step in the
ISAPI Extension Wizard
process is to set filter
parameters.

Writing a filter from this shell is quite simple. You have been provided with a stub function to
react to each event for which notification was requested. For example, the filter class has a
function called OnEndOfNetSession() which is called when a client's session with this server is
ending. You add code to this function to log, monitor, or otherwise react to this event. When
the filter is complete, you edit the Registry by hand so that the server will run your DLL.

To write an extension, add one or more functions to your DLL. Each function will be passed a
CHttpContext pointer, which can be used to gather information such as the user's IP address.
If the function is invoked from an HTML form, additional parameters such as values of other
fields on the form will also be passed to the function.

The details of what the function does depend on your application. If you are implementing an
online ordering system, the functions involved will be lengthy and complex. Other extensions
will be simpler.

When the function is complete, you place the DLL in the executable folder for the server—
usually the folder where CGI programs are kept—and adjust your Web pages so that they
include links to your DLL, like this:

```
Now you can <A HREF=http://www.company.com/exec/orders.dll>
place an order</A> online!
```

For more information on ISAPI programming, be sure to read Que's *Special Edition Using ISAPI*, included in its entirety on this book's CD-ROM. You will learn how ISAPI applications can make your Web site dynamic and interactive, learn how to write filters and extensions, and cover advanced topics including debugging ISAPI applications and writing multi-threaded applications.

From Here...

Adding the Internet to your applications is an exciting trend. It's going to make lots of work for programmers and create some powerful products that simplify the working life of anyone with an Internet connection. Just a year ago, writing Internet applications meant getting your fingernails dirty with sockets programming, memorizing TCP/IP ports, and reading RFCs. The new WinInet and ISAPI classes, as well as improvements to the old MAPI support, mean that today you can add amazing power to your application with just a few lines of code or by selecting a box on an AppWizard dialog box.

To learn more about using the APIs introduced in this chapter and building other specific kinds of applications refer to:

- Chapter 19, "Internet Programming with the WinInet Classes," lets you work through an example program built with the WinInet classes.

- Chapter 22, "Database Access," covers the basics of database manipulation.

Part

VI

App

18

Internet Programming with the WinInet Classes

Chapter 18, "Sockets, MAPI, and the Internet," introduced the WinInet classes you can use to build Internet client applications at a fairly high level. This chapter develops an Internet application that demonstrates a number of these classes. The application also serves a useful function: You can use it to learn more about the Internet presence of a company or organization. You don't need to learn about sockets or handle the details of Internet protocols to do this. ■

Designing the Internet Query Application

Imagine that you have someone's e-mail address (**kate@gregcons.com**, for example) and you'd like to know more about the domain (**gregcons.com** in this example). Or perhaps you have a great idea for a domain name and want to know if it's taken already. This application, Query, will try connecting to **gregcons.com** (or **greatidea.org**, or any other domain name that you specify) in a variety of different ways and will report the result of those attempts to the user.

This application will have a simple user interface. The only piece of information the user needs to supply is the domain name to be queried, and there is no need to keep this information in a document. You might want a menu item called Query that brings up a dialog box in which to specify the name of the site, but a better approach is to use a dialog-based application and incorporate a Query button into the dialog box.

Dialog-based applications, as discussed in the "A Dialog-Based Application" section of Chapter 1, "Building Your First Application," have no document and no menu. The application displays a dialog box at all times; closing the dialog box closes the application. You build the dialog box for this application like any other, with Developer Studio.

To build the shell of this application, choose File, New from within Developer Studio and then click the Project tab. Highlight MFC AppWizard(exe), name the application Query, and in Step 1, choose a dialog-based application, as shown in Figure 19.1. Click Next to move to Step 2 of AppWizard.

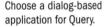
FIG. 19.1

Choose a dialog-based application for Query.

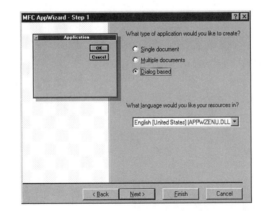

In Step 2 of AppWizard, request an About box, no context-sensitive help, 3-D controls, no Automation or ActiveX control support, and no sockets support. (This application won't be calling socket functions directly.) Give the application a sensible title for the dialog box. The AppWizard choices should be as summarized in Figure 19.2. Click Next to move to Step 3 of AppWizard.

The rest of the AppWizard process should be familiar by now: You want comments, you want to link to the MFC libraries as a shared DLL, and you don't need to change any of the class names suggested by AppWizard. When the AppWizard process is complete, you are ready to build the heart of the Query application.

FIG. 19.2
This application does not need help, Automation, ActiveX controls, or sockets.

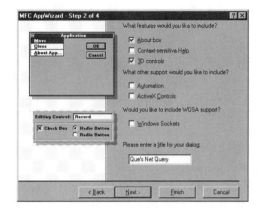

Building the Query Dialog Box

AppWizard produces an empty dialog box for you to start with, as shown in Figure 19.3. To edit this dialog box, switch to the resource view, expand the Query resources, expand the Dialogs section, and double-click the IDD_QUERY_DIALOG resource. The following steps will transform this dialog box into the interface for the Query application.

FIG. 19.3
AppWizard generates an empty dialog box for you.

Part
VI

Ch
19

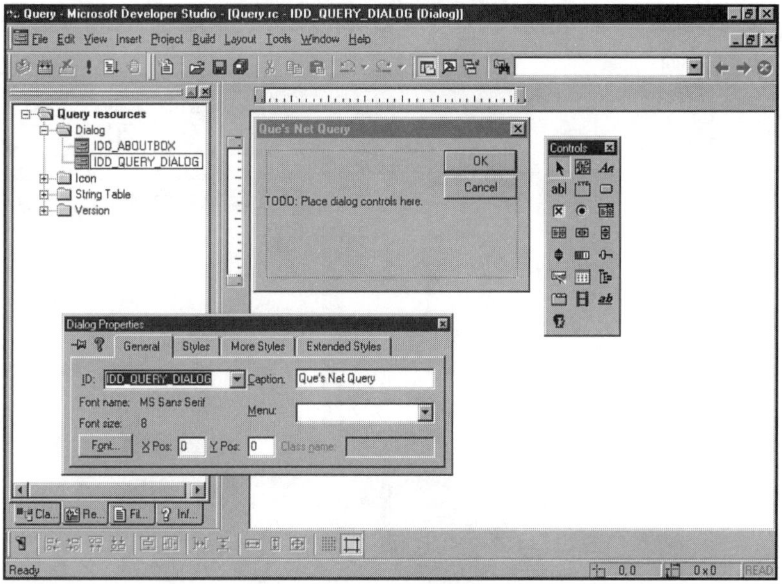

T I P If working with dialog boxes is still new to you, be sure to read Chapter 2, "Dialog Boxes and Controls."

1. Change the caption on the OK button to Query.

2. Change the caption on the Cancel button to Close.

3. Delete the TODO static text.

4. Grab a sizing handle on the right edge of the dialog box and stretch it so that the dialog box is 300 pixels wide, or more. (The size of the currently selected item is at the lower right corner of the screen.)

5. At the top of the dialog box, add an edit box with the resource ID IDC_HOST. Stretch the edit box as wide as possible.

6. Add a static label next to the dialog box. Set the text to Site name.

7. Grab a sizing handle along the bottom of the dialog box and stretch it longer, so that dialog box is 150 pixels high, or more.

8. Add another edit box and resize it to fill as much of the bottom part of the dialog box as possible.

9. Give this edit box the resource ID IDC_OUT.

10. Click the Styles tab on the Properties box and select the Multi-line, Horizontal scroll, Vertical scroll, Border, and Read-only check boxes. Make sure all the other check boxes are deselected.

The finished dialog box, and the Style properties of the large edit box, should resemble Figure 19.4.

FIG. 19.4
Build the Query user interface as a single dialog box.

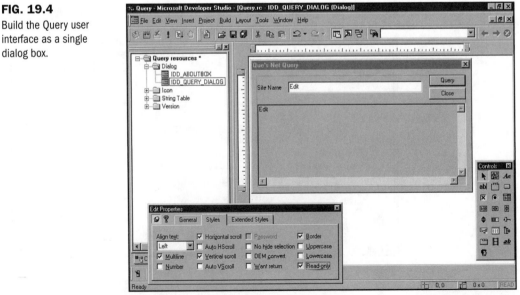

When the user clicks the Query button, this application should somehow query the site. The last step in the building of the interface is to connect the Query button to code with ClassWizard. Follow these steps to make that connection:

1. Choose View, Class Wizard to bring up ClassWizard.

2. There are three possible classes that could catch the command generated by the button click, but CQueryDlg is the logical choice because the host name will be known by that class. Make sure that CQueryDlg is the class selected in the Class name drop-down list box.

3. Highlight ID_OK (you did not change the resource ID of the OK button when you changed the caption) in the left list box, and BN_CLICKED in the right list box.

4. Click Add Function to add a function that will be called when the Query button is clicked.

5. ClassWizard suggests the name OnOK; change it to OnQuery, as shown in Figure 19.5, and then click OK.

FIG. 19.5

Add a function to handle a click on the Query button, whose ID is still IDOK.

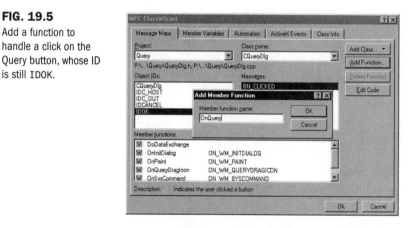

6. Click the Member Variables tab to prepare to connect the edit controls on the dialog box to member variables of the dialog class.

7. Highlight IDC_HOST and click Add Variable. As shown in Figure 19.6, you will connect this control to a CString member variable of the dialog class called m_host.

8. Connect IDC_OUT to m_out, also a CString.

Click OK to close ClassWizard. Now all that remains is to write CQueryDlg::OnQuery(), which will use the value in m_host to produce lines of output for m_out.

Part

VI

Ch

19

FIG. 19.6

Connect IDC_HOST to CQueryDlg::m_host.

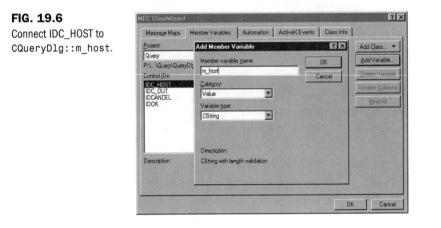

Querying HTTP Sites

The first kind of connection to try when investigating a domain's Internet presence is HTTP, because so many sites have Web pages. The simplest way to make a connection using HTTP is to use the WinInet class CInternetSession and call its OpenURL() function. This will return a file, and you can display the first few lines of the file in m_out. First, add this line at the beginning of QueryDlg.cpp:

```
#include "afxinet.h"
```

This gives your code access to the WinInet classes. Because this application will try a number of URLs, add a function to CQueryDlg called TryURL(). It takes a CString parameter called URL and returns void. Right-click CQueryDlg in the ClassView and choose Add Function to add TryURL() as a protected member function. The new function, TryURL(), will be called from CQueryDlg::OnQuery() as shown in Listing 19.1. Edit OnQuery() to add this code.

Listing 19.1   QueryDlg.cpp—*CQueryDlg::OnQuery()*

```
void CQueryDlg::OnQuery()
{
    const CString http = "http://";

    UpdateData(TRUE);
    m_out = "";
    UpdateData(FALSE);

    TryURL(http + m_host);

    TryURL(http + "www." + m_host);
}
```

The call to UpdateData(TRUE) fills m_host with the value that the user typed. The call to UpdateData(FALSE) fills the IDC_OUT read-only edit box with the newly cleared m_out. Then come two calls to TryURL(). If, for example, the user typed **microsoft.com**, the first call would try **http://microsoft.com** and the second would try **http://www.microsoft.com**. TryURL() is shown in Listing 19.2.

Listing 19.2 QueryDlg.cpp—*CQueryDlg::TryURL()*

```
void CQueryDlg::TryURL(CString URL)
{
    CInternetSession session;

    m_out += "Trying " + URL + "\r\n";
    UpdateData(FALSE);

    CInternetFile* file = NULL;
    try
    {
        //We know for sure this is an Internet file,
        //so the cast is safe
        file = (CInternetFile*) session.OpenURL(URL);
    }
    catch (CInternetException* pEx)
    {
        //if anything went wrong, just set file to NULL
        file = NULL;
        pEx->Delete();
    }
    if (file)
    {
        m_out += "Connection established. \r\n";
        CString line;

        for (int i=0; i < 20 && file->ReadString(line); i++)
        {
            m_out += line + "\r\n";
        }
        file->Close();
        delete file;
    }
    else
    {
        m_out += "No server found there. \r\n";
    }

    m_out += "-------------------------\r\n";
    UpdateData(FALSE);
}
```

Part
VI

Ch
19

The remainder of this section presents this code again, a few lines at a time. First, establish an Internet session by constructing an instance of CInternetSession. There are a number of parameters to this constructor, but they all have default values that will be fine for this application.

The parameters follow:

- **LPCTSTR pstrAgent**   The name of your application. If NULL, it's filled in for you using the name that you gave to AppWizard.

- **DWORD dwContext**   The context identifier for the operation. For synchronous sessions, this is not an important parameter.

- **DWORD dwAccessType**   The access type, one of INTERNET_OPEN_TYPE_PRECONFIG (default), INTERNET_OPEN_TYPE_DIRECT, or INTERNET_OPEN_TYPE_PROXY.

- **LPCTSTR pstrProxyName**   The name of your proxy, if access is INTERNET_OPEN_TYPE_PROXY.

- **LPCTSTR pstrProxyBypass**   A list of addresses to be connected directly rather than through the proxy server, if access is INTERNET_OPEN_TYPE_PROXY.

- **DWORD dwFlags**   Options that can be OR'ed together. The available options are INTERNET_FLAG_DONT_CACHE, INTERNET_FLAG_ASYNC, and INTERNET_FLAG_OFFLINE.

dwAccessType defaults to using the value in the Registry. Obviously, an application that insists on direct Internet access or proxy Internet access is less useful than one that allows users to configure that information. But making users set their Internet access type outside this program may be confusing. To set your default Internet access, double-click the My Computer icon on your desktop, then on the Control Panel, and then on the Internet tool in the Control Panel. Choose the Connection tab, shown in Figure 19.7, and complete the dialog box as appropriate for your setup.

FIG. 19.7

Set your Internet connection settings once, and all applications can retrieve them from the Registry.

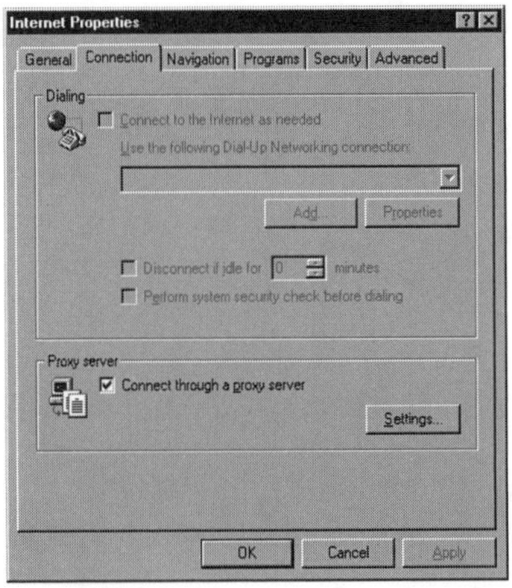

- If you dial up to the Internet, select the Dial check box and fill in the parameters in the top half of the page.

- If you connect to the Internet through a proxy server, select the Proxy check box and click the Settings button to identify your proxy addresses and ports.

- If you are connected directly to the Internet, leave both check boxes unselected.

If you want to set up an *asynchronous* (non-blocking) session, for the reasons discussed in the "Using Windows Sockets" section of Chapter 18, "Sockets, MAPI, and the Internet," your options in dwFlags must include INTERNET_FLAG_ASYNC. In addition, you must call the member function EnableStatusCallback() to set up the callback function. When a request is made through the session—such as the call to OpenURL() that occurs later in TryURL()—and the response will not be immediate, a non-blocking session returns a pseudo error code, ERROR_IO_PENDING. When the response is ready, these sessions automatically invoke the callback function.

For this simple application, there is no need to allow the user to do other work or interact with the user interface while waiting for the session to respond, so the session is constructed as a blocking session and all the other default parameters are also used:

```
CInternetSession session;
```

Having constructed the session, TryURL() goes on to add a line to m_out that echoes the URL passed in as a parameter. The "\r\n" characters are return and newline, and they separate the lines added to m_out. UpdateData(FALSE) gets that onto the screen:

```
m_out += "Trying " + URL + "\r\n";
UpdateData(FALSE);
```

Next is a call to the session's OpenURL() member function. This function returns a pointer to one of several different file types, because the URL might have been to one of four protocols:

- file:// opens a file. The function constructs a CStdioFile and returns a pointer to it.
- ftp:// goes to an FTP site and returns a pointer to a CInternetFile object.
- gopher:// goes to a Gopher site and returns a pointer to a CGopherFile object.
- http:// goes to a World Wide Web site and returns a pointer to a CHttpFile object.

Because CGopherFile and CHttpFile both inherit from CInternetFile, and because you can be sure that TryURL() will not be passed a file:// URL, it is safe to cast the returned pointer to a CInternetFile.

Part
VI

Ch
19

T I P There is some confusion in Microsoft's online documentation whenever example URLs are shown. A backslash (\) character will never appear in an URL. In any Microsoft example that includes backslashes, use forward slashes (/) instead.

If the URL would not open, file will be NULL or OpenURL()_ will throw an exception. (For background on exceptions, see Chapter 26, "Exceptions, Templates, and the Latest Additions to C++.") While in a normal application, it would be a serious error if an URL didn't open; in this application you are making up URLs to see if they work or not, and it's to be expected that some of them won't. As a result, you should catch these exceptions yourself and do just enough to prevent runtime errors. In this case, it's enough to make sure that file is NULL when an exception is thrown. To delete the exception and prevent memory leaks, call CException::Delete(), which is not mentioned in the online documentation but does exist and safely deletes the exception. The block of code containing the call to OpenURL() is in Listing 19.3.

Listing 19.3   QueryDlg.cpp—*CQueryDlg::TryURL()*

```
CInternetFile* file = NULL;
try
{
    //We know for sure this is an Internet file,
    //so the cast is safe
    file = (CInternetFile*) session.OpenURL(URL);
}
catch (CInternetException* pEx)
{
    //if anything went wrong, just set file to NULL
    file = NULL;
    pEx->Delete();
}
```

If file is not NULL, this routine will display some of the Web page that was found. It first echoes another line to m_out. Then in a for loop, the routine calls CInternetFile::ReadString() to fill the CString line with the characters in file up to the first \r\n, which are stripped off. This code simply tacks line (and another \r\n) onto m_out. If you would like to see more or less than the first 20 lines of the page, adjust the number in this for loop. When the first few lines have been read, TryURL() closes and deletes the file. That block of code is shown in Listing 19.4.

Listing 19.4   QueryDlg.cpp—*CQueryDlg::TryURL()*

```
if (file)
{
    m_out += "Connection established. \r\n";
    CString line;

    for (int i=0; i < 20 && file->ReadString(line); i++)
    {
        m_out += line + "\r\n";
    }
    file->Close();
    delete file;
}
```

If the file could not be opened, a message to that effect is echoed onto m_out:

```
else
{
    m_out += "No server found there. \r\n";
}
```

Then whether the file existed or not, a line of dashes is tacked onto m_out to indicate the end of this attempt, and one last call to UpdateData(FALSE) gets the new m_out onto the screen:

```
    m_out += "------------------------\r\n";
    UpdateData(FALSE);
}
```

You can now build and run this application. If you enter **microsoft.com** in the text box and click Query, you will discover that there are Web pages at both **http://microsoft.com** and **http://www.microsoft.com**. Figure 19.8 shows the results of that query.

FIG. 19.8
Query can find
Microsoft's Web sites.

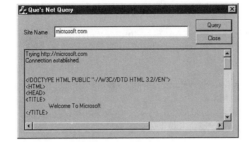

If Query doesn't find Web pages at either the domain name you provided or **www.** plus the domain name, it doesn't mean that the domain doesn't exist or even that the organization that owns the domain name doesn't have a Web page. It does make it less likely, however, that the organization both exists and has a Web page. If you see a stream of HTML, then you know for certain that the organization exists and has a Web page. You may be able to read the HTML yourself, but even if you cannot, you can now connect to the site with a Web browser such as Microsoft's Internet Explorer.

Querying FTP Sites

As part of an investigation of a site name, you should check to see if there is an FTP site, too. Most FTP sites have names like **ftp.company.com**, though some older sites do not have names of that form. Checking for these sites is not as simple as just calling TryURL() again, because TryURL() assumes that the URL leads to a file, and URLs like **ftp.greatidea.org** lead to a list of files that cannot simply be opened and read. Rather than making TryURL() even more complicated, add a function to the class called TryFTPSite(CString host). (Right-click CQueryDlg in the ClassView and choose Add Function to add the function. It can return void.)

TryFTPSite() has to establish a connection within the session, and if the connection is established, it has to get some information that can be added to m_out to show the user that the connection has been made. Getting a list of files is reasonably complex, so because this is just an illustrative application, the simpler task of getting the name of the default FTP directory is the way to go. The code is in Listing 19.5.

Listing 19.5 QueryDlg.cpp—CQueryDlg::TryFTPSite()

```
void CQueryDlg::TryFTPSite(CString host)
{
    CInternetSession session;

    m_out += "Trying FTP site " + host + "\r\n";
```

continues

Listing 19.5   Continued

```
    UpdateData(FALSE);

    CFtpConnection* connection = NULL;
    try
    {
        connection = session.GetFtpConnection(host);
    }
    catch (CInternetException* pEx)
    {
        //if anything went wrong, just set connection to NULL
        connection = NULL;
        pEx->Delete();
    }
    if (connection)
    {
        m_out += "Connection established. \r\n";
        CString line;

        connection->GetCurrentDirectory(line);
        m_out += "default directory is " + line + "\r\n";

        connection->Close();
        delete connection;
    }
    else
    {
        m_out += "No server found there. \r\n";
    }

    m_out += "------------------------\r\n";
    UpdateData(FALSE);
}
```

This code is very much like `TryURL()`, except that instead of opening a file with `session.OpenURL()`, it opens an FTP connection with `session.GetFtpConnection()`. Again, exceptions are caught and essentially ignored, with the routine just making sure that the connection pointer won't be used. The call to `GetCurrentDirectory()` returns the directory on the remote site in which sessions start. The rest of the routine is just like `TryURL()`.

Add two lines at the end of `OnQuery()` to call this new function:

```
TryFTPSite(m_host);
TryFTPSite("ftp." + m_host);
```

Build the application and try it. Figure 19.9 shows Query finding no FTP site at **microsoft.com** and finding one at **ftp.microsoft.com**. You may find the delay until results start to appear a little disconcerting. You could correct this by using asynchronous sockets, or *threading,* so that early results could be added to the edit box while later results are still coming in over the wire, but for a simple demonstration application like this, just wait patiently until the results appear. It may take several minutes, depending on network traffic between your site and Microsoft's, your line speed, and so on.

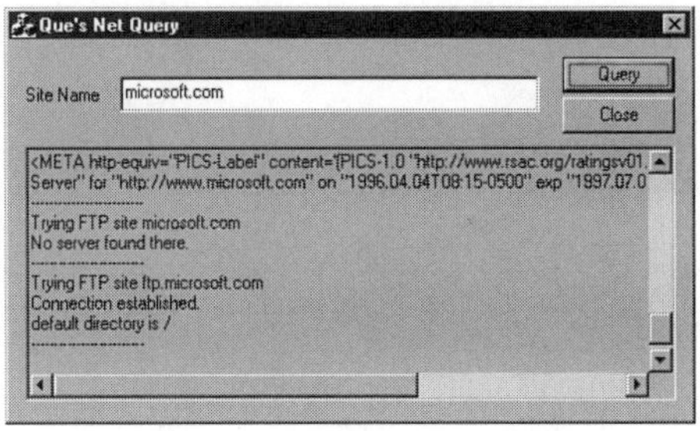

FIG. 19.9
Query finds one
Microsoft FTP site.

If Query doesn't find Web pages or FTP sites, perhaps this domain does not exist at all, or does not have any Internet services other than e-mail, but there are a few more investigative tricks available. The results of these investigations will definitely add to your knowledge of existing sites.

Querying Gopher Sites

As was the case with FTP, TryURL() won't work for querying a Gopher site like **gopher.company.com**, because this returns a list of file names rather than a single file. The solution is to write a function called TryGopherSite() that is almost identical to TryFTPSite(), except that it opens a CGopherConnection, and instead of a single line describing the default directory, it echoes a single line describing the Gopher locator associated with the site. Add TryGopherSite to CQueryDlg by right-clicking the class name in ClassView and choosing Add Function, as you did for TryFTPSite(). The code for TryGopherSite() is in Listing 19.6.

Part
VI

Ch
19

Listing 19.6   QueryDlg.cpp—*CQueryDlg::TryGopherSite()*

```
void CQueryDlg::TryGopherSite(CString host)
{
    CInternetSession session;

    m_out += "Trying Gopher site " + host + "\r\n";
    UpdateData(FALSE);

    CGopherConnection* connection = NULL;
    try
    {
        connection = session.GetGopherConnection(host);
    }
    catch (CInternetException* pEx)
    {
        //if anything went wrong, just set connection to NULL
        connection = NULL;
        pEx->Delete();
    }
    if (connection)
    {
        m_out += "Connection established. \r\n";
```

continues

Listing 19.6   Continued

```
        CString line;

        CGopherLocator locator = connection->CreateLocator(NULL, NULL,
GOPHER_TYPE_DIRECTORY);
        line = locator;
        m_out += "first locator is " + line + "\r\n";

        connection->Close();
        delete connection;
    }
    else
    {
        m_out += "No server found there. \r\n";
    }

    m_out += "-------------------------\r\n";
    UpdateData(FALSE);
}
```

The call to `CreateLocator()` takes three parameters. The first is the file name, which may include wild cards. `NULL` means any file. The second parameter is a selector that can be `NULL`. The third is one of the following types:

GOPHER_TYPE_TEXT_FILE	GOPHER_TYPE_GIF
GOPHER_TYPE_DIRECTORY	GOPHER_TYPE_IMAGE
GOPHER_TYPE_CSO	GOPHER_TYPE_BITMAP
GOPHER_TYPE_ERROR	GOPHER_TYPE_MOVIE
GOPHER_TYPE_MAC_BINHEX	GOPHER_TYPE_SOUND
GOPHER_TYPE_DOS_ARCHIVE	GOPHER_TYPE_HTML
GOPHER_TYPE_UNIX_UUENCODED	GOPHER_TYPE_PDF
GOPHER_TYPE_INDEX_SERVER	GOPHER_TYPE_CALENDAR
GOPHER_TYPE_TELNET	GOPHER_TYPE_INLINE
GOPHER_TYPE_BINARY	OPHER_TYPE_UNKNOWN
GOPHER_TYPE_REDUNDANT	GOPHER_TYPE_ASK
GOPHER_TYPE_TN3270	GOPHER_TYPE_GOPHER_PLUS

Normally, you don't build locators for files or directories; instead, you ask the server for them. The locator that will be returned from this call to `CreateLocator()` describes the locator associated with the site you are investigating.

Add a pair of lines at the end of `OnQuery()` that call this new `TryGopherSite()` function:

```
TryGopherSite(m_host);
TryGopherSite("gopher." + m_host);
```

Build and run the program again. You may have to wait several minutes for the results. Figure 19.10 shows that Query has found two Gopher sites for **harvard.edu**. In both cases, the locator describes the site itself. This is enough to prove that there is a Gopher site at **harvard.edu**, which is all that Query is supposed to do.

FIG. 19.10

Query finds two Harvard Gopher sites.

T I P Gopher is an older protocol that has been almost entirely supplemented by the World Wide Web. As a general rule, if a site has a Gopher presence, it's been on the Internet since before the World Wide Web existed (1989) or at least before the huge upsurge in popularity began (1992). What's more, the site was probably large enough in the early 1990s to have an administrator who would set up the Gopher menus and text.

Part
VI

Ch

19

Using Gopher to Send a Finger Query

There is another protocol that can give you information about a site. It's one of the oldest protocols on the Internet, and it's called Finger. You can finger a single user or an entire site, and though many sites have disabled Finger, many more will provide you with useful information in response to a Finger request.

There is no MFC class or API function with the word *finger* in its name, but that doesn't mean you can't use the classes already presented. This section relies on a trick—and on knowledge of the Finger and Gopher protocols. While the WinInet classes are a boon to new Internet programmers who don't know quite how the Internet works, they also have a lot to offer to old-timers who know what's going on under the hood.

As discussed in the "Using Windows Sockets" section of Chapter 18, "Sockets, MAPI, and the Internet," all Internet transactions involve both a host and a port. Well-known services use standard port numbers. For example, when you call `CInternetSession::OpenURL()` with an URL that starts **http://**, the code behind the scenes connects to port 80 on the remote host. When you call `GetFtpConnection()`, the connection is made to port 21 on the remote host. Gopher uses port 70. If you look at Figure 19.10, you will see that the locator that describes the **gopher.harvard.edu** site includes a mention of port 70.

The Gopher documentation makes this clear: If you build a locator with a host name, port 70, Gopher type 0 (`GOPHER_TYPE_TEXT_FILE` is defined to be 0), and a string with a file name, any Gopher client simply sends the string, whether it's a file name or not, to port 70. The Gopher server listening on that port responds by sending the file.

Now, Finger is a simple protocol, too. If you send a string to port 79 on a remote host, the Finger server that is listening there will react to the string by sending a Finger reply. If the string is only `\r\n`, the usual reply is a list of all the users on the host and some other information about them, such as their real names. (Many sites consider this an invasion of privacy or a security risk, and they disable Finger. But many other sites deliberately make this same information available on their Web pages.)

Putting this all together, if you build a Gopher locator using port 79—rather than the default 70—and an empty file name, you can do a Finger query using the MFC WinInet classes. First, add another function to `CQueryDlg` called `TryFinger()`, which takes a `CString host` and returns `void`. The code for this function is very much like `TryGopherSite()`, except that the connection is made to port 79:

```
connection = session.GetGopherConnection(host,NULL,NULL,79);
```

Once the connection is made, a text file locator is created:

```
CGopherLocator locator = connection->CreateLocator(NULL, NULL,
➥GOPHER_TYPE_TEXT_FILE);
```

This time, rather than simply casting the locator into a `CString`, use it to open a file:

```
CGopherFile* file = connection->OpenFile(locator);
```

Then echo the first 20 lines of this file, just as `TryURL()` echoed the first 20 lines of the file returned by a Web server. The code to do this is in Listing 19.7.

Listing 19.7 QueryDlg.cpp—*CQueryDlg::TryFinger()* Excerpt

```
if (file)
{
    CString line;

    for (int i=0; i < 20 && file->ReadString(line); i++)
    {
        m_out += line + "\r\n";
```

```
        }
        file->Close();
        delete file;
}
```

Putting it all together, `TryFinger()` is shown in Listing 20.8.

Listing 19.8 QueryDlg.cpp—*CQueryDlg::TryFinger()*

```
void CQueryDlg::TryFinger(CString host)
{
    CInternetSession session;

    m_out += "Trying to Finger " + host + "\r\n";
    UpdateData(FALSE);

    CGopherConnection* connection = NULL;

    try
    {
        connection = session.GetGopherConnection(host,NULL,NULL,79);
    }
    catch (CInternetException* pEx)
    {
        //if anything went wrong, just set connection to NULL
        connection = NULL;
        pEx->Delete();
    }
    if (connection)
    {
        m_out += "Connection established. \r\n";

        CGopherLocator locator = connection->CreateLocator(NULL, NULL,
        ➥GOPHER_TYPE_TEXT_FILE);

        CGopherFile* file = connection->OpenFile(locator);
        if (file)
        {
            CString line;

            for (int i=0; i < 20 && file->ReadString(line); i++)
            {
                m_out += line + "\r\n";
            }
            file->Close();
            delete file;
        }

        connection->Close();
        delete connection;
```

Part

VI

Ch

19

continues

Listing 19.8   Continued

```
    }
    else
    {
        m_out += "No server found there. \r\n";
    }

    m_out += "-----------------------\r\n";
    UpdateData(FALSE);

}
```

Add a line at the end of OnQuery() that calls this new function:

```
TryFinger(m_host);
```

Now, build and run the application. Figure 19.11 shows the result of a query on the site **whitehouse.gov**, scrolled down to the Finger section.

FIG. 19.11

Query gets e-mail addresses from the White House Finger server.

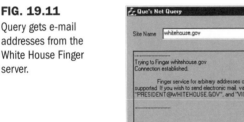

> **N O T E**   If the site you are investigating is not running a Finger server, there will be a longer than usual delay, and a message box will appear telling you the connection timed out. Click OK on the message box if it appears. ■

Using Gopher to Send a Whois Query

One last protocol provides information about sites. It, too, is an old protocol not supported directly by the WinInet classes. It is called Whois, and it's a service offered by only a few servers on the whole Internet. The servers that offer this service are maintained by the organizations that register domain names. For example, domain names that end in **.com** are registered through an organization called InterNIC, and it runs a Whois server called **rs.internic.net** (the *rs* stands for Registration Services). Like Finger, Whois responds to a string sent on its own port; the Whois port is 43. Unlike Finger, you don't send an empty string in the locator; you send the name of the host you want to look up. You connect to **rs.internic.net** every time. (Dedicated Whois servers offer users a chance to change this, but in practice, no one ever does.)

Add a function called TryWhois(); as usual, it takes a CString host and returns void. The code is in Listing 19.9.

Listing 19.9 QueryDlg.cpp—*CQueryDlg::TryWhois()*

```
void CQueryDlg::TryWhois(CString host)
{
    CInternetSession session;

    m_out += "Trying Whois for " + host + "\r\n";
    UpdateData(FALSE);

    CGopherConnection* connection = NULL;
    try
    {
        connection = session.GetGopherConnection("rs.internic.net",NULL,NULL,43);
    }
    catch (CInternetException* pEx)
    {
        //if anything went wrong, just set connection to NULL
        connection = NULL;
        pEx->Delete();
    }
    if (connection)
    {
        m_out += "Connection established. \r\n";
        CGopherLocator locator = connection->CreateLocator(NULL, host,
GOPHER_TYPE_TEXT_FILE);
        CGopherFile* file = connection->OpenFile(locator);
        if (file)
        {
            CString line;
            for (int i=0; i < 20 && file->ReadString(line); i++)
            {
                m_out += line + "\r\n";
            }
            file->Close();
            delete file;
        }
        connection->Close();
        delete connection;
    }
    else
    {
        m_out += "No server found there. \r\n";
    }
    m_out += "-------------------------\r\n";
    UpdateData(FALSE);
}
```

Part

VI

Ch

19

Add a line at the end of OnQuery() to call it:

```
TryWhois(m_host);
```

Build and run the application one last time. Figure 19.12 shows the Whois part of the report for **mcp.com**—this is the domain for Macmillan Computer Publishing, Que's parent company.

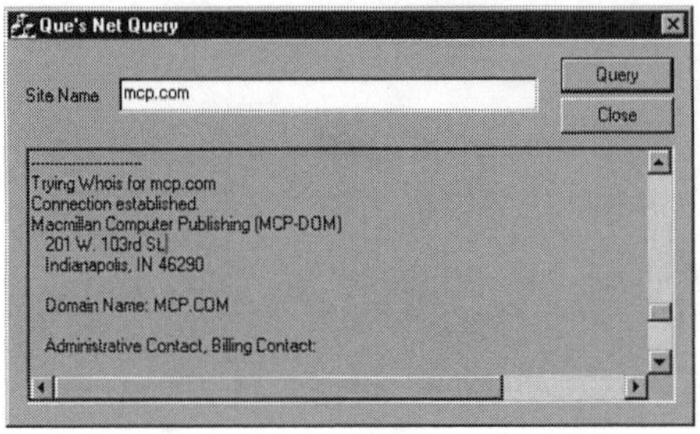

FIG. 19.12

Query gets real-life addresses and names from the InterNIC Whois server.

Adding code after the Finger portion of this application means that you can no longer ignore the times when the Finger code cannot connect. When the call to OpenFile() in TryFinger() tries to open a file on a host that is not running a Finger server, an exception is thrown. Control will not return to OnQuery(), and TryWhois() will never be called. To prevent this, you must wrap the call to OpenFile() in a try and catch block. Listing 19.10 shows the changes to make.

Listing 19.10   QueryDlg.cpp—Changes to *TryFinger()*

```
//replace this line:
        CGopherFile* file = connection->OpenFile(locator);
//with these lines:
        CGopherFile* file = NULL;
        try
        {
            file = connection->OpenFile(locator);
        }
        catch (CInternetException* pEx)
        {
            //if anything went wrong, just set file to NULL
            file = NULL;
            pEx->Delete();
        }
```

Change TryFinger(), build Query again, and query a site that does not run a Finger server, such as **microsoft.com**. You should successfully reach the Whois portion of the application.

Future Work

The Query application built in this chapter does a lot, but it could do much more. There are e-mail and news protocols that could be reached by stretching the WinInet classes a little more and using them to connect to the standard ports for these other services. You could also connect to some well-known Web search engines and submit queries by forming URLs according to the pattern used by those engines. In this way, you can automate the sort of poking around on the Internet that most of us do when we're curious about a domain name or an organization.

If you'd like to learn more about Internet protocols, port numbers, and what's happening when a client connects to a server, you might want to read Que's *Building Internet Applications with Visual C++*. The book was written for Visual C++ 2.0, and though all the applications in the book compile and run under later versions of MFC, they would be much shorter and easier to write now. Still, the insight into the way the protocols work is valuable.

The WinInet classes can do much more than you've seen here, too. Query doesn't use them to retrieve real files over the Internet. There are two WinInet sample applications included with Visual C++ 5.0 that do a fine job of showing how to retrieve files:

- FTPTREE builds a tree list of the files and directories on an FTP site.
- TEAR brings back a page of HTML from a Web site.

There are a lot more Microsoft announcements coming over the next few months, as well. Keep an eye on its Web site, **www.microsoft.com**, for libraries and software development kits that will make Internet software development even easier and faster.

From Here...

This chapter introduced you to the WinInet classes as one way to write Internet programs. Some related chapters that may interest you include the following:

- Chapter 1, "Building Your First Application," compares dialog-based applications to the MDI or SDI applications that AppWizard can also generate for you.
- Chapter 18, "Sockets, MAPI, and the Internet," introduces you to the concepts involved in Internet programming.
- Chapter 20, "Building an Internet ActiveX Control," discusses small, efficient controls designed to run quickly and smoothly in an Internet Web page.

Part
VI

Ch
19

Building an Internet ActiveX Control

In Chapter 17, "Building an ActiveX Control," you learned how to build your own controls and include them in forms-based applications written in Visual Basic, Visual C++, and the VBA macro language. There's one other place those controls can go—on a web page. But the ActiveX controls generated by older versions of Visual C++ were too big and slow to put on a web page. This chapter shows how to get these controls onto your web pages, and how to write faster, sleeker controls that will make your pages a pleasure to use. ■

How Microsoft Explorer loads ActiveX controls

When you see a web page with an ActiveX control in it, your jaw will drop!

How Netscape Navigator loads ActiveX controls

Yes, it's true, Netscape Navigator can display an ActiveX control. This section points you to the plug-in your users will need.

ActiveX controls versus Java applets

There's more than one way to allow a user to interact with a web page. We compare ActiveX controls to Java applets.

AppWizard's Advanced Control options

AppWizard's ActiveX ControlWizard can add some nice optimizations to your controls.

Asynchronous properties

The last thing you want your control to do is slow down your web page. The second to last thing you want is for your control to be boring.

Embedding an ActiveX Control into a Microsoft Explorer Web Page

It's a remarkably simple matter to put an ActiveX control onto a web page that you know will be loaded by Microsoft Explorer 3.0. You use the <OBJECT> tag, a relatively new addition to HTML that describes a wide variety of objects that you might want to insert into a web page: a moving video clip, a sound, a Java applet, an ActiveX control, and many more kinds of information and ways of interacting with a user. Listing 20.1 shows the HTML source for a page that displays the Dieroll control from Chapter 17, "Building an ActiveX Control."

Listing 20.1 fatdie.html—Using <OBJECT>

```
<HEAD>
<TITLE>A Web page with a rolling die</TITLE>
</HEAD>
<BODY>
<OBJECT ID="Dieroll1"
CLASSID="CLSID:46646B43-EA16-11CF-870C-00201801DDD6"
CODEBASE="dieroll.cab#Version=1,0,0,1"
WIDTH="200"
HEIGHT="200">
<PARAM NAME="ForeColor" VALUE="0">
<PARAM NAME="BackColor" VALUE="16777215">
If you see this text, your browser does not support the OBJECT tag.
<BR>
</OBJECT>
<BR>
Here is some text after the die
</BODY>
</HTML>
```

The only ugly thing here is the CLSID, and the easiest way to get that, since you're a software developer, is to cut and paste it from dieroll.odl, the Object Description Library. Use FileView to open dieroll.odl quickly. Here's the section in dieroll.odl that includes the CLSID:

```
//  Class information for CDierollCtrl

[ uuid(46646B43-EA16-11CF-870C-00201801DDD6),
  helpstring("Dieroll Control"), control ]
```

This section is at the end of dieroll.odl—the earlier CLSIDs do not refer to the whole control, only to portions of it. Copy the uuid from inside the brackets into your HTML source.

T I P Microsoft has a product called the Control Pad that gets CLSIDs from the Registry for you and makes life easier for web page builders who are intimidated by instructions like "open the ODL file" or who don't have the ODL file, since it's not shipped with the control. Since you're building this control, and know how to open files in Developer Studio, this chapter will not describe the Control Pad tool. If you're curious, see Microsoft's Control Pad Web page at **http://www.microsoft.com/workshop/author/ cpad/** for more details.

The CODEBASE attribute of the OBJECT tag specifies where the OCX file is kept, so that if the user does not have a copy of the ActiveX control, one will be downloaded automatically. The use of the CLSID means that if this user has already installed this ActiveX control, there is no download time, the control is simply used right away. You can simply specify an URL to the OCX file, but in order to automate the DLL downloading, this CODEBASE attribute points to a CAB file. Putting your control into a CAB file will cut your download time to as little as half what it otherwise would be. You can learn more about CAB technology at **http://www.microsoft.com/ intdev/cab/**. That page is written for Java developers, but the technology works just as well to cut the download time for ActiveX controls.

T I P   If you don't have access to a Web server in which you can put controls while you're developing them, use a file:// URL in the CODEBASE attribute that points to the location of the control on your hard drive.

The remainder of the attributes of the OBJECT tag should be fairly intuitive if you've built a Web page before: ID is used by other tags on the page to refer to this control, WIDTH and HEIGHT specify the size, in pixels, that the control should appear, and HSPACE and VSPACE are horizontal and vertical blank spaces, in pixels, around the entire control.

Everything after the <OBJECT ...> tag and before the </OBJECT> tags is ignored by browsers that understand the OBJECT tag. (The <OBJECT...> tag is usually many lines long and contains all the information to describe the object.) Browsers that do not understand the OBJECT tag ignore the <OBJECT ...> tag and the </OBJECT> tag and display the HTML between them (in this case, a line of text pointing out that this browser does not support the tag). This is part of the specification for a Web browser: It should ignore tags it doesn't understand.

Figure 20.1 shows this page displayed in Microsoft Explorer 3.0. Clicking the die rolls it, and everything works beautifully. Things certainly look simple and amazing, but two flaws appear immediately:

■ Not all browsers support the OBJECT tag.

■ It can take a long time to download the control.

Figure 20.2 shows the same page displayed in Netscape Navigator 2.0. It doesn't support the OBJECT tag, so it doesn't show the die. And Netscape Navigator is used by well over half of the people who browse the Web! Does that mean it's not worth writing ActiveX controls for Web pages? Not at all. As you'll see in the very next section, there's a way that Navigator users can use the same controls as Explorer users.

The size issue is a bigger worry. The release version of the Dieroll control, as built for Chapter 17, "Building an ActiveX Control," is 26K. Many designers put a 50K limit per Web page for graphics and other material to be downloaded, and this simple control uses half that limit. A more powerful control would easily exceed it. The majority of this chapter deals with ways to

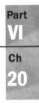

Part
VI

Ch
20

reduce that size or otherwise minimize the download time for ActiveX controls. Web page designers will then be able to tap the controls' full power without worrying that users will label their pages as "slow," one of the worst knocks against any Web site.

FIG. 20.1

Microsoft Internet Explorer can show ActiveX controls.

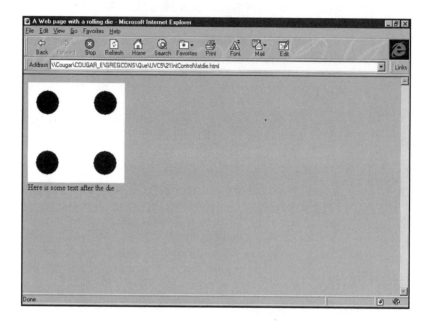

FIG. 20.2

Netscape Navigator cannot show ActiveX controls.

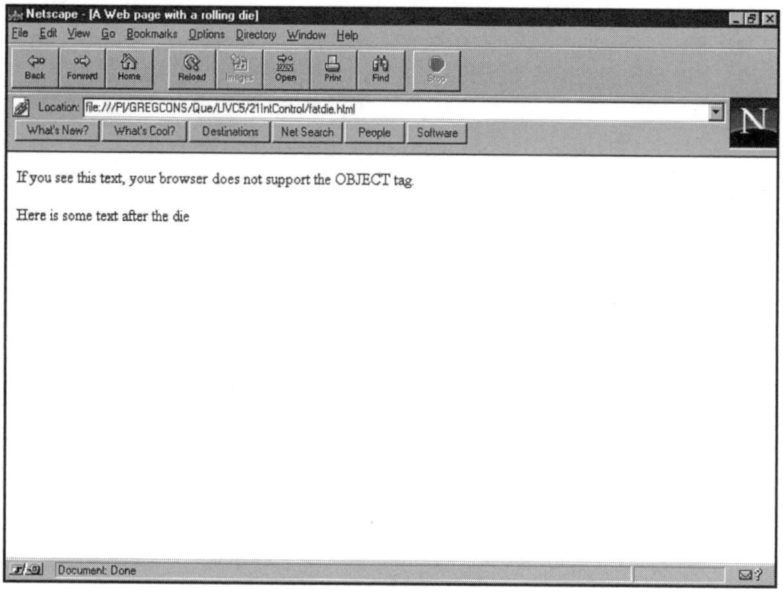

There's a third flaw that you won't notice because you have Visual C++ installed on your computer. The control requires the MFC DLL. The user must download it and install it before the controls can run. The mechanism that automatically downloads and installs controls does not automatically download and install this DLL, though using a CAB file as discussed earlier can make it possible.

TIP

For an example of a Web page that includes a cab file for the Dieroll control and the MFC DLLs, come to **http://www.gregcons.com/dieroll.htm**.

N O T E   It might occur to you to try linking the MFC Library statically into your control. It seems easy enough to do: Choose Build Settings, and on the General tab there is a drop-down list box inviting you to choose static linking. If you do that and build, you'll get hundreds of linker errors: The `COleControl` and `CPropPage` functions are not in the DLL that is linked statically. (That's because Microsoft felt it would be foolish to link the MFC functions statically into a control.) Setting up another library to link in those functions is beyond the scope of this chapter, especially since all this work would lead to an enormous (over 1M) control that would take far too long to download the first time. ■

Embedding an ActiveX Control into a Netscape Navigator Web Page

NCompass Labs (**www.ncompasslabs.com**) has produced a Netscape plug-in, called ControlActive, that allows you to embed an ActiveX control into a page that will be read with Netscape Navigator. Just look at Figure 20.3, which shows the Dieroll in Netscape. The HTML for this page is shown in Listing 20.2. (Resist the temptation to load this HTML into Netscape yourself until you have registered the control as safe for initializing and scripting in the next section.)

On the CD

Listing 20.2   fatdie2.html—Using <OBJECT> and <EMBED>

```
<HTML>
<HEAD>
<TITLE>A Web page with a rolling die</TITLE>
</HEAD>
<BODY>
<OBJECT ID="Dieroll1"
CLASSID="CLSID:46646B43-EA16-11CF-870C-00201801DDD6"
CODEBASE="dieroll.cab#Version=1,0,0,1"
WIDTH="200"
HEIGHT="200">
<PARAM NAME="ForeColor" VALUE="0">
<PARAM NAME="BackColor" VALUE="16777215">
<PARAM NAME="Image" VALUE="beans.bmp">
<EMBED LIVECONNECT NAME="Dieroll1"
```

Part
VI

Ch
20

continues

Listing 20.2   Continued

```
WIDTH="200"
HEIGHT="200"
CLASSID="CLSID:46646B43-EA16-11CF-870C-00201801DDD6"
TYPE="application/oleobject"
CODEBASE="dieroll.cab#Version=1,0,0,1"
PARAM_ForeColor="0"
PARAM_BackColor="16777215">
</OBJECT>
<BR>
Here is some text after the die
</BODY>
</HTML>
```

FIG. 20.3

ActiveX controls can be displayed in Netscape Navigator with the NCompass Labs plug-in.

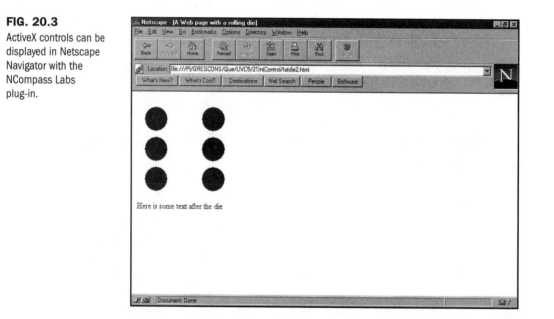

It is the <EMBED> tag that brings up the plug-in. Because it's inside the <OBJECT>...</OBJECT> tag, Microsoft Internet Explorer and other browsers that know the OBJECT tag will ignore the EMBED tag. This means that this HTML source will display the control equally well in Netscape Navigator and in Explorer. You will probably want to include a link on your page to the NCompass page to help your readers get and learn about the plug-in.

Microsoft is committed to establishing ActiveX controls as a cross-platform, multi-browser solution that will, in the words of its slogan, "Activate the Internet." The ActiveX control specification is no longer a proprietary document, but has been released to a committee that will maintain the standard. So don't pay any attention to people who suggest you should only build these controls if your readers use Internet Explorer!

Registering as Safe for Scripting and Initializing

For any of your readers who operate with a Medium Safety level, the control should be registered as safe for scripting and initializing. This assures anyone who wants to view a page containing the control that no matter what functions are called from a script, or what parameters are initialized through the PARAM attribute, nothing unsafe will happen. For an example of a control that is not safe, think of a control that deletes a file on your machine when it executes. The default file is one you won't miss or that probably won't exist. A page that put this control in a script, or that initialized the file name with PARAM attributes, might order the control to delete a very important file or files, based on guesses about where most people keep documents. It would be simple to delete C:\MSOFFICE\WINWORD\WINWORD.EXE, for example, and that would be annoying for Word users. Figure 20.4 shows the error message displayed in Explorer when you are using the Medium safety level and load a page featuring a control that is not registered as script-safe or init-safe. The NCompassLabs plug-in, ControlActive, also refuses to load controls that are not registered as script-safe and init-safe.

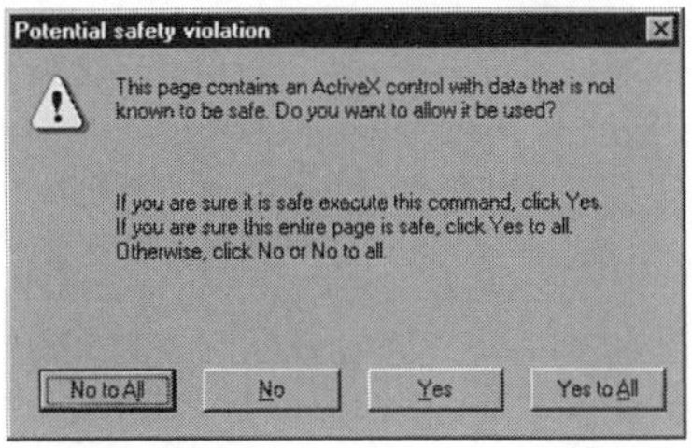

FIG. 20.4
Explorer alerts you to controls that might run amok.

First, you need to add three functions to DierollCtl.cpp. (These come unchanged from the ActiveX SDK.) These functions are called by code presented later in this section. Don't forget to add declarations of the these functions to the header file too. The code is in Listing 20.3.

Listing 20.3   DierollCtl.cpp—New Functions to Mark the Control as Safe

```
/////////////////////////////////////////////////////////////////
// Copied from the ActiveX SDK
// This code is used to register and unregister a
// control as safe for initialization and safe for scripting

HRESULT CreateComponentCategory(CATID catid, WCHAR* catDescription)
{
    ICatRegister* pcr = NULL ;
    HRESULT hr = S_OK ;

    hr = CoCreateInstance(CLSID_StdComponentCategoriesMgr,
            NULL, CLSCTX_INPROC_SERVER, IID_ICatRegister, (void**)&pcr);
    if (FAILED(hr))
            return hr;

    // Make sure the HKCR\Component Categories\{..catid...}
```

Part
VI

Ch
20

continues

Listing 20.3   Continued

```
            // key is registered
            CATEGORYINFO catinfo;
            catinfo.catid = catid;
            catinfo.lcid = 0x0409 ; // english

            // Make sure the provided description is not too long.
            // Only copy the first 127 characters if it is
            int len = wcslen(catDescription);
            if (len>127)
                    len = 127;
            wcsncpy(catinfo.szDescription, catDescription, len);
            // Make sure the description is null terminated
            catinfo.szDescription[len] = '\0';

            hr = pcr->RegisterCategories(1, &catinfo);
            pcr->Release();

            return hr;
}

HRESULT RegisterCLSIDInCategory(REFCLSID clsid, CATID catid)
{
    // Register your component categories information.
    ICatRegister* pcr = NULL ;
    HRESULT hr = S_OK ;
    hr = CoCreateInstance(CLSID_StdComponentCategoriesMgr,
            NULL, CLSCTX_INPROC_SERVER, IID_ICatRegister, (void**)&pcr);
    if (SUCCEEDED(hr))
    {
            // Register this category as being "implemented" by
            // the class.
            CATID rgcatid[1] ;
            rgcatid[0] = catid;
            hr = pcr->RegisterClassImplCategories(clsid, 1, rgcatid);
    }

    if (pcr != NULL)
            pcr->Release();

    return hr;
}

HRESULT UnRegisterCLSIDInCategory(REFCLSID clsid, CATID catid)
{
    ICatRegister* pcr = NULL ;
    HRESULT hr = S_OK ;
    hr = CoCreateInstance(CLSID_StdComponentCategoriesMgr,
            NULL, CLSCTX_INPROC_SERVER, IID_ICatRegister, (void**)&pcr);
    if (SUCCEEDED(hr))
    {
        // Unregister this category as being "implemented" by
        // the class.
        CATID rgcatid[1] ;
        rgcatid[0] = catid;
```

```
      hr = pcr->UnRegisterClassImplCategories(clsid, 1, rgcatid);
   }

   if (pcr != NULL)
   pcr->Release();

   return hr;
}
```

Second, add two #include statements at the top of DierollCtl.cpp:

```
#include "comcat.h"
#include "objsafe.h"
```

Finally, modify UpdateRegistry() in DierollCtl.cpp to call these new functions. The new code calls CreateComponentCategory() to create a category called "CATID_SafeForScripting," then adds this control to that category. Then it creates a category called "CATID_SafeForInitializing" and adds the control to that category as well. Listing 20.4 shows the new version of UpdateRegistry().

Listing 20.4 DierollCtl.cpp—
CDierollCtrl::CDierollCtrlFactory::UpdateRegistry()

```
BOOL CDierollCtrl::CDierollCtrlFactory::UpdateRegistry(BOOL bRegister)
{
   // TODO: Verify that your control follows apartment-model threading rules.
   // Refer to MFC TechNote 64 for more information.
   // If your control does not conform to the apartment-model rules, then
   // you must modify the code below, changing the 6th parameter from
   // afxRegInsertable ¦ afxRegApartmentThreading to afxRegInsertable.

   if (bRegister)
   {
       HRESULT hr = S_OK ;

       // register as safe for scripting
       hr = CreateComponentCategory(CATID_SafeForScripting,
               L"Controls that are safely scriptable");

       if (FAILED(hr))
           return FALSE;

       hr = RegisterCLSIDInCategory(m_clsid, CATID_SafeForScripting);

       if (FAILED(hr))
           return FALSE;

       // register as safe for initializing
       hr = CreateComponentCategory(CATID_SafeForInitializing,
               L"Controls safely initializable from persistent data");

       if (FAILED(hr))
```

continues

Listing 20.4   Continued

```
            return FALSE;

    hr = RegisterCLSIDInCategory(m_clsid, CATID_SafeForInitializing);

    if (FAILED(hr))
        return FALSE;

    return AfxOleRegisterControlClass(
        AfxGetInstanceHandle(),
        m_clsid,
        m_lpszProgID,
        IDS_DIEROLL,
        IDB_DIEROLL,
        afxRegInsertable | afxRegApartmentThreading,
        _dwDierollOleMisc,
        _tlid,
        _wVerMajor,
        _wVerMinor);
    else
    {
    HRESULT hr = S_OK ;
    hr = UnRegisterCLSIDInCategory(m_clsid, CATID_SafeForScripting);

    if (FAILED(hr))
        return FALSE;

    hr = UnRegisterCLSIDInCategory(m_clsid, CATID_SafeForInitializing);

    if (FAILED(hr))
        return FALSE;

        return AfxOleUnregisterClass(m_clsid, m_lpszProgID);
    }
}
```

To confirm that this works, open Explorer and set your safety level to Medium. Load the HTML page that uses the control; it should warn you the control is unsafe. Then make these changes, build the control, and reload the page. The warning will not reappear.

Choosing Between ActiveX and Java

Java is an application development language as well as an applet development language, which means you can develop ActiveX controls in Java if you choose to, using a tool like Microsoft's Visual J++ integrated into Developer Studio. But when most people frame a showdown like "ActiveX versus Java," they mean ActiveX versus Java *applets*, which are little tightly contained applications that run on a Web page and cannot run stand-alone.

Many people are concerned about the security of running an application they did not code, when they do not know the person or organization supplying the application. The Java approach attempts to restrict the actions that applets can perform, so that even malicious applets cannot do any real damage. But regular announcements of flaws in the restriction approach are damaging the credibility of Java. Even if a Java applet was guaranteed to be safe, these same restrictions keep applets from doing certain useful tasks.

The approach taken by Microsoft with ActiveX is the trusted supplier approach, which is extendable to Java and any other code that can run. Code is digitally signed so that you are sure who provided it, and that it has not been changed since it was signed. This won't prevent bad things from happening if you run the code, but will guarantee that you know who is to blame if bad things do occur. This is just the same as buying shrink-wrapped software from the shelf in the computer store. For more details, look at **http://www.microsoft.com/ie/most/howto/ trusted.htm** and follow some of the links from that page.

Probably the biggest difference between the ActiveX approach and the Java applet approach is downloading. Java code is downloaded every time you load the page that contains it. ActiveX code is downloaded once, unless you already have the control installed some other way (perhaps a CD was sent to you in a magazine, for example) and then never again. A copy is stored on the user's machine and entered into the Registry. The Java code that is downloaded is small, because most of the code that's involved is in the Java Virtual Machine installed on your computer, probably as part of your browser.

The ActiveX code that's downloaded can be much larger, though the optimizations discussed in the next section can reduce the size significantly by relying on DLLs and other code already on the user's computer. If users will come to this page once and never again, they may be annoyed to find ActiveX controls cluttering up their disk and Registry. On the other hand, if they come to the same page repeatedly, they will be pleased to find that there is no download time: The control simply activates and runs.

There are still other differences. Java applets cannot fire events to notify the container that something has happened. Java applets cannot be licensed, and often don't distinguish between design-time and run-time use. Java applets can't be used in Visual Basic forms or VC++ programs or Word documents in the same way that ActiveX controls can. ActiveX controls are about 10 times faster than Java applets. In their favor, Java applets are genuinely multi-platform and typically smaller than the equivalent ActiveX control.

Part
VI

Ch
20

Using AppWizard to Create Faster ActiveX Controls

Microsoft did not develop OCX controls to be placed into Web pages, and changing their name to ActiveX controls didn't magically make them smaller or faster to load. So the AppWizard that comes with Visual C++ has a number of options available to achieve those ends. This chapter will change these options in the Dieroll control that was already created just to show how it's done. Since Dieroll is a fairly lean control already, and loads quickly, these simple changes won't make much difference. It's worth learning the techniques, though, for your own controls, which will surely be fatter than Dieroll.

The first few options to reduce the size of your control have always been available on Step 2 of the ActiveX Control Wizard:

- Activates when visible
- Invisible at runtime
- Available in Insert Object dialog box
- Has an About box
- Acts as a simple frame control

If you are developing your control entirely for the Web, many of these settings won't matter anymore. For example, it doesn't matter whether or not your control has an About box; users won't be able to bring it up when they are viewing the control in a Web page.

The Activates When Visible option is very important. Activating a control takes a lot of over-head activity, and should be postponed as long as possible so that your control appears to load quickly. If your control activates as soon as it is visible, you will add to the time it takes to load your control. To deselect this option in the existing Dieroll code, open the Dieroll project in Developer Studio, and open DierollCtl.cpp with FileView. Look for a block of code like the one in Listing 20.5.

Listing 20.5   Excerpt from DierollCtl.cpp—Setting Activates when Visible

```
/////////////////////////////////////////////////////////////////////////
// Control type information

static const DWORD BASED_CODE _dwDierollOleMisc =
    OLEMISC_ACTIVATEWHENVISIBLE |
    OLEMISC_SETCLIENTSITEFIRST |
    OLEMISC_INSIDEOUT |
    OLEMISC_CANTLINKINSIDE |
    OLEMISC_RECOMPOSEONRESIZE;

IMPLEMENT_OLECTLTYPE(CDierollCtrl, IDS_DIEROLL, _dwDierollOleMisc)
```

Delete the OLEMISC_ACTIVATEWHENVISIBLE line. Build a release version of the application. Though the size of the Dieroll OCX file is unchanged, Web pages with this control should load more quickly, since the window is not created until the user first clicks the die. If you reload the Web page with the die in it, you'll see the first value immediately, even though the control is inactive. The window is created to catch mouse clicks, not to display the die roll.

There are more optimizations available. Figure 20.5 shows the list of advanced options for ActiveX Control Wizard, reached by clicking the Advanced button on Step 2. You can choose each of these options when you first build the application through the Control Wizard. They can also be changed in an existing application, saving you the trouble of redoing AppWizard and adding your own functionality again. The options are:

- Windowless Activation
- Unclipped Device Context

- Flicker-free Activation
- Mouse Pointer Notifications When Inactive
- Optimized Drawing Code
- Loads Properties Asynchronously

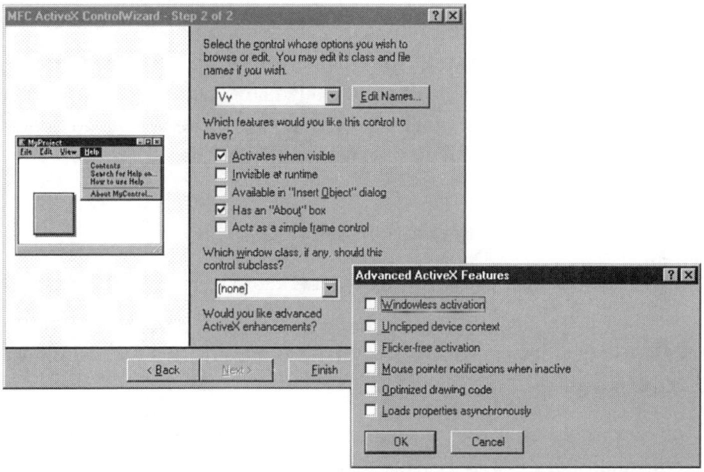

FIG. 20.5

The Advanced button on Step 2 of the ActiveX Control Wizard leads to a choice of optimizations.

Windowless Activation is going to be very popular because of the benefits it provides. If you want a transparent control or one that is not a rectangle, you must use Windowless Activation. However, because it reduces code size and speeds execution, every control should consider using this option. Modern containers will provide the functionality for the control. In older containers, the control will create the window anyway, denying you the savings but ensuring the control still works.

To implement the Windowless Activation option in Dieroll, override `CDierollCtrl::GetControlFlags()` like this:

```
DWORD CDierollCtrl::GetControlFlags()
{
    return COleControl::GetControlFlags()| windowlessActivate;
}
```

Add the function quickly by right-clicking `CDierollCtrl` in Class View and choosing Add Function. If you do this to Dieroll, build it, and reload the Web page that uses it, you will notice no apparent effect, because Dieroll is such a lean control. You will at least notice that it still functions perfectly, and doesn't mind not having a window.

The next two options, Unclipped Device Context and Flicker-free Activation, are not available to windowless controls. In a control with a window, choosing Unclipped Device Context means that you are completely sure that you never draw outside the client rectangle of the control. Skipping the checks that make sure you don't means your control runs faster, though it could mean trouble if you have an error in your draw code. If you were to do this in Dieroll, the override of `GetControlFlags()` would look like this:

Part

VI

Ch

20

```
DWORD CDierollCtrl::GetControlFlags()
{
    return COleControl::GetControlFlags()& ~clipPaintDC;
}
```

Don't try to combine this with windowless activation: It doesn't do anything.

Flicker free activation is useful for controls which draw their inactive and active views identically. (Think back to Chapter 15, "Building an ActiveX Server Application," in which the server object was drawn in dimmed colors when the objects were inactive.)If there is no need to redraw, because the drawing code is the same, you can select this option and skip the second draw. Your users won't see an annoying flicker as the control activates, and activation will be a tiny bit quicker. If you were to do this in Dieroll, the GetControlFlags()override would be:

```
DWORD CDierollCtrl::GetControlFlags()
{
    return COleControl::GetControlFlags()¦ noFlickerActivate;
}
```

Like unclipped device context, don't try to combine this with windowless activation: It doesn't do anything.

Mouse pointer notifications, when inactive, enable more controls to turn off the activate when visible option. If the only reason to be active is to have a window to process mouse interactions, this option will divert those interactions to the container through an IPointerInactive interface. To enable this option in an application that is already built, you override GetControlFlags()again:

```
 DWORD CDierollCtrl::GetControlFlags()
{
    return COleControl::GetControlFlags()¦ pointerInactive;
}
```

Now your code will receive WM_SETCURSOR and WM_MOUSEMOVE messages through message map entries, even though you have no window. The container, whose window your control is using, will send these messages to you through the IPointerInactive interface.

The other circumstance under which you might want to process window messages while still inactive, and so without a window, is if the user drags something over your control and drops it. The control needs to activate at that moment, so that it has a window to be a drop target. You can arrange that with an override to GetActivationPolicy():

```
DWORD CDierollCtrl::GetActivationPolicy()
{
    return POINTERINACTIVE_ACTIVATEONDRAG;
}
```

Don't bother doing this if your control isn't a drop target, of course.

The problem with relying on the container to pass on your messages through the IPointerInactive interface is that the container may have no idea such an interface exists, and have no plans to pass your messages on with it. If you think your control might end up in such a container, then don't remove the `OLEMISC_ACTIVATEWHENVISIBLE` flag from the block of code, like the one in Listing 20.6

Listing 20.6 Excerpt from DierollCtl.cpp—Finetuning Activates when Visible

```
/////////////////////////////////////////////////////////////////////////
// Control type information

static const DWORD BASED_CODE _dwDierollOleMisc =
    OLEMISC_ACTIVATEWHENVISIBLE ¦
    OLEMISC_SETCLIENTSITEFIRST ¦
    OLEMISC_INSIDEOUT ¦
    OLEMISC_CANTLINKINSIDE ¦
    OLEMISC_RECOMPOSEONRESIZE;

IMPLEMENT_OLECTLTYPE(CDierollCtrl, IDS_DIEROLL, _dwDierollOleMisc)
```

Instead, combine another flag, `OLEMISC_IGNOREACTIVATEWHENVISIBLE`, with these flags using the bitwise *or* operator. This oddly named flag is meaningful to containers that understand `IPointerInactive`, and means, in effect "I take it back, don't activate when visible after all." Containers that don't understand `IPointerInactive` don't understand this flag either, and your control will activate when visible, and thus be around to catch mouse messages in these containers.

Optimized drawing code is only useful to controls that will be sharing the container with a number of other drawing controls. As you may recall from Chapter 6, "Drawing On the Screen," the typical pattern for drawing a view of any kind is to set the brush, pen, or other GDI object to a new value, saving the old, then use the GDI object, then restore it to the saved value. If there are a number of controls doing this in turn, all those restore steps could be skipped in favor of one restore at the end of all the drawing. The container saves all the GDI object values before instructing the controls to redraw and restores them all afterwards.

If you would like your control to take advantage of this, there are two changes to be made. First, if a pen or other GDI object is to remain connected between draw calls, it must not go out of scope. That means any local pens, brushes, and fonts should be converted to member variables so that they stay in scope between function calls. Second, the code to restore the old objects should be surrounded by an if statement that calls `COleControl::IsOptimizedDraw()` to see if the restoration is necessary. A typical draw routine would set up the colors, then proceed like this:

```
...
if(!m_pen.m_hObject)
{
    m_pen.CreatePen(PS_SOLID, 0, forecolor);
}
if(!m_brush.m_hObject)
{
    m_brush.CreateSolidBrush(backcolor);
}
```

Part

VI

Ch

20

```
CPen* savepen = pdc->SelectObject(&m_pen);
CBrush* savebrush = pdc->SelectObject(&m_brush);

...
// use device context
...
if(!IsOptimizedDraw())
{
    pdc->SelectObject(savepen);
    pdc->SelectObject(savebrush);
}
...
```

The device context has the addresses of the member variables, so when it lets go of them at the direction of the container, their m_hObject member becomes NULL. As long as it is not NULL there is no need to reset the device context, and if this container supports optimized drawing code there is no need to restore it either.

If you select this optimized drawing code option with AppWizard, the if statement with the call to IsOptimizedDraw() is added to your draw code, with some comments to remind you what to do.

The last of the optimization options loads properties asynchronously and is covered in the next section.

Speeding Control Codes with Asynchronous Properties

Asynchronous refers to spreading out activities over time, and not insisting that one activity be complete before another can begin. In the context of the Web, it's worth harking back to the features that made Netscape Navigator better than Mosaic, way back when it was first released. The number one benefit cited by people who were on the Web then was that the Netscape browser, unlike Mosaic, could display text while pictures were still loading. This is classic asynchronous behavior. You don't have to wait until the huge image files have transferred to see what the words on the page are and whether the images are worth waiting for.

Faster Internet connections and more compact image formats have lessened some of the concerns about waiting for images. Still, being asynchronous is a good thing. For one thing, waiting for video clips, sound clips, and executable code has made many Web users long for the good old days when they only had to wait 30 seconds for pages to find all their images.

Properties

The die that comes up in your Web page is the default die appearance. There's no way for the user to access the properties of the control. The Web page developer can, using the <PARAM> tag inside the <OBJECT> tag. (Browsers that ignore OBJECT also ignore PARAM.) Here's the PARAM tag to add to your HTML between <OBJECT> and </OBJECT> to include a die with a number rather than dots:

```
<PARAM NAME="Dots" value="0">
```

The PARAM tag has two attributes: NAME provides a name that matches the external ActiveX name (Dots in this case) and value provides the value (0, or FALSE, in this case). The die displays with a number.

In order to demonstrate the value of asynchronous properties, Dieroll needs to have some big properties. So, since this is a demonstration application, the next step is to add a big property. A natural choice is to give the user more control over the appearance of the die. The user (which means the Web page designer if the control is being used in a Web page) can specify an image file and use that as the background for the die. Before you see how to make that happen, imagine what the Web page reader will have to wait for when loading a page that uses Dieroll:

- The HTML has to be loaded from the server
- The browser lays out the text and non-text elements and starts to display text
- The browser searches the Registry for the CLSID of the control
- If necessary, the control is downloaded, using the CODEBASE parameter
- The control properties are initialized using the PARAM tags
- The control runs and draws itself

When Dieroll gains another property, an image file that might be quite large, there will be another delay while the image file is retrieved from wherever it is kept. If nothing happens in the meantime, the Web page reader will eventually tire of staring at an empty square and go away to another page. Using asynchronous properties means that the control can draw itself roughly and start to be useful, even while the large image file is still being downloaded. For Dieroll, drawing the dots on a plain background using GetBackColor() will do until the image file is ready.

Using BLOBs

A BLOB is a Binary Large OBject. It's a generic name for things like the image file we are about to add to the Dieroll control. The way a control talks to a BLOB is through a moniker. That's not new, it's just that monikers have always been hidden away inside OLE. If you already understand them, you will have a great deal more to learn about them, because things are changing with the introduction of asynchronous monikers. If you've never heard of them before, no problem. Eventually there will be all sorts of asynchronous monikers, but at the moment, only URL monikers have been implemented. These are ways for ActiveX to connect BLOB properties to URLs. If you're prepared to trust ActiveX to do this for you, you can achieve some amazing things. The remainder of this subsection explains how to work with URL monikers to load BLOB properties asynchronously.

Remember, the idea here is that the control will start drawing itself even before it has all of its properties. Your OnDraw() code will be structured like this:

```
// prepare to draw
if(AllPropertiesAreLoaded)
```

Part
VI

Ch
20

```
{
    // draw using the BLOB
}
else
{
    // draw without the BLOB
}
//cleanup after drawing
```

There are two problems to solve here. First, what will be the test to see if all the properties are loaded? And second, how can you arrange to have OnDraw called again when the properties are ready, if it's already been called, and has already drawn the control the "BLOBless" way?

The first problem has been solved by adding two new functions to `COleControl`. `GetReadyState()` returns one of these values:

- `READYSTATE_UNINITIALIZED` means the control is completely unitialized
- `READYSTATE_LOADING` means the control properties are loading
- `READYSTATE_LOADED` means the properties are all loaded
- `READYSTATE_INTERACTIVE` means the control can talk to the user but isn't fully loaded yet
- `READYSTATE_COMPLETE` means there is nothing more to wait for

The function `InternalSetReadyState()` sets the ready state to one of these values.

The second problem, getting a second call to `OnDraw()` after the control has already been drawn without the BLOB, has been solved by a new class called `CDataPathProperty`, and its derived class `CCachedDataPathProperty`. These classes have a member function called `OnDataAvailable()` which catches the Windows message generated when the property has been retrieved from the remote site. The `OnDataAvailable()` function invalidates the control, forcing a redraw.

Changing Dieroll

Make a copy of the Dieroll folder you created in Chapter 17, "Building an ActiveX Control," (or the Chapter 17 code from the CD) and change it to windowless activation as described earlier in this chapter. Now you're ready to begin. There is a lot to be done to implement asynchronous properties, but each step is quite straightforward.

Add the *CDierollDataPathProperty* class   Bring up Class Wizard, click the Automation tab, and click the Add Class button. From the drop-down menu that appears under the button, choose New. This brings up the Create New Class dialog box. Name the class `CDierollDataPathProperty`. Click the drop-down box for Base class and choose `CCachedDataPathProperty`. The dialog box should resemble Figure 20.6. Click OK to create the class and add it to the project.

The reason that the new class should inherit from `CCachedDataProperty` is that it will load the property information into a file, and that is an easier way to handle the bitmap. If the control has a property that was downloaded because it changed often (for example, current weather) then `CDataPathProperty` would be a better choice.

FIG. 20.6
Create a new class to handle asynchronous properties.

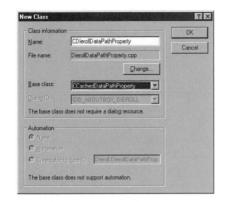

Add the Image Property to *CDierollCtrl*   With the new CDierollDataPathProperty class added to the Dieroll control, add the property to the original CDierollCtrl class that you copied, like this: in Class Wizard, on the Automation tab, make sure that CDierollCtrl is selected in the rightmost drop-down box. Click Add Property, and fill out the dialog as shown in Figure 20.7. The external name you choose is the one that will appear in the HTML: Image is simple and doesn't require a lot of typing. The type should be OLE_BSTR—that choice won't be in the drop-down box for type until you change the Implementation to Get/Set method.

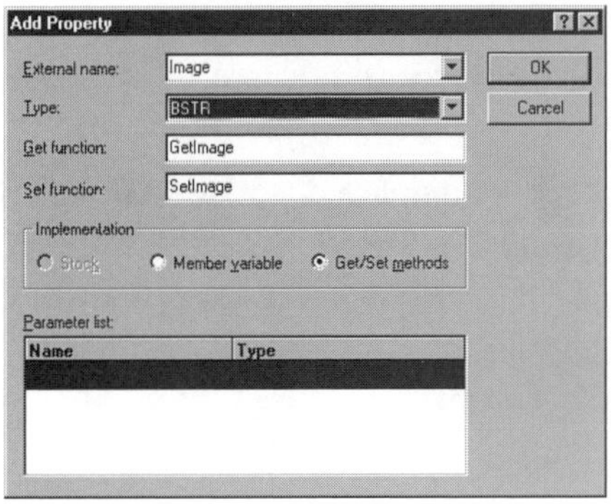

FIG. 20.7
The image file is added as a BSTR property.

Class Wizard adds the Get and Set functions to your control class, but the TODO comments (see Listing 20.7) are a little cryptic.

Part
VI

Ch
20

Listing 20.7   DierollCtl.cpp—Get and Set Functions

```
BSTR CDierollCtrl::GetImage()
{
    CString strResult;
    // TODO: Add your property handler here

    return strResult.AllocSysString();
```

continues

Listing 20.7 Continued

```
}

void CDierollCtrl::SetImage(LPCTSTR lpszNewValue)
{
    // TODO: Add your property handler here

    SetModifiedFlag();
}
```

As with other Get and Set properties, you will have to add a member variable to the control class, and add code to these functions to get or set its value. It is an instance of the new CDierollDataPathProperty class. Right-click onCDierollCtrl in Class View and choose Add Member Variable. Figure 20.8 shows how to fill in the dialog box to declare the member variable mdpp_image. (The dpp in the name is to remind you that this is a data path property.)

FIG. 20.8

The image file member variable is an instance of the new class.

Now you can finish the Get and Set functions, as shown in Listing 20.8.

Listing 20.8 DierollCtl.cpp—Completed Get and Set Functions

```
BSTR CDierollCtrl::GetImage()
{
    CString strResult;
    strResult = mdpp_image.GetPath();
    return strResult.AllocSysString();
}

void CDierollCtrl::SetImage(LPCTSTR lpszNewValue)
{
    Load(lpszNewValue, mdpp_image);
    SetModifiedFlag();
}
```

At the top of the header file for CDierollCtrl, add this include statement:

```
#include "DierollDataPathProperty.h"
```

Now there are some bits and pieces to deal with because you are changing an existing control rather than turning on asynchronous properties when you first built Dieroll. First, in CDierollCtrl::DoPropExchange(), arrange persistence and initialization for mdpp_image by adding this line:

```
PX_DataPath( pPX, _T("Image"), mdpp_image);
```

Second, add a line to the stub of CDierollCtrl::OnResetState() that Class Wizard provided, to reset the data path property when the control is reset. The function is shown in Listing 20.9.

Listing 20.9 DierollCtl.cpp—*CDierollCtrl::OnResetState()*

```
////////////////////////////////////////////////////////////////////////
// CDierollCtrl::OnResetState - Reset control to default state

void CDierollCtrl::OnResetState()
{
    COleControl::OnResetState();   // Resets defaults found in DoPropExchange

    mdpp_image.ResetData();
}
```

Add the ReadyStateChange Event and the ReadyState Property   Use Class Wizard to add the stock event ReadyStateChange. In Class Wizard, click the ActiveX Events tab, then the Add Event button. Choose ReadyStateChange from the drop-down box and click OK. Figure 20.9 shows the Add Event dialog box for this event. Events, as discussed in Chapter 17, notify the container of the control that something has happened within the control. In this case, what has happened is that the rest of the control's data has arrived and the control's state of readiness has changed.

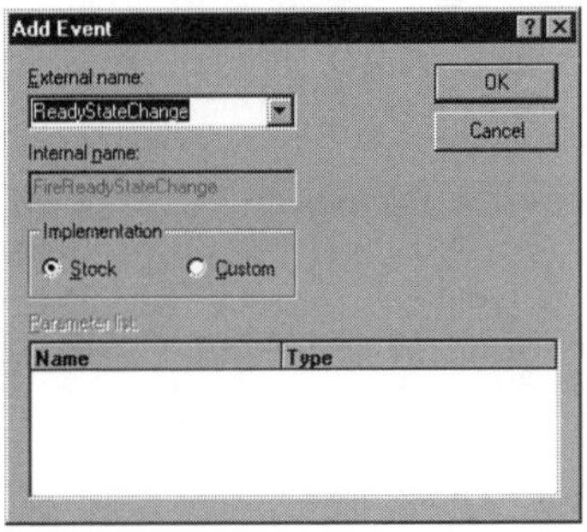

FIG. 20.9
Add a stock event to notify the container of a change in the readiness of the control.

Use Class Wizard to add a property to CDierollCtrl for the ready state. In Class Wizard, click the Automation tab, then the Add Property button. Choose ReadyState from the drop-down box, and since this is a stock property, the rest of the dialog box is filled in for you, as shown in Figure 20.10. ClassWizard doesn't add a stub function for GetReadyState()because CDierollCtrl will inherit this from COleControl.

Add code to the constructor to connect the cached property to this control and to initialize the member variable in COleControl that is used in COleControl::GetReadyState() and set by COleControl::InternalSetReadyState(). Since the control can be used right away, the readiness state should start at READYSTATE_INTERACTIVE. Listing 20.10 shows the new constructor:

Part

VI

Ch

20

FIG. 20.10
Add a stock property to track the readiness of the control.

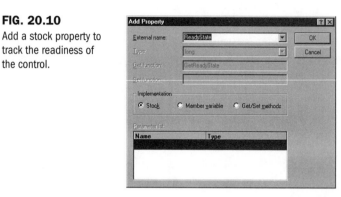

Listing 20.10   DierollCtl.cpp—*CDierollCtrl::GetImage()*

```
CDierollCtrl::CDierollCtrl()
{
    InitializeIIDs(&IID_DDieroll, &IID_DDierollEvents);
    mdpp_image.SetControl(this);
    m_lReadyState = READYSTATE_INTERACTIVE;
}
```

Implement *CDierollDataPathProperty*   There is some work to do in
CDierollDataPathProperty before changing CDierollCtrl::OnDraw(). This class loads a
bitmap, and this chapter is not going to explain most of what's involved in reading a .BMP file
into a CBitmap object. The most important function is OnDataAvailable(), which is in Listing
20.11. Add this function to the class by right-clicking CDierollCtrl in ClassView and choosing
Add Virtual Function. Select OnDataAvailable from the list on the left, and click Add and Edit,
then type in this code.

Listing 20.11   DierollDataPathProperty.cpp—*OnDataAvailable()*

```
void CDierollDataPathProperty::OnDataAvailable(DWORD dwSize, DWORD grfBSCF)
{
    CCachedDataPathProperty::OnDataAvailable(dwSize, grfBSCF);

    if(grfBSCF & BSCF_LASTDATANOTIFICATION)
    {
        m_Cache.SeekToBegin();
        if (ReadBitmap(m_Cache))
        {
            BitmapDataLoaded = TRUE;
            // safe because this control has only one property:
            GetControl()->InternalSetReadyState(READYSTATE_COMPLETE);
            GetControl()->InvalidateControl();
        }
    }
}
```

Every time a block of data is received from the remote site, this function is called. The first line of code uses the base class version of the function to deal with that block and set the flag called grfBSCF. If, after dealing with the latest block, the download is complete, the ReadBitmap() function is called to read the cached data into a bitmap object that can be displayed as the control background. The code for ReadBitmap() will not be presented or discussed here, though it is on the CD for those who would like to read it. Once the bitmap has been read, the control's ready state is complete and the call to InvalidateControl() arranges for a redraw.

Revise *CDierollCtrl::OnDraw()* The structure of CDierollCtrl::OnDraw()was laid out long ago. The background is filled in before the code that checks whether to draw dots or a number, in this block of code:

```
COLORREF back = TranslateColor(GetBackColor());
CBrush backbrush;
backbrush.CreateSolidBrush(back);
pdc->FillRect(rcBounds, &backbrush);
```

Replace that block with the one in Listing 20.12.

Listing 20.12   DierollDataPathProperty.cpp—New Code for *OnDraw()*

```
CBrush backbrush;
BOOL drawn = FALSE;
if (GetReadyState() == READYSTATE_COMPLETE)
{
    CBitmap* image = mdpp_image.GetBitmap(*pdc);
    if (image)
    {
        CDC memdc;
        memdc.CreateCompatibleDC(pdc);
        memdc.SelectObject(image);
        BITMAP bmp;                 //just for height and width
        image->GetBitmap(&bmp);
        pdc->StretchBlt(0,             //upper left
                    0,                 //upper right
                    rcBounds.Width(), // target width
                    rcBounds.Height(), // target height
                    &memdc,            // the image
                    0,                 //offset into image -x
                    0,                 //offset into image -y
                    bmp.bmWidth, // width
                    bmp.bmHeight, // height
                    SRCCOPY);     //copy it over

        drawn = TRUE;
    }
}
if (!drawn)
{
    COLORREF back = TranslateColor(GetBackColor());
    backbrush.CreateSolidBrush(back);
    pdc->FillRect(rcBounds, &backbrush);
}
```

Part
VI

Ch
20

The BOOL variable drawn ensures that if the control is complete, but something goes wrong with the attempt to use the bitmap, the control will be drawn the old way. If the control is complete, the image is loaded into a CBitmap*, and then drawn into the device context. Bitmaps can only be selected into a memory device context, and then copied over to an ordinary device context. Using StretchBlt()will stretch the bitmap during the copy, though a sensible Web page designer will have specified a bitmap that matches the HEIGHT and WIDTH attributes of the OBJECT tag. The old drawing code is still here, used if drawn remains FALSE.

Testing and Debugging Dieroll

Having made all those changes, build the control, which will register it. One way to test it would be to bring up that HTML page in Explorer again, but you may prefer to debug the control. It is possible to debug a control even though you cannot run it stand-alone. Normally, a developer would arrange to debug the control in the Test Container, but you can use any application that can contain the control.

In Developer Studio, choose Project Settings. Click the Debug tab, and make sure that all the lines in the leftmost list box are selected. Select General in the top drop-down box, and in the edit box labeled Executable for debug session, enter the full path to Microsoft Internet Explorer on your computer. (Figure 20.11 shows an example.) Now when you choose Build Go, or click the Go toolbar button, Explorer will launch. Open a page of HTML that loads the control, and the control will run in the debugger. You can set breakpoints, step through code, and examine variables just as with any other application.

FIG. 20.11

Arrange to run Explorer when you debug the control.

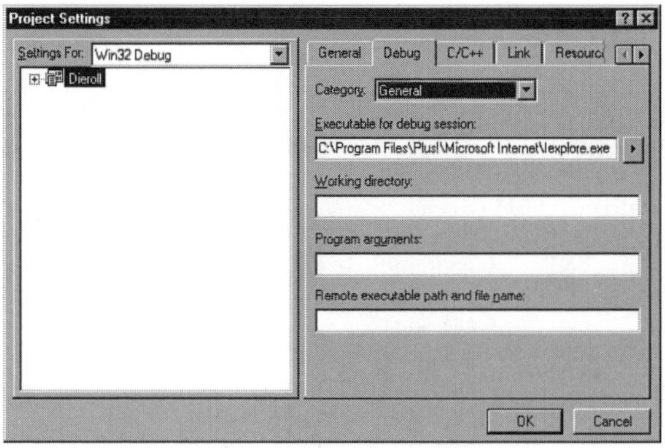

Here's the syntax for an OBJECT tag that sets the Image property:

```
<OBJECT
CLASSID="clsid:46646B43-EA16-11CF-870C-00201801DDD6"
CODEBASE="http://www.gregcons.com/test/dieroll.ocx"
ID=die1
WIDTH=200
HEIGHT=200
ALIGN=center
HSPACE=0
```

```
VSPACE=0
>
<PARAM NAME="Dots" VALUE="1">
<PARAM NAME="Image" VALUE="http://www.gregcons.com/test/beans.bmp">
If you see this text, your browser does not support the OBJECT tag. </BR>
</OBJECT>
```

TIP Remember, don't just copy these HTML samples to your own machine if you are bulding Dieroll yourself. You need to use your own CLSID, an URL to the location of your copy of the OCX, and the image file you are using.

Figure 20.12 shows the control with a background image of jelly beans. It takes 30 seconds to a minute to load this 40K image through the Web, and while it is loading, the control is perfectly usable as a plain die with no background image. That's the whole point of asynchronous properties, and that's what all the effort of the previous sections achieves.

FIG. 20.12
Now the die displays on a field of jelly beans, or any other image you choose.

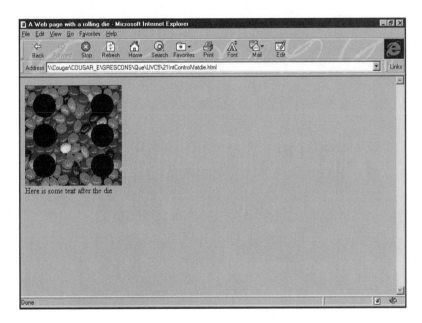

From Here...

ActiveX controls are changing fast. Watch for more announcements from Microsoft of development kits and other add-ons to make building Internet-ready controls faster and easier.

If you'd like to read more background about ActiveX programming, be sure to check the electronic copy of "ActiveX Programming with Visual C++", which is included in its entirety on the CD included with this book.

If you'd like to learn more about programming for the Internet, try one of these chapters:

- Chapter 18, "Sockets, MAPI, and the Internet," introduces you to some of the ways you can write your own Internet programs rather than writing a control that is delivered over the Internet.

- Chapter 19, "Internet Programming with the WinInet Classes," introduces the latest MFC classes, and shows you how quickly you can build a truly useful (and unique) Internet application.

- Chapter 21, "The Active Template Library," teaches you how to build an ActiveX control without using MFC.

The Active Template Library

The Active Template Library, ATL, is a collection of C++ class templates that you can use to build ActiveX controls. These small controls generally do not use MFC at all. Writing an ActiveX control with ATL requires a lot more knowledge of COM and interfaces than writing an MFC ActiveX control, because MFC protects you from a lot of low-level COM concepts. Using ATL is not for the timid, but it pays dividends in smaller, tighter controls. This chapter will rewrite the Dieroll control of Chapter 17, "Building an ActiveX Control," and Chapter 20, "Building an Internet ActiveX Control," by using ATL. You will learn the important COM/ActiveX concepts that were skimmed over while you were using MFC. For a more complete examination of these concepts, be sure to read the electronic copy of "ActiveX Programming with Visual C++," which is included in its entirety on the CD that comes with this book. ∎

What is the Active Template Library?

Using MFC makes controls easy to write, but big. The power of templates lets you leave MFC behind.

ATL wizards

An AppWizard to create the project and an ObjectWizard to create a control or a property page make getting started simple.

Properties and persistence

Exposing properties in an ATL control is a job for your custom interface.

Events

Your control can notify the application using it that something important has happened.

Using the control

Microsoft's Control Pad is an easy way to test your control. So is Internet Explorer.

Why use the ATL?

Building an ActiveX Control with MFC is quite simple, as you saw in Chapters 17, "Building an ActiveX Control," and 20, "Building an Internet ActiveX Control." You can get by without really knowing what a COM interface is, or how to use a type library. Your control can use all sorts of handy MFC classes, like CString and CWnd, can draw itself using CDC member functions, and more. The only downside is that users of your control need the MFC DLLs, and if those DLLs aren't on their system already, the delay while 700K or so of CAB file downloads will be significant.

The alternative is to get the ActiveX functionality from the Active Template Library (ATL) and to call Win32 SDK functions, just as C programmers did when writing for Windows in the days before Visual C++ and MFC. The Win32 SDK is a lot to learn, and won't be covered fully in this chapter. The good news is, if you're familiar with major MFC classes, like CWnd and CDC, you'll recognize a lot of these SDK functions even if you've never seen them before: Many of the MFC member functions are just wrappers for SDK functions.

How much download time can you save? The MFC control from Chapter 20, "Building an Internet ActiveX Control," is about 30K, plus of course the MFC DLLs. The ATL control built in this chapter is at most 100K and is fully self-contained. With a few tricks you could get it down to 50K of control and 20K for the ATL DLL—one-tenth the size of the total control and DLL from Chapter 20!

Using AppWizard to Get Started

There's an AppWizard that knows how to make ATL controls, and it makes your job quite a bit simpler than it would have been without the wizard. As always, choose File, New and click the Projects tab on the New dialog box. Fill in an appropriate directory and name the project DieRollControl, as shown in Figure 21.1. Click OK.

FIG. 21.1

AppWizard makes creating an ATL control simple.

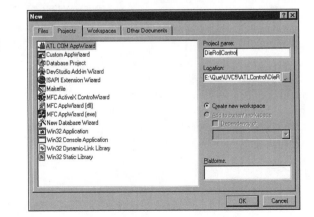

N O T E It's tempting to name the project DieRoll, but later in this process you will be inserting a
control into the project—that control will be called DieRoll, so to avoid name conflicts,
choose a longer name for the project. ▩

There is only one step in the ATL COM AppWizard and it is shown in Figure 21.2. The default
choices—DLL control, no merging proxy/stub code, no MFC support—are the right ones for
this project. The file extension will be DLL rather than OCX as it was for MFC controls, but
that's not an important difference. Click Finish.

FIG.21.2

Create a DLL control.

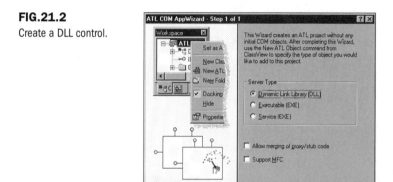

The New Project Information dialog box, shown in Figure 21.3, confirms the choices you have
made. Click OK to create the project.

FIG. 21.3

Your ATL choices are
summarized before you
create the project.

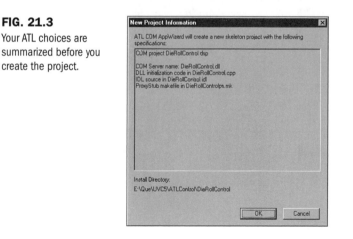

Using the Object Wizard

The ATL COM AppWizard created seven files, but you don't have a skeleton control yet. First you have to follow the instructions included in the Step 1 dialog box, and insert an ATL object into the project.

Adding a Control to the Project

Choose Insert, New ATL Object from the menu bar. This brings up the ATL Object Wizard, shown in Figure 21.4.

FIG. 21.4

Add an ATL Control to your project.

There are several kinds of ATL objects you can add to your project, but at the moment you are interested only in controls, so select Controls in the list box on the left. The choices in the list box on the left become Full Control, Internet Explorer Control, or Property Page. If you know for certain that this control would be used only in Internet Explorer, perhaps as part of an intranet project, you could choose Internet Explorer Control and save a little space. This dieroll control might end up in any browser, in a VB app, or anywhere else for that matter, so a Full Control is the way to go. You'll add a property page later in this chapter. Select Full Control and click Next.

Naming the Control

Now the ATL Object Wizard Properties Dialog box appears. The first tab is the Names tab. Here you can customize all the names used for this control. Enter DieRoll for the short name of DieRoll and the rest will default to names based on it, as shown in Figure 21.5. You could change these names if you wanted, but there is no need to. Note that the Type name, DieRoll Class, is the name that will appear in the Insert Object dialog box of most containers. Since the MFC version of DieRoll is probably already in your Registry, having a different name for this version is actually a good thing. On other projects you might consider changing the type name.

Setting Control Attributes

Click the Attributes tab. Leave the default values: Apartment Threading Model, Dual Interface, and Yes for Aggregation. Select the check boxes Support ISupportErrorInfo and Support Connection Points. Leave Free Threaded Marshaler deselected, as shown in Figure 21.6. Each of these choices is discussed in the paragraphs that follow.

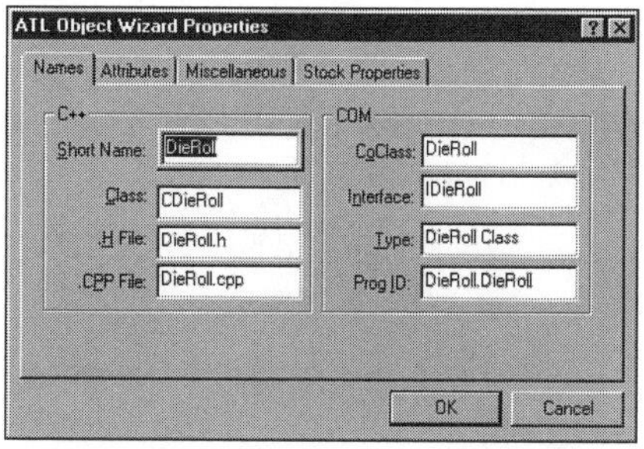

FIG. 21.5
Set the names of the
files and the control.

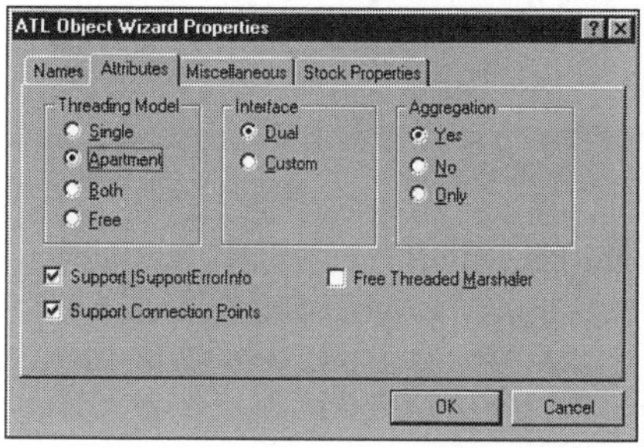

FIG. 21.6
Set the COM properties
of your control.

Threading models   Avoid selecting the Single-Thread model even if your controls do not have
any threading. In order to be sure that no two functions of such a control are running at the
same time, all calls to methods of a single-threaded control must be marshalled through a
proxy, which slows execution significantly. The Apartment setting is a better choice for new
controls.

The Apartment model refers to STA, or Single-Threaded Apartment model. This means that
access to any resources shared by instances of the control (globals and statics) is through
serialization. Instance data—local automatic variables and objects dynamically allocated on the
heap—does not need this protection. This makes STA controls faster than single-threaded
controls. Internet Explorer exploits STA in controls it contains.

TIP   If the design for your control includes a lot of globals and statics, it may be a great deal of work to use
the Apartment model. This is not a good reason to write a single-threaded control; it is a good reason
to redesign your control as a more object-oriented system.

The Free threading (Multithreaded Apartment or MTA) model refers to controls that are
threaded and that already include protection against thread collisions. While it might seem like
a great idea to write a multithreaded control, using such a control in a nonthreaded or STA
container will result in marshalling again, this time to protect the container against having two
functions called at once. This, too, introduces inefficiencies. As well, there will be significant
extra work for you, the developer, to create a free-threaded control, since you must add the
thread collision protection.

Part
VI

Ch
21

The Both option in the threading column asks the wizard to make a control that can be STA or MTA, avoiding inefficiences when used in a container that is single-threaded or STA, and exploiting the power of MTA models when available. You will have to add the threading-protection work, just as when you write an MTA control.

At the moment, controls for Internet Explorer should be STA. DCOM controls that may be accessed by several connections at once can benefit from being MTA.

Dual and Custom interfaces   COM objects communicate through *interfaces*, a collection of function names that describe the possible behavior of a COM object. To use an interface, you get a pointer to it and then call a member function of the interface. All Automation servers and ActiveX controls have an IDispatch interface in addition to any other interfaces that may be specific to what the server or control is for. To call a method of a control, you can use the In-voke() method of the IDispatch interface, passing in the dispid of the method you wish to invoke. (This technique was developed so that methods could be called from Visual Basic and other pointerless languages.)

Simply put, a *dual-interface* control lets you call methods both ways: by using a member function of a custom interface, or by using IDispatch. MFC controls only use IDispatch, but this is slower than using a custom interface. The Interface column on this dialog box lets you choose Dual or Custom: Custom leaves IDispatch out of the picture altogether. Select Dual so that the control can be used from Visual Basic if necessary.

Aggregation   The third column, Aggregation, governs whether or not a COM class can use this COM class by containing a reference to an instance of it. Choosing Yes means that other COM objects may use this class; No means they cannot; Only means they must: this object cannot stand alone.

Other control settings   Selecting support for ISupportErrorInfo means that your control will be able to return richer error information to the container. Selecting support for Connection Points is vital for a control, like this one, that will fire events. Selecting Free-Threaded Marshaler is not required for an STA control.

Click the Miscellaneous tab and examine all the settings, which can be left at their default values (see Figure 21.7). The control should be opaque, with a solid background, and should use a normalized DC even though that's slightly less efficient, because your draw code will be much easier to write.

TIP   If you'd like to see how a DC is normalized for an ATL control, remember that all the ATL source is available to you, just as the MFC source is. In Program Files\DevStudio\VC\atl\include\ATLCTL.CPP, you will find CComControlBase::OnDrawAdvanced(), which normalizes a DC and calls OnDraw() for you.

FIG. 21.7
Leave the Miscellaneous properties at the defaults.

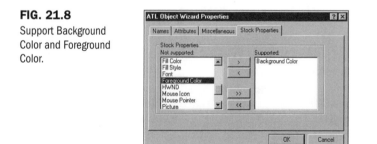

Supporting Stock Properties

Click the Stock Properties tab to specify which stock properties the control will support. To add support for a stock property, select it in the left Not Supported list box, then click the > button and it will be moved to the Supported list on the right. Add support for Background Color and Foreground Color, as shown in Figure 21.8. If you plan to support a lot of properties, use the >> button to move them all to the supported list and then move back the ones you don't want to support.

FIG. 21.8
Support Background Color and Foreground Color.

Click OK on the Object Wizard to complete the control creation. At this point you can build the project if you wish, though the control does nothing at the moment.

Adding Properties to the Control

The MFC versions of Dieroll featured three stock properties: `BackColor`, `ForeColor`, and `ReadyState`. The first two have been added already, but the `ReadyState` stock properties must be added by hand. As well there are two custom properties, `Number` and `Dots`, and an asynchronous property, `Image`.

Part
VI

Ch
21

Code From Object Wizard

A COM class that implements or uses an interface does so by inheriting from a class representing that interface. Listing 21.1 shows all the classes that CDieRoll inherits from.

Listing 21.1   Excerpt from DieRollControl.h—Inheritance

```
class ATL_NO_VTABLE CDieRoll :
    public CComObjectRootEx<CComSingleThreadModel>,
    public CComCoClass<CDieRoll, &CLSID_DieRoll>,
    public CComControl<CDieRoll>,
    public CStockPropImpl<CDieRoll, IDieRoll, &IID_IDieRoll,
    ➥&LIBID_DIEROLLCONTROLLib>,
    public IProvideClassInfo2Impl<&CLSID_DieRoll, NULL,
    ➥&LIBID_DIEROLLCONTROLLib>,
    public IPersistStreamInitImpl<CDieRoll>,
    public IPersistStorageImpl<CDieRoll>,
    public IQuickActivateImpl<CDieRoll>,
    public IOleControlImpl<CDieRoll>,
    public IOleObjectImpl<CDieRoll>,
    public IOleInPlaceActiveObjectImpl<CDieRoll>,
    public IViewObjectExImpl<CDieRoll>,
    public IOleInPlaceObjectWindowlessImpl<CDieRoll>,
    public IDataObjectImpl<CDieRoll>,
    public ISupportErrorInfo,
    public IConnectionPointContainerImpl<CDieRoll>,

    public ISpecifyPropertyPagesImpl<CDieRoll>
```

Now you can see where the T in ATL comes in: All these classes are template classes. (If you aren't familiar with templates, read Chapter 26, "Exceptions, Templates, and the Latest Additions to C++.") You add support for an interface to a control by adding another entry to this list of interface classes from which it inherits.

N O T E   Notice the names follow the pattern `IxxxImpl`: that means that this class implements the `Ixxx` interface. Classes inheriting from `IxxxImpl` inherit code as well as function names. For example, `CDieRoll` inherits from `ISupportErrorInfo`, not `ISupportErrorInfoImpl<CDieRoll>`, even though such a template does exist. That is because the code in that template implementation class is not appropriate for an ATL control, so the control only inherits the names of the functions from the original interface, and provides code for them in the source file as you will shortly see. ■

Further down the header file you will find the COM map, shown in Listing 21.2.

Listing 21.2   Excerpt from DieRollControl.h—COM Map

```
BEGIN_COM_MAP(CDieRoll)
    COM_INTERFACE_ENTRY(IDieRoll)
    COM_INTERFACE_ENTRY(IDispatch)
    COM_INTERFACE_ENTRY_IMPL(IViewObjectEx)
    COM_INTERFACE_ENTRY_IMPL_IID(IID_IViewObject2, IViewObjectEx)
    COM_INTERFACE_ENTRY_IMPL_IID(IID_IViewObject, IViewObjectEx)
    COM_INTERFACE_ENTRY_IMPL(IOleInPlaceObjectWindowless)
    COM_INTERFACE_ENTRY_IMPL_IID(IID_IOleInPlaceObject,
    ➥IOleInPlaceObjectWindowless)
    COM_INTERFACE_ENTRY_IMPL_IID(IID_IOleWindow, IOleInPlaceObjectWindowless)
    COM_INTERFACE_ENTRY_IMPL(IOleInPlaceActiveObject)
```

```
        COM_INTERFACE_ENTRY_IMPL(IOleControl)
        COM_INTERFACE_ENTRY_IMPL(IOleObject)
        COM_INTERFACE_ENTRY_IMPL(IQuickActivate)
        COM_INTERFACE_ENTRY_IMPL(IPersistStorage)
        COM_INTERFACE_ENTRY_IMPL(IPersistStreamInit)
        COM_INTERFACE_ENTRY_IMPL(ISpecifyPropertyPages)
        COM_INTERFACE_ENTRY_IMPL(IDataObject)
        COM_INTERFACE_ENTRY(IProvideClassInfo)
        COM_INTERFACE_ENTRY(IProvideClassInfo2)
        COM_INTERFACE_ENTRY(ISupportErrorInfo)
        COM_INTERFACE_ENTRY_IMPL(IConnectionPointContainer)
    END_COM_MAP()
```

This COM map is the connection between IUnknown::QueryInterface() and all the interfaces supported by the control. All COM objects must implement IUnknown, and QueryInterface() can be used to determine what other interfaces the control supports and obtain a pointer to them. The macros connect the Ixxx interfaces to the IxxxImpl classes from which CDieRoll inherits.

Looking back at the inheritance list for CDieRoll, most of the templates take only one parameter, the name of this class, and came from AppWizard. This entry came from ObjectWizard:

```
public CStockPropImpl<CDieRoll, IDieRoll, &IID_IDieRoll,
    ➥&LIBID_DIEROLLCONTROLLib>,
```

This line is how ObjectWizard arranged for support for stock properties. Notice there is no indication which properties are supported. Further down the header file, two member variables have been added to CDieRoll:

```
OLE_COLOR m_clrBackColor;
OLE_COLOR m_clrForeColor;
```

The ObjectWizard also updated DieRollControl.idl, the interface definition file, to show these two stock properties, as shown in Listing 21.3.

Listing 21.3 Excerpt From DieRollControl.idl—Stock Properties

```
[
    object,
    uuid(2DE15F32-8A71-11D0-9B10-0080C81A397C),
    dual,
    helpstring("IDieRoll Interface"),
    pointer_default(unique)
]
interface IDieRoll : IDispatch
{
[propput, id(DISPID_BACKCOLOR)]
    HRESULT BackColor([in]OLE_COLOR clr);
[propget, id(DISPID_BACKCOLOR)]
    HRESULT BackColor([out,retval]OLE_COLOR* pclr);
[propput, id(DISPID_FORECOLOR)]
    HRESULT ForeColor([in]OLE_COLOR clr);
[propget, id(DISPID_FORECOLOR)]
```

Part

VI

Ch

21

continues

> **Listing 21.3   Continued**
>
> ```
>     HRESULT ForeColor([out,retval]OLE_COLOR* pclr);
> };
> ```

This class will provide all the support for the get and put functions and will notify the container when one of these properties changes.

Adding the ReadyState Stock Property

Although ReadyState was not on the stock property list in the ATL Object Wizard, it is supported by CStockPropImpl. You can add another stock property by editing the header and idl files. In the header file, immediately after the lines that declared m_clrBackColor and m_clrForeColor, declare another member variable:

```
    long m_nReadyState;
```

This property will be used in the same way as the ReadyState property in the MFC version of Dieroll: to implement Image as an asynchronous property. In DieRollControl.idl, add these lines to the IDispatch block, after the lines for BackColor and ForeColor:

```
[propget, id(DISPID_READYSTATE)]
HRESULT ReadyState([out,retval]long* pclr);
```

You don't need to add a pair of lines to implement put for this property, since external objects cannot update ReadyState. Save the header and idl files to update ClassView—if you do not, you will not be able to add more properties with ClassView. Expand CDieRoll and IDieRoll in ClassView to see that the member variable has been added to CDieRoll and a ReadyState() function has been added to IDieRoll.

Adding Custom Properties

To add custom properties, you will use an ATL tool similar to the MFC ClassWizard. Right-click IDieRoll (the top-level one, not the one under CDieRoll) in ClassView to bring up the shortcut menu shown in Figure 21.9, and choose Add Property.

FIG. 21.9
ATL projects have a different ClassView shortcut menu than MFC projects.

The Add Property to Interface dialog box, shown in Figure 21.10, appears. Choose short for the type and fill in Number for the name. Deselect Put Function since containers will not need to change the number showing on the die. Leave the rest of the settings unchanged and click OK to add the property.

FIG. 21.10

Add Number as a
Read-Only Property.

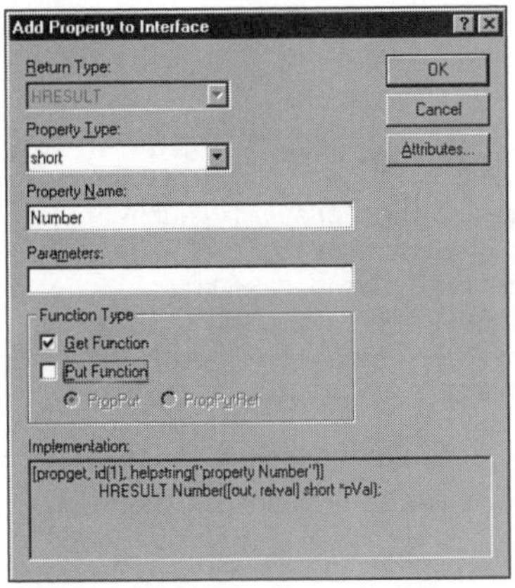

Repeat this process for the BOOL Dots, which should have both get and put functions. (Leave the put radio button at PropPut.) The ClassView now shows entries under both CDieRoll and IDieRoll related to these new properties. Try double-clicking the new entries. For example, double-clicking get_Dots() under the IDieRoll that is under CDieRoll opens the source (cpp) file scrolled to the get_Dots() function. Double-clicking Dots() under the top-level IDieRoll opens the IDl file scrolled to the propget entry for Dots.

Although a number of entries have been added to CDieRoll, no member variables have been added. Only you can add the member variables that correspond to the new properties. While in many cases it's safe to assume that the new properties are simply member variables of the control class, they might not be. For example, Number might have been the dimension of some array kept within the class rather than a variable of its own.

Add to the header file, after the declarations of m_clrBackColor, m_clrForeColor, and m_nReadyState:

```
short m_sNumber;
BOOL m_bDots;
```

In the idl file, the new propget and propput entries use hard coded dispids of 1 and 2, like this:

```
[propget, id(1), helpstring("property Number")]
    HRESULT Number([out, retval] short *pVal);
[propget, id(2), helpstring("property Dots")]
    HRESULT Dots([out, retval] BOOL *pVal);
[propput, id(2), helpstring("property Dots")]
    HRESULT Dots([in] BOOL newVal);
```

Part
VI

Ch

21

To make the code more readable, use an `enum` of `dispids`. Adding the declaration of the enum to the idl file will make it usable in both the idl and header file. Add these lines to the beginning of DieRollControl.idl:

```
typedef enum propertydispids
    {
        dispidNumber = 1,
    dispidDots = 2,
    }PROPERTYDISPIDS;
```

Now you can change the propget and propput lines:

```
[propget, id(dispidNumber), helpstring("property Number")]
    HRESULT Number([out, retval] short *pVal);
[propget, id(dispidDots), helpstring("property Dots")]
    HRESULT Dots([out, retval] BOOL *pVal);
[propput, id(dispidDots), helpstring("property Dots")]
    HRESULT Dots([in] BOOL newVal);
```

The next step is to code the `get` and `set` functions to use the member variables. Listing 21.4 shows the completed functions. (If you can't see these in ClassView, expand the `IDieRoll` under `CDieRoll`.)

Listing 21.4   Excerpt from DieRoll.cpp—*Get* and *Set* Functions

```
STDMETHODIMP CDieRoll::get_Number(short * pVal)
{
    *pVal = m_sNumber;
    return S_OK;
}

STDMETHODIMP CDieRoll::get_Dots(BOOL * pVal)
{
    *pVal = m_bDots;
    return S_OK;
}

STDMETHODIMP CDieRoll::put_Dots(BOOL newVal)
{
    if (FireOnRequestEdit(dispidDots) == S_FALSE)
    {
        return S_FALSE;
    }
    m_bDots = newVal;
    SetDirty(TRUE);
    FireOnChanged(dispidDots);
    FireViewChange();

    return S_OK;
}
```

The code in the two `get` functions is simple and straightforward. The `put_dots()` code is a little more complex, because it fires notifications. `FireOnRequestEdit()` notifies all the

IPropertyNotifySink interfaces that this property is going to change. Any one of these interfaces can deny the request, and if one does then this function will return S_FALSE to forbid the change.

Assuming the change is allowed, the member variable is changed and the control is marked as modified ("dirty") so that it will be saved. The call to FireOnChange() notifies the IPropertyNotifySink interfaces that this property has changed, and the call to FireViewChange() tells the container to redraw the control.

Initializing the Properties

Having added the code to get and set these properties, you should now change the CDieRoll constructor to initialize all the stock and custom properties, as shown in Listing 21.5. A stub for the constructor is in the header file for you to edit.

Listing 21.5   Excerpt from DieRoll.h—Constructor

```
CDieRoll()
{
    srand( (unsigned)time( NULL ) );
    m_nReadyState = READYSTATE_INTERACTIVE;
    m_clrBackColor = 0x80000000 | COLOR_WINDOW;
    m_clrForeColor = 0x80000000 | COLOR_WINDOWTEXT;
    m_sNumber = Roll();
    m_bDots = TRUE;
}
```

At the top of the header, add this line to bring in a declaration of the time() function:

```
#include "time.h"
```

Just as you did in the MFC version of this control, you initialize m_sNumber to a random number between 1 and 6, returned by the Roll() function. Add this function to CDieRoll by right-clicking the class name in ClassView and choosing Add Member Function from the shortcut menu. Roll() is protected, takes no parameters, and returns a short. The code for Roll() is in Listing 21.6, and was explained in Chapter 17, "Building an ActiveX Control."

Listing 21.6   *CDieRoll::Roll()*

```
short CDieRoll::Roll()
{
    double number = rand();
    number /= RAND_MAX + 1;
    number *= 6;
    return (short)number + 1;
}
```

Part

VI

Ch

21

Adding the Asynchronous Property

Just as in Chapter 20, "Building an Internet ActiveX Control," the Image property represents a bitmap to be loaded asynchronously and used as a background image. Add the property to the interface just as Number and Dots were added. Use BSTR for the type and Image for the name. Update the enum in the idl file, so that dispidImage is 3, and edit the propget and propput lines in the idl file to use the enum value:

```
[propget, id(dispidImage), helpstring("property Image")]
    HRESULT Image([out, retval] BSTR *pVal);
[propput, id(dispidImage), helpstring("property Image")]
    HRESULT Image([in] BSTR newVal);
```

Add a member variable, m_bstrImage, to the class:

```
CComBSTR m_bstrImage;
```

CComBSTR is an ATL wrapper class with useful member functions for manipulating a BSTR.

A number of other member variables must be added to handle the bitmap and the asynchronous loading. Add these lines to DieRoll.h:

```
HBITMAP hBitmap;
BITMAPINFOHEADER bmih;
char *lpvBits;
BITMAPINFO *lpbmi;
HGLOBAL hmem1;
HGLOBAL hmem2;
BOOL BitmapDataLoaded;
char *m_Data;
unsigned long m_DataLength;
```

The first six of these new variables are used to draw the bitmap and will not be discussed. The last three combine to achieve the same behavior as the data path property used in the MFC version of this control.

Add these three lines to the constructor:

```
m_Data = NULL;
m_DataLength = 0;
BitmapDataLoaded = FALSE;
```

Add a destructor to CDieRoll (in the header file) and add the code in Listing 21.7.

Listing 21.7   *CDieRoll::~CDieRoll()*

```
~CDieRoll()
{
    if (BitmapDataLoaded)
    {
        GlobalUnlock(hmem1);
        GlobalFree(hmem1);
        GlobalUnlock(hmem2);
        GlobalFree(hmem2);
        BitmapDataLoaded = FALSE;
    }
```

```
    if (m_Data != NULL)
    {
        delete m_Data;
    }
}
```

The Image property has get and put functions. Code them as in Listing 21.8.

Listing 21.8   DieRoll.cpp—*get_Image()* and *put_Image()*

```
STDMETHODIMP CDieRoll::get_Image(BSTR * pVal)
{
    *pVal = m_bstrImage.Copy();
    return S_OK;
}

STDMETHODIMP CDieRoll::put_Image(BSTR newVal)
{
    USES_CONVERSION;

    if (FireOnRequestEdit(dispidImage) == S_FALSE)
    {
        return S_FALSE;
    }

// if there was an old bitmap or data, delete them
    if (BitmapDataLoaded)
    {
        GlobalUnlock(hmem1);
        GlobalFree(hmem1);
        GlobalUnlock(hmem2);
        GlobalFree(hmem2);
        BitmapDataLoaded = FALSE;
    }

    if (m_Data != NULL)
    {
        delete m_Data;
    }

    m_Data = NULL;
    m_DataLength = 0;

    m_bstrImage = newVal;
    LPSTR string = W2A(m_bstrImage);

    if (string != NULL && strlen(string) > 0)
    {
        // not a null string so try to load it
        BOOL relativeURL = FALSE;
        if (strchr(string, ':') == NULL)
        {
            relativeURL = TRUE;
```

Part
VI

Ch
21

continues

Listing 21.8   Continued

```
        }

        m_nReadyState = READYSTATE_LOADING;

        HRESULT ret = CBindStatusCallback<CDieRoll>::Download(this,
            OnData, m_bstrImage, m_spClientSite, relativeURL);
    }     else
    {
        // was a null string so don't try to load it
        m_nReadyState = READYSTATE_INTERACTIVE;
    }

    SetDirty(TRUE);
    FireOnChanged(dispidImage);
    return S_OK;
}
```

As with Numbers and Dots, the get function is straightforward, and the put function is a bit more complicated. The beginning and end of the function is like put_Dots(), firing notifications to check if the variable can be changed, then other notifications that it was changed. In between is the code unique to an asynchronous property.

To start the download of the asynchronous property, this function will call CBindStatusCallback<CDieRoll>::Download() but first it needs to determine whether the URL in m_bstrImage is a relative or absolute URL. Use the ATL macro W2A to convert the wide BSTR to an ordinary C string so that the C function strchr() can be used to search for a : character in the URL. An URL with no : in it is assumed to be a relative URL.

N O T E   A BSTR is a wide (double-byte) character on all 32-bit Windows platforms. It is a narrow (single-byte) string on a PowerMac. ■

In the MFC version of the dieroll control with an asynchronous image property, whenever a block of data came through, the OnDataAvailable() function was called. The call to Download() arranges for a function called OnData() to be called when data arrives. You will write the OnData() function. Add it to the class with the other public functions and add the implementation shown in Listing 21.9 to DieRoll.cpp.

Listing 21.9   DieRoll.cpp—*CDieRoll::OnData()*

```
void CDieRoll::OnData(CBindStatusCallback<CDieRoll>* pbsc,
                      BYTE * pBytes, DWORD dwSize)
{

    char *newData = new char[m_DataLength + dwSize];

    memcpy(newData, m_Data, m_DataLength);
    memcpy(newData+m_DataLength, pBytes, dwSize);
    m_DataLength += dwSize;
```

```
        delete m_Data;
        m_Data = newData;

        if (ReadBitmap())
        {
            m_nReadyState = READYSTATE_COMPLETE;
    }
    }
```

Since there is no `realloc()` when using new, this function uses `new` to allocate enough `chars` to hold the data that has already been read (`m_DataLength`) and the new data that is coming in (`dwSize`), then copies `m_Data` to this block, and the new data (`pBytes`) after `m_Data`. It then attempts to convert the data that has been received so far into a bitmap: If this succeeds, the download must be complete and the call to `FireViewChange()` sends a notification to the container to redraw the view. You can get the `ReadBitmap()` function from the CD and add it to your project: It's much like the MFC version but it does not use any MFC classes like `Cfile`.

Drawing the Control

Now that all the properties have been added, you can code `OnDraw()`. While the basic structure of this function is the same as in the MFC version of Chapter 20, "Building an Internet ActiveX Control," there is a lot more work to be done because you cannot rely on MFC to do some of it for you.

The structure of `OnDraw()` is:

```
HRESULT CDieRoll::OnDraw(ATL_DRAWINFO& di)
// if the bitmap is ready, draw it
// else draw a plan background using BackColor
// if !Dots draw a number in ForeColor
// else draw the dots
```

First, you need to test if the bitmap is ready, and draw it if possible. This code is in Listing 21.10: Add it to the existing `OnDraw()` in place of the code left for you by AppWizard. Notice that if `ReadyState` is `READYSTATE_COMPLETE` but the call to `CreateDIBitmap()` doesn't result in a valid bitmap handle, the bitmap member variables are cleared away to make subsequent calls to this function give up a little faster. This chapter will not discuss how to draw bitmaps.

Listing 21.10   CDieRoll::OnDraw()—Use the Bitmap

```
int width = (di.prcBounds->right - di.prcBounds->left + 1);
int height = (di.prcBounds->bottom - di.prcBounds->top + 1);

BOOL drawn = FALSE;
if (m_nReadyState == READYSTATE_COMPLETE)
{
    if (BitmapDataLoaded)
    {
```

Part VI
Ch
21

continues

Listing 21.10 Continued

```
hBitmap = ::CreateDIBitmap(di.hdcDraw, &bmih, CBM_INIT, lpvBits,
    lpbmi, DIB_RGB_COLORS);

if (hBitmap)
{
    HDC hmemdc;
    hmemdc = ::CreateCompatibleDC(di.hdcDraw);
    ::SelectObject(hmemdc, hBitmap);
    DIBSECTION ds;
    ::GetObject(hBitmap,sizeof(DIBSECTION),(LPSTR)&ds);
    ::StretchBlt(di.hdcDraw,
                    di.prcBounds->left, // left
                    di.prcBounds->top,  // top
                    width, // target width
                    height, // target height
                    hmemdc,          // the image
                    0,               //offset into image -x
                    0,               //offset into image -y
                    ds.dsBm.bmWidth, // width
                    ds.dsBm.bmHeight, // height
                    SRCCOPY);     //copy it over

    drawn = TRUE;
    ::DeleteObject(hBitmap);
    hBitmap = NULL;
    ::DeleteDC(hmemdc);
}
else
{
    GlobalUnlock(hmem1);
    GlobalFree(hmem1);
    GlobalUnlock(hmem2);
    GlobalFree(hmem2);
    BitmapDataLoaded = FALSE;
}
    }
}
```

If the bitmap was not drawn, either because ReadyState was not READYSTATE_COMPLETE yet or because there was a problem with the bitmap, OnDraw() draws a solid background by using the BackColor property, as shown in Listing 21.11. Add this code to OnDraw(). The SDK calls are very similar to the MFC calls used in the MFC version of DieRoll: for example ::OleTranslateColor() corresponds to TranslateColor().

Listing 21.11 *CDieRoll::OnDraw()—Draw a Solid Background*

```
if (!drawn)
{
    COLORREF back;
    ::OleTranslateColor(m_clrBackColor, NULL, &back);
```

```
    HBRUSH backbrush = ::CreateSolidBrush(back);
    ::FillRect(di.hdcDraw, (RECT *)di.prcBounds, backbrush);
    ::DeleteObject(backbrush);
}
```

With the background drawn, either as a bitmap image or a solid color, OnDraw() must now tackle the foreground. Getting the foreground color is quite simple. Add these two lines to OnDraw():

```
COLORREF fore;
::OleTranslateColor(m_clrForeColor, NULL, &fore);
```

If Dots is FALSE, the die should be drawn with a number on it. Add the code in Listing 21.12 to OnDraw(). Again the SDK functions do the same job as the similarly named MFC functions used in the MFC version of DieRoll.

Listing 21.12 *CDieRoll::OnDraw()*—Draw a Number

```
if (!m_bDots)
{
    _TCHAR val[20]; //character representation of the short value
    _itot(m_sNumber, val, 10);
        ::SetTextColor(di.hdcDraw, fore);
    ::ExtTextOut(di.hdcDraw, 0, 0, ETO_OPAQUE,
        (RECT *)di.prcBounds, val, _tcslen(val), NULL );
}
```

The code that draws dots is in Listing 21.13. Add it to OnDraw() to complete the function. This code is long, but was explained in Chapter 17, "Building an ActiveX Control." As in the rest of OnDraw(), MFC function calls have been replaced with SDK calls.

Listing 21.13 *CDieRoll::OnDraw()*—Draw Dots

```
    else
    {
        //dots are 4 units wide and high, one unit from the edge
        int Xunit = width/16;
        int Yunit = height/16;
        int Xleft = width%16;
        int Yleft = height%16;

        // adjust top left by amount left over
        int Top = di.prcBounds->top + Yleft/2;
        int Left = di.prcBounds->left + Xleft/2;

        HBRUSH forebrush;
        forebrush = ::CreateSolidBrush(fore);

        HBRUSH savebrush = (HBRUSH)::SelectObject(di.hdcDraw, forebrush);
```

Part
VI

Ch
21

continues

Listing 21.13 Continued

```
switch(m_sNumber)
{
case 1:
    ::Ellipse(di.hdcDraw, Left+6*Xunit, Top+6*Yunit,
                    Left+10*Xunit, Top + 10*Yunit); //center
    break;
case 2:
    ::Ellipse(di.hdcDraw, Left+Xunit, Top+Yunit,
                    Left+5*Xunit, Top + 5*Yunit);   //upper left
    ::Ellipse(di.hdcDraw, Left+11*Xunit, Top+11*Yunit,
                    Left+15*Xunit, Top + 15*Yunit); //lower right
    break;
case 3:
    ::Ellipse(di.hdcDraw, Left+Xunit, Top+Yunit,
                    Left+5*Xunit, Top + 5*Yunit);   //upper left
    ::Ellipse(di.hdcDraw, Left+6*Xunit, Top+6*Yunit,
                    Left+10*Xunit, Top + 10*Yunit); //center
    ::Ellipse(di.hdcDraw, Left+11*Xunit, Top+11*Yunit,
                    Left+15*Xunit, Top + 15*Yunit); //lower right
    break;
case 4:
    ::Ellipse(di.hdcDraw, Left+Xunit, Top+Yunit,
                    Left+5*Xunit, Top + 5*Yunit);   //upper left
    ::Ellipse(di.hdcDraw, Left+11*Xunit, Top+Yunit,
                    Left+15*Xunit, Top + 5*Yunit);  //upper right
    ::Ellipse(di.hdcDraw, Left+Xunit, Top+11*Yunit,
                    Left+5*Xunit, Top + 15*Yunit);  //lower left
    ::Ellipse(di.hdcDraw, Left+11*Xunit, Top+11*Yunit,
                    Left+15*Xunit, Top + 15*Yunit); //lower right
    break;
case 5:
    ::Ellipse(di.hdcDraw, Left+Xunit, Top+Yunit,
                    Left+5*Xunit, Top + 5*Yunit);   //upper left
    ::Ellipse(di.hdcDraw, Left+11*Xunit, Top+Yunit,
                    Left+15*Xunit, Top + 5*Yunit);  //upper right
    ::Ellipse(di.hdcDraw, Left+6*Xunit, Top+6*Yunit,
                    Left+10*Xunit, Top + 10*Yunit); //center
    ::Ellipse(di.hdcDraw, Left+Xunit, Top+11*Yunit,
                    Left+5*Xunit, Top + 15*Yunit);  //lower left
    ::Ellipse(di.hdcDraw, Left+11*Xunit, Top+11*Yunit,
                    Left+15*Xunit, Top + 15*Yunit); //lower right
    break;
case 6:
    ::Ellipse(di.hdcDraw, Left+Xunit, Top+Yunit,
            Left+5*Xunit, Top + 5*Yunit);   //upper left
    ::Ellipse(di.hdcDraw, Left+11*Xunit, Top+Yunit,
            Left+15*Xunit, Top + 5*Yunit);  //upper right
    ::Ellipse(di.hdcDraw, Left+Xunit, Top+6*Yunit,
            Left+5*Xunit, Top + 10*Yunit);  //center left
    ::Ellipse(di.hdcDraw, Left+11*Xunit, Top+6*Yunit,
              Left+15*Xunit, Top + 10*Yunit); //center right
    ::Ellipse(di.hdcDraw, Left+Xunit, Top+11*Yunit,
            Left+5*Xunit, Top + 15*Yunit);  //lower left
```

```
            ::Ellipse(di.hdcDraw, Left+11*Xunit, Top+11*Yunit,
                Left+15*Xunit, Top + 15*Yunit); //lower right
            break;
        }

        ::SelectObject(di.hdcDraw, savebrush);
        ::DeleteObject(forebrush);
    }
    return S_OK;
}
```

Persistence and a Property Page

The properties have been added to the control and used in the drawing of the control. Now all that remains is to make the properties persistent and to add a property page.

Adding a Property Page

Choose Insert, New ATL Object from the menu bar to bring up the ATL Object Wizard. Select Controls in the left pane and Property Page in the right pane, then click Next. On the Names tab, enter DieRollPPG for the Short Name, and click the Strings tab (the settings on the Attributes tab will not be changed.) Enter General for the Title and DieRoll Property Page for the Doc String. Blank out the Helpfile Name. Click OK to add the property page to the project.

Switch to ResourceView in the Workspace pane, and open the dialog IDD_DIEROLLPPG. Add a check box with the resource ID IDC_DOTS and the caption Display Dot Pattern and an edit box with the resource ID IDC_IMAGE labelled Image URL, as shown in Figure 21.12.

At the top of DieRollPPG.h, add this line:

```
#include "DieRollControl.h"
```

You need to connect the controls on this property page to properties of the dieroll control. The first step is to add three lines to the message map in DieRollPPG.h so that it resembles Listing 21.14.

Listing 21.14   DieRollPPG.h—Message Map

```
BEGIN_MSG_MAP(CDieRollPPG)
    MESSAGE_HANDLER(WM_INITDIALOG, OnInitDialog)
    COMMAND_HANDLER(IDC_DOTS, BN_CLICKED, OnDotsChanged)
    COMMAND_HANDLER(IDC_IMAGE, EN_CHANGE, OnImageChanged)
    CHAIN_MSG_MAP(IPropertyPageImpl<CDieRollPPG>)
END_MSG_MAP()
```

Part VI
Ch 21

These new lines ensure that OnInitDialog() will be called when the dialog box is initialized, and OnDotsChanged() or OnImageChanged() will be called whenever Dots or Image are changed (the other properties don't have put methods and so can't be changed.)

FIG. 21.12
Add two controls to the
property page.

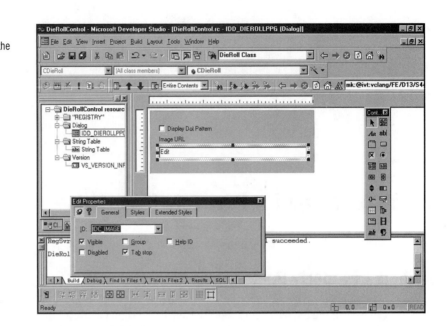

Add the code in Listing 21.15 to the header file to declare and implement OnInitDialog().

Listing 21.15   DieRollPPG.h—CDieRollPPG::OnInitDialog()

```
LRESULT OnInitDialog(UINT uMsg, WPARAM wParam, LPARAM lParam,
                     BOOL & bHandled)
{
    USES_CONVERSION;

    CComQIPtr<IDieRoll, &IID_IDieRoll> pDieRoll(m_ppUnk[0]);

    BOOL dots;
    pDieRoll->get_Dots(&dots);
    ::SendDlgItemMessage(m_hWnd, IDC_DOTS, BM_SETCHECK, dots, 0L);

    BSTR image;
    pDieRoll->get_Image(&image);
    LPTSTR image_URL = W2T(image);
    SetDlgItemText(IDC_IMAGE, image_URL);

    return TRUE;
}
```

This code starts by declaring a pointer to an IDieRoll interface using the CComQIPtr template
class and initializing it to the first element of the m_ppUnk array in this class, CDieRollPPG. (A
property page can be associated with multiple controls.) The constructor for the CComQIPtr
template class uses the QueryInterface() method of the IUnknown pointer that was passed in

to the constructor to find a pointer to an `IDieRoll` interface. Now you can call member functions of this interface to access the properties of the `DieRoll` control.

Getting the value of the `Dots` property of the `CDieRoll` object is simple enough: just call `get_Dots()`. To use that value to initialize the check box on the property page, send a message to the control using the SDK function `::SendDlgItemMessage()`. The `BM_SETCHECK` parameter indicates that you are setting whether the box is checked (selected) or not. Passings `dots` as the fourth parameter ensures that `IDC_DOTS` will be selected if `dots` is TRUE and deselected if `dots` is FALSE. Similarly, get the URL for the image with `get_Image()`, convert it from wide characters, then use `SetDlgItemText()` to set the edit box contents to that URL.

`OnDotsChanged()` and `OnImageChanged()` are quite simple: add the code in Listing 21.16 to the header file, after `OnInitDialog()`.

Listing 21.16   DieRollPPG.h—The OnChanged Functions

```
LRESULT OnDotsChanged(WORD wNotify, WORD wID, HWND hWnd, BOOL& bHandled)
{
    SetDirty(TRUE);
    return FALSE;
}

LRESULT OnImageChanged(WORD wNotify, WORD wID, HWND hWnd, BOOL& bHandled)
{
    SetDirty(TRUE);
    return FALSE;
}
```

The calls to `SetDirty()` in these functions ensure that the `Apply()` function will be called when the user clicks OK on the property page.

The ObjectWizard generated a simple `Apply()` function, but it doesn't affect the Dots or Number properties. Edit Apply() so that it resembles Listing 21.17.

Listing 21.17   DieRollPPG.h—CDieRollPPG::Apply()

```
STDMETHOD(Apply)(void)
{
    USES_CONVERSION;
    BSTR image = NULL;
    GetDlgItemText(IDC_IMAGE, image);

    BOOL dots = (BOOL)::SendDlgItemMessage(m_hWnd, IDC_DOTS,
            BM_GETCHECK, 0, 0L);

    ATLTRACE(_T("CDieRollPPG::Apply\n"));
    for (UINT i = 0; i < m_nObjects; i++)
    {
        CComQIPtr<IDieRoll, &IID_IDieRoll> pDieRoll(m_ppUnk[i]);
```

Part

VI

Ch

21

continues

Listing 21.17   Continued

```
        if FAILED(pDieRoll->put_Dots(dots))
        {
            CComPtr<IErrorInfo> pError;
            CComBSTR            strError;
            GetErrorInfo(0, &pError);
            pError->GetDescription(&strError);
            MessageBox(OLE2T(strError), _T("Error"), MB_ICONEXCLAMATION);
            return E_FAIL;
        }

        if FAILED(pDieRoll->put_Image(image))
        {
            CComPtr<IErrorInfo> pError;
            CComBSTR            strError;
            GetErrorInfo(0, &pError);
            pError->GetDescription(&strError);
            MessageBox(OLE2T(strError), _T("Error"), MB_ICONEXCLAMATION);
            return E_FAIL;
        }
    }
    m_bDirty = FALSE;
    return S_OK;
}
```

Apply starts by getting dots and image from the dialog box. Notice in the call to
::SendDlgItemMessage() that the third parameter is BM_GETCHECK, so this call gets the selected
state (TRUE or FALSE) of the check box. Then a call to ATLTRACE prints a trace message to
aid debugging. Like the trace statements discussed in Chapter 24, "Improving Your
Application's Performance," this statement disappears in a release build.

The majority of Apply() is a for loop that is executed once for each control associated with this
property page. It gets an IDieRoll interface pointer just as in OnInitDialog(), and tries calling
the put_Dots() and put_Image() member functions of that interface. If either call fails, a message box informs the user of the problem. After the loop, the m_bDirty member variable can be
set to FALSE.

Connecting the Property Page to CDieRoll

The changes to CDieRollPPG are complete. There are some changes to be made to CDieRoll
to connect it to the property page class. Specifically, the property map needs some more entries. Edit it until it looks like Listing 21.18.

Listing 21.18   DieRollPPG.h—*CDieRollPPG::Apply()*

```
BEGIN_PROPERTY_MAP(CDieRoll)
    PROP_ENTRY( "Dots", dispidDots, CLSID_DieRollPPG)
    PROP_ENTRY( "Image", dispidImage, CLSID_DieRollPPG)
    PROP_ENTRY( "Fore Color", DISPID_FORECOLOR, CLSID_StockColorPage )
    PROP_ENTRY( "Back Color", DISPID_BACKCOLOR, CLSID_StockColorPage )
END_PROPERTY_MAP()
```

For Dots and Image the entries are new: for Fore Color and Back Color, replacing the PROP_PAGE macro supplied by ObjectWizard with PROP_ENTRY macros ensures that the properties will persist, that is they will be saved with the control.

Persistence in a Property Bag

There are a number of different ways that Internet Explorer can get property values out of some HTML and into a control wrapped in an <OBJECT> tag. With stream persistence, provided by default, you use a DATA attribute in the <OBJECT> tag. If you would like to use <PARAM> tags, which are far more readable, the control must support property bag persistence through the IPersistPropertyBag interface.

Add another class to the list of base classes at the start of the CDieRoll class:

```
public IPersistPropertyBagImpl<CDieRoll>,
```

Add this line to the COM map:

```
COM_INTERFACE_ENTRY_IMPL(IPersistPropertyBag)
```

Now you can use <PARAM> tags to set properties of the control.

Using the Control in Control Pad

You've added a lot of code to CDieRoll and CDieRollPPG, and it's time to build the control. After fixing any typos or minor errors, you can actually use the control.

You are going to build the HTML to display this control in Microsoft's Control Pad. If you don't have Control Pad, it's freely downloadable from **http://www.microsoft.com/workshop/author/cpad/download.htm**. If you have a copy of Control Pad from before January 1997, get the latest one. If you use the old version, the init safe and script safe work you'll do later in this chapter will appear not to function properly.

When you start Control pad it makes an empty HTML document. With the cursor between <BODY> and </BODY>, choose Edit, Insert ActiveX Control. The Insert ActiveX Control dialog appears: Choose DieRoll Class from the list (you may recall from Figure 21.5 that the type name for this control is DieRoll Class) and click OK. The control and a Properties dialog, appear. Click the Image property and enter the full path to the file **beans.bmp** (available on the CD) in the edit box at the top of the Properties dialog. Click Apply, and the control redraws with a background of jelly beans, as shown in Figure 21.13. Close the Properties dialog and the Edit ActiveX Control dialog and you will see the HTML generated for you, including the <PARAM> tags that were added because Control Pad could determine that DieRoll supports the IPersistPropertyBag interface.

The control does not have its full functionality yet: It does not roll itself when you click it. The next section will add events.

Part
VI

Ch
21

FIG. 21.13

Inserting the control into Control Pad displays it for you.

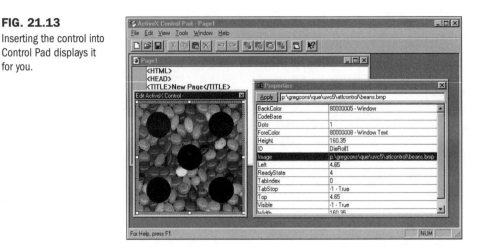

Adding Events

There are two events to be added: one when the user clicks the control, and one when the ready state changes. The Click event was discussed in Chapter 17, "Building an ActiveX Control," and the ReadyStateChanged event was discussed in Chapter 20, "Building an Internet ActiveX Control."

Editing the idl file

There is no ATL Add Event dialog: You will add the events entirely by hand. First, you will need a guid for the event interface. This is a globally unique identifier and should be generated on your own machine with the guidgen utility. Choose Start, Run, enter guidgen, and click OK. The Create GUID dialog box, shown in Figure 21.14, appears. Select Registry Format, which is closest to the format used in idl files, then Click Copy to copy the new guid into the clipboard. Click Exit, and return to Developer Studio.

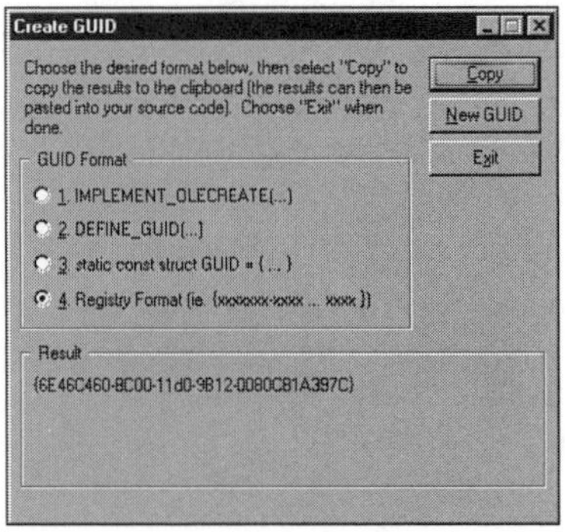

FIG. 21.14

Generate a guid for your event interface.

You will add the lines in Listing ATL. to the idl file, in the library section, after the two `importlib` statements. Paste in your new guid in place of the one you see in Listing 21.19.

Listing 21.19   DieRoll.idl—Lines to Add to the Library Section

```
[
    uuid(6E46C460-8C00-11d0-9B12-0080C81A397C),
    helpstring("Event interface for DieRoll")
]
dispinterface _DieRollEvents
{
    properties:
    methods:
    [id(DISPID_CLICK)] void Click();
    [id(DISPID_READYSTATECHANGE)] void ReadyStateChange();
};
```

A few lines further down, in the coclass block for DieRoll, add this line:

```
[default, source] dispinterface _DieRollEvents;
```

A Wrapper Class for the *IConnectionPoint* Interface

In order to fire events, you will implement the `IConnectionPoint` interface. The ATL Proxy component gets you started. First, save the idl file and build the project so that the typelib associated with the project is up to date.

Choose Project, Add to Project, Components and Controls. The Components and Controls Gallery dialog comes up. Double click Developer Studio Components. Select ATL Proxy Generator, as shown in Figure 21.15, and click Insert. Click OK when asked if you want to insert the component or not.

Click the ... button to browse for the typelib file. Select DieRollControl.tlb and click Open. In the Not Selected listbox on the left, click _DieRollEvents, then click > to move it to the Selected pane. Select Connection Point for Proxy Type, as shown in Figure 21.16, and click Insert.

FIG. 21.15

Insert an ATL Proxy Generator component.

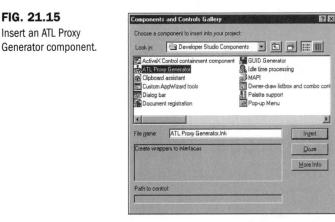

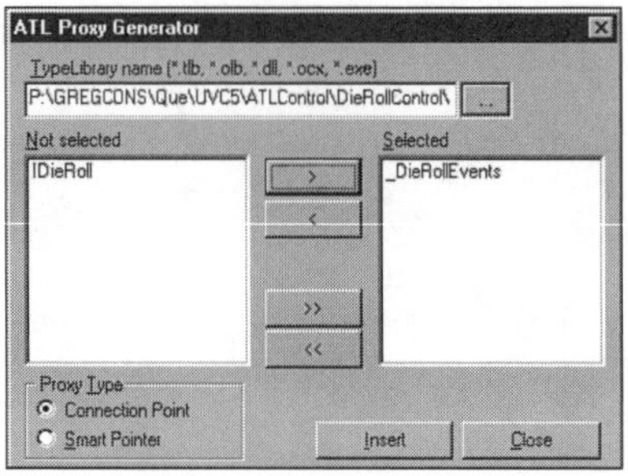

FIG. 21.16

Select the new interface component, then click Insert.

A save dialog will come up and prompt you to save it in CPDieRollControl.h. Click Save. Click OK on the "Successfully generated proxy." message, and close the ATL Proxy Generator dialog, then close the Components and Controls Gallery dialog.

The proxy generator created a wrapper class, `CProxy_DieRollEvents`, in CPDieRollControl.h. Add this include statement to DieRoll.h:

```
#include "CPDieRollControl.h"
```

To add this interface to CDieRoll, add it to the inheritance list at the top of the class:

```
public CProxy_DieRollEvents<CDieRoll>,
```

The new connection point must be added to the empty connection point map. It should look like this:

```
BEGIN_CONNECTION_POINT_MAP(CDieRoll)
    CONNECTION_POINT_ENTRY(DIID__DieRollEvents)
END_CONNECTION_POINT_MAP()
```

The general preparation is complete.

Firing the Click Event

When the user clicks the control, it should fire a Click event. Add an entry to the message map:

```
MESSAGE_HANDLER(WM_LBUTTONDOWN, OnLButtonDown)
```

Add the member function `OnLButtonDown()` to CDieRoll and add the code shown in Listing 21.20.

Listing 21.20   *CDieRoll::OnLButtonDown()*

```
LRESULT CDieRoll::OnLButtonDown(UINT uMsg, WPARAM wParam, LPARAM lParam, BOOL &
bHandled)
{
    m_sNumber = Roll();
    FireOnChanged(dispidNumber);
    Fire_Click();
    FireViewChange();
    return 0;
}
```

This code rolls the die, fires a notification that `Number` has changed, fires a `Click` event, and notifies the container that the control should be redrawn.

Firing the *ReadyStateChange* Event

`put_Image()` and `OnData()` can now fire events when the ready state changes. Look for a line in `put_Image()` like this:

```
m_nReadyState = READYSTATE_LOADING;
```

Add immediately after that line:

```
Fire_ReadyStateChange();
```

Then find this line:

```
m_nReadyState = READYSTATE_INTERACTIVE;
```

Add the call to `Fire_ReadyStateChange()` after this line as well. In OnData(), find this line:

```
m_nReadyState = READYSTATE_COMPLETE;
```

Build the control again, and insert it into a new page in Control Pad. Click the die in the Edit ActiveX Control window, and it will roll a new number each time that you click. As another test, bring up the ActiveX Control Test container (available from the Tools menu in Developer Studio) and insert a control, then use the event log to confirm that Click and ReadyStateChange events are being fired.

Exposing the *DoRoll( )* Function

The next stage in the development of this control is to expose a function that will allow the container to roll the die. One use for this is to arrange for the container to roll one die whenever the other is clicked. Right-click the `IDieRoll` interface in ClassView and choose Add Method. Enter DoRoll for Method Name, and leave the parameters section blank. Click OK.

Functions have a `dispid` just as properties do. Add an entry to the enum of `dispid`s in the idl file, so that `dispidDoRoll` is 4. This ensures that if you add another property later, you won't collide with the `dispid` for `DoRoll()`. When you added the function to the interface, a line was added after the get and put entries for the properties. Change it to use the new `dispid`, so it looks like this:

```
[id(dispidDoRoll), helpstring("method DoRoll")] HRESULT DoRoll();
```

The code for DoRoll() is in Listing 21.21. Add it to DieRoll.cpp.

Listing 21.21   *CDieRoll::DoRoll()*

```
STDMETHODIMP CDieRoll::DoRoll()
{
    m_sNumber = Roll();
    FireOnChanged(dispidNumber);
    FireViewChange();
    return S_OK;
}
```

Part
VI

Ch
21

This code is just like OnLButtonDown but does not fire a Click event.

Registering as Init Safe and Script Safe

In Chapter 20, "Building an Internet ActiveX Control," you added Registry entries to indicate that the control was safe to accept parameters in a Web page and to interact with a script. For an ATL control you can achieve this by supporting the IObjectSafety interface. A container will query this interface to see if the control is safe.

Add this following line to the inheritance list for CDieRoll:

```
public IObjectSafetyImpl<CDieRoll>,
```

Add this line to the COM map:

```
COM_INTERFACE_ENTRY_IMPL(IObjectSafety)
```

This will automatically make the control script safe. The default behavior in ATL does not make controls init safe. To make this control init safe, you will override the default definition of IObjectSafetyImpl::GetInterfaceSafetyOptions() and IObjectSafetyImpl::SetInterfaceSafetyOptions().

The code for these functions, modified from the default ATL source in DevStudio\VC\ATL\INCLUDE\ATLCTL.H, is in Listing 21.22 and 21.23. Add these functions after the destructor in DieRoll.h.

Listing 21.22   *CDieRoll::GetInterfaceSafetyOptions()*

```
STDMETHOD(GetInterfaceSafetyOptions)(REFIID riid,
     DWORD *pdwSupportedOptions, DWORD *pdwEnabledOptions)
{
    ATLTRACE(_T("IObjectSafetyImpl::GetInterfaceSafetyOptions\n"));
    if (pdwSupportedOptions == NULL || pdwEnabledOptions == NULL)
       return E_POINTER;
    *pdwSupportedOptions = INTERFACESAFE_FOR_UNTRUSTED_CALLER
      || INTERFACESAFE_FOR_UNTRUSTED_DATA;
    *pdwEnabledOptions = INTERFACESAFE_FOR_UNTRUSTED_CALLER
      || INTERFACESAFE_FOR_UNTRUSTED_DATA;
    return S_OK;
}
```

Listing 21.23   *CDieRoll::DoRoll()*

```
STDMETHOD(SetInterfaceSafetyOptions)(REFIID riid,
                                     DWORD dwOptionSetMask,
                                     DWORD dwEnabledOptions)
{
    ATLTRACE(_T("IObjectSafetyImpl::SetInterfaceSafetyOptions\n"));
    return S_OK;
}
```

The changes here are that the supported and enabled options are
INTERFACESAFE_FOR_UNTRUSTED_DATA and INTERFACESAFE_FOR_UNTRUSTED_CALLER instead
of just INTERFACESAFE_FOR_UNTRUSTED_CALLER. Instead of restricting these options to only
the IDispatch interface, this code reports the control is safe to all interfaces.

Preparing the Control for Use in Design Mode

When a developer is building a form or dialog box in an application like Visual Basic or Visual
C++, a control palette makes it simple to identify the controls to be added. Building the icon
used on that palette is the next step in completing this control.

Create a bitmap resource by choosing Insert, Resource and double-clicking Bitmap. Choose
View, Properties and set both the height and width to 16. Change the resource ID to
IDB_DIEROLL and draw the icon shown in Figure 21.17.

The Registry Script for this control refers to this icon by resource number. To discover what
number has been assigned to IDB_DIEROLL, choose View, Resource Symbols and note
the numeric value associated with IDB_DIEROLL. (On the machine where this sample was
written, it is 202.) Open DieRoll.rgs (the script file) from FileView and look for this line:

```
ForceRemove 'ToolboxBitmap32' = s '%MODULE%, 1'
```

Change it to:

```
ForceRemove 'ToolboxBitmap32' = s '%MODULE%, 202'
```

FIG. 21.17
Draw an icon for the
control.

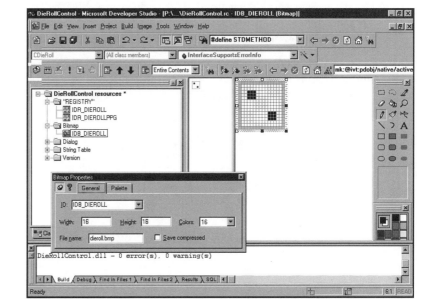

Part
VI

Ch
21

Be sure to use your value rather than 202. Build the control again. Run the Control Pad again and choose File, New HTML Layout Control. Select the Additional tab on the Toolbox palette and then right-click the page. From the shortcut menu that appears, choose Additional Controls. Find DieRoll Class on the list and select it, then click OK. The new icon appears on the Additional tab, as shown in Figure 21.18.

FIG. 21.18

Add the DieRoll class to the HTML Layout toolbox.

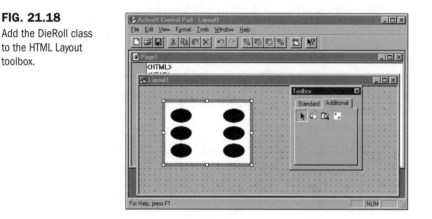

Minimizing Executable Size

Up until now, you have been building debug versions of the control. Dieroll.dll is about 300K. While that's a lot smaller than the 700K of cab file for the MFC DLLs that the MFC version of dieroll might require, it's a lot larger than the 30K or so that the release version of dieroll.ocx takes up. With development complete, it's time to build a release version.

Choose Build, Set Active Configuration to bring up the Set Active Configuration dialog box shown in Figure 21.19. You will notice that there are twice as many release versions in an ATL project as in an MFC project: In addition to choosing whether or not you suport Unicode, you must choose "MinSize" or "MinDependency."

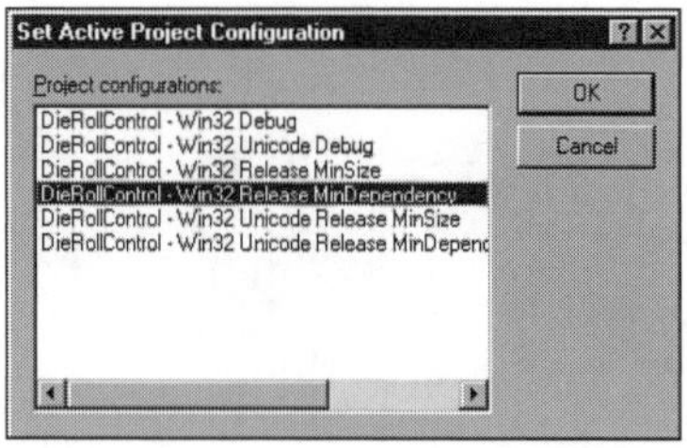

FIG. 21.19

Choose a build type from the Set Active Configuration dialog box.

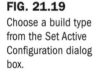

The minimum size release version makes the control as small as possible by linking dynamically to an ATL DLL and the ATL Registrar. The minimum dependencies version links to these statically, which makes the control larger but self-contained. If you choose minimum size, you will need to set up cab files for the control and the DLLs as discussed in Chapter 20,"Building an Internet ActiveX Control," for the MFC DLLs. At this early stage of ATL acceptance, it's probably better to choose minimum dependencies.

If you choose minimum dependency and build, you will get these error messages from the linker:

```
Linking...
   Creating library ReleaseMinDependency/DieRollControl.lib and
➥object ReleaseMinDependency/DieRollControl.exp
LIBCMT.lib(crt0.obj) : error LNK2001: unresolved external symbol _main
ReleaseMinDependency/DieRollControl.dll :
➥fatal error LNK1120: 1 unresolved externals
Error executing link.exe.

DieRollControl.dll - 2 error(s), 0 warning(s)
```

This error is not because of any mistake you may have made. By default, ATL release builds use a tiny version of the C runtime library (CRT) so that they will build as small a DLL as possible. This minimal CRT does not include the time(), rand(), and srand() functions used to roll the die. The linker finds these functions in the full-size CRT, but that library expects a main() function in your control. Since there isn't one, the link fails.

This behavior is controlled with a linker setting. Choose Project, Settings. From the drop-down box at the upper left, choose Win32 Release MinDependency. Click the C/C++ tab on the right. Click in the Preprocessor Definitions box and press END to move to the end of the box. Remove the _ATL_MIN_CRT flag, highlighted in Figure 21.20, and the comma immediately before it. Build the project again, and the linker errors disappear.

FIG. 21.20
Turn off the flag that links in only a tiny version of the C runtime library.

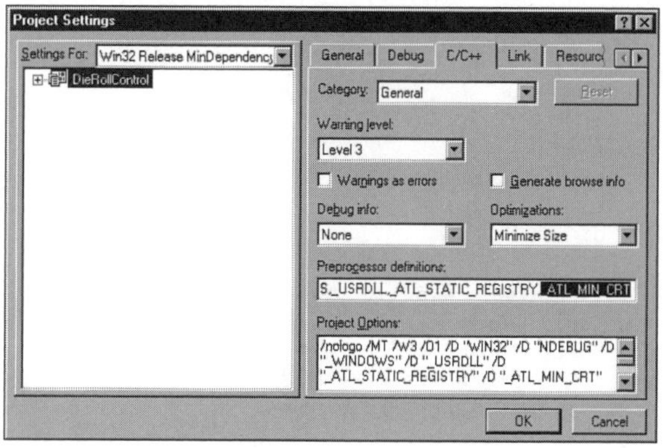

If you comment out the calls to rand(), srand(), and time(), so that the control no longer works, it will link with _ATL_MIN_CRT into a 48K DLL. With _ATL_MIN_CRT removed, it is 104K—a significant increase, but still substantially smaller than the MFC control and its DLLs. A minimum size release build with _ATL_MIN_CRT removed is 98K: The savings is hardly worth the trouble to package up the ATL DLLs. With rand(), srand(), and time() commented out, a minimum size release build with _ATL_MIN_CRT left in is only 45K.

Removing the _ATL_MIN_CRT flag increases the size of the control by over 50K. Although there is no way to rewrite this control so that it doesn't need the rand(), srand(), and time() functions, you could write your own versions of them and include them in the project so that the control would still link with the _ATL_MIN_CRT flag. You can find algorithms for random number generators and their seed functions in books of algorithms. The SDK GetSystemTime() function can substitute for time(). If you were writing a control that would be used for the first time by many users in a time sensitive application, this extra work might be worth it. Remember that the second time a user comes to a web page with an ActiveX control, the control does not need to be downloaded again.

T I P You can find a version of the ATL Dieroll control with rand() and srand() functions included so that the C runtime isn't required by following the link on the support page at **http://www.gregcons.com/ uvc50.htm**.

Using the Control in a Web Page

This control has a slightly different name and different CLSID than the MFC version built in Chapter 20, "Building an Internet ActiveX Control." You can use them both together in a single web page to compare them. Listing 21.21 is some HTML that puts the two controls in a table. (Use your own CLSID values when you create this page—you may want to use Control Pad as described earlier.) Figure 21.21 shows this page in Explorer. If you want to load the page in Netscape Navigator, run dieroll.htm through the NCompassLabs converter as discussed in Chapter 20.

Listing 21.24   dieroll.htm

```
</HEAD>
<BODY>
<TABLE CELLSPACING=15>
<TR>
<TD>
Here's the MFC die:<BR>
<OBJECT ID="MFCDie"
 CLASSID="CLSID:46646B43-EA16-11CF-870C-00201801DDD6"
 WIDTH="200" HEIGHT="200">
    <PARAM NAME="ForeColor" VALUE="0">
    <PARAM NAME="BackColor" VALUE="16777215">
    <PARAM NAME="Image" VALUE="beans.bmp">
If you see this text, your browser does not support the OBJECT tag.
</OBJECT>
</TD>
<TD>
Here's the ATL die:<BR>
<OBJECT ID="ATLDie" WIDTH=200 HEIGHT=200
 CLASSID="CLSID:2DE15F35-8A71-11D0-9B10-0080C81A397C">
    <PARAM NAME="Dots" VALUE="1">
    <PARAM NAME="Image" VALUE="beans.bmp">
```

```
            <PARAM NAME="Fore Color" VALUE="2147483656">
            <PARAM NAME="Back Color" VALUE="2147483653">
    </OBJECT>
    </TD>
    </TR>
    </TABLE>
    </BODY>
    </HTML>
```

 You can edit HTML files in Developer Studio as easily as source files, and with syntax coloring too. Simply choose File, New then select HTML Page from the list on the File tab. When you have typed in the HTML, right-click in the editor area and choose Preview to have InfoViewer show you the page just as Explorer would.

FIG. 21.21
The ATL control can be used wherever the MFC control was used.

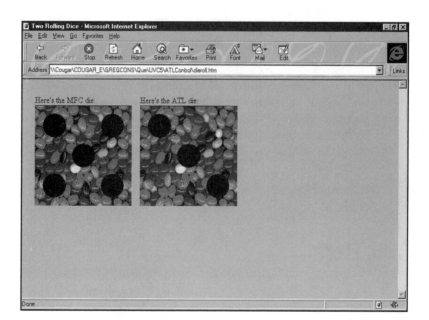

Fixing Flicker

When you use the two controls side-by-side like this, you may notice a tiny difference between them. When the die rolls and redraws, the MFC die does not redraw the background. The ATL die draws a white background before redrawing the bitmap. This tiny flicker is noticeable and annoying. If you load any of the sample ATL controls included with Visual C++ 5.0, you will see the same momentary flicker and you might conclude this is an unavoidable defect of ATL. It is not, and you can eliminate the flicker.

Part
VI

Ch
21

You are going to override the FireViewChange() function that was called by OnData(). Listing 21.25 shows the code from the base class.

Listing 21.25   dieroll.htm

```
HRESULT CComControlBase::FireViewChange()
{
    if (m_bInPlaceActive)
    {
        // Active
        if (m_hWndCD != NULL)
            return ::InvalidateRect(m_hWndCD, NULL, TRUE); // Window based
        if (m_spInPlaceSite != NULL)
            return m_spInPlaceSite->InvalidateRect(NULL, TRUE); // Windowless
    }
    // Inactive
    SendOnViewChange(DVASPECT_CONTENT);
    return S_OK;
}
```

FireViewChange() features calls two different InvalidateRect() functions, depending on whether your control is window based or windowless. Both InvalidateRect() functions have a parameter that determines whether the background should be erased before the control is redrawn. It is the last parameter in these calls, and is TRUE in the base class code.

Add the function FireViewChange() to CDieRoll() and copy in the code from CComControlBase::FireViewChange() (you can find it in Program Files\DevStudio\VC\atl\include\ATLCTL.CPP,) then change each TRUE to FALSE. Rebuild the project and reload the page with the two controls side-by-side—the flicker should be gone.

From Here...

This chapter introduced you to the Active Template Library, which makes use of template technology to simplify building ActiveX controls without MFC. It's a lot more work to build a control this way, and you can't ignore the underlying COM concepts as you can when using MFC, but you can build controls that are small, so that they download quickly, yet have all the functionality of MFC controls.

Some other chapters that may interest you are:

- Chapter 13, "ActiveX Concepts," introduces the concepts that this chapter expanded on.
- Chapter 24, "Improving Your Application's Performance," explores the differences between debug and release builds.
- Chapter 26, "Exceptions, Templates, and the Latest Additions to C++," shows how templates work and how to use them.

PART VII

Advanced Programming Techniques

CHAPTER 22

Database Access

Without a doubt, databases are one of the most popular computer applications. Virtually every business uses databases to keep track of everything from their customer list to the company payroll. Unfortunately, there are many different types of database applications, each of which defines its own file layouts and rules. In the past, programming database applications was a nightmare, because it was up to the programmer to figure out all the intricacies of accessing the different types of database files.

Now, however, Visual C++ includes classes that are built upon the ODBC (Open Database Connectivity) and DAO (Data Access Objects) systems. Believe it or not, by using AppWizard, you can create a simple database program without writing even a single line of C++ code. More complex tasks do require some programming, but not as much as you might think.

In this chapter, you get an introduction to programming with Visual C++'s ODBC classes. You'll also learn about the similarities and differences between ODBC and DAO. Along the way, you create a database application that can not only display records in a database, but also update, add, delete, sort, and filter records. ■

Basic database concepts

Regardless of what type of database you want to access, the basic concepts, like records and fields, remain the same.

How the flat and relational database models differ

Flat model databases are the simplest type of databases, but relational databases are the most efficient and powerful.

MFC's ODBC database classes

The ODBC classes enable you to access databases without all the hassles previously associated with database programming.

How to use AppWizard to create a basic ODBC application

AppWizard is an amazing tool for getting your database application up and running quickly and easily.

How to implement add, delete, update, sort, and filter abilities to your database program

Although AppWizard can create a functional database program for you, you have to do a little programming to incorporate more sophisticated database commands into your application.

Understanding Database Concepts

Before you can write database applications, you have to know a little about how databases work. Databases have come a long way since their invention, so there's much you can learn about them. This section provides a quick introduction to basic database concepts, including the two main types of databases: flat and relational.

Using the Flat Database Model

Simply put, a *database* is a collection of records. Each record in the database is comprised of fields, and each field contains information that's related to that specific record. For example, suppose you have an address database. In this database, you have one record for each person. Each record contains six fields: the person's name, street address, city, state, ZIP Code, and phone number. So, a single record in your database might look like this:

```
NAME: Ronald Wilson
STREET: 16 Tolland Dr.
CITY: Hartford
STATE: CT
ZIP: 06084
PHONE: 860-555-3542
```

Your entire database will contain many records like this one, with each record containing information about a different person. To find a person's address or phone number, you search for the name. When you find the name, you also find all the information that's included in the record with the name.

This type of database system uses the *flat database model*. For home use or for small businesses, the simple flat database model can be a powerful tool. However, for large databases that must track dozens, or even hundreds, of fields of data, a flat database can lead to repetition and wasted space. Suppose you run a large department store and want to track some information about your employees, including their names, departments, manager's names, and so on. If you have 10 people in Sporting Goods, the name of the Sporting Goods manager will be repeated in each of those 10 records. When Sporting Goods gets a new manager, all 10 records will have to be updated. It would be much simpler if each employee record could be *related* to another database of departments and manager names.

Using the Relational Database Model

A *relational database* is like several flat databases linked together. Using a relational database, you cannot only search for individual records as you can with a flat database, but you can also relate one set of records to another. This enables you to store data much more efficiently. Each set of records in a relational database is called a *table*. The links are accomplished through *keys*, values that define a record. (For example, the employee ID might be the key to an employee table.)

The example relational database that you use in this chapter was created using Microsoft Access. The database is a simple system for tracking employees, managers, and the departments for which they work. Figures 22.1, 22.2, and 22.3 show the tables: the Employees table contains information about each of the store's employees, the Managers table contains information about each store department's manager, and the Departments table contains information about the departments themselves. (This database is very simple and probably not usable in the real world.)

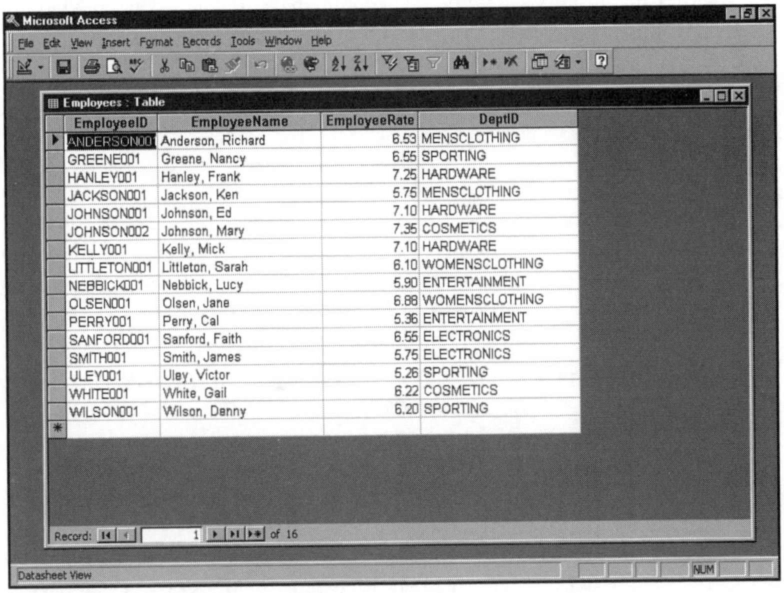

EmployeeID	EmployeeName	EmployeeRate	DeptID
ANDERSON001	Anderson, Richard	6.53	MENSCLOTHING
GREENE001	Greene, Nancy	6.55	SPORTING
HANLEY001	Hanley, Frank	7.25	HARDWARE
JACKSON001	Jackson, Ken	5.76	MENSCLOTHING
JOHNSON001	Johnson, Ed	7.10	HARDWARE
JOHNSON002	Johnson, Mary	7.35	COSMETICS
KELLY001	Kelly, Mick	7.10	HARDWARE
LITTLETON001	Littleton, Sarah	6.10	WOMENSCLOTHING
NEBBICK001	Nebbick, Lucy	5.90	ENTERTAINMENT
OLSEN001	Olsen, Jane	6.88	WOMENSCLOTHING
PERRY001	Perry, Cal	5.36	ENTERTAINMENT
SANFORD001	Sanford, Faith	6.55	ELECTRONICS
SMITH001	Smith, James	5.75	ELECTRONICS
ULEY001	Uley, Victor	5.26	SPORTING
WHITE001	White, Gail	6.22	COSMETICS
WILSON001	Wilson, Denny	6.20	SPORTING

FIG. 22.1 The Employees table contains data fields for each store employee.

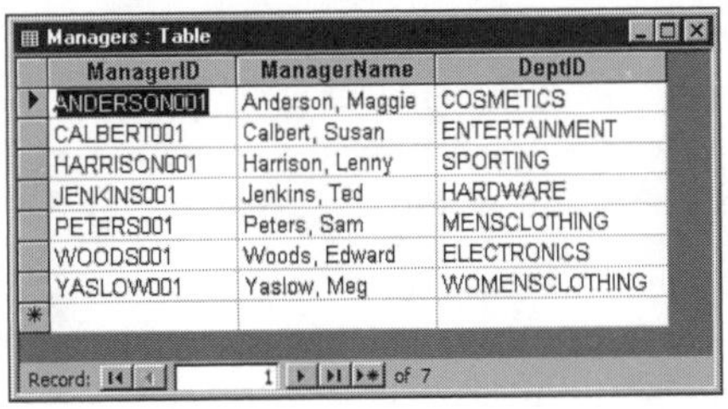

ManagerID	ManagerName	DeptID
ANDERSON001	Anderson, Maggie	COSMETICS
CALBERT001	Calbert, Susan	ENTERTAINMENT
HARRISON001	Harrison, Lenny	SPORTING
JENKINS001	Jenkins, Ted	HARDWARE
PETERS001	Peters, Sam	MENSCLOTHING
WOODS001	Woods, Edward	ELECTRONICS
YASLOW001	Yaslow, Meg	WOMENSCLOTHING

FIG. 22.2 The Managers table contains information about each store department's manager.

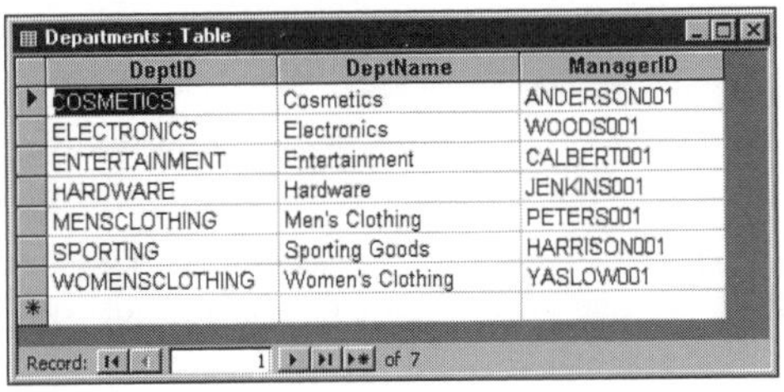

DeptID	DeptName	ManagerID
COSMETICS	Cosmetics	ANDERSON001
ELECTRONICS	Electronics	WOODS001
ENTERTAINMENT	Entertainment	CALBERT001
HARDWARE	Hardware	JENKINS001
MENSCLOTHING	Men's Clothing	PETERS001
SPORTING	Sporting Goods	HARRISON001
WOMENSCLOTHING	Women's Clothing	YASLOW001

FIG. 22.3 The Departments table contains data about each store department.

Accessing a Database

Relational databases are accessed using some sort of database scripting language. The most commonly used database language is *SQL*, which is used not only to manage databases on desktop computers but also on the huge databases used by banks, schools, corporations, and other institutions with sophisticated database needs. By using a language like SQL, you can compare information in the various tables of a relational database and extract results that are made up of data fields from one or more tables combined.

 TIP   Most developers pronounce SQL as "Sequel."

Learning SQL, though, is a large task, one that is way beyond the scope of this book (let alone this chapter). In fact, entire college-level courses are taught on the design, implementation, and manipulation of databases. Because there isn't space in this chapter to cover relational databases in any useful way, you'll use the Employee table (refer to Figure 22.1) of the Department Store database in the sample database program you'll soon develop. When you're finished creating the application, you'll have learned one way you can update the tables of a relational database without learning even a word of SQL. (Those of you who live and breathe SQL will enjoy Chapter 23, "Enterprise Edition.")

The Visual C++ ODBC Classes

When you create a database program with Visual C++'s AppWizard, you end up with an application that draws extensively upon the various ODBC classes that have been incorporated into MFC. The most important of these classes are CDatabase, CRecordset, and CRecordView.

AppWizard automatically generates the code needed to create an object of the CDatabase class. This object represents the connection between your application and the data source that you'll be accessing. In most cases, using the CDatabase class in an AppWizard-generated program is transparent to you, the programmer. All the details are handled by the framework.

AppWizard also generates the code needed to create a CRecordset object for the application. The CRecordset object represents the actual data that's currently selected from the data source, and its member functions manipulate the data from the database.

Finally, the CRecordView object in your database program takes the place of the normal view window you're used to using in AppWizard-generated applications. A CRecordView window is like a dialog box that's being used as the application's display. This dialog box-type of window retains a connection to the application's CRecordset object, hustling data back and forth between the program, the window's controls, and the recordset. When you first create a new database application with AppWizard, it's up to you to add edit controls to the CRecordView window. These edit controls must be bound to the database fields they represent, so the application framework knows where to display the data you want to view.

In the next section, you'll see how these various database classes fit together as you build the Employee application step-by-step.

Creating an ODBC Database Program

Although creating a simple ODBC database program is easy with Visual C++, there are number of steps you must complete:

1. Register the database with the system.

2. Use AppWizard to create the basic database application.

3. Add code to the basic application in order to implement features not automatically supported by AppWizard.

In the following sections, you'll see how to perform these steps as you create the Employee application, which enables you to add, delete, update, sort, and view records in the Employees table of the sample department store database.

Registering the Database

Before you can create a database application, you must register the database that you want to access as a data source that you can access through the ODBC driver. Follow these steps to accomplish this important task:

1. Create a folder called **Database** on your hard disk, and copy the file named DeptStore.mdb from this book's CD-ROM to the new Database folder.

   The DeptStore.mdb file is a database created with Microsoft Access. You'll be using this database as the data source for the Employee application.

2. From the Windows 95 Start menu, run Control Panel. When Control Panel appears, double-click the 32-Bit ODBC icon. The Data Sources dialog box appears, as shown in Figure 22.4.

FIG. 22.4

Connecting a data source to your application starts with the ODBC Data Source Administrator.

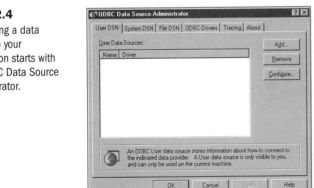

3. Click the A<u>d</u>d button. The Create New Data Source dialog box appears. Select the Microsoft Access Driver from the list of drivers as shown in Figure 22.5 and click Finish.

The Microsoft Access Driver is now the ODBC driver that will be associated with the data source you'll be creating for the Employee application.

FIG. 22.5

Creating a new data source is as simple as choosing Access from a list of drivers.

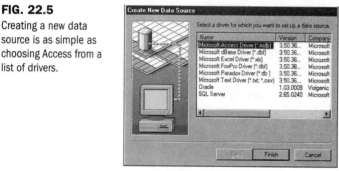

4. When the ODBC Microsoft Access 7.0 Setup dialog box appears, enter **Department Store** into the Data Source <u>N</u>ame text box, and enter **Department Store Sample** in the <u>D</u>escription text box, as shown in Figure 22.6.

The datasource name is simply a way of identifying the specific data source that you're creating. The Description field enables you to include more specific information about the data source.

5. Click the <u>S</u>elect button. The Select Database file selector appears. Use the selector to locate and select the DeptStore.mdb file (see Figure 22.7).

FIG. 22.6

Name your data source whatever you like.

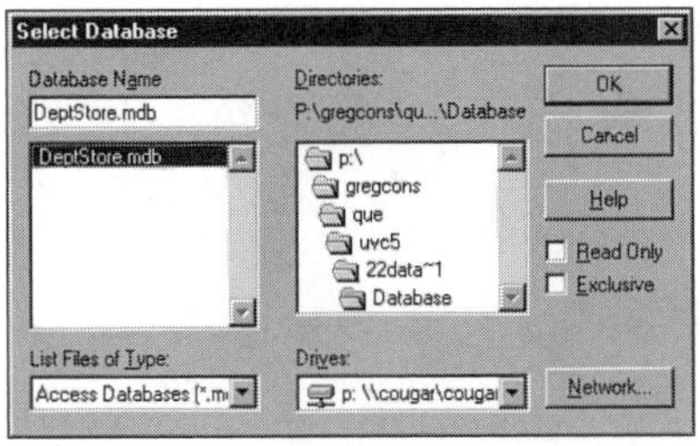

FIG. 22.7

Browse your way to the .mdb file that holds your data.

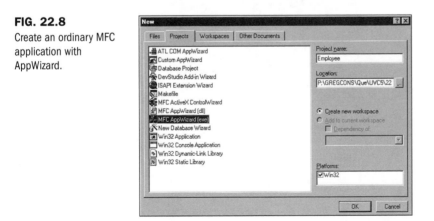

6. Click OK to finalize the database selection, and then in the ODBC Microsoft Access 97 Setup dialog box, click OK to finalize the data-source creation process. Finally, click OK in the ODBC Data Source Administrator dialog box.

Your system is now set up to access the DeptStore.mdb database file with the Microsoft Access ODBC driver.

Creating the Basic Employee Application

Now that you have your data source created and registered, it's time to create the basic Employee application. The steps that follow lead you through this process. After you've completed these steps, you'll have an application that can access and view the Employees table of the Department Store database:

1. Select File, New from Developer Studio's menu bar. Click the Projects tab.

2. Select MFC AppWizard (exe) and type **Employee** into the Name box, as shown in Figure 22.8. Click OK. The Step 1 dialog box appears.

FIG. 22.8

Create an ordinary MFC application with AppWizard.

3. Select Single Document, as shown in Figure 22.9, to ensure that the Employee application will not allow more than one window to be open at a time. Click Next.

FIG. 22.9

Create a Single
Document application.

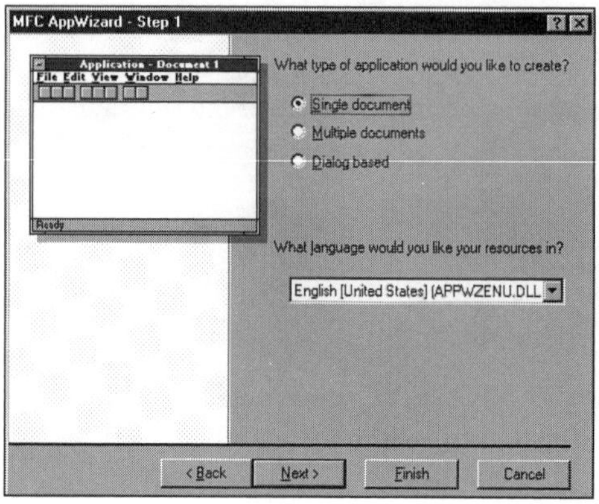

4. Select the <u>D</u>atabase View Without File Support option, as shown in Figure 22.10, so that AppWizard will generate the classes you need to view the contents of a database. This application will not use any supplemental files besides the database, so it doesn't need file (serializing) support. Click the Data <u>S</u>ource button to connect the application to the data source you set up earlier.

FIG. 22.10

Arrange for a Database
View, but no other file
support.

5. In the Database Options dialog box, drop down the ODBC list and select the Department Store data source, as shown in Figure 22.11. Click OK.

FIG. 22.11

Choose your Depart-
ment Store data source.

6. In the Select Database Tables dialog box, select the Employees table, as shown in Figure 22.12, and click OK. The Step 2 dialog box reappears, filled in as shown in Figure 22.13.

   You've now associated the Employees table of the Department Store data source with the Employee application. Click Next to move to step 3.

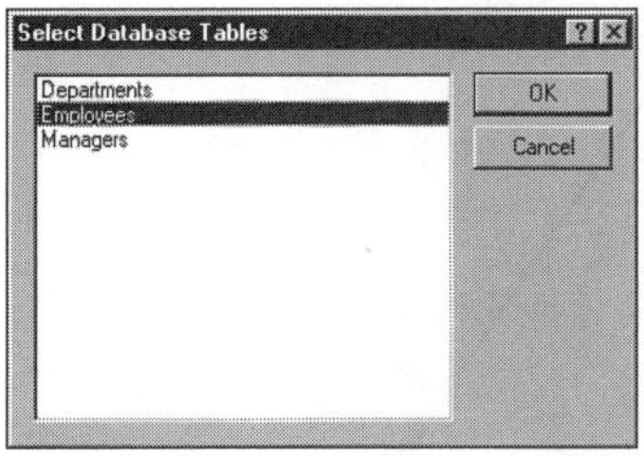

FIG. 22.12

Select which tables from the data source you want to use in this application.

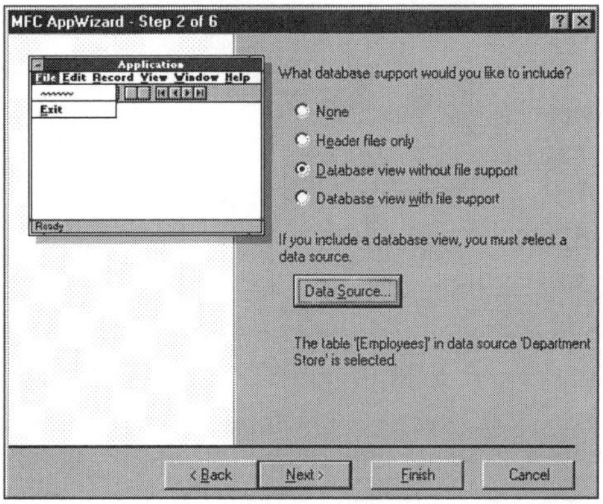

FIG. 22.13

After selecting the data source, the Step 2 dialog box should look like this.

7. Accept the default, No Compound Document Support, and click Next.

8. In the Step 4 dialog box, turn off the Printing and Print Preview option so that the dialog box resembles Figure 22.14. Click Next.

FIG. 22.14

Turn off print support.

9. Accept the defaults for step 5 by clicking Next. In step 6, just click Finish to finalize your selections for the Employee application. The New Project Information dialog box that appears should look like Figure 22.15.

FIG. 22.15

The application summary mentions the data source as well as the usual information.

10. Click OK, and AppWizard creates the basic Employee application.

At this point, you can compile the application by clicking the Build button on Developer Studio's toolbar, by selecting the Build, Build command from the menu bar, or by pressing F7 on your keyboard. After the program has compiled, select the Build, Execute command from the menu bar or press Ctrl+F5 to run the program. When you do, you see the window shown in Figure 22.16. You can use the database controls in the application's toolbar to navigate from one record in the Employee table to another. However, nothing appears in the window because you've yet to associate controls with the fields in the table that you want to view. You'll do that in the following section.

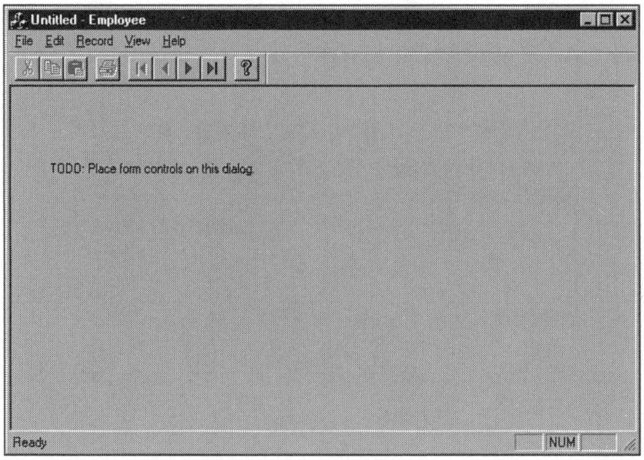

FIG. 22.16

The basic Employee application looks nice but doesn't do much.

Creating the Database Display

The next step in creating the Employee database application is to modify the form that displays data in the application's window. Because this form is just a special type of dialog box, it's easy to modify with Developer Studio's resource editor, as you'll discover as you complete the following steps:

1. Select the Resource View tab to display the application's resources.

2. Open the resource tree by clicking + next to the Employee Resources folder. Then, open the Dialog resource folder the same way. Double-click the IDD_EMPLOYEE_FORM dialog box ID to open the dialog box into the resource editor, as shown in Figure 22.17.

FIG. 22.17

Open the dialog box in the resource editor.

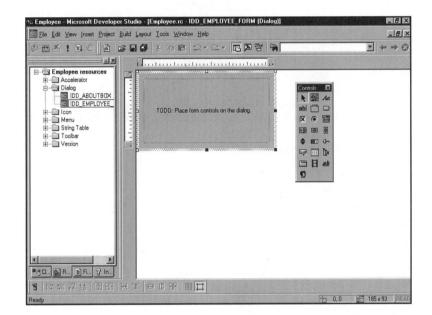

3. Click the static string in the center of the dialog box to select it, and then press Delete to remove the string from the dialog box.

4. Use the dialog box editor's tools to create the dialog box shown in Figure 22.18 by adding edit boxes and static labels. (Editing dialog boxes is introduced in Chapter 2, "Dialogs and Controls.") Give the edit boxes the following IDs: **IDC_EMPLOYEE_ID**, **IDC_EMPLOYEE_NAME, IDC_EMPLOYEE_RATE**, and **IDC_EMPLOYEE_DEPT**. Set the Read-Only style (found on the Styles page of the Edit Properties property sheet) of the IDC_EMPLOYEE_ID edit box.

Each of these edit boxes will represent a field of data in the database. The first edit box is read-only because it will hold the database's primary key, which should never be modified.

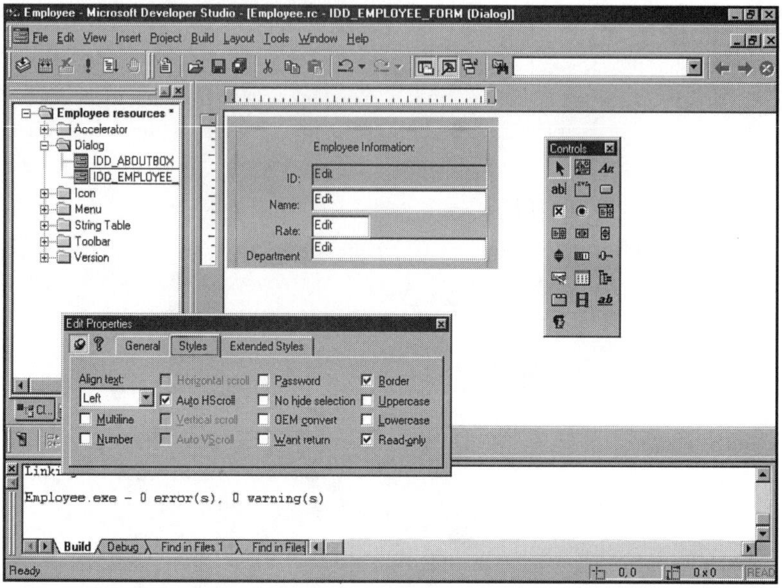

FIG. 22.18

Create a dialog box to be used in your database form.

5. Choose View, ClassWizard to bring up ClassWizard, and click the Member Variables tab.

6. With the IDC_EMPLOYEE_DEPT resource ID selected, click the Add Variable button. The Add Member Variable dialog box appears.

7. Click the arrow next to the Member Variable Name drop-down list, and select m_pSet->m_DeptID, as shown in Figure 22.19.

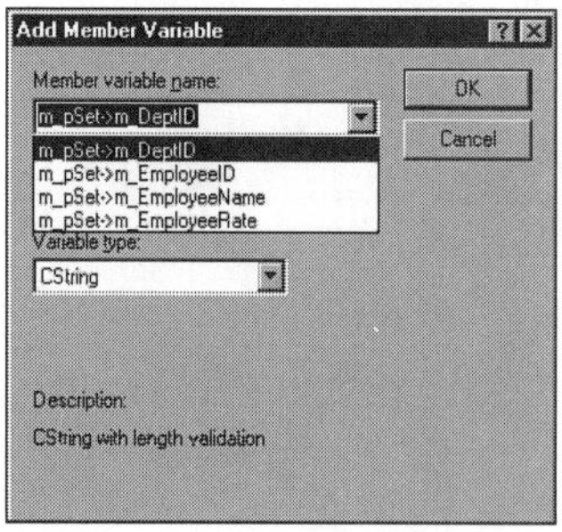

FIG. 22.19

Connect the IDC_EMPLOYEE_DEPT control with the m_DeptID member variable of the recordset.

8. Associate other member variables (m_pSet->EmployeeID, m_pSet->EmployeeName, and m_pSet->EmployeeRate) with the edit controls in the same way. When you're finished, the Member Variables page of the MFC ClassWizard property sheet should look like Figure 22.20.

By selecting member variables of the application's CEmployeeSet class (derived from MFC's CRecordset class) as member variables for the controls in Database view, you're establishing a connection through which data can flow between the controls and the data source.

FIG. 22.20

All four controls are connected to member variables.

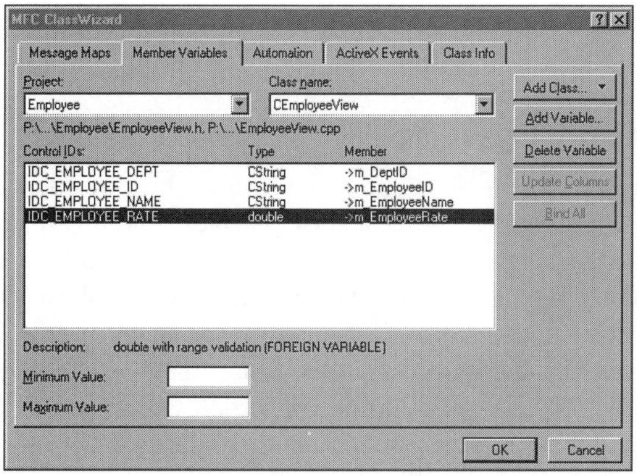

9. Click the OK button in the MFC ClassWizard property sheet in order to finalize your changes.

You've now created a data-display form for the Employee application. Build and execute the program again, and you see the window shown in Figure 22.21. Now the application displays the contents of records in the Employee database table. Use the database controls in the application's toolbar to navigate from one record in the Employee table to another.

FIG. 22.21

The Employee application now displays data in its window.

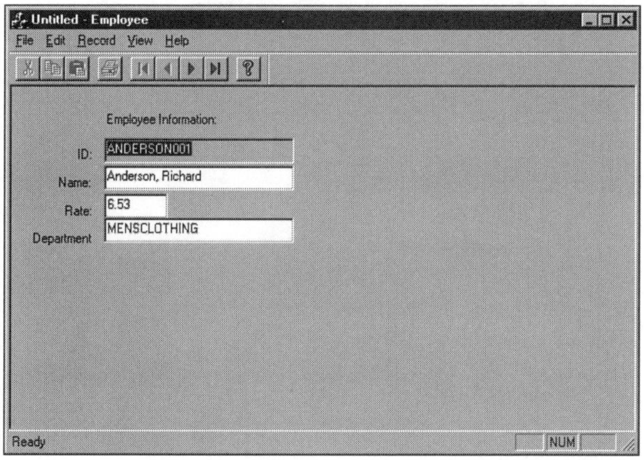

After you've examined the database, try updating a record. To do this, simply change one of the record's fields (except the employee ID, which is the table's primary key and can't be edited). When you move to another record, the application automatically updates the modified record. The commands in the application's Record menu also enable you to navigate through the records in the same manner as the toolbar buttons.

Notice that you've created a fairly sophisticated database-access program without writing a single line of C++ code—a pretty amazing feat. Still, the Employee application is limited.

For example, it can't add or delete records. As you may have guessed, that's the next piece of the database puzzle that you'll add.

Adding and Deleting Records

Once you can add and delete records from a database table, you'll have a full-featured program for manipulating a flat (that is, not a relational) database. In this case, the "flat database" is the Employees table of the department store relational database. Adding and deleting records in a database table is an easier process than you might believe, thanks to Visual C++'s CRecordView and CRecordSet classes, which provide all the member functions you need to accomplish these common database tasks. You'll need to add some menu items to the application, as first discussed in Chapter 9, "Building a Complete Application: ShowString." Follow these steps to include add and delete commands in the Employee application:

1. Select the ResourceView tab, open the Menu folder, and double-click the IDR_MAINFRAME menu ID. The menu editor appears, as shown in Figure 22.22.

FIG. 22.22

Developer Studio's menu editor is in the pane on the right.

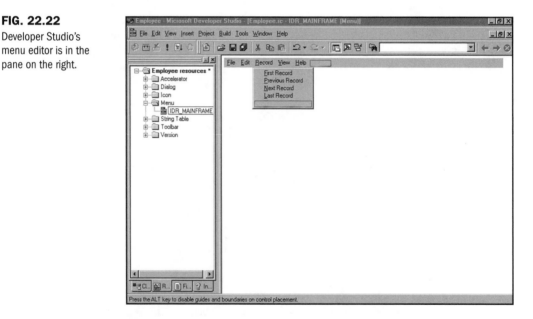

2. Click the Record menu item to open it, and click the blank menu item at the bottom of the menu. Choose View, Properties and pin the Properties dialog box in place.

3. In the ID edit box, enter **ID_RECORD_ADD**, and in the Caption box, enter **&Add Record**, as shown in Figure 22.23. This adds a new command to the Record menu.

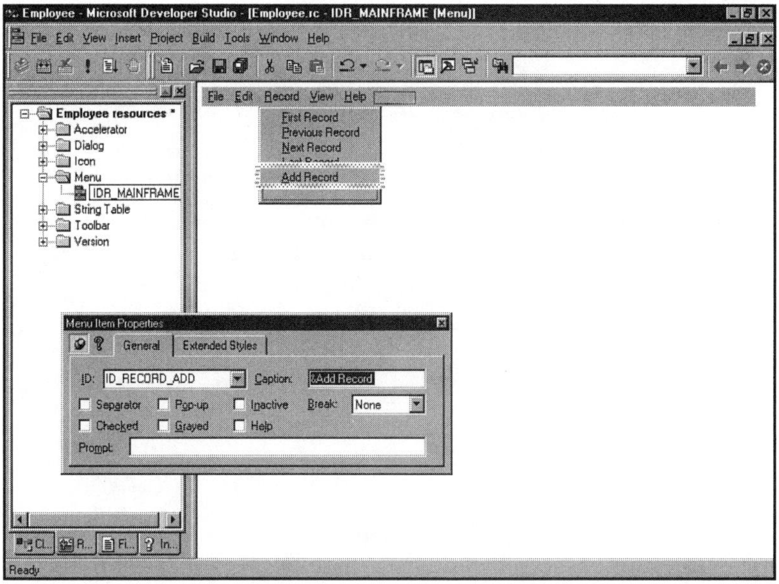

FIG. 22.23

Add a menu item to add a record.

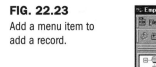

4. In the next blank menu item, add a delete command with the ID ID_RECORD_DELETE and the caption **&Delete Record**.

Next, you will connect these commands to toolbar buttons, as first discussed in Chapter 10, "Toolbars and Status Bars." Follow these steps:

1. In the ResourceView pane, open the Toolbar folder, and then double-click the IDR_MAINFRAME ID. The application's toolbar appears in the resource editor.

2. Click the blank toolbar button to select it, and then use the editor's tools to draw a blue + on the button.

3. Double-click the new button in the toolbar. The Toolbar Button Properties property sheet appears. Select ID_RECORD_ADD in the ID box, as shown in Figure 22.24.

4. Select the blank button again and draw a red minus sign, giving the button the ID_RECORD_DELETE ID, as you can see in Figure 22.25. Drag and drop the Add and Delete buttons to the left of the Help (question mark) button.

FIG. 22.24
Add a button and
connect it to the menu
item.

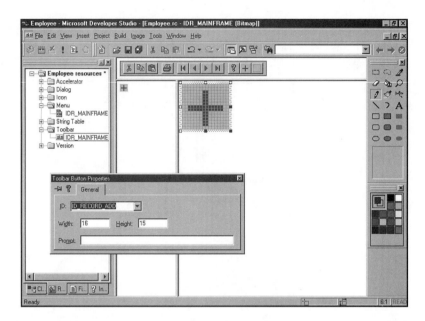

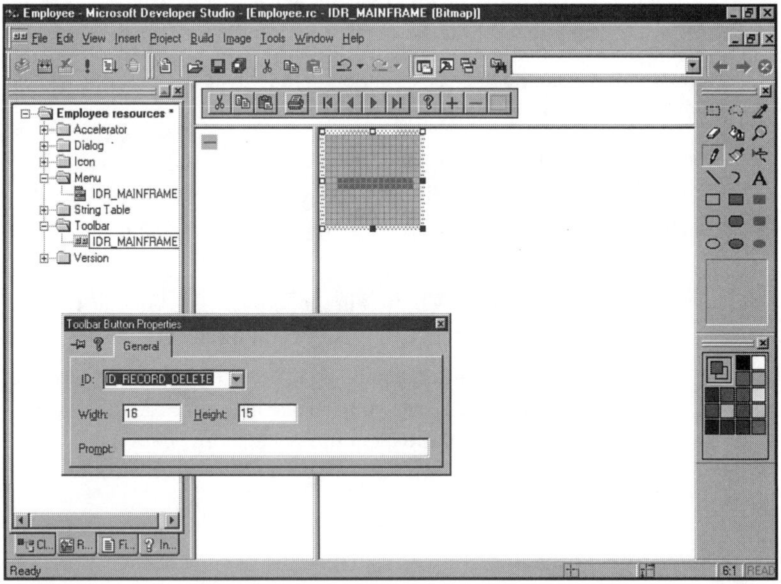

FIG. 22.25
The minus-sign button
will control the Delete
function.

Now that you have added the menu items and the toolbar buttons, you need to arrange for code to "catch" the command message that is sent when the user clicks the button or chooses the menu item. Background information on this process is in Chapter 4, "Messages and Commands;" Chapter 9, "Building a Complete Application: ShowString;" and Chapter 10, "Status Bars and Toolbars." Because it is the view that is connected to the database, the view will catch these messages. Follow these steps:

1. Bring up ClassWizard and select the Message Maps tab.

2. Set the Class Name box to CEmployeeView, click the ID_RECORD_ADD ID in the Object IDs box, and then double-click COMMAND in the Messages box. The Add Member Function dialog box appears, as shown in Figure 22.26.

FIG. 22.26
Add a function to catch the message.

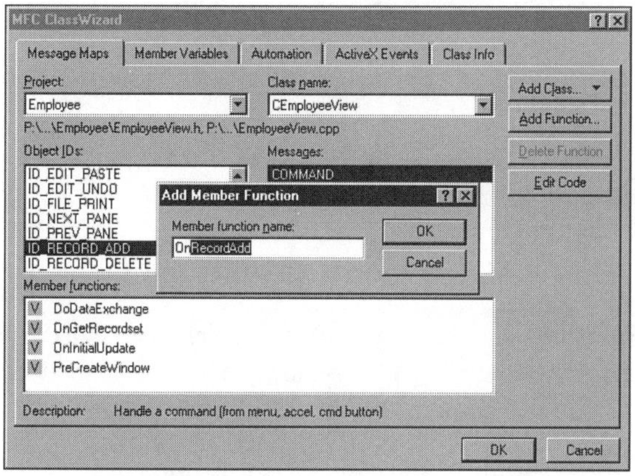

3. Click the OK button to accept the default name for the new function. The function appears in the Member Functions box at the bottom of the ClassWizard dialog box.

4. Add a member function for the ID_RECORD_DELETE command in the same way. The list of functions should resemble Figure 22.27. Click OK to close ClassWizard.

FIG. 22.27
The new functions appear in the Member Functions box.

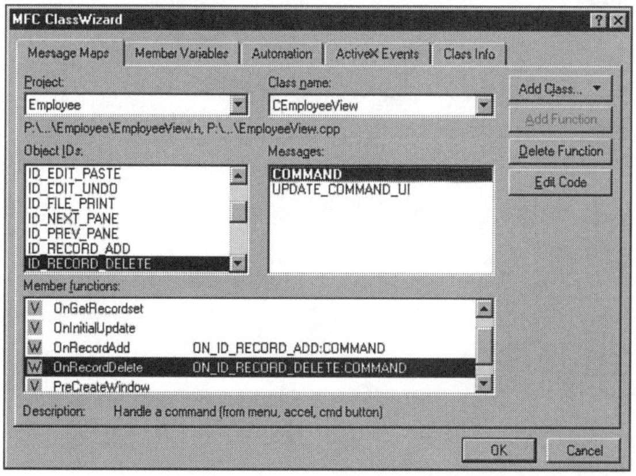

5. Open the EmployeeView.h file by double-clicking CEmployeeView in the ClassView pane. In the Attributes section of the class's declaration, add the following lines:

```
protected:
  BOOL m_bAdding;
```

6. Double-click the CEmployeeView constructor in ClassView to edit it, and add this line at the bottom of the function:

```
m_bAdding = FALSE;
```

7. Double-click the OnRecordAdd() function and edit it so that it looks like Listing 22.1. This code is explained in the next section.

Listing 22.1   *CEmployeeView::OnRecordAdd()*

```
void CEmployeeView::OnRecordAdd()
{
    m_pSet->AddNew();
    m_bAdding = TRUE;
    CEdit* pCtrl = (CEdit*)GetDlgItem(IDC_EMPLOYEE_ID);
    int result = pCtrl->SetReadOnly(FALSE);
    UpdateData(FALSE);
}
```

8. Right-click CEmployeeView in ClassView and choose Add Virtual Function. Select OnMove from the list on the left, as shown in Figure 22.28, then click Add and Edit to add the function and edit the skeleton code immediately.

FIG. 22.28

Override the *OnMove()* function.

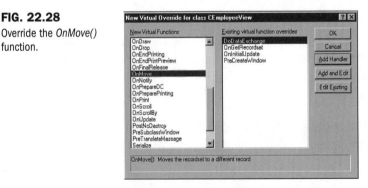

9. Edit OnMove() function so that it has the code in Listing 22.2. This code is explained in the next section.

Listing 22.2 *CEmployeeView::OnMove()*

```
BOOL CEmployeeView::OnMove(UINT nIDMoveCommand)
{
    if (m_bAdding)
    {
        m_bAdding = FALSE;
        UpdateData(TRUE);
        if (m_pSet->CanUpdate())
            m_pSet->Update();
        m_pSet->Requery();
        UpdateData(FALSE);
        CEdit* pCtrl = (CEdit*)GetDlgItem(IDC_EMPLOYEE_ID);
        pCtrl->SetReadOnly(TRUE);
        return TRUE;
    }
    else
        return CRecordView::OnMove(nIDMoveCommand);
}
```

10. Double-click the `OnRecordDelete()` function and edit it so that it looks like Listing 22.3. This code is explained in the next section.

Listing 22.3 *CEmployeeView::OnRecordDelete()*

```
void CEmployeeView::OnRecordDelete()
{
    m_pSet->Delete();
    m_pSet->MoveNext();

    if (m_pSet->IsEOF())
        m_pSet->MoveLast();
    if (m_pSet->IsBOF())
        m_pSet->SetFieldNull(NULL);

    UpdateData(FALSE);
}
```

You've now modified the Employee application so that it can add and delete—as well as update—records. After compiling the application, run it by selecting the Build, Execute command from Developer Studio's menu bar or by pressing Ctrl+F5. When you do, you see the Employee application's main window, which doesn't look any different than it did in the previous section. Now, however, you can add new records by clicking the Add button on the toolbar (or by selecting the Record, Add Record command in the menu bar) and delete records by clicking the Delete button (or by clicking the Record, Delete Record command).

When you click the Add button, the application displays a blank record. Fill in the fields for the record; then when you move to another record, the application automatically updates the database with the new record. To delete a record, just click the Delete button. The current record (the one on the screen) vanishes and is replaced by the next record in the database.

Examining the *OnRecordAdd()* Function

You now may be wondering how the C++ code you added to the application works. OnRecordAdd() starts with a call to the AddNew() member function of CEmployeeSet, the class derived from CRecordSet. This sets up a blank record for the user to fill in, but the new blank record doesn't appear on the screen until the view window's UpdateData() function is called. Before that happens, you have a few other things to tackle.

After the user has created a new record, the database will need to be updated. By setting a flag in this routine, the move routine will be able to determine whether the user is moving away from an ordinary database record or a newly added one. That's why m_bAdding is set to TRUE here.

Now, because the user is entering a new record, it should be possible to change the contents of the Employee ID field, which is currently set to read-only. To change the read-only status of the control, the program first gets a pointer to the control with GetDlgItem() and then calls the control's SetReadOnly() member function to set the read-only attribute to FALSE.

Finally, the call to UpdateData() will display the new blank record.

Examining the *OnMove()* Function

Now that the user has a blank record on the screen, it is a simple matter to fill in the edit controls with the necessary data. To actually add the new record to the database, the user most move to a new record, an action that forces a call to the view window's OnMove() member function. Normally, OnMove() does nothing more than display the next record. Your override will save new records as well.

When OnMove() is called, the first thing the program does is check the Boolean variable m_bAdding in order to see whether the user is in the process of adding a new record. If m_bAdding is FALSE, the body of the if statement is skipped and the else clause is executed. In the else clause, the program calls the base class (CRecordView) version of OnMove(), which simply moves to the next record.

If m_bAdding is TRUE, the body of the if statement is executed. There, the program first resets the m_bAdding flag, then calls UpdateData() to transfer data out of the view window's controls and into the recordset. A call to the recordset's CanUpdate() method determines if it's okay to update the data source, after which a call to the recordset's Update() member function adds the new record to the data source.

In order to rebuild the recordset, the program must call the recordset's `Requery()` member function, and then a call to the view window's `UpdateData()` member function transfers new data to the window's controls. Finally, the program sets the Employee ID field back to read-only, with another call to `GetDlgItem()` and to `SetReadOnly()`.

Examining the *OnRecordDelete()* Function

Deleting a record is quite simple. `OnRecordDelete()` just calls the recordset's `Delete()` function. Once the record is deleted, a call to the recordset's `MoveNext()` arranges for the record that follows to be displayed.

A problem might arise, though, when the deleted record was in the last position or when the deleted record was the only record in the recordset. A call to the recordset's `IsEOF()` function will determine whether the recordset was at the end. If the call to `IsEOF()` returns TRUE, the recordset needs to be repositioned on the last record. The recordset's `MoveLast()` function takes care of this task.

When all records have been deleted from the recordset, the record pointer will be at the beginning of the set. The program can test for this situation by calling the recordset's `IsBOF()` function. If this function returns TRUE, the program sets the current record's fields to NULL.

Finally, the last task is to update the view window's display with another call to `UpdateData()`.

Sorting and Filtering

In many cases when you're accessing a database, you want to change the order in which the records are presented, or you may even want to search for records that fit certain criteria. MFC's ODBC database classes feature member functions that enable you to sort a set of records on any field. You can also call member functions in order to limit the records displayed to those whose fields contain given information, such as a specific name or ID. This latter operation is called *filtering*. In this section, you'll add sorting and filtering to the Employee application. Just follow these steps:

1. Add a Sort menu to the application's menu bar, as shown in Figure 22.29. Let Developer Studio set the command IDs.

2. Use ClassWizard to arrange for `CEmployeeView` to catch the four new sorting commands, using the function names suggested by ClassWizard. Figure 22.30 shows the resultant ClassWizard property sheet.

3. Add a Filter menu to the application's menu bar, as shown in Figure 22.31. Let Developer Studio set the command IDs.

4. Use ClassWizard to arrange for `CEmployeeView` to catch the four new filtering commands, using the function names suggested by ClassWizard.

FIG. 22.29
The Sort menu has four commands for sorting the database.

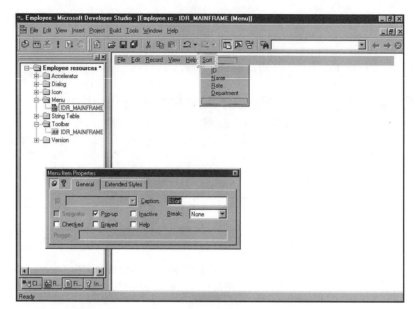

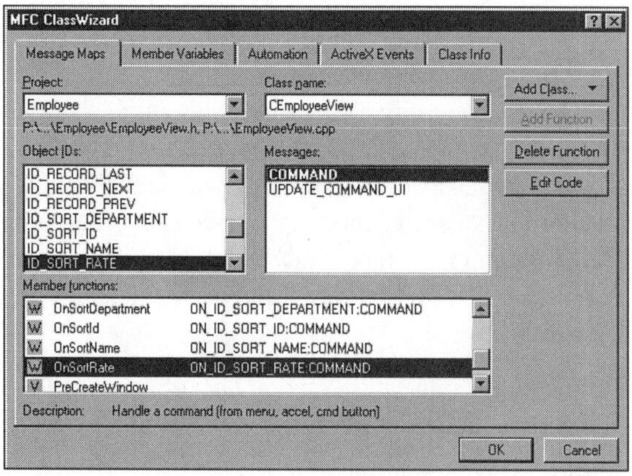

FIG. 22.30
After you add the four new functions, ClassWizard should look like this.

5. Create a new dialog box by choosing Insert, Resource and double-clicking Dialog, then edit the dialog so it resembles the dialog box shown in Figure 22.32. Give the edit control the ID **ID_FILTERVALUE**.

6. Start ClassWizard while the new dialog box is on the screen. The Adding a Class dialog box appears. Select the Create a New Class option and click OK.

FIG. 22.31
The Filter menu has
four commands.

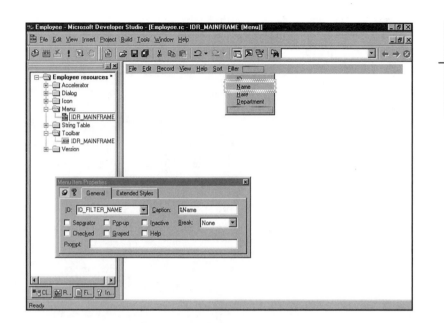

FIG. 22.32
Create a filter
dialog box.

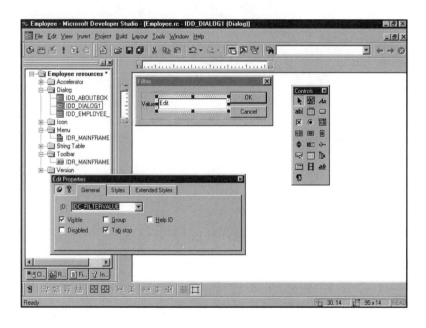

7. The Create New Class dialog box appears. In the Name box, type **CFilterDlg**, as shown in Figure 22.33.

FIG. 22.33

Create a dialog class for the Filter dialog box.

8. Click ClassWizard's Member Variables tab. Connect the IDC_FILTERVALUE control to a member variable called m_filterValue. Click the OK button to dismiss ClassWizard.

Now that the menus and dialogs have been created and connected to skeleton functions, it's time to add some code to those functions. Double-click OnSortDepartment() in ClassView and edit it to look like Listing 22.4.

Listing 22.4   *CEmployeeView::OnSortDepartment()*

```
void CEmployeeView::OnSortDepartment()
{
        m_pSet->Close();
        m_pSet->m_strSort = "DeptID";
        m_pSet->Open();
        UpdateData(FALSE);
}
```

Double-click OnSortID() in ClassView and edit it to look like Listing 22.5. Double-click OnSortName() in ClassView and edit it to look like Listing 22.6. Double-click OnSortRate() in ClassView and edit it to look like Listing 22.7.

Listing 22.5 *CEmployeeView::OnSortId()*

```
void CEmployeeView::OnSortId()
{
        m_pSet->Close();
        m_pSet->m_strSort = "EmployeeID";
        m_pSet->Open();
        UpdateData(FALSE);
}
```

Listing 22.6 *CEmployeeView::OnSortName()*

```
void CEmployeeView::OnSortName()
{
        m_pSet->Close();
        m_pSet->m_strSort = "EmployeeName";
        m_pSet->Open();
        UpdateData(FALSE);
}
```

Listing 22.7 LST14_07.TXT—Code for the *OnSortRate()* Function

```
void CEmployeeView::OnSortRate()
{
        m_pSet->Close();
        m_pSet->m_strSort = "EmployeeRate";
        m_pSet->Open();
        UpdateData(FALSE);
}
```

At the top of EmployeeView.cpp, add the following line after the other #include directives:

```
#include "FilterDlg.h"
```

Edit OnFilterDepartment(),OnFilterID(), OnFilterName(), and OnFilterRate() using Listing 22.8.

Listing 22.8 The Four Filtering Functions

```
void CEmployeeView::OnFilterDepartment()
{
        DoFilter("DeptID");
}

void CEmployeeView::OnFilterId()
{
        DoFilter("EmployeeID");
}
```

continues

Listing 22.8   Continued

```
void CEmployeeView::OnFilterName()
{
        DoFilter("EmployeeName");
}

void CEmployeeView::OnFilterRate()
{
        DoFilter("EmployeeRate");
}
```

These four functions all call DoFilter(). You will write this function to filter the database records represented by the record set class. Right-click CEmployeeView in ClassView and choose Add Member Function. The type is void and the declaration is DoFilter(CString col). It's a protected member function, because it's only called from other member functions of CEmployeeView. Double-click DoFilter() in ClassView and add the code from Listing 22.9.

Listing 22.9   *CEmployeeView::DoFilter()*

```
void CEmployeeView::DoFilter(CString col)
{
    CFilterDlg dlg;
    int result = dlg.DoModal();

    if (result == IDOK)
    {
        CString str = col + " = '" + dlg.m_filterValue + "'";
        m_pSet->Close();
        m_pSet->m_strFilter = str;
        m_pSet->Open();
        int recCount = m_pSet->GetRecordCount();

        if (recCount == 0)
        {
            MessageBox("No matching records.");
            m_pSet->Close();
            m_pSet->m_strFilter = "";
            m_pSet->Open();
        }

        UpdateData(FALSE);
    }

}
```

You've now added the ability to sort and filter records in the employee database. Build the application and run it. When you do, the application's main window appears, looking the same as before. Now, however, you can sort the records on any field, just by selecting a field from the Sort menu. You can also filter the records by selecting a field from the Filter menu, and then typing the filter string into the Filter dialog box that appears. You can tell how the records are sorted or filtered by moving through them one at a time. Try sorting by department, or rate, for example. Then try filtering on one of the departments you saw scroll by.

Examining the *OnSortDept()* Function

The sorting functions all have the same structure. They close the recordset, set its `m_strSort` member variable, open it again, and then call `UpdateData()` to refresh the view with the values from the newly sorted recordset. You don't see any calls to a member function with `Sort` in its name. So when does the sort happen? When the recordset is reopened.

A `CRecordset` object (or any object of a class derived from `CRecordset`, such as this program's `CEmployeeSet` object) uses a special string, called `m_strSort`, to determine how the records should be sorted. When the recordset is being created, the object checks this string and sorts the records accordingly.

Examining the *DoFilter()* Function

Whenever the user selects a command from the Filter menu, the framework calls the appropriate member function, either `OnFilterDept()`, `OnFilterID()`, `OnFilterName()`, or `OnFilterRate()`. Each of these functions does nothing more than call the local member function `DoFilter()` with a string representing the field on which to filter.

`DoFilter()` displays the same dialog box no matter which filter menu item was chosen, by creating an instance of the dialog box class and calling its `DoModal()` function.

If `result` does not equal `IDOK`, the user must have clicked Cancel: the entire `if` statement gets skipped over and the `DoFilter()` function does nothing but return.

Inside the `if` statement, the function first creates the string that will be used to filter the database. Just as you set a string to sort the database, so too do you set a string to filter the database. In this case, the string is called `m_strFilter`. The string you use to filter the database must be in a form like this:

```
ColumnID = 'ColumnValue'
```

The column ID was provided to `DoFilter()` as a `CString` parameter, and the value was provided by the user. So if, for example, the user chooses to filter by department and types **hardware** in the filter value box, `DoFilter()` would set `str` to `DeptID = 'hardware'`.

With the string constructed, the program is ready to filter the database. Just as with sorting, the recordset must first be closed, then `DoFilter()` sets the recordset's filter string, then it reopens the recordset.

What happens when the given filter results in no records being selected? Good question. The `DoFilter()` function handles this by getting the number of records in the new recordset and comparing them to zero. If the record set is empty, the program displays a message box telling the user of the problem. Then the program closes the recordset, resets the filter string to an empty string, and reopens the recordset. This restores the recordset to include all the records in the Employees table.

Finally, whether the filter resulted in a subset of records or the recordset had to be restored, the program must redisplay the data, by calling UpdateData(), as always.

Choosing Between OBDC and DAO

In the previous section, you read an introduction to Visual C++'s ODBC classes and how they're used in an AppWizard-generated application. Visual C++ also features a complete set of DAO classes that you can use to create database applications. DAO is, in many ways, almost a superset of the ODBC classes, containing most of the functionality of the OBDC classes and adding a great deal of its own. Unfortunately, although DAO can read ODBC data sources for which ODBC drivers are available, it's not particularly efficient at the task. For this reason, the DAO classes are best suited for programming applications that manipulate Microsoft's .mdb database files, which are created by Microsoft Access. Other file formats that DAO can read directly are those created by Fox Pro and Excel.

The DAO classes, which use the Microsoft Jet Database Engine, are so much like the ODBC classes that you can often convert a ODBC program to DAO simply by changing the class names in the program: CDatabase becomes CDaoDatabase, CRecordset becomes CDaoRecordset, and CRecordView becomes CDaoRecordView. One big difference between ODBC and DAO, however, is the way in which the system implements the libraries. ODBC is implemented as a set of DLLs, whereas DAO is implemented as OLE objects. Using OLE objects makes DAO a bit more up-to-date, at least as far as architecture goes, than ODBC.

Although DAO is implemented as OLE objects, you don't have to worry about dealing with those objects directly. The MFC DAO classes handle all the details for you, providing data and function members that interact with the OLE objects. The CDaoWorkspace class provides more direct access to the DAO database-engine object through static member functions. Although MFC handles the workspace for you, you can access its member functions and data members in order to explicitly initialize the database connection.

Another difference is that the DAO classes feature a more powerful set of methods that you can use to manipulate a database. These more powerful member functions enable you to perform sophisticated database manipulations without having to write a lot of complicated C++ code or SQL statements.

- ODBC and DAO can both manipulate ODBC data sources. However, DAO is less efficient at this task because it is best used with .mdb database files.

- AppWizard can create a basic database application based on either the ODBC or DAO classes. Which type of application you want to create depends—at least in some part—on the type of databases with which you'll be working.

- ODBC and DAO both use objects of an MFC database class to provide a connection to the database being accessed. In ODBC, this database class is called CDatabase, whereas in DAO the class is called CDaoDatabase. Although these classes have different names, the DAO database class contains some similar members to those found in the ODBC class.

- ODBC and DAO both use objects of a recordset class to hold the currently selected records from the database. In ODBC, this recordset class is called `CRecordset`, whereas in DAO the class is called `CDaoRecordset`. Although these classes have different names, the DAO recordset class contains not only almost the same members as the ODBC class but also a large set of additional member functions.

- ODBC and DAO use similar procedures for viewing the contents of a data source. That is, in both cases, the application must create a database object, create a recordset object, and then call member functions of the appropriate classes to manipulate the database.

Some differences between ODBC and DAO include:

- Although both ODBC and DAO MFC classes are similar (very similar in some cases), some similar methods have different names. In addition, the DAO classes feature many member functions not included in the ODBC classes.

- ODBC uses macros and enumerations to define options that can be used when opening recordsets. DAO, on the other hand, defines constants for this purpose.

- Under ODBC, snapshot recordsets are the default, whereas under DAO, dynamic recordsets are the default.

- The many available ODBC drivers make ODBC useful for many different database file formats, whereas DAO is best suited to applications that will need to access only .mdb files.

- ODBC is implemented as a set of DLLs, whereas DAO is implemented as OLE objects.

- Under ODBC, an object of the `CDatabase` class transacts directly with the data source. Under DAO, a `CDaoWorkspace` object sits between the `CDaoRecordset` and `CDaoDatabase` objects, thus enabling the workspace to transact with multiple database objects.

OLE DB

OLE DB is a collection of OLE (ActiveX) interfaces that simplify access to data stored in non-database applications such as e-mail mailboxes or flat files. An application using OLE DB can integrate information from DBMS systems like Oracle, SQL Server, or Access with information from non-database systems using the power of OLE (ActiveX).

A full treatment of OLE DB is outside the scope of this chapter. You need to be comfortable with OLE interfaces to use this powerful tool. If you have only created OLE (ActiveX) applications with MFC and AppWizard, you may be in for a shock when you see what Microsoft considers "simplified." There are lots of calls to `QueryInterface()`, and lots of variables with names like `pIColsInfo` or `rgColInfo`. Still, when you wander down through all the interfaces and all the setting up, you can call a function like `GetData()` and take information out of a non-database application just as though it was a database, and that can be a big time-saver.

There is an OLE DB Programmer's Reference in the Visual C++ online documentation. Once you are familiar with OLE and ActiveX concepts, that's a great place to start.

From Here...

There's no doubt that using AppWizard and MFC's database classes makes writing database applications infinitely easier than the old-fashioned, roll-up-your-sleeves method. In fact, AppWizard can generate a fully functional database browser with very little help from you. Even when you have to get your hands dirty, though, implementing additional database commands in your application is just a matter of calling a few member functions. And, although the ODBC classes are adequate for most database projects, the DAO classes are newer, more powerful, and best suited for manipulating .mdb files, such as those created by Microsoft Access.

For more information on related topics, please consult the following chapters:

- Chapter 2, "Dialog Boxes and Controls," teaches you about MFC's many control classes and how you can incorporate them into your own programs.
- Chapter 4, "Messages and Commands," shows how MFC's message-routing system works and how you can adapt that system to your own menus and commands.
- Chapter 9, "Building a Complete Application: ShowString," combines menus, dialog boxes, and code into a complete working application.
- Chapter 23, "Enterprise Edition," tackles another sort of database programming: large scale enterprise SQL programming.

New Enterprise Edition

The Enterprise Edition of Visual C++ was developed for those of you who are integrating SQL databases and C++ programs, especially if you use stored procedures. It is sold as a separate edition of the product: Y

 can buy a copy of the Enterprise Edition instead of the Professional Edition. If you already own a Professional or Subscription Edition, you can upgrade to the Enterprise Edition for a reduced price. ■

SQL

SQL, Structured Query Language, allows you to retrieve, update, or add records to or from a relational database.

SQL from C++

Calling a SQL-stored procedure from C++ is not a difficult task.

The DataView

Look at and change the structure and contents of your database, build queries on-the-fly, and edit and debug stored procedures, all in one powerful new view.

New Database tools

Query Designer, Database Designer, and Database Diagrams are all designed to simplify the job of dealing with database and with SQL.

Microsoft Transaction Server

If your database work involves transactions, you need to learn about MTS and what it can do for you.

Visual Source Safe

This revision control system is important to any developer, even if your applications don't involve databases at all. It comes with the Enterprise Edition.

Understanding SQL

Structured Query Language, SQL, is a way to access databases, interactively or in a program, that is designed to read as though it were English. Most SQL statements are queries, requests for information from one or more databases, but it is also possible to use SQL to add, delete, and change information. As mentioned in Chapter 22, "Database Access," SQL is an enormous topic. This section reviews the most important SQL commands, so that even if you haven't used it before you can understand these examples and see how powerful these tools can be.

> **N O T E**   The Enterprise Edition comes with a Developer Edition of Microsoft SQL Server 6.5. The SQL
> Server Books Online included with the product contains an excellent SQL Reference. ■

SQL is used to access a relational database, which contains several *tables*. A table is made up of rows, and a row is made up of columns. Table 23.1 lists some names used in database research or in some other kinds of databases for tables, rows, and columns.

Table 23.1   Database Terminology

SQL	Also known as
Table	Entity
Row	Record, Tuple
Column	Field, Attribute

Here's a sample SQL statement:

```
SELECT au_fname, au_lname FROM authors
```

It produces a list of author first and last names from a table called authors. (This table is included in the sample pubs database that comes with SQL Server that you'll be using in this chapter.) Here's a far more complicated SQL statement:

```
SELECT item, SUM(amount) total, AVG(amount) average FROM ledger
   WHERE action = 'PAID'
   GROUP BY item
having AVG(amount) > (SELECT avg(amount) FROM ledger
                      WHERE action = 'PAID')
```

A SQL statement is put together from keywords, table names, and column names. The keywords include:

- ■ SELECT: returns specific column of the database. Secondary keywords including FROM, WHERE , LIKE, NULL, and ORDER BY restrict the search to certain records within each table.

- ■ DELETE: removes records. The secondary keyword WHERE specifies which records to delete.

- ■ UPDATE: changes the value of columns (specified with SET), in records specified with WHERE. Can be combined with a SELECT statement.

- INSERT: inserts a new record into the database.
- COMMIT: saves any changes you have made to the database.
- ROLLBACK: undoes all your changes back to the most recent COMMIT.
- EXEC: calls a stored procedure.

Like C++, SQL supports two kinds of comments:

```
/* This comment has begin and end symbols */
— This is a from-here-to-end-of-line comment
```

Working with SQL Databases from C++

As you saw in Chapter 22, "Database Access," an ODBC program using CDatabase and CRecordset can already access a SQL Server database, or any database that supports SQL queries. What's more, with the ExecuteSQL function of CDatabase, you can execute any line of SQL at all from within your program. Most of the time, the line of SQL that you execute is a stored procedure, a collection of SQL statements stored with the database and designed to be executed on-the-fly.

There are lots of reasons not to hard-code your SQL into your C++ program. The three most compelling are:

- Reuse
- Skill separation
- Maintainability

Many programmers accessing a SQL database from a C++ application are building on the work of other developers who have been building the database and its stored procedures for years. Copying those procedures into your code would be foolish indeed. Calling them from within your code lets you build slick user interfaces, simplify Internet access, or take advantage of the speed of C++, while retaining all the power of the stored procedures that have already been written.

Highly skilled professionals are always in demand, and sometimes the demand exceeds the supply. Many companies find it hard to recruit solid C++ programmers and just as hard to recruit experienced database administrators who can learn the structure of a database and write in SQL. Imagine how hard it would be to find a single individual who can do both. Almost as difficult as it would be to expect two developers to work on the parts of the program that called SQL from C++. A much better approach is to have the C++ programmer call well-documented SQL stored procedures, and the SQL developer build those stored procedures and keep the database running smoothly.

Separating the C++ and SQL parts of your application has another benefit: Changes to one may not affect the other. For example, a minor C++ that doesn't involve the SQL will compile and link more quickly since the C++ part of the application is a little bit smaller without the SQL statements in it. Changes to the SQL stored procedure, if they don't involve the parameters to the function or the values it returns, will not take effect without compiling and linking the C++ program.

There is a downside, however. It can be very difficult to track down problems when you are not sure whether they are in the C++ or the SQL part of your program. When one developer is doing both parts, learning two different tools and switching between them makes the job harder than it would be in a single tool. The tools available for working with SQL have not had many of the features that Visual C++ has offered C++ programmers.

Now with the Enterprise Edition of Visual C++, you can have the best of both worlds. You can separate your C++ and SQL for reuse and maintenance, but use the editor, syntax coloring, and even the debugger from Visual C++ to work on your SQL stored procedures.

Exploring the Publishing Application

One of the sample databases that comes with SQL Server is called pubs. It tracks the sales of books and the royalties paid to their authors. In this chapter, you will write a new stored procedure and display the records returned by it in a simple record view dialog box. SQL Server should be up and running before you start to build the application.

Building the Application Shell

Bring up Developer Studio and choose File, New, then click the Projects tab. Select MFC AppWizard (exe), and name the project Publishing, as shown in Figure 23.1. Click OK to start the AppWizard process.

FIG. 23.1
Start AppWizard in the usual way.

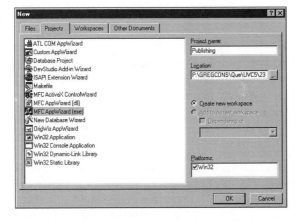

In step 1 of AppWizard, choose an SDI application. Click Next to move to step 2 of AppWizard. As shown in Figure 23.2, select the Database view without file support option. Click Data Source to connect a data source to your application.

FIG. 23.2
This application needs database support but will not have a document.

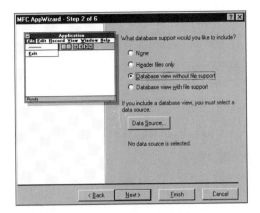

Select the ODBC option, and select Local Server from the drop-down box next to it, as shown in Figure 23.3. Leave the Recordset type as Snapshot, and click OK to specify the exact data source.

FIG. 23.3
Your data source is a local ODBC database.

The SQL Server login dialog box appears. Click the Options button to show the enlarged dialog box of Figure 23.4. Choose pubs from the Database: drop-down box, and enter your login ID and password at the top of the dialog box. Click OK.

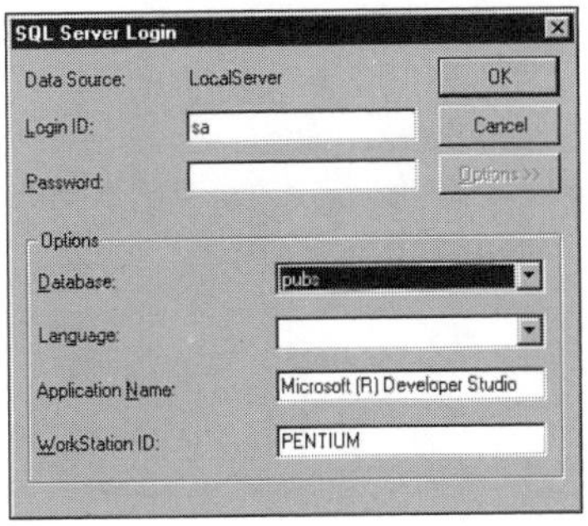

FIG. 23.4
Connect to the sample pubs database.

The Select Database Tables dialog box, shown in Figure 23.5, appears. Click dbo.authors, dbo.titleauthor, and dbo.titles. Click OK.

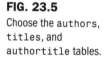

FIG. 23.5

Choose the authors, titles, and authortitle tables.

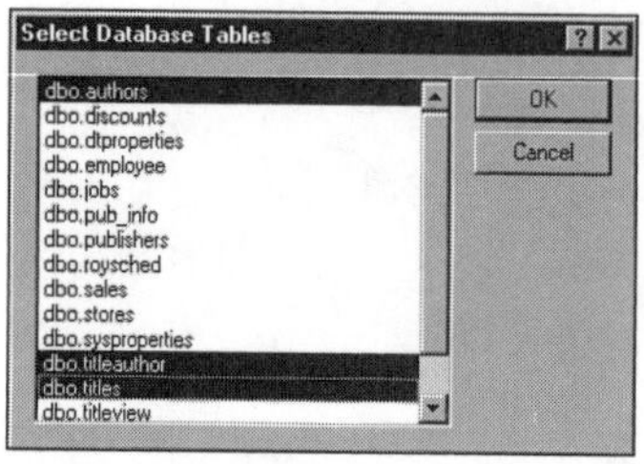

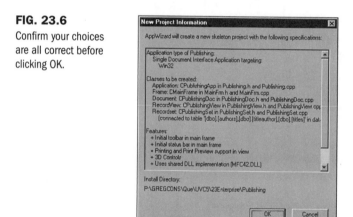

You are back to Step 2 of AppWizard. Click Next to move to Step 3. Choose no support for compound documents or ActiveX controls, and click Next to move to Step 4. Click Next to accept the Step 4 defaults, then Next again to accept the Step 5 defaults. On Step 6, click Finish. The New Project Information summary, shown in Figure 23.6, appears. Click OK to create the project.

FIG. 23.6

Confirm your choices are all correct before clicking OK.

You have now completed a shell of an application that displays database values in a record view, much like the one discussed in Chapter 22, "Database Access." Nothing you have done so far has been specific to the Enterprise Edition. That is about to change.

Making a Data Connection

The database tables you specified are connected to your record set, but they are not available for use with the SQL features of the Enterprise Edition. You need to make a data connection to connect the database to your application. Follow these steps to make the connection:

1. Choose Project, Add to Project, New
2. Click the Projects tab.

3. As shown in Figure 23.7, select a Database Project, name it PubDB, and select the Add to current workspace radio button. Click OK.

FIG. 23.7
Create a subproject
within this project.

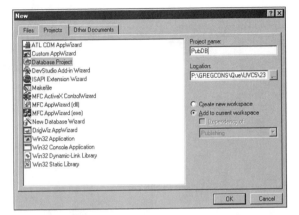

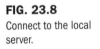

Part
VII

Ch
23

4. The Select Data Source dialog box appears. Choose LocalServer, as shown in Figure 23.8, and click OK.

FIG. 23.8
Connect to the local
server.

5. The SQL Server Login dialog box appears. As before, specify your Login-ID and password, and make sure the pubs database is selected. Click OK to complete the data connection.

In the Workspace pane on the left of the screen, a new tab has appeared. Figure 23.9 shows the new DataView. Expand the Tables section, and expand Authors to show the columns within the table. Double-click the Authors table and you can see your data, on the right in Figure 23.9.

FIG. 23.9
The DataView shows you the database structure, and can display your data in the working area.

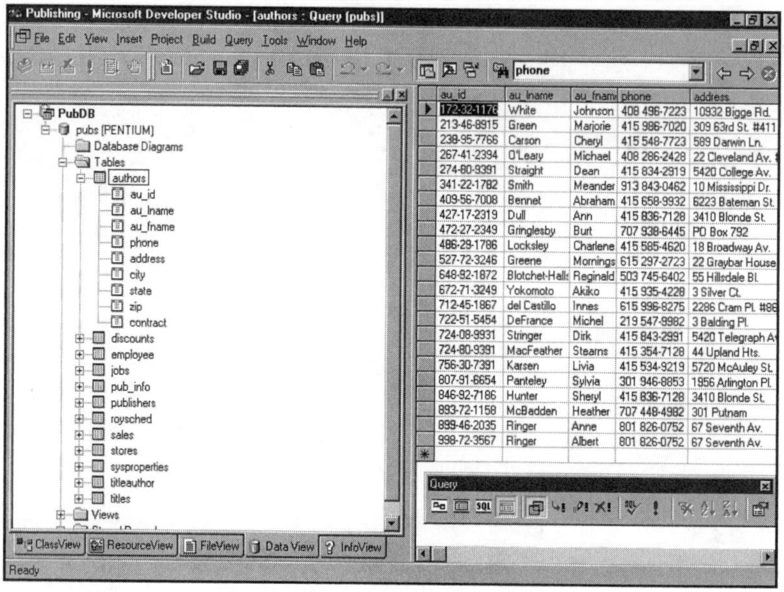

Also featured in Figure 23.9 is the Query toolbar, with the following buttons:

- **Show Diagram Pane**—Toggles the Query designer diagram pane, discussed in the next section
- **Show Grid Pane**—Toggles the Query designer grid pane, discussed in the next section
- **Show SQL Pane**—Toggles the Query designer SQL pane, discussed in the next section
- **Show Results Pane**—Toggles the Query designer results pane, discussed in the next section
- **Create Select Query**—Builds a SELECT query in the four panes of Query designer
- **Create Insert Query**—Builds an INSERT query in the four panes of Query designer
- **Create Update Query**—Builds an UPDATE query in the four panes of Query designer
- **Create Delete Query**—Builds a DELETE query in the four panes of Query designer
- **Verify SQL Syntax**—Checks the syntax of the SQL you have written
- **Run**—Executes your SQL
- **Remove Filter**—Shows all the records instead of just those that meet the filter specifications

- **Sort Ascending**—Displays records from low value of a selected column to high
- **Sort Descending**—Displays records from high value of a selected column to low
- **Properties**—Displays information about a column or table

Working with Query Designer

When you double-click a table name, such as `authors`, in the DataView to display all the columns and all the records, you are actually executing a simple SQL query, as follows:

```
SELECT authors.* FROM authors
```

The results of this query appear in the results pane, which by default is the only one of the four Query Designer panes to be displayed. This query was built for you by Query Designer, and means "show all the columns and records of the `authors` table." Figure 23.10 shows the four panes of Query Designer as they appear when you first make the data connection. To see all four panes, use the toolbar buttons to toggle them on. You can adjust the vertical size of each pane, but not the horizontal.

Part
VII

Ch
23

FIG. 23.10

The DataView shows you the database structure, and can display your data in the working area.

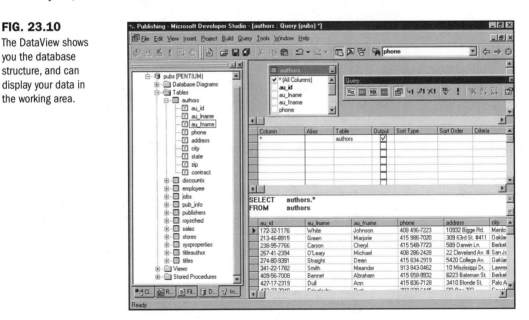

To change your query, deselect * (All Columns) in the diagram pane (at the top of Figure 23.10) and then select au_lname, au_fname, and phone. The values in the results pane go gray to remind you that these are not the results of the query you are now building. As you make these selections in the diagram pane, the other panes update automatically, as shown in Figure 23.11.

FIG. 23.11

You can build simple queries even if you don't know SQL.

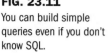

Highlight phone in the diagram pane and click the Sort Ascending button on the Query toolbar. This will sort the results by phone number. Click the Run button on the Query toolbar to execute the SQL that has been built for you. Figure 23.12 shows what you should see, including the new values in the Results pane.

FIG. 23.12

Running your SQL queries is a matter of a single click.

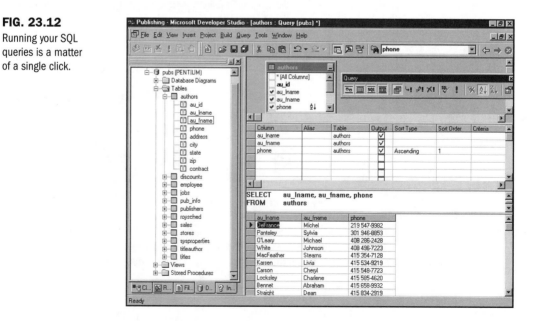

N O T E After you have been looking at your Results pane for a while, a message like the one in Figure 23.13 will appear. If you don't need the results any more, click No. If you are still looking at them, click Yes. If you click neither (for example if another application has focus and you ignore the alert sound that acompanies the message) the results pane will be cleared after another minute. You can get the results back by running the query again. ■

FIG. 23.13

Results take up space and are cleared as soon as possible.

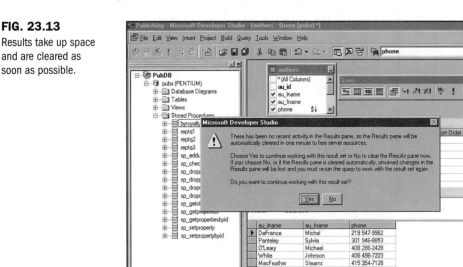

Stored Procedures

The capability to create simple SQL queries quickly, even if your SQL skills are not strong, is an amazing aspect of the Enterprise Edition. But using stored procedures is where the real payoff of this software displays itself.

Collapse the tables section in the DataView, and expand the Stored Procedures section. This shows all the stored procedures that are kept in the database and are available for you to use. Double-click reptq2 to display the procedure, and you should see something like Figure 23.14.

One thing you probably noticed immediately was the syntax coloring in the editor window. The colors used are:

- ■ Blue: for keywords such as PRINT and SELECT
- ■ Green: for both styles of comment
- ■ Black: for other kinds of text

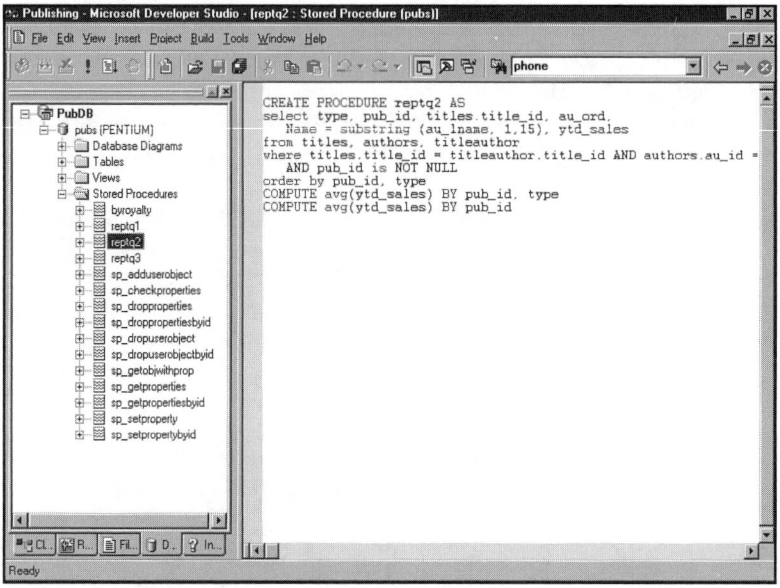

FIG. 23.14

Using the Developer Studio editor to work with SQL means no learning curve for you.

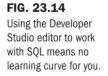

To run a stored procedure, choose <u>T</u>ools, <u>R</u>un, or right-click the stored procedure name in DataView and choose <u>R</u>un, or right-click in the editor and choose <u>R</u>un. The results appear in the Results pane of the Output window—don't confuse this with the Results pane of Query Designer. Figure 23.15 shows the Output window stretched very large to show some of the results of reptq2.

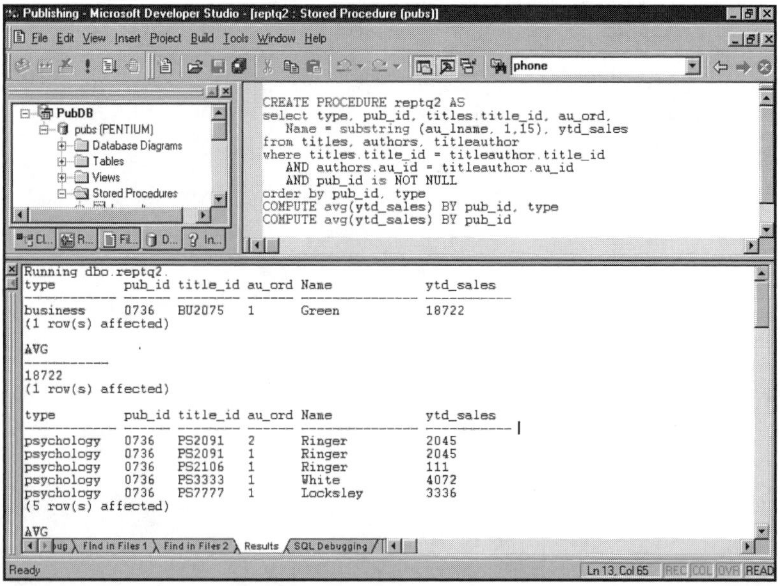

FIG. 23.15

You can see the results of any stored procedure from within Developer Studio.

Some stored procedures take parameters. For example, double-click reptq3; its code looks like this:

```
CREATE PROCEDURE reptq3 @lolimit money, @hilimit money,
@type char(12)
AS
select pub_id, type, title_id, price
from titles
where price >@lolimit AND price <@hilimit AND type = @type
      OR type LIKE '%cook%'
order by pub_id, type
COMPUTE count(title_id) BY pub_id, type
```

This stored procedure takes three parameters: lolimit, hilimit, and type. If you run it, the dialog box shown in Figure 23.16 appears: Enter parameter values and click OK to run the procedure and see the results in the Output window.

FIG. 23.16
Providing parameters
to stored procedures
is simple.

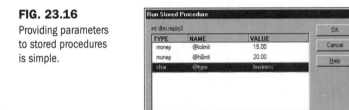

It might be nice if the type parameter was a drop-down box, allowing you to see all the type values in the table before submitting the query. That sort of capability is just what you can build into a C++ program that uses SQL stored procedures. To see how, in the next section you will write a new stored procedure and call it from your C++ program.

Writing a New Stored Procedure

To create a new stored procedure, right-click Stored Procedures in DataView and choose New Stored Procedure. This code appears in the editor:

```
Create Procedure /*Procedure_Name*/
As
     return (0)
```

Edit this code so that it looks like Listing 23.1. Save the stored procedure and its name appears in the DataView.

Listing 23.1   author_ytd—the New Stored Procedure

```
CREATE PROCEDURE author_ytd @sales int
AS
SELECT authors.au_lname, titles.title, ytd_sales
   FROM authors, titles, titleauthor
```

continues

Listing 23.1   Continued

```
    WHERE ytd_sales > @sales
        AND authors.au_id = titleauthor.au_id
        AND titleauthor.title_id = titles.title_id
    ORDER BY ytd_sales DESC
```

This SQL code gathers information from three tables, using the au_id and title_id columns to connect authors to titles. It takes one parameter, sales, which is an integer value. Run the procedure to see the results immediately. Listing 23.2 shows the results using 4000 as the value for sales:

Listing 23.2   author_ytd—Results (@Sales = 4000)

```
Running Stored Procedure dbo.author_ytd ( @sales = 4000 ).
au_lname         au_fname   title                                               ytd_sales
—————————        ————————   ————————————————————————————————                    —————————
DeFrance         Michel     The Gourmet Microwave                               22246
Ringer           Anne       The Gourmet Microwave                               22246
Green            Marjorie   You Can Combat Computer Stress!                     18722
Blotchet-Halls   Reginald   Fifty Years in Buckingham Palace Kitchens           15096
Carson           Cheryl     But Is It User Friendly?                            8780
Green            Marjorie   The Busy Executive's Database Guide                 4095
Bennet           Abraham    The Busy Executive's Database Guide                 4095
Straight         Dean       Straight Talk About Computers                       4095
Dull             Ann        Secrets of Silicon Valley                           4095
Hunter           Sheryl     Secrets of Silicon Valley                           4095
O'Leary          Michael    Sushi, Anyone?                                      4095
Gringlesby       Burt       Sushi, Anyone?                                      4095
Yokomoto         Akiko      Sushi, Anyone?                                      4095
White            Johnson    Prolonged Data Deprivation: Four Case Studies 4072
 (14 row(s) affected)
Finished running dbo.author_ytd.
RETURN_VALUE = 0
```

Connecting the Stored Procedure to C++ Code

At the moment, you have an empty C++ application that uses a recordset and would display members of that recordset in a record view if you added fields to the dialog to do so. The recordset contains all the columns from the three tables (authors, titleauthor, and titles) that you specified during the AppWizard process. That's arranged by a function called CPublishingSet::GetDefaultSQL() that AppWizard wrote for you. It's shown in Listing 23.3.

Listing 23.3   *CPublishingSet::GetDefaultSQL() from AppWizard*

```
CString CPublishingSet::GetDefaultSQL()
{
    return _T("[dbo].[authors],[dbo].[titleauthor],[dbo].[titles]");
}
```

You are going to change this default SQL so that it calls your stored procedure, which is now part of the pubs database. First, choose Project, Set Active Project and select Publishing. Switch to ClassView in the Workspace pane, expand CPublishingSet, and double-click GetDefaultSQL() to edit it. Replace the code with that in Listing 23.4.

Listing 23.4 CPublishingSet::GetDefaultSQL() to Call Your Stored Procedure

```
CString CPublishingSet::GetDefaultSQL()
{
    return _T("{CALL author_ytd(4000)}");
}
```

N O T E Normally you would not hard-code the parameter value like this. Adding member variables to the class to hold parameters and passing them to the SQL is a topic you can explore in the online help once you are more familiar with the Enterprise Edition. ■

The records returned from this query will go into your recordset. The query returns four columns (au_lname, au_fname, title, and ytd_sales) but the recordset is expecting far more than that. You can use ClassWizard to edit your recordset definition. Follow these steps:

1. Bring up ClassWizard by choosing View, ClassWizard.

2. Click the Member Variables tab. You should see something like Figure 23.17, showing all the member variables of the record set connected to table columns.

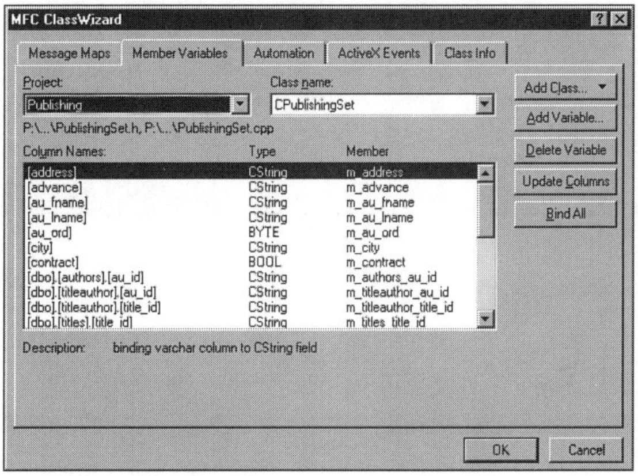

FIG. 23.17

ClassWizard manages your record set definition.

3. Highlight [address] and click Delete Variable.

4. In the same way, delete all the variables except au_lname, au_fname, title, and ytd_sales.

5. Click OK to close ClassWizard.

Your application would compile and run now, but until you edit the record view dialog box you won't be able to see the records and columns that are returned by another query. Editing the dialog box was covered in Chapter 22, "Database Access," and uses skills first demonstrated in Chapter 2, "Dialog Boxes and Controls," so the description here will be brief.

Click on the ResourceView tab, expand the resources, expand Dialogs, and double-click IDD_PUBLISHING_FORM. This dialog box was created for you by AppWizard but has no controls on it yet. Delete the static text reminding you to add controls, and add four edit boxes and their labels so that the dialog box resembles Figure 23.18. Use sensible resource IDs for the edit boxes, not the defaults provided by Developer Studio. Name them IDC_QUERY_LNAME, IDC_QUERY_FNAME, IDC_QUERY_TITLE, and IDC_QUERY_YTDSALES.

FIG. 23.18

Edit your record view dialog box.

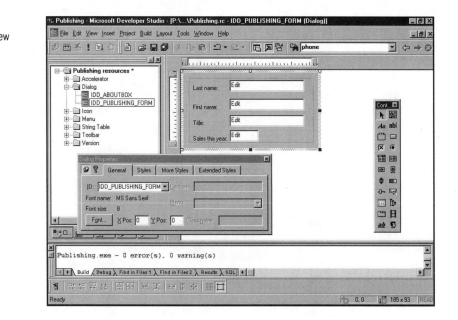

There is one task left: to connect these fields to member variables. Here's how to make that connection:

1. Bring up ClassWizard while this dialog box has focus.

2. Click the Member Variables tab.

3. Select IDC_QUERY_FNAME and click Add Variable to bring up the Add Member Variable dialog box.

4. From the drop-down box labelled Member Variable name, choose m_pSet->m_au_fname and click OK.

5. In the same way, connect IDC_QUERY_LNAME to m_pSet->m_au_lname, IDC_QUERY_TITLE to m_pSet->m_title, and IDC_QUERY_YTDSALES to m_pSet->m_ytd_sales.

6. Figure 23.19 shows the ClassWizard dialog box when all four controls have been connected. Click OK to close ClassWizard.

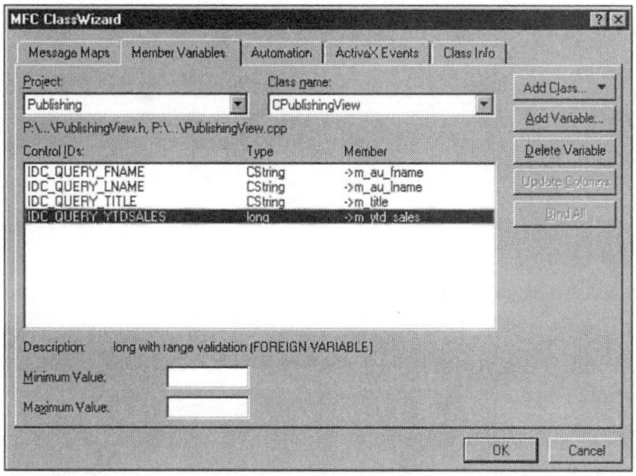

FIG. 23.19
Connect the record view controls to member variables of the record set.

Build your project and run it. You should see a record view like Figure 23.20 (you may have to go through the SQL login procedure again first) and if you scroll through the record view with the arrow buttons, you should see every author from the report in Listing 23.2.

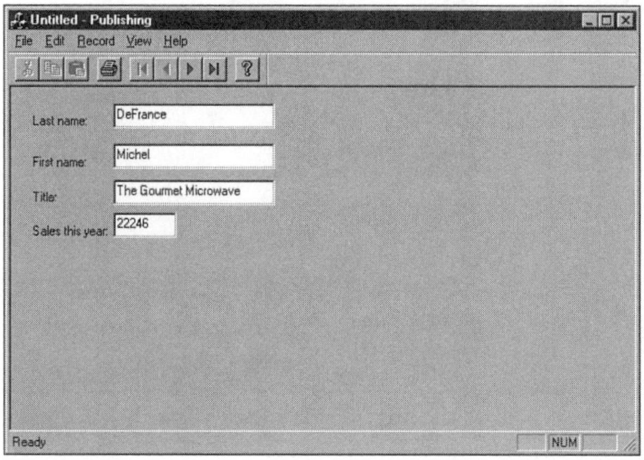

FIG. 23.20
Your application displays the results of the query in your stored procedure.

> **TIP** Make sure you have saved the SQL stored procedure before you build. Because the stored procedures are in a subproject of Publishing, building Publishing will not trigger any saves in the subproject.

This application doesn't do much at the moment: It just calls a stored procedure and presents the results neatly. With a little imagination, you can probably see how your SQL-based C++ programs can wrap stored procedures in user-friendly interfaces, and just how easy it is to develop and maintain those stored procedures using Developer Studio. You can even debug your SQL by using the Developer Studio debugger.

Working with Your Database

The DataView gives you full control over not just the contents of your SQL database, but its design. A raft of graphical tools makes it easy to see how the database works, or to change any aspect of it.

Database Designer

Return to the DataView, right-click the authors table, and choose Design. With the Database Designer, shown in Figure 23.21, you can change the key column, adjust the width, apply constraints on valid values and more.

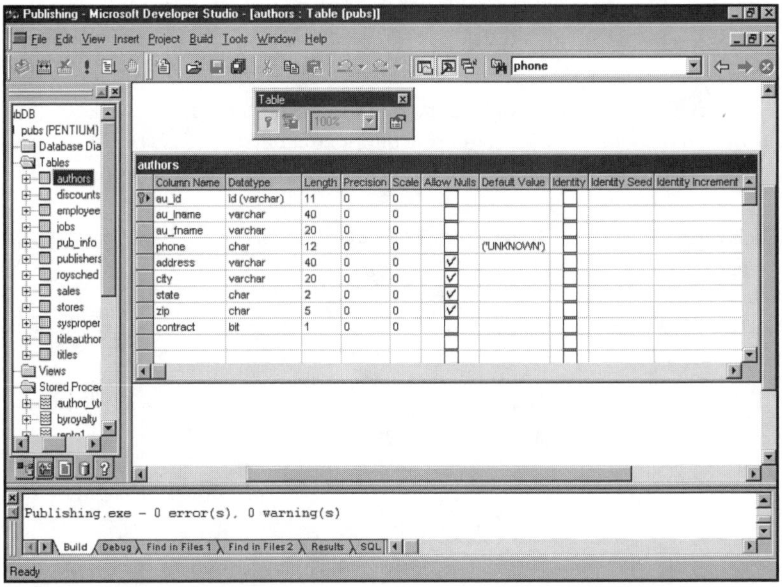

FIG. 23.21

The Database Designer lets you change any aspect of the design of your database.

For example, click the Properties button at the rightmost end of the Table toolbar while au_id is selected to bring up the property sheet shown in Figure 23.22. The constraint shown here means that au_id must be a nine-digit number. Clicking the Relationship tab, shown in Figure 23.23, shows that au_id is used to connect the authors table to the titleauthor table.

FIG. 23.22
It's simple to specify column constraints.

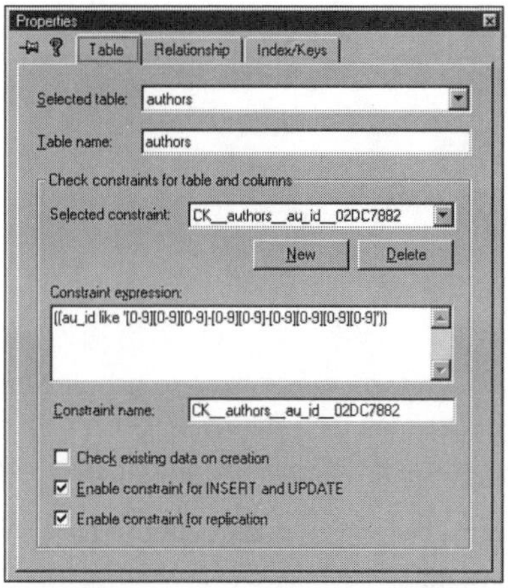

FIG. 23.23
The Relationships tab makes it simple to see how tables are related.

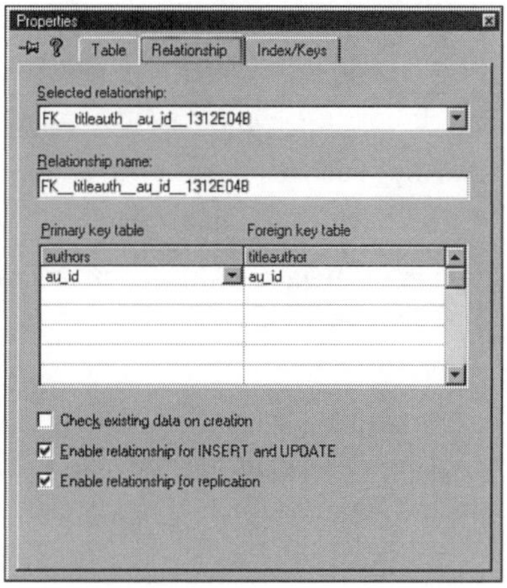

If you're a database developer, you probably can't wait to open your own database in the Database Designer and get to work. Be sure to take advantage of the many shortcut menus available for you. For example, Figure 23.24 shows the menu that pops up when you right-click anywhere in the authors grid. The first item, Column Properties, is drawn with a pushed-in button to show it's selected. Select Column Names and the grid becomes much smaller—bring back the shortcut menu and choose Column Properties to return to the large grid of properties. Select Keys to see just those columns that are keys, and Name Only to shrink the grid to a tiny column showing only the name of the table.

FIG. 23.24
Shortcut menus make
common tasks easy to
select.

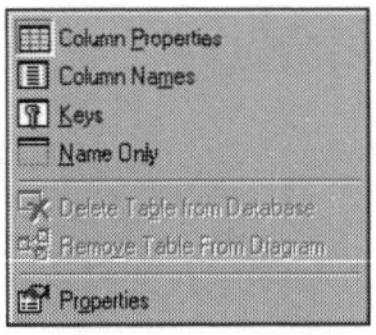

Database Diagrams

One of the easiest ways to get a lot of information across to people quickly is with a diagram. Figure 23.25 shows a diagram that explains the relationships between the three tables used throughout this chapter. To create the same diagram yourself, follow these steps:

1. Right-click Database Diagrams in DataView, and choose New Diagram.
2. Click authors and drag it into the working area.
3. Click titleauthor and drag it into the working area. Wait a moment for a link between authors and titleauthor to appear.
4. Click titles and drag it into the working area. Wait for the link to appear.
5. Rearrange the tables so that their keys are aligned as in Figure 23.25.
6. Drag the links up or down until they run from one key to another as they do in Figure 23.25.

If you wish, you can save this diagram in the database. Just click the Save button on the Standard toolbar and provide a name. The diagrams will be available to any other developers who use the Enterprise Edition to access this database.

To change any design decision about these tables, bring up the shortcut menu and choose Column Properties, then edit these properties just as you could in the Database Designer. How's that for an easy way to design and administer a SQL database?

FIG. 23.25

A picture is worth a thousand words when it's time to explain your database design.

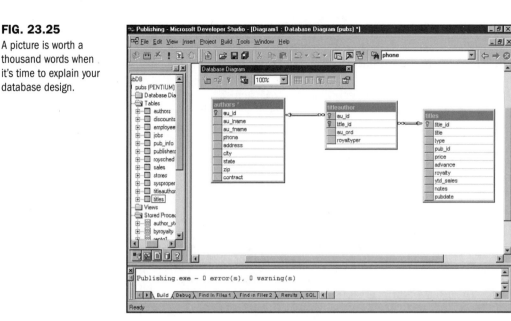

Understanding Microsoft Transaction Server

Microsoft Transaction Server is a completely separate product that comes with the Enterprise Edition of Visual C++ but is not integrated with it. MTS enables you to use a collection of COM objects called components to securely implement distributed transactions within enterprise-scale database applications. Applications that use MTS can be written in any language that can produce ActiveX applications, including Visual C++, Visual J++, and Visual Basic.

To work with MTS, you must be comfortable doing under-the-hood ActiveX and COM programming, working directly with interfaces. If you've always relied on MFC to hide interfaces from you, you should probably read Chapter 21, "The Active Template Library," to gain an introduction to the way interfaces are used. There's more information in the electronic copy of "ActiveX Programming with Visual C++," which is included in its entirety on the CD that comes with this book

You can use MTS with almost any kind of database, including ordinary file systems, just as you can use ODBC with almost any kind of database. Certainly, SQL databases will work with MTS, but so will a huge variety of other resource managers. This allows you access to the power of MTS without having to change your database system at all.

An MTS component is a COM object. It can do any specific task within your system, and often several components will be involved in a given *transaction*. Components are gathered together into packages installed as a unit onto your system.

Part

VII

Ch

23

A transaction is a unit of work that should succeed or fail as a whole. For example, if a customer is transferring money from one bank account to another, the money should be withdrawn from one account and deposited to the other. It does not make sense for one step in this process to fail and the other to proceed to completion. That would either take money away from customers unfairly, or give money to customers unfairly. Database programmers have long realized this, and developed ways of rolling back transactions that were partially completed when a step failed, or of pre-checking conditions to be sure that all the steps will succeed before starting. But these techniques are much more difficult to implement in a large, distributed system—too difficult to implement by hand.

For example, imagine two systems are about to take money (say, $100) from a customer's bank account. The first system checks the balance and there is enough money. Both systems are connected through a network to the system that keeps the balance for that account. The first system asks for the balance and gets the reply: $150. Moments later, the second asks and is also told $150. The first confidently sends the request for $100 and succeeds, the second asks just a fraction of a second later for $100 and fails. Any portions of a transaction involving this customer that were already completed by the second system will now have to be rolled back. A transactional system like MTS makes this process much simpler for developers by providing system services to support these tasks.

Sound good? Then install the product and get going in the online help. There are two good sample systems included: a simple banking application and a game. You can also check out Microsoft's Transaction Server Web site at **http://www.microsoft.com/transaction**.

Using Visual SourceSafe

If you work as part of a team of developers, a revision control system isn't just a nicety, it's a necessity. For too many teams the revision control system consists of sticking your head into the hall and telling your fellow programmers that you'll be working on fooble.h and fooble.cpp for a while, and to leave them alone. Or perhaps it is more about demanding to know who saved their changes to fooble.h over your changes because you both had the file open at once, and somebody saved after you did. There is a better way.

Revision control systems are not a new idea. They all implement these concepts:

- **Check out a file**—By bringing a copy of a file down to your desktop from a central library or repository, you mark the file as unavailable to others who might want to change it. (Some systems allow changes by several developers at once to source files and can merge them later.)
- **Check in a file**—When your changes are complete, you return the file to the library. You provide a brief description of what you've done, and the RCS adds your name, the date, and other files affected by this change automatically.
- **Merge changes**—Some RCS systems can accept check-ins by different developers on the same file, and will make sure that both sets of changes appear in the central file.

- ■ **Change tracking**—Some RCS systems can reconstruct earlier versions of a file by working backwards through a change log.

- ■ **History**—The information added at check-in can form a nice summary of what was done to each file, when and why.

Microsoft's Visual Source Safe is a good revision control system that many developers use to keep their code in order. What sets Visual SourceSafe apart from other RCS systems? It's project-oriented, it hooks into Visual C++ (through the new SCCI interface, some other RCS systems can also hook in,) and it comes with the Enterprise Edition of Visual C++.

When you install Visual SourceSafe, choose a custom installation and select Enable SourceSafe Integration. Doing this adds a cascading menu to Developer Studio's Project menu, shown in Figure 23.26.

FIG. 23.26

Installing Visual SourceSafe adds a cascading menu to the Project menu.

The items on the menu are as follows:

- ■ **Get Latest Version**—For selected files, replace your copies with newer copies from the library.

- ■ **Check Out**—Start to work on a file

- ■ **Check In**—Finish working on a file and make your changed versions available to everyone

- ■ **Undo Check Out**—Give back a file without making any changes or an entry in the history

- ■ **Add To Source Control**—Enable source control for this project

- ■ **Remove From Source Control**—Disable source control for this project

- ■ **Show History**—Display the changes made to selected files

- ■ **Show Differences**—Display the differences between old and new files

- ■ **SourceSafe Properties**—See information SourceSafe keeps about your files

- ■ **Share From SourceSafe**—Allow other developers to work on selected files

- ■ **Refresh Status**—Update your display with status changes made by other developers

- ■ **Source Safe**—Run Visual SourceSafe to see reports and summaries

You must have an account and password set up in Visual SourceSafe before you can put a project under source control and use these features. Run Visual SourceSafe from this menu to perform any administrative tasks that have not already been taken care of for you.

Unless you are the only developer who will work on your project, you simply must use a revision control system. Visual SourceSafe is good, it works from within Developer Studio, and if you have the Enterprise Edition of Visual C++, it's free. What more could you want? Install it, learn it, use it. You won't regret it.

TIP Revision control systems work as well on Web pages, database contents, documentation, bug lists, and spreadsheets as they do on code and program files. Once you get the habit and see the benefits, you just won't stop.

From Here...

This chapter has introduced you to the Enterprise Edition of Visual C++. You've seen how easy it is to integrate C++ and SQL programming, even if your SQL is weak. The sample application in this chapter calls a simple stored procedure, and you can use this technique to call stored procedures written by SQL developers and wrap them in a friendly interface. You've also briefly met the Microsoft Transaction Server and Visual SourceSafe, two stand-alone products that come with the Enterprise Edition.

For information on related topics, try these chapters:

- Chapter 2, "Dialog Boxes and Controls," introduces the steps involved in adding controls to a dialog box.
- Chapter 21, "The Active Template Library," pulls back the MFC covers to reveal the COM interfaces that power ActiveX.
- Chapter 22, "Database Access," covers the fundamentals of record sets, record views, and ODBC.
- Chapter 25, "Achieving Reuse with the Gallery and Your Own AppWizards," discusses some other ways that developers can share their work to produce amazing applications more quickly than ever before.

CHAPTER 24

Improving Your Application's Performance

When developing a new application, there are various hurdles developers need to overcome. You have to get your application to compile and run without blowing up, and you have to be sure that it does what you want it to do. On some projects, there is time to determine if your application can run faster or use less memory, or if you can have a smaller executable file. The performance improvement techniques discussed in this chapter can prevent your program from blowing up, and prevent the kind of "thinkos" that result in a program calculating or reporting the wrong numbers. These improvements are not just final tweaks and touch-ups on a finished product.

You should get in the habit of adding "an ounce of prevention" to your code as you write, and of using the debugging capabilities provided to you by Developer Studio to be sure of what's going on in your program. If you save all your testing to the end, both the testing and the bug-fixing will be much harder than if you had been testing all along. And, of course, any bug you manage to prevent will never have to be fixed at all! ■

Employing ASSERT and TRACE

Assertions prevent trouble, and trace statements show you what's going on. These macros belong in every program.

Memory leaks

When your application allocates memory but never frees it, you have a memory leak. See what causes them, how to find them, and how to eliminate them.

Optimization

You can produce faster or smaller code today, simply by asking the compiler to optimize for you. Learn what options are available and how to make your decision.

Profiling

Too many programmers sweat bullets trying to speed up code that is rarely called, while ignoring slow code that is causing a bottleneck. Profiling shows you where to spend your energy.

ASSERT and *TRACE*

The concepts of asserting and tracing were not invented by the developers of Visual C++. Other languages support these ideas, and they are taught in many computer science courses. What is exciting about the Visual C++ implementation of these concepts is the clear way your results are presented, and the ease with which you can suppress assertions and trace statements in release versions of your application.

ASSERT: Detecting Logic Errors

The ASSERT macro allows you to check a condition that you logically believe should always be true. For example, imagine you are about to access an array like this:

```
array[i] = 5;
```

You want to be sure that the index, i, is not less than zero and is not larger than the number of elements allocated for the array. Presumably you have already written code to calculate i, and if that code has been written properly, i must be between 0 and the array size. An ASSERT statement will verify that:

```
ASSERT( i > 0 && i < ARRAYSIZE)
```

N O T E   There is no semicolon (;) at the end of the line because ASSERT is a macro, not a function. Older C programs may call a function named assert(), but you should replace these calls with the ASSERT macro, because ASSERT disappears during a release build, as discussed later in this section. ■

ASSERT statements are ways for you to check your own logic. They should never be used to check for user input errors or bad data in a file. Whenever the condition inside an ASSERT statement is false, program execution halts with a message telling you which assertion failed. At this point, you know you have a logic error, or a developer error, that you need to correct. Here's another example:

```
// Calling code must pass a non-null pointer
void ProcessObject( Foo * fooObject )
{
       ASSERT( fooObject )
       // process object
}
```

This code can de-reference the pointer in confidence, knowing execution will be halted if the pointer is null.

You probably already know that Developer Studio makes it simple to build debug and release versions of your programs. The Debug version #defines a constant, _DEBUG, and macros and other pre-processor code can check this constant to determine the build type. When _DEBUG is not defined, the ASSERT macro does nothing. This means there is no speed constraint in the final code as there would be if you added if statements yourself to test for logic errors. There is no need for you to go through your code removing ASSERT statements when you release your application, and in fact it's better to leave them there to help the developers who work on version 2. In addition, ASSERT cannot help you if there is a problem with the release version of your code because it is used to find logic and design errors before you release version 1.0 of your product.

TRACE: Isolating Problems Areas in Your Program

As discussed in Reference Chapter C, "Debugging," the power of the Developer Studio debugger is considerable. You can step through your code one line at a time, or run to a breakpoint, and you can see the values of any of your variables in watch windows as you move through the code. This can be slow, however, and many developers use TRACE statements as a way of speeding up this process and zeroing in on the problem area. Then they turn to more traditional step-by-step debugging to isolate the bad code.

In the old days, isolating bad code meant adding lots of print statements to your program, which is problematic in a Windows application. So before you start to think up workarounds, like printing to a file, relax, because the TRACE macro does everything you want. And like ASSERT, it magically goes away in release builds.

There are actually several TRACE macros: TRACE, TRACE0, TRACE1, TRACE2, and TRACE3. The number-suffix indicates the number of parametric arguments beyond a simple string, working much like printf. The different versions of TRACE were implemented to save data segment space.

When you generate an application with AppWizard, many ASSERT and TRACE statements are added for you. Here's a TRACE example:

```
if (!m_wndToolBar.Create(this)
    || !m_wndToolBar.LoadToolBar(IDR_MAINFRAME))
{
    TRACE0("Failed to create toolbar\n");
    return -1;      // fail to create
}
```

If the creation of the toolbar fails, this routine will return -1, which signals to the calling program that something is wrong. This will happen in both debug and release builds. But in debug builds, a trace output will be sent that should help the programmer understand what went wrong.

All of the TRACE macros write to afxDump, which is usually the debug window, but can be set to stderr for console applications. The number-suffix indicates the parametric argument count, and you use the parametric values within the string to indicate the passed data type. For example, to send a TRACE statement that includes the value of an integer variable:

```
TRACE1("Error Number: %d\n", -1 );
```

Or, to pass two arguments, maybe a string and an integer:

```
TRACE2("File Error %s, error number: %d\n", __FILE__, -1 );
```

The most difficult part of tracing is making it a habit. Sprinkle TRACE statements anywhere you return error values: before ASSERT statements, and in areas where you are not quite sure you constructed your code correctly. When confronted with unexpected behavior, add TRACE statements first so that you understand more of what is going on before you start debugging.

Debug Only Features

If the idea of code that is not included in a release build appeals to you, you may want to arrange for some of your own code to be included in debug builds but not in release builds. It's easy. Just wrap the code in a test of the _DEBUG constant, like this:

```
#ifdef _DEBUG
    // debug code here
#endif
```

In release builds, this code will not be compiled at all.

You can also use different settings for debug and release builds. For example, many developers use different compiler warning levels. All of the settings and configurations of the compiler and linker are kept separately for debug and release builds, and can be changed independently. For example, to bump your Warning Level to 4 for debug builds only, follow these steps:

1. Choose Project, Settings, which opens the Project Settings dialog box, shown in Figure 24.1.

2. Choose Debug or Release from the drop-down list box at the upper left. If you choose All Configurations you will change debug and release settings simultaneously.

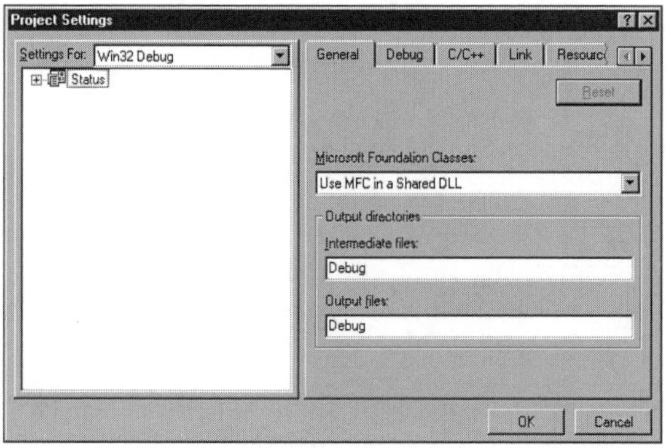

FIG. 24.1

The Project Settings dialog box enables you to set configuration items for different phases of development.

3. Click the C/C++ tab and set the Warning Level to Level 4, as shown in Figure 24.2. The default is Level 3, which we will use for the release version (see Figure 24.3).

FIG. 24.2
Warning levels can be
set higher during
development.

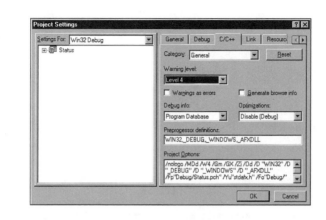

FIG. 24.3
Warning levels are
usually lower in a
production release.

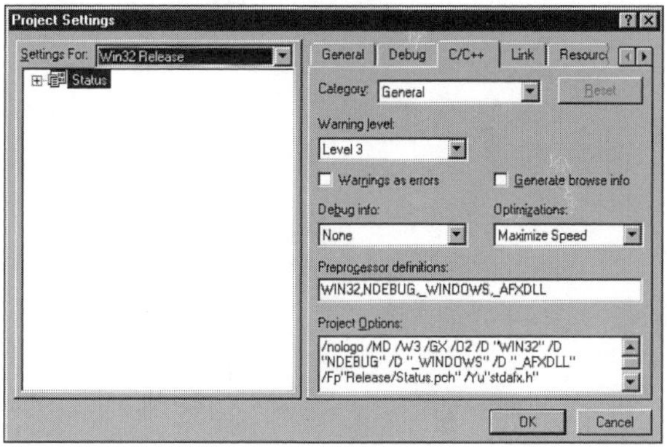

Sealing Memory Leaks

A memory leak can be the most pernicious of errors. Small leaks may not cause any execution
errors in your program until it is run for an exceptionally long time or with a larger-than-usual
data file. Because most programmers test with tiny data files, or run the program for only a few
minutes when they are experimenting with parts of it, memory leaks may not reveal themselves in everyday testing. Alas, memory leaks may well reveal themselves to your users when
the program crashes or otherwise misbehaves.

Common Causes of Memory Leaks

What does it mean when your program has a memory leak? It means that your program allocated memory and never released it. One very simple cause is calling new to allocate an object
or an array of objects on the heap, and never calling delete. Another cause of memory leaks is
changing the pointer kept in a variable without deleting the memory the pointer was pointing
to. More subtle memory leaks arise when a class with a pointer as a member variable calls new
to assign the pointer, but doesn't have a copy constructor, assignment operator, or destructor.
Listing 24.1 illustrates some ways that memory leaks are caused.

Listing 24.1 Causing Memory Leaks

```
// simple pointer leaving scope
{
  int * one = new int;
  *one = 1;
} // one is out of scope now, and wasn't deleted

// mismatched new and delete: new uses delete and new[] uses delete[]
{
float * f = new float[10];
// use array
delete f; // Oops! Deleted f[0] correct version is delete [] f;
}

// pointer of new memory goes out of scope before delete
{
    const char * DeleteP = "Don't forget P";
    char * p = new char[strlen(DeleteP) + 1];
    strcpy( p, DeleteP );
} // scope ended before delete[]

class A
{
   public:
      int * pi;
}

A::A()
{
    pi = new int();
    *pi = 3;
}

//  ..later on, some code using this class..

A firsta;    //allocates an int for first.pi to point to
B seconda;   //allocates another int for seconda.pi

seconda=firsta;

// will perform a bitwise copy. Both objects have
// a pi that points to the first int allocated. The
// pointer to the second int allocated is gone forever.
```

The code fragments all represent ways memory can be allocated and the pointer to that memory lost before deallocation. Once the pointer goes out of scope, you cannot reclaim the memory and no one else can use it either. Things get even worse when you consider exceptions, discussed in Chapter 26, "Exceptions, Templates, and the Latest Additions to C++," because if an exception is thrown, your flow of execution may leave a function before reaching the delete at the bottom of the code. Because destructors are called for objects that are going out of scope as the stack unwinds, you can prevent some of these problems by putting delete calls in destructors. This is also discussed in more detail in Chapter 26, in the "Placing the Catch Block" section.

Like all bugs, the secret to dealing with memory leaks is to prevent them, or to detect them as early as possible when they occur. You can develop some good habits to help you:

- If a class contains a pointer, and allocates that pointer with new, be sure to code a destructor that deletes the memory. Also code a copy constructor and an operator (=).

- If a function will allocate memory and return something to let the calling program access that memory, it must return a pointer rather than a reference. You cannot delete a reference.

- If a function will allocate memory and then delete it later in the same function, allocate the memory on the stack if at all possible, so that you do not forget to delete it.

- Never change the value of a pointer unless you have first deleted the object or array it was pointing to. Never increment a pointer that was returned by new.

Debug *new* and *delete*

MFC has a lot to offer the programmer who is looking for memory leaks. In debug builds, whenever you use new and delete you are actually using special debug versions, that track the file number and line on which each allocation occurred, and that match up deletes with their news. If memory is left over as the program ends, you get a warning message in the output section, as shown in Figure 24.4.

FIG. 24.4

Memory leaks are detected automatically in debug builds.

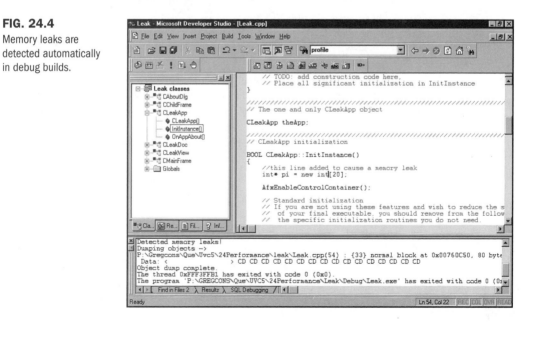

To see this for yourself, create an AppWizard MDI application called Leak, accepting all the defaults. In the `InitInstance()` function of the application class (`CLeakApp` in this example), add this line:

```
int* pi = new int[20];
```

Build a debug version of the application and run it by choosing <u>B</u>uild, Start <u>D</u>ebug, <u>G</u>o, or click the Go button on the Build mini-bar. You should see output like Figure 24.4. Notice that the file name (Leak.cpp) and line number where the memory was allocated are provided in the error message. The editor window displays Leak.cpp with the cursor on line 54. (The coordinates in the lower-right corner remind you what line number you are on at all times.) If you were writing a real application you would now know what the problem was. The next problem to tackle is where to fix it (more specifically, where to put `delete`).

Automatic Pointers

When a program is executing within a particular scope, like a function, all variables allocated in that function are allocated on the stack. The *stack* is a temporary storage space that shrinks and grows, like an accordion. The stack is used to store the current execution address prior to a function call, the arguments passed to the function, and the local function objects and variables.

When the function returns, the *stack pointer* is reset to that location where the prior execution point was stored. This makes the stack space after the reset location available to whatever else needs it, which means those elements allocated on the stack in the function are gone. This process is referred to as *stack unwinding*.

N O T E Objects or variables defined with the keyword `static` are not allocated on the stack. ■

Stack unwinding also happens when an exception occurs. To reliably restore the program to its state before an exception occurred in the function, the stack is unwound. Stack-wise variables are gone and the destructors for stack-wise objects are called and are also gone. Unfortunately, the same is *not* true for dynamic objects. The handles (for example, pointers) are unwound but `delete` is not called by the unwinding process. This causes a memory leak.

In some cases, the solution is to add `delete` statements to the destructors of objects you know will be destructed as part of the unwinding, so that they can use these pointers before they go out of scope. A more general approach is to replace simple pointers with a C++ class that can be used just like a pointer, but contains a destructor that deletes any memory at the location where it points. Don't worry; you don't have to write such a class: One is included in the Standard Template Library, which comes with Visual C++. Listing 24.2 is a heavily edited version of the `auto_ptr` class definition, presented to demonstrate the key concepts.

  T I P   If you haven't seen template code before, it's explained in Chapter 26, "Exceptions, Templates, and the Latest Additions to C++."

Listing 24.2 A Scaled-Down Version of the *auto_ptr* Class

```
// This class is not complete. Use the complete definition in
//the Standard Template Library.
 template <class T>
 class auto_ptr
 {
 public:
        auto_ptr( T *p = 0) : rep(p) {}
        // store pointer in the class
        ~auto_ptr(){ delete rep; }              // delete internal rep
        // include pointer conversion members
        inline T* operator->() const { return rep; }
        inline T& operator*() const { return *rep; }
  private:
        T * rep;
 };
```

The class has one member variable, a pointer to whatever type it is you want a pointer to. It has a one argument constructor to build an auto_ptr from an int* or a Truck* or any other pointer type. The destructor deletes the memory pointed to by the internal member variable. Finally, the class overrides -> and *, the dereferencing operators, so that dereferencing an auto_ptr feels just like dereferencing an ordinary pointer.

If there is some class C to which you want to make an automatic pointer called p, all you do is this:

```
auto_ptr<C> p(new C());
```

Now you can use p just as though it were a C*. For example:

```
p->Method();    // calls C::Method()
```

You never have to delete the C object that p points to, even in the event of an exception, because p was allocated on the stack. When it goes out of scope, its destructor is called and the destructor calls delete on the C object that was allocated in the new statement.

Part
VII

Ch
24

Optimization

There was a time when programmers were expected to optimize their code themselves. Many a night was spent arguing about the order in which to test conditions, or which variables should be register rather than automatic storage. These days, compilers come with optimizers that can speed execution or shrink program size far beyond what a typical programmer can accomplish by hand.

Here's a simple example of how optimizers work. Imagine you have written a piece of code like this:

```
for (i=0;i<10;i++)
{
    y=2;
    x[i]=5;
}
for (i=0; i<10; i++)
{
    total += x[i];
}
```

Your code will run faster, with no impact on the final results, if the y=2 is moved to before the first loop. In addition, the two loops can easily be combined into a single loop. If you do that, it's faster to add 5 to total each time than it is to calculate the address of x[i] in order to retrieve the value just stored into it. Really bright optimizers may even realize that total can be calculated outside the loop as well. The revised code may look like this:

```
y=2;
for (i=0;i<10;i++)
{
    x[i]=5;
}
    total += 50;
```

Optimizers do far more than this, of course, but this example gives you an idea of what's going on behind the scenes. It's up to you whether the optimizer focuses on speed, occasionally at the expense of memory usage, or tries to minimize memory usage, perhaps at a slighter lower speed.

To set the optimization options for your project, select the Project, Settings command from Developer Studio's menu bar. The Project Settings property sheet, first shown in Figure 24.1, appears. Click the C/C++ tab and make sure you are looking at the Release settings, then select Optimizations in the Category box. Optimization should be turned off for debug builds, since the code in your source files and the code being executed won't match line for line, which will confuse you and the debugger. You should turn on some kind of optimization for release builds. Choose from the drop-down list box, as shown in Figure 24.5.

If you select the Customize option in the Optimizations box, you can select from the list of individual optimizations, including Assume No Aliasing, Global Optimizations, Favor Fast Code, Generate Intrinsic Functions, Frame-Pointer Omission, and more. However, as you can tell from the names of these optimizations, you really have to know what you're doing before you set up a custom optimization scheme. For now, accept the schemes that have been laid out for you.

FIG. 24.5
Select the type of
optimization you want.

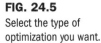

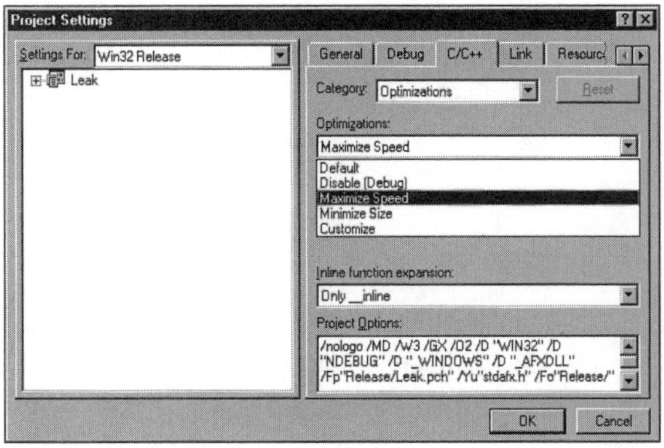

If aren't sure what any of the radio buttons on this dialog box mean, click the ? (question

Profiling

Profiling an application lets you discover bottlenecks, pieces of code that are slowing your application's execution and deserve special attention. It's pointless to hand-optimize a routine if you don't know that the routine is called often enough for its speed to matter.

Another use of a profiler is to see whether the test cases you have put together result in every one of your functions being called, or in each line of your code being executed. You may think you have selected test inputs that guarantee this; however, the profiler can confirm it for you.

Visual C++ includes a profiler integrated with the IDE: all you need to do is use it. First, adjust your project settings to include profiler information. Bring up the Project Settings property sheet as you did in the preceeding section and click the Link tab. Check the Enable Profiling check box. Click OK and rebuild your project. Links will be slower now, because you cannot do an incremental link when you are planning to profile, but you can go back to your old settings once you've learned a little about the way your program runs. Choose Build, Profile, and the Profile dialog box, shown in Figure 24.6, appears.

FIG. 24.6
A profiler can gather
many kinds of
information.

If you aren't sure what any of the radio buttons on this dialog box mean, click the ? (question mark) in the upper-right corner and then click the radio button. You will receive a short explanation of the option. (If you would like to add this kind of context-sensitive help to your own applications, be sure to read Chapter 11, "Help.")

Part
VII

Ch
24

You don't profile as a way to catch bugs, but it can help to validate your testing, or show you the parts of your application that need work, which makes it a vital part of the developer's toolbox. Get in the habit of profiling all of your applications at least once in the development cycle.

From Here...

MFC provides you with powerful tools to help ensure that your programs are bug-free and fast. ASSERT statements protect you against errors in logic. TRACE statements let you follow your application's progress without having to use the debugger. The debug new and delete make memory leaks easier to track. All of these features disappear in release builds, which means they cannot slow down or bloat the code your users get—though the impact of using these techniques in development can be a significantly positive one. Finally, the optimizer can speed or shrink your code, and the profiler can draw your attention to specific functions that need attention. Programmers who use the techniques presented in this chapter will produce faster, neater code with fewer bugs and no mysterious hangs from memory leaks.

To learn about other techniques and tools, see these chapters:

- Chapter 9, "Building a Complete Application: ShowString," provides the information you need to build menus, dialog boxes, and other user interface elements.
- Chapter 11, "Help," shows you how to add Help to your application.
- Chapter 26, "Exceptions, Templates, and the Latest Additions to C++," discusses exceptions and templates.

CHAPTER 25

Achieving Reuse with the Gallery and Your Own AppWizards

Reuse and why you want it

The fastest way to write working, tested code is to already have it.

How to add components to Component Gallery

Reusable components can be anything from a dialog box to an OLE control. Component Gallery organizes components so that you can add them to your projects with a couple of mouse clicks.

About creating custom AppWizards

Generate your own kinds of projects, customized for the way your team (even if it's a team of one) likes to work.

In these days of complex programs, reusability has become more than just a buzzword. It's become a survival technique for programmers who find themselves with the awesome task of creating hundreds of thousands of lines of working source code in a minimum amount of time. Visual C++ is packed with ways to let you reuse the work of programmers who have gone before you, like AppWizard, ClassWizard, and of course MFC, the Microsoft Foundation Classes. The tools discussed in this chapter let you be the one who contributes code to the future, ready to be reused quickly and easily by some future coworker—or better yet, by you. ■

Reviewing the Benefits of Writing Reusable Code

If you have a job to do, it's easy to see how reusing someone else's code, dialog boxes, or design will make your work simpler and get you finished faster. As long as you can trust the provider of material you will reuse, the more you can reuse, the better. That means there's a market for reusable bits and pieces of programs.

In fact there are two markets: one formal one, with vendors selling project parts such as controls or templates; and another informal one within many large companies, with departments developing reusable parts for "brownie points" or bragging rights, or other intangibles. Some companies even have a "reuse budget" to which you can charge the time you spend making parts of your project reusable, or award "reuse credits" if someone else in the company reuses one of your parts. If yours doesn't, maybe it should: reuse can save as much as 60 percent of your software budget, but only if someone is noble or charitable enough to develop with reuse in mind, or if company policy inspires everyone to develop with reuse in mind.

Most newcomers to reuse think only of reusing code, but there are other parts of a project that can save you far more time than you can save with code reuse only. These include the following:

- **Design**. The Document/View paradigm, first discussed in Chapter 5, "Documents and Views," is a classic example of a design decision that is reused in project after project.

- **Interface Resources**. You can reuse controls, icons, menus, toolbars, or entire dialog boxes and reduce training time for your users as well as development time for your programmers.

- **Project Settings**. Whether it's an obscure linker setting or the perfect arrangement of toolbars, your working environment must be right for you, and getting it right is faster on every project you do, because you reuse the decisions you made last time.

- **Documentation**. As you read in Chapter 11, "Help," help text for standard commands like File, Open is generated for you by AppWizard. You can reuse your own help text from project to project and save even more time.

Using Component Gallery

Component Gallery is one way that Developer Studio helps support reuse. Component Gallery gives you instant access to everything from reusable classes and OLE controls to wizards. You can even create your own components and add them to Component Gallery. In fact, in its default installation, Developer Studio automatically adds a category to Component Gallery for new AppWizard applications that you create.

Adding a Component to the Gallery

Suppose you have a dialog box that you use frequently in projects. You can create this dialog box just once, add it to Component Gallery, and then merge it into new projects whenever you need it. To see how this might work, follow these steps:

1. Start a new AppWizard project workspace called App1. (Just click Finish on Step 1 to use all the default AppWizard settings, then click OK to create the project.)

2. Add a new dialog box to the project by choosing Insert, Resource and double-clicking Dialog.

3. Using the techniques first presented in Chapter 2, "Dialog Boxes and Controls," build the dialog-box resource shown in Figure 25.1, giving the dialog box the resource ID `IDD_NAMEDLG`.

FIG. 25.1

Build a dialog box to add to Component Gallery.

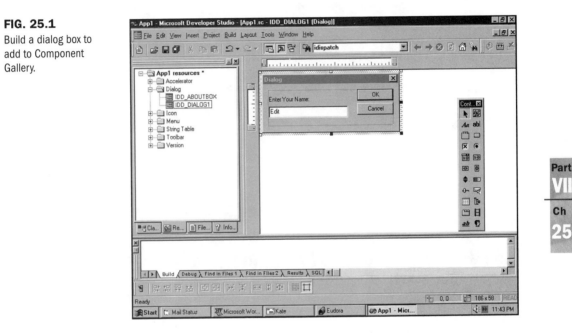

4. While the dialog box has focus, bring up ClassWizard and agree to create a new class. Call the new class `CNameDlg`.

5. Close ClassWizard.

6. Right-click `CNameDlg` in ClassView and choose Add To Gallery from the shortcut menu.

Although it appears that nothing has happened, the class `CNameDlg` and the associated resource have been added to the Gallery. Minimize Developer Studio and browse your hard drive, starting at My Computer, until you are displaying C:\Program Files\DevStudio\SharedIDE\Gallery (if you installed Visual C++ into another directory, look in that directory for the SharedIDE folder and continue down from there). As you can see in Figure 25.2, there is now an App1 folder in the Gallery.

FIG. 25.2

The Gallery uses your project name as the folder name when you add a class.

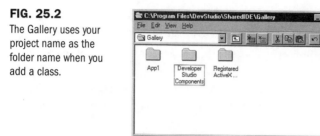

Double-click the App1 folder and you'll see it contains one file, Name Dlg.ogx, as shown in Figure 25.3. The .ogx extension signifies a Gallery component.

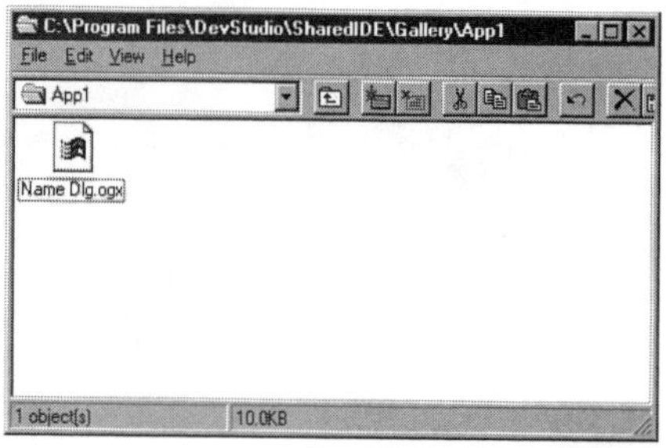

FIG. 25.3

The file name for your Gallery component is based on the class name.

Using Gallery Components in Your Projects

Now that you've added the resource and associated class to the Gallery, a logical next step is to make another project that will use them. Create another application with AppWizard called App2 and again click Finish on Step 1 to accept all the defaults, then OK to create the project.

Click the ClassView tab and expand the App2 classes. There are six: CAboutDlg, CApp2App, CApp2Doc, CApp2View, CChildFrame, and CMainFrame.

Choose Project, Add To Project, Components and Controls. The Components and Controls Gallery dialog box, shown in Figure 25.4, appears.

Double click App1 and you will see Name Dlg.ogx again. Double-click it. When prompted, confirm that you want to insert this component into your project. Click Close to close the Gallery.

Look at ClassView again. CNameDlg has been added. Check in FileView and you'll see that NameDlg.cpp and NameDlg.h have been added to the project. Switch to ResourceView to confirm that the dialog IDD_NAMEDLG has been added. You can use this resource in App2 in just the way you used it in App1.

FIG. 25.4

Gallery components are arranged in folders.

Exploring the Gallery

You can use Component Gallery to manage many other types of components, including those that you might get from a friend or buy from a third-party supplier. Component Gallery can add, delete, import, and edit components in a variety of ways, depending upon the type of component with which you're working. Take some time to experiment with Component Gallery, and you'll quickly see how easy it is to use.

Figure 25.5 shows the contents of the Registered ActiveX Controls folder. Both the ATL and MFC versions of the Dieroll control are here: DieRoll Class was built in Chapter 21, "The Active Template Library," and Dieroll Control was built in Chapter 17, "Building an ActiveX Control." Before this shot was taken, Grid Control was highlighted and the More Info button was clicked. Components can be bundled with a help file that is reached from the More Info button.

FIG. 25.5

All ActiveX controls are available through the Gallery.

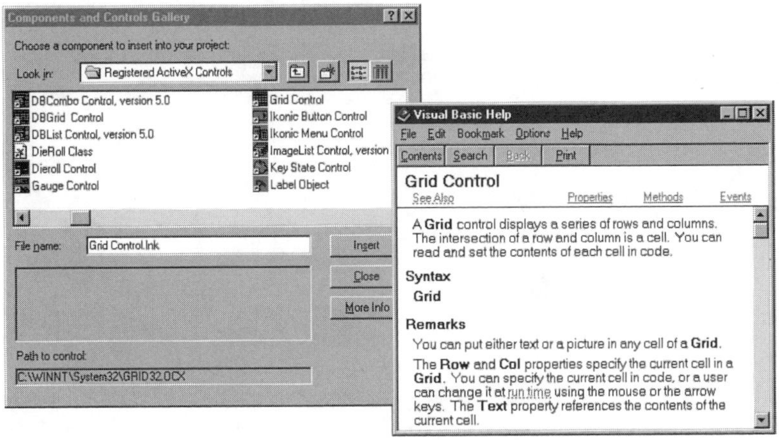

Part
VII

Ch
25

Introducing Custom AppWizards

AppWizard is a sensational tool for getting projects started quickly and easily. However, because of its general nature, AppWizard makes many assumptions about the way you want a new project created. Sometimes, you may need a special type of AppWizard project that isn't supported by the default AppWizard. If this special project is a one-time deal, you'd probably just go ahead and create the project by hand. However, if you need to use this custom project type again and again, you might want to consider creating a custom AppWizard.

You can create a custom AppWizard in three ways: using the existing AppWizard steps as a starting point, using an existing project as a starting point, or starting completely from scratch. However, no matter what method you choose, creating a custom AppWizard can be a complicated task, requiring that you understand and be able to write script files by using the macros and commands provided by Visual C++ for this purpose.

The following tackles the very simplest case first, creating an AppWizard that can reproduce an existing project with a different name. Follow these steps:

1. Create a project in the usual way. Call it Original and click Finish on Step 1 to accept all the AppWizard defaults.

2. Edit the About Original dialog box to resemble Figure 25.6.

FIG. 25.6

Customize your About box.

3. Choose File, New, and click the Projects tab. Select Custom AppWizard and enter OrigWiz, as shown in Figure 25.7. Click OK.

FIG. 25.7

Create a Custom AppWizard.

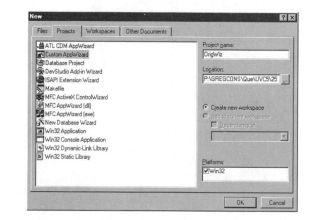

4. The first of two custom AppWizard dialogs appears, as shown in Figure 25.8. Select An existing project to base your wizard on the project you created in steps 1 and 2. Do not edit the name of the wizard. Click Next.

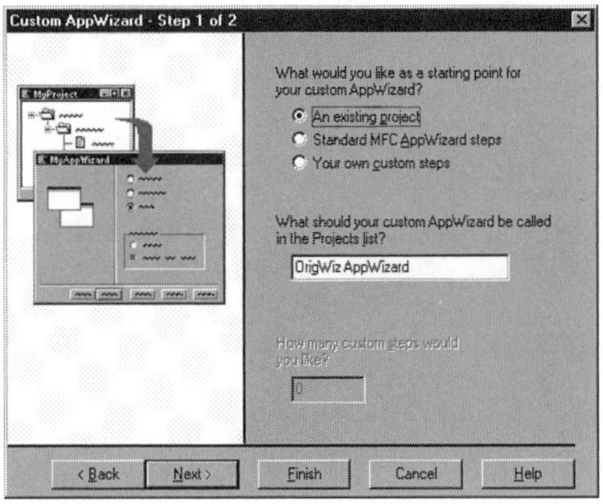

FIG. 25.8
Base your wizard on an existing project.

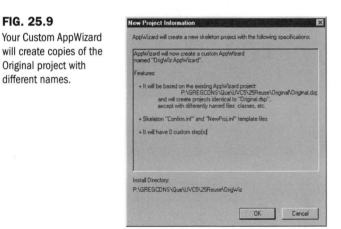

5. The second custom AppWizard dialog box appears. Browse to the project file for the Original project. Click Finish.

6. The New Project Information dialog box, shown in Figure 25.9, confirms your choices. Click OK.

FIG. 25.9
Your Custom AppWizard will create copies of the Original project with different names.

Part
VII
Ch
25

You are now working on the OrigWiz project, and in many cases you would add code at this point. Since this is a sample, just build the project immediately.

To use your custom AppWizard, choose File, New again and click the Projects tab. As shown in Figure 25.10, OrigWizard has been added to the list of choices on the left. Select it and enter App3 for the name of the project. Click OK.

FIG. 25.10

Your Custom AppWizard has been added to the list of AppWizards.

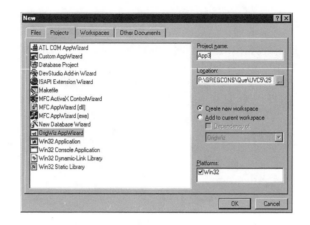

N O T E When you compile the custom AppWizard, Developer Studio creates the final files and stores them in your C:\Program Files\DevStudio\SharedIDE\Template directory. The next time you choose to start a new project workspace, your custom AppWizard will be listed in the project types. To remove the custom AppWizard, delete the wizard's .awx and .pdb files from your C:\Program Files\DevStudio\SharedIDE\Template directory.

Figure 25.11 shows one of the tasks that you normally complete before you build the AppWizard: generating the text for the New Project Information dialog box. Click OK.

FIG. 25.11

You have to write the text for the New Project Information dialog.

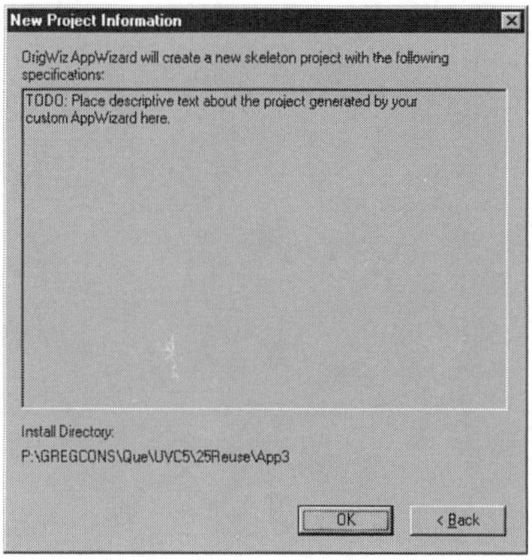

Look at the class names and the code—App3 looks like any of the projects created in this chapter that accept all the AppWizard defaults, but you didn't have to go through any dialog steps. Switch to ResourceView and edit IDD_ABOUTBOX. As Figure 25.12 shows, it contains the extra text (Based on Original 1.0) you added, but the application name on the top line of the box has been correctly changed to App3. This is one smart wizard.

FIG. 25.12
Your custom About box was copied to the new project by your AppWizard.

When you build a wizard from an existing project, all the classes, resources, and code that you added will be incorporated in the new projects you generate with the wizard. It's a great timesaver.

You can also build custom AppWizards that present dialogs for you to fill out. Before you do that, you should be comfortable writing wizards that are not AppWizards, like the ones discussed in Chapter 12, "Property Pages and Sheets and Wizards." You should also have generated lots of different types of applications so that you have a feel for the sort of work AppWizard does. When you're ready, check the section in the online help titled "Creating Custom AppWizards."

From Here...

This whole book has shown you the value of using other people's designs, classes, code, controls, dialog boxes, and other project parts. This chapter has shown two simple ways that you can arrange for other people (or your future self) to reuse your code. This can bring real benefits to your customers or employer by saving significant development time. And it can make your job more fun, by taking care of the repetitive tasks like building a dialog and associating it with a class, freeing you to do the fun stuff.

For more information on related topics, please refer to the following chapters:

- Chapter 1, "Building Your First Application," introduces AppWizard.
- Chapter 12, "Property Pages and Sheets and Wizards," teaches you how to build wizard dialog boxes with Next and Back buttons.
- Chapter 17, "Building an ActiveX Control," describes one type of component you can add to Component Gallery.

Part
VII

Ch
25

Exceptions, Templates, and the Latest Additions to C++

C++ is an evolving language, and frequently undergoes review and improvement. New power features that have been added to C++ in the recent past are exceptions, templates, Run-Time Type Information (RTTI), namespace support, and some new keywords and data types. While most programmers delay learning these concepts until they have six months to a year of Visual C++ programming experience, you should consider learning it now. These concepts are not much more difficult than the ones covered earlier in this book, and can add real power to your programs. ■

How to catch, throw, and define exception objects

Exceptions are a better way of handling runtime errors in your programs than using old-fashioned error-handling techniques.

About function templates

Function templates enable you to create a general blueprint for a function. The compiler can then create different versions of the function for you.

How to create and use class templates

Class templates are similar to function templates, except that they act as a blueprint for classes rather than for functions.

About Run-Time Type Infor-mation

Run-Time Type Information (RTTI) adds to C++ the ability to safely downcast polymorphic-object pointers, as well as to get information about objects at runtime.

How to define and use namespaces

Identifier scope can be a hassle when you have to include several external libraries in your project. Namespaces help you avoid identifier-name conflict.

Understanding Exceptions

When you write applications by using Visual C++, sooner or later you're going to run into error-handling situations that don't seem to have a solution. Perhaps you are writing a function that returns a numeric value, and need a way to send back an error response. Sometimes you can come up with one special return value, perhaps 0 or -1, that indicates a problem. Other times, there doesn't seem to be a way to signal trouble. Or perhaps you use special return values, but find yourself writing code that starts out like this:

```
while (somefunction(x))
{
    for (int i=0; i<limit; i++)
    {
        y = someotherfunction(i);
    }
}
```

Now you realize that if `someotherfunction()` returns -1, you should not move on to the next i, and you should leave the `while` loop. Your code becomes the following:

```
int timetostop = 0;
while (somefunction(x) && !timetostop)
{
    for (int i=0; i<limit && !timetostop; i++)
    {
        if ( (y = someotherfunction(i)) == -1)
            timetostop = 1;
    }
}
```

This isn't bad, though it's getting hard to read. If there are two or three things that could go wrong, your code gets unmanageably complex.

Exceptions are designed to handle just these sorts of problems. The exception mechanism allows programs to signal each other about serious and unexpected problems. There are three places in your code that participate in most exceptions:

- The *try block* marks the code you believe might run into difficulty.
- The *catch block*, immediately following the try block, holds the code that deals with the problem.
- The *throw statement* is how the code with a problem notifies the calling code.

Simple Exception Handling

The mechanism used by exception-handling code is really pretty simple. You place the source code that you want guarded against errors inside a try block. You then construct a catch program block that acts as the error handler. If the code in the try block (or any code called from the try block) throws an exception, the try block immediately ceases execution and the program continues inside the catch block.

For example, memory allocation is one place in a program where you might expect to run into trouble. Listing 26.1 shows a nonsensical little program that allocates some memory and then immediately deletes it. Because memory allocation could fail, the code that allocates the memory is enclosed in a try program block. If the pointer returned from the memory allocation is NULL, the try block throws an exception. In this case, the exception object is a string.

N O T E The sample applications in this chapter are console applications, which can run from a DOS prompt and don't have a graphical interface. This keeps them small enough to be shown in their entirety in the listings. To try them yourself, create a console application as discussed in Chapter 28, "Future Explorations," add a file to the project, and add the code shown here. ▪

Listing 26.1 EXCEPTION1.CPP—Simple Exception Handling

```cpp
#include <iostream.h>

int main()
{
    int* buffer;

    try
    {
        buffer = new int[256];

        if (buffer == NULL)
            throw "Memory allocation failed!";
        else
            delete buffer;
    }
    catch(char* exception)
    {
        cout << exception << endl;
    }

    return 0;
}
```

Part
VII

Ch
26

When the program throws the exception, program execution jumps to the first line of the catch program block. (The remainder of the code inside the try block is not executed.) In the case of Listing 26.1, this line just prints out a message, after which the function's return line is executed and the program ends.

If the memory allocation is successful, the program executes the entire try block, deleting the buffer. Then program execution skips over the catch block completely, in this case, going directly to the return statement.

N O T E The catch program block does more than direct program execution. It actually catches the exception object thrown by the program. For example, in Listing 26.1, you can see the exception object being caught inside the parentheses following the catch keyword. This is very similar to a parameter being received by a method. In this case, the type of the "parameter" is char* and the name of the parameter is exception. ■

Exception Objects

The beauty of C++ exceptions is that the exception object thrown can be just about any kind of data structure you like. For example, you might want to create an exception class for certain kinds of exceptions that occur in your programs. Listing 26.2 shows a program that defines a general-purpose exception class called MyException. In the case of a memory-allocation failure, the main program creates an object of the class and throws it. The catch block catches the MyException object, calls the object's GetError() member function to get the object's error string, and then displays the string on the screen.

Listing 26.2   EXCEPTION2.CPP—Creating an Exception Class

```
#include <iostream.h>

class MyException
{
protected:
    char* m_msg;

public:
    MyException(char *msg) { m_msg = msg; }

    ~MyException(){}

    char* GetError() {return m_msg; };
};

int main()
{
    int* buffer;

    try
    {
        buffer = new int[256];

        if (buffer == NULL)
        {
            MyException* exception =
                new MyException("Memory allocation failed!");
            throw exception;
        }
        else
            delete buffer;
    }
    catch(MyException* exception)
    {
        char* msg = exception->GetError();
        cout << msg << endl;
```

```
    }

    return 0;
}
```

An exception object can be as simple as an integer error code or as complex as a fully developed class. MFC provides a number of exception classes, including CException and several classes derived from it. The abstract class CException has a constructor and three member functions: Delete(), which deletes the exceptions, GetErrorMessage(), which returns a string describing the exception, and ReportError(), which reports the error in a message box.

Placing the *catch* Block

The catch program block doesn't have to be in the same function as the one in which the exception is thrown. When an exception is thrown, the system starts "unwinding the stack," looking for the nearest catch block. If the catch block is not found in the function that threw the exception, the system looks in the function that's called the throwing function. This search continues on up the function-call stack. If the exception is never caught, the program halts.

Listing 26.3 is a short program that demonstrates this concept. The program throws the exception from the AllocateBuffer() function but catches the exception in main(), which is the function from which AllocateBuffer() is called.

Listing 26.3   EXCEPTION3.CPP—Catching Exceptions Outside of the Throwing Function

```
#include <iostream.h>

class MyException
{
protected:
    char* m_msg;

public:
    MyException(char *msg) { m_msg = msg;}
    ~MyException(){}
    char* GetError() {return m_msg;}
};

class BigObect
{
private:
    int* intarray;
public:
    BigObject() {intarray = new int[1000];}
    ~BigObject() {delete intarray;}
}

int* AllocateBuffer();
```

continues

Part

VII

Ch

26

Listing 26.3 Continued

```
int main()
{
    int* buffer;

    try
    {
        buffer = AllocateBuffer();
        delete buffer;
    }
    catch (MyException* exception)
    {
        char* msg = exception->GetError();
        cout << msg << endl;
    }

    return 0;
}

int* AllocateBuffer()
{
    BigObject huge;
    float* floatarray = new float[1000];
    int* buffer = new int[256];

    if (buffer == NULL)
    {
        MyException* exception =
            new MyException("Memory allocation failed!");
        throw exception;
    }

    delete floatarray;
    return buffer;
}
```

When the exception is thrown in `AllocateBuffer()`, the remainder of the function is not executed. The dynamically allocated `floatarray` will not be deleted. The BigObject that was allocated on the stack will go out of scope and its destructor will be executed, deleting the `intarray` member variable that was allocated with `new` in the constructor. This is an important concept to grasp: objects created on the stack will be destructed as the stack unwinds. Objects created on the heap will not. Your code must take care of these. For example, `AllocateBuffer()` should include code to delete `floatarray` before throwing the exception, like this:

```
if (buffer == NULL)
    {
        MyException* exception =
            new MyException("Memory allocation failed!");
        delete floatarray;
        throw exception;
    }
```

In many cases, using an object with a carefully written destructor can save you significant code duplication when you are using exceptions. If you are using objects allocated on the heap, you may need to catch and rethrow exceptions just so that you can delete them. Consider the code in Listing 26.4, in which the exception is thrown right past an intermediate function up to the catching function.

Listing 26.4 EXCEPTION4.CPP—Unwinding the Stack

```
#include <iostream.h>

class MyException
{
protected:
    char* m_msg;

public:
    MyException(char *msg) { m_msg = msg;}
    ~MyException(){}
    char* GetError() {return m_msg;}
};

class BigObject
{
private:
    int* intarray;
public:
    BigObject() {intarray = new int[1000];}
    ~BigObject() {delete intarray;}
};

int* AllocateBuffer();
int* Intermediate();

int main()
{
    int* buffer;

    try
    {
        buffer = Intermediate();
        delete buffer;
    }
    catch (MyException* exception)
    {
        char* msg = exception->GetError();
        cout << msg << endl;
    }

    return 0;
}

int* Intermediate()
{
```

continues

Listing 26.4   Continued

```
    BigObject bigarray;
    float* floatarray = new float[1000];
    int* retval = AllocateBuffer();
    delete floatarray;
    return retval;
}

int* AllocateBuffer()
{
    int* buffer = new int[256];

    if (buffer == NULL)
    {
        MyException* exception =
            new MyException("Memory allocation failed!");
        throw exception;
    }

    return buffer;
}
```

Now if the exception is thrown, execution of AllocateBuffer() is abandoned immediately. The stack unwinds. Since there is no catch block in Intermediate(), execution of that function will be abandoned after the call to AllocateBuffer(). The delete for floatarray will not happen, but the destructor for bigarray will be executed. Listing 26.5 shows a way around this problem.

Listing 26.5   Rethrowing Exceptions

```
int* Intermediate()
{
    BigObject bigarray;
    float* floatarray = new float[1000];
    int* retval = NULL;
    try
    {
        retval = AllocateBuffer();
    }
    catch (MyException e)
    {
        delete floatarray;
        throw;
    }
    delete floatarray;
    return retval;
}
```

This revised version of Intermediate() catches the exception just so that it can delete floatarray, and then throws it further up to the calling function. (Notice that the name of the exception is not in this throw statement: it can throw only the exception it just caught.) There are a few things you should notice about this revised code:

- The line that deletes `floatarray` has been duplicated.
- The declaration of `retval` has had to move out of the `try` block so that it will still be in scope after the `try` block.
- `retval` has been initialized to a default value.

This is really starting to get ugly. Through all of this, the `BigObject` called `bigarray` has been quietly handled properly and easily, with an automatic call to the destructor no matter which function allocated it or where the exception was called. When you write code that uses exceptions, wrapping all your heap-allocated objects in classes like `BigObject` makes your life easier. `BigObject` implements a *managed pointer*: when a `BigObject` object like `bigarray` goes out of scope, the memory it pointed to is deleted. A very flexible approach to managed pointers is described at the end of the Template section in this chapter.

Handling Multiple Types of Exceptions

Because it's often the case that a block of code generates more than one type of exception, you can use multiple `catch` blocks with a `try` block. You might, for example, need to be on the lookout for both `CException` and `char*` exceptions. Because a `catch` block must receive a specific type of exception object, you need two different `catch` blocks to watch for both `CException` and `char*` exception objects. You can also set up a `catch` block to catch whatever type of exception hasn't been caught yet, by placing ellipses (...) in the parentheses, rather than a specific argument. The problem with this sort of multipurpose `catch` block is that you have no access to the exception object received and so must handle the exception in some general way.

Listing 26.6 is a program that generates three different types of exceptions based on a user's input. (In a real program, you shouldn't use exceptions to deal with user errors. It's a slow mechanism, and checking what the user typed can usually be handled more efficiently another way.)

When you run the program, you're instructed to enter a value between 4 and 8, except for 6. If you enter a value less than 4, the program throws a `MyException` exception; if you enter a value greater than 8, the program throws a `char*` exception; and, finally, if you happen to enter 6, the program throws the entered value as an exception.

Although the program throws the exceptions in the `GetValue()` function, the program catches them all in `main()`. The `try` block in `main()` is associated with three `catch` blocks. The first catches the `MyException` object, the second catches the `char*` object, and the third catches any other exception that happens to come down the pike.

N O T E Just as with `if-else` statements, the order in which you place `catch` program blocks can have a profound effect on program execution. You should always place the most specific `catch` blocks first. For example, in Listing 26.6, if the `catch(...)` block was first, none of the other `catch` blocks would ever be called. This is because the `catch(...)` is as general as you can get, catching every single exception that the program throws. In this case (as in most cases), you want to use `catch(...)` to receive only the leftover exceptions. ■

Listing 26.6   EXCEPTION6.CPP—Using Multiple *catch* Blocks

```cpp
#include <iostream.h>

class MyException
{
protected:
    char* m_msg;

public:
    MyException(char *msg) { m_msg = msg;}
    ~MyException(){}
    char* GetError() {return m_msg;}
};

int GetValue();


int main()
{
    try
    {
        int value = GetValue();
        cout << "The value you entered is okay." << endl;
    }
    catch(MyException* exception)
    {
        char* msg = exception->GetError();
        cout << msg << endl;
    }
    catch(char* msg)
    {
        cout << msg << endl;
    }
    catch(...)
    {
        cout << "Caught unknown exception!" << endl;
    }

    return 0;
}

int GetValue(){
    int value;

    cout << "Type a number from 4 to 8 (except 6):" << endl;
    cin >> value;

    if (value < 4)
    {
        MyException* exception =
            new MyException("Value less than 4!");
        throw exception;
    }
    else if (value > 8)
```

```
    {
        throw "Value greater than 8!";
    }
    else if (value == 6)
    {
        throw value;
    }
    return value;
}
```

The Old Exception Mechanism

Before `try`, `catch`, and `throw` were added to Visual C++, there was a rudimentary form of exception handling available to both C and C++ programmers through macros called TRY, CATCH, and THROW. These macros are a little slower than the standard exception mechanisms, and can only throw exceptions that are objects of a class derived from `CException`. Don't use these in your programs. If you have an existing program that uses them, you may want to convert to the new mechanism. There's a helpful article on this topic in the Visual C++ documentation: search for TRY and you'll find it.

Exploring Templates

It's a good guess that, at one time or another, you wished you could develop a single function or class that could handle any kind of data. Sure, you can use function overloading to write several versions of a function, or you can use inheritance to derive several different classes from a base class. But, in these cases, you still end up writing many different functions or classes. If only there was a way to make functions and classes a little smarter, so that you could write just one that handled any kind of data you wanted to throw at it. There is a way to accomplish this seemingly impossible task. You need to use something called *templates,* which are the focus of this section.

Part
VII

Ch
26

Introducing Templates

A *template* is a kind of blueprint for a function or class. You write the template in a general way, supplying placeholders, called *parameters*, for the data objects that the final function or class will manipulate. A template always begins with the keyword `template` followed by a list of parameters between angle brackets, like this:

```
template<class Type>
```

You can have as many parameters as you need, and you can name them whatever you like, but each must begin with the `class` keyword and must be separated by commas, like this:

```
template<class Type1, class Type2, class Type3>
```

As you may have guessed from the previous discussion, there are two types of templates: function and class. The following sections describe how to create and use both types of templates.

Creating Function Templates

A function template starts with the `template` line you just learned about, followed by the function's declaration, as shown in Listing 26.7. The `template` line specifies the types of arguments that will be used when calling the function, whereas the function's declaration specifies how those arguments are to be received as parameters by the function. Every parameter specified in the `template` line must be used by the function declaration. Notice the `Type1` immediately before the function name. `Type1` is a placeholder for the function's return type, which will vary depending upon how the template is used.

Listing 26.7   The Basic Form of a Function Template

```
template<class Type1, class Type2>
Type1 MyFunction(Type1 data1, Type1 data2, Type2 data3)
{
    // Place the body of the function here.
}
```

An actual working example will help you understand how function templates become functions. A common example is a `Min()` function that can accept any type of arguments. Listing 26.6 is a short program that defines a template for a `Min()` function and then uses that function in `main()`. When you run the program, the program displays the smallest value of whatever data is sent as arguments to `Min()`. This works because the compiler takes the template and creates functions for each of the data types that are compared in the program.

Listing 26.8   TEMPLATE1.CPP—Using a Typical Function Template

```
#include <iostream.h>

template<class Type>
Type Min(Type arg1, Type arg2)
{
    Type min;

    if (arg1 < arg2)
        min = arg1;
    else
        min = arg2;

    return min;
}

int main()
{
    cout << Min(15, 25) << endl;
    cout << Min(254.78, 12.983) << endl;
    cout << Min('A', 'Z') << endl;

    return 0;
}
```

NOTE Notice how, in Listing 26.8, the `Min()` template uses the data type `Type` not only in its parameter list and function argument list, but also in the body of the function, in order to declare a local variable. This illustrates how you can use the parameter types just as you would use any specific data type such as `int` or `char`. ▪

Because function templates are so flexible, they can often lead to trouble. For example, in the `Min()` template, you have to be sure that the data types you supply as parameters can be compared. If you tried to compare two classes, your program would not compile unless the classes overloaded the < and > operators.

Another way you can run into trouble is when the arguments you supply to the template are not used as you think. For example, what if you added the following line to `main()` in Listing 26.6?

```
cout << Min("APPLE", "ORANGE") << endl;
```

If you don't think about what you're doing in the previous line, you may jump to the conclusion that the returned result will be APPLE. The truth is, however, that the preceding line may or may not give you the result you expect. Why? Because the `"APPLE"` and `"ORANGE"` string constants result in pointers to `char`. This means that the program will compile fine, with the compiler creating a version of `Min()` that compares `char` pointers. But there's a big difference between comparing two pointers and comparing the data to which the pointers point. If `"ORANGE"` happens to be stored at a lower address than `"APPLE"`, the preceding call to `Min()` results in `"ORANGE"`.

A way to avoid this problem is to provide a specific replacement function for `Min()` that defines exactly how you want the two string constants compared. When you provide a specific function, the compiler uses that function instead of creating one from the template. Listing 26.9 is a short program that demonstrates this important technique. When the program needs to compare the two strings, it doesn't call a function created from the template but instead uses the specific replacement function.

Part
VII
Ch
26

Listing 26.9 TEMPLATE2.CPP—Using a Specific Replacement Function

```cpp
#include <iostream.h>
#include <string.h>

template<class Type>
Type Min(Type arg1, Type arg2)
{
    Type min;

    if (arg1 < arg2)
        min = arg1;
    else
        min = arg2;
```

continues

Listing 26.9   Continued

```
    return min;
}

char* Min(char* arg1, char* arg2)
{
    char* min;

    int result = strcmp(arg1, arg2);

    if (result < 0)
        min = arg1;
    else
        min = arg2;

    return min;
}

int main()
{
    cout << Min(15, 25) << endl;
    cout << Min(254.78, 12.983) << endl;
    cout << Min('A', 'Z') << endl;
    cout << Min("APPLE", "ORANGE") << endl;

    return 0;
}
```

Creating Class Templates

Just as you can create abstract functions with function templates, so too can you create abstract classes with class templates. A class template represents a class, which in turn represents an object. When you define a class template, the compiler takes the template and creates a class. You then declare (instantiate) objects of the class. As you can see, class templates add another layer of abstraction to the concept of classes.

You define a class template much as you define a function template, by supplying the `template` line followed by the class's declaration, as shown in Listing 26.10. Notice that, just as with a function template, you use the abstract data types given as parameters in the `template` line in the body of the class in order to define member variables, return types, and other data objects.

Listing 26.10   Defining a Class Template

```
template<class Type>
class CMyClass
{
protected:
    Type data;

public:
```

```
        CMyClass(Type arg) { data = arg; }
        ~CMyClass() {};
};
```

When you're ready to instantiate objects from the template class, you must supply the data type that will replace the template parameters. For example, to create an object of the CMyClass class, you might use a line like this:

```
CMyClass<int> myClass(15);
```

The previous line creates a CMyClass object that uses integers in place of the abstract data type. If you wanted the class to deal with floating-point values, you'd create an object of the class something like this:

```
CMyClass<float> myClass(15.75);
```

For a more complete example, suppose you want to create a class that stores two values and has member functions that compare those values. Listing 26.11 is a program that does just that. First, the listing defines a class template called CCompare. This class stores two values that are supplied to the constructor. The class also includes the usual constructor and destructor, as well as member functions for determining the larger or smaller of the values, or to determine whether the values are equal.

Listing 26.11   TEMPLATE3.CPP—Using a Class Template

```
#include <iostream.h>

template<class Type>
class CCompare
{
protected:
    Type arg1;
    Type arg2;

public:
    CCompare(Type arg1, Type arg2)
    {
        CCompare::arg1 = arg1;
        CCompare::arg2 = arg2;
    }

    ~CCompare() {}

    Type GetMin()
    {
        Type min;

        if (arg1 < arg2)
            min = arg1;
        else
            min = arg2;
```

continues

Listing 26.11   Continued

```
        return min;
    }

    Type GetMax()
    {
        Type max;

        if (arg1 > arg2)
            max = arg1;
        else
            max = arg2;

        return max;
    }

    int Equal()
    {
        int equal;

        if (arg1 == arg2)
            equal = 1;
        else
            equal = 0;

        return equal;
    }
};

int main()
{
    CCompare<int> compare1(15, 25);
    CCompare<double> compare2(254.78, 12.983);
    CCompare<char> compare3('A', 'Z');

    cout << "THE COMPARE1 OBJECT" << endl;
    cout << "Lowest: " << compare1.GetMin() << endl;
    cout << "Highest: " << compare1.GetMax() << endl;
    cout << "Equal: " << compare1.Equal() << endl;
    cout << endl;

    cout << "THE COMPARE2 OBJECT" << endl;
    cout << "Lowest: " << compare2.GetMin() << endl;
    cout << "Highest: " << compare2.GetMax() << endl;
    cout << "Equal: " << compare2.Equal() << endl;
    cout << endl;

    cout << "THE COMPARE2 OBJECT" << endl;
    cout << "Lowest: " << compare3.GetMin() << endl;
    cout << "Highest: " << compare3.GetMax() << endl;
    cout << "Equal: " << compare3.Equal() << endl;
    cout << endl;

    return 0;
}
```

The main program instantiates three objects from the class template, one that deals with integers, one that uses floating-point values, and one that stores and compares character values. After creating the three CCompare objects, main() calls the objects' member functions in order to display information about the data stored in each object. Figure 26.1 shows the program's output.

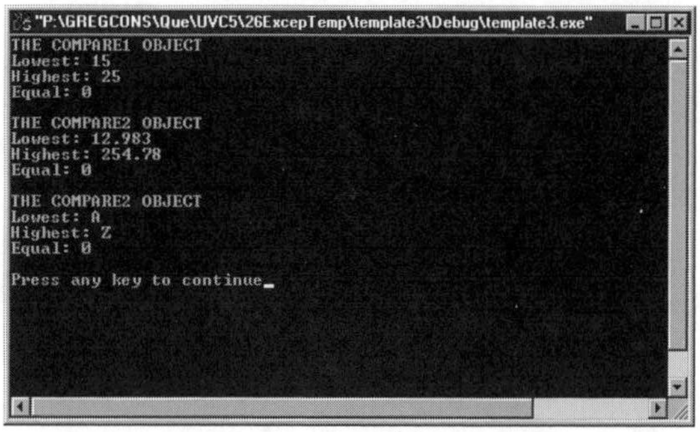

FIG. 26.1

The Template3 program creates three different objects from a class template.

You can, of course, pass as many parameters as you like to a class template, just as you can with a function template. Listing 26.12 shows a class template that uses two different types of data.

Listing 26.12 Using Multiple Parameters with a Class Template

```
template<class Type1, class Type2>
class CMyClass
{
protected:
    Type1 data1;
    Type2 data2;

public:
    CMyClass(Type1 arg1, Type2 arg2)
    {
        data1 = arg1;
        data2 = arg2;
    }

    ~CMyClass() {}
};
```

Part
VII

Ch
26

To instantiate an object of the CMyClass class, you might use a line like this:

```
CMyClass<int, char> myClass(15, 'A');
```

Finally, you can use specific data types, as well as the placeholder data types, as parameters in a class template. You just add the specific data type to the parameter list, just as you add any other parameter. Listing 26.13 is a short program that creates an object from a class template that uses two abstract parameters and one specific data type.

Listing 26.13   Using Specific Data Types as Parameters in a Class Template

```
#include <iostream.h>

template<class Type1, class Type2, int num>
class CMyClass
{
protected:
    Type1 data1;
    Type2 data2;
    int data3;

public:
    CMyClass(Type1 arg1, Type2 arg2, int num)
    {
       data1 = arg1;
       data2 = arg2;
       data3 = num;
    }

    ~CMyClass() {}
};

int main()
{
    CMyClass<int, char, 0> myClass(15, 'A', 10);

    return 0;
}
```

The Standard Template Library

Before you run off to write templates that implement linked lists, binary trees, sorting, and other common tasks, you might like to know that somebody else already has. Visual C++ incorporates the Standard Template Library (STL), which includes hundreds of function and class templates to tackle common tasks. Would you like a stack of ints or a stack of floats? Don't write lots of different stack classes, don't even write one stack class template, just use the stack template included in the STL. The same is true for almost every common data structure and operation.

Earlier in this chapter, you saw applications that use exceptions and allocate memory on the heap (dynamic allocation with new) can run into trouble when exceptions are thrown and the delete statement for that memory gets bypassed. If there was an object on the stack whose destructor called delete for the memory, you would prevent this problem. STL implements a managed pointer like this: it's called auto-ptr. Here's the declaration for auto_ptr:

```
template<class T>
    class auto_ptr {
public:
    typedef T element_type;
    explicit auto_ptr(T *p = 0) ;
```

```
auto_ptr(const auto_ptr<T>& rhs) ;
auto_ptr<T>& operator=(auto_ptr<T>& rhs);
~auto_ptr();
T& operator*() const ;
T *operator->() const;
T *get() const ;
T *release() const;
};
```

Once you create a pointer to an `int`, `float`, `Employee`, or any other type of object, you can make an `auto_ptr` and use that just like a pointer. For example, imagine a code fragment like this:

```
// ...
    Employee* emp = new Employee(stuff);
    emp->ProcessEmployee;
    delete emp;
// ...
```

When you realize that `ProcessEmployee()` might throw an `EmployeeException`, you might change this code to read like this:

```
// ...
    Employee* emp = new Employee(stuff);
    try
    {
        emp->ProcessEmployee;
    }
    catch (EmployeeException e)
    {
        delete emp;
        throw;
    }
    delete emp;
// ...
```

But you think this is ugly and hard to maintain, so you go with an `auto_ptr` instead:

```
#include <memory>
// ...
    auto_ptr<Employee> emp (new Employee(stuff));
    emp->ProcessEmployee;
// ...
```

This looks just like the first example, but it works just like the second: whether you leave this code snippet normally or because of an exception, `emp` will go out of scope, and when it does the `Employee` object that was allocated on the heap will be deleted for you automatically. No extra `try` or `catch` blocks, and as an extra bonus you don't even have to remember to `delete` the memory in the routine at all—it's taken care of for you.

Look again at the functions declared in the template: a constructor, a copy constructor, an address-of (&) operator, a destructor, a contents of (*) operator, a dereferencing (->) operator, and functions called `get()` and `release()`. These work together to ensure that you can treat your pointer exactly as though it was an ordinary pointer. It's neat stuff.

Part
VII

Ch
26

Using Run-Time Type Information

Run-Time Type Information (RTTI) was added to C++ so that programmers could obtain information about objects at runtime. This capability is especially useful when you're dealing with polymorphic objects, because it enables your program to determine at runtime what exact type of object it's currently working with. Later in this section, you'll see how important this type of information can be when you're working with class hierarchies. RTTI can also be used to safely downcast an object pointer. In this section, you'll discover how RTTI works and why you'd want to use it.

 Polymorphism is discussed in Chapter 4, "Messages and Commands," in a sidebar in the "Message Maps" section.

Introducing RTTI

The RTTI standard introduces three new elements to the C++ language. The `dynamic_cast` operator performs downcasting of polymorphic objects; the `typeid` operator retrieves information (in the form of a `type_info` object) about an object; and the `type_info` class stores information about an object, providing member functions that can be used to extract that information.

The public portion of the `type_info` class is defined in Visual C++ and shown in Listing 26.14.

Listing 26.14 The *type_info* Class, Defined by Visual C++

```
class type_info {
public:
     virtual ~type_info();
     int operator==(const type_info& rhs) const;
     int operator!=(const type_info& rhs) const;
     int before(const type_info& rhs) const;
     const char* name() const;
     const char* raw_name() const;
};
```

As you can see, the class provides member functions that can compare objects for equality, and return the object's name, both as a readable text string and as a raw decorated object name. The `before()` member function remains a bit mysterious and poorly documented. According to Microsoft, the Visual C++ implementation of `before()` is used "to determine the collating sequence of types." Microsoft further states that "there is no link between the collating order of types and inheritance relationships."

Performing Safe Downcasts

Once you start writing a lot of OOP programs, you'll run into times when you need to downcast one type of object to another. *Downcasting* is the act of converting a base-class pointer to a derived-class pointer (a *derived class* being a class that's derived from the base class). You use `dynamic_cast` to downcast an object, like this:

```
Type* ptr = dynamic_cast<Type*>(Pointer);
```

In the preceding example, `Type` is the type to which the object should be cast, and `Pointer` is a pointer to the object. If the pointer cannot be safely downcast, the `dynamic_cast` operator returns 0.

Suppose, for example, that you have a base class called `CBase` and a class derived from `CBase` called `CDerived`. Because you want to take advantage of polymorphism, you obtained a pointer to `CDerived`, like this:

```
CBase* derived = new CDerived;
```

Notice that, although you're creating a `CDerived` object, the pointer is of the base-class type, `CBase`. This is a typical scenario in programs that take advantage of OOP polymorphism.

Now suppose that you want to safely downcast the `CBase` pointer to a `CDerived` pointer. You might use `dynamic_cast`, as follows:

```
CDerived* ptr = dynamic_cast<CDerived*>(derived);
```

If the cast returns 0, the downcast was not allowed.

Getting Object Information

As mentioned previously, you can use the `typeid` operator to obtain information about an object. Although the `dynamic_cast` operator applies only to polymorphic objects, you can use `typeid` on any type of data object. For example, to get information about the `int` data object, you could use lines like these:

```
const type_info& ti = typeid(int);
cout << ti.name();
```

In the first line, you can see that the `typeid` operator returns a reference to a `type_info` object. You can then use the object's member functions to extract information about the data object. In the preceding example, the `cout` object will output the word `int`. The `typeid` operator's single argument is the name of the data object for which you want a `type_info` object.

Of course, a better use for `typeid` is to compare and get information about classes that you have defined in your program. Listing 26.15 is a short program that prints out information about the classes it defines.

Listing 26.15 RTTI.CPP—Using the *typeid* Operator

```
#include <iostream.h>
#include <typeinfo.h>

class CBase
{
public:
```

continues

Listing 26.15 Continued

```
    CBase() {};
    ~CBase() {};
};

class CDerived : public CBase
{
public:
    CDerived() {};
    ~CDerived() {};
};

int main()
{
    CBase* base = new CBase;
    CBase* derived = new CDerived;

    const type_info& ti1 = typeid(CBase);
    const type_info& ti2 = typeid(CDerived);

    cout << "First object's name: " << ti1.name() << endl;
    cout << "First object's raw name: " << ti1.raw_name() << endl;
    cout << endl;

    cout << "Second object's name: " << ti2.name() << endl;
    cout << "Second object's raw name: " << ti2.raw_name() << endl;
    cout << endl;

    if (ti1 == ti2)
        cout << "The two objects are equal." << endl;
    else
        cout << "The two objects are not equal." << endl;

    cout << endl;

    delete base;
    delete derived;

    return 0;
}
```

Listing 26.15 first defines a base class called CBase. The program then derives a second class, called CDerived, from the base class. In main(), the program instantiates an object from each class, the objects being called base and derived. Then the program calls typeid to obtain type_info objects for each class. Finally, the program calls the type_info member functions to extract information about the classes, as well as to compare the classes for equality. Figure 26.2 shows the program's output. If you have trouble running the RTTI program shown in Listing 26.15, jump ahead to the next section, which tells you how to enable RTTI.

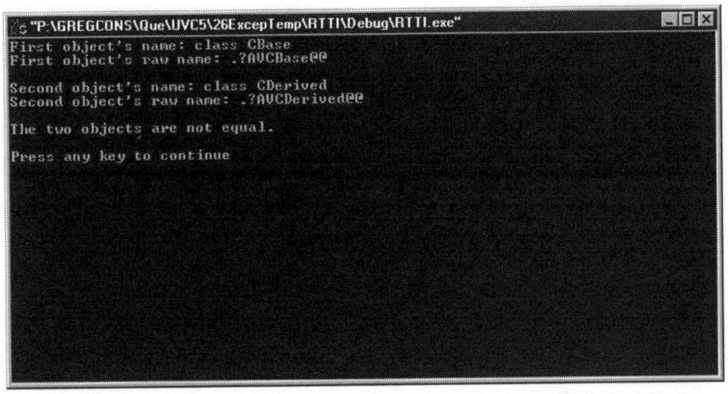

FIG. 26.2

This is Listing 26.15 in action.

Preparing to Use RTTI

If you got a strange error message or warning when you tried to compile the RTTI program, you probably don't yet have RTTI enabled. To enable RTTI, use the following procedure:

1. Select the Project, Settings command from Developer Studio's menu bar. The Project Settings dialog box appears.

2. Click the C/C++ tab. The C/C++ setting-options page appears.

3. In the Category box, select the C++ Language item. The C++ language options appear (see Figure 26.3).

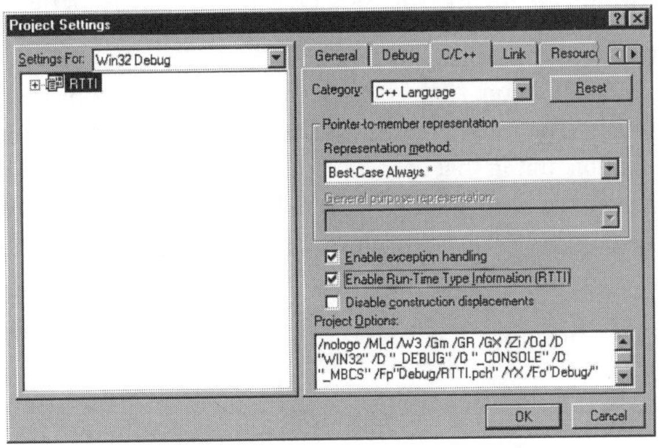

FIG. 26.3

The C/C++ options page controls Run-Time Type Identification.

Part

VII

Ch

26

4. Select the Enable Run-Time Type Information (RTTI) option and then click OK to finalize your choices.

Also, be sure that you include the TYPEID.H header file in any source-code file that calls the `typeid` operator. If you don't, your program will not compile.

Understanding Namespaces

A *namespace* defines a scope in which duplicate identifiers cannot be used. For example, you already know that you can have a global variable named `value` and then also define a function with a local variable called `value`. Because the two variables are in different namespaces, your program knows that it should use the local `value` when inside the function and the global `value` everywhere else.

Namespaces, however, do not extend far enough to cover some very thorny problems. One example is duplicate names in external classes or libraries. This issue crops up when a programmer is using several external files within a single project. None of the external variables and functions can have the same name as other external variables or functions. To avoid this type of problem, third-party vendors frequently add prefixes or suffixes to variable and function names in order to reduce the likelihood of some other vendor using the same name.

Obviously, the C++ gurus have come up with a solution to such scope-resolution problems. (Otherwise, we wouldn't be having this discussion.) The solution is user-defined namespaces, about which you'll study in this section.

Defining a Namespace

To accommodate user-defined namespaces, the keyword `namespace` was added to the C++ language. In its simplest form, a namespace is not unlike a structure or a class. You start the namespace definition with the `namespace` keyword, followed by the namespace's name and the declaration of the identifiers that will be valid within the scope of that namespace.

Listing 26.16 shows a namespace definition. The namespace is called A and includes two identifiers, `i`, and `j`, and a function, `Func()`. Notice that the `Func()` function is completely defined within the namespace definition. You can also choose to define the function outside of the namespace definition, but in that case, you must preface the function definition's name with the namespace's name, much as you would preface a class's member-function definition with the class's name. Listing 26.17 shows this form of namespace function definition.

Listing 26.16   Defining a Namespace

```
namespace A
{
    int i;
    int j;

    int Func()
    {
        return 1;
    }
}
```

Listing 26.17   Defining a Function Outside of the Namespace Definition

```
namespace A
{
    int i;
    int j;

    int Func();
}

int A::Func()
{
    return 1;
}
```

N O T E   Namespaces must be defined at the file level of scope or within another namespace definition. They cannot be defined, for example, inside a function. ▪

Namespace Scope Resolution

Namespaces add a new layer of scope to your programs, but this means that you need some way of identifying that scope. The identification is, of course, the namespace's name, which you must use in your programs to resolve references to identifiers. For example, to refer to the variable i in namespace A, you'd write something like this:

```
A::i = 0;
```

You can, if you like, nest one namespace definition within another, as shown in Listing 26.18. In the case shown in the listing, however, you have to use more complicated scope resolutions in order to differentiate between the i variable declared in A and B, like this:

```
A::i = 0;
A::B::i = 0;
```

Part **VII**

Ch **26**

Listing 26.18   Nesting Namespace Definitions

```
namespace A
{
    int i;
    int j;

    int Func()
    {
        return 1;
    }

    namespace B
    {
        int i;
    }
}
```

If you're going to frequently reference variables and functions within namespace A, you can avoid using the A:: resolution by preceding the program statements with a using line, as shown in Listing 26.19.

Listing 26.19   Resolving Scope with the *using* Keyword

```
using namespace A;
i = 0;
j = 0;
int num1 = Func();
```

Unnamed Namespaces

Just to be sure that you're thoroughly confused, Visual C++ allows you to have unnamed namespaces. You define an unnamed namespace exactly as you would any other namespace, except you leave off the name. Listing 26.20 shows the definition of an unnamed namespace. This lets you arrange variables whose names are only valid within one namespace, and cannot be accessed from elsewhere, because no other code can know the name of the unnamed namespace.

Listing 26.20   Defining an Unnamed Namespace

```
namespace
{
    int i;
    int j;

    int Func()
    {
        return 1;
    }
}
```

You refer to the identifiers in the unnamed namespace without any sort of extra scope resolution, like this:

```
i = 0;
j = 0;
int num1 = Func();
```

Namespace Aliases

There may be times when you run into namespaces that have long names. In these cases, having to use that long name over and over in your program in order to access the identifiers defined in the namespace can be a major chore. To solve this problem, Visual C++ enables you to create *namespace aliases*, which are just replacement names for a namespace. You create an alias like this:

```
namespace A = LongName;
```

LongName is the original name of the namespace, and A is the alias. After the preceding line executes, you can access the LongName namespace using either A or LongName. You can think of an alias as a nickname or short form. Listing 26.21 is a short program that demonstrates namespace aliases.

Listing 26.21 Using a Namespace Alias

```
namespace ThisIsANamespaceName
{
    int i;
    int j;

    int Func()
    {
        return 2;
    }
}

int main()
{
    namespace ns = ThisIsANamespaceName;

    ns::i = 0;
    ns::j = 0;
    int num1 = ns::Func();

    return 0;
}
```

Reviewing New Keywords and Data Types

Visual C++ has added a number of keywords in accordance with recommendations from the ANSI committee working on Standard C++. These are bool, true, false, mutable, typename, and explicit.

The *bool* Data Type

The new data type bool is special integer type that can have the values true or false only. It's a formal replacement for the informal #define and typedefs most C++ programmers have been using for years. Most conditional expressions, like (i ! =0) or (a < b) now return a bool rather than an int.

The *mutable* Keyword

The mutable keyword is used to make an exception to the const status of an object. For example, imagine you have an Account class that needs to make a single big calculation at the beginning of all of its member functions. You decide to cache the result of this calculation in the object as a private member variable. The class looks something like this:

```
class Account
{
private:
// lots of data
    float value;
    bool valueok;
public:
    void PrintStatement(CTime starttime);
    float GetValue();
    void CreditSalesRep(SalesRep& owner);
    void Deposit (float amt);
    // and so on
private:
    void UpdateValue();
};

void Account::PrintStatement(CTime startttime)
{
    if (!valueok)
    {
        UpdateValue();
        valueok = true;
    }
    //rest of function
}

void Account::Deposit(float amt)
{
    valueok=false;
    //rest of function
}
// more functions
```

Typically, a class isn't written like this at first. Probably each function just called UpdateValue() every time, until someone noticed a problem with execution speed and decided to cache value in the object so that UpdateValue() wouldn't have to be called so often. This is a private implementation change and won't affect any of the rest of the code that uses this object.

There is one catch though: what if some of these member functions were const member functions? PrintStatement(), for example, doesn't really change an Account object at all, or at least it didn't until the decision to cache value. But the compiler will balk if you try to declare PrintAccount() as const now, because it changes valueok. If you move the line valueok = true to the bottom of UpdateValue(), and declare UpdateValue() to be a const member function, then PrintAccount() will compile, but the line valueok = true (and the line that sets value) will generate an error message when you compile UpdateValue().

In days of yore, programmers got around this with a process referred to as casting away const, which was dangerous and hard to read. Now you simply declare value and valueok to be mutable:

```
private:
// lots of data
```

```
mutable float value;
mutable bool valueok;
```

This says that the rules of const don't apply to these member variables, and they can be changed even in a const function. This enables you to preserve "conceptual constness" and keeps your programs more readable.

The *typename* Keyword

This keyword belongs only in template code, and it means that the name you are about to give is the name of a type rather than the name of a variable. It can also replace the word class in a template definition.

The *explicit* Keyword

You may have seen this keyword in the declaration of the auto_ptr class template earlier in this chapter. It can be used only on constructors, and is present only in the declaration, such as shown in the following:

```
class Foo
{
    explicit Foo() {data=0;}    //fine
    explicit Foo(int i);        //fine
    //rest of class
};
explicit Foo::Foo(int I)        //not allowed
{
    data = i;
}
Foo::Foo(int I)  //fine, it's explicit because
                 //class declaration said so
{
    data = i;
}
```

What does it mean if a constructor is explicit? It means that it cannot be used to do the sort of invisible conversions that compilers do all the time. Consider this code snippet:

```
void func(Foo f);
//...
    f(3);
//...
```

In order to compile this code, the compiler looks around for a way to make a Foo from an integer. You can imagine that it creates code something like this:

```
{
Foo compiler_temporary (3);
func(compiler_temporary);
}
```

If you add trace statements (see Chapter 24, "Improving Your Application's Performance,") to your constructor and destructor, you will see just how often the compiler makes implicit conversions like this. It happens a lot.

The explicit keyword says that this constructor is not to be used in these implicit conversions. Since the Foo constructor that takes an int is explicit, the compiler can't make the conversion and the call to func will not compile.

Why would you want to write code that will not compile? When compiling it would make things far worse. If Foo was a managed pointer, when compiler_temporary went out of scope the memory it pointed to would be deleted and your program would have a serious bug. If you want to call func, make a Foo object yourself and pass it down, and you avoid the bug.

From Here...

You've covered a lot of ground in this chapter. The techniques covered here, although fairly new to C++ programming, are rapidly becoming must-know techniques for all C++ programmers. Exceptions and templates, especially, are things that you'll run into often when you examine other programmers' code—or, more importantly, when you apply for that programmer's job.

For more information on related topics, please refer to the following chapters:

- Chapter 19, "Internet Programming with the WinInet Classes," shows the use of exceptions in a real application.

- Chapter 24, "Improving Your Application's Performance," discusses finding bottlenecks, preventing memory leaks, and using trace statements.

- Chapter 28, "Future Explorations," introduces console applications like the ones used in this chapter.

CHAPTER 27

Multitasking with Windows Threads

When using Windows 95 (and other modern operating systems), you know that you can run several programs simultaneously. This ability is called *multitasking*. What you may not know is that many of today's operating systems also allow *threads,* which are separate processes that are not complete applications. A thread is a lot like a subprogram. An application can create several threads—several different flows of execution—and run them concurrently. Threads give you the ability to have multitasking inside multitasking. The user knows that he or she can run several applications at a time. The programmer knows that each application can run several threads at a time. In this chapter, you'll learn how to create and manage threads in your applications. ■

How to create and run threads

Writing a thread and getting it started is easy under MFC. In fact, one function call is all it takes to get your thread running.

About inter-thread communication

Although threads are like self-contained subprograms, they still need to communicate with other threads, including the main program. There are several ways of doing this, the best of which is Windows messages and event objects.

About synchronizing threads with critical sections

You often have to ensure that data can be accessed by only one thread at a time. Critical sections help you accomplish this type of data protection.

How to use mutexes to synchronize threads

Mutexes are a lot like critical sections in that they enable you to guard data against thread corruption.

Understanding Simple Threads

A thread is a path of execution through a program. In a multi-threaded program, each thread has its own stack, and operates independently of any other threads that may be running within the same program. MFC distinguishes between *UI threads*, which have a message pump and typically perform user interface tasks, and *worker threads*, which do not.

N O T E Any application always has at least one thread, which is the program's primary or main thread. You can start and stop as many additional threads as you need, but the main thread keeps running as long as the application is active. ■

To create a thread by using MFC, all you have to do is write a function that you wish to run parallel with the rest of your application then call `AfxBeginThread()` to start a thread that will execute your function. The thread remains active as long as the thread's function is executing: When the thread function exits, the thread is destroyed. A simple call to `AfxBeginThread()` looks like this:

```
AfxBeginThread(ProcName, param, priority);
```

In the previous line, `ProcName` is the name of the thread's function, `param` is any 32-bit value you want to pass to the thread, and `priority` is the thread's priority, which is represented by a number of predefined constants. Those constants and their descriptions are shown in Table 27.1.

Table 27.1 Thread Priority Constants

Constant	Description
THREAD_PRIORITY_ABOVE_NORMAL	Sets a priority one point higher than normal.
THREAD_PRIORITY_BELOW_NORMAL	Sets a priority one point lower than normal.
THREAD_PRIORITY_HIGHEST	Sets a priority two points above normal.
THREAD_PRIORITY_IDLE	Sets a base priority of 1. For a REALTIME_PRIORITY_CLASS process, sets a priority of 16.
THREAD_PRIORITY_LOWEST	Sets a priority two points below normal.
THREAD_PRIORITY_NORMAL	Sets normal priority.
THREAD_PRIORITY_TIME_CRITICAL	Sets a base priority of 15. For a REALTIME_PRIORITY_CLASS process, sets a priority of 30.

N O T E A thread's priority determines how often the thread takes control of the system relative to the other running threads. Generally, the higher the priority, the more running time the thread gets, which is why the value of THREAD_PRIORITY_TIME_CRITICAL is so high. ■

In order to see a simple thread in action, build the Thread application as detailed in the following steps.

1. Start a new AppWizard project workspace called Thread, as shown in Figure 27.1.

FIG. 27.1

Start an AppWizard project workspace called Thread.

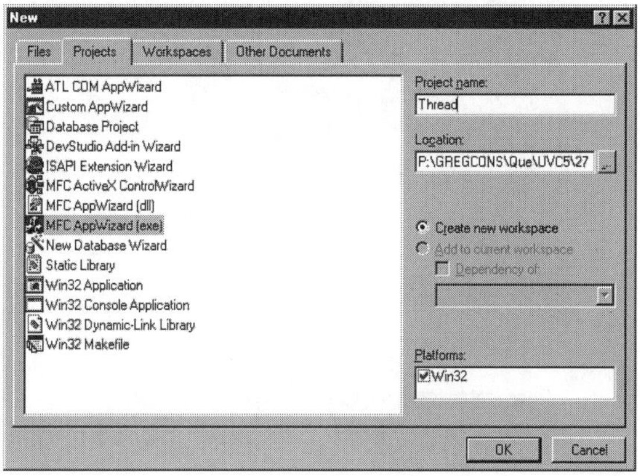

2. Give the new project the following settings in the AppWizard dialog boxes. The New Project Information dialog box should then look like Figure 27.2.

           Step 1: Single document

           Step 2: Default settings

           Step 3: Default settings

           Step 4: Turn off all options

           Step 5: Default settings

           Step 6: Default settings

FIG. 27.2

These are the AppWizard settings for the Thread project.

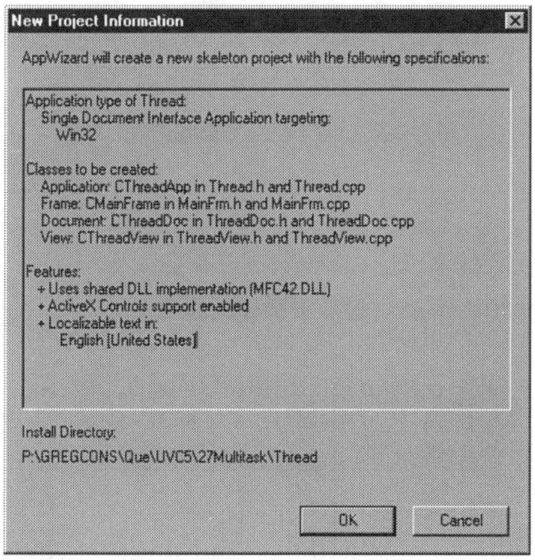

Part

VII

Ch

27

3. Use the resource editor to add a Thread menu to the application's IDR_MAINFRAME menu. Give the menu one command called Start Thread with a command ID of ID_STARTTHREAD, and enter a sensible prompt and ToolTip, as shown in Figure 27.3.

FIG. 27.3

Add a Thread menu with a Start Thread command.

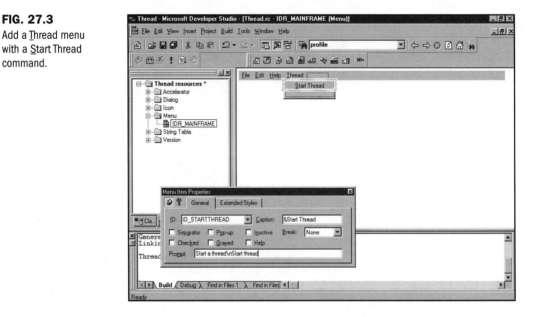

4. Use ClassWizard to associate the ID_STARTTHREAD command with the OnStartthread() message-response function, as shown in Figure 27.4. Make sure that you have CThreadView selected in the Class Name box before you add the function.

FIG. 27.4

Add the OnStartthread() message-response function to the view class.

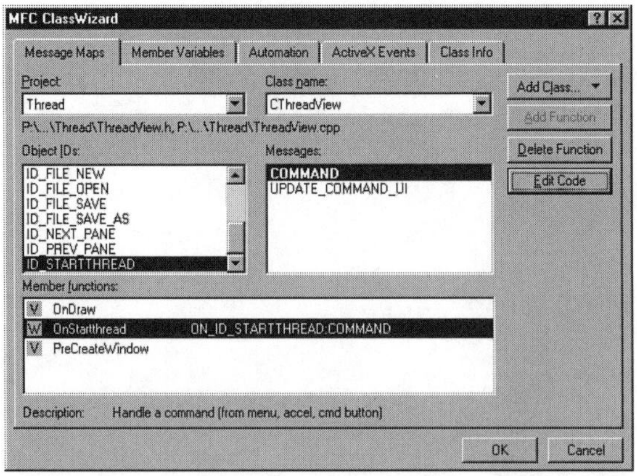

5. Click the Edit Code button and then add the following lines to the new OnStartthread() function, replacing the TODO: Add your command handler code here comment:

```
HWND hWnd = GetSafeHwnd();
AfxBeginThread(ThreadProc, hWnd, THREAD_PRIORITY_NORMAL);
```

This code will call a function called ThreadProc within a thread of its own. Next, add ThreadProc, shown in Listing 27.1, to ThreadView.cpp, placing it right before the OnStartthread() function. Note that ThreadProc() is a global function and not a member function of the CThreadView class, even though it is in the view class's implementation file.

Listing 27.1 ThreadView.cpp—*ThreadProc()*

```
UINT ThreadProc(LPVOID param)
{
    ::MessageBox((HWND)param, "Thread activated.", "Thread", MB_OK);

    return 0;
}
```

This threaded function doesn't do much, just reports that it was started. The SDK function MessageBox() is very much like AfxMessageBox(), but since this is not a member function of a class derived from CWnd, you cannot use AfxMessageBox().

T I P   The double colons in front of a function name indicate a call to a global function, rather than an MFC class member function. For Windows programmers this usually means an API or SDK call. For example, inside an MFC window class, you can call MessageBox("Hi, There!") to display "Hi, There!" to the user. This form of MessageBox() is a member function of the MFC window classes. To call the original Windows version , you'd write something like ::MessageBox(0, "Hi, There!", "Message", MB_OK). Notice the colons in front of the function name and the additional arguments.

When you run the Thread program, the main window appears. Select the Thread, Start Thread command, and the system starts the thread represented by the ThreadProc() function and displays a message box, as shown in Figure 27.5.

FIG. 27.5

The simple secondary thread in the Thread program displays a message box and then ends.

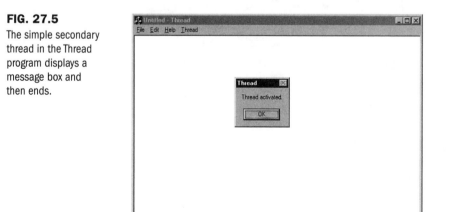

Understanding Thread Communication

Usually, a secondary thread performs some sort of task for the main program, which implies that there needs to be a channel of communication between the program (which is also a thread) and its secondary threads. There are several ways to accomplish these communications tasks: using global variables, using event objects, and using messages. In this section, you'll explore these thread-communication techniques.

Communicating with Global Variables

Suppose you want your main program to be able to stop the thread. You need a way, then, to tell the thread when to stop. One way to do this is to set up a global variable and then have the thread monitor the global variable for a value that signals the thread to end. To see how this technique works, modify the Thread application.

First, use the resource editor to add a Stop Thread command to the application's Thread menu. Give this new command the ID_STOPTHREAD ID, as shown in Figure 27.6.

FIG. 27.6

Add a Stop Thread command to the Thread menu.

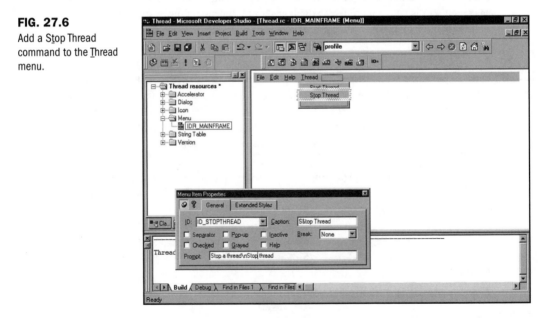

Use ClassWizard to associate the ID_STOPTHREAD command with the OnStopthread() message-response function, as shown in Figure 27.7. Make sure that you have CThreadView selected in the Class Name box before you add the function. Add the following line to the OnStopthread() function, replacing the TODO: Add your command handler code here comment:

```
threadController = 0;
```

FIG. 27.7
Add the
OnStopthread()
message-response
function.

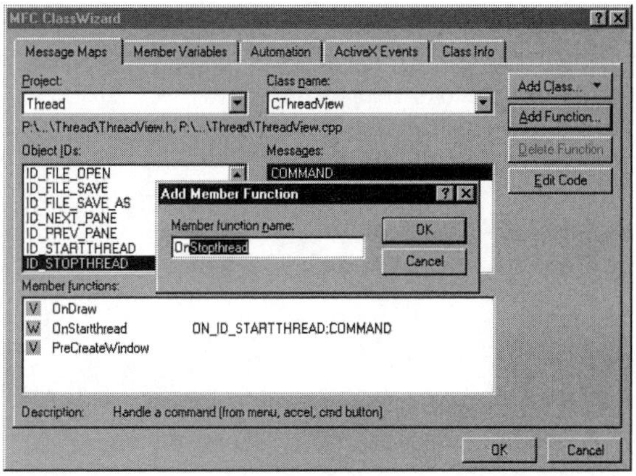

This refers to a new global variable you are about to declare. Add the following line to the top of the ThreadView.cpp file, right after the `endif` directive:

```
volatile int threadController;
```

The `volatile` keyword means that you expect this variable will be changed from outside a thread that uses it. The keyword requests that the compiler not cache the variable in a register or in any way count on the value staying unchanged just because code in one thread doesn't seem to change it.

Add the following line to the `OnStartthread()` function, before the two lines you added earlier:

```
threadController = 1;
```

By now perhaps you've guessed that the value of threadController determines whether the thread will continue or not. Replace the `ThreadProc()` function with the one shown in Listing 27.2.

Listing 27.2 The New *ThreadProc()* Function

```
UINT ThreadProc(LPVOID param)
{
    ::MessageBox((HWND)param, "Thread activated.", "Thread", MB_OK);

    while (threadController == 1)
    {
        ;
    }

    ::MessageBox((HWND)param, "Thread stopped.", "Thread", MB_OK);

    return 0;
}
```

Part

VII

Ch

27

Now the thread first displays a message box, telling the user that the thread is starting. Then a `while` loop continues to check the threadController global variable, waiting for its value to change to 0. Although this `while` loop is trivial, it is here that you would place the code that performs whatever task you want the thread to perform, being sure not to tie things up for too long before rechecking the value of `threadController`.

Try a test: Build and run the program, and choose Thread, Start Thread to start the secondary thread. When you do, a message box appears telling you that the new thread was started. To stop the thread, select the Thread, Stop Thread command. Again, a message box appears, this time telling you that the thread is stopping.

> **CAUTION**
>
> Using global variables to communicate between threads is, to say the least, an unsophisticated approach to thread communication and can be a dangerous technique if you're not sure how C++ handles variables from an assembly-language level. Other thread-communication techniques are safer and more elegant.

Communicating with User-Defined Messages

Now you have a simple, albeit unsophisticated, method for communicating information from your main program to your thread. How about the reverse? That is, how can your thread communicate with the main program? The easiest method to accomplish this communication is to incorporate user-defined Windows messages into the program.

The first step is to define a user message, which you can do easily, like this:

```
const WM_USERMSG = WM_USER + 100;
```

The `WM_USER` constant, defined by Windows, holds the first available user-message number. Because other parts of your program may use some of the user messages for their own purposes, the preceding line sets `WM_USERMSG` to `WM_USER+100`.

After defining the message, you call `::PostMessage()` from the thread in order to send the message to the main program whenever you need to. (Message handling was discussed in Chapter 4, "Messages and Commands." Sending your own messages allows you take advantage of the message-handling facility built into MFC.) A typical call to `::PostMessage()` might look like this:

```
::PostMessage((HWND)param, WM_USERMSG, 0, 0);
```

`PostMessage()`'s four arguments are the handle of the window to which the message should be sent, the message identifier, and the message's `WPARAM` and `LPARAM` parameters.

Modify the Thread application according to the next steps in order to see how to implement posting user messages from a thread.

1. Add the following line to the top of the ThreadView.h header file, right before the beginning of the class declaration:

   ```
   const WM_THREADENDED = WM_USER + 100;
   ```

2. Still in the header file, add the following line to the message map, right after the AFX_MSG comment and before DECLARE_MESSAGE_MAP:

```
afx_msg LONG OnThreadended(WPARAM wParam, LPARAM lParam);
```

3. Switch to the ThreadView.cpp file and add the following line to the class's message map, making sure to place it right *after* the }}AFX_MSG_MAP comment:

```
ON_MESSAGE(WM_THREADENDED, OnThreadended)
```

4. Replace the ThreadProc() function with the one shown in Listing 27.3.

Listing 27.3   The Message-Posting *ThreadProc()*

```
UINT ThreadProc(LPVOID param)
{
    ::MessageBox((HWND)param, "Thread activated.", "Thread", MB_OK);

    while (threadController == 1)
    {
        ;
    }

    ::PostMessage((HWND)param, WM_THREADENDED, 0, 0);

    return 0;
}
```

5. Add the function shown in Listing 27.4 to the end of the ThreadView.cpp file.

Listing 27.4   *CThreadView::OnThreadended()*

```
LONG CThreadView::OnThreadended(WPARAM wParam, LPARAM lParam)
{
    AfxMessageBox("Thread ended.");
    return 0;
}
```

Part
VII

Ch
27

When you run the new version of the Thread program, select the Thread, Start Thread command to start the thread. When you do, a message box appears telling you that the thread has started. To end the thread, select the Thread, Stop Thread command. Just as with the previous version of the program, a message box appears, telling you that the thread has ended.

Although this version of the Thread application seems to run identically to the previous version, there's a subtle difference. Now the program displays the message box that signals the end of the thread in the main program rather that from inside the thread. The program can do this because, when the user selects the Stop Thread command, the thread sends a WM_THREADENDED message to the main program. When the program receives that message, it displays the final message box.

Communicating with Event Objects

A slightly more sophisticated method of signaling between threads is to use *event objects,* which under MFC are represented by the CEvent class. An event object can be in one of two states: signaled and nonsignaled. Threads can watch for events to be signaled and so perform their operations at the appropriate time. Creating an event object is as easy as declaring a global variable, like this:

```
CEvent threadStart;
```

Although the CEvent constructor has a number of optional arguments, you can usually get away with creating the default object, as shown in the previous line of code. Upon creation, the event object is automatically in its nonsignaled state. To signal the event, you call the event object's SetEvent() member function, like this:

```
threadStart.SetEvent();
```

After the preceding line executes, the threadStart event object will be in its signaled state. Your thread should be watching for this signal, so that the thread knows it's okay to get to work. How does a thread watch for a signal? By calling the Windows API function, WaitForSingleObject():

```
::WaitForSingleObject(threadStart.m_hObject, INFINITE);
```

This function's two arguments are:

- The handle of the event for which to check (stored in the event object's m_hObject data member)
- How long the function should wait for the event

The predefined INFINITE constant tells WaitForSingleObject() not to return until the specified event is signaled. In other words, if you place the preceding line at the beginning of your thread, the system suspends the thread until the event is signaled. Even though you've started the thread execution, it's halted until whatever you need to have happen happens. When your program is ready for the thread to perform its duty, you call the SetEvent() function, as described a couple of paragraphs ago.

Once the thread is no longer suspended, it can go about its business. But, if you want to signal the end of the thread from the main program, the thread must watch for this next event to be signaled. The thread can do this by polling for the event. To poll for the event, you again call WaitForSingleObject(), only this time you give the function a wait time of 0, like this:

```
::WaitForSingleObject(threadend.m_hObject, 0);
```

In this case, if WaitForSingleObject() returns WAIT_OBJECT_0, the event has been signaled. Otherwise, the event is still in its nonsignaled state.

To better see how event objects work, follow these steps to further modify the Thread application:

1. Add the following line to the top of the ThreadView.cpp file, right after the line `#include "ThreadView.h"`:

   ```
   #include "afxmt.h"
   ```

2. Add the following lines near the top of the ThreadView.cpp file, after the `volatile int threadController` line that you placed there previously:

   ```
   CEvent threadStart;
   CEvent threadEnd;
   ```

3. Delete the `volatile int threadController` line from the file.

4. Replace the `ThreadProc()` function with the one shown in Listing 27.5.

Listing 27.5   Yet Another *ThreadProc()*

```
UINT ThreadProc(LPVOID param)
{
    ::WaitForSingleObject(threadStart.m_hObject, INFINITE);
    ::MessageBox((HWND)param, "Thread activated.",
        "Thread", MB_OK);

    BOOL keepRunning = TRUE;
    while (keepRunning)
    {
        int result =
            ::WaitForSingleObject(threadEnd.m_hObject, 0);
        if (result == WAIT_OBJECT_0)
            keepRunning = FALSE;
    }

    ::PostMessage((HWND)param, WM_THREADENDED, 0, 0);

    return 0;
}
```

5. Replace all of the code in the `OnStartthread()` function with the following line:

   ```
   threadStart.SetEvent();
   ```

6. Replace the code in the `OnStopthread()` function with the following line:

   ```
   threadEnd.SetEvent();
   ```

7. Use ClassWizard to add an `OnCreate()` function that handles the `WM_CREATE` message, as shown in Figure 27.8. Make sure that you have `CThreadView` selected in the Class Name box before you add the function.

8. Add the following lines to the `OnCreate()` function, replacing the `TODO: Add your specialized creation code here` comment:

   ```
   HWND hWnd = GetSafeHwnd();
   AfxBeginThread(ThreadProc, hWnd);
   ```

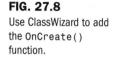

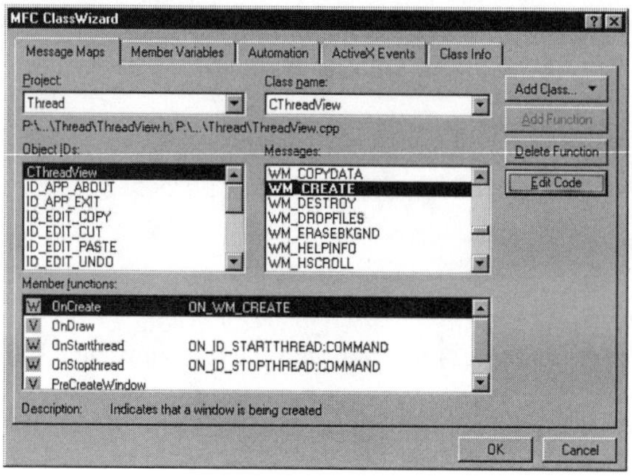

FIG. 27.8
Use ClassWizard to add
the `OnCreate()`
function.

Again, this new version of the program seems to run just like the previous version. However, the program is now using both event objects and user-defined Windows messages to communicate between the main program and the thread. No more messing with clunky global variables.

One big difference from previous versions of the program is that the secondary thread gets started in the `OnCreate()` function, which is called when the application first runs and creates the view. However, because the first line of the thread function is the call to `WaitForSingleObject()`, the thread immediately suspends execution and waits for the `threadStart` event to be signaled.

When the `threadStart` event object is signaled, the thread is free to display the message box and then enter its `while` loop, where it polls the `threadEnd` event object. The `while` loop continues to execute until `threadEnd` is signaled, at which time the thread sends the `WM_THREADENDED` message to the main program and exits. Because the thread is started in `OnCreate()`, once the thread ends, it cannot be restarted.

Using Thread Synchronization

Using multiple threads can lead to some interesting problems. For example, how do you prevent two threads from accessing the same data at the same time? What if, for example, one thread is in the middle of trying to update a data set when another thread tries to read that data? The second thread will almost certainly read corrupted data, since only some of the data set will have been updated.

Trying to keep threads working together properly is called *thread synchronization*. Event objects, about which you just learned, are actually a form of thread synchronization. In this section, you'll learn about *critical sections, mutexes,* and *semaphores*—thread synchronization objects that make your thread programming even safer.

Using Critical Sections

Critical sections are an easy way to ensure that only one thread at a time can access a data set. When you use a critical section, you give your threads an object that they have to share between them. Whichever thread possesses the critical-section object has access to the guarded data. Other threads have to wait until the first thread releases the critical section, after which another thread can grab the critical section in order to access the data in turn.

Because the guarded data is represented by a single critical-section object, and because only one thread can own the critical section at any given time, the guarded data can never be accessed by more than a single thread at a time.

To create a critical-section object in an MFC program, you create an instance of the CCriticalSection class, like this:

```
CCriticalSection criticalSection;
```

Then, when program code is about to access the data that you want to protect, you call the critical-section object's Lock() member function, like this:

```
criticalSection.Lock();
```

If another thread doesn't already own the critical section, Lock() gives the object to the calling thread. That thread can then access the guarded data, after which it calls the critical-section object's Unlock() member function:

```
criticalSection.Unlock();
```

Unlock() releases the ownership of the critical-section object so that another thread can grab it and access the guarded data.

The best way to implement something like critical sections is to build the data you want to protect into a thread-safe class. When you do this, you no longer have to worry about thread synchronization in the main program; the class handles it all for you. As an example, look at Listing 27.6, which is the header file for a thread-safe array class.

Listing 27.6   COUNTARRAY.H—The *CCountArray* Class's Header File

```
#include "afxmt.h"

class CCountArray
{
private:
    int array[10];
    CCriticalSection criticalSection;

public:
    CCountArray() {};
    ~CCountArray() {};

    void SetArray(int value);
    void GetArray(int dstArray[10]);
};
```

Part
VII

Ch
27

The header file starts off by including the MFC header file, afxmt.h, which gives the program access to the CCriticalSection class. Within the CCountArray class declaration, the file declares a ten-element integer array, which is the data that the critical section will guard, and declares the critical-section object, here called criticalSection. The CCountArray class's public member functions include the usual constructor and destructor, as well as functions for setting and reading the array. It's these latter two member functions that must deal with the critical-section object, because it's those functions that access the array.

Listing 27.7 is the CCountArray class's implementation file. Notice that, in each member function, the class takes care of locking and unlocking the critical-section object. This means that any thread can call these member functions without worrying about thread synchronization. For example, if thread one calls SetArray(), the first thing SetArray() does is call criticalSection.Lock(), which gives the critical-section object to thread one. The complete for loop then executes, without any fear of being interrupted by another thread. If thread two calls SetArray() or GetArray(), the call to criticalSection.Lock() suspends thread two until thread one releases the critical-section object, which it does when SetArray() finishes the for loop and executes the criticalSection.Unlock() line. Then the system wakes up thread two and gives it the critical-section object. In this way, all threads have to wait politely for their chance to access the guarded data.

Listing 27.7   COUNTARRAY.CPP—The *CCountArray* Class's Implementation File

```
#include "stdafx.h"
#include "CountArray.h"

void CCountArray::SetArray(int value)
{
    criticalSection.Lock();

    for (int x=0; x<10; ++x)
        array[x] = value;

    criticalSection.Unlock();
}

void CCountArray::GetArray(int dstArray[10])
{
    criticalSection.Lock();

    for (int x=0; x<10; ++x)
        dstArray[x] = array[x];

    criticalSection.Unlock();
}
```

Now that you've had a chance to see what a thread-safe class looks like, it's time to put the class to work. Perform the following steps, which modify the Thread application to test the CCountArray class:

1. Use the File, New command to add a new C++ header file called CountArray.h to the project, as shown in Figure 27.9. Enter the code from Listing 27.6.

FIG. 27.9

Add CountArray.h to the Thread project.

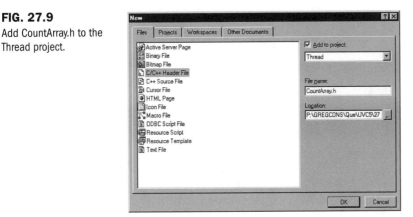

2. Again choose File, New, and create a new C++ source file called CountArray.cpp in this project. Enter the code from Listing 27.7.

3. Switch to ThreadView.cpp and then add the following line near the top of the file, after the line `#include "afxmt.h"`, which you placed there previously:

   ```
   #include "CountArray.h"
   ```

4. Add the following line near the top of the file, after the `CEvent threadEnd` line you placed there previously:

   ```
   CCountArray countArray;
   ```

5. Delete the `CEvent threadStart` and `CEvent threadEnd` lines from the file.

6. Delete the lines `ON_MESSAGE(WM_THREADENDED, OnThreadended)`, `ON_COMMAND(ID_STOPTHREAD, OnStopthread)`, and `ON_WM_CREATE()` from the message map.

7. Replace the `ThreadProc()` function with the thread functions shown in Listing 27.8.

Part
VII

Ch
27

Listing 27.8 *mdWriteThreadProc()* and *ReadThreadProc()*

```
UINT WriteThreadProc(LPVOID param)
{
    for(int x=0; x<10; ++x)
    {
        countArray.SetArray(x);
        ::Sleep(1000);
    }

    return 0;
}
```

continues

Listing 27.8 Continued

```
UINT ReadThreadProc(LPVOID param)
{
    int array[10];

    for (int x=0; x<20; ++x)
    {
        countArray.GetArray(array);
        char str[50];
        str[0] = 0;
        for (int i=0; i<10; ++i)
        {
            int len = strlen(str);
            wsprintf(&str[len], "%d ", array[i]);
        }
        ::MessageBox((HWND)param, str, "Read Thread", MB_OK);
    }

    return 0;
}
```

8. Replace all of the code in the `OnStartthread()` function with the following lines:
```
HWND hWnd = GetSafeHwnd();
AfxBeginThread(WriteThreadProc, hWnd);
AfxBeginThread(ReadThreadProc, hWnd);
```

9. Delete the `OnStopthread()`, `OnThreadended`, and `OnCreate()` functions from the file.

10. Switch to the ThreadView.h file and delete the line const `WM_THREADENDED = WM_USER + 100` from the listing.

11. Also in ThreadView.h, delete the lines `afx_msg LONG OnThreadended(WPARAM wParam, LPARAM lParam)`, `afx_msg void OnStopthread()` and `afx_msg int OnCreate(LPCREATESTRUCT lpCreateStruct)` from the message map.

12. Using the resource editor, remove the Stop Thread command from the Thread menu.

Now build and run the new version of the Thread application. When you do, the main window appears. Select the Thread, Start Thread command to gets things hopping. The first thing you'll then see is a message box (see Figure 27.10) displaying the current values in the guarded array. Each time you dismiss the message box, it reappears with the new contents of the array. The message box will reappear 20 times. The values you see listed in the message box depend upon how often you dismiss the message box. The first thread is writing new values into the array once a second, even as you're viewing the array's contents in the second thread.

The important thing to notice is that at no time does the second thread interrupt when the first thread is changing the values in the array. You can tell that this is true because the array always contains ten identical values. If the first thread was interrupted as it modified the array,

FIG. 27.10

This message box displays the current contents of the guarded array.

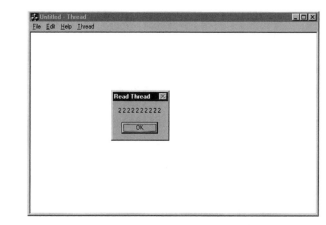

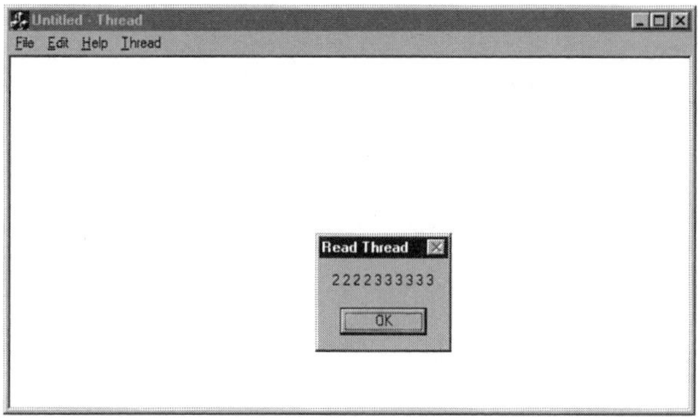

the ten values in the array would not be identical, as shown in Figure 27.11.

If you examine the source code carefully, you'll see that the first thread, named WriteThreadProc(), is calling the array class's SetArray() member function ten times within a for loop. Each time through the loop, SetArray() gives the thread the critical-section object, changes the array contents to the passed number, and then takes the critical-section object away again. Note the call to the Sleep() function, which suspends the thread for the number of milliseconds given as the function's single argument.

The second thread, named ReadThreadProc(), is also trying to access the same critical-section object in order to construct a display string of the values contained in the array. But if WriteThreadProc() is currently trying to fill the array with new values, ReadThreadProc() has to wait. The inverse is also true. That is, WriteThreadProc() can't access the guarded data until it can regain ownership of the critical section from ReadThreadProc().

If you really want to prove that the critical-section object is working, remove the criticalSection.Unlock() line from the end of the CCountArray class's SetArray() member function. Then compile and run the program. This time when you start the threads, no message box appears. Why? Because WriteThreadProc() takes the critical-section object and

Part

VII

Ch

27

FIG. 27.11

Without thread synchronization, you might see something like this in the message box.

never lets it go, which forces the system to suspend `ReadThreadProc()` forever (or at least until you exit the program).

Using Mutexes

Mutexes are a lot like critical sections but are a little more complicated, because they enable safe sharing of resources not only between threads in the same application, but also between threads of different applications. Although synchronizing threads of different applications is beyond the scope of this chapter, you can get a little experience with mutexes by using them in place of critical sections.

Listing 27.9 is the `CCountArray2` class's header file. Except for the new class name and the mutex object, this header file is identical to the original CountArray.h. Listing 27.10 is the modified class's implementation file. As you can see, the member functions look a lot different when they are using mutexes instead of critical sections, even though both objects provide essentially the same type of services.

Listing 27.9 CCOUNTARRAY2.H—The *CCountArray2* Class's Header File

```
#include "afxmt.h"

class CCountArray2
{
private:
    int array[10];
    CMutex mutex;

public:
    CCountArray2() {};
    ~CCountArray2() {};

    void SetArray(int value);
    void GetArray(int dstArray[10]);
};
```

Listing 27.10 COUNTARRAY2.CPP—The *CCountArray2* Class's Implementation File

```
#include "stdafx.h"
#include "CountArray2.h"

void CCountArray2::SetArray(int value)
{
    CSingleLock singleLock(&mutex);
    singleLock.Lock();

    for (int x=0; x<10; ++x)
        array[x] = value;
```

```
    }

void CCountArray2::GetArray(int dstArray[10])
{
    CSingleLock singleLock(&mutex);
    singleLock.Lock();

    for (int x=0; x<10; ++x)
        dstArray[x] = array[x];
}
```

In order to access a mutex object, you must create a CSingleLock or CMultiLock object, which performs the actual access control. The CCountArray2 class uses CSingleLock objects, because this class is dealing with only a single mutex. When the code is about to manipulate guarded resources (in this case, the array), you create a CSingleLock object, like this:

```
CSingleLock singleLock(&mutex);
```

The constructor's argument is a pointer to the thread-synchronization object that you want to control. Then, to gain access to the mutex, you call the CSingleLock object's Lock() member function:

```
singleLock.Lock();
```

If the mutex is unowned, the calling thread becomes the owner. If another thread already owns the mutex, the system suspends the calling thread until the mutex is released, at which time the waiting thread is awakened and takes control of the mutex.

To release the mutex, you call the CSingleLock object's Unlock() member function. However, if you create your CSingleLock object on the stack (rather than on the heap, using the new operator) as shown in Listing 29.10, you don't have to call Unlock() at all. When the function exits, the object goes out of scope, which causes its destructor to execute. The destructor automatically unlocks the object for you.

To try out the new CCountArray2 class in the Thread application, add new CountArray2.h and CountArray.cpp files to the Thread project and then delete the original CountArray.h and CountArray.cpp files. Finally, in ThreadView.cpp, change all references to CCountArray to CCountArray2. Because all the thread synchronization is handled in the CCountArray2 class, no further changes are necessary in order to use mutexes rather than critical sections. Convenient, eh?

Part VII
Ch 27

Using Semaphores

Although semaphores are used like critical sections and mutexes in an MFC program, they serve a slightly different function. Rather than allowing only one thread to access a resource at a time, semaphores allow multiple threads to access a resource, but only to a point. That is, semaphores allow a maximum number of threads to access a resource simultaneously.

When you create the semaphore, you tell it how many threads should be allowed simultaneous access to the resource. Then, each time a thread grabs the resource, the semaphore decrements its internal counter. When the counter reaches 0, no further threads are allowed access to the guarded resource until another thread releases the resource, which increments the semaphore's counter.

You create a semaphore by supplying the initial count and the maximum count, like this:

```
CSemaphore Semaphore(2, 2);
```

Because, in this section, you'll be using a semaphore to create a thread-safe class, it's actually more convenient to declare a CSemaphore pointer as a data member of the class and then create the CSemaphore object dynamically in the class's constructor, like this:

```
semaphore = new CSemaphore(2, 2);
```

You should do this because you have to initialize a data member in the constructor rather than at the time you declare it. With the critical-section and mutex objects, you didn't have to supply arguments to the class's constructors, so you were able to create the object at the same time you declared it.

Once you have the semaphore object created, it's ready to start counting resource access. To implement the counting process, you first create a CSingleLock (or CMultiLock, if you're dealing with multiple thread-synchronization objects) object, giving it a pointer to the semaphore you want to use, like this:

```
CSingleLock singleLock(semaphore);
```

Then, to decrement the semaphore's count, you call the CSingleLock object's Lock() member function:

```
singleLock.Lock();
```

At this point, the semaphore object has decremented its internal counter. This new count remains in effect until the semaphore object is released, which you can do explicitly by calling the object's Unlock() member function:

```
singleLock.Unlock();
```

Alternatively, if you've created the CSingleLock object locally on the stack, you can just let the object go out of scope, which not only automatically deletes the object but also releases the hold on the semaphore. In other words, both calling Unlock() and deleting the CSingleLock object increments the semaphore's counter, enabling a waiting thread to access the guarded resource.

Listing 27.11 is the header file for a class called CSomeResource. CSomeResource is a mostly useless class whose only calling is to demonstrate the usage of semaphores. The class has a single data member, which is a pointer to a CSemaphore object. The class also has a constructor and destructor, as well as a member function called UseResource(), which is where the semaphore will be used.

Listing 27.11 SOMERESOURCE.H

```
#include "afxmt.h"

class CSomeResource
{
private:
    CSemaphore* semaphore;

public:
    CSomeResource();
    ~CSomeResource();

    void UseResource();
};
```

Listing 27.12 shows the CSomeResource class's implementation file. You can see that the CSemaphore object is constructed dynamically in the class's constructor and deleted in the destructor. The UseResource() member function simulates accessing a resource by attaining a count on the semaphore and then sleeping for five seconds, after which the hold on the semaphore is released when the function exits and the CSingleLock object goes out of scope.

Listing 27.12 SOMERESOURCE.CPP

```
#include "stdafx.h"
#include "SomeResource.h"

CSomeResource::CSomeResource()
{
    semaphore = new CSemaphore(2, 2);
}

CSomeResource::~CSomeResource()
{
    delete semaphore;
}

void CSomeResource::UseResource()
{
    CSingleLock singleLock(semaphore);
    singleLock.Lock();

    Sleep(5000);
}
```

Part

VII

Ch

27

If you modify the Thread application to use the CSomeResource object, you can watch semaphores at work. Follow these steps:

1. Delete any CountArray files that are still in the project.
2. Create the new empty SomeResource.h and SomeResource.cpp files in the project.

3. Add the code from Listings 27.11 and 27.12 to these empty files.

4. Load ThreadView.cpp and replace the line #include "CountArray2.h" with the following:

```
#include "SomeResource.h"
```

5. Replace the line CCountArray2 countArray with the following:

```
CSomeResource someResource;
```

6. Replace the WriteThreadProc() and ReadThreadProc() functions with the functions shown in Listing 27.13.

Listing 27.13 **ThreadProc1(), ThreadPrco2(), and ThreadProc3()**

```
UINT ThreadProc1(LPVOID param)
{
    someResource.UseResource();

    ::MessageBox((HWND)param,
        "Thread 1 had access.", "Thread 1", MB_OK);

    return 0;
}

UINT ThreadProc2(LPVOID param)
{
    someResource.UseResource();

    ::MessageBox((HWND)param,
        "Thread 2 had access.", "Thread 2", MB_OK);

    return 0;
}

UINT ThreadProc3(LPVOID param)
{
    someResource.UseResource();

    ::MessageBox((HWND)param,
        "Thread 3 had access.", "Thread 3", MB_OK);

    return 0;
}
```

7. Replace the code in the OnStartthread() function with that shown in Listing 27.14.

Listing 27.14 **LST27_14.TXT—New Code for the OnStartthread() Function**

```
HWND hWnd = GetSafeHwnd();
AfxBeginThread(ThreadProc1, hWnd);
AfxBeginThread(ThreadProc2, hWnd);
AfxBeginThread(ThreadProc3, hWnd);
```

Now compile and run the new version of the Thread application. When the main window appears, select the Thread, Start Thread command. In about five seconds, two message boxes will appear informing you that Thread one and Thread two had access to the guarded resource. About five seconds after that, a third message box will appear, telling you that Thread three also had access to the resource. Thread three took five seconds longer because Thread one and Thread two grabbed control of the resource first. The semaphore is set to allow only two simultaneous resource accesses, so Thread three had to wait for Thread one or Thread two to release its hold on the semaphore.

N O T E Although the sample programs in this chapter have demonstrated using a single thread-synchronization object, you can have as many synchronization objects as you need in a single program. You can even use critical sections, mutexes, and semaphores all at once in order to protect different data sets and resources in different ways. ▪

From Here...

For complex applications, threads offer the ability to keep data processing moving along fast and efficiently. You no longer have to wait for one part of the program to finish its task before moving on to something else. For example, a spreadsheet application could use one thread to update the calculations while the main thread continues accepting entries from the user. Using threads, however, leads to some interesting problems, not the least of which is the need to control access to shared resources. Writing a threaded application requires some thought and careful consideration of how the threads will be used and what resources they'll access.

For more information on related topics, please refer to the following chapters:

- Chapter 4, "Messages and Commands," can give you some review on how MFC applications process Windows messages with message maps.
- Chapter 24, "Improving Your Application's Performance," offers a number of techniques for writing faster and more robust programs.

Part
VII

Ch
27

CHAPTER 28

Future Explorations

There are a number of topics that have not been covered elsewhere in this book, but that are well known to experienced Visual C++ programmers. They are best explored once you have experience with Developer Studio, MFC, and C++ programming. This chapter has just enough to show you how interesting these topics are, and to encourage you to explore them yourself in the months and years to come. ■

Creating console applications

A console application is not a Window program. It runs a character-based, non-GUI interface.

32-bit Dlls

Follow the example program to see how easy writing and using 32-bit DLLs can be.

Sending messages and commands

An integral part of an event driven operating system like Windows is its Messaging capability. This section shows how to extend that capability with messages of your own devising.

International issues and the Unicode standard

Unicode is a 2-byte character set standard enabling programs to work with international languages whose alphabet requires more than 8-bits of storage. MFC makes support for Unicode easy, and this section shows how.

Creating Console Applications

A console application looks very much like a DOS application, though it runs in a resizable window. It has a strictly character-based interface with cursor keys rather than mouse movement. You use the Console API and character based I/O functions like `printf()` and `scanf()` to interact with the user.

Creating a Console Executable

A console application is still executed from the DOS command line or by choosing Start, Run and typing the full name of the application. Console applications are probably still among the easiest programs to create and this version of the compiler supports them directly.

Let's walk together through the few steps necessary to create a basic console application and then we'll explore some beneficial uses of creating these kinds of applications. The first console application we'll create is a spin on the classic 'Hello, World!' that Kernighan and Ritchie (the creators of C++'s ancestor C) created in the 1970s.

Open the Microsoft Developer Studio and follow these steps to create a console application:

1. In the Microsoft Developer Studio, select File, New.
2. In the New dialog box, click the Projects tab to bring up the now familiar New Project dialog box. (If it isn't familiar, go back to Chapter 1, "Building Your First Application.")
3. Name the project HelloWorld, set an appropriate folder for the project, and choose `Win32 Console Application` from the list on the left.
4. Click OK.

The project is created immediately: no wizard dialog boxes appear and there are no further questions to answer. Now you need to create source and header files and add them to the project. This sample will all fit in one file. Follow these steps:

1. Select File, New from the file menu and click the File tab.
2. Leave the Add To Projectbox selected; the new file will be added to the project.
3. Choose C++ Source File from the box on the left.
4. Enter HelloWorld as the filename—the extension .cpp will be added automatically.
5. The New dialog box should resemble Figure 28.1. Click OK.

A blank text file is created and named for you, and added to the project, all in one step. This is a big improvement from previous versions of Visual C++, where you created a file with a name like Text1, renamed it to HelloWorld.cpp (or whatever name you wished) and then added it to the project.

Add the code in Listing 28.1 to the new file.

FIG. 28.1
Create a C++ source file for your console application.

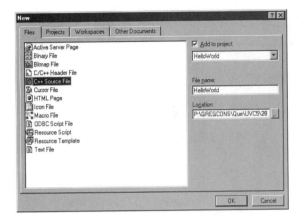

Listing 28.1 HelloWorld.Cpp

```cpp
#include <iostream.h>
int main()
{
    cout << "Hello from the console!"<< endl;
    return 0;
}
```

Choose Build, Go to compile, link, and execute the program. You should see a DOS box appear that resembles Figure 28.2. The line `Press any key to continue` is generated by the system and gives you a chance to read your output before the DOS box disappears.

FIG. 28.2
Your application appears to be a DOS program.

Part
VII

Ch
28

Writing an Object-Oriented Console Application

The HelloWorld application is clearly C++ and would not compile in a C compiler, which does not support stream based I/O with cout, but it's not object oriented—there's not an object in it. Replace the code in HelloWorld.cpp with the lines in Listing 28.2.

Listing 28.2   HelloWorld.Cpp—With Objects

```
// HelloWorld.cpp
//

#include <iostream.h>
#include <afx.h>

class Hello
{
private:
    CString message;

public:
    Hello();
    void display();
};

Hello::Hello()
{
    message = "Hello from the console!";
}

void Hello::display()
{
    cout << message << endl;
}

int main()
{
    Hello hello;
    hello.display();

    return 0;

}
```

Now this is an object-oriented program, and what's more it uses CString, an MFC class. To do so it must include <afx.h>. If you build the project now, you will get linker error messages that refer to _beginthreadex and _endthreadex. By default, console applications are single-threaded, but MFC is multithreaded. By including afx.h and bringing in MFC, this application is making itself incompatible with the single-threaded default. To fix this, choose Project Settings and click the C/C++ tab. From the drop-down box at the top of the dialog box, choose Code Generation. In the drop-down list box labeled Use Runtime Library, choose Debug Multithreaded. (The completed dialog box is shown in Figure 28.3.) Click OK, and rebuild the project.

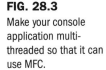

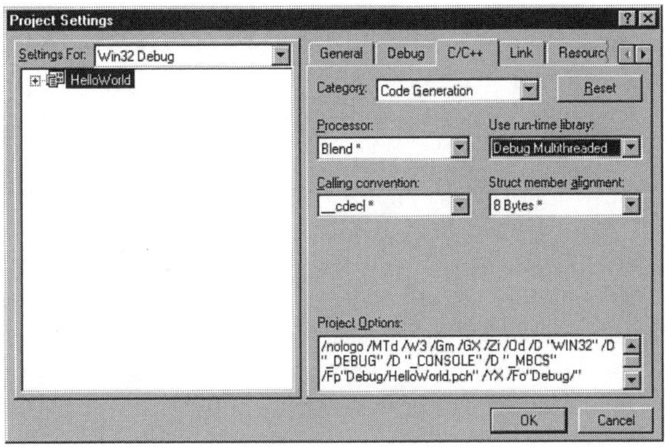

FIG. 28.3

Make your console application multi-threaded so that it can use MFC.

The output of this object-oriented program is just like that of the previous program—this is just a sample. But you see that console applications can use MFC, can be built around objects, and can be quite small. They must have a `main()` function and it is this function that is called by the operating system when you run the application.

NOTE Although this application is small, Visual C++ creates a lot of overhead files. The Debug directory occupies about 6.5M, of which almost a full megabyte is HelloWorld.exe. The rest is the MFC libraries—they aren't small. ■

Scaffolding Discrete Algorithms

The best argument for anyone to build a DOS application these days is to *scaffold* small code fragments or single objects. This refers to building a temporary framework around the code you want to test. (Some developers call this a *test harness*.) The simplest possible framework is a console application like the one you just built.

To scaffold an object or function, you should do the following:

1. Create a new console application just for the scaffolding process.
2. Add a `main()` function to the .CPP file you plan to scaffold.
3. Include the header file for the object or function to be tested.
4. Write code that exercises the function or object in a variety of test cases and include it in `main()`.

Having followed those steps, you can now test the code thoroughly, focusing only on the performance characteristics and correctness of this small piece of your large project. Scaffolding holds true to the canon of software development which states: "Design in the large and program in the small."

By applying a scaffold to any algorithm you are helping to ensure the accuracy in the small. Remember there are additional benefits involved too: by placing the scaffold code directly into the module you are clearly documenting that the code has been tested, and how to use it. You make it available for further testing, debugging, or extending at a later date.

Part
VII

Ch
28

Creating and Using a 32-Bit Dynamic Link-Library

Dynamic-link libraries (DLLs) are the backbone of the Windows 95 and Windows NT operating systems. Windows 95 uses Kernel32.Dll, User32.Dll, and Gdi32.Dll to perform the vast majority of its work, and you can use them as well. The Microsoft Visual C++ On-line Books are a good source of information for API functions found in these three DLLs.

Another tool for poking around in Windows applications is the DumpBin utility in \MSDEV\BIN. This utility is a command line program that shows you the imports and exports of executable files and dynamic link libraries. The following listing is an excerpted example of the output produced when using DumpBin to examine the executable file for Spy++, one of the utilities provided with Visual C++.

Listing 28.3   Output from Dumpbin

```
dumpbin -imports spyxx.exe
Microsoft (R) COFF Binary File Dumper Version 3.00.5270
Copyright (C) Microsoft Corp 1992-1995. All rights reserved.

Dump of file spyxx.exe

File Type: EXECUTABLE IMAGE

        Section contains the following Imports

            USER32.dll
                167    LoadCursorA
                135    GetWindowTextA
                1DF    SetDlgItemTextW
                153    IsChild
                 D7    GetClassLongA
                 D8    GetClassLongW
                 C5    FillRect
                165    LoadBitmapA
                16B    LoadIconA
                 E6    GetDC
                1F4    SetRectEmpty
                15B    IsRectEmpty
                1F3    SetRect
                141    InflateRect
                1FE    SetTimer
                162    KillTimer
                1CF    SetActiveWindow
                249    wsprintfA
                 80    DeleteMenu
                122    GetSystemMenu
                1A1    PeekMessageA
                100    GetLastActivePopup
                  2    AdjustWindowRectEx
                  4    AppendMenuA
                 51    CreatePopupMenu
                 C1    EnumWindows
```

B1	EnumChildWindows
188	MessageBoxA
206	SetWindowPlacement
A	BringWindowToTop
197	OffsetRect
132	GetWindowPlacement
13A	GetWindowWord
15E	IsWindowUnicode
243	WinHelpA
DF	GetClipboardFormatNameA
12F	GetWindowDC
160	IsZoomed
1B9	ReleaseDC
D0	GetCapture
33	ClientToScreen
246	WindowFromPoint
1D8	SetCursor
237	UpdateWindow
12D	GetWindow
15F	IsWindowVisible
E8	GetDesktopWindow
204	SetWindowLongA
1B8	ReleaseCapture
1D0	SetCapture
1A8	PtInRect
F0	GetFocus
120	GetSysColor
CB	FrameRect
9B	DrawFocusRect
F9	GetKeyState
187	MessageBeep
22C	TranslateMessage
8C	DispatchMessageA
159	IsIconic
1	AdjustWindowRect
133	GetWindowRect
1BF	ScreenToClient
C2	EqualRect
148	InvalidateRect
DC	GetClientRect
123	GetSystemMetrics
15C	IsWindow
D9	GetClassNameA
130	GetWindowLongA
D3	GetClassInfoA
1A3	PostMessageA
20E	SetWindowsHookExA
22E	UnhookWindowsHookEx
7D	DefWindowProcA
139	GetWindowThreadProcessId
1AF	RegisterClipboardFormatA
DB	GetClassWord
86	DestroyWindow
1AB	RegisterClassA
52	CreateWindowExA

Part

VII

Ch

28

continues

Listing 28.3   Continued

```
            AB    EnableWindow
            1C6   SendMessageA
            115   GetParent
            1E2   SetForegroundWindow
            232   UnpackDDElParam
            216   ShowWindow
Summary

    10000  .data
     3000  .idata
     8000  .rdata
     8000  .reloc
     F000  .rsrc
    36000  .text
```

As you can see, the utility program Spy++ uses the User32.Dll extensively.

You can call the Windows DLLs in any of your programs and more importantly, you can write DLLs of your own.

Making a 32-Bit DLL

There are two kinds of DLLs in Visual C++: those that use MFC and those that do not. Each kind of DLL has its own AppWizard, as you will see shortly.

If you gather three or four functions into a DLL, your DLL *exports* those functions for other programs to use. Quite often a DLL will also *import* functions from other DLLs to get its work done.

Importing and Exporting Functions   To designate a symbol as exportable, use the following syntax:

```
__declspec(dllexport) data_type int var_name; // for variables
```

or

```
__declspec(ddlexport) return_type func_name( [argument_list ] ); // for functions
```

Importing functions is almost identical: simply replace the keyword tokens,
`__declspec(dllexport)` with `__declspec(dllimport)`. Using an actual function and variable to demonstrate the syntax this time:

```
__declspec(dllimport) int referenceCount;
__declspec(dllimport) void DiskFree( lpStr Drivepath );
```

T I P   Two underscores precede the keyword `__declspec`.

By convention Microsoft uses a header file and a preprocessor macro to make the inclusion of DLL declarations much simpler. The technique simply requires that you make a preprocessor token using a unique token—the header file name works easily, and requires very little in the way of memorization—and define a macro which will replace the token with the correct import or export statement. Thus, assuming a header file named DISKFREE.H, the preprocessor macro in the header file would be as follows:

Listing 28.4 Diskfree.h

```
// DISKFREE.H - Contains a simpler function for returning the
amount of free disk space.
// Copyright (c) 1996. All Rights Reserved.
// By Paul Kimmel. Okemos, MI USA
#ifndef __DISKFREE_H
#define __DISKFREE_H

#ifndef __DISKFREE__
#define DISKFREELIB __declspec(dllimport)
#else
#define DISKFREELIB __declspec(dllexport)
#endif
// Use the macro to control an import or export declaration.
DISKFREELIB unsigned long DiskFree( unsigned int drive ); // (e.g.
o = A:, 1 = B:, 2 = C:
#endif
```

Simply by including the header file you can let the preprocessor decide whether DiskFree is being imported or exported. Now you can share the header file for the DLL developer and the DLL user, and that means less maintenance headaches.

Creating the DiskFree DLL   The DiskFree utility provides a simple way to determine the amount of free disk space for any given drive. The underlying functionality is the `GetDiskFreeSpace()` function found in Kernel32.Dll.

To create a non-MFC DLL, choose File, New, click the Projects tab, select Win32 DLL from the list on the left, and enter DiskFree for the project name, as shown in Figure 28.4. Click OK and the project is created with no files in it.

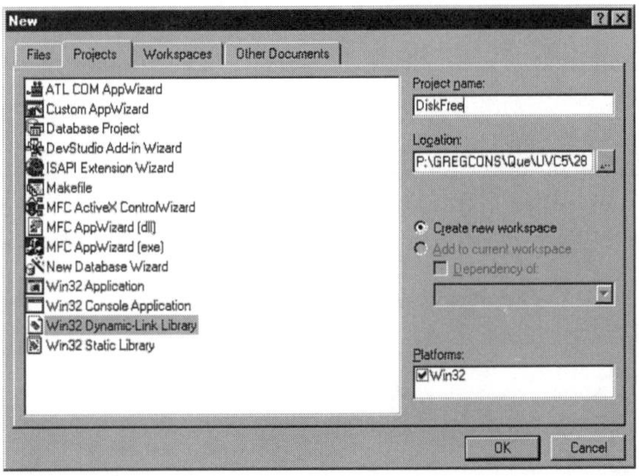

FIG. 28.4
Creating a non-MFC DLL project is a one-step process.

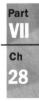

Part
VII

Ch
28

Add a C++ header file called DiskFree.h and type in the code from Listing 28.5. Add a C++ source file called DiskFree.cpp and type in the code from Listing 28.6 (or copy these files from the CD.)

Listing 28.5   DiskFree.h

```
#ifndef __DISKFREE_H
#define __DISKFREE_H
#ifndef __DISKFREE__
#define __DISKFREELIB__ __declspec(dllimport)
#else
#define __DISKFREELIB__ __declspec(dllexport)
#endif
// Returns the amount of free space on drive number (e.g. 0 = A:,
1= B:, 2 = c:)
__DISKFREELIB__ unsigned long DiskFree( unsigned int drive );
#endif
```

Listing 28.6   DiskFree.Cpp

```
#include <afx.h>
#include <winbase.h>      // Contains the kernel32 GetDiskFreeSpace declaration.
#define __DISKFREE__      // Define the token before the inclusion of the library
#include "diskfree.h"
// Returns the amount of free space on drive number (e.g. 0 = A:, 1= B:, 2 = c:)
__DISKFREELIB__ unsigned long DiskFree( unsigned int drive )
{
    unsigned long bytesPerSector, sectorsPerCluster,
        freeClusters, totalClusters;
    char DrivePath[4] = { char( drive + 65 ), ':', '\\', '\0' };
    if( GetDiskFreeSpace( DrivePath, &sectorsPerCluster,
        &bytesPerSector, &freeClusters, &totalClusters ))
    {
        return sectorsPerCluster * bytesPerSector * freeClusters;
    }
    else
    {
        return 0;
    }
}
```

Change the Code Generation settings to Multithreaded Debug as discussed in the Console Applications section earlier in this chapter, and build the DLL. In the next section you will see how to use 32-bit DLLs in general, and how Windows finds DLLs on your system.

The most common use of a DLL is to provide extended, reusable functionality and let Windows implicitly load the DLL. Topics that will not be discussed in this book, that you might want to explore for yourself, include:

- Dynamic versus static linking of MFC.
- Implicit versus explicit DLL loading, which requires the use of LoadLibrary and FreeLibrary.
- Multithreading DLLs.
- Sharing data across DLL boundaries.
- Calling conventions for DLLs that will be used by other languages (__stdcall, WINAPI, …).

In this chapter you are going to use a default compile of DiskFree, using an implicit DllMain (the compiler added one), and an implicit loading of the DLL, allowing Windows to manage loading and unloading the library.

Using 32-Bit DLLs

Many DLLs are loaded implicitly and their loading and unloading is managed by Windows. Libraries loaded in this fashion are searched for like executables: first the directory of the application loading the DLL is searched, followed by the current directory, the Windows\System directory, the Windows directory and finally each directory specified in the PATH.

It is a common practice to place a DLL in the Windows or Windows\System directories once the application is shipped, but in the meantime you may use the development directory of the executable for temporary storage. One thing to safeguard against is that you do not end up with multiple versions of the DLL in each of the Windows, Windows\System, or project directories.

Using a DLL   Implicitly loading and using a DLL is about as simple as using any other function. This is especially true if you created the header file as described in the "Creating the DiskFree DLL" section. When you compile your DLL, Microsoft Visual C++ creates a .LIBfile. (So, DISKFREE.DLL has a DISKFREE.LIB created by the compiler.) The library (.LIB) file is used to resolve the load address of the DLL and specify the full pathname of the dynamic link library, and the header file provides the declaration.

All you have to do is include the header in the file using the DLL functionality and add the .LIB name to the Project, Settings dialog box, on the Link tab (see Figure 28.5), in the Object/library modules edit field.

Part
VII

Ch
28

FIG. 28.5

Add your LIB file to the project settings.

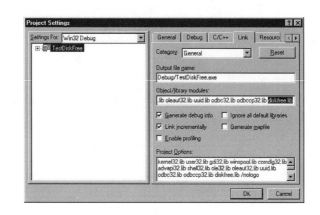

To test the DiskFree DLL, create a console application called TestDiskFree and add a C++ source file called TestDiskFree.cpp. Add the code from Listing 28.7 to this file. Copy DiskFree.h to this folder and add it to the project by choosing Project, Add To Project, Files, and selecting DiskFree.h. Copy DiskFree.Dll and DiskFree.Lib to the TestDiskFree folder also. (You'll find them in DiskFree\Debug.) Change the project settings as just described, and build the project.

Listing 28.7   TestDiskFree.Cpp

```
#include <afx.h>
#include <iostream.h>
#include "diskfree.h"
#define CodeTrace(arg) \
     cout << #arg << endl;\
     arg
int main()
{
     CodeTrace( cout << DiskFree(2) << endl );
     return 0;
}
```

This code brings in the DLL by including diskfree.h, and then uses it. The CodeTrace macro simply prints out a line of code before executing it. All that this application does is call the DiskFree() function to ask how much space is free on drive 2. Drive 0 is a:, drive 1 is b: and drive 2 is c:. If you build and execute the program you should see output like Figure 28.6.

According to TestDiskFree, the C: drive on the machine used for these samples has almost 400 M of free disk space. This number is correct. Now you can write real functions in a DLL, and use them or make them available to other people to use.

FIG. 28.6

Your little application calls the DLL.

Sending Messages and Commands

As discussed in Chapter 4, "Messages and Commands," messages are the heart of Windows. Everything that happens in a Windows application happens because a message showed up to make it happen. When you move your mouse and click a button, a huge number of messages are generated, including WM_MOUSEMOVE for each movement of the mouse, WM_LBUTTONDOWN when the button goes down, WM_LBUTTONCLICK when the button is released, and higher level, more abstract messages like the WM_COMMAND message with the button's resource ID as one of its parameters. You can ignore the lower-level messages if you wish and many programmers do.

What you may not know is that *you* can generate messages, too. There are two functions that generate messages: CWnd::SendMessage() and CWnd::PostMessage(). Each of these gets a message to an object that inherits from CWnd. An object that wants to send a message to a window using one of these functions must have a pointer to the window, and the window must be prepared to catch the message. A very common approach to this situation is to have a member variable in the sending object that stores a pointer to the window that will receive the message and another that stores the message to be sent:

```
CWnd* m_messagewindow;
UINT m_message;
```

Messages are represented by unsigned integers. They appear to have names only because names like WM_MOUSEMOVE are connected to integers with #define statements.

The sending class has a member function to set these member variables, typically very short:

```
void Sender::SetReceiveTarget(CWnd *window, UINT message)
{
    m_messagewindow = window;
    m_message = message;
}
```

When the sending class needs to get a message to the window, it calls SendMessage:

```
m_messagewindow->SendMessage(m_message, wparam, lparam);
```

Or PostMessage:

```
m_messagewindow->PostMessage(m_message, wparam, lparam);
```

Part
VII

Ch
28

The difference between sending and posting a message is that SendMessage() does not return until the message has been handled by the window that received it, but PostMessage() just adds the message to the message queue and returns right away. If, for example, you build an object, pass that object's address as the lparam, and then delete the object, you should choose SendMessage(), because you can't delete the object until you are sure that the message-handling code has finished with it. If you are not passing pointers you can probably use PostMessage() and move on as soon as the message has been added to the queue.

The meaning of the wparam and lparam values depends on the message you are sending. If it is a defined system message like WM_MOUSEMOVE, you can read the online documentation to learn what the parameters are. If, as is more likely, you are sending a message that you have invented, the meaning of the parameters is entirely up to you. You are the one who is inventing this message, and writing the code to handle it when it arrives at the other window.

To invent a message, add a defining statement to the header file of the class that will catch it:

```
#define WM_HELLO WM_USER + 300
```

WM_USER is an unsigned integer that marks the start of the range of message numbers available for user defined messages. In this release of MFC, its value is 0x4000, though you should not depend on that. User defined messages have message numbers between WM_USER and 0x7FFF.

Then add a line to the message map, in both the header and source file, outside the ClassWizard comments. The source file message map might look like this:

```
BEGIN_MESSAGE_MAP(CMainFrame, CMDIFrameWnd)
    //{{AFX_MSG_MAP(CMainFrame)
        // NOTE - the ClassWizard will add and remove mapping macros here.
        //    DO NOT EDIT what you see in these blocks of generated code !
    //}}AFX_MSG_MAP
    ON_MESSAGE(WM_HELLO, OnHello)
END_MESSAGE_MAP()
```

The entry added outside the //AFX_MSG_MAP comments catches the WM_HELLO message and arranges for the OnHello() function to be called. The header file message map might look like this:

```
// Generated message map functions
protected:
    //{{AFX_MSG(CMainFrame)
    afx_msg int OnCreate(LPCREATESTRUCT lpCreateStruct);
        // NOTE - the ClassWizard will add and remove member functions here.
        //    DO NOT EDIT what you see in these blocks of generated code!
    //}}AFX_MSG
    afx_msg LRESULT OnHello(WPARAM wParam, LPARAM lParam);
    DECLARE_MESSAGE_MAP()
```

Then you add an implementation of OnHello() to the source file to complete the process.

Considering International Software Development Issues

International boundaries are shrinking at incredible rates. As access to wider serial communications widens and the preponderance of discrete resalable components continues, more and more demands for pieces built by vendors world-wide will grow. Even in-house software development will less frequently be able to ignore international markets. The rise in popularity of the Internet has expanded the reach of many developers into countries where languages other than English and character sets other than ASCII predominate. This means your applications should be able to communicate with users in languages other than English, and in characters sets other than the typical Western character set.

Microcomputers were created in the United States which explains why we have 8-bit character based operating systems. There are only 26 letters in our alphabet and ten digits, which leaves plenty of room (about 220 characters worth) for punctuation and other miscellaneous characters. But countries like Japan and China require a character set in the thousands.

Unicode is one way to tackle the character set problem. The Unicode standard was developed and is supported by a consortium of some of the biggest players in the international computing markets. Among these are Adobe, Aldus, Apple, Borland, Digital, IBM, Lotus, Microsoft, Novell, and Xerox.

Unicode uses two bytes for each character, whereas ASCII uses only one. One byte (8-bits) can represent 2^8 or 256 characters. Two bytes (16-bits) can represent 65,536 characters. This is enough not just for one language, but for all the character sets in general use. For example, the Japanese character set, one of the largest, needs about 5000 characters. Most require far less. The Unicode specification sets aside different ranges for different character sets and can cover almost every language on Earth in one universal code—a Unicode.

MFC has full Unicode support, with Unicode versions of almost every function. For example, consider the function CWnd::SetWindowText(). It takes a string and sets the title of the window, or the caption of a button, to that string. What kind of string it takes depends on whether you have Unicode support turned on in your application. In reality, there are two different functions to set the window text one, a Unicode version and a non-Unicode version, and in WINUSER.H, the block of code shown in Listing 28.8 changes the function name that you call to SetWindowTextA if you are not using Unicode, or SetWindowTextW if you are.

Listing 28.8   Microsoft's WINUSER.H Implementing Unicode Support

```
WINUSERAPI BOOL WINAPI SetWindowTextA(HWND hWnd, LPCSTR lpString);
WINUSERAPI BOOL WINAPI SetWindowTextW(HWND hWnd, LPCWSTR lpString);

#ifdef UNICODE
#define SetWindowText   SetWindowTextW
#else
#define SetWindowText   SetWindowTextA
#endif // !UNICODE
```

Part

VII

Ch

28

The difference between these two functions is the type of the second parameter: LPCSTR for the A version and LPCWSTR for the W (Wide) version.

If you are using Unicode, whenever you pass a literal string (like "Hello") to a function, wrap it in the _T macro, like this:

```
pWnd->SetWindowText(_T("Hello"));
```

If you can deal with the annoyance of wrapping all text strings in _T macros, just like that your application is Unicode aware. When you prepare your Greek or Japanese version of the application, life will be much simpler.

N O T E Windows 95 was built on old Windows, so it was not built using Unicode. This means that if you use Unicode in your Windows 95 programs, you are going to suffer performance penalties because the Windows 95 kernel will have to convert Unicode strings back to ordinary strings. Windows NT was designed at Microsoft from scratch, so is completely compatible with Unicode.

If you are developing for several platforms with C++ and using Unicode, your Win95 version may seem sluggish in comparison to the Windows NT version. ▓

From Here...

This chapter demonstrated the way to build a console application, with or without MFC. You also learned how to use a dynamic-link library (DLL) and how to create your own DLL, and how to send custom messages to another part of your application. Finally, you learned how to ready your applications for the international market with Unicode.

To learn about related topics see:

- ▓ Chapter 4, "Messages and Commands," for an introduction to the importance of messages and how message maps work.
- ▓ Chapter 26, "Exceptions, Templates, and the Latest Additions to C++" for other advanced programming topics.

Appendixes

Windows Programming Review and a Look Inside *CWnd*

**The Microsoft Foundation Classes were written for one single purpose: to make Windows programming easier by providing classes with methods and data that handle tasks common to all Windows programs. The classes that are in MFC are designed to be useful to a Windows programmer specifically. The methods within each class perform tasks that Windows programmers often need to perform. Many of the classes have a close correspondence to structures and "window classes" in the old Windows sense of the word class. Many of the methods correspond closely to API (Application Programming Interface) functions that are already familiar to Windows programmers. ■

Windows programming review
A brief review of Windows programming in C for those who haven't done it recently.

API functions: what they are, why you should care
The useful functions provided to Windows C programmers are still used by C++ programmers, but they are wrapped up inside MFC classes that call the API functions for you.

The MFC classes arranged by category
An overview of the chapters that discuss various categories of MFC classes.

Programming for Windows

If you've programmed for Windows in C, you know that the word *class* was used to describe the definition of a window long before C++ programming came to Windows. A window class is vital to any Windows C program. A standard structure holds the data that describes this window class, and a number of standard window classes are provided by the operating system. A programmer usually builds a new window class for each program and registers it by calling an API function, `RegisterClass()`. Windows that appear on the screen can then be created, based on that class, by calling another API function, `CreateWindow()`.

A C-style windows class

The WNDCLASS structure, which describes the window class, is equivalent to the WNDCLASSA structure, shown in Listing A.1.

Listing A.1   *WNDCLASSA* Structure from WINUSER.H

```
typedef struct tagWNDCLASSA {
    UINT        style;
    WNDPROC     lpfnWndProc;
    int         cbClsExtra;
    int         cbWndExtra;
    HINSTANCE   hInstance;
    HICON       hIcon;
    HCURSOR     hCursor;
    HBRUSH      hbrBackground;
    LPCSTR      lpszMenuName;
    LPCSTR      lpszClassName;
} WNDCLASSA, *PWNDCLASSA, NEAR *NPWNDCLASSA, FAR *LPWNDCLASSA;
```

WINUSER.H sets up two very similar window class structures, WNDCLASSA for programs that use normal strings, and WNDCLASSW for Unicode programs. Unicode programs are covered in Chapter 28, "Future Explorations," in the "Unicode" section.

 T I P   WINUSER.H is code supplied with Developer Studio. It's typically in the folder \Program Files\DevStudio\VC\include.

If you were creating a Windows program in C, you would need to fill a WNDCLASS structure. The members of the WNDCLASS structure are as follows:

- `style`—A number made by combining standard styles, represented with `constants` like `CS_GLOBALCLASS` or `CS_OWNDC`, with the bitwise OR operator (|). A perfectly good class can be registered with a style value of 0; the other styles are for exceptions to normal procedure.

- ▓ `lpfnWndProc`—A pointer to a function that is the Windows Procedure (generally called the WindProc) for the class. This function is discussed in Chapter 4, "Messages and Commands."

- ▓ `cbClsExtra`—How many extra bytes to add to the window class. Usually 0, but C programmers would sometimes build a window class with extra data in it.

- ▓ `cbWndExtra`—How many extra bytes to add to each instance of the window. Usually 0.

- ▓ `hInstance`—A handle to an instance of an application, the running program that is registering this window class. For now, just think of this as a way that the window class can reach the application that uses it.

- ▓ `hIcon`—An icon to be drawn when the window is minimized. Typically this is set with a call to another API function, `LoadIcon()`.

- ▓ `hCursor`—The cursor to be displayed when the mouse is over the screen window associated with this window class. Typically this is set with a call to the API function `LoadCursor()`.

- ▓ `hbrBackground`—The brush to be used for painting the background of the window. The API call `GetStockObject()` is the usual way to set this variable.

- ▓ `lpszMenuName`—A long pointer to a string that is zero terminated and contains the name of the menu for the window class.

- ▓ `lpszClassName`—The name for this window class, to be used by `CreateWindow()`, when a window (an instance of the window class) is created. You would make a name up.

Window Creation

If you've never written a Windows program before, you might be quite intimidated by having to fill out a `WNDCLASS` structure. But this is the first step in Windows programming in C. However, you can always find simple sample programs to copy, like this one:

```
WNDCLASS wcInit;

wcInit.style = 0;
wcInit.lpfnWndProc = (WNDPROC)MainWndProc;
wcInit.cbClsExtra = 0;
wcInit.cbWndExtra = 0;
wcInit.hInstance = hInstance;
wcInit.hIcon = LoadIcon (hInstance, MAKEINTRESOURCE(ID_ICON));
wcInit.hCursor = LoadCursor (NULL, IDC_ARROW);
wcInit.hbrBackground = GetStockObject (WHITE_BRUSH);
wcInit.lpszMenuName = "DEMO";
wcInit.lpszClassName ="NewWClass";

return (RegisterClass (&wcInit));
```

Hungarian Notation

You might wonder what kind of variable name `lpszClassName` is. You also might wonder why it is `wcInit` and not just `Init`. Microsoft programmers use a variable naming convention called *Hungarian Notation*. It is so named because it was popularized at Microsoft by a Hungarian programmer named Charles Simonyi, and probably because at first glance, the variable names seem to be written in another language.

In Hungarian Notation, the variable is given a descriptive name, like `Count` or `ClassName`, that starts with a capital letter. If it is a multi-word name, each word is capitalized. Then, before the descriptive name, letters are added to indicate the type of the variable—for example, `nCount` for an integer, or `bFlag` for a Boolean (True or False) variable. In this way the programmer should never forget a variable type, or do something foolish like passing a signed variable to a function that is expecting an unsigned value.

The style has gained widespread popularity, though some people hate it. If you long for the good old days of arguing where to put the brace brackets, or better still whether to call them brace, face, or squiggle brackets, but can't find anyone to rehash those old wars any more, you can probably find somebody to argue about Hungarian Notation instead. The arguments in favor boil down to "you catch yourself making stupid mistakes" and the arguments against to "it's ugly and hard to read." But the practical truth is that the structures used by the API and the classes defined in MFC all use Hungarian Notation, so you might as well get used to it. You'll probably find yourself doing it for your own variables too. The prefixes are as follows:

Prefix	Variable Type	Comment
a	Array	
b	Boolean	
d	Double	
h	Handle	
i	Integer	"index into"
l	Long	
lp	Long pointer to	
lpfn	Long pointer to function	
m_	Member variable	
n	Integer	"number of"
p	Pointer to	
s	String	
sz	Zero terminated string	
u	Unsigned integer	
C	Class	

Many people add their own type conventions to variable names; the `wc` in `wcInit` stands for window class.

Filling the `wcInit` structure and calling RegisterClass is fairly standard stuff, registering a class called `NewWClass` with a menu called DEMO and a WindProc called MainWndProc. Everything else about it is ordinary to an experienced Windows C programmer. After registering the class, when those old-time Windows programmers wanted to create a window on the screen, out popped some code like this:

```
HWND hWnd;
hInst = hInstance;
hWnd = CreateWindow (
"NewWClass",
"Demo 1",
WS_OVERLAPPEDWINDOW,
CW_USEDEFAULT,
CW_USEDEFAULT,
CW_USEDEFAULT,
CW_USEDEFAULT,
NULL,
NULL,
hInstance,
NULL);

if (! hWnd)
return (FALSE);

ShowWindow (hWnd, nCmdShow);
UpdateWindow (hWnd);
```

This code calls `CreateWindow()`, then `ShowWindow()`, and `UpdateWindow()`. The parameters to the API function `CreateWindow()` are as follows:

- `lpClassName`—A pointer to the class name that was used in the `RegisterClass()` call.

- `lpWindowName`—The window name. You make this up.

- `dwStyle`—The window style, made by combining `#define` constants with the | operator. For a primary application window like this one, `WS_OVERLAPPEDWINDOW` is standard.

- `x`—The horizontal position of the window. `CW_USEDEFAULT` lets the operating system calculate sensible defaults based on the user's screen settings.

- `y`—The vertical position of the window. `CW_USEDEFAULT` lets the operating system calculate sensible defaults based on the user's screen settings.

- `nWidth`—The width of the window. `CW_USEDEFAULT` lets the operating system calculate sensible defaults based on the user's screen settings.

- `nHeight`—The height of the window. `CW_USEDEFAULT` lets the operating system calculate sensible defaults based on the user's screen settings.

- `hWndParent`—The handle of the parent or owner window. (Some windows are created by other windows, which own them.) `NULL` means there is no parent to this window.

- `hMenu`—The handle to a menu or child-window identifier, in other words a window owned by this window. `NULL` means there are no children.

■ `hInstance`—The handle of application instance that is creating this window.

■ `lpParam`—A pointer to any extra parameters. None are needed in this example.

`CreateWindow()` returns a window handle—everybody calls their window handles `hWnd`—and this handle is used in the rest of the standard code. If it's `NULL`, the window creation failed. If the handle returned has any non-`NULL` value, the creation succeeded and the handle is passed to `ShowWindow()` and `UpdateWindow()`, which together draw the actual window on the screen.

Handles

A *handle* is more than just a pointer. Windows programs refer to resources like windows, icons, cursors, and so on with a handle. Behind the scenes there is a handle table that tracks the address of the resource as well as information about the resource type. It's called a handle because a program uses it as a way to "get hold of" a resource. Handles are typically passed around to functions that need to use resources, and returned from functions that allocate resources.

There are a number of basic types of handles: `hWnd` for a window handle, `HICON` for an icon handle, and so on. No matter what kind of handle is being used, remember it's a way to reach a resource so that you can use it.

Encapsulating the Windows API

API functions create and manipulate windows on the screen, handle drawing, connect programs to Help files, facilitate threading, manage memory, and much more. When these functions are encapsulated into MFC classes, your programs can accomplish these same basic Windows tasks, with less work on your part.

There are literally thousands of API functions, and it can take six months to a year to get a good handle on the API, so this book does not attempt to present a mini-tutorial on the API. In the "Programming for Windows" section earlier in this chapter you were reminded about two API functions, `RegisterClass()` and `CreateWindow()`. These form a good illustration of what was difficult about C Windows programming with the API, and how the MFC classes make it easier. Documentation on the API functions is available from inside Visual C++: Click the InfoViewer tab in the Workspace pane, and expand the Platform SDK topic. Within that topic, expand Reference, Functions, and finally Win32 Functions to display a list of alphabetical categories such as ArrangeIconicWindows to CloseClipboard. Functions are arranged alphabetically within these categories. There are also index entries that will lead to specific functions.

Inside *CWnd*

`CWnd` is a hugely important MFC class. Roughly a third of all the MFC classes use it as a base class—classes like `CDialog`, `CEditView`, `CButton`, and many more. It serves as a wrapper for the old style windows class and the API functions that create and manipulate window classes. For example, the only public member variable is `m_hWnd`, the member variable that stores the window handle. This variable is set by the member function `CWnd::Create()` and used by almost all the other member functions when they call their associated API functions.

You might think that the call to the API function CreateWindow() would be handled automatically in the CWnd constructor, CWnd::CWnd, so that when the constructor is called to initialize a CWnd object the corresponding window on the screen is created. This would save you, the programmer, a good deal of effort, because you can't forget to call a constructor. In fact, that's not what Microsoft has chosen to do. The constructor looks like this:

```
CWnd::CWnd()
{
 AFX_ZERO_INIT_OBJECT(CCmdTarget);
}
```

AFX_ZERO_INIT_OBJECT is just a macro, expanded by the C++ compiler's preprocessor, that uses the C function memset to zero out every byte of every member variable in the object, like this:

```
#define AFX_ZERO_INIT_OBJECT(base_class) [ccc]
 memset(((base_class*)this)+1, 0, sizeof(*this) [ccc]
 - sizeof(class base_class));
```

The reason why Microsoft chose not to call CreateWindow() in the constructor is that constructors cannot return a value. If something goes wrong with the window creation, there are no elegant or neat ways to deal with it. Instead, the constructor does almost nothing, a step that essentially cannot fail, and the call to CreateWindow() is done from within the member function Cwnd::Create(), or the closely related CWnd::CreateEx(), which looks like the one in Listing A.2:

Listing A.2 CWnd::CreateEx() from WINCORE.CPP

```
BOOL CWnd::CreateEx(DWORD dwExStyle, LPCTSTR lpszClassName,
 LPCTSTR lpszWindowName, DWORD dwStyle,
 int x, int y, int nWidth, int nHeight,
 HWND hWndParent, HMENU nIDorHMenu, LPVOID lpParam)
{
 // allow modification of several common create parameters
 CREATESTRUCT cs;
 cs.dwExStyle = dwExStyle;
 cs.lpszClass = lpszClassName;
 cs.lpszName = lpszWindowName;
 cs.style = dwStyle;
 cs.x = x;
 cs.y = y;
 cs.cx = nWidth;
 cs.cy = nHeight;
 cs.hwndParent = hWndParent;
 cs.hMenu = nIDorHMenu;
 cs.hInstance = AfxGetInstanceHandle();
 cs.lpCreateParams = lpParam;

 if (!PreCreateWindow(cs))
 {
 PostNcDestroy();
 return FALSE;
 }
```

Listing A.2 Continued

```
AfxHookWindowCreate(this);
HWND hWnd = ::CreateWindowEx(cs.dwExStyle, cs.lpszClass,
cs.lpszName, cs.style, cs.x, cs.y, cs.cx, cs.cy,
cs.hwndParent, cs.hMenu, cs.hInstance, cs.lpCreateParams);

#ifdef _DEBUG
 if (hWnd == NULL)
 {
 TRACE1("Warning: Window creation failed: [ccc]
 GetLastError returns 0x%8.8X\n",
 GetLastError());
 }
#endif

 if (!AfxUnhookWindowCreate())
 PostNcDestroy();
 // cleanup if CreateWindowEx fails too soon

 if (hWnd == NULL)
 return FALSE;
 ASSERT(hWnd == m_hWnd); // should have been set in send msg hook
 return TRUE;
 }
```

> **TIP**
> WINCORE.CPP is code supplied with Developer Studio. It's typically in the folder \Program Files\DevStudio\VC\mfc\src.

This sets up a `CREATESTRUCT` structure very much like a `WNDCLASS`, and fills it with the parameters that were passed to `CreateEx()`. It calls `PreCreateWindow`, `AfxHookWindowCreate()`, `::CreateWindow()`, and `AfxUnhookWindowCreate()` before checking `hWnd` and returning.

> **TIP**
> The AFX prefix on many useful MFC functions dates back to the days when Microsoft's internal name for their class library was Application Framework. The `::` in the call to `CreateWindow` identifies it as an API function, sometimes referred to as an SDK function in this context. The other functions are member functions of `CWnd` that set up other background boilerplates for you.

So, on the face of it, there doesn't seem to be any savings here. You declare an instance of some `CWnd` object, call its `Create()` function, and have to pass just as many parameters as you did in the old C way of doing things. What's the point? Well, `CWnd` is really a class from which to inherit. Things get much simpler in the derived classes. Take `CButton`, for example, a class that encapsulates the concept of a button on a dialog box. A button is just a tiny little window, but its behavior is constrained — for example the user cannot resize a button. Its `Create()` member function looks like this:

```
BOOL CButton::Create(LPCTSTR lpszCaption, DWORD dwStyle,
 const RECT& rect, CWnd* pParentWnd, UINT nID)
{
```

```
CWnd* pWnd = this;
return pWnd->Create(_T("BUTTON"), lpszCaption, dwStyle, rect, pParentWnd, nID);
}
```

Those are a lot fewer parameters. If you want a button, you create a button, and let the class hierarchy fill in the rest.

Getting a Handle on all These MFC Classes

There are over 200 MFC classes. Why so many? What do they do? How can any normal human keep track of them and know which one to use for what? Good questions. Questions that will take a pretty large piece of this book to answer. The first half of this book presents the most commonly used MFC classes. This section looks at some of the more important base classes.

CObject

Figure A.1 shows a high-level overview of the inheritance tree for the classes in MFC. Only a handful of MFC classes do not inherit from CObject. Cobject contains the basic functionality that all the MFC classes (and most of the new classes you create) will be sure to need, like persistence support and diagnostic output. As well, classes derived from CObject can be contained in the MFC container classes, discussed in Reference E, "Useful Classes."

FIG. A.1
Almost all the classes in MFC inherit from CObject.

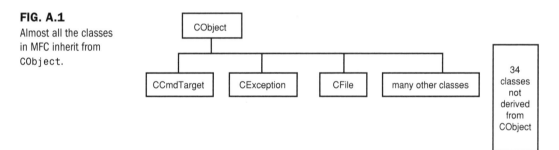

CCmdTarget

Some of the classes that inherit from CObject, like CFile and CException and their derived classes, do not need to interact directly with the user and the operating system through messages and commands. All the classes that do need to receive messages and commands inherit from CCmdTarget. Figure A.2 shows a bird's eye view of CCmdTarget's derived classes, generally called command targets.

CWnd

As already mentioned, CWnd is a hugely important class. Only classes derived from CWnd can receive messages; threads and documents can receive commands but not messages.

FIG. A.2
Any class that will
receive a command
must inherit from
CCmdTarget.

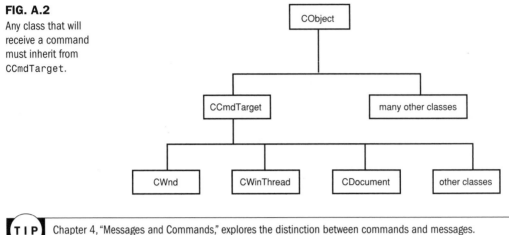

> **TIP** Chapter 4, "Messages and Commands," explores the distinction between commands and messages.
> Chapter 5, "Documents and Views," explains documents, and Chapter 27, "Multitasking with Windows
> Threads," explains threads.

Cwnd provides window-oriented functionality like calls to CreateWindow and DestroyWindow,
functions to handle painting the window in the screen, processing messages, talking to the
Clipboard, and much more—almost 250 member functions in all. Only a handful of these will
need to be overridden in derived classes. Figure A.3 shows the classes that inherit from CWnd;
there are so many control classes that to list them all would clutter up the diagram, so they are
lumped together as control classes.

All Those Other Classes

So you've seen ten classes so far on these three figures. What about the other 200+? You'll meet
them in context, throughout the book. If there's a specific class you were wondering about,
check the index. Check the online help, too, because every class is documented there. And
don't forget, the full source for MFC is included with every copy of Visual C++. Reading the
source is a hard way to figure out how a class works, but sometimes you need that level of
detail.

FIG. A.3
Any class that will
receive a message
must inherit from
CWnd, which provides
lots of window-related
functions.

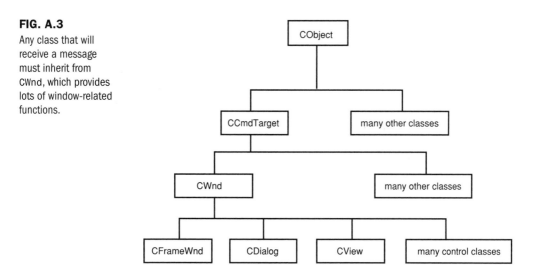

The Developer Studio User Interface

When you buy Microsoft Visual C++, you actually get Microsoft Developer Studio with the Visual C++ component activated. Developer Studio is far more than just a compiler, and you have far more to learn than you may think. The interface is very visual, which means that there are many possibilities greeting you when you first run Visual C++. ■

The components of Developer Studio

Developer Studio is more than just a compiler.

The project workspace window

This tabbed window makes it simple and fast to access any part of your application.

The Info view

Find your way around Books Online.

The Resource view

Access menus, dialog boxes, bitmaps, and other user interface resources.

The Class view

See all your classes and their variables and functions. See at a glance whether a variable is public or private, or double-click a function to jump to its source code.

The File view

Organize your files and open them easily.

The output window and status bar

At the bottom of the screen, these areas inform you and provide results.

The code editor

This is where the work gets done: You type in code, fix mistakes, and watch your application take shape.

Reviewing Developer Studio: An Integrated Development Environment

Microsoft Visual C++ is one component of the Microsoft Developer Studio. The capabilities of this one piece of software are astonishing. It is called an *integrated development environment* (IDE) because within a single tool, you can perform the following:

■ Read documentation and Books Online.

■ Generate starter applications without writing code.

■ View a project several different ways.

■ Edit source and include files.

■ Build the visual interface (menus and dialog boxes) of your application.

■ Compile and link.

■ Debug an application while it runs.

Visual C++ is, technically speaking, just one component of Developer Studio. You can buy, for example, Microsoft's Visual J++ compiler and use it in Developer Studio as well. Looking at it another way, Visual C++ is more than just Developer Studio, because the *Microsoft Foundation Classes* (MFC) that are becoming the standard for C++ Windows programming are a class library and not related to the development environment. In fact, the major C++ compilers all use MFC now. However, for most people, Visual C++ and Developer Studio mean the same thing, and in this book the names are used interchangeably.

Choosing a View

The user interface of Developer Studio is very visual, encouraging you to move from view to view of your project: looking at your resources, classes, and files, or checking the online documentation. The main screen is divided into panes that you can resize to suit your own needs. There are many shortcut menus, reached by right-clicking different places on the screen, to simplify common tasks.

With Visual C++, you work on a single application as a project. A *project* is a collection of files: source, headers, resources, settings, and configuration information. Developer Studio is designed to enable work on all aspects of a single project at once. You create a new application by creating a new project. When you want to work on your application, you open the project (a file with the extension .dsw) rather than opening each code file independently. The interface of Developer Studio, shown in Figures B.1 and B.2, is designed to work with a project and is divided into several zones.

FIG. B.1

The Developer Studio interface presents a lot of information. The Project Workspace window is on the left.

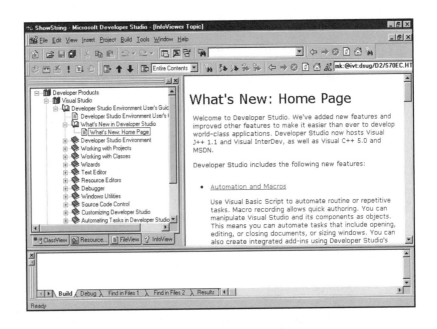

FIG. B.2

When the Project Workspace window is narrowed, the words on the tabs are replaced with icons.

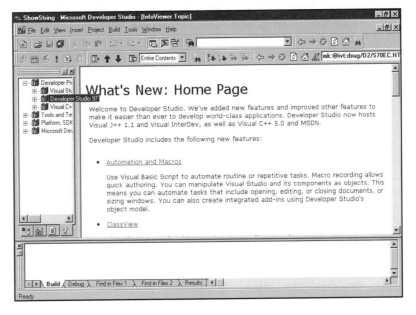

The zones that make up the Developer Studio interface are as follows:

- Across the top: menus and toolbars. These are discussed in the second half of this chapter.

- On the left: the Project Workspace window.

■ On the right: your main working area where you edit files or read documentation.

■ Across the bottom: the output window and status bar.

TIP Open Developer Studio and try to resize the panes and follow along as functions are described in this chapter.

The Project Workspace window determines which way you look at your project, and what is in the main working area: documentation, code files, or resources (menus, icons, and dialog boxes). Each of these views is discussed in detail in a separate section in this chapter, including the following:

■ The InfoView is discussed in the "Looking at Documentation" section.

■ The ResourceView is discussed in the "Looking at Interface Elements" section.

■ The ClassView is discussed in the "Looking at Your Code, Arranged by Class" section.

■ The FileView is discussed in the "Looking at Your Code, Arranged by File" section.

Developer Studio uses two different files to keep track of all the information about your project. The *project workspace file*, with a .dsw extension, contains the names of all the files in the project, what directories they are in, compiler and linker options, and other information required by everyone who may work on the project. There is also a *project file*, with a .dsp extension, for each project within the workspace. The *workspace options file*, with a .opt extension, contains all your personal settings for Developer Studio—colors, fonts, toolbars, which files are open and how their MDI windows are sized and located, breakpoints from your most recent debugging session, and so on. If someone else is going to work on your project, you give that person a copy of the project workspace file and project file but not the project options file.

To open the project, open the project workspace file. The other files are opened automatically.

NOTE Earlier versions of Visual C++ used .mdp files to store project information. When you open an old file, you are asked if it should be converted to the new format. The conversion process creates .dsw, .dsp, and .opt files for you and does not delete your old files. ■

Looking at Documentation

When you first start Developer Studio and no project is open, the only tab in the Project Workspace window is the InfoView tab. When a project is open, there are other tabs to choose from. Clicking the InfoView tab brings a table of contents into the Project Workspace window and an InfoViewer topic window into the main working area, as shown in Figures B.1 and B.2. The table of contents is an outline that can be expanded or collapsed. Double-clicking an entry in the table of contents displays that entry in the InfoViewer topic window.

TIP If your Project Workspace window is too narrow for reading the topic headings in the table of contents, you can scroll the window with the horizontal scroll bar. You can also pause the mouse cursor over any topic heading, and a small box like a ToolTip appears showing the full heading for the topic.

Within the InfoViewer topic window, documentation is displayed as hypertext. Words and phrases that are highlighted act as links; clicking a link displays different information. The documentation is written in HTML and is displayed just as it would be in Microsoft Internet Explorer, the Web browser from Microsoft. While most of the links lead to other help topics on your hard drive or CD, some of them lead out onto the Internet for the very latest information.

App

B

TIP Your settings in Microsoft Internet Explorer affect how InfoViewer in Developer Studio displays documentation. For example, if you turn off image display in Explorer, images will not be displayed in InfoViewer until you click them.

By default, the InfoViewer window is maximized to fill the entire working area, and the title bar of Developer Studio has InfoViewer Topic added to it. By clicking the Restore button under the main Restore button for all of Developer Studio, you can arrange the InfoViewer MDI window within the main working area. This allows you to compare two help topics or a help topic and a piece of code. Figure B.3 shows the InfoViewer window restored. The topic window can also be minimized.

FIG. B.3

The InfoViewer topic window does not have to be maximized.

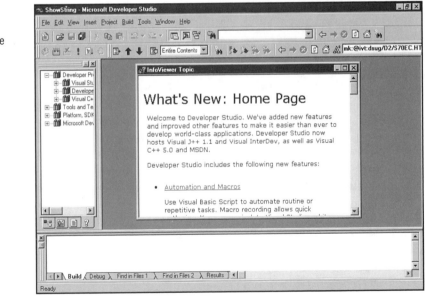

FIG. B.4

The InfoViewer topic window has a number of shortcuts available on the right-click menu.

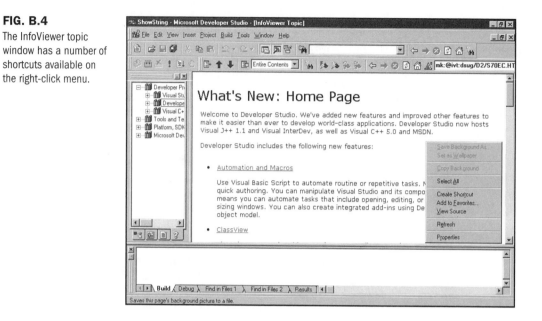

Many InfoViewer commands are on the Help menu or the InfoViewer toolbar, both discussed in the second half of this chapter. There is a shortcut menu, reached by right-clicking anywhere within the InfoViewer topic window. As shown in Figure B.4, it features commands that are commonly used when looking at a page of HTML in Microsoft Internet Explorer, and is not very useful while using Visual C++.

Looking at Interface Elements

Clicking the ResourceView tab in the Project Workspace window brings up an expandable and collapsible outline of the visual elements of your program: accelerators, dialog boxes, icons, menus, the string table, toolbars, and version information. These resources define the way users interact with your program. Chapter 2, "Dialog Boxes and Controls;" Chapter 9, "Building a Complete Application: ShowString;" and Chapter 10, "Status Bars and Toolbars" cover the work involved in creating and editing these resources. The next few sections cover the way in which you can look at completed resources.

TIP Open one of the projects on the CD that comes with this book, or a sample project from Visual C++, and follow along as functions are described in this section. ShowString, the sample application from Chapter 9, "Building a Complete Application: ShowString," is a good choice since it uses most of the features described in this section.

Accelerators

Accelerators associate key combinations with menu items. Figure B.5 shows an accelerator resource created by AppWizard. All of these accelerator combinations are made for you when you create a new application. You can add hot keys for specific menu items, if necessary.

FIG. B.5
Accelerators associate key combinations with menu items.

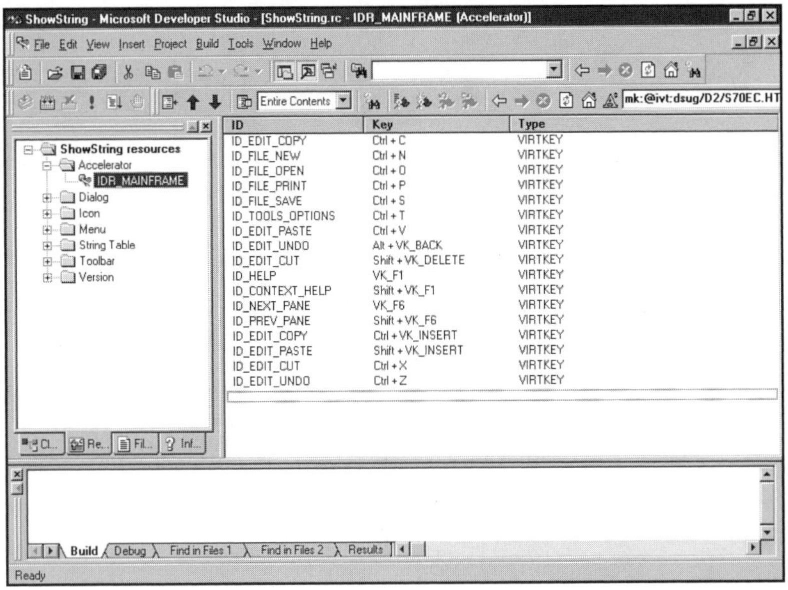

Dialog Boxes

Dialog boxes are the way your application gets information from users. When a dialog resource is being displayed in the main working area, as in Figure B.6, a control palette floats over the working area. (If it's not displayed, right-click the menu bar and check Controls to display it.) Each small icon on the palette represents a control (edit box, list box, button, and so on) that can be inserted onto your dialog box. By choosing View, Properties, the Properties box shown in Figure B.6 is displayed. Here the behavior of a control or of the whole dialog box can be controlled.

> **TIP** Click the pushpin at the top left of the Properties box to keep it displayed even when a different item is highlighted. The box displays the properties of each item you click.

This method of editing dialog boxes is one of the reasons for the name Visual C++. In this product, if you want a button to be a little lower on a dialog box, you click it with the mouse, drag it to the new position, and release the mouse button. Similarly, if you want the dialog box larger or smaller, grab a corner or edge and drag it to the new size just like any other sizable window. Before Visual C++ was released, the process would have involved coding and pixel counting and taken many minutes rather than just a few seconds. This visual approach to dialog box building made Windows programming accessible to many more programmers.

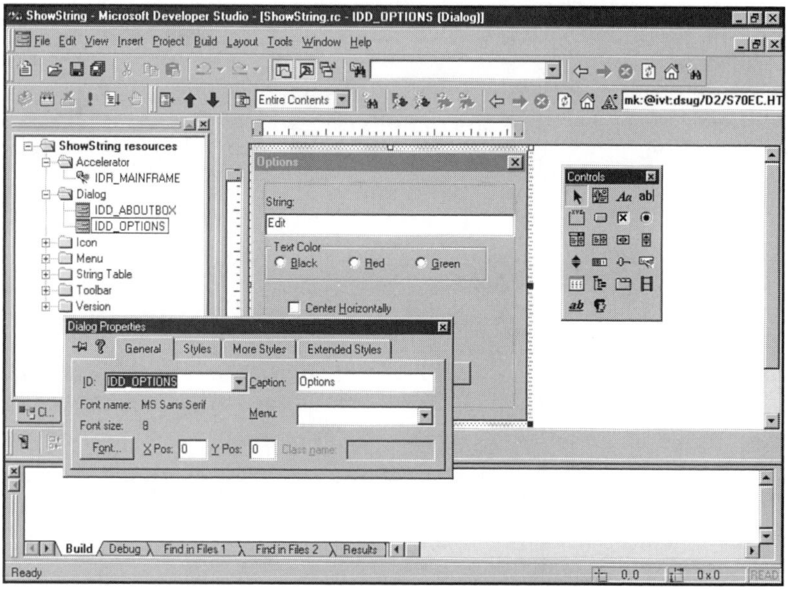

FIG. B.6

Dialog boxes get information from the user.

Icons

Icons are small bitmaps that represent your program or its documents. For example, when a program is minimized, an icon is used to represent it. A larger version of that icon is used to represent both the program and its documents within an Explorer window. And when an MDI window is minimized within your application, the minimized window is represented by an icon. Figure B.7 shows the default icon provided by AppWizard for minimized MDI windows. One of your first tasks after building any application is to replace this with an icon that more clearly represents the work your program performs.

An icon is a 32×32 pixel bitmap that can be edited with any number of drawing tools, including the simple bitmap editor included in Developer Studio. The interface is very similar to Microsoft Paint or Microsoft Paintbrush in Zoom mode. You can draw one pixel at a time by clicking, or freehand lines by clicking and dragging. You can work on the small or zoomed versions of the icon and see the effects at once in both places.

FIG. B.7

Icons represent your application and its documents.

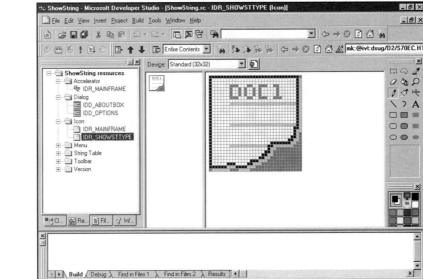

Menus

Menus are the way that users tell your program what to do. *Keyboard shortcuts* (accelerators) are linked to menu items, as are toolbar buttons. AppWizard creates the standard menus for a new application, and you edit those and create new ones in this view. Later, you'll use ClassWizard to connect menu items to functions within your code. Figure B.8 shows a menu displayed in the resource view. Choose <u>V</u>iew, Pro<u>p</u>erties to display the properties box for the menu item. Every menu item has the following three components:

- *Resource ID*. This uniquely identifies this menu item. Accelerators and toolbar buttons are linked to resource IDs. The convention is to build the ID from the menu choices that lead to the item. In Figure B.8, the resource ID is ID_FILE_OPEN.

- *Caption*. This is the text that appears for a menu choice. In Figure B.8, the caption is &Open...\tCtrl+O. The & means that the O will appear underlined, and the menu item can be selected by typing <u>O</u> when the menu is displayed. The \t is a tab, and the Ctrl+O is the accelerator for this menu item, as defined in Figure B.5.

- *Prompt*. A prompt appears in the status bar when the highlight is on the menu item or the cursor is over the associated toolbar button. In Figure B.8, the prompt is Open an existing document\nOpen. Only the portion before the newline (\n) is displayed in the status bar. The second part of the prompt, Open, is the text for the tool tip that appears if the user pauses the mouse over a toolbar button with this resource ID. All of this functionality is provided for you automatically by the framework of Visual C++ and MFC.

FIG. B.8

Menus are the way your application receives commands.

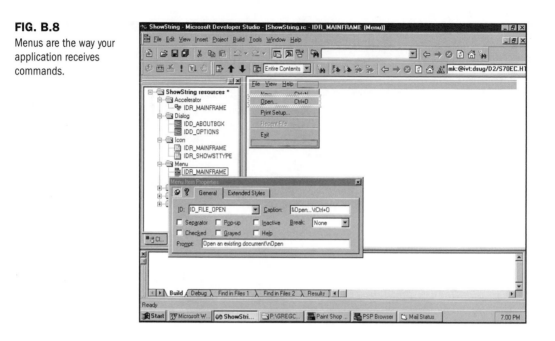

The String Table

The *string table* is a list of strings within your application. Many strings, such as the static text on dialog boxes or the prompts for menu items, can be accessed in far simpler ways than through the string table, but some are reached only through it. For example, a default name or value can be kept in the string table and changed without recompiling any code, though the resources will have to be compiled and the project linked. Each of these could be hard coded into the program, but then changes would require a full recompile.

Figure B.9 shows the string table for a sample application. To change a string, bring up the Properties dialog box and change the caption. Strings cannot be changed within the main working area.

FIG. B.9

The string table stores all the prompts and text in your application.

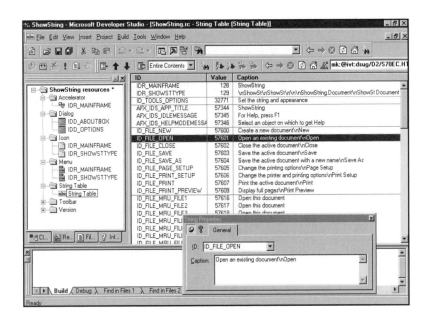

Toolbars

Toolbars are the lines of small buttons typically located directly underneath the menus of an application. Each button is linked to a menu item, and its appearance depends on the state of the menu item. If a menu item is grayed, the corresponding toolbar button is grayed as well. If a menu item is checked, the corresponding toolbar button is typically drawn as a pushed-in button. In this way, toolbar buttons serve as indicators as well as mechanisms for giving commands to the application.

A toolbar button has two parts: a bitmap of the button and a resource ID. When a user clicks the button, it is just as though the menu item with the same resource ID was chosen. Figure B.10 shows a typical toolbar and the properties of the File, Open button on that toolbar. In this view, you can change the resource ID of any button, and edit the bitmap with the same tools used to edit icons.

FIG. B.10

Toolbar buttons are associated with menu items through a resource ID.

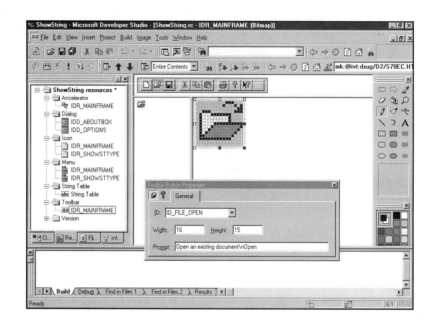

Version Information

Good installation programs use the version information resource when installing your application on a user's machine. For example, if a user is installing an application that has already been installed, the installation program may not have to copy as many files. It may alert the user if an old version is being installed over a new version, and so on.

When you create an application with AppWizard, version information like that in Figure B.11 is generated for you automatically. Before attempting to change any of it, make sure you understand how installation programs use it.

FIG. B.11
Version information
is used by install
programs.

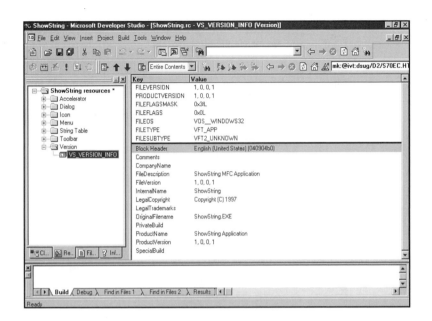

Looking at Your Code, Arranged by Class

The ClassView shows the classes in your application. Under each class, the member variables
and functions are shown, as demonstrated in Figure B.12. Member functions are shown first
with a purple icon next to them, followed by member variables with a turquoise icon. Protected
members have a key next to the icon, while private members have a padlock.

FIG. B.12
The ClassView shows
the functions and
variables in each class
of your application.

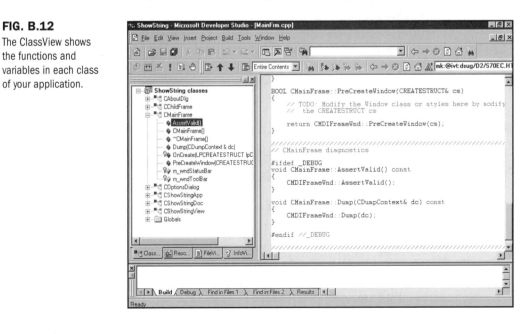

Double-clicking a function name brings up the source for that function in the main working area. Double-clicking a variable name brings up the header file in which the variable is declared.

Right-clicking a class name brings up a shortcut menu, shown in Figure B.13, with these items:

FIG. B.13

Common commands related to classes are on the ClassView shortcut menu for a class.

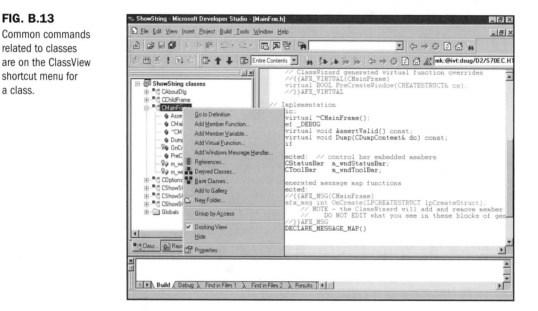

- *Go to Definition*. Opens the header (.h) file at the definition of this class.

- *Add Member Function*. Opens the Add Member Function dialog box shown in Figure B.14. This adds a declaration of the function to the header file and the stub of a definition to the source file.

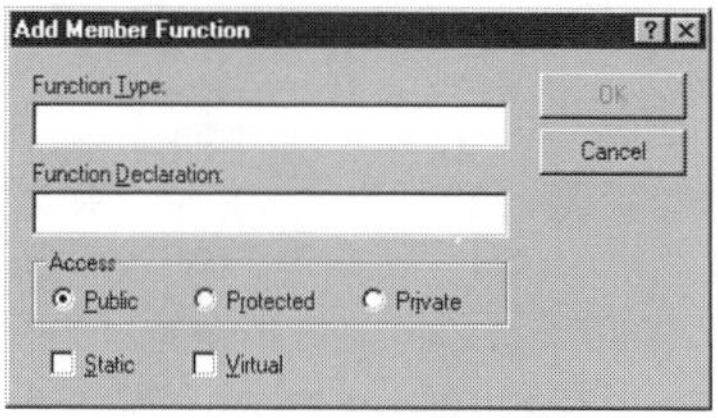

FIG. B.14

Never again forget to add part of a function declaration or definition when you use the Add Member Function shortcut.

- *Add Member Variable*. Opens the Add Member Variable dialog box shown in Figure B.15. This adds a declaration of the variable to the header file.

- *Add Virtual Function*. Opens the New Virtual Override dialog, discussed in Chapter 4, "Messages and Commands."

- *Add Windows Message Handler*. Opens the New Windows Message Handler dialog box, discussed in Chapter 4, "Messages and Commands."

FIG. B.15
Simplify adding
member variables
with this shortcut.

■ *References*. Brings up a list of the places where the class name is mentioned within your application. Typically the class name occurs in declarations of instances of the class, but this will also find places where the class name is passed as a parameter to a function or macro.

■ *Derived Classes*. Brings up a list of all the member functions and member variables of this class, a list of other classes that use this class as a base class, and the references information.

■ *Base Classes*. Brings up a list of all the member functions and member variables of this class, a list of the base classes of this class, and the references information.

■ *Add to Gallery*. Adds this class to the Component Gallery, discussed in Chapter 25, "Achieving Reuse with the Gallery and your own AppWizards."

■ *New Folder*. Creates a folder you can drag classes into. This helps to organize projects with large numbers of classes.

■ *Group by Access*. Rearranges the order of the list. By default, functions are listed in alphabetical order, followed by data members in alphabetical order. With this option toggled on, functions come first (public, then protected, then private functions, alphabetically in each section) followed by data members (again public, then protected, then private data members, alphabetically in each section).

■ *Docking View*. Keeps the project workspace window docked at the side of the main working area.

■ *Hide*. Hides the project workspace window. To redisplay it, choose View, Workspace.

■ *Properties*. Displays the properties of the class (name, base class).

> **TIP** Menu items that appear on a toolbar have their toolbar icon next to them on the menu. Make note of the icon; the next time you want to choose that item, perhaps you can use a toolbar instead.

Right-clicking the name of a member function brings up a substantial shortcut menu, with the following menu items:

■ *Go To Definition*. Opens the source (.cpp) file at the code for this function.

■ *Go To Declaration*. Opens the header (.h) file at the declaration of this function.

■ *Set Breakpoint*. Sets a breakpoint. Breakpoints are discussed in Appendix C, "Debugging."

■ *References*. Brings up a list of the places where the function is called within your application.

■ *Calls.* Displays a collapsible and expandable outline of all the functions that this function calls. Figure B.16 shows a sample Call Graph window.

FIG. B.16

The Call Graph window lists all the functions that your function calls, and all the functions they call, and so on.

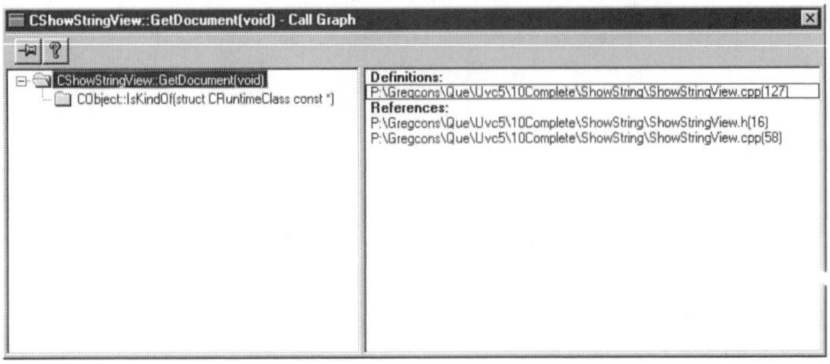

■ *Called By.* Displays a Callers Graph listing the functions this function is called by.

■ *New Folder.* Creates a folder you can drag classes into. This helps to organize projects with large numbers of classes.

■ *Group by Access.* Rearranges the order of the list. By default, functions are listed in alphabetical order, followed by data members in alphabetical order. With this option toggled on, functions come first (public, then protected, then private functions, alphabetically in each section) followed by data members (again public, then protected, then private data members, alphabetically in each section).

■ *Docking View.* Keeps the project workspace window docked at the side of the main working area.

■ *Hide.* Hides the project workspace window. To redisplay it, choose View, Project Workspace.

■ *Properties.* Displays the properties of the function (name, return type, parameters).

Right-clicking the name of a member variable brings up a shortcut menu with less menu items. The items are as follows:

■ *Go To Definition.* Opens the header (.h) file at the declaration of this variable.

■ *References.* Brings up a list of the places where the variable is used within your application.

■ *New Folder.* Creates a folder you can drag classes into. This helps to organize projects with large numbers of classes.

■ *Group by Access.* Rearranges the order of the list. By default, functions are listed in alphabetical order, followed by data members in alphabetical order. With this option toggled on, functions come first (public, then protected, then private functions, alphabetically in each section) followed by data members (again public, then protected, then private data members, alphabetically in each section).

- *Docking View*. Keeps the project workspace window docked at the side of the main working area.

- *Hide*. Hides the project workspace window. To redisplay it, choose <u>V</u>iew, <u>P</u>roject Workspace.

- *Properties*. Displays the properties of the variable (name and type).

When the main working area is displaying a source or header file, you can edit your code as described in the later section "Editing Your Code."

Looking at Your Code, Arranged by File

The FileView is much like the ClassView in that you can display and edit source and header files (see Figure B.17). However, it gives you access to parts of your file that are outside of class definitions, and makes it easy to open non-code files like resources and plain text.

The project workspace window contains a tree view of the source files in your project. The default categories used are Source Files, Header Files, Resource Files, and Help Files (if your project has Help). You can add your own categories by right-clicking anywhere in the FileView and choosing Ne<u>w</u> Folder, then specifying which file extensions belong in the new category.

FIG. B.17

The FileView displays source and header files.

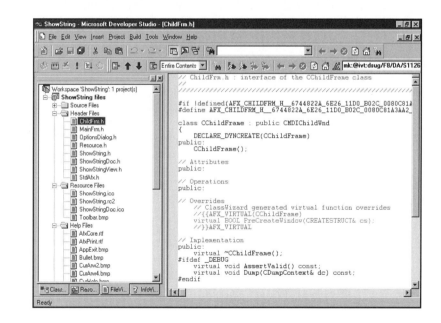

Double-clicking a file name displays that file in the main working area. You can then edit the file (even if it is not a source or header file) as described in the later section "Editing Your Code."

Output and Error Messages

Across the bottom of the Developer Studio screen is the Output view. This is a tabbed view that shows output and error messages from a variety of Developer Studio functions.

 TIP   If there is no Output view on your screen, choose <u>V</u>iew, <u>O</u>utput from the menu to restore the view.

The five tabs in the Output View are the following:

- *Build*. Displays the results of compiling and linking.
- *Debug*. Used when debugging, as discussed in Reference Appendix C, "Debugging."
- *Find in Files 1*. Displays the results of the Find in Files search, discussed later in this chapter.
- *Find in Files 2*. An alternate display window for Find in Files results, so that you can preserve earlier results.
- *Results*. Displays results of tools like the profiler, discussed in Chapter 24, "Improving Your Application's Performance."

If you have installed the Enterprise Edition of Visual C++, there is a sixth tab, SQL Debugging. For more information, see Chapter 23, "Enterprise Edition."

Editing Your Code

For most people, editing code is the most important task you do in a development environment. If you've used any other editor or word processor before, you can handle the basics of the Developer Studio editor right away. You should be able to type in code, fix your mistakes, and move around in source or header files just by using the basic Windows techniques you would expect to be able to use. But because this is a programmer's editor, there are some nice features you should know about.

Basic Typing and Editing

To add text into a file, click where you want the text to go and start typing. By default, the editor is in *Insert mode*, which means your new text pushes the old text over. To switch to *Overstrike mode*, press the Insert key. Now your text types over the text that is already there. The OVR indicator on the status bar reminds you that you are in Overstrike mode. Pressing Insert again puts you back in Insert mode. Move around in the file by clicking with the mouse or use the cursor keys. To move a page or more at a time, use the Page Up and Page Down keys or the scroll bar at the right-hand side of the main working area.

By default, the window for the file you are editing is maximized within the main working area. You can click the Restore button at the top right, just under the Restore button for all of Developer Studio, to show the file in a smaller window. If you have several files open at once, you can arrange them so that you can see them side-by-side, as shown in Figure B.18.

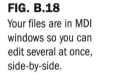

FIG. B.18
Your files are in MDI windows so you can edit several at once, side-by-side.

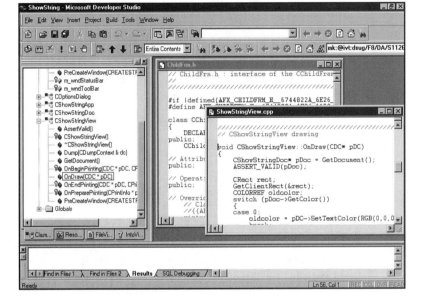

Working with Blocks of Text

Much of the time, you will want to perform an action on a block of text within the editor. First, you select the block by clicking at one end of it and, holding the mouse button down, moving the mouse to the other end of the block, then releasing the mouse button. This should be familiar from so many other Windows applications. Not surprisingly, at this point you can copy or cut the block to the Clipboard, replace it with text you type, replace it with with the current contents of the Clipboard, or delete it.

TIP To select columns of text, as shown in Figure B.19, hold down the Alt key as you select the block.

Syntax Coloring

You may have noticed the color scheme used to present your code. Developer Studio highlights the elements of your code with *syntax coloring*. By default, your code is black, with comments in green and keywords (reserved words in C++ like `public`, `private`, `new`, or `int`) in blue. You can also arrange for special colors for strings, numbers, or operators (like + and -) if you want, using the Format tab of the Options dialog box, reached by choosing Tools, Options.

FIG. B.19
Selecting columns makes fixing indents much simpler. Hold down the Alt key as you select the block.

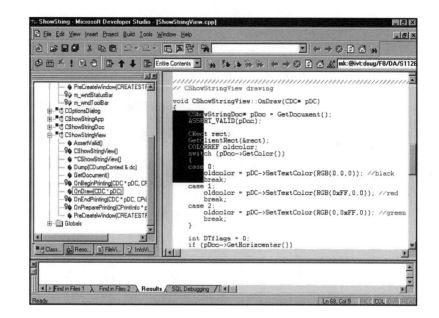

Syntax coloring can help you spot silly mistakes. If you forget to close a C-style comment, the huge swath of green in your file points out the problem right away. If you type **inr** where you meant to type **int**, the inr isn't blue, and that alerts you to a mistyped keyword. This means you can prevent most compiler errors before you even compile.

T I P If you build Web pages and still use Notepad from time to time so that you can see the tags, you're in for a pleasant surprise. Open an HTML file in Developer Studio and see HTML syntax coloring in action. You'll never go back to Notepad.

Shortcut Menu

Many of the actions you are likely to perform are available on the shortcut menu that appears when you right-click within a file you are editing. The items on that menu are as follows:

- *Cut.* Cuts the selected text to the Clipboard.
- *Copy.* Copies the selected text to the Clipboard.
- *Paste.* Replaces the selected text with the Clipboard contents, or if no text is selected, inserts the Clipboard contents at the cursor.
- *Insert File Into Project.* Adds the file you are editing to the project you have open.
- *Open.* Opens the file whose name is under the cursor. Especially useful for header files, because you don't need to know what folder they are in.

- *Go To Definition.* Opens the file where the item under the cursor is defined (header for a variable, source for a function) and positions the cursor at the definition of the item.
- *Go To Reference.* Positions the cursor at the next reference to the variable or function whose name is under the cursor.
- *Insert/Remove Breakpoint.* Inserts a breakpoint at the cursor, or removes one that is already there.
- *Enable Breakpoint.* Enables a disabled breakpoint (breakpoints are discussed in Appendix C, "Debugging").
- *ClassWizard.* Brings up ClassWizard.
- *Properties.* Brings up the property sheet.

App
B

Not all the items are enabled at once—for example, Cut and Copy are only enabled when there is a selection. Insert File into Project is only enabled when the file you are editing is not in the project you have open. All of these actions have menu and toolbar equivalents and are discussed more fully later in this chapter.

Learning the Menu System

Developer Studio has many menus. Some commands are three or four levels deep under the menu structure. In most cases, there are far quicker ways to accomplish the same task, but for a new user, the menus are an easier way to learn because you can rely on reading the menu items as opposed to memorizing shortcuts. There are nine menus on the Developer Studio menu bar, as follows:

- *File.* For actions related to entire files, such as opening, closing, and printing.
- *Edit.* For copying, cutting, pasting, searching, and moving about.
- *View.* For changing the appearance of Developer Studio, including toolbars and subwindows like the Workspace window.
- *Insert.* For adding files or components to your project.
- *Project.* For dealing with your entire project.
- *Build.* For compiling, linking, and debugging.
- *Tools.* For customizing the Developer Studio and accessing stand-alone utilities.
- *Window.* To change which window is maximized or has focus.
- *Help.* To use the InfoViewer system (not the usual online help).

The following section presents each Developer Studio menu in turn, and mentions keyboard shortcuts and toolbar buttons where they exist.

Using File Menu

The File menu, shown in Figure B.20, collects most of the commands that affect entire files or the entire project.

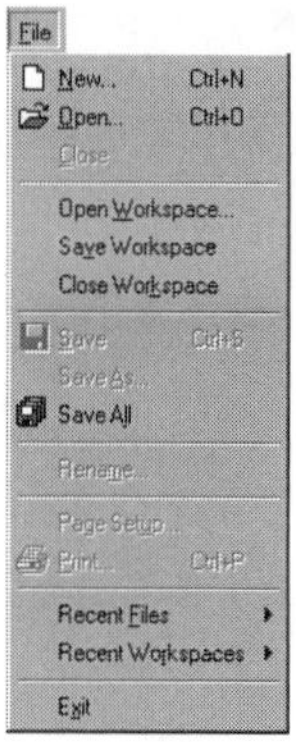

FIG. B.20

The File menu has actions for files like Open, Close, and Print.

File New (Ctrl+N)   Choosing this menu item brings up the New dialog box, shown in Figure B.21. This tabbed dialog box is used to create new files, projects, workspaces, or other documents. The Project tab is used to start AppWizard, discussed for the first time in Chapter 1, "Building Your First Application."

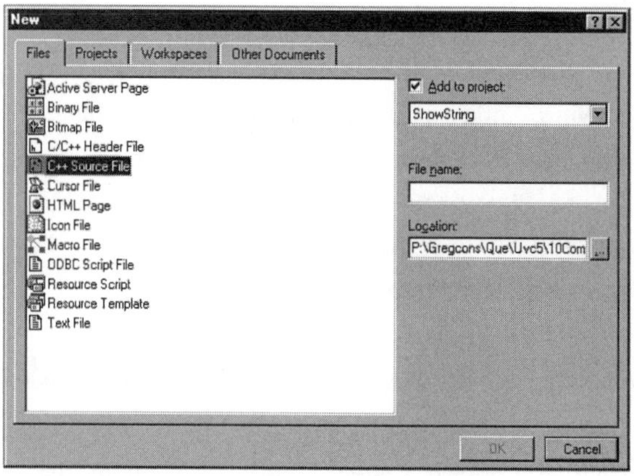

FIG. B.21

The New dialog box is used to create new files or workspaces.

This dialog box is an easy way to create a blank file, give it a name, and insert it into your project all in one step.

File Open (Ctrl+O)   Choosing this item brings up the Open dialog box, as shown in Figure B.22. (It's the standard Windows File Open dialog box, so it should be pretty familiar.) The file type defaults to Common Files with .c, .cpp, .cxx, .h, or .rc extensions. By clicking the drop-down box, you can open almost any kind of file, including executables and workspaces.

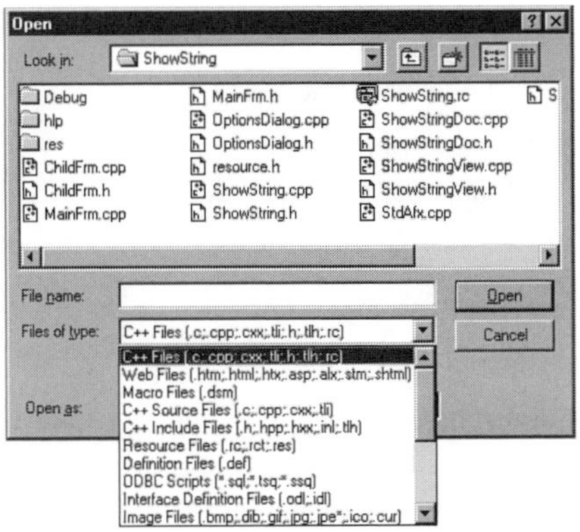

FIG. B.22

The familiar File Open
dialog box is used
to open a variety of
file types.

 TIP Don't forget the list of recently opened files further down the File menu. That can save a lot of typing or
clicking.

File Close   Choosing the File, Close item closes the file that has focus; if no file has focus, the
item is grayed. You can also close a file by clicking the cancel button, depicted by an X, in the
top-right corner. You may also close the window by double-clicking the icon in the upper-right
corner. (The icon used to be the system menu, shown with a minus on a button.)

File Open Workspace   Use this item to open a workspace. (You can use File, Open and change
the file type to Project Workspace, but using File, Open Workspace is quicker.)

File Close Workspace   Use this item to close a workspace. The current workspace is closed
automatically when you create a new project or open another workspace, so you won't use this
menu item very often.

File Save (Ctrl+S)   Use this item to save the file that has focus at the moment; if no file has
focus, the item is grayed. There is a Save button on the Standard toolbar as well.

File Save As   Use this item to save a file and change its name at the same time. It saves the
file that has focus at the moment; if no file has focus, the item is grayed.

File Save All   This item saves all the files that are currently open. All files are saved just
before a compile and when the application is closed, but if you aren't compiling very often and
are making a lot of changes, it's a good idea to save all your files every 15 minutes or so. (You
can do it less often if the idea of losing that amount of work doesn't bother you.)

File Rename   Use this item to change the name of a file without leaving a copy under the
old name.

File Page Setup   This item brings up the Page Setup dialog box, shown in Figure B.23. Here
you specify the header, footer, and margins—left, right, top, and bottom. The header and footer
can contain any text including one or more special fields, which you add by clicking the arrow
next to the edit box or entering the codes yourself.

The codes are:

- *Filename*. The name of the file being printed (&f).
- *Page Number*. The current page number (&p).
- *Current Time*. The time the page was printed (&t).
- *Current Date*. The date the page was printed (&d).
- *Left Align*. Align this portion to the left (&l).
- *Right Align*. Align this portion to the right (&c).
- *Center*. Center this portion (this is the default alignment)—(&c).

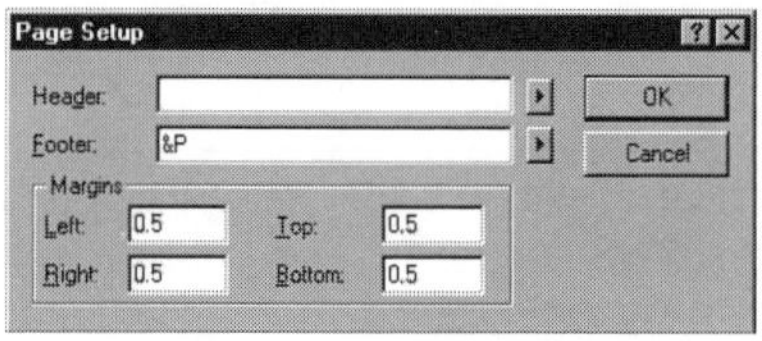

FIG. B.23

The Page Setup dialog
box lays out your printed
pages the way you want.

File Print (Ctrl+P)   Choosing this item prints the file with focus according to your Page Setup settings. (The item is grayed if no file has focus.) The Print dialog box, shown in Figure B.24, has you confirm the printer you want to print on. If you have some text highlighted, the Selection radio button is enabled. Choosing it lets you print just the selected text; otherwise, only the All radio button is enabled, which prints the entire file. If you forget to set the headers, footers, and margins before choosing File, Print, the Setup button brings up the Page Setup dialog box discussed in the previous section. There is no way to print only certain pages or to cancel printing once it has started.

FIG. B.24

The Print dialog box
confirms your choice
to print a file.

Recent Files and Workspaces   The recent files and workspaces items, between Print and Exit, each lead to a cascading menu. The items on the secondary menus are the names of files and workspaces which have been opened most recently, up to the last four of each. These are real time-savers if you work on several projects at once. Whenever you want to open a file, before you click that toolbar button and prepare to point and click your way to the file, think first if it might be on the File menu. Menus aren't always the slower way to go.

File Exit   Probably the most familiar Windows menu item of all, this closes Developer Studio. You can also click the X in the top-right corner, or double-click what used to be the system menu in the top left. If you have made changes without saving, you get a chance to save each file on your way out.

Edit

The Edit menu, shown in Figure B.25, collects actions related to changing text in a source file.

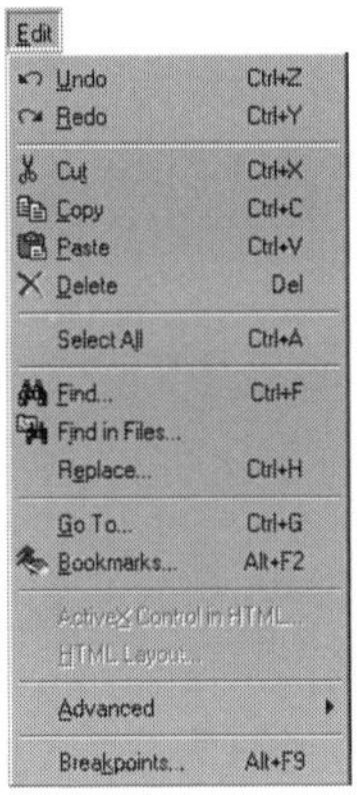

FIG. B.25
The Edit menu holds items that change the text in a file.

```
Edit
 Undo            Ctrl+Z
 Redo            Ctrl+Y
 Cut             Ctrl+X
 Copy            Ctrl+C
 Paste           Ctrl+V
 Delete          Del
 Select All      Ctrl+A
 Find...         Ctrl+F
 Find in Files...
 Replace...      Ctrl+H
 Go To...        Ctrl+G
 Bookmarks...    Alt+F2
 ActiveX Control in HTML...
 HTML Layout...
 Advanced        ▶
 Breakpoints...  Alt+F9
```

Edit Undo (Ctrl+Z)   The Undo item reverses whatever you just did. Most operations, like text edits and deleting text, can be undone. When Undo is disabled, it is an indication that nothing needs to be undone or you cannot undo the last operation.

There is an Undo button on the Standard toolbar. Clicking the button displays a stack (reverse order list from most recent to least recent) of operations that can be undone. You must select a contiguous range of undo items including the first, second, and so on. You cannot pick and choose.

Edit Redo (Ctrl+Y)   As you undo actions, the name given to the operations moves from the Undo to the Redo list (Redo is next to Undo on the toolbar). If you undo a little too much, choose Edit, Redo to un-undo them (if that makes sense).

Edit Cut (Ctrl+X)   This item cuts the currently highlighted text to the Clipboard. That means a copy of it goes to the Clipboard, and the text itself is deleted from your file. The Cut button (represented as scissors) is on the Standard toolbar.

Edit Copy (Ctrl+C)   Editing buttons on the toolbar are grouped next to the scissors (Cut). Edit, Copy copies the currently selected text or item to the Windows Clipboard.

Edit Paste (Ctrl+V)   Choosing this item copies the Clipboard contents at the cursor, or replaces the highlighted text with the Clipboard contents if any text is highlighted. The Paste item and button are disabled if there is nothing in the Clipboard in a format appropriate for pasting to the focus window. In addition to text, you can copy and paste menu items, dialog box items, and other resources. The Paste button is on the Standard toolbar.

Edit Delete (Delete)   Edit, Delete clears the selected text or item. If what you deleted is undeletable, then the Undo button is enabled and the last operation is added to the Undo button combo box. Deleted material does not go to the Clipboard and cannot be retrieved except by undoing the delete.

Edit Select All (Ctrl+A)   This item selects everything in the file with focus that can be selected. For example, if a text file has focus, the entire file is selected. If a dialog box has focus, every control on it is selected.

To select many items on a dialog box, you can click the first item and then Ctrl+click each of the remaining items. It is often faster to use Edit, Select All to select everything, and then Ctrl+click to unselect the few items you do not want highlighted.

Edit Find (Ctrl+F)   The Find dialog box shown in Figure B.26 enables you to search for text within the file that currently has the focus. Enter a word or phrase into the Find what edit box. The following check boxes set the options for the search:

- *Match Whole Word Only.* If this is checked, `table` in the Find What box matches only `table`, not `suitable` or `tables`.

- *Match Case.* If this is checked, `Chapter` in the Find What box matches only `Chapter`, not `chapter` or `CHAPTER`. Upper- and lowercase must match.

- *Regular Expression.* The Find What box is treated as a regular expression if this box is checked.

- *Search All Open Documents.* Expands your search to all the documents you have open at the moment.

- *Direction.* Choose the Up radio button to search backwards, and the Down radio button to search forwards through the file.

FIG. B.26

The Find dialog box is used to find a string within the file that has focus.

TIP   If you highlight a block of text before selecting Edit, Find, that text is put into the Find What box for you. If no text is highlighted, the word or identifier under the cursor is put into the Find What box.

A typical use for the Find dialog box is to enter some text and click the Find Next button until you find the precise occurrence of the text for which you are searching. But you may want to combine the Find feature with bookmarks (discussed a little later in this section), and put a bookmark on each line that has an occurrence of the string. Click the Mark All button in the Find dialog box to add temporary, unnamed bookmarks on match lines; they are indicated with a blue oval in the margin.

There is a Find edit box on the Standard toolbar. Enter the text you want to search for in the box and press Enter to search forward. Regular expressions are used if you have turned them on using the Find dialog box. To repeat a search, click the Find Next or Find Previous buttons on the Standard toolbar (these are icons with binoculars with clockwise and counter-clockwise arrows, respectively).

Regular Expressions

Many of the find and replace operations within Developer Studio can be made more powerful with regular expressions. For example, if you want to search for a string only at the end of a line, or one of several similar strings, you can do so by constructing an appropriate regular expression, entering it in the Search dialog box, and instructing Developer Studio to use regular expressions for the search. A regular expression is some text, combined with special characters that represent things that can't be typed, like "the end of a line" or "any number" or "three capital letters."

When regular expressions are being used, some characters give up their usual meaning and instead stand in for one or more other characters. Regular expressions in Developer Studio are built from ordinary characters mixed in with these special entries, shown in Table B.1.

You don't have to type these in if you have trouble remembering them. Next to the Find What box is an arrowhead pointing to the right. Click there to bring up a shortcut menu of all these fields, and click any one of them to insert it into the Find What box. (You need to be able to read these symbols to understand what expression you are building, and there's no arrowhead on the toolbar's Find box.) Remember to select the Regular Expressions box so that these regular expressions are evaluated properly.

Here are some examples of regular expressions:

- `^test$` matches only `test` alone on a line.
- `doc[1234]` matches doc1, doc2, doc3, or doc4 but not doc5.
- `doc[1-4]` matches the same strings as above but requires less typing.
- `doc[^56]` matches doca, doc1, and anything else that starts with doc and is not doc5 or doc6.
- If the Find What box contains `(\Good\) morning` and the replace box is `\1 afternoon`, then `Good morning` is changed to `Good afternoon`.
- `H\~ello` matches `Hillo` and `Hxllo` (and lots more) but not `Hello`.
- `\{x\!y\}z` matches `xz` and `yz`.
- `New *York` matches `New York` but also `NewYork` and `New  York`.
- `New +York` matches `New York` and `New  York` but not `NewYork`.
- `New.*k` matches `Newk`, `Newark`, and `New York`, plus lots more.
- `\:n` matches `0.123`, `234`, and `23.45` (among others) but not `-1C`.
- `World$` matches `World` at the end of a line but `World\$` matches only `World$` anywhere on a line.

Table B.1   Regular Expression Entries

Entry	Matches
[af]	Start of the line.
$	End of the line.

continues

Table B.1   Continued

Entry	Matches
.	Any single character.
[ ]	Any one of the characters within the brackets (use - for a range, [af] for "except").
\~	Anything except the character that follows next.
*	Zero or more of the next character.
+	One or more of the next character.
\(\)	Doesn't match especially, but saves part of the match string to be used in the replacement string. Up to nine portions can be tagged like this.
\{\!\}	Either of the characters within the {}.
{\\}	Just like [].
\:a	A single letter or number.
\:b	White space (tabs or spaces).
\:c	A single letter.
\:d	A single numerical digit.
\:n	An unsigned number.
\:z	An unsigned integer.
\:h	A hexadecimal number.
\:i	A string of characters that meets the rules for C++ identifiers (starts with a letter, number, or underscore).
\:w	A string of letters only.
\:q	A quoted string surrounded by double or single quotes.
\	Removes the special meaning from the character that follows.

Edit Find in Files   This useful command searches for a word or phrase within a large number of files at once. In its simplest form, shown in Figure B.27, you enter a word or phrase into the Find What edit box, restrict the search to certain types of files in the In Files of Type box, and choose the folder to conduct the search within the In Folder edit box. The following check boxes in the bottom half of the dialog box set the options for the search:

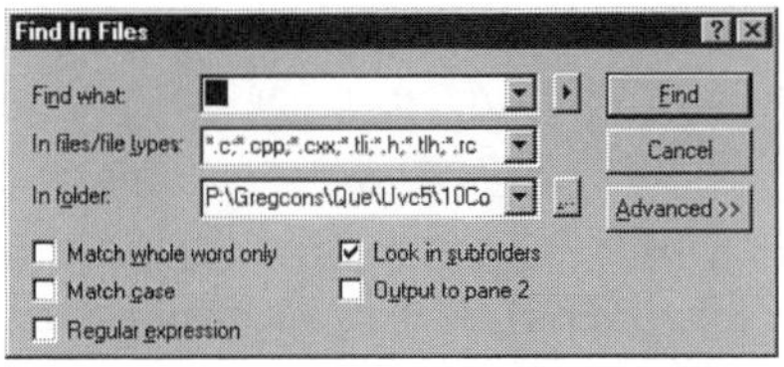

FIG. B.27

The simplest Find in Files approach searches for a string within a folder and its subfolders.

Find In Files

Find what:	▮ ▾ ▸	Find
In files/file types:	*.c;*.cpp;*.cxx;*.tli;*.h;*.tlh;*.rc ▾	Cancel
In folder:	P:\Gregcons\Que\Uvc5\10Co ▾ ...	Advanced >>

☐ Match whole word only ☑ Look in subfolders
☐ Match case ☐ Output to pane 2
☐ Regular expression

■ *Match Whole Word Only.* If this is checked, `table` in the Find What box matches only `table`, not `suitable` or `tables`.

■ *Match Case.* If this is checked, `Chapter` in the Find What box matches only `Chapter`, not `chapter` or `CHAPTER`. Upper- and lowercase must match.

■ *Regular Expression.* The Find What box is treated as a regular expression (see the previous sidebar "Regular Expressions") if this box is checked.

■ *Look in Subfolders.* Work through all the subfolders of the chosen folder if this is checked.

■ *Output to Pane 2.* Sends the results to the Find in Files 2 pane of the output window, so as not to wipe out the results of an earlier search.

Using Advanced Text Finding Features At the bottom right of the Find in Files dialog box is the Advanced button. Clicking it expands the dialog box shown in Figure B.28 and allows you to search several different folders at once.

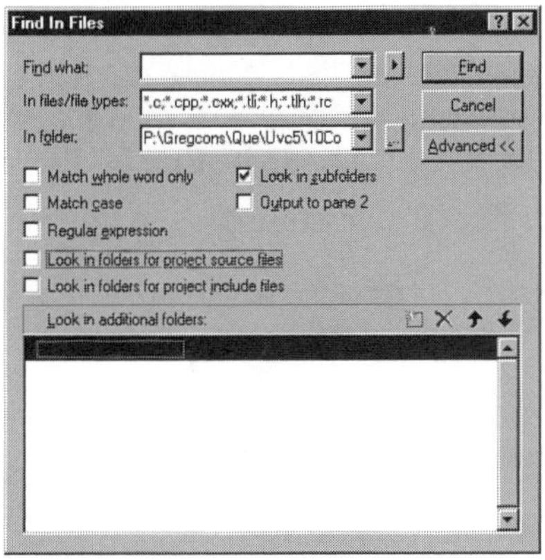

FIG. B.28

Advanced Find in Files searches for a string within several folders and their subfolders.

Find In Files

Find what:	▾ ▸	Find
In files/file types:	*.c;*.cpp;*.cxx;*.tli;*.h;*.tlh;*.rc ▾	Cancel
In folder:	P:\Gregcons\Que\Uvc5\10Co ▾ ...	Advanced <<

☐ Match whole word only ☑ Look in subfolders
☐ Match case ☐ Output to pane 2
☐ Regular expression
☐ Look in folders for project source files
☐ Look in folders for project include files

Look in additional folders: ☐ ✕ ↑ ↓

TIP If you highlight a block of text before selecting Find in Files, that text is put into the Find What box for you. If no text is highlighted, the word or identifier under the cursor is put into the Find What box.

The results of the Find in Files command appear in the Find in Files 1 tab (unless you ask for pane 2) of the output window; the output window will be visible after this operation if it was not already. You can resize this window like any other window, by holding the mouse over the border until it becomes a sizing cursor, and you can scroll around within the window in the usual way. Double-clicking a file name in the output list opens that file with the cursor on the line where the match was found.

Edit Replace (Ctrl+H)   This item brings up the Replace dialog box, shown in Figure B.29. It is very similar to the Find dialog box but is used to replace the found text with new text. Enter one string into the Find What edit box and the replacement string into the Replace With edit box. The three check boxes—Regular Expression, Match Case, and Match Whole Word Only—have the same meaning as on the Find dialog box (discussed in the previous section). The Replace In radio buttons allow you to restrict the search-and-replace operation to a block of highlighted text, if you prefer.

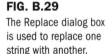

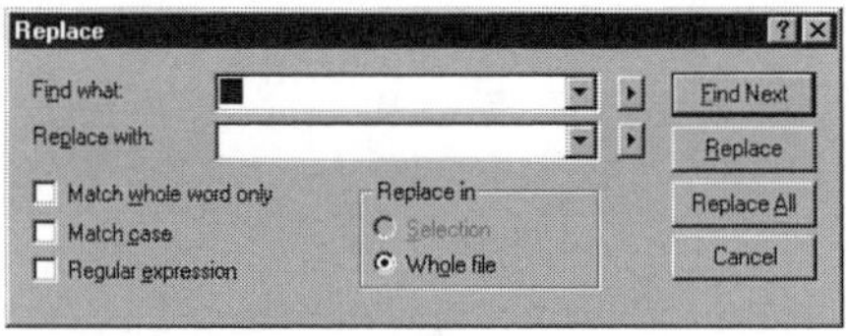

FIG. B.29

The Replace dialog box is used to replace one string with another.

To see the next match before you agree to replace it, click Find Next. To replace the next match or the match you have just found, click Replace. If you are confident that there won't be any false matches, you can click Replace All to do the rest of the file all at once. (If you realize after you click Replace All that you were wrong, there is always Edit, Undo.)

Edit Go To (Ctrl+G)   The Go To dialog box (see Figure B.30) is a central navigation point. It enables you to go to a particular line number (the default), address, reference, or bookmark, among other things. To use the Go To dialog box, select something from the Go To What list on the left; if Line is selected enter a line number, if Bookmark is selected pick the particular bookmark from the combo box, and so on.

FIG. B.30

The Go To dialog box moves you around within your project.

The Go To What box contains the following choices:

- *Address*. In the Memory or Disassembly windows, as explained in Appendix C, "Debugging," you can go to an address given by a debugger expression.

- *Bookmark*. In a text file, you can go to a bookmark, though you are more likely to choose Edit, Bookmarks or the bookmark-related buttons on the Edit toolbar.

- *Definition*. If the cursor is over the name of a function, this opens the source (.cpp) file at its definition. If the cursor is over a variable, it opens the include (.h) file.

- *Error/Tag.* After a compile, you can move from error to error by double-clicking them within the output window by using this dialog box or (most likely) by pressing F4.
- *InfoViewer Bookmark.* This is one way to cycle through your InfoViewer bookmarks, but most of the time the InfoViewer toolbar is a better way.
- *Line.* This is the default selection. The line number that is filled in for you is your current line.
- *Offset.* Enter an offset address (in hexadecimal).
- *Reference.* Enter a name, like a function or object name, and the cursor will be placed on the line of code where the name is defined, in your code or in the MFC libraries.

App

B

TIP The pushpin in the upper-left corner of this dialog box is used to "pin" it to the screen so that it stays in place after you have gone to the requested location. Click the pin to unpin the dialog box from the screen so that it goes away after the jump.

Edit Bookmarks (Alt+F2) This item is used to manage the bookmarks within your text files, which are completely independent of any InfoViewer bookmarks you may have set. The bookmark list is shown in Figure B.31. Note that temporary bookmarks set by the Find command are not included in this list.

FIG. B.31
The Bookmarks dialog box manages the bookmarks you have set in text files.

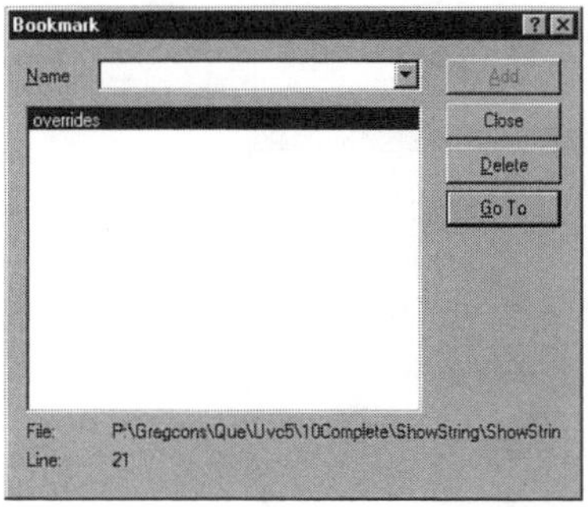

To add a named bookmark for the line you are on and have it saved with the file, type a name in the Name box and click Add. To go to a named bookmark, choose it from the list box and click Go To. There are buttons on the Edit toolbar to add or delete a bookmark at the cursor, move to the next or previous bookmark, and clear all bookmarks in the file.

Edit ActiveX Control in HTML If you have Visual InterDev installed and are working with an ActiveX control, this menu item will let you edit its settings. Building ActiveX controls is discussed in Chapter 17, "Building an ActiveX Control."

Edit HTML Layout This item is used to edit an HTML layout with Visual InterDev.

Edit Advanced   Choosing this item brings up a cascading menu with the following items:

- *Incremental Search*. This is a faster search than bringing up the Find dialog box discussed earlier. You enter your search string on the status bar. As you type each letter, Developer Studio finds the string you have built so far. For example, in a header file, if you choose Edit, Advanced, Incremental Search then type **p**, the cursor will jump to the first instance of the letter p, probably in the keyword `public`. If you go on to type **r**, the cursor will jump to the first pr, probably in the keyword `protected`. This can save you from typing the entire word you are looking for.

- *Format Selection*. This item adjusts the indenting of a selection using the same rules that apply when you are entering code.

- *Tabify Selection*. Converts spaces to tabs.

- *Untabify Selection*. Converts tabs to spaces.

- *Make Selection Uppercase*. Converts the selected text to capital letters.

- *Make Selection Lowercase*. Converts the selected text to lowercase letters.

- *View Whitespace*. Inserts small placeholder characters (. for space and >> for tab) to show all the whitespace in your document.

Edit Breakpoints (Alt+F9)   A *breakpoint* pauses program execution. The Edit, Breakpoints item displays the Breakpoints dialog box, shown in Figure B.32 and discussed in Appendix C, "Debugging."

FIG. B.32

The Breakpoints dialog box is used in debugging your application.

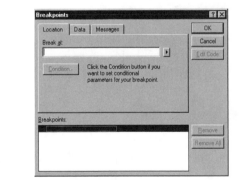

Using the View Menu

The View menu, shown in Figure B.33, collects actions that are related to the appearance of Developer Studio—which windows are open, what toolbars are visible, and so on.

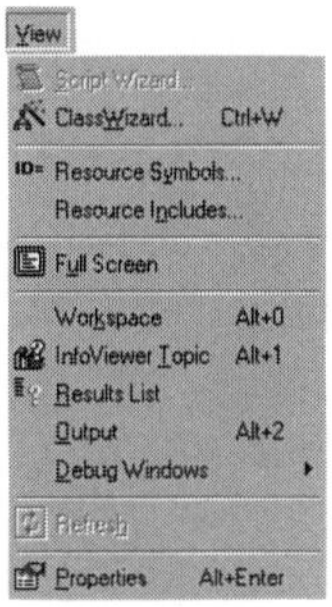

FIG. B.33

The View menu controls the appearance of Developer Studio.

View ScriptWizard   This InterDev-related command is used to edit Web page scripts.

View ClassWizard (Ctrl+W)   ClassWizard is probably the most-used tool in Developer Studio. Whenever you add a resource (menu, dialog box, control, and so on), you connect it to your code with ClassWizard. When you are working with ActiveX, you use ClassWizard to set up properties, methods, and events. If you use custom messages, you use ClassWizard to arrange for them to be caught. You learn how to use ClassWizard starting in Chapter 2, "Dialog Boxes and Controls."

> **CAUTION**
>
> All changed files are saved when you bring up ClassWizard, just as they are saved before a compile. If you have been making changes that you may not want saved, don't bring up ClassWizard.

View Resource Symbols   This item brings up the Resource Symbols dialog box, shown in Figure B.34. It displays the resource IDs, such as ID_EDIT_COPY, used in your application. The large list box at the top of the dialog box lists resource IDs, and the smaller box below it reminds you where this resource is used—on a menu, in an accelerator, in the string table, and so on. The buttons along the right side are used to make changes. Click New to create a new resource ID, Delete to delete this resource ID (if it is not in use), Change to change the ID (if it is in use by only one resource), and View Use to open the resource (menu, string table, and so on) that is highlighted in the lower list.

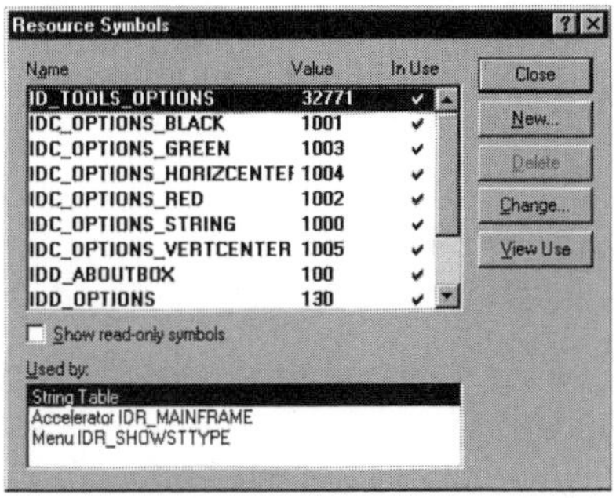

FIG. B.34

The Resource Symbols dialog box displays resource IDs.

View Resource Includes Choosing this item brings up the Resource Includes dialog box, as shown in Figure B.35. It is unusual for you to need to change this generated material. In the rare cases where the resource.h file generated for you is not quite what you need, you can add extra lines with this dialog box.

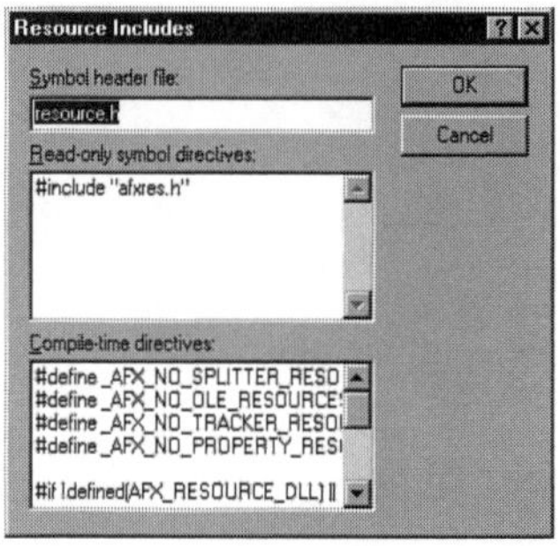

FIG. B.35

The Resource Includes dialog box lets you insert extra instructions into the file that describes the resources of your project.

View Full Screen This item hides all the toolbars, menus, Output window, and Project Workspace window, giving you your entire screen as the main working area. One small toolbar appears whose only button is Toggle Full Screen. Click that button to restore the menus, toolbars, and windows.

View Workspace (Alt+0) Choosing this item brings up the Workspace window, if it is hidden. It does not take away the Project Workspace window. To hide it, right-click the window and choose Hide, or press Shift+Esc while the window has focus. There is a Workspace button on the Standard toolbar which hides or displays the window.

View InfoViewer Topic (Alt+1) This item re-opens your most recently viewed InfoViewer topic.

View Results List Choosing this item brings up a tabbed window of lists relevant to InfoViewer, like that shown in Figure B.36. The tabs are Search, Lookup, See Also, and History.

View Output (Alt+2) This item brings up the Output window, if it is hidden. To hide the Output window, right-click it and choose Hide, or press Shift+Esc while the window has focus. The Output window opens automatically when you build your project or use Find in Files.

View Debug Windows This cascading menu deals with windows used while debugging, which are discussed in Appendix C, "Debugging." It contains the following items:

- Watch
- Call Stack
- Memory
- Variables
- Registers
- Disassembly

View Properties (Alt+Enter) Choosing this item brings up a property sheet. The property sheets for different items vary widely, as shown in Figures B.37, B.38, and B.39, which illustrate the property sheet for an entire source file, an accelerator table selected in the Project Workspace window, and one key in that accelerator table, respectively.

FIG. B.36

The InfoViewer Results tabbed dialog box collects InfoViewer lists in one spot.

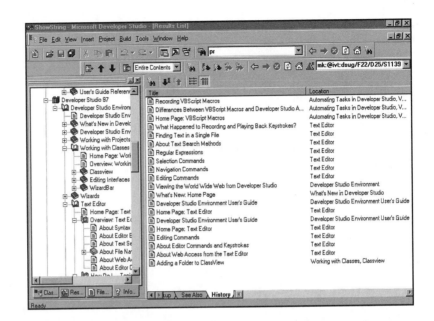

FIG. B.37

The property sheet for a source file reminds you of the name and size, and lets you set the language (used for syntax coloring) and tab size.

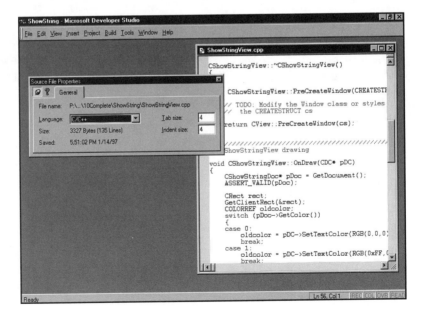

FIG. B.38

The property sheet for an accelerator table is where you set the language, enabling you to include multiple tables in one application.

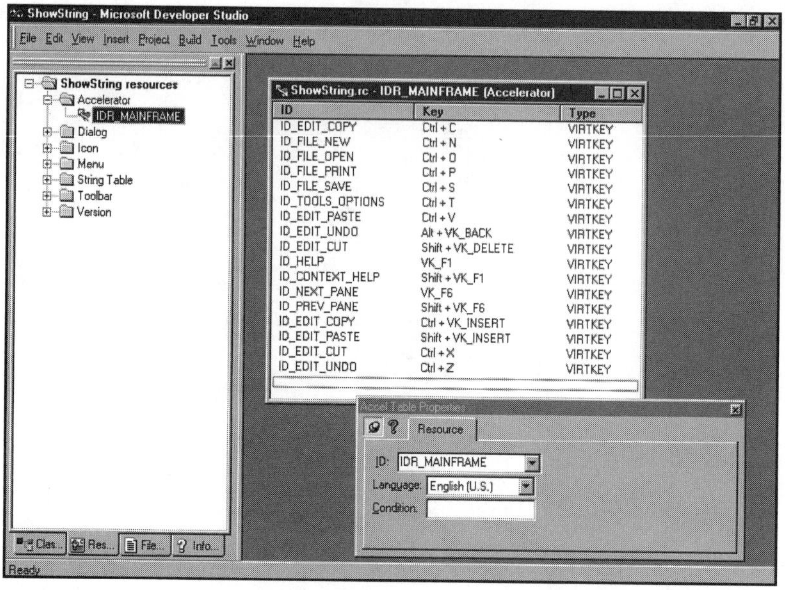

FIG. B.39

The property sheet for an entry in an accelerator table gives you full control over the keystrokes associated with the resource ID.

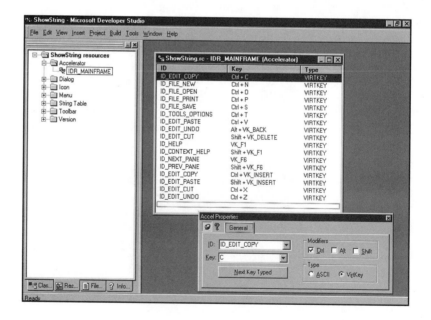

Property sheets are a powerful way of editing non-source file entities, such as resources. For functions and variables, however, it's usually easier to make the changes in the source file. Some rather obscure effects can only be achieved through property sheets. For example, to turn off syntax coloring for a file, use the property sheet to set the language to None. (The effect will be observed after the window is repainted by Windows.)

TIP The property normally disappears as soon as you click something else. If you click the pushpin button in the top-left corner, it stays "pinned" to the screen as you work, displaying the properties of all the entities you are working with.

Insert

The Insert menu, shown in Figure B.40, collects actions related to inserting something into your project or one of its files.

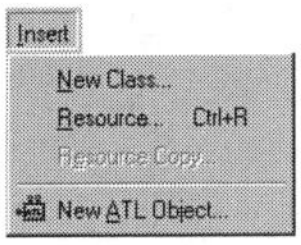

FIG. B.40

The Insert menu is one way to add items to a project or a file.

App

B

Insert New Class   Use this item to create a header and source file for a new class and add it to this project. The New Class dialog box is shown in Figure B.41. Note the drop-down box that makes specifying the base class simpler.

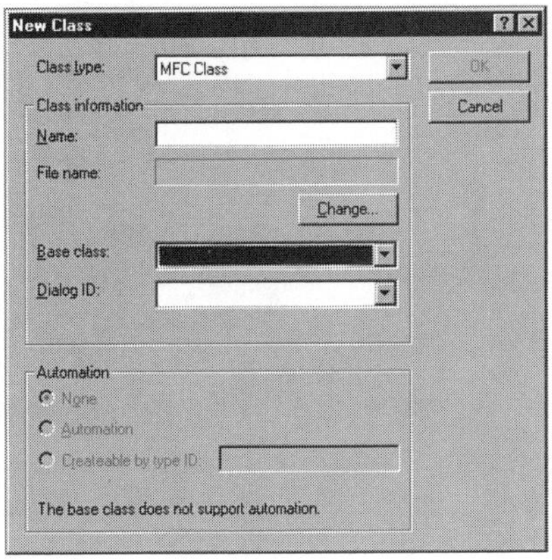

FIG. B.41

The New Class dialog box simplifies creating a new class.

Insert Resource (Ctrl+R)   Use this item to add a new resource to your project. The Insert Resource dialog box, shown in Figure B.42, appears. Choose the type of resource to be added and click OK.

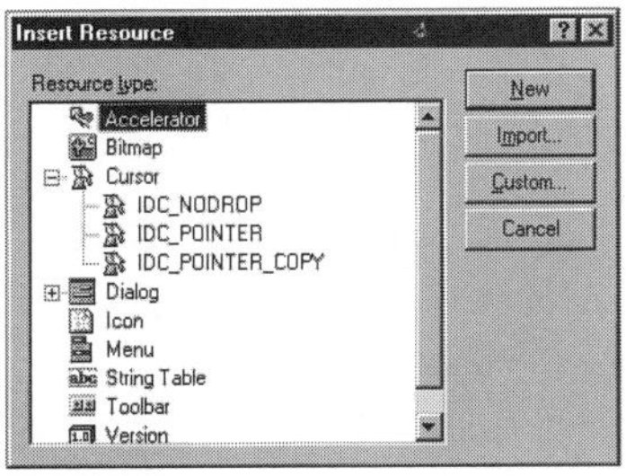

FIG. B.42

The Insert Resource dialog box is one way to add resources to your project.

There are buttons on the Resource toolbar to add a new dialog box, menu, cursor, icon, bitmap, toolbar, accelerator, string table, or version.

Insert Resource Copy   Use this item to copy an existing resource, changing only the *language* (for example, from US English to Canadian French) or the *condition* (for example, building a debug version of a dialog box). Your project will have different language versions of the resource, allowing you to use compiler directives to determine which resource is compiled into the executable.

Insert New ATL Object   When you are creating an ActiveX control with the Active Template Library (ATL), use this item to insert ATL objects into your project. See Chapter 21, "The Active Template Library."

Project

The Project menu, shown in Figure B.43, holds items associated with project maintenance. The items in this menu are:

FIG. B.43
The Project menu simplifies project maintenance.

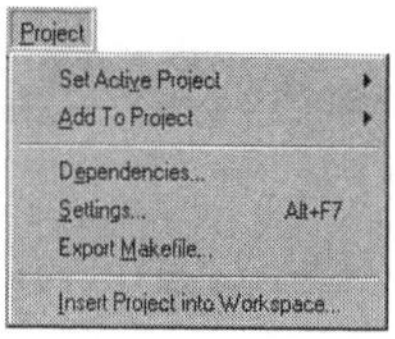

Project Set Active Project   If you have several projects in your workspace, this item sets which project is active.

Project Add to Project   This item brings up a cascading menu with the following choices:

- *New*. Brings up the same dialog box as File, New with the Add to Project box selected.
- *New Folder*. Creates a new folder to organize the classes in the project.
- *Files*. Brings up the Insert Files Into Project dialog box shown in Figure B.44.
- *Data Connection*. Available in the Enterprise Edition discussed in Chapter 23, "Enterprise Edition," this item connects your project to a data source.
- *Components and Controls*. Brings up the Components and Controlled Gallery, discussed in Chapter 25, "Achieving Reuse with the Gallery and Your Own AppWizards."

Project Dependencies   This item allows you to make one project dependent on another so that when one project is changed, its dependents are rebuilt.

Project Settings (Alt+F7)   This item brings up the Project Settings dialog box, which has the following eight tabs:

- *General*. Change the static versus shared DLL choice you made when AppWizard built this project, and change the directory where intermediate (source and object) or output (EXE, DLL, OCX) files are kept (see Figure B.45).

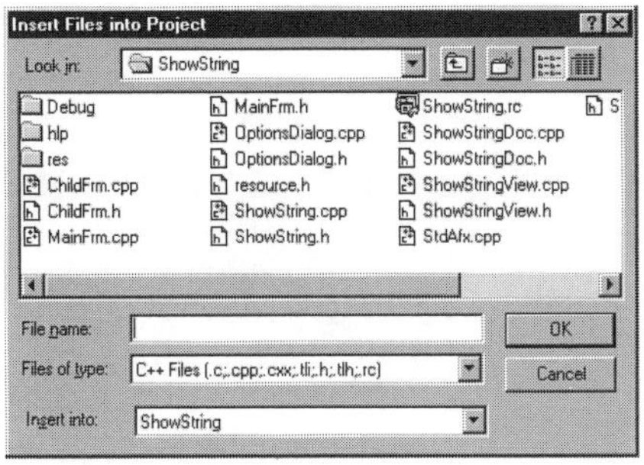

FIG. B.44

The Insert Files into Project dialog box looks very much like a File Open dialog box.

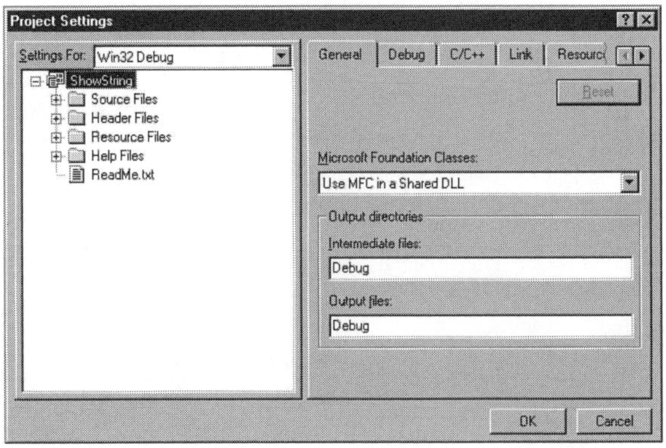

FIG. B.45

The General tab of the Project Settings dialog box governs where files are kept.

■ *Debug*. These settings are discussed in Appendix C, "Debugging."

■ *C/C++*. These are your compiler settings. The Category combo box has General selected by default. To change the settings category, select a category from the combo box. Figure B.46 shows the General category. You can change the optimization criteria (your choices are Maximize Speed, Minimize Size, Customize, or Disable if your debugging is being thrown off by the optimizer) or the warning level. This tab is discussed in more detail in Chapter 24, "Improving your Application's Performance."

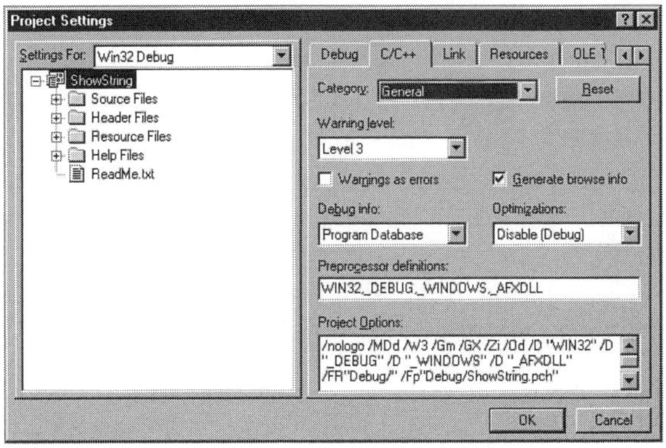

FIG. B.46

The C/C++ tab of the Project Settings dialog box governs compiler settings in eight categories, starting with General.

■ *Link*. This tab controls link options, which you are unlikely to need to change. The settings are divided into five categories; the General category is shown in Figure B.47.

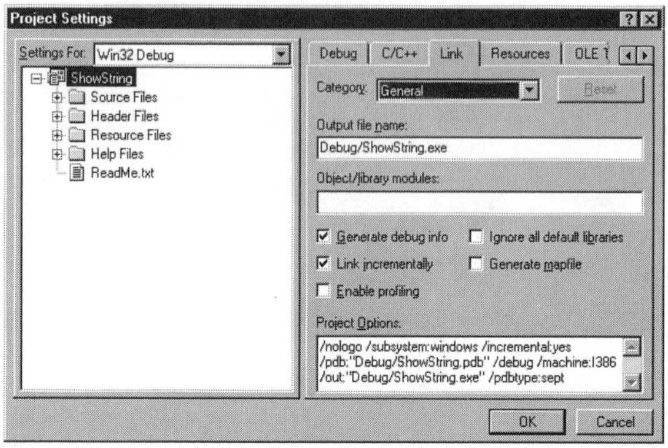

FIG. B.47

The Link tab of the Project Settings dialog box governs linker settings in five categories, starting with General.

■ *Resources*. This tab, shown in Figure B.48, is used to change the language you are working in. This tab enables you to change which resources are compiled into your application, and other resource settings.

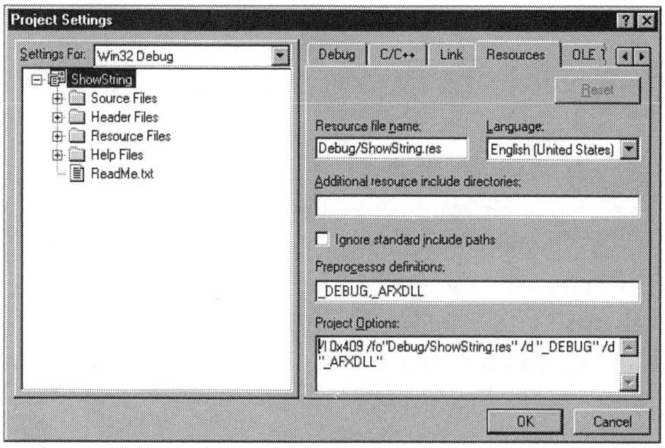

FIG. B.48

The Resources tab of the Project Settings dialog box governs resources settings, including language.

■ *OLE Types*. This tab is used by programmers who are building a type library (TLB) from a object description (ODL) file. ODL files are discussed in Chapter 16, "Building an Automation Server."

■ *Browse Info*. This tab, shown in Figure B.49, controls the Browse Info (.bsc) file used for the Go To Definition, Go To Declaration, and similar menu items. If you never use these, your links will be quicker if you don't generate browse information. If you want browse information, in addition to checking Build Browse info file on this tab check Generate Browse Info in the General category of the C/C++ tab.

FIG. B.49

The Browse Info tab of the Project Settings dialog box turns on or off the powerful browse feature.

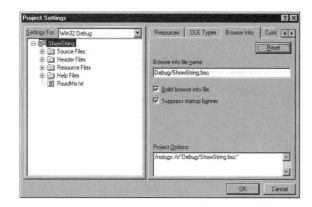

■ *Custom Build.* These settings allow you to add your own steps to be performed as part of every build process.

■ *Pre-Link Step.* You can add your own steps just before the link step.

■ *Post-Build Step.* You can add your own steps to be performed after everything else has successfully completed.

To see the last few tabs, click the right-pointing arrow at the end of the list of tabs. You can adjust the settings for each configuration (Debug, Release, and so on) separately or all at once. Many of the panes have a Reset button that restores the settings to those you chose when you first created the project.

Build

The Build menu, shown in Figure B.50, holds all the actions associated with compiling, running, and debugging your application.

FIG. B.50

The Build menu is used to compile, link, and debug your application.

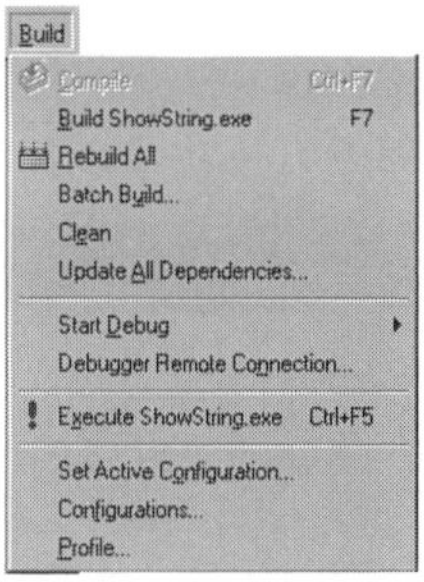

The Build menu will be a hub of activity when your are ready to compile and debug. The Build menu item names are:

Build Compile (Ctrl+F7)   Choosing this item compiles the file with focus. This is a very useful thing to do when you are expecting to find errors or warnings, such as the first time you compile after a lot of changes. For example, if there is an error in a header file that is included in many source files, a typical build produces error messages related to that header file over and over again as each source file is compiled. If there are warnings in one of your source files, a typical build links the project, but you might prefer to stop and correct the warnings. There is a Compile button on the Project toolbar, represented by a stack of papers with an arrow pointing downward.

Build Build (F7)   This item compiles all the changed files in the project and then links them. There is a Build button on the Project toolbar.

Build Rebuild All   This item compiles all files in the project, even those that have not been changed since the last build, and then links them. There are times when a typical build misses a file that should be recompiled, and using this item corrects the problem.

Build Batch Build   Typically a project contains at least two *configurations*: Debug and Release. Usually you work with the Debug configuration, changing, building, testing, and changing the project again until it is ready to be released, and then build a Release version. If you ever need to build several configurations at once, use this menu item to bring up the Batch Build dialog box shown in Figure B.51. Choose Build to compile only changed files, and Rebuild All to compile all files. If the compiles are successful, links follow.

FIG. B.51
The Batch Build dialog box builds several configurations of your project at once.

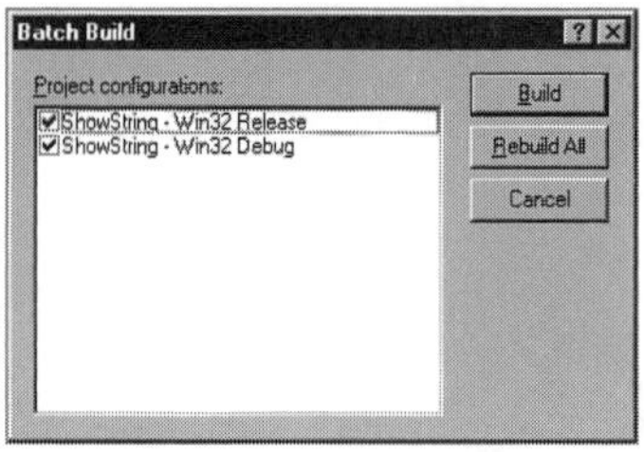

Build Clean   This item deletes all the intermediate and output files so that your project directory contains only source files.

Build Update All Dependencies   The list of dependencies tracks which files use (depend on) other files within your project. If a header file changes, all the source files that include that header file must be compiled during a build. When header files include other header files, or when files are added to a project, the list of dependencies can get messed up. This item regenerates the list and gets everything running smoothly again.

Build Start Debug   Debugging is a lengthy topic, discussed in Appendix C, "Debugging."

Build Debugger Remote Connection   It is possible to run a program on one computer and debug it on another. As part of that process, you use this menu item to connect the two computers. This is discussed in Appendix C, "Debugging."

Build Execute (Ctrl+F5)   Choosing the Build, Execute item runs your application without bringing up the debugger.

Build Set Active Configuration   The Set Active Project Configuration dialog box, shown in Figure B.52, sets which of your configurations is active (typically Debug and Release). The active configuration is built by the Build commands.

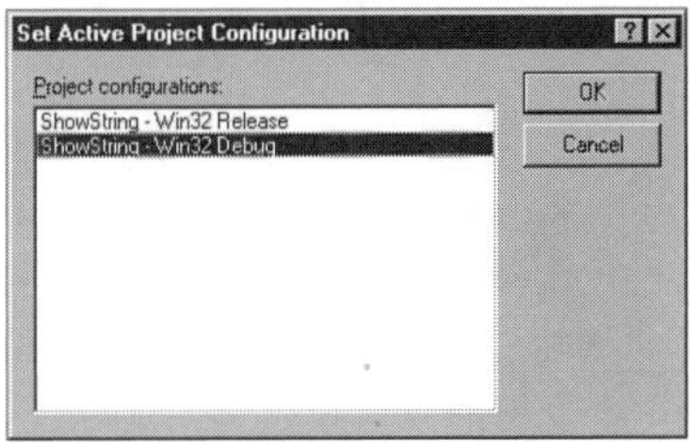

App

B

FIG. B.52

The Set Active Project Configuration dialog box sets the default configuration.

Build Configurations   Choosing this item brings up the Configurations dialog box, shown in Figure B.53. Here you can add or remove configurations. Use Project Settings to change the settings for the new configuration.

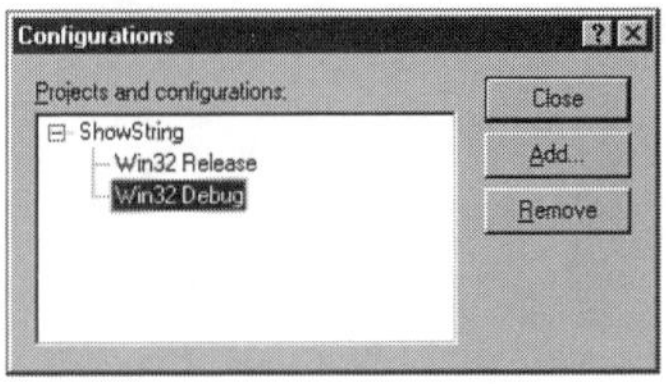

FIG. B.53

The Configurations dialog box lets you add to the standard Debug and Release configurations.

Build Profiler   The profiler is a powerful tool to identify bottlenecks in your applications. It is discussed in Chapter 24, "Improving Your Application's Performance."

Tools

The Tools menu, shown in Figure B.54, simplifies access to add-in tools, and holds some odds-and-ends leftover commands that don't fit on any other menu.

FIG. B.54

The Tools menu organizes add-in tools.

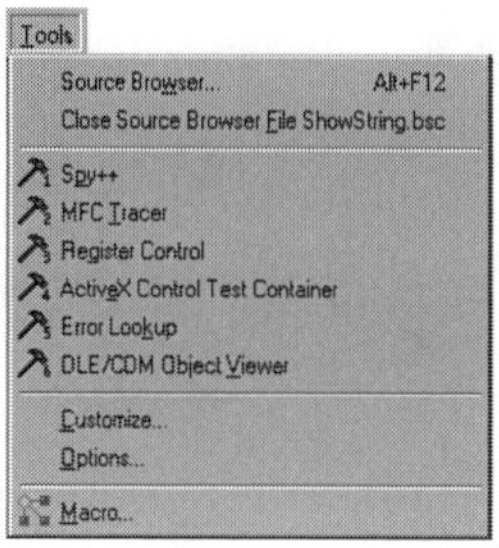

Tools Source Browser (Alt+F12)   The browser is a very powerful addition to Developer Studio; you use it whenever you go to a definition or reference, check a call graph, or otherwise explore the relationships among the classes, functions, and variables in your project. However, it's unusual to access the browser through this menu item, which brings up the Browse dialog box shown in Figure B.55. You are more likely to use Edit, Go To, a Go To item from the right-click menu, or one of the 11 buttons on the Browse toolbar.

FIG. B.55

The Browse dialog box is a less-common way to browse your objects, functions, and variables.

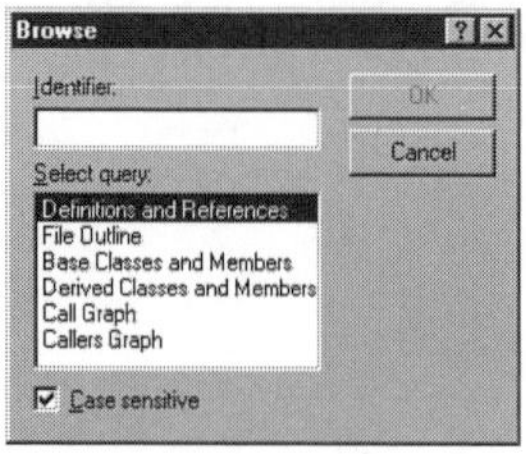

Tools Close Source Browser File   Whenever you rebuild your project, your browse file is rebuilt, too. If you rebuild your project outside Developer Studio with a tool like NMAKE, you should close the browse file first via the menu choice so that it can be updated by that tool.

Accessory Tools   A number of tools are added to the Tools menu when you install Visual C++, and you can add more tools with the Customize menu item, discussed next.

Tools Customize   Choosing this option brings up the Customize dialog box. The Commands pane of that dialog box is shown in Figure B.56 with the File buttons showing. The nine buttons correspond to items on the File menu, and if you would like one of those items on any toolbar, simply drag it from the dialog box to the appropriate place on the toolbar and release it. The list box on the left side of the Toolbar tab lets you choose other menus, each with a collection of toolbar buttons you can drag to any toolbar. Remember that the menu bar is now a toolbar to which you can drag buttons, if you want.

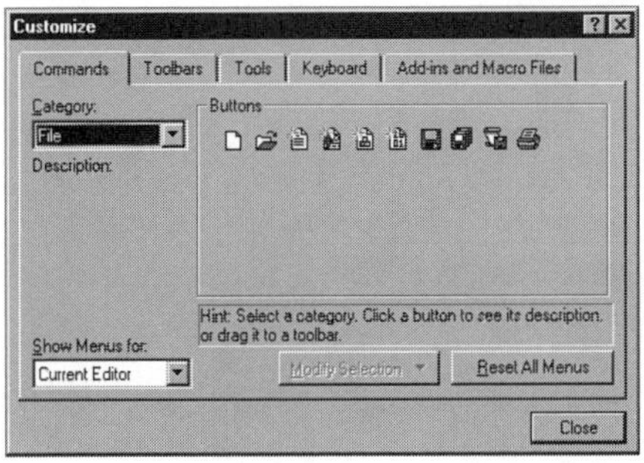

FIG. B.56

The Commands pane of the Customize dialog box lets you build your own toolbars.

> **TIP** If your toolbars are all messed up, with extra buttons or missing buttons or both, the Reset All Menus button on this dialog returns objects to their normal state.

The Toolbars pane, shown in Figure B.57, is one way to control which toolbars are displayed. As you can see, you can also suppress ToolTips if they annoy you, or turn on larger toolbar buttons if you have the space for them. (The Standard toolbar in Figure B.57 has large buttons.)

FIG. B.57

The Toolbars tab of the Customize dialog box is one way to turn a toolbar on or off, and the only way to govern ToolTips and button size.

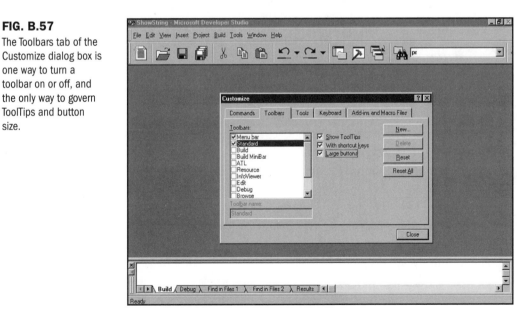

The Tools tab lets you add programs to the Tools menu, and the Keyboard tab lets you change the keyboard shortcuts for commands, or add shortcuts for commands without them. The new Add-Ins and Macro Files tab lets you add *macros*, which are written in VBScript and can automate many Developer Studio tasks, or *add-ins*, which can be written in any language and also automate Developer Studio tasks, to your workspace.

Tools Options This item gathers up a great number of settings and options that relate to Developer Studio itself. For example, Figure B.58 shows the Editor tab of the Options dialog box. If there is a feature of Developer Studio you don't like, you can almost certainly change it within this large dialog box.

FIG. B.58

The Editor tab of the Options dialog box is where you change editor settings.

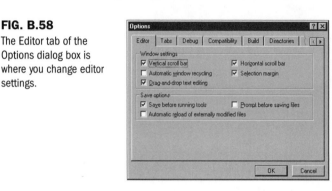

The tabs are as follows:

- *Editor.* Choose scroll bars, enable drag and drop, and set automatic saving and loading.
- *Tabs.* Sets options related to tabs (inserted when you press the Tab key) and indents (inserted by the editor on new lines after language elements such as braces).
- *Debug.* Determines what information is displayed during debugging.
- *Compatibility.* Lets you choose to emulate another editor (Brief or Epsilon) or just one portion of that editor's interface.
- *Build.* Generate an external makefile or a build log.
- *Directories.* Sets directories in which to look for include, executable, library, and source files.
- *Workspace.* Shown in Figure B.59, sets docking windows, status bar, and project reloading.
- *Data View.* (Enterprise Edition only) Governs the appearance of the DataView.
- *Macros.* Sets the rules for reloading a changed macro.
- *Format.* Sets the color scheme, including syntax coloring, for source, InfoViewer, and other windows.
- *InfoViewer.* Determines the behavior and appearance of InfoViewer.

TIP If you work on the same project all the time, check the Reload Last Project at Startup box on the Workspace tab of the Option dialog box. Loading the Developer Studio and the last project then becomes a one-step process; simply loading the Developer Studio will load the last project, too. If you work on a variety of different projects, uncheck this box so that Developer Studio comes up more quickly.

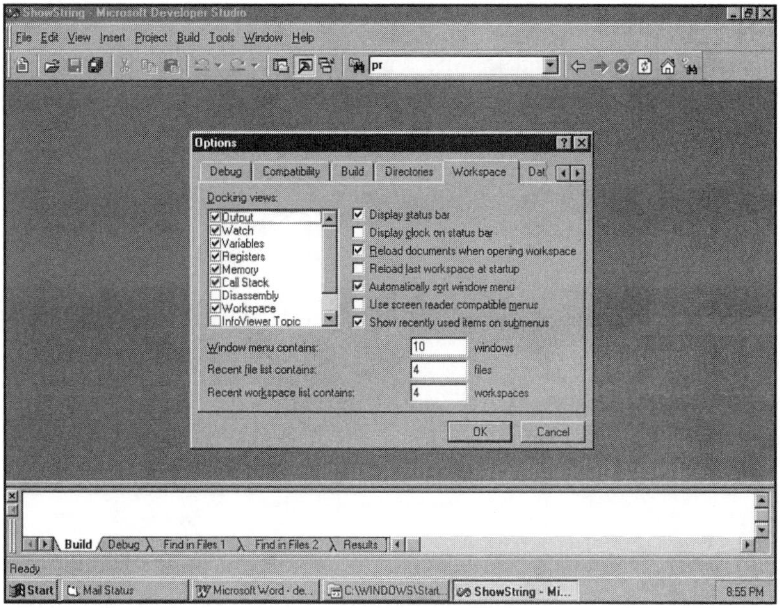

FIG. B.59

The Workspace tab of the Options dialog box sets which views dock and which float as well as reload options.

Tools Macro   This item brings up the Macro dialog box, shown in Figure B.60. Here you can record or play back simple macros, or edit a set of recorded keystrokes by adding VBScript statements.

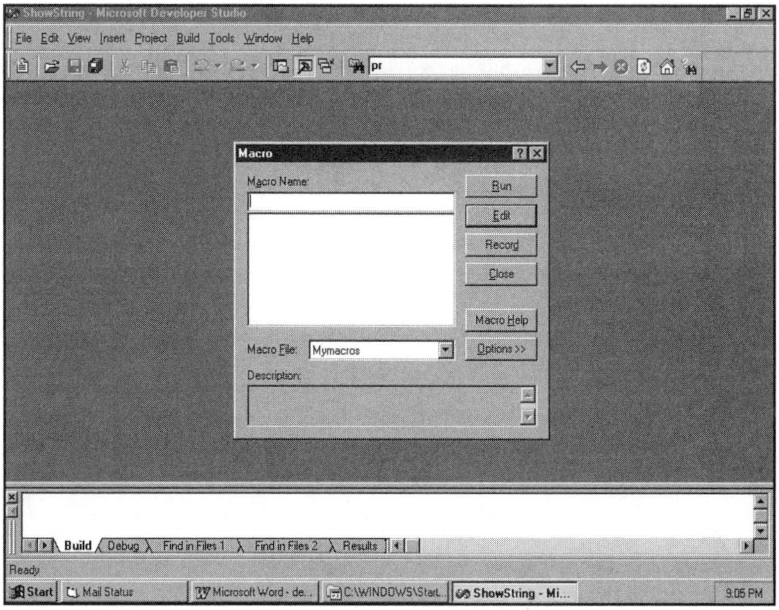

FIG. B.60

The Macro dialog box is the nerve center for creating, editing, and using macros.

Window

The Window menu, shown in Figure B.61, controls the windows in the main working area of Developer Studio.

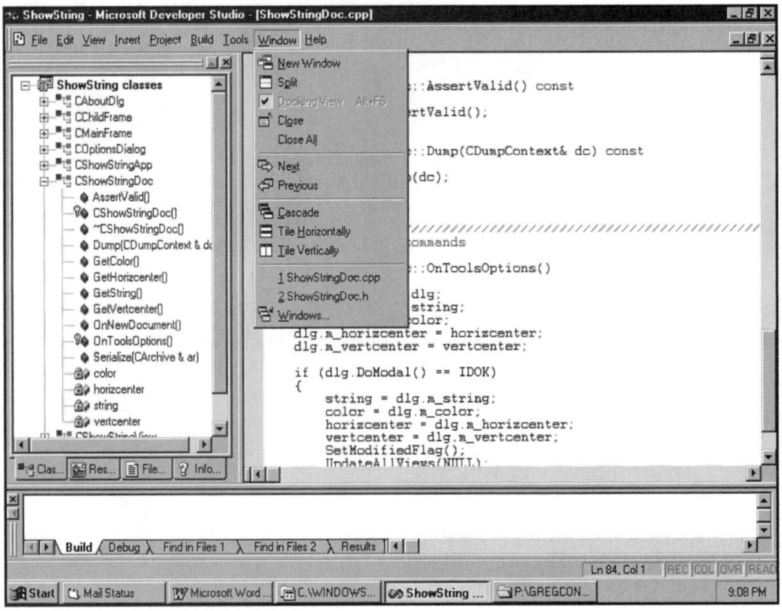

FIG. B.61

The Window menu controls the windows in the main working area.

Window New Window   Choosing this item opens another window containing the same source file as the window with focus. The first window's title bar is changed, with :1 added after the file name; in the new window, :2 is added after the file name. Changes made in one window are immediately reflected in the other. The windows can be scrolled, sized, and closed independently.

Window Split   Choosing this window puts cross hairs over the file with focus; when you click the mouse, the window is split into four panes along the lines of these cross hairs. You can drag these boundaries around in the usual way if they are not in the right place. Scrolling one pane scrolls its companion pane as well, so that the views stay in sync. To unsplit a window, drag a boundary right to the edge of the window, and it disappears. Drag away both the horizontal and vertical boundaries, and the window is no longer split.

Window Docking View   This menu item governs whether the window with focus is a docking view or not. It is disabled when the main working area has focus.

Window Close   Choosing this item closes the window with focus and its associated file. If you have any unsaved changes, you are asked whether to save them or not.

Window Close All   Choosing this item closes all the windows in the main working area. If you have any unsaved changes, you are asked whether to save them or not.

Window Next   This item switches focus to the next window. The order of the windows can be determined by looking at the list of open windows at the bottom of the menu.

Window Previous   This item switches focus to the previous window.

Window Cascade   This item arranges all the windows in the main working area in the familiar cascade pattern, like the one shown in Figure B.62. Minimized windows are not restored and cascaded.

App

B

FIG. B.62
Arranging windows in a cascade makes it easy to switch between them.

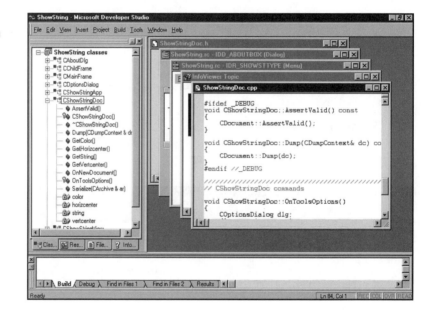

Window Tile Horizontally   This item arranges all the windows in the main working area so that each is the full width of the working area, as shown in Figure B.63. The file that had focus when you chose this item is at the top.

FIG. B.63

When windows are tiled horizontally, each is the full width of the main working area.

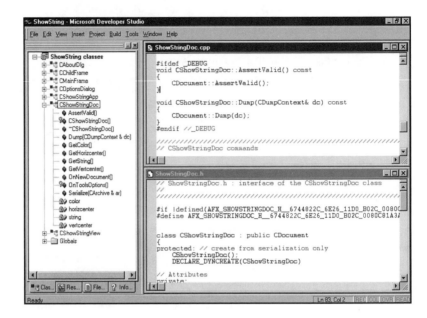

Window Tile Vertically   This item arranges all the windows in the main working area so that each is the full height of the working area, as shown in Figure B.64. The file that had focus when you chose this item is at the left.

FIG. B.64

When windows are tiled vertically, each is the full height of the main working area.

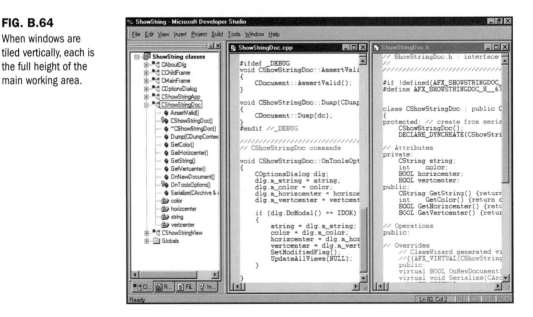

Open Windows   The bottom section of this menu lists the windows in the main working area so that you can move among them even when they are maximized. If there are more than nine open windows, only the first nine are listed. The rest can be reached by choosing Window, Windows.

Window Windows   This item brings up the Windows dialog box, shown in Figure B.65. From here you can close, save, or activate any window.

FIG. B.65

The Windows dialog box allows access to any window in the main working area.

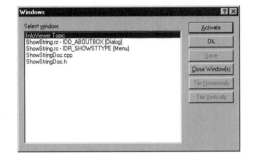

Help

There are two Help systems for Developer Studio. One is InfoViewer; the other the standard Windows Help system. Pressing F1 in most dialog boxes brings up the standard Help, but choosing items on this menu, shown in Figure B.66, activates InfoViewer.

FIG. B.66

The Help menu is your doorway to the InfoViewer system.

Help Contents   This item opens the Workspace window if it is hidden, switches to the InfoViewer tab, and displays the table of contents.

Help Search   This item brings up the Search dialog box, which can be used as an index or for queries. With the Index tab, shown in Figure B.67, you type all or part of an index term, and, as you type, the list of index terms scrolls. To open the InfoViewer topic, select a term, click List Books, then select a book from the lower list box and click Display.

FIG. B.67

The Index tab of the Search dialog box uses the index to find InfoViewer topics.

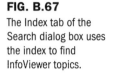

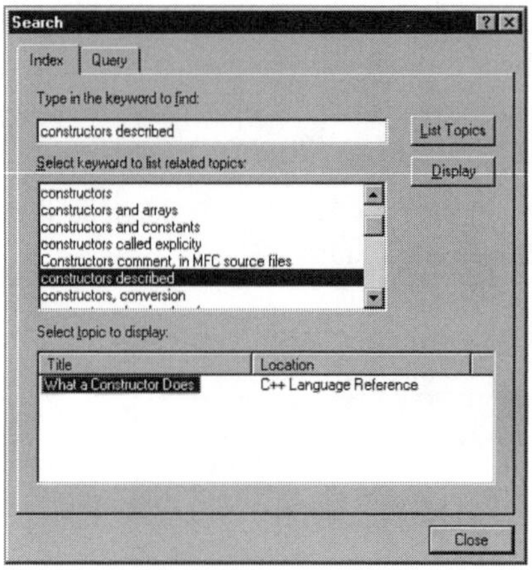

With the Query tab, shown in Figure B.68, you enter one or more keywords, then submit the query. Results are gathered into a query results list like that shown in Figure B.69. Double-click any topic to display it.

FIG. B.68

The Query tab of the Search dialog box is the way to submit queries that search through the entire InfoViewer text.

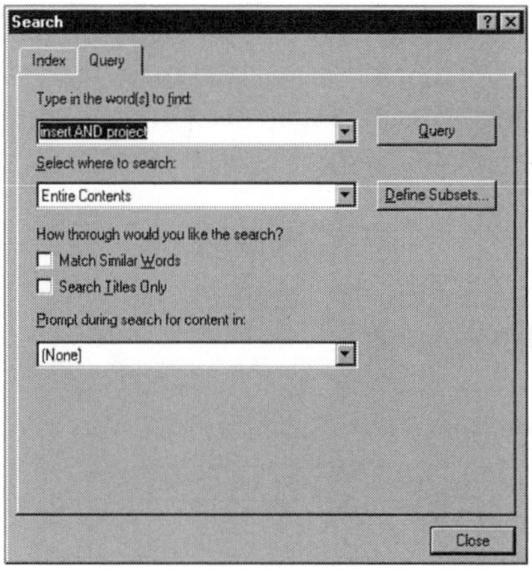

Help Documentation Home Page   This menu item brings up the Developer Studio home page, which has links to a number of other useful InfoViewer topics or Web pages.

Help InfoViewer Bookmarks   You can set bookmarks on any InfoViewer topic to help you find it again when you need it. While most people use the toolbar buttons to set, delete, and go to InfoViwer bookmarks, you can also use this menu item, which brings up the dialog box shown in Figure B.70.

FIG. B.69
The Query Results list shows the topics that match your query.

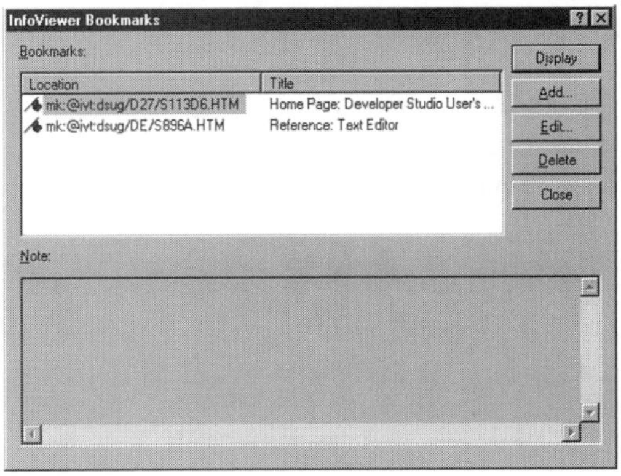

FIG. B.70
The InfoViewer Bookmarks dialog box lets you add, edit, or delete bookmarks as well as jump to them.

Help Synchronize Contents   When you move from one InfoViewer topic to another by following a link, the table of contents in the Workspace pane is not adjusted. Sometimes you can lose track of where you have jumped to. Choosing this item will redisplay the table of contents with the current topic highlighted.

Help Define Subsets   Searches through the entire InfoViewer text can be slow, and can produce too many false hits. You can restrict your use of InfoViewer to selected books within InfoViewer, called a *subset*. Choosing this item brings up the Define Subset dialog box, shown in Figure B.71.

Define Subsets
Subset Name:
Empty Subset
Save
Delete
Close
Options
Nodes to Choose From
Developer Products
Tools and Technologies
Platform, SDK, and DDK Documentation
Microsoft Developer Network Visual Studio Edition
Add
Add All
Remove
Remove All
Nodes in Subset
Include New Topics Only

FIG. B.71
The Define Subset dialog box is used to narrow the topics used within InfoViewer.

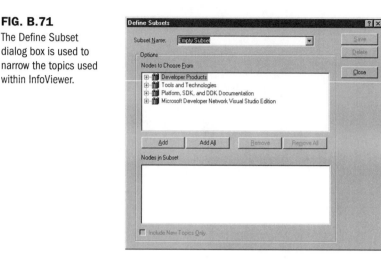

Help Select Subsets Once one or more subsets of InfoViewer have been defined, choose this item to set one of them to the default, used in query and index searches and the table of contents display.

Help Keyboard Map This item does not involve InfoViewer. Choosing it brings up the Help Keyboard dialog box, shown in Figure B.72. Use the drop-down box at the top to choose the commands for which you want to see keystrokes: Bound commands (those with keystrokes assigned), All commands, or commands from the File, Edit, View, Insert, Build, Debug, Tools, Window, or Help menus. Commands related to Images and Layout are also available.

Help Keyboard
Edit
Cate Command Keys Description
Edit SelectCharInclusive Starts inclusive character selection mode
Edit SelectColumn Ctrl+Shift+F8 Selects a columnar block of text
Edit SelectHighlight Highlights the region between the cursor and the mark
Edit SelectLine Ctrl+F8 Selects lines of text
Edit SelectPara Selects the current paragraph
Edit SelectSwapAnchor Swaps the anchor and the cursor in a selection
Edit SelectionFormat Alt+F8 Formats the selection using the smart indent settings
Edit SelectionLowercase Ctrl+U Makes the selection all lowercase
Edit SelectionTabify Replaces spaces with tabs in the selection
Edit SelectionUntabify Replaces tabs with spaces in the selection
Edit SelectionUppercase Ctrl+Shift+U Makes the selection all uppercase
Edit SentenceCut Alt+Shift+L Deletes the remainder of the sentence

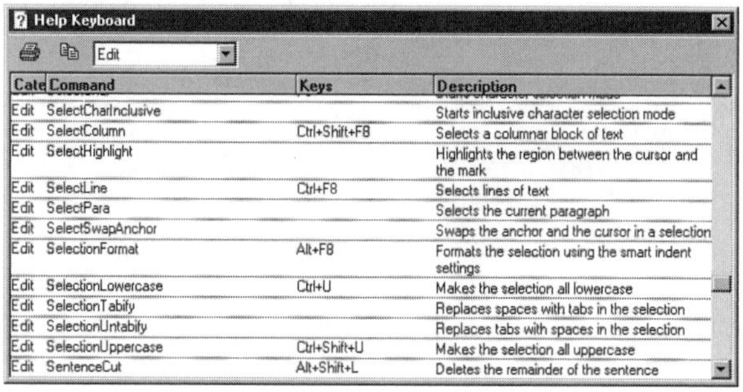

FIG. B.72
The Help Keyboard dialog box displays the keystrokes associated with commands.

Click the title bars across the top of the table to sort the display by that column. Keystrokes cannot be changed here; choose Tools, Customize and use the Keyboard tab to change keystrokes.

Help Tip of the Day Choosing this item brings up the Tip of the Day, like that in Figure B.73. Some are Windows tips; others are specific to Developer Studio. If you can't wait to see a new tip each time you open Developer Studio, click Next Tip to scroll through the list. If you are annoyed by these tips on startup, deselect the Show Tips at Startup box.

FIG. B.73
The Tip of the Day
is a great way to learn
more about Developer
Studio.

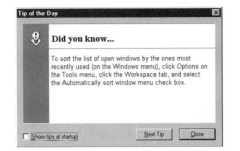

App

B

Help Technical Support   If you think you need technical support, start here. Not only do you learn how to get that support, but you may find the answer to your question.

Help Microsoft on the Web   One of the ways Microsoft supplies information about Developer Studio and other products is through the World Wide Web. Choosing this item brings up a cascading menu with a list of Web sites. Choosing any these displays the pages within InfoViewer by default. You can arrange to launch another browser if you prefer: choose Tools, Options, click the InfoViewer tab, and unselect Use Infoviewer for Microsoft on the Web. Now your default browser will be used.

Help About Developer Studio   Choosing this item brings up the About box for Developer Studio, which includes, among other information, your Product ID.

Reviewing Toolbars

After you are familiar with the types of actions you are likely to request of Developer Studio, the toolbars save you a lot of time. Instead of choosing File, Open, which takes two clicks and a mouse move, it is simpler to just click the Open button on the toolbar. There are, however, 11 toolbars plus a menu bar in this product, and that means a lot of little icons to learn. In this section, you will see each toolbar and which menu items the buttons correspond to.

Figure B.74 shows all the toolbars that are available in Developer Studio. The quickest way to turn several toolbars on and off is with the Toolbars dialog box, which you can also use to turn ToolTips on or off, and set whether the tips include the shortcut keys for the command. Any of these toolbars can dock against any of the four edges of the working area, as shown in Figure B.75. To move a docked toolbar, drag it by the *wrinkles*—the two vertical bars at the far right. You move an undocked toolbar like any other window. When it nears the edge of the main working area, the shape change shows you it will dock. Take some time to experiment moving toolbars around until you find a configuration that suits you.

FIG. B.74
Developer Studio has
12 toolbars, shown
here floating.

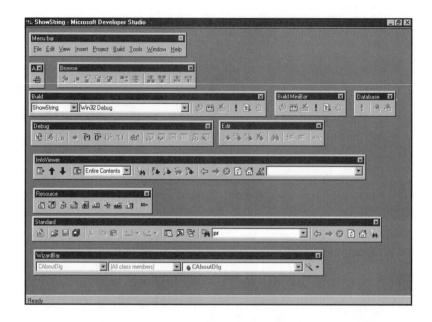

FIG. B.75
Developer Studio
toolbars can dock
against any edge.

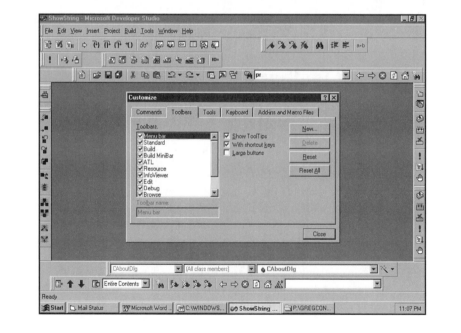

Two of the most important toolbars are the Standard and the Build Mini-Bar. These are discussed in the sections that follow. For a full description of what each button does, refer to the section earlier in this chapter for the corresponding menu item.

Standard Toolbar

The Standard Toolbar helps you maintain and edit text and files in your workspace. Table B.2 names each Standard tool button and its equivalent menu operation.

Table B.2   Standard Toolbar Buttons and Equivalent Menu Operations

Button Name	Menu Equivalent
New Text File	File, New
Open	File, Open
Save	File, Save
Save All	File, Save All
Cut	Edit, Cut
Copy	Edit, Copy
Paste	Edit, Paste
Undo	Edit, Undo
Redo	Edit, Redo
Workspace	View, Workspace
Output	View, Output
Window List	Window, Windows
Find in Files	Edit, Find in Files
Find	Edit, Find
Back	N/A
Forward	N/A
Stop	N/A
Refresh	View, Refresh
Home	Help, Documentation Home Page
Search	Help, Search
ClassWizard	View, ClassWizard

Build Mini-bar

The names for the Build Mini-Bar buttons, which are related to compiling and debugging, are defined in Table B.3.

Table B.3   Build Mini-Bar Buttons and Equivalent Menu Commands

Button Name	Menu Equivalent
Compile	Build, Compile
Build	Build, Build
Stop Build	Build, Stop Build
Execute	Build, Execute
Go	Build, Start Debug, Go
Insert/Remove Breakpoint	N/A

Using Other Toolbars

You can display any or all of the toolbars, add and remove buttons to them, and generally make Developer Studio into a product that works the way you work. Experiment and see what simplifies your software development effort. ●

Debugging

Debugging is a vital part of programming. Whenever a program doesn't do what you expect, even if it doesn't blow up, you should turn to the debugger to see what's really going on. Some of the philosophies and techniques of debugging have been explained elsewhere in this book, especially in Chapter 24, "Improving Your Application's Performance." This appendix concentrates on the nuts and bolts of how to use the debugger: the menus, toolbars, and windows that were not covered in Appendix B, "The Developer Studio Interface." ■

Debugging vocabulary

What's a breakpoint? What's the difference between Go and Restart? You'll see.

Debugging commands and windows

There's a lot of information available to you when you're debugging an application. Get a handle on it all.

Tracing

The system will tell you what's happening if you just ask it to.

Dump functions

In case of an error, get your objects to describe themselves so you can see what's wrong.

Debugging Vocabulary

Probably the most important word in debugging is *breakpoint*. A breakpoint is a spot in your program, a single line of code, where you would like to pause. Perhaps you are wondering how many times a loop gets executed, or whether control transfers inside a certain `if` statement, or whether a function even gets called. Setting a breakpoint on a line will make execution stop when that line is about to be executed. At that point, you may want the program to be off and running again, or to move through your code a line or so at a time. You may want to know the values of some of your variables, or see how control transferred to this point by examining the call stack.

When it's time to move along, there are a number of ways you might like execution to resume. These are explained in the following list:

- *Go*—Execute to the next breakpoint or, if there are no more breakpoints, until the program completes.
- *Restart*—Start all over again from the beginning.
- *Step Over*—Execute just the next statement, then pause again. If it is a function call, run the whole function and pause after returning from it.
- *Step Into*—Execute just the next statement, but if it is a function, go into it and pause before executing the first statement in the function.
- *Step Out*—Execute all the rest of the current function, and pause in the function that called this one.
- *Run To Cursor*—Start running, and stop a few lines from now, where the cursor is positioned.

Most of the information made available to you by the debugger is in the form of new windows. These are discussed in the following sections.

Debugging Commands and Windows

Developer Studio has a powerful debugger with a rich interface. There are menu items, toolbar buttons, and windows (output areas) that are used only when debugging.

Menu Items

The user interface for debugging starts with items on some ordinary menus that are used only in debugging and were not discussed in Appendix B. These include:

- Edit, Breakpoints
- View, Debug Windows, Watch
- View, Debug Windows, Call Stack
- View, Debug Windows, Memory

- View, Debug Windows, Variables
- View, Debug Windows, Registers
- View, Debug Windows, Disassembly
- Build, Start Debug, Go
- Build, Start Debug, Step Into
- Build, Start Debug, Run to Cursor
- Build, Start Debug, Attach to Process
- Build, Debugger Remote Connection

These are not the only menu items you will use, of course. For example, the Edit, Go To dialog box can be used to scroll the editor to a specific breakpoint as easily as a line, bookmark, or address. Many of the menu items you already learned about are useful during debugging.

Once you have started debugging, the Build menu disappears and a Debug menu appears. The items on that menu are as follows:

- Debug, Go
- Debug, Restart
- Debug, Stop Debugging
- Debug, Break
- Debug, Step Into
- Debug, Step Over
- Debug, Step Out
- Debug, Run to Cursor
- Debug, Step Into Specific Function
- Debug, Exceptions
- Debug, Threads
- Debug, Show Next Statement
- Debug, QuickWatch

As you can see, some of the items from the Build, Start Debug cascading menu are also on the Debug menu, along with many other items. The individual items will be discussed in the sections that follow.

Setting Breakpoints

Probably the easiest way to set a simple breakpoint is to place the cursor on the line of code where you would like to pause. Then, toggle a breakpoint by pressing F9 or by clicking the Insert/Remove breakpoint button on the Build Mini-bar, which looks like an upraised hand (you're supposed to think "Stop!"). A red dot appears in the margin to indicate you have placed a breakpoint here, as shown in Figure C.1.

FIG. C.1

The F9 key toggles a
breakpoint on the line
containing the cursor.

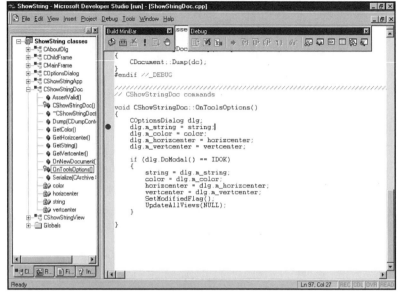

N O T E The application being debugged throughout this reference chapter is ShowString, as built in
Chapter 9, "Building a Complete Application: ShowString." ■

Choosing Edit, Breakpoints displays a tabbed dialog box to set simple or conditional
breakpoints. For example, you may want to pause whenever a certain variable's value changes.
Searching through your code for lines that change that variable's value and setting breakpoints
on them all is tiresome. Instead, use the Data tab of the Breakpoints dialog box, shown in Figure C.2. When the value of the variable changes, a message box tells you why execution is
pausing, then you can look at code and variables as described in Figure C.2.

FIG. C.2

You can arrange for
execution to pause
whenever a variable or
expression changes
value.

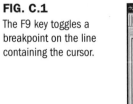

You can also set conditional breakpoints, such as "break on this line when i exceeds 100," that
spare you from mindlessly clicking Go, Go, Go until you have been through a loop 100 times.

Examining Variable Values

When you set a breakpoint and debug the program, everything proceeds normally until the breakpoint line of code is about to execute. Then Developer Studio comes up on top of your application, with some extra windows in the display and a yellow arrow in the red margin dot that indicated your breakpoint, as shown in Figure C.3. This shows you the line of code that is about to execute.

FIG. C.3

A yellow arrow indicates the line of code about to execute.

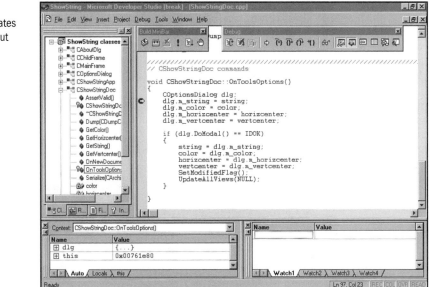

App

C

Move the mouse over a variable name, like `color` or `horizcenter`. A DataTip appears, telling you the current value of this variable. You can check as many local variables as you want like this, then continue executing and check them again. But there are other ways to examine variable values.

You could click the variable and choose Debug, QuickWatch, or click the QuickWatch button (a pair of glasses) on the toolbar. This brings up the QuickWatch window, which shows you the value of a variable or expression and lets you add it to the watch window if you wish. You're probably wondering why anyone uses this feature now that DataTips will show you a variable's value without even clicking. DataTips can't handle expressions, even simple ones like `dlg.m_horizcenter`, but QuickWatch can, as you see in Figure C.4. You can also change a variable's value with this dialog box, to recover from horrible errors and see what happens.

Figure C.5 shows a debug session after running forward a few lines from the original breakpoint (you'll see how to do that in a moment.) The Watch and Variable windows have been undocked to show more clearly which is which, and two watches have been added: one for `horizcenter` and one for `dlg.m_horizcenter`. The program is paused immediately after the user clicked OK on the Options dialog box, and in this case the user changed the string, the color, and both kinds of centering.

FIG. C.4

The QuickWatch dialog box evaluates expressions. You can add them to the Watch window by clicking Add Watch.

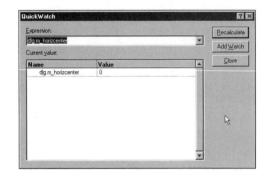

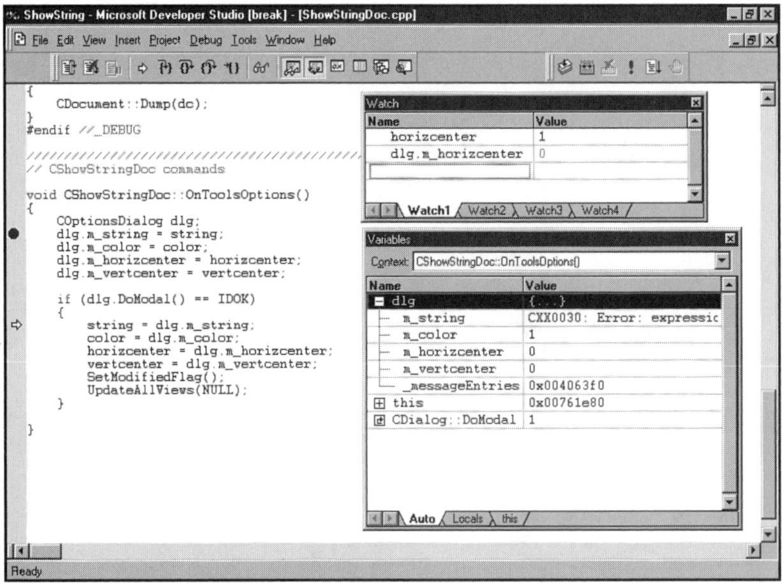

FIG. C.5

The Watch window and the Variable window make it easy to know the values of all your variables.

The Watch window simply shows the values of the two variables that were added to it. horizcenter is still true (1), because the line of code that sets it has not yet been executed. dlg.m_horizcenter is false (0), because the user deselected the check box associated with the member variable. (Dialogs boxes, controls, and associating controls with member variables are all discussed in Chapter 2, "Dialog Boxes and Controls.")

The Variables window has a lot more information in it, which sometimes makes it harder to use. The local variable dlg, and the pointer to the object for whom this member function was invoked, this, are both in the Variables window in tree form: click a + to expand the tree and a - to collapse it. In addition, the return value from DoModal, 1, is displayed.

At the top of the Variables window is a drop-down box labeled Context. Dropping it down shows how control got here: It lists the names of a series of functions. The top entry is the function in which the line about to be executed is contained,

CShowStringDoc::OnToolsOptions(). The second entry is the function that called this one, DispatchCmdMsg, which dispatches command messages. Chapter 4, "Messages and Commands," introduces commands and messages and discusses the way that control passes to a message-handling function like OnToolsOptions. Here, the debugger gives proof of this process right before your eyes. Double-click any function name in the drop-down box and the code for that function is displayed, you can look at variables local to that function, and so on.

The Call Stack window, shown in Figure C.6, is a little easier to examine than the drop-down box in the Variables window, and it shows the same information. As well as the function names, you can see the parameters that were passed to each function. You may notice the number 32771 recurring in most of the function calls. Choose View, Resource Symbols and you'll see that 32771 means ID_TOOLS_OPTIONS, the resource ID associated with the menu item Tools, Options in ShowString (see Figure C.7).

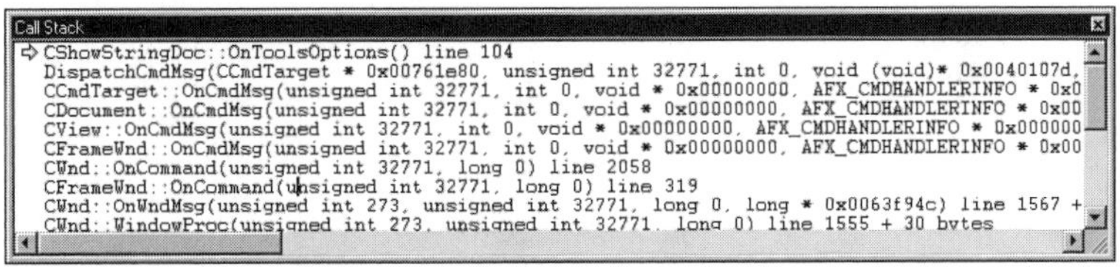

FIG. C.6

The Call Stack window shows how you got here.

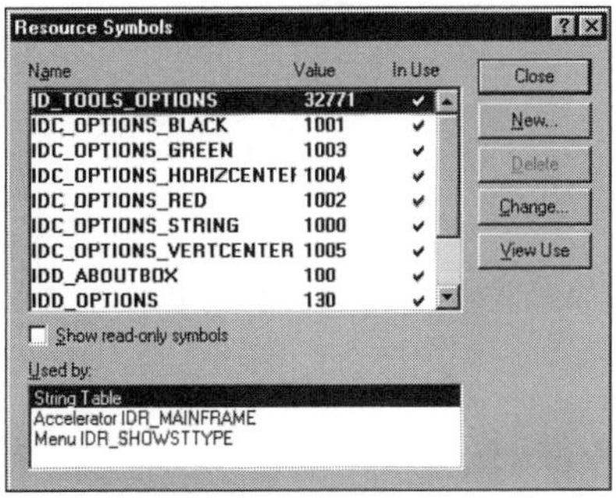

```
Call Stack                                                                    x
⇨ CShowStringDoc::OnToolsOptions() line 104
  DispatchCmdMsg(CCmdTarget * 0x00761e80, unsigned int 32771, int 0, void (void)* 0x0040107d,
  CCmdTarget::OnCmdMsg(unsigned int 32771, int 0, void * 0x00000000, AFX_CMDHANDLERINFO * 0x00
  CDocument::OnCmdMsg(unsigned int 32771, int 0, void * 0x00000000, AFX_CMDHANDLERINFO * 0x00
  CView::OnCmdMsg(unsigned int 32771, int 0, void * 0x00000000, AFX_CMDHANDLERINFO * 0x000000
  CFrameWnd::OnCmdMsg(unsigned int 32771, int 0, void * 0x00000000, AFX_CMDHANDLERINFO * 0x00
  CWnd::OnCommand(unsigned int 32771, long 0) line 2058
  CFrameWnd::OnCommand(unsigned int 32771, long 0) line 319
  CWnd::OnWndMsg(unsigned int 273, unsigned int 32771, long 0, long * 0x0063f94c) line 1567 +
  CWnd::WindowProc(unsigned int 273, unsigned int 32771, long 0) line 1555 + 30 bytes
```

FIG. C.7

The number 32771 corresponds to ID_TOOLS_OPTIONS.

```
Resource Symbols                                              ? X
Name                          Value      In Use    [ Close ]
ID_TOOLS_OPTIONS              32771         ✓
IDC_OPTIONS_BLACK             1001          ✓       [ New... ]
IDC_OPTIONS_GREEN             1003          ✓
IDC_OPTIONS_HORIZCENTEF       1004          ✓       [ Delete ]
IDC_OPTIONS_RED               1002          ✓
IDC_OPTIONS_STRING            1000          ✓       [ Change... ]
IDC_OPTIONS_VERTCENTER        1005          ✓
IDD_ABOUTBOX                  100           ✓       [ View Use ]
IDD_OPTIONS                   130           ✓

☐ Show read-only symbols
Used by:
String Table
Accelerator IDR_MAINFRAME
Menu IDR_SHOWSTTYPE
```

Stepping Through Code

Double-clicking a function name in the call stack or the context drop-down box of the Variables window doesn't make any code execute: it simply gives you a chance to examine the local variables of the functions that called the function that is now executing. After you've looked at all the variables you want to look at, it's time to move on. While there are items on the Debug menu to Step Over, Step Into, and so on, most developers use the toolbar buttons or the keyboard shortcuts. The Debug can be seen in Figures C.1, C.3, and C.5. Pause your mouse over each button to see the command it is connected to and a reminder of the keyboard shortcut. For example, the button showing an arrow going down into a pair of brace brackets is Step Into, and the shortcut key is F11.

As you move through code, the yellow arrow in the margin moves with you, to show which line is about to execute. Whenever the program is paused you can add or remove breakpoints, examine variables, or resume execution. These are the mechanics of debugging.

Other Debug Windows

Three debug windows have not yet been discussed: Memory, Registers, and Disassembly. These windows provide a level of detail rarely required in ordinary debugging. With each release of Visual C++, the circumstances under which these windows are needed dwindle. For example, the Registers window used to be the only way to see the value just returned from a function call. Now that information is in the Variables window in a more accessible format.

The Memory Window   This window, shown in Figure C.8, shows you the hex values in every byte of the memory space from 0x00000000 to 0xFFFFFFFF. It's a very long list, which makes the dialog box hard to scroll in—use the Address box to enter an address that interests you. Typically, these addresses are copied (through the clipboard, not by hand) from the Variables window. It is a handy way to look through a large array or to track down subtle platform-dependent problems.

FIG. C.8

You can examine raw memory, though you'll rarely need to.

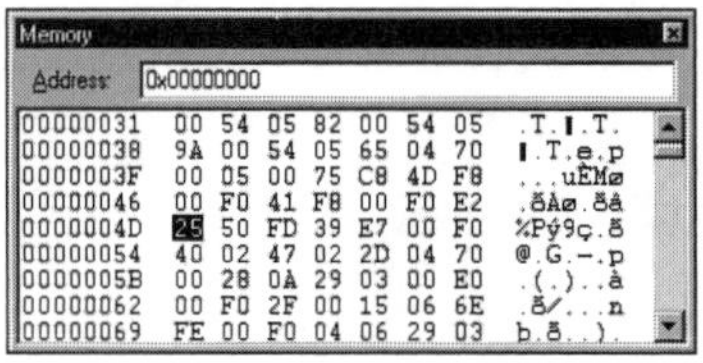

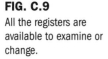

The Registers Window   If you are debugging at the assembler level, it may be useful to examine the registers. Figure C.9 shows the Registers window. This shot was taken at the same point of execution as Figure C.5, and you can see that the EAX register contains the value 1, which is the return value from DoModal().

FIG. C.9

All the registers are available to examine or change.

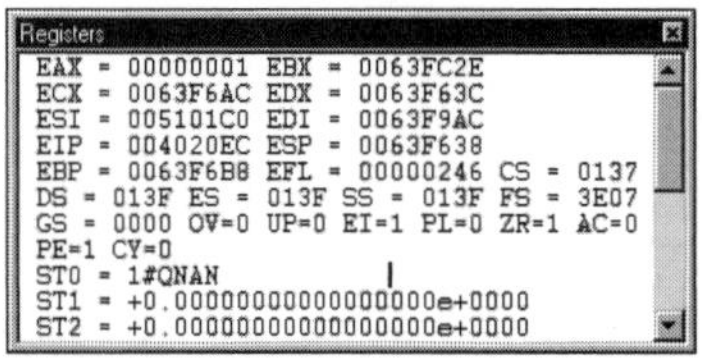

The Disassembly window   By default, the Disassembly window comes up full screen, replacing the C++ code in the main working area. You can see the assembly language statements generated for your C++ code, as shown in Figure C.10. Debugging at the assembly level is beyond the scope of this book.

FIG. C.10

You can debug the assembler that was generated for you.

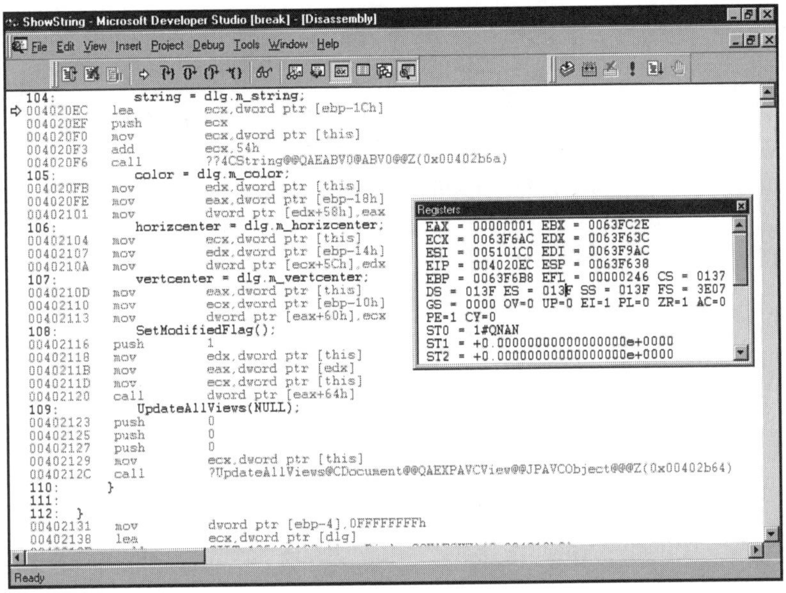

Using MFC Tracer

The MFC Tracer utility is a stand-alone application with an integrated menu item in the Developer Studio. To run it, choose Tools, MFC Tracer. Figure C.11 shows the Tracer dialog box that appears.

FIG. C.11

A stand-alone utility simplifies setting trace flags.

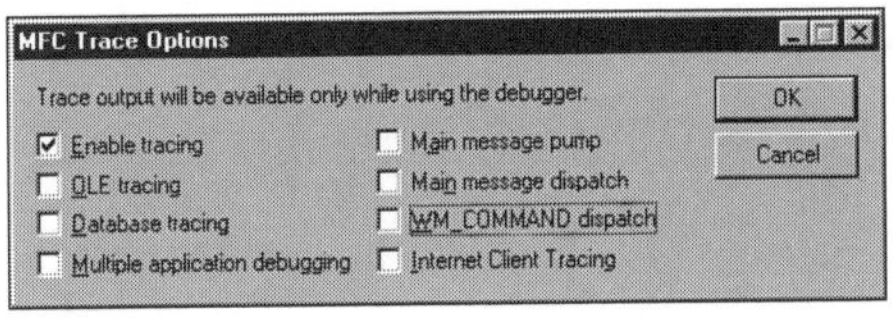

Tracer doesn't do very much: it's just an easy way to set trace flags that govern the kind of debug output you get. Try setting all the flags on and running ShowString, simply starting it up and shutting it down. Turn off a few flags and see how the output you get changes.

With all the trace flags on, your application will be slow. Use Tracer to set only the ones you're interested in, while you're interested in them. It's much easier than changing a variable on-the-fly.

Defining a *Dump* Member Function

All MFC classes have a Dump() member function. When things go wrong, some error-handling code calls this function to show you the contents of the object. You can write Dump() functions for your objects, too.

App

C

MFC classes inherit Dump() from Cobject, where it is defined like this:

```
virtual void Dump(CDumpContext& dc ) const;
```

The keyword virtual suggests you should override the method in your derived classes, and const indicates that Dump() will not modify the object state.

Like trace and assert statements, the Dump() member function disappears in a release build. This saves users seeing output they can't deal with, and makes a smaller, faster, release version for you. You have to make this happen yourself for any Dump() function you write, with conditional compilation.

In the header file, declare Dump() like this:

```
class CNewClass : public CObject
{
public:
     // other class stuff
     #ifdef _DEBUG
     virtual void Dump( CDumpContext& dc) const
     #endif
     // ...
};
```

And in the implementation file, the definition, which includes a code body, might look like this:

```
#include "cnewclass.h"

#ifdef _DEBUG
void CNewClass::Dump( CDumpContext& dc ) const
{
     CObject::Dump( dc );       // Dump parent;
     // perhaps dump individual members, works like cout
     dc << "member: " << /* member here */ endl;
}

#endif
```

As you see in the code for the Dump() function, writing the code is much like writing to standard output with the cout object, or serializing to an archive. You are provided with a CDumpContext object called dc, and you send text and values to that object with the << operator. If this is unfamiliar to you, read Chapter 8, "Persistence and File I/O."

A Sample Using *CDumpContext*, *CFile*, and *axfDump*

The sample application in this section uses the MFC debugging class CDumpContext and the global axfDump object. The debug window output from this demo and the output CFile code are in Listing C.1. To run this application yourself, create a console application as described in Chapter 28, "Future Explorations," and create an empty C++ source file called Dump.cpp. Enter this code, build, and run a debug version of the project.

 T I P The Dump project is on the CD in the RefC folder.

**Listing C.1   Dump.Cpp—Demonstrates the MFC Debugging Class
CDumpContext and *CFile***

```cpp
#include <afx.h>
// _DEBUG defined for debug build

class CPeople : public CObject
{
public:
    // constructor
        CPeople( const char * name );
        // destructor
        virtual ~CPeople();
        #ifdef _DEBUG
            virtual void Dump(CDumpContext& dc) const;
        #endif
    private:
        CString * person;
    };

    // constructor
    CPeople::CPeople( const char * name) : person( new CString(name)) {};
    // destructor
    CPeople::~CPeople(){ delete person; }

#ifdef _DEBUG
    void CPeople::Dump( CDumpContext& dc ) const
    {
        CObject::Dump(dc);
        dc << person->GetBuffer( person->GetLength() + 1);
    }
#endif

int main()
    {
        CPeople person1("Kate Gregory");
        CPeople person2("Clayton Walnum");
        CPeople person3("Paul Kimmel");

        // Use existing afxDump with virtual dump member function
        person1.Dump( afxDump );

        // Instantiate a CFile object
        CFile dumpFile("dumpout.txt", CFile::modeCreate |
            CFile::modeWrite);

        if( !dumpFile )
        {
            afxDump << "File open failed.";
        }
        else
        {
            // Dump with other CDumpContext
            CDumpContext context(&dumpFile);
```

continues

Listing C.1   Continued

```
        person2.Dump(context);
    }

    return 0;
}
```

This single file contains a class definition, all the code for the member functions of the class, and a main() function to run as a console application. Each of these parts of the file is explained in the next few paragraphs. The class is a simple wrapper around a CString pointer, which allocates the CString with new in the constructor and deletes it in the destructor. It's so simple it's actually useless for anything other than demonstrating the Dump() function.

First, the <afx.h> header file is included, which contains the CObject class definition and provides access to afxDump.

Next, this code defines a class CPeople derived from CObject. Notice the placement of the override of the virtual Dump() method and the conditional compiler wrap. (Any calls to Dump() should be wrapped in just the same way.)

After the constructor and destructor comes the code for CPeople::Dump(). Notice how it, too, is wrapped in conditional compiler directives. The call to CObject::Dump() takes advantage of the work done by the MFC programmers, dumping information all objects keep.

Finally, the main() function exercises this little class. It creates three instances of the CPeople class, and dumps the first one.

For the second CPeople object, this code creates and opens a CFile object by passing a text string to the constructor. If the open succeeds, it creates a CDumpContextObject from the file, and passes this context to Dump rather than the usual afxDump().

If you run this program, you will see output like that in Figure C.12. The file **dumpout.txt** will contain these lines:

```
a CObject at $71FDE4
Kate Gregory
```

The first line of the output, both to the debug window and to the file, came from CObject::Dump() and gives you the object type and the address. The second line is from your own code and is simply the CString kept within each CPeople.

If you get error messages when linking a Debug version of this product that refer to _beginthreadex and _endthreadex, you need to change some settings. By default, console applications are single-threaded, but MFC is multithreaded. By including afx.h and bringing in MFC, this application is making itself incompatible with the single-threaded default. To fix this, choose Project Settings and click the C/C++ tab. From the drop-down box at the top of the dialog box, choose Code Generation. In the drop-down box labelled Use Runtime Library, choose Debug Multithreaded. (The completed dialog box is shown in Figure C.13.) Click OK, and rebuild the project. You should usually change the settings for Release as well, but since the calls to Dump() aren't surrounded by tests of _DEBUG, this code won't compile a Release version anyway.

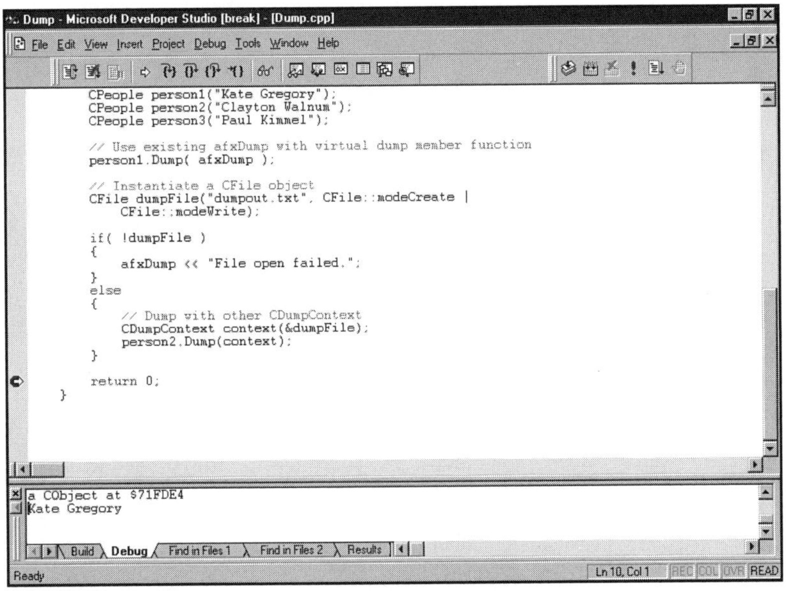

FIG. C.12

Using the *afxDump* context sends your output to the Debug window.

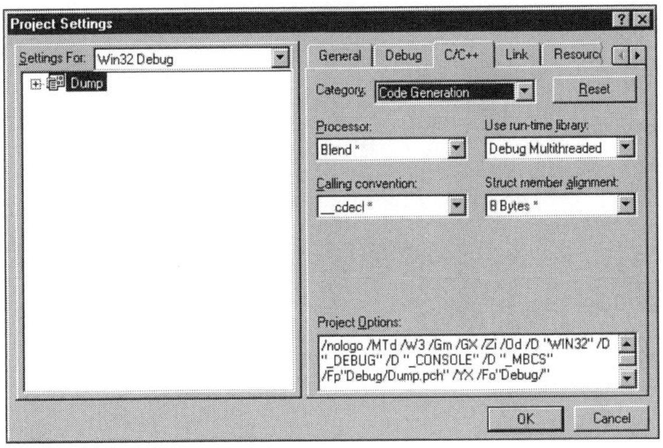

```
CPeople person1("Kate Gregory");
CPeople person2("Clayton Walnum");
CPeople person3("Paul Kimmel");

// Use existing afxDump with virtual dump member function
person1.Dump( afxDump );

// Instantiate a CFile object
CFile dumpFile("dumpout.txt", CFile::modeCreate |
    CFile::modeWrite);

if( !dumpFile )
{
    afxDump << "File open failed.";
}
else
{
    // Dump with other CDumpContext
    CDumpContext context(&dumpFile);
    person2.Dump(context);
}

return 0;
}
```

```
a CObject at $71FDE4
Kate Gregory
```

App

C

FIG. C.13

To use MFC in a console application, change to the multi-threaded runtime library.

Project Settings

Settings For: Win32 Debug

Dump

General | Debug | C/C++ | Link | Resource

Category: Code Generation   Reset

Processor: Use run-time library:
Blend *   Debug Multithreaded

Calling convention: Struct member alignment:
__cdecl *   8 Bytes *

Project Options:
/nologo /MTd /W3 /Gm /GX /Zi /Od /D "WIN32" /D
"_DEBUG" /D "_CONSOLE" /D "_MBCS"
/Fp"Debug/Dump.pch" /YX /Fo"Debug/"

OK   Cancel

Now that you've seen the basic tools of debugging in action, you'll be ready to put them to work in your own applications. You'll find errors quickly, understand other people's code, and see with your own eyes just how message-routing and other behind-the-scenes magic really occurs. If you find yourself actually enjoying debugging, don't worry: No one else has to know! ●

MFC Macros and Globals

When you're writing programs, there are many types of data and operations that you must use again and again. Sometimes, you have to do something as simple as creating a portable integer data type. Other times, you need to do something a little more complex, like extracting a word from a long word value or storing the position of the mouse pointer. As you may know, when you compile your program with Visual C++ there are many constants and variables already defined. You can use these in your programs to save time writing code and to make your programs more portable and more readable by other programmers. In the following tables, you'll get a look at the most important of these globally available constants, macros, and variables. ■

Application Information and Management Functions

Use global functions that return frequently needed information about the application in different places in a program.

ClassWizard Comment Delimiters

Learn how ClassWizard uses delimiters to keep track of what it's doing.

Collection Class Helpers

MFC defines collection classes that enable you to get these common data structures initialed quickly and manipulated easily.

Data Types

Learn about the most commonly used data types devined by Visual C++ for Windows 95 and NT.

Using Diagnostic Services

Test your program by using diagnostic macros, functions, and global variables.

Ten Categories of Macros and Global Variables

Because there are so many constants, macros, and global variables, it is helpful to divide them into ten categories, listed below. The following sections describe each of these categories and the symbols they define:

- Application information and management
- ClassWizard comment delimiters
- Collection class helpers
- CString formatting and message-box display
- Data types
- Diagnostic services
- Exception processing
- Message maps
- Runtime object model services
- Standard command and window IDs

Application Information and Management Functions

Because a typical Visual C++ application contains only one application object but many other objects created from other MFC classes, you frequently need to get information about the application in different places in a program. Visual C++ defines a set of global functions that return this information to any class in a program. These functions, which are listed in Table D.1, can be called from anywhere within an MFC program. For example, you frequently need to get a pointer to an application's main window. The following function call accomplishes that task:

```
CWnd* pWnd = AfxGetMainWnd();
```

Table D.1   Application Information and Management

Function	Description
AfxBeginThread()	Creates a new thread. (See Chapter 27, "Multitasking with Windows Threads.")
AfxEndThread()	Terminates a thread.
AfxGetApp()	Gets the application's CWinApp pointer.
AfxGetAppName()	Gets the application's name.
AfxGetInstanceHandle()	Gets the application's instance handle.
AfxGetMainWnd()	Gets a pointer to the application's main window.
AfxGetResourceHandle()	Get the application's resource handle.

Function	Description
AfxGetThread()	Gets a pointer to a CWinThread object.
AfxRegisterClass()	Registers a window class in an MFC DLL.
AfxRegisterWndClass()	Registers a Windows window class in an MFC application.
AfxSetResourceHandle()	Sets the instance handle that determines where to load the application's default resources.
AfxSocketInit()	Initializes Windows Sockets. (See Chapter 18, "Sockets, MAPI, and the Internet.")

ClassWizard Comment Delimiters

Visual C++ defines a number of delimiters that ClassWizard uses to keep track of what it's doing, as well as to locate specific areas of source code. Although you'll rarely, if ever, use these macros yourself, you will see them embedded in your AppWizard applications, so you might like to know exactly what they do. Table D.2 fills you in.

Table D.2 ClassWizard Delimiters

Delimiter	Description
AFX_DATA	Starts and ends member variable declarations in header files that are associated with dialog data exchange.
AFX_DATA_INIT	Starts and ends dialog data exchange variable initialization in a dialog class's constructor.
AFX_DATA_MAP	Starts and ends dialog data exchange function calls in a dialog class's DoDataExchange() function.
AFX_DISP	Starts and ends Automation declarations in header files.
AFX_DISP_MAP	Starts and ends Automation mapping in implementation files.
AFX_EVENT	Starts and ends ActiveX event declarations in header files.
AFX_EVENT_MAP	Starts and ends ActiveX events in implementation files.
AFX_FIELD	Starts and ends member variable declarations in header files that are associated with database record field exchange.
AFX_FIELD_INIT	Starts and ends record field exchange member variable initialization in a record set class's constructor.
AFX_FIELD_MAP	Starts and ends record field exchange function calls in a record set class's DoFieldExchange() function.
AFX_MSG	Starts and ends ClassWizard entries in header files for classes that use message maps.

App

D

continues

Table D.2 Continued	
Delimiter	**Description**
AFX_MSG_MAP	Starts and ends message map entries.
AFX_VIRTUAL	Starts and ends virtual function overrides in header files.

Collection Class Helpers

Because certain types of data structures are so commonly used in programming, MFC defines collection classes that enable you to get these common data structures initialized quickly and manipulated easily. MFC includes collection classes for arrays, linked lists, and mapping tables. Each of these types of collections contain elements that represent the individual pieces of data that compose the collection. To make it easier to access these elements, MFC defines a set of functions created from templates (see Chapter 26, "Exceptions, Templates, and the Latest Additions to C++.") The functions are shown in Table D.3, and you provide the implementation for each particular data type.

For example, if you want to keep a sorted list, the functions that insert new items into the list must be able to compare two Truck objects or two Employee objects to decide where to put a new Truck or Employee. You implement CompareElements() for the Truck class or Employee class, and then the collection class code can use this function to decide where to put new additions to the collection.

Table D.3 Collection Class Helper Functions	
Function	**Description**
CompareElements()	Checks elements for equality.
ConstructElements()	Constructs new elements (works similar to a class constructor).
DestructElements()	Destroys elements (works similar to a class destructor).
DumpElements()	Provides diagnostic output in text form.
HashKey()	Calculates hashing keys.
SerializeElements()	Saves or loads elements to or from an archive.

CString Formatting and Message-Box Display

If you've done much Visual C++ programming, you know that MFC features a special string class, called CString, that makes string handling under C++ less cumbersome. CString objects are used extensively throughout MFC programs, and are discussed in Appendix E, "Useful Classes." There are times when CString is not the right class though, such as when dealing with strings in a resource's string table. These global functions, which replace format characters in string tables, provide the CString Format() capability for resource strings. There's also a global function for displaying a message box (see Table D.4).

Table D.4   *CString* Formatting and Message-Box Functions

Function	Description
AfxFormatString1()	Replaces the format characters (such as %1) in a string resource with a given string.
AfxFormatString2()	Replaces the format characters "%1" and "%2" in a string resource with the given strings.
AfxMessageBox()	Displays a message box.

Data Types

The most commonly used constants are those that define a portable set of data types. You've seen tons of these constants, which are named by using all uppercase letters, used in Windows programs. You'll recognize many of these from the Windows SDK. Others are included only as part of Visual C++. You use these constants exactly as you would any other data type. For example, to declare a Boolean variable, you'd write something like this:

```
BOOL flag;
```

Table D.5 lists the most commonly used data types defined by Visual C++ for Windows 95 and NT. Searching in the help index on any one of these types will lead you to a page in the online help that lists all the data types used in MFC and the Windows SDK.

Table D.5   Commonly Used Data Types

Constant	Data Type
BOOL	Boolean value.
BSTR	32-bit pointer to character data.
BYTE	8-bit unsigned integer.
COLORREF	32-bit color value.
DWORD	32-bit unsigned integer.
LONG	32-bit signed integer.
LPARAM	32-bit window-procedure parameter.
LPCRECT	32-bit constant RECT structure pointer.
LPCSTR	32-bit string-constant pointer.

App
D

continues

Table D.5   Continued

Constant	Data Type
LPSTR	32-bit string pointer.
LPVOID	32-bit void pointer.
LRESULT	32-bit window-procedure return value.
POSITION	The position of an element in a collection.
UINT	32-bit unsigned integer.
WNDPROC	32-bit window-procedure pointer.
WORD	16-bit unsigned integer.
WPARAM	32-bit window-procedure parameter.

Using Diagnostic Services

Once you have your program written, you're far from done. Then comes the grueling task of testing, which means rolling up your sleeves, cranking up your debugger, and weeding out all the gotchas hiding in your code. Luckily, Visual C++ provides many macros, functions, and global variables that you can use to incorporate diagnostic abilities into your projects. Using these tools, you can print output to a debugging window, check the integrity of memory blocks, and much more. Table D.6 lists these valuable diagnostic macros, functions, and global variables.

Table D.6   Diagnostic Macros, Functions, and Global Variables

Symbol	Description
AfxCheckMemory()	Verifies the integrity of allocated memory.
AfxDoForAllClasses()	Calls a given iteration function for all classes that are derived from CObject and that incorporate runtime type checking.
AfxDoForAllObjects()	Calls a given iteration function for all objects that were derived from CObject and that were allocated with the new operator.
afxDump	A global CDumpContext object that enables a program to send information to the debugger window.
AfxDump()	Dumps an object's state during a debugging session.
AfxEnableMemoryTracking()	Toggles memory tracking.
AfxIsMemoryBlock()	Checks that memory allocation was successful.

Symbol	Description
`AfxIsValidAddress()`	Checks that a memory address range is valid for the program.
`AfxIsValidString()`	Checks string pointer validity.
`afxMemDF`	A global variable that controls memory-allocation diagnostics. Can be set to `allocMemDF`, `DelayFreeMemDF`, or `checkAlwaysMemDF`.
`AfxSetAllocHook()`	Sets a user-defined hook function that is called whenever memory allocation is performed.
`afxTraceEnabled`	A global variable that enables or disables TRACE output.
`afxTraceFlags`	A global variable that enables the MFC reporting features.
ASSERT	Prints a message and exits the program if the assert expression is false. (See Chapter 24, "Improving Your Application's Performance.")
ASSERT_VALID	Validates an object by calling the object's `AssertValid()` function.
DEBUG_NEW	Used in place of the `new` operator in order to trace memory-leak problems. (See Chapter 24, "Improving Your Application's Performance.")
TRACE	Creates formatted strings for debugging output. (See Chapter 24, "Improving Your Application's Performance.")
TRACE0	Same as TRACE but requires no arguments in the format string.
TRACE1	Same as TRACE but requires one argument in the format string.
TRACE2	Same as TRACE but requires two arguments in the format string.
TRACE3	Same as TRACE but requires three arguments in the format string.
VERIFY	Like ASSERT, but VERIFY evaluates the assert expression in both the Debug and Release versions of MFC. If the assertion fails, a message is printed and the program halted only in the Debug version.

App
D

Exception Processing

One of the newest elements of the C++ language is *exceptions*, which give a program greater control over how errors are handled. (See Chapter 26, "Exceptions, Templates, and the Latest Additions to C++.") Before exceptions were part of the language, MFC developers used macros to achieve the same results. Now that exceptions are firmly established in Visual C++, a number of functions make it easier to throw exceptions of various types. These macros and functions are listed in Table D.7.

Table D.7   Exception Macros and Functions

Symbol	Description
`AfxAbort()`	Terminates an application upon a fatal error.
`AfxThrowArchiveException()`	Throws an archive exception.
`AfxThrowDAOException()`	Throws a `CDaoException`.
`AfxThrowDBException()`	Throws a `CDBException`.
`AfxThrowFileException()`	Throws a file exception.
`AfxThrowMemoryException()`	Throws a memory exception.
`AfxThrowNotSupportedException()`	Throws a not-supported exception.
`AfxThrowOleDispatchException()`	Throws an OLE automation exception.
`AfxThrowOleException()`	Throws an OLE exception.
`AfxThrowRe-sourceException()`	Throws a resource-not-found exception.
`AfxThrowUserException()`	Throws an end-user exception.
AND_CATCH	Begins code that will catch specified exceptions not caught in the preceding TRY block.
AND_CATCH_ALL	Begins code that will catch all exceptions not caught in the preceding TRY block.
CATCH	Begins code for catching an exception.
CATCH_ALL	Begins code for catching all exceptions.
END_CATCH	Ends CATCH or AND_CATCH code blocks.
END_CATCH_ALL	Ends CATCH_ALL code blocks.
THROW	Throws a given exception.
THROW_LAST	Throws the most recent exception to the next handler.
TRY	Starts code that will accommodate exception handling.

Using Message-Map Macros

Windows is an event-driven operating system, which means that every Windows application must handle a flood of messages that flow between an application and the system. MFC does away with the clunky `switch` statements that early Windows programmers had to construct in order to handle messages and replaces those statements with a message map. A *message map* is nothing more than a table that matches a message with its message handler (see Chapter 4, "Messages and Commands"). In order to simplify the declaration and definition of these tables, Visual C++ defines a set of message-map macros. Many of these macros, which are listed in Table D.8, will already be familiar to experienced MFC programmers.

Table D.8   Message-Map Macros

Macro	Description
BEGIN_MESSAGE_MAP	Begins a message-map definition.
DECLARE_MESSAGE_MAP	Starts a message-map declaration.
END_MESSAGE_MAP	Ends a message-map definition.
ON_COMMAND	Begins a command-message message-map entry.
ON_COMMAND_RANGE	Begins a command-message message-map entry that maps multiple messages to a single handler.
ON_CONTROL	Begins a control-notification message-map entry.
ON_CONTROL_RANGE	Begins a control-notification message-map entry that maps multiple control IDs to a single handler.
ON_MESSAGE	Begins a user-message message-map entry.
ON_REGISTERED_MESSAGE	Begins a registered user-message message-map entry.
ON_UPDATE_COMMAND_UI	Begins a command-update message-map entry.
ON_UPDATE_COMMAND_UI_RANGE	Begins a command-update message-map entry that maps multiple command-update messages to a single handler.

App
D

Runtime Object Model Services

Frequently in your programs you need access to information about classes at runtime. MFC supplies a macro for obtaining this type of information in a `CRuntimeClass` structure. In addition, the MFC application framework relies on a set of macros to declare and define runtime abilities (such as object serialization and dynamic object creation). If you've used AppWizard at all, you've seen these macros used in the generated source-code files. If you're an advanced MFC programmer, you may have even used these macros yourself. Table D.9 lists the runtime macros and their descriptions.

Table D.9 Runtime Services Macros

Macro	Description
DECLARE_DYNAMIC	Used in a class declaration to enable runtime class information access.
DECLARE_DYNCREATE	Used in a class declaration to allow the class (derived from CObject) to be created dynamically. Also, allows runtime class information access.
DECLARE_OLECREATE	Used in a class declaration to allow object creation with OLE automation.
DECLARE_SERIAL	Used in a class declaration to allow object serialization, as well as runtime class information access.
IMPLEMENT_DYNAMIC	Used in a class implementation to enable runtime class information access.
IMPLEMENT_DYNCREATE	Used in a class implementation to allow dynamic creation of the object and runtime information access.
IMPLEMENT_OLECREATE	Used in a class implementation to enable object creation with OLE.
IMPLEMENT_SERIAL	Used in a class implementation to allow object serialization and runtime class information access.
RUNTIME_CLASS	Returns a CRuntimeClass structure for the given class.

Standard Command and Window IDs

There are myriad standard messages that can be generated by a user of a Windows application. For example, whenever the user selects a menu command from a standard menu like File or Edit, the program sends a message. Each of these standard commands is represented by an ID. In order to relieve the programmer of having to define the dozens of IDs that are often used in a Windows application, Visual C++ defines these symbols in a file called AFXRES.H. Some of these IDs have obvious purposes (for example, ID_FILE_OPEN), but many others are used internally by MFC for everything from mapping standard Windows messages to their handlers to defining string-table IDs to assigning IDs to toolbar and status-bar styles.

There are far too many of these identifiers to list here. However, if you're interested in seeing them, just load the AFXRES.H file from your Visual C++ installation folder. ●

Useful Classes

MFC includes a lot more than classes for programming the Windows graphical user interface. It also features many utility classes for handling such things as lists, arrays, times and dates, and mapped collections. By using these classes, you can gain extra power over data in your programs, as well as simplify many operations involved in using complex data structures such as lists.

For example, because MFC's array classes can change their size dynamically, you are relieved of creating over-sized arrays in an attempt to ensure that the arrays are large enough for the application. In this way, you save memory. The other collection classes provide many other similar conveniences. ■

How to create array, list, and map collection objects

By using MFC's ready-to-use collection classes, you gain more power over mundane data structures.

How to add, remove, and modify collection elements

The MFC collection classes provide member functions for modifying the contents of a collection.

How to iterate over collections

When you need to search through a collection, use these iteration member functions.

How to create your own type of collection class

You're not limited to MFC's collection classes. You can roll your own any time you need them.

How to use CString

When you need to work with character strings, MFC's CString class is the one for you!

How to use the time classes

Many programs need to manage the time and date. MFC's Date class is perfect for this task.

The Array Classes

MFC's array classes enable you to create and manipulate one-dimensional array objects that can hold virtually any type of data. These array objects work much like the standard arrays that you're used to using in your programs, except that MFC can enlarge or shrink an array object dynamically at runtime. This means that you don't have to be concerned with dimensioning your array just right when it's declared. Because MFC's arrays can grow dynamically, you can forget about the memory waste that often occurs with conventional arrays, which must be dimensioned to hold the maximum number of elements that may be needed in the program, whether or not you actually use every element.

The array classes include CByteArray, CDWordArray, CObArray, CPtrArray, CUIntArray, CWordArray, and CStringArray. As you can tell from the class names, each class is designed to hold a specific type of data. For example, the CUIntArray, which will be used in this section's examples, is an array class that can hold unsigned integers. The CPtrArray class, on the other hand, represents an array of pointers to void, and the CObArray class represents an array of objects. The array classes are all almost identical, differing only in the type of data that they store. Once you've learned to use one of the array classes, you've learned to use them all. Table E.1 lists the member functions of the array classes and their descriptions.

Table E.1   Member Functions of the Array Classes

Function	Description
Add()	Appends a value to the end of the array, increasing the size of the array as needed.
ElementAt()	Gets a reference to an array element's pointer.
FreeExtra()	Releases unused array memory.
GetAt()	Gets the value at the specified array index.
GetSize()	Gets the number of elements in the array.
GetUpperBound()	Gets the array's *upper bound*, which is the highest valid index at which a value can be stored.
InsertAt()	Inserts a value at the specified index, shifting existing elements upward as necessary to accommodate the insert.
RemoveAll()	Removes all the array's elements.
RemoveAt()	Removes the value at the specified index.
SetAt()	Places a value at the specified index. Because this function will not increase the size of the array, the index must be currently valid.

Function	Description
SetAtGrow()	Places a value at the specified index, increasing the size of the array as needed.
SetSize()	Sets the array's initial size and the amount by which it grows when needed. By allocating more than one element's worth of space at a time, you save time but could waste memory.

Introducing the Array Application

To illustrate how the array classes work, this chapter includes the Array application. After a brief tour of the application, you'll see how to build it yourself in the sections that follow. When you run the program, you see the window shown in Figure E.1. The window displays the current contents of the array. Because the application's array object (which is an instance of CUIntArray) starts off with ten elements, the values for these elements (indexed as 0 through 9) are displayed on the screen. The application enables you to change, add, or delete elements in the array and see the results.

T I P This application is on the CD in the RefE folder.

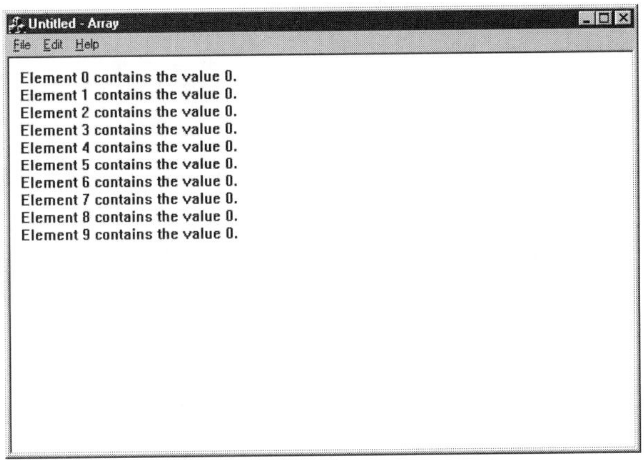

FIG. E.1

The Array Demo application enables you to experiment with MFC's array classes.

```
Untitled - Array                                    _ □ ×
File  Edit  Help

Element 0 contains the value 0.
Element 1 contains the value 0.
Element 2 contains the value 0.
Element 3 contains the value 0.
Element 4 contains the value 0.
Element 5 contains the value 0.
Element 6 contains the value 0.
Element 7 contains the value 0.
Element 8 contains the value 0.
Element 9 contains the value 0.
```

App

E

You can add an element to the array in several ways. To see these choices, click in the application's window. The dialog box shown in Figure E.2 appears. Type an array index in the Index box and the new value in the Value box. Then select whether you want to set, insert, or add the element. When you choose Set, the value of the element you specify in the Index field gets changed to the value in the Value field. The Insert operation creates a new array element at the location specified by the index, pushing succeeding elements forward. Finally, the Add operation just tacks the new element onto the end of the array. In this case, the program ignores the Index field of the dialog box.

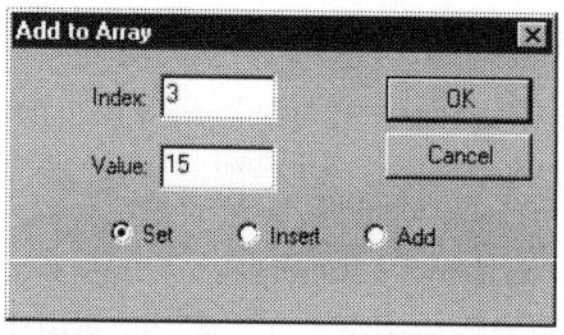

FIG. E.2

The Add to Array dialog box enables you to add elements to the array.

Suppose, for example, that you enter **3** into the dialog box's Index field and **15** into the Value field, leaving the Set radio button selected. Figure E.3 shows the result: the program has placed the value 15 into element **3** of the array, overwriting the value that was there previously. Now type **2** into Index, **25** into Value, select the Insert radio button, and click OK. Figure E.4 shows the result: the program stuffs a new element into the array, shoving the other elements forward.

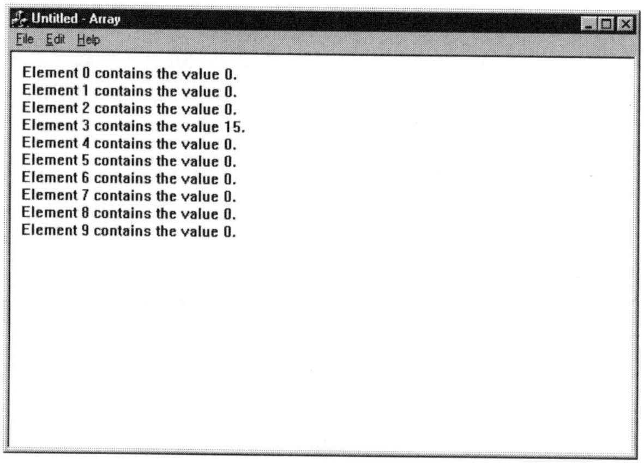

FIG. E.3

The value of 15 has been placed into array element 3.

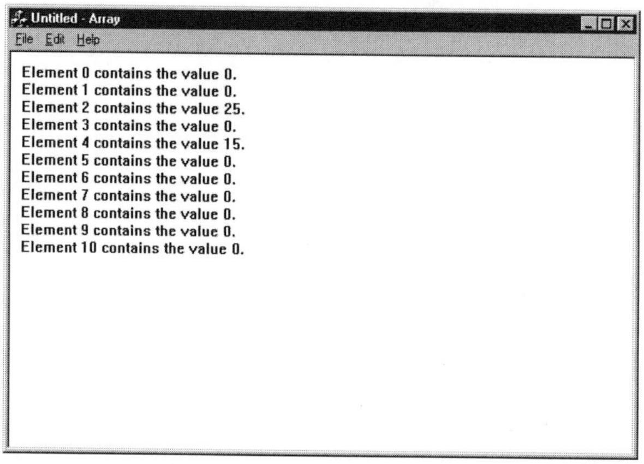

FIG. E.4

The screen now shows the new array elements, giving 11 elements in all.

An interesting thing to try—something that really shows how dynamic MFC's arrays are—is to set an array element beyond the end of the array. For example, given the program's state shown in Figure E.4, if you type **20** in Index and **45** in Value and then choose the Set radio button, you get the results shown in Figure E.5. Because there was no element 20, the array class created the new elements that it needed to get to 20. You don't need to keep track of how many elements are in the array. Try that with an old-fashioned array.

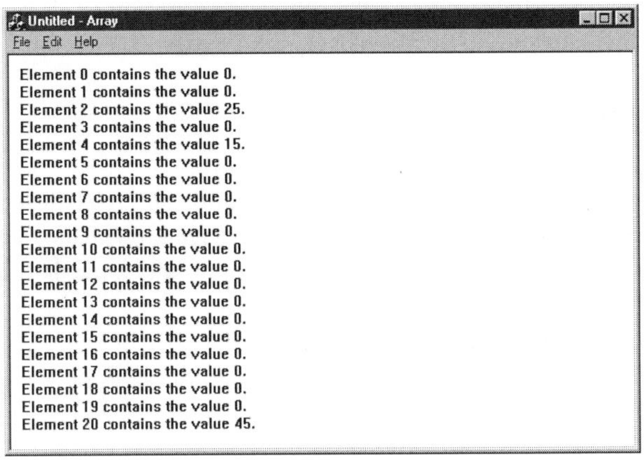

FIG. E.5

The array class has added the elements needed in order to set element 20.

Besides adding new elements to the array, you can also delete elements in one of two ways. To do this, first right-click in the window. When you do, you see the dialog box shown in Figure E.6. If you type an index into the Remove field and then click OK, the program deletes the selected element from the array. This is the opposite of the effect of Insert command, because the Remove command shortens the array rather than lengthening it. If you want, you can select the Remove All option in the dialog box. Then the program deletes all elements from the array, leaving it empty.

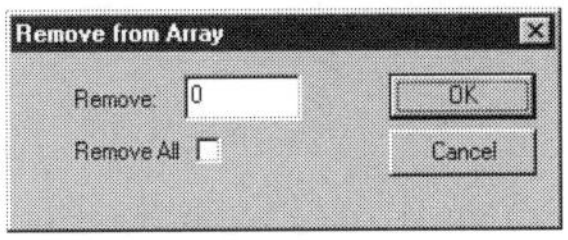

App
E

FIG. E.6

The Remove from Array dialog box enables you to delete elements from the array.

Declaring and Initializing the Array

Now you'd probably like to see how all this array trickery works. It's really pretty simple. First, the program declares the array object as a data member of the view class, like this:

```
CUIntArray array;
```

Then, in the view class's constructor, the program initializes the array to 10 elements:

```
array.SetSize(10, 5);
```

The SetSize() function takes as parameters the number of elements to give the array initially and the number of elements by which the array should grow whenever it needs to. You don't need to call SetSize() in order to use the array class. However, if you fail to do so, MFC adds elements to the array one at a time, as needed, which is a slow process (although, unless you're doing some heavy processing, you're not likely to notice any difference in speed.) If your application doesn't add elements to its arrays often, and you are concerned about memory consumption, don't use SetSize(). If your application repeatedly adds elements, and you have lots of memory available, using SetSize() to arrange for many elements to be allocated at once will reduce the number of allocations performed, giving you a faster application.

Adding Elements to the Array

After setting the array size, the program waits for the user to click the left or right mouse buttons in the window. When the user does, the program springs into action, displaying the appropriate dialog box and processing the values entered into the dialog box. Listing E.1 shows the Array Demo application's OnLButtonDown() function, which handles the left mouse button clicks.

> **TIP** Chapter 4, "Messages and Commands," shows you how to catch mouse clicks and arrange for a message-handler like OnLButtonDown() to be called.

Listing E.1   CArrayView::OnLButtonDown()

```
void CArrayView::OnLButtonDown(UINT nFlags, CPoint point)
{
    ArrayAddDlg dialog(this);
    dialog.m_index = 0;
    dialog.m_value = 0;
    dialog.m_radio = 0;
    int result = dialog.DoModal();
    if (result == IDOK)
    {
        if (dialog.m_radio == 0)
            array.SetAtGrow(dialog.m_index, dialog.m_value);
        else if (dialog.m_radio == 1)
            array.InsertAt(dialog.m_index, dialog.m_value, 1);
        else
            array.Add(dialog.m_value);
        Invalidate();
    }
    CView::OnLButtonDown(nFlags, point);
}
```

This code starts by creating a dialog object and initializing it, as discussed in Chapter 2, "Dialog Boxes and Controls." If the user exits the dialog box by clicking the OK button, the OnLButtonDown() function checks the value of the dialog box's m_radio data member. A value of 0 means that the first radio button (Set) is selected, 1 means that the second button (Insert) is selected, and 2 means that the third button (Add) is selected.

Chapter 2, "Dialog Boxes and Controls," discusses displaying dialog boxes and getting values from them.

If the user wants to set an array element, the program calls SetAtGrow(), giving the array index and the new value as arguments. Unlike the regular SetAt() function, which you can use only with a currently valid index number, SetAtGrow() will enlarge the array as necessary in order to set the specified array element. That's how the extra array elements were added when you chose to set element 20.

When the user has selected the Insert radio button, the program calls the InsertAt() function, giving the array index and new value as arguments. This causes MFC to create a new array element at the index specified, shoving the other array elements forward. Finally, when the user has selected the Add option, the program calls the Add() function, which adds a new element to the end of the array. This function's single argument is the new value to place in the added element. The call to Invalidate() forces the window to redraw the data display with the new information.

Reading Through the Array

So that you can see what's happening as you add, change, and delete array elements, the Array Demo application's OnDraw() function reads through the array, displaying the values that it finds in each element. The code for this function is shown in Listing E.2.

Chapter 6, "Drawing on the Screen," shows you how to write an OnDraw() function and how it gets called.

Listing E.2   CArrayView::OnDraw()

```
void CArrayView::OnDraw(CDC* pDC)
{
    CArrayDoc* pDoc = GetDocument();
    ASSERT_VALID(pDoc);

    // Get the current font's height.
    TEXTMETRIC textMetric;
    pDC->GetTextMetrics(&textMetric);
    int fontHeight = textMetric.tmHeight;
    // Get the size of the array.
    int count = array.GetSize();
    int displayPos = 10;
    // Display the array data.
    for (int x=0; x<count; ++x)
    {
        UINT value = array.GetAt(x);
        char s[81];
        wsprintf(s, "Element %d contains the value %u.", x, value);
        pDC->TextOut(10, displayPos, s);
        displayPos += fontHeight;
    }
}
```

App
E

Here, the program first gets the height of the current font so that it can properly space the lines of text that it displays in the window. It then gets the number of elements in the array, by calling the array object's `GetSize()` function. Finally, the program uses the element count to control a `for` loop, which calls the array object's `GetAt()` member function to get the value of the currently indexed array element. The program converts this value to a string for display purposes.

Removing Elements from the Array

Because it is a right-button click in the window that brings up the Remove From Array dialog box, it is the program's `OnRButtonDown()` function that handles the element-deletion duties. That function is shown in Listing E.3.

Listing E.3   CArrayView::OnRButtonDown()

```
void CArrayView::OnRButtonDown(UINT nFlags, CPoint point)
{
    ArrayRemoveDlg dialog(this);
    dialog.m_remove = 0;
    dialog.m_removeAll = FALSE;
    int result = dialog.DoModal();
    if (result == IDOK)
    {
        if (dialog.m_removeAll)
            array.RemoveAll();
        else
            array.RemoveAt(dialog.m_remove);
        Invalidate();
    }

    CView::OnRButtonDown(nFlags, point);
}
```

In this function, after displaying the dialog box, the program checks the value of the dialog box's `m_removeAll` data member. A value of TRUE means that the user has checked this option and wants to delete all elements from the array. In this case, the program calls the array object's `RemoveAll()` member function. Otherwise, the program calls `RemoveAt()`, whose single argument specifies the index of the element to delete. The call to `Invalidate()` forces the window to redraw the data display with the new information.

The List Classes

Lists are like fancy arrays. The MFC list classes implement *linked lists*, which use pointers to link their elements (called *nodes*) rather than depending upon contiguous memory locations to order values, lists are a better data structure to use when you need to be able to insert and delete items quickly. However, finding items in a list can be slower than finding items in an array, because a list often needs to be traversed sequentially in order to follow the pointers from one item to the next.

When using lists, you need to know some new vocabulary. Specifically, you need to know that the *head* of a list is the first node in the list, and the *tail* of the list is the last node in the list (see Figure E.7.) Each node knows how to reach the *next* node, the one after it in the list. You'll see these terms used often as you explore MFC's list classes.

FIG. E.7

A linked list has a head and a tail, with the remaining nodes in between.

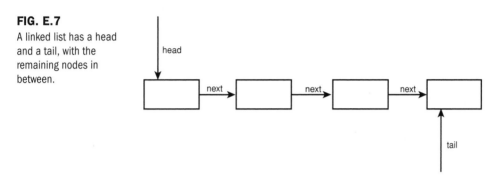

MFC provides three list classes that you can use to create your lists. These classes are CObList (which represents a list of objects), CPtrList (which represents a list of pointers), and CStringList (which represents a list of strings). Each of these classes has similar member functions, and the classes differ in the type of data that they can hold in their lists. Table E.2 lists and describes the member functions of the list classes.

Table E.2 Member Functions of the List Classes

Function	Description
AddHead()	Adds a node to the head of the list, making the node the new head.
AddTail()	Adds a node to the tail of the list, making the node the new tail.
Find()	Searches the list sequentially to find the given object pointer. Returns a POSITION value.
FindIndex()	Scans the list sequentially, stopping at the node indicated by the given index. Returns a POSITION value for the node.
GetAt()	Gets the node at the specified position.
GetCount()	Gets the number of nodes in the list.
GetHead()	Gets the list's head node.
GetHeadPosition()	Gets the head node's position.
GetNext()	Gets the next node in the list when iterating over a list.
GetPrev()	Gets the previous node in the list when iterating over a list.

App

E

continues

Table E.2   Continued

Function	Description
GetTail()	Gets the list's tail node.
GetTailPosition()	Gets the tail node's position.
InsertAfter()	Inserts a new node after the specified position.
InsertBefore()	Inserts a new node before the specified position.
IsEmpty()	Returns TRUE if the list is empty and returns FALSE otherwise.
RemoveAll()	Removes all of a list's nodes.
RemoveAt()	Removes a single node from a list.
RemoveHead()	Removes the list's head node.
RemoveTail()	Removes the list's tail node.
SetAt()	Sets the node at the specified position.

Introducing the List Application

As you've no doubt guessed, now that you know a little about list classes and their member functions, you're going to get a chance to see lists in action, in the List Application. When you run the application, you see the window shown in Figure E.8. The window displays the values of the single node with which the list begins. Each node in the list can hold two different values, both of which are integers.

TIP   This application is on the CD in the RefE folder.

FIG. E.8

The List Demo application starts off with one node in its list.

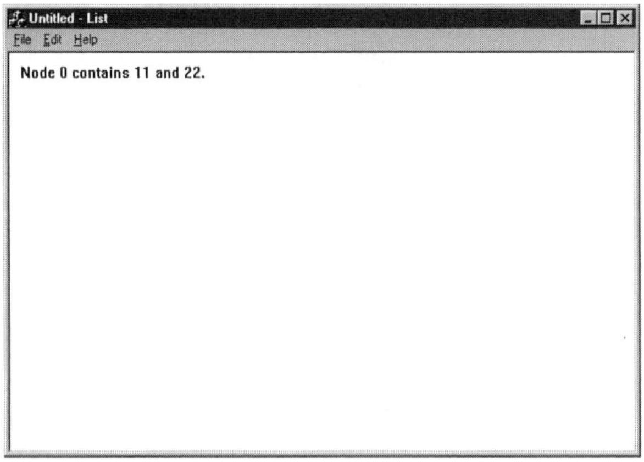

```
Untitled - List                                    _ □ ✕
File  Edit  Help

Node 0 contains 11 and 22.
```

Using the List Demo application, you can experiment with adding and removing nodes from a list. To add a node, left-click in the application's window. You then see the dialog box shown in Figure E.9. Enter the two values that you want the new node to hold and then click OK. When you do, the program adds the new node to the tail of the list and displays the new list in the window. For example, if you enter the values 55 and 65 into the dialog box, you see the display shown in Figure E.10.

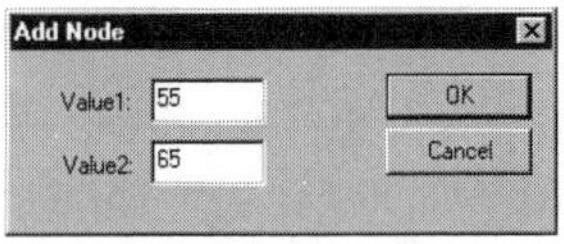

FIG. E.9

A left-click in the window brings up the Add Node dialog box.

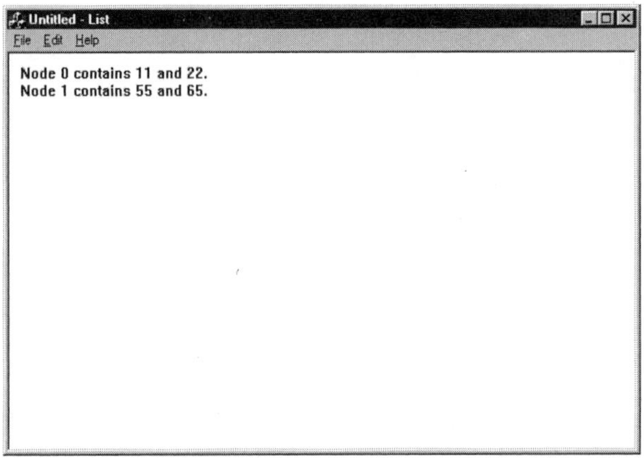

FIG. E.10

Each node you add to the list can hold two different values.

You can also delete nodes from the list. To do this, right-click in the window to display the Remove Node dialog box (see Figure E.11). Using this dialog box, you can choose to remove the head or tail node. If you exit the dialog box by clicking OK, the program deletes the specified node and displays the resulting list in the window.

N O T E If you try to delete nodes from an empty list, the List Demo application displays a message box, warning you of your error. If the application didn't catch this possible error, the program could crash when it tries to delete a nonexistent node.

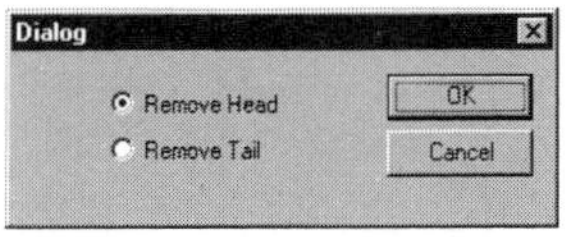

FIG. E.11

Right-click in the window to delete a node.

Declaring and Initializing the List

Declaring a list is as easy as declaring any other data type. Just include the name of the class you're using, followed by the name of the object. For example, the List Demo application declares its list like this:

```
CPtrList list;
```

Here, the program is declaring an object of the `CPtrList` class. This class holds a linked list of pointers, which means that the list can reference just about any type of information.

Although there's not much you need to do to initialize an empty list, you do need to decide what type of information will be pointed to by the pointers in the list. That is, you need to declare exactly what a node in the list will look like. The List Demo application declares a node as shown in Listing E.4.

Listing E.4   *CNode* Structure

```
struct CNode
{
    int value1;
    int value2;
};
```

Here, a node is defined as a structure holding two integer values. However, you can create any type of data structure you like for your nodes. To add a node to a list, you use the `new` operator to create a node structure in memory, and then you add the returned pointer to the pointer list. The List Demo application begins its list with a single node, which is created in the view class's constructor, as shown in Listing E.5.

Listing E.5   *CMyListView* Constructor

```
CMyListView::CMyListView()
{
    CNode* pNode = new CNode;
    pNode->value1 = 11;
    pNode->value2 = 22;
    list.AddTail(pNode);
}
```

In Listing E.5, the program first creates a new `CNode` structure on the heap and then sets the node's two members. After initializing the new node, a quick call to the list's `AddTail()` member function adds the node to the list. Because the list was empty, adding a node to the tail of the list is the same as adding the node to the head of the list. That is, the program could have also called `AddHead()` to add the node. In either case, the new single node is now both the head and tail of the list.

Adding a Node to the List

Although you can insert nodes into a list at any position, the easiest way to add to a list is to add a node to the head or tail, making the node the new head or tail. In the List Demo application, you left-click in the window to bring up the Add Node dialog box, so you'll want to examine the OnLButtonDown() function, which looks like Listing E.6.

Listing E.6 *CMyListView::OnLButtonDown()*

```
void CMyListView::OnLButtonDown(UINT nFlags, CPoint point)
{
    // Create and initialize the dialog box.
    AddNodeDlg dialog;
    dialog.m_value1 = 0;
    dialog.m_value2 = 0;
    // Display the dialog box.
    int result = dialog.DoModal();
    // If the user clicked the OK button...
    if (result == IDOK)
    {
        // Create and initialize the new node.
        CNode* pNode = new CNode;
        pNode->value1 = dialog.m_value1;
        pNode->value2 = dialog.m_value2;
        // Add the node to the list.
        list.AddTail(pNode);
        // Repaint the window.
        Invalidate();
    }
    CView::OnLButtonDown(nFlags, point);
}
```

In Listing E.6, after displaying the dialog box, the program checks whether the user exited the dialog with the OK button. If so, the user wants to add a new node to the list. In this case, the program creates and initializes the new node, just as it did previously for the first node that it added in the view class's constructor. The program adds the node in the same way, too, by calling the AddTail(). If you want to modify the List Demo application, one thing you could try is giving the user a choice between adding the node at the head or the tail of the list, instead of just at the tail.

App

E

Deleting a Node from the List

Deleting a node from a list can be easy or more complicated, depending on where in the list you want to delete the node. As with adding a node, dealing with nodes other than the head or tail requires that you first locate the node that you want and then get its position in the list. You'll learn about node positions in the next section, which demonstrates how to iterate over a list. To keep things simple, however, this program enables you to delete nodes only from the head or tail of the list, as shown in Listing E.7.

Listing E.7   *CMyListView::OnRButtonDown()*

```
void CMyListView::OnRButtonDown(UINT nFlags, CPoint point)
{
    // Create and initialize the dialog box.
    RemoveNodeDlg dialog;
    dialog.m_radio = 0;
    // Display the dialog box.
    int result = dialog.DoModal();
    // If the user clicked the OK button...
    if (result == IDOK)
    {
        CNode* pNode;
        // Make sure the list isn't empty.
        if (list.IsEmpty())
            MessageBox("No nodes to delete.");
        else
        {
            // Remove the specified node.
            if (dialog.m_radio == 0)
                pNode = (CNode*)list.RemoveHead();
            else
                pNode = (CNode*)list.RemoveTail();
            // Delete the node object and repaint the window.
            delete pNode;
            Invalidate();
        }
    }
    CView::OnRButtonDown(nFlags, point);
}
```

Here, after displaying the dialog box, the program checks whether the user exited from the dialog box via the OK button. If so, the program must then check whether the user wants to delete a node from the head or tail of the list. If the Remove Head radio button was checked, the dialog box's m_radio data member will be 0. In this case, the program calls the list class's RemoveHead() member function. Otherwise, the program calls RemoveTail(). Both of these functions return a pointer to the object that was removed from the list. Before calling either of these member functions, however, notice how the program calls IsEmpty() in order to determine whether the list contains any nodes. You can't delete a node from an empty list.

N O T E   Notice that, when removing a node from the list, the List Demo application calls delete on the pointer returned by the list. It's important to remember that, when you remove a node from a list, the node's pointer is removed from the list, but the object to which the pointer points is still in memory, where it stays until you delete it. ■

Iterating Over the List

Often, you'll want to *iterate over* (read through) a list. You might, for example, as is the case with List, want to display the values in each node of the list, starting from the head of the list and working your way to the tail. The List application does exactly this in its OnDraw() function, as shown in Listing E.8.

Listing E.8 *CMyListView::OnDraw()*

```
void CMyListView::OnDraw(CDC* pDC)
{
    CListDoc* pDoc = GetDocument();
    ASSERT_VALID(pDoc);
// Get the current font's height.
    TEXTMETRIC textMetric;
    pDC->GetTextMetrics(&textMetric);
    int fontHeight = textMetric.tmHeight;
    // Initialize values used in the loop.
    POSITION pos = list.GetHeadPosition();
    int displayPosition = 10;
    int index = 0;
    // Iterate over the list, displaying each node's values.
    while (pos != NULL)
    {
        CNode* pNode = (CNode*)list.GetNext(pos);
        char s[81];
        wsprintf(s, "Node %d contains %d and %d.",
            index, pNode->value1, pNode->value2);
        pDC->TextOut(10, displayPosition, s);
        displayPosition += fontHeight;
        ++index;
    }
}
```

App

E

In Listing E.8, the program gets the position of the head node by calling the GetHeadPosition() member function. The position is a value that many of the list class's member functions use to quickly locate nodes in the list. You must have this starting position value in order to iterate over the list.

In the while loop, the iteration actually takes place. The program calls the list object's GetNext() member function, which requires as its single argument the position of the node to retrieve. The function returns a pointer to the node and sets the position to the next node in the list. When the position is NULL, the program has reached the end of the list. In Listing E.8, this NULL value is the condition that's used to terminate the while loop.

Cleaning Up the List

There's one other time when you need to iterate over a list. That's when the program is about to terminate and you need to delete all the objects pointed to by the pointers in the list. The List Demo application performs this task in the view class's destructor, as shown in Listing E.9.

Listing E.9   *CMyListView* destructor

```
CMyListView::~CMyListView()
{
    // Iterate over the list, deleting each node.
    while (!list.IsEmpty())
    {
        CNode* pNode = (CNode*)list.RemoveHead();
        delete pNode;
    }
}
```

The destructor in Listing E.9 iterates over the list in a `while` loop until the `IsEmpty()` member function returns `TRUE`. Inside the loop, the program removes the head node from the list (which makes the next node in the list the new head) and deletes the node from memory. When the list is empty, all the nodes that the program allocated have been deleted.

CAUTION

Don't forget that you're responsible for deleting every node that you create with the new operator. If you fail to delete nodes, you could cause a memory leak. In a small program like this, a few wasted bytes don't matter, but in a long-running program adding and deleting hundreds or thousands of list nodes, you could create serious errors in your program. It's always good programming practice to delete any objects you allocate in memory.

TIP   Chapter 24, "Improving Your Application's Performance," discusses memory management and preventing memory leaks.

The Map Classes

You can use MFC's mapped collection classes for creating lookup tables. For example, you might want to convert digits into the words that represent the numbers. That is, you might want to use the digit 1 as a key in order to find the word *one*. A mapped collection is perfect for this sort of task. Thanks to the many MFC map classes, you can use various types of data for keys and values.

The MFC map classes are `CMapPtrToPtr`, `CMapPtrToWord`, `CMapStringToOb`, `CMapStringToPtr`, `CMapStringToString`, `CMapWordToOb`, and `CMapWordToPtr`. The first data type in the name is the key, and the second is the value type. So, for example, CMapStringToOb uses strings as keys and objects as values, whereas CMapStringToString, which this section uses in its examples, uses strings as both keys and values. All the map classes are similar, and so have similar member functions, which are listed and described in Table E.3.

Table E.3 Functions of the Map Classes

Function	Description
GetCount()	Gets the number of map elements.
GetNextAssoc()	Gets the next element when iterating over the map.
GetStartPosition()	Gets the first element's position.
IsEmpty()	Returns TRUE if the map is empty and returns FALSE otherwise.
Lookup()	Finds the value associated with a key.
RemoveAll()	Removes all the map's elements.
RemoveKey()	Removes an element from the map.
SetAt()	Adds a map element or replaces an element with a matching key.

Introducing the Map Application

This section's example program, Map, displays the contents of a map and enables you to retrieve values from the map by giving the program the appropriate key. When you run the program, you see the window shown in Figure E.12.

T I P This application is on the CD in the RefE folder.

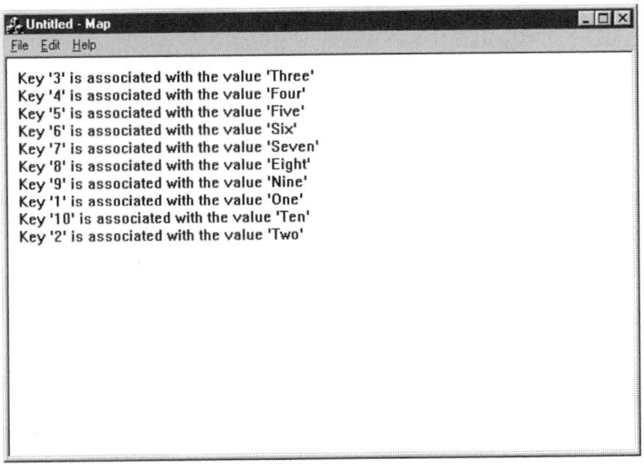

App
E

FIG. E.12

The Map application displays the contents of a map object.

```
Untitled - Map                                           _ □ ×
File  Edit  Help

  Key '3' is associated with the value 'Three'
  Key '4' is associated with the value 'Four'
  Key '5' is associated with the value 'Five'
  Key '6' is associated with the value 'Six'
  Key '7' is associated with the value 'Seven'
  Key '8' is associated with the value 'Eight'
  Key '9' is associated with the value 'Nine'
  Key '1' is associated with the value 'One'
  Key '10' is associated with the value 'Ten'
  Key '2' is associated with the value 'Two'
```

The window displays the contents of the application's map object, in which digits are used as keys to access the words that represent the numbers. To retrieve a value from the map, click in the window. You then see the dialog box shown in Figure E.13. Type the digit that you want to use for a key and then click OK. The program finds the matching value in the map and displays it in another message box. For example, if you type 8 as the key, you see the message box shown in Figure E.14. If the key doesn't exist, the program's message box tells you so.

FIG. E.13
The Get Map Value
dialog box enables you
to match a key with the
key's value in the map.

FIG. E.14
This message box
displays the requested
map value.

Creating and Initializing the Map

The Map Demo application starts off with a ten-element map. The map object is declared as a data member of the view class, like this:

```
CMapStringToString map;
```

This is an object of the CMapStringToString class, which means that the map uses strings as keys and strings as values.

Declaring the map object doesn't, of course, fill it with values. You have to do that on your own, which the Map Demo application does in its view class constructor, shown in Listing E.10.

Listing E.10   *CMapView* Constructor

```
CMapView::CMapView()
{
    map.SetAt("1", "One");
    map.SetAt("2", "Two");
    map.SetAt("3", "Three");
    map.SetAt("4", "Four");
    map.SetAt("5", "Five");
    map.SetAt("6", "Six");
    map.SetAt("7", "Seven");
    map.SetAt("8", "Eight");
    map.SetAt("9", "Nine");
    map.SetAt("10", "Ten");
}
```

The `SetAt()` function takes as parameters the key and the value to associate with the key in the map. If the key already exists, the function replaces the value associated with the key with the new value given as the second argument.

Retrieving a Value from the Map

When you click in Map's window, the Get Map Value dialog box appears, so it's probably not surprising that the view class `OnLButtonDown()` member function comes into play somewhere. Listing E.11 shows this function.

Listing E.11 *CMapView::OnLButtonDown()*

```
void CMapView::OnLButtonDown(UINT nFlags, CPoint point)
{
// Initialize the dialog box.
    GetMapDlg dialog(this);
    dialog.m_key = "";
    // Display the dialog box.
    int result = dialog.DoModal();
    // If the user exits with the OK button...
    if (result == IDOK)
    {
        // Look for the requested value.
        CString value;
        BOOL found = map.Lookup(dialog.m_key, value);
        if (found)
            MessageBox(value);
        else
            MessageBox("No matching value.");
    }
    CView::OnLButtonDown(nFlags, point);
}
```

In `OnLButtonDown()`, the program displays the dialog box in the usual way, checking to see whether the user exited the dialog box by clicking the OK button. If the user did, the program calls the map object's `Lookup()` member function, using the key that the user entered into the dialog box as the first argument. The second argument is a reference to the string into which the function can store the value it retrieves from the map. If the key can't be found, the `Lookup()` function returns FALSE; otherwise, it returns TRUE. The program uses this return value in order to determine whether it should display the string value retrieved from the map or a message box indicating an error.

Iterating Over the Map

In order to display the keys and values used in the map, the program must iterate over the map, moving from one entry to the next, retrieving and displaying the information for each map element. As with the array and list examples, the Map Demo application accomplishes this in its `OnDraw()` function, which is shown in Listing E.12.

Listing E.12   *CMapView::OnDraw()*

```
void CMapView::OnDraw(CDC* pDC)
{
    CMapDoc* pDoc = GetDocument();
    ASSERT_VALID(pDoc);
    TEXTMETRIC textMetric;
    pDC->GetTextMetrics(&textMetric);
    int fontHeight = textMetric.tmHeight;
    int displayPosition = 10;
    POSITION pos = map.GetStartPosition();
    CString key;
    CString value;
    while (pos != NULL)
    {
        map.GetNextAssoc(pos, key, value);
        CString str = "Key '" + key +
            "' is associated with the value '" +
            value + "'";
        pDC->TextOut(10, displayPosition, str);
        displayPosition += fontHeight;
    }
}
```

Much of this OnDraw() function is similar to other versions that you've seen in this chapter. The map iteration, however, begins when the program calls the map object's GetStartPosition() member function, which returns a position value for the first entry in the map (not neces- sarily the first entry that you added to the map). Inside a while loop, the program calls the map object's GetNextAssoc() member function, giving the position returned from GetStartPosition() as the single argument. GetNextAssoc() retrieves the key and value at the given position and then updates the position to the next element in the map. When the position value becomes NULL, the program has reached the end of the map.

Collection Class Templates

MFC includes class templates that you can use to create your own special types of collection classes. (For more information on templates, please refer to the section "Templates" in Chapter 26, "Exceptions, Templates, and the Latest Additions to C++.") Although the subject of tem- plates can be complex, using the collection class templates is easy enough. For example, suppose that you want to create an array class that can hold structures of the type shown in Listing E.13.

Listing E.13   A Sample Structure

```
struct MyValues
{
    int value1;
    int value2;
    int value3;
};
```

The first step is to use the template to create your class, like this:

```
CArray<MyValues, MyValues&> myValueArray;
```

Here, `CArray` is the template you use for creating your own array classes. The template's two arguments are the type of data to store in the array and the type of data that the new array class's member functions should use as arguments where appropriate. In this case, the type of data to store in the array is structures of the `MyValues` type. The second argument specifies that class member functions should expect references to `MyValues` structures as arguments where needed.

To build your array, you optionally set the array's initial size:

```
myValueArray.SetSize(10, 5);
```

Then you can start adding elements to the array, like this:

```
MyValues myValues;
myValueArray.Add(myValues);
```

Once you create your array class from the template, you use the array just as you do any of MFC's array classes, as described earlier in this chapter. Other collection class templates you can use are `CList` and `Cmap`. This means you can take advantage of all the design work put in by the MFC team to create an array of Employee objects, or a linked list of Order objects, or a map linking names to Customer objects.

App
E

The String Class

There are few programs that don't have to deal with text strings of one sort or another. Unfortunately, C++ is infamous for its weak string-handling capabilities, while languages like BASIC and Pascal have always enjoyed superior power when it came to these ubiquitous data types. MFC's `CString` class addresses C++'s string problems by providing member functions that are as handy to use as those found in other languages. Table E.4 lists the commonly used member functions of the `CString` class.

Table E.4   Commonly Used Member Functions of the *CString* Class

Function	Description
Compare()	Case-sensitive compare of two strings.
CompareNoCase()	Case-insensitive compare of two strings.
Empty()	Clears a string.
Find()	Locates a substring.
Format()	"Print" variables into a CString much like the C sprintf function.
GetAt()	Gets a character at a specified position in the string.
GetBuffer()	Gets a pointer to the string's contents.
GetLength()	Gets the number of characters in the string.
IsEmpty()	Returns TRUE if the string holds no characters.
Left()	Gets the left segment of a string.
MakeLower()	Lowercases a string.
MakeReverse()	Reverses the contents of a string.
MakeUpper()	Uppercases a string.
Mid()	Gets the middle segment of a string.
Right()	Gets the right segment of a string.
SetAt()	Sets a character at a specified position in the string.
TrimLeft()	Removes leading white-space characters from a string.
TrimRight()	Removes trailing white-space characters from a string.

Besides the functions listed in the table, the CString class also defines a full set of operators for dealing with strings. Using these operators, you can do things like *concatenate* (join together) strings with the plus sign (+), assign values to a string object with the equal sign (=), access the string as a C-style string with the LPCTSTR operator, and more.

Creating a string object is quick and easy, like this:

```
CString str = "This is a test string";
```

Of course, there are lots of ways to construct your string object. The previous example is only one possibility. You can create an empty string object and assign characters to it later, you can create a string object from an existing string object, and you can even create a string from a repeating character.

Once you have the string object created, you can call its member functions and manipulate the string in a number of ways. For example, to convert all the characters in the string to uppercase, you'd make a function call like this:

```
str.MakeUpper();
```

To lengthen a string, use the + or += operators, like this:

```
CString sentence = "hello " + str;
sentence += " there."
```

Or, to compare two strings, you'd make a function call something like this:

```
str.Compare("Test String");
```

You can also compare two CString objects:

```
CString testStr = "Test String";
str.Compare(testStr);
```

Or neater still:

```
if (testStr == str)
```

If you peruse your online documentation, you'll find that most of the other CString member functions are equally easy to use.

The Time Classes

If you've ever tried to manipulate time values returned from a computer, you'll be pleased to learn about MFC's CTime and CTimeSpan classes, which represent absolute times and elapsed times, respectively. The use of these classes is pretty straightforward, so there's no sample program for this section. However, the following sections get you started with these handy classes. Before you start working with the time classes, however, look over Table E.5, which lists the member functions of the CTime class, and Table E.6, which lists the member functions of the CTimeSpan class.

App

E

Table E.5   Member Functions of the *CTime* Class

Function	Description
Format()	Constructs a string representing the time object's time.
FormatGmt()	Constructs a string representing the time object's GMT (or UTC) time. This is the Greenwich mean time.
GetCurrentTime()	Creates a CTime object for the current time.
GetDay()	Gets the time object's day as an integer.

continues

Table E.5 Continued

Function	Description
GetDayOfWeek()	Gets the time object's day of the week, starting with 1 for Sunday.
GetGmtTm()	Gets a time object's second, minute, hour, day, month, year, day of the week, and day of the year as a tm structure.
GetHour()	Gets the time object's hour as an integer.
GetLocalTm()	Gets a time object's local time, returning the second, minute, hour, day, month, year, day of the week, and day of the year in a tm structure.
GetMinute()	Gets the time object's minutes as an integer.
GetMonth()	Gets the time object's month as an integer.
GetSecond()	Gets the time object's second as an integer.
GetTime()	Gets the time object's time as a time_t value.
GetYear()	Gets the time object's year as an integer.

Table E.6 Member Functions of the *CTimeSpan* Class

Function	Description
Format()	Constructs a string representing the time-span object's time.
GetDays()	Gets the time-span object's days.
GetHours()	Gets the time-span object's hours for the current day.
GetMinutes()	Gets the time-span object's minutes for the current hour.
GetSeconds()	Gets the time-span object's seconds for the current minute.
GetTotalHours()	Gets the time-span object's total hours.
GetTotalMinutes()	Gets the time-span object's total minutes.
GetTotalSeconds()	Gets the time-span object's total seconds.

Using a *CTime* Object

Creating a CTime object for the current time is a simple matter of calling the GetCurrentTime() function, like this:

```
CTime time = CTime::GetCurrentTime();
```

Because `GetCurrentTime()` is a static member function of the `CTime` class, you can call it without actually creating a `CTime` object. You do, however, have to include the class's name as part of the function call, as shown in the preceding code. As you can see, the function returns a `CTime` object. This object represents the current time. If you wanted to display this time, you could call upon the `Format()` member function, like this:

```
CString str = time.Format("DATE: %A, %B %d, %Y");
```

The `Format()` function takes as its single argument a format string that tells the function how to create the string representing the time. The previous example creates a string that looks something like this:

```
DATE: Saturday, April 20, 1996
```

The format string used with `Format()` is not unlike the format string used with functions like the old DOS favorite `printf()` or the Windows conversion function `wsprintf()`. That is, you specify the string's format by including literal characters along with control characters. The literal characters, such as the "DATE:" and the commas in the previous string example, are added to the string exactly as you type them, whereas the format codes are replaced with the appropriate values. For example, the `%A` in the previous code example will be replaced by the name of the day and the `%B` will be replaced by the name of the month. Although the format-string concept is the same as that used with `printf()`, the `Format()` function has its own set of format codes, which are listed in Table E.7.

Table E.7   Format Codes for the *Format()* Function

Code	Description
%a	Day name, abbreviated (such as Sat for Saturday).
%A	Day name, no abbreviation.
%b	Month name, abbreviated (such as Mar for March).
%B	Month name, no abbreviation.
%c	Localized date and time (for the U.S., that would be something like 03/17/96 12:15:34).
%d	Day of the month as a number (01–31).
%H	Hour in the 24-hour format (00–23).
%I	Hour in the normal 12-hour format (01–12).
%j	Day of the year as a number (001–366).
%m	Month as a number (01–12).
%M	Minute as a number (00–59).
%p	Localized A.M./P.M. indicator for 12-hour clock.

App

E

continues

Table E.7   Continued

Code	Description
%S	Second as a number (00–59).
%U	Week of the year as a number (00–51, considering Sunday to be the first day of the week).
%w	Day of the week as a number (0–6, with Sunday being 0).
%W	Week of the year as a number (00–51, considering Monday to be the first day of the week).
%x	Localized date representation.
%X	Localized time representation.
%y	Year without the century prefix as a number (00–99).
%Y	Year with the century prefix as a decimal number (such as 199).
%z	Name of time zone, abbreviated.
%Z	Name of time zone, no abbreviation.
%%	Percent sign.

Other `CTime` member functions like `GetMinute()`, `GetYear()`, and `GetMonth()` are obvious in their usage. However, you may like an example of using a function like `GetLocalTm()`, which is what the following shows:

```
struct tm* timeStruct;
timeStruct = time.GetLocalTm();
```

The first line of the previous code declares a pointer to a `tm` structure. (The `tm` structure is defined by Visual C++ and shown in Listing E.14.) The second line sets the pointer to the `tm` structure created by the call to `GetLocalTm()`.

Listing E.14   The *tm* Structure

```
struct tm {
        int tm_sec;     /* seconds after the minute - [0,59] */
        int tm_min;     /* minutes after the hour - [0,59] */
        int tm_hour;    /* hours since midnight - [0,23] */
        int tm_mday;    /* day of the month - [1,31] */
        int tm_mon;     /* months since January - [0,11] */
        int tm_year;    /* years since 1900 */
        int tm_wday;    /* days since Sunday - [0,6] */
        int tm_yday;    /* days since January 1 - [0,365] */
        int tm_isdst;   /* daylight savings time flag */
        };
```

N O T E The CTime class features a number of overloaded constructors, enabling you to create CTime objects in various ways and using various times. ▨

Using a *CTimeSpan* Object

A CTimeSpan object is nothing more complex than the difference between two times. You can use CTime objects in conjunction with CTimeSpan objects to easily determine the amount of time that's elapsed between two absolute times. To do this, first create a CTime object for the current time. Then, when the time you're measuring has elapsed, create a second CTime object for the current time. Subtracting the old time object from the new one gives you a CTimeSpan object representing the amount of time that has elapsed. The example in Listing E.15 shows how this process works.

Listing E.15 Calculating a Time Span

```
CTime startTime = CTime::GetCurrentTime();
    //.
    //. Time elapses...
    //.
CTime endTime = CTime::GetCurrentTime();
CTimeSpan timeSpan = endTime - startTime;
```

App
E

F

Visual Basic Script Quick Reference

Visual Basic Script (VBScript) syntax and commands are divided into several categories depending on their use and function.

- **Objects are the building blocks of VBScript.**

  They're used to return and modify the status of forms, pages, the browser, and programmer-defined variables. An easy way to think about an object is as a noun. Cat, car, house, computer, and form are all nouns and can be represented as objects (see the later entry "Objects").

- **You use properties to differentiate between objects of the same class—for example, all objects that are a cat.**

  Properties are adjectives and refer to items that might make the object different from other objects. In the cat example, properties might be weight, color, breed, disposition, or current activity (see the later entry "Properties").

- **You use methods to pass messages to the object and sometimes to change its properties.**

  You could use one method, for example, to change the cat's current activity from eating to sleeping, whereas you could use another to changes its weight from heavy to really heavy (see the later entry "Methods").

The following is a list of the objects, properties, and methods used in VBScript.

+ (Addition)

Syntax `result = operand1 + operand2`

Type Arithmetic Operator

Synopsis Adds two operands together.

Description If either operand has the Null value, `result` is Null. Operands that have the Empty value are equivalent to zero.

See Also Operators, Subtraction

/ (Division)

Syntax `result = operand1 / operand2`

Type Arithmetic Operator

Synopsis Divides `operand1` by `operand2`.

Description If either operand has the Null value, `result` is Null. Operands that have the Empty value are equivalent to zero. And, of course, division by zero results in a runtime error.

See Also On Error, Operators

= (Equality)

Syntax `operand1 = operand2`

Type Comparison Operator

Synopsis Returns True if `operand1` is equal to `operand2`.

Description If either operand has the Null value, `result` is Null. Operands with the Empty value are equivalent to zero.

The equality operator is frequently used in conditional expressions for If, Do, and For statements.

Example

```
' In this If statement, the equality operator
' is used in the conditional expression.
if intNumPages = 15 Then
 Alert "Ok"
End If

' In the third assignment statement below, the
' equality operator is used to give a value of
' False to intTest.
intA = 10
intB = 5
intTest = (intA = intB) ' intTest equals False.
```

See Also Operators

^ (Exponentiation)

Syntax `result = operand1 ^ operand2`

Type Arithmetic Operator

Synopsis Raises *operand1* to the power of *operand2*.

Description If either operand has the Null value, *result* is Null. Operands that have the Empty value are equivalent to zero.

See Also Operators

> (Greater Than)

Syntax `operand1 > operand2`

Type Comparison Operator

Synopsis Returns True if *operand1* is greater than *operand2*.

Description If either operand has the Null value, *result* is Null. Operands with the Empty value are equivalent to zero.

The greater-than operator is frequently used in conditional expressions for If, Do, and For statements.

Example

```
' In this If statement, the greater than operator
' is used in the conditional expression.
if intNumPages > 15 Then
 Alert "Ok"
End If

' In the third assignment statement below, the
' greater than operator is used to give a value of
' True to intTest.
intA = 10
intB = 5
intTest = (intA > intB)
```

See Also Operators

>= (Greater Than or Equal To)

Syntax `operand1 >= operand2`

Type Comparison Operator

Synopsis Returns True if *operand1* is greater than or equal to *operand2*.

Description If either operand has the Null value, *result* is Null. Operands with the Empty value are equivalent to zero.

The greater than or equal to operator is frequently used in conditional expressions for If, Do, and For statements.

App

F

Example

```
' In this If statement, the >= operator
' is used in the conditional expression.
if intNumPages >= 15 Then
 Alert "Ok"
End If

' In the third assignment statement below, the
' >= operator is used to give a value of
' True to intTest.
intA = 10
intB = 5
intTest = (intA >= intB)
```

See Also   Operators

<> (Inequality)

Syntax   *operand1 <> operand2*

Type   Comparison Operator

Synopsis   Returns True if *operand1* doesn't equal *operand2*.

Description   If either operand has the Null value, *result* is Null. Operands with the Empty value are equivalent to zero.

The inequality operator is frequently used in conditional expressions for If, Do, and For statements.

Example

```
' In this If statement, the inequality operator
' is used in the conditional expression.
if intNumPages <> 15 Then
 Alert "Ok"
End If

' In the third assignment statement below, the
' inequality operator is used to give a value of
' True to intTest.
intA = 10
intB = 5
intTest = (intA <> intB)
```

See Also   Operators

\ (Integer Division)

Syntax   *result = operand1 \ operand2*

Type   Arithmetic Operator

Synopsis   Divides one number by another and rounds the result to the nearest whole number.

Description   If either operand has the Null value, *result* is Null. Operands with the Empty value are equivalent to zero. And, of course, division by zero results in a runtime error.

See Also   On Error, Operators

< (Less Than)

Syntax   *operand1* < *operand2*

Type   Comparison Operator

Synopsis   Returns True if *operand1* is less than *operand2*.

Description   If either operand has the Null value, *result* is Null. Operands with the Empty value are equivalent to zero.

The less-than operator is frequently used in conditional expressions for If, Do, and For statements.

Example

```
' In this If statement, the less than operator
' is used in the conditional expression.
if intNumPages < 15 Then
 Alert "Ok"
End If

' In the third assignment statement below, the
' less than operator is used to give a value of
' False to intTest.
intA = 10
intB = 5
intTest = (intA < intB)
```

See Also   Operators

<= (Less Than Or Equal To)

Syntax   *operand1* < *operand2*

Type   Comparison Operator

Synopsis   Returns True if *operand1* is less than or equal to *operand2*.

Description   If either operand has the Null value, *result* is Null. Operands with the Empty value are equivalent to zero.

The less-than-or-equal-to operator is frequently used in conditional expressions for If, Do, and For statements.

Example

```
' In this If statement, the <= operator
' is used in the conditional expression.
if intNumPages <= 15 Then
 Alert "Ok"
End If
```

App

F

```
' In the third assignment statement below, the
' <= operator is used to give a value of
' False to intTest.
intA = 10
intB = 5
intTest = (intA <= intB)
```

See Also   Operators

* (Multiplication)

Syntax   *result = operand1 * operand2*

Type   Arithmetic Operator

Synopsis   Multiplies one number by another.

Description   If either operand has the `Null` value, *result* is `Null`. Operands with the `Empty` value are equivalent to zero.

See Also   Operators

– (Negation)

Syntax   *- operand*

Type   Arithmetic Operator

Synopsis   Negates the value of *operand*.

Example

```
intA = 10 ' intA equals positive 10.
intB = -10 ' intB equals negative 10.
```

See Also   Operators

& (String Concatenation)

Syntax   *result = string1 & string2*

Type   String Concatenation Operator

Synopsis   Appends *string2* to *string1*.

Description   Although you also can use the + operator to concatenate two character strings, you should use the & operator for concatenation instead. The & operator eliminates ambiguity and provides self-documenting code.

See Also   Operators

– (Subtraction)

Syntax   *result = operand1 - operand2*

Type   Arithmetic Operator

Synopsis   Subtracts *operand2* from *operand1*.

Description If one of the operands contains the Null value, the result is Null. If one of the operands contains the Empty value, it's treated as though it were zero.

See Also Operators

Abs

Syntax *Abs(number)*

Type Intrinsic Conversion and Math Function

Synopsis Returns the absolute value of *number*.

Example

```
intTemp = abs(-2) ' intTemp equals 2.
intTemp - abs(2) ' intTemp equals 2.
```

See Also Atn, Conversion Functions, Cos, Exp, Log, Math Functions, Randomize, Rnd, Sin, Sqr, Tan

Action

Syntax 1 *form.Action*

Syntax 2 *form.Action = string*

Type Property

Synopsis Gets or sets the address that does the form's action.

Description The *string* parameter is usually an URL that represents a CGI script. It can also be a script procedure or an e-mail address. If no URL is specified for a form's action, the base URL is used.

Addition (+)

Syntax *result = operand1 + operand2*

Type

Arithmetic Operator

Synopsis Adds two operands together.

Description If either operand has the Null value, *result* is Null. Operands with the Empty value are equivalent to zero.

See Also Operators, Subtraction

Alert

Syntax *window.alert(string)*

Type Method

Synopsis Displays a message dialog box.

App
F

Description If *window* isn't specified, the current Window object is used.

Example

```
<!-- This document shows how to use the
 Alert method.
-->
<HTML>
 <HEAD>
 <TITLE>VBScript Example Page</TITLE>
 <SCRIPT LANGUAGE="VBScript">
 <!--
 Alert("This is an Alert message box.")
 -->
 </SCRIPT>
 </HEAD>
 <BODY>
 <H1>VBScript Example Page</H1>
 Did you like the Alert message?<P>
 </BODY>
</HTML>
```

Figure F.1 shows the message box displayed by the example HTML page.

FIG. F.1

An Alert message box.

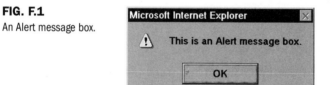

aLinkColor

Syntax 1 *document*.aLinkColor = *rgbValue*

Syntax 2 *document*.aLinkColor = *string*

Type Property

Synopsis Gets or sets the active link color for *document*.

Description You can set the color by specifying an RGB value in hexadecimal or by specify-ing a color name. The "Color Names" entry lists all the color names you can use.

A link is active when the mouse pointer is positioned over it, and the mouse button is pressed and held down.

You can set this property only while the document is being parsed. An OnLoad event handler procedure is a good place to set document properties.

N O T E Internet Explorer doesn't support the aLinkColor property. It's part of the browser's object module for compatibility reasons. ■

Anchor

Type   Object

Synopsis   Represents a hyperlink in a document.

Description   Table F.1 lists the sole property of an Anchor object. See the "Anchors" entry for more information.

Table F.1   Properties of an *Anchor* Object

Property	Page Number	Description
Name	868	Gets or sets the name of an anchor.

Anchors

Syntax   *document*.Anchors[*index*]

Type   Read-Only Property

Synopsis   Returns an array of anchors, or you can specify an index to retrieve a single anchor.

Description   You can find out how many anchors *document* has by using the sample code in the "Example" section. Figure F.2 shows the results of the sample HTML document. Notice that the number of links in the document changes as the document is parsed.

FIG. F.2
The number of anchors in a document depends a great deal on when the anchors are counted.

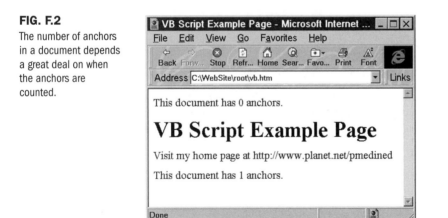

App

F

Example

```
<!-- This document shows how to determine
 the number of anchors in a document.
-->
<HTML>
 <HEAD>
  <TITLE>VBScript Example Page</TITLE>
```

```
<SCRIPT language="VBScript">
<!--
Sub dispAnchors
intNumAnchors = Document.Anchors.Length
Document.Open
Document.Write "This document has " &
intNumAnchors &
" anchors.<P>"
Document.Clear
End Sub

dispAnchors
-->
</SCRIPT>
</HEAD>
<BODY LANGUAGE="VBScript">
<H1>VBScript Example Page</H1>
    Visit my home page at
<A NAME="Home Page">http://www.planet.net/pmedined</A>
<P>
<SCRIPT language="VBScript">
<!--
dispAnchors
-->
</SCRIPT>
</BODY>
</HTML>
```

And

Syntax   *result = operand1* And *operand2*

Type   Operator

Synopsis   Returns True if both operands are true.

Description   If one operand is True and the second is Null, or if both operands are Null, *result* is Null. If the operands are numeric, a bitwise comparison is made.

Example

```
intHasCold = blnFever And blnSniffling
```

See Also   Operators

AppCodeName

Syntax   *navigator*.AppCodeName

Type   Read-Only Property

Synopsis   The code name of the current application.

Description   This property returns Mozilla when you're using Microsoft Internet Explorer version 3.0 (4.70.1158).

Example

```
' Display the application code name.
Alert Navigator.AppCodeName
```

AppName

Syntax   *navigator*.AppName

Type   Read-Only Property

Synopsis   The name of the current application.

Description   This property returns `Microsoft Internet Explorer` when you're using Microsoft Internet Explorer version 3.0 (4.70.1158).

Example

```
' Display the application name.
Alert Navigator.AppName
```

AppVersion

Syntax   *navigator*.AppVersion

Type   Read-Only Property

Synopsis   The version number of the current application.

Description   This property returns `2.0 (compatible; MSIE 3.0A; Windows 95)` when you're using Microsoft Internet Explorer version 3.0 (4.70.1158).

Example

```
' Display the application version
Alert Navigator.AppVersion
```

Array Variables

Type   Definition

Description   An array variable can contain a collection or series of values. Array variables can have more than one dimension. You can use a two-dimensional array, for example, to hold values generated by this formula: $y = .5 + x$. Each x, y pair of values is another element in the array. Three-dimensional arrays are also useful when doing mathematics. Although VBScript supports up to 60 dimensions, few programmers use more than three or four.

If you don't know in advance how big the array should be, use a *dynamic* array, which you create by using empty parentheses. When your script knows the correct size, the `ReDim` keyword resizes the array.

The lower bound of an array variable is always zero. This means that an array always holds one more element than is declared in the `Dim` statement. The example should make this concept clear.

Table F.2 lists the functions and keywords related to arrays.

App

F

Table F.2   VBScript Array Functions and Keywords

Function	Description
Dim	Declares script-level or procedure-level variables
Erase	Reinitializes fixed-size arrays and frees memory associated with dynamic arrays
IsArray	Tests a variable to see whether it's an array
LBound	Returns the smallest subscript for a given dimension of an array
ReDim	Declares or modifies the bounds for dynamic arrays
UBound	Returns the largest subscript for dimension of an *arrayname*

Example

```
<SCRIPT LANGUAGE="VBScript">
<!--
' Declare a vector of integer - a one-dimensional
' array.
Dim aryInt_A(20)

' assign a value to the fifth element.
aryInt_A(4) = 23;

' retrieve the eighth element of the array.
lngNumBooks = aryInt_A(7)

' Declare a 66-element two-dimensional array of
' long integers. It will have 11 rows and 6 columns.
Dim aryLng_B(10, 5)

' assign a value to the first element
aryLng_B(0, 0) = 2343412

' Declare a dynamic array.
Dim ary_C()

' Define the bounds of the dynamic array.
ReDim ary_C(10, 10)

-->
</SCRIPT>
```

See Also   Dim, IsArray, ReDim

Asc

Syntax   Asc(*string*)

Type   Intrinsic Conversion and String Function

Synopsis   Returns the ANSI code of the first character in *string*.

Description   If *string* contains no characters, a runtime error occurs.

Example

```
intTemp = Asc("ABCDE") ' intTemp equals 65.
```

See Also   AscB, AscW, Chr, ChrB, ChrW, Conversion Functions, InStr, InStrB, Len, LenB, Left, LeftB, LCase, LTrim, Mid, MidB, Right, RightB, Space, StrComp, String, String Functions, Trim, UCase

AscB

Syntax   `AscB(string)`

Type   Intrinsic Conversion and String Function

Synopsis   Returns the first byte in *string*.

Description   You should use `AscB` when *string* contains byte data.

See Also   Asc, AscW, Chr, ChrB, ChrW, Conversion Functions, InStr, InStrB, Len, LenB, Left, LeftB, LCase, LTrim, Mid, MidB, Right, RightB, Space, StrComp, String, String Functions, Trim, UCase

AscW

Syntax   `AscW(string)`

Type   Intrinsic String Function

Synopsis   Returns the first Unicode character (32 bits) in *string*.

Description   You should use `AscW` when *string* contains Unicode data.

See Also   Asc, AscB, Chr, ChrB, ChrW, Conversion Functions, InStr, InStrB, Len, LenB, Left, LeftB, LCase, LTrim, Mid, MidB, Right, RightB, Space, StrComp, String, String Functions, Trim, UCase

Atn

Syntax   `Atn(number)`

Type   Intrinsic Math Function

Synopsis   Returns the arctangent of *number*.

Description   The *number* parameter is the ratio of two sides of a right triangle. `Atn` returns the corresponding angle in radians. The range of the result is $-\pi/2$ to $\pi/2$ radians. You can change radians to degrees by multiplying radians by $180/\pi$.

See Also   Abs, Cos, Exp, Log, Math Functions, Randomize, Rnd, Sin, Sqr, Tan

Back

Syntax   `history.Back(number)`

Type   Method

App
F

Synopsis   Moves backward in the history list, exactly as though the browser's Back button is clicked.

Example

```
' Move backward five times.
History.Back(5)
```

BgColor

Syntax 1   `document.BgColor = rbgValue`

Syntax 2   `document.BgColor = string`

Type   Method; applies to `History` objects

Synopsis   Gets or sets the background color of `document`.

Description   You can set the color by specifying an RGB value in hexadecimal or by specifying a color name. The "Color Names" entry later lists all the color names you can use.

You can set this property only while the document is being parsed. An `OnLoad` event handler procedure is a good place to set document properties.

Example

```
' Set the background color to gold.
Document.BgColor = &HFFD700
```

See Also   FgColor

Blur

Syntax   `element.Blue`

Type   Method

Synopsis   Clears the focus from `element`.

Description   This method causes the `OnBlur` event.

Boolean Variables

Type   Definition

Description   Boolean variables have only two values: `True` (1) or `False` (0). If you use the `CBool` function to convert a variable into the `Boolean` subtype, anything that isn't zero becomes `True`.

VBScript functions and Web browser functions sometimes handle Boolean variables in different ways. The "Example" section highlights these differences. In real-world use, however, you rarely display the value of Boolean values. They almost always indicate status. For example, did the mail arrive? or has the check box been selected?

Example

```
blnTemp = True ' using a constant
blnTemp = CByte(1) ' using a conversion function
```

```
Alert blnTemp ' displays "-1"
MsgBox blnTemp ' displays "True"
```

Byte Variables

Type   Definition

Description   Byte variables can have whole-number values ranging from 0 to 255, inclusive.

Example

```
bytTemp = CBool(234)
```

Call

Syntax   Call *name*([*argumentlist*])

Type   Keyword

Synopsis   Runs a Sub or Function procedure.

Description   In most cases, the Call keyword is optional. If you do use it, however, you must also enclose the procedure parameters with parentheses. If you don't use Call, you must also omit the enclosing parentheses. Any return value from functions invoked by using Call are ignored.

Example

```
Call myFunction(parameterOne, parameterTwo)
myFunction parameterOne, parameterTwo
```

See Also   Function, Procedure, Sub

CBool

Syntax   CBool(*expression*)

Type   Intrinsic Conversion Function

Synopsis   Converts *expression* into a Boolean subtype.

Description   If *expression* is zero, False is returned; otherwise, True is returned. If *expression* isn't numeric, a runtime error occurs.

Example

```
blnBigBook = CBool(numPages > 500)
```

See Also   CByte, CDate, CDbl, CInt, CLng, Conversion Functions, CSng, CStr

CByte

Syntax   CByte(*expression*)

Type   Intrinsic Conversion Function

Synopsis   Converts *expression* into a Byte subtype.

Description   If *expression* can't be converted into a Byte value, a runtime error occurs.

See Also   CBool, CDate, CDbl, CInt, CLng, Conversion Functions, CSng, CStr

App
F

CDate

Syntax   CDate(*expression*)

Type   Intrinsic Conversion Function

Synopsis   Converts *expression* into a Date subtype.

Description   You can specify date and time literals or a variable as *expression*. When you're converting a number to a date, the whole-number portion is converted to a date. Any fractional part of the number is converted to a time of day, starting at midnight. CDate usually recognizes only date formats that correspond to the locale setting of your system. The correct order of day, month, and year may not be determined if it's provided in a format other than one of the recognized date settings.

Example

```
myBirthday = CDate("9-20-96")
```

See Also   CBool, CByte, CDbl, CInt, CLng, Conversion Functions, CSng, CStr, IsDate

CDbl

Syntax   CDbl(*expression*)

Type   Intrinsic Conversion Function

Synopsis   Converts *expression* into a Double subtype.

See Also   CBool, CByte, CDate, CInt, CLng, Conversion Functions, CSng, CStr

Checked

Syntax 1   *element*.Checked

Syntax 2   *element*.Checked = *status*

Type   Property

Synopsis   Gets or sets the checked state of *element*.

Description   If you're testing the checked state, 1 is returned if *element* is checked; otherwise, 0 is returned. If you're setting the checked state, *status* can be either 1 or 0.

Chr

Syntax   Chr(*charcode*)

Type   Intrinsic Conversion Function

Synopsis   Returns the character associated with *charcode*.

Description   The ANSI standard assigns a number to each alphanumeric character. The numbers from 0 to 31 are associated with various control functions. The tab character is 9, for example, and the carriage return character is 13.

See Also   Asc, AscB, AscW, ChrB, ChrW, Conversion Functions, InStr, InStrB, Len, LenB, Left, LeftB, LCase, LTrim, Mid, MidB, Right, RightB, Space, StrComp, String, String Functions, Trim, UCase

ChrB

Syntax   ChrB(*charcode*)

Type   Intrinsic Conversion Function

Synopsis   Returns the byte associated with *charcode*.

Description   ChrB is used for strings with byte data.

See Also   Asc, AscB, AscW, Chr, ChrW, Conversion Functions, InStr, InStrB, Len, LenB, Left, LeftB, LCase, LTrim, Mid, MidB, Right, RightB, Space, StrComp, String, String Functions, Trim, UCase

ChrW

Syntax   ChrW(*charcode*)

Type   Intrinsic Conversion Function

Synopsis   Returns the Unicode character associated with *charcode*.

Description   ChrW is used for strings with byte data. Unicode characters are 32 bits wide.

See Also   Asc, AscB, AscW, Chr, ChrB, Conversion Functions, InStr, InStrB, Len, LenB, Left, LeftB, LCase, LTrim, Mid, MidB, Right, RightB, Space, StrComp, String, String Functions, Trim, UCase

CInt

Syntax   CInt(*expression*)

Type   Intrinsic Conversion Function

Synopsis   Converts *expression* into an Integer subtype.

Description   Use CInt when you need to force integer math. If *expression* lies outside the acceptable range for the Integer subtype, an error occurs. The CInt function rounds the value of *expression*; it doesn't truncate it like Fix and Int do. Fractional values of .5 and higher cause CInt to round up to the nearest even number.

Example

```
a = CInt(0.5) ' a will equal 0
b = CInt(1.5) ' b will equal 2
```

See Also   CBool, CByte, CDate, CDbl, CLng, Conversion Functions, CSng, Cstr

Clear

Syntax 1   *document*.Clear

Syntax 2   *err*.Clear

App
F

Type   Method

Synopsis   Closes *document* and updates the display, or clears the property settings for *err*.

Document Object Description   The Microsoft documentation is unclear about the necessity of calling the Clear method. Most of the documentation refers solely to the Close method. The Close method, however, doesn't actually close the document; it simply updates the display according to that same documentation. My best advice is to ignore the Clear method and solely use Close. I hope that Microsoft rectifies this confusing situation soon.

Error Object Description   You should call the Clear method to clear the Err object when an error has been handled. The Err object is automatically cleared after On Error Resume Next, Exit Sub, and Exit Function statements.

clearTimeout

Syntax   *window*.clearTimeout(*timerId*)

Type   Method; applies to Window objects

Synopsis   Clears a timeout timer so that it doesn't go off.

Description   If *window* isn't specified, the current Window object is used.

Example

```
' Set up a time so that the Send button is clicked in
' five seconds.
clickTimer = setTimeout ("btnSend_OnClick", 5000, "VBScript")

' Clear the timer to avoid automatically clicking
' the Send button.
clearTimer(clickTimer)
```

See Also   setTimeout

Click

Syntax   *element*.Click

Type   Method

Synopsis   Emulates the user clicking *element*.

Description   This method causes an OnClick event.

CLng

Syntax   CLng(*expression*)

Type   Intrinsic Conversion Function

Synopsis   Converts *expression* into a Long subtype.

Description   You use CLng when you need to force integer math. The CLng function rounds the value of *expression*; it doesn't truncate it like Fix or Int does. Fractional values of .5 and higher cause CLng to round up to the nearest whole number.

Example

```
a = CLng(0.5) ' a will equal 0
b = CLng(1.5) ' b will equal 2
```

See Also   CBool, CByte, CDate, CDbl, CInt, Conversion Functions, CSng, CStr

Close

Syntax 1   *document*.Close

Syntax 2   window.Close

Type   Method

Synopsis   Closes *document* and updates the display, or closes *window*.

Description   If *window* isn't specified, the current Window object is used. If you simply see a Close method without an attached object, a window is being closed.

Color Names

Type   Definition

Description   Table F.3 lists all the color names that you can use in VBScript. Although you normally specify the RGB value as one six-digit hexadecimal number, the table displays the numbers as separate red, green, and blue two-digit numbers to make understanding the numbers easier.

Table F.3   VBScript's Color Names

Color/String Literal	Red	Green	Blue
aliceblue	F0	F8	FF
antiquewhite	FA	EB	D7
aqua	00	FF	FF
aquamarine	7F	FF	D4
azure	F0	FF	FF
beige	F5	F5	DC
bisque	FF	E4	C4
black	00	00	00
blanchedalmond	FF	EB	CD
blue	00	00	FF
blueviolet	8A	2B	E2
brown	A5	2A	2A

App

F

continues

Table F.3 Continued

Color/String Literal	Red	Green	Blue
burlywood	DE	B8	87
cadetblue	5F	9E	A0
chartreuse	7F	FF	00
chocolate	D2	69	1E
coral	FF	7F	50
cornflowerblue	64	95	ED
cornsilk	FF	F8	DC
crimson	DC	14	3C
cyan	00	FF	FF
darkblue	00	00	8B
darkcyan	00	8B	8B
darkgoldenrod	B8	86	0B
darkgray	A9	A9	A9
darkgreen	00	64	00
darkkhaki	BD	B7	6B
darkmagenta	8B	00	8B
darkolivegreen	55	6B	2F
darkorange	FF	8C	00
darkorchid	99	32	CC
darkred	8B	00	00
darksalmon	E9	96	7A
darkseagreen	8F	BC	8F
darkslateblue	48	3D	8B
darkslategray	2F	4F	4F
darkturquoise	00	CE	D1
darkviolet	94	00	D3
deeppink	FF	14	93
deepskyblue	00	BF	FF
dimgray	69	69	69

Color/String Literal	Red	Green	Blue
dodgerblue	1E	90	FF
firebrick	B2	22	22
floralwhite	FF	FA	F0
forestgreen	22	8B	22
fuchsia	FF	00	FF
gainsboro	DC	DC	DC
ghostwhite	F8	F8	FF
gold	FF	D7	00
goldenrod	DA	A5	20
gray	80	80	80
green	00	80	00
greenyellow	AD	FF	2F
honeydew	F0	FF	F0
hotpink	FF	69	B4
indianred	CD	5C	5C
indigo	4B	00	82
ivory	FF	FF	F0
khaki	F0	E6	8C
lavender	E6	E6	FA
lavenderblush	FF	F0	F5
lawngreen	7C	FC	00
lemonchiffon	FF	FA	CD
lightblue	AD	D8	E6
lightcoral	F0	80	80
lightcyan	E0	FF	FF
lightgoldenrodyellow	FA	FA	D2
lightgreen	90	EE	90
lightgrey	D3	D3	D3
lightpink	FF	B6	C1

continues

App
F

Table F.3   Continued

Color/String Literal	Red	Green	Blue
lightsalmon	FF	A0	7A
lightseagreen	20	B2	AA
lightskyblue	87	CE	FA
lightslategray	77	88	99
lightsteelblue	B0	C4	DE
lightyellow	FF	FF	E0
lime	00	FF	00
limegreen	32	CD	32
linen	FA	F0	E6
magenta	FF	00	FF
maroon	80	00	00
mediumaquamarine	66	CD	AA
mediumblue	00	00	CD
mediumorchid	BA	55	D3
mediumpurple	93	70	DB
mediumseagreen	3C	B3	71
mediumslateblue	7B	68	EE
mediumspringgreen	00	FA	9A
mediumturquoise	48	D1	CC
mediumvioletred	C7	15	85
midnightblue	19	19	70
mintcream	F5	FF	FA
mistyrose	FF	E4	E1
moccasin	FF	E4	B5
navajowhite	FF	DE	AD
navy	00	00	80
oldlace	FD	F5	E6
olive	80	80	00
olivedrab	6B	8E	23

Color/String Literal	Red	Green	Blue
orange	FF	A5	00
orangered	FF	45	00
orchid	DA	70	D6
palegoldenrod	EE	E8	AA
palegreen	98	FB	98
paleturquoise	AF	EE	EE
palevioletred	DB	70	93
papayawhip	FF	EF	D5
peachpuff	FF	DA	B9
peru	CD	85	3F
pink	FF	C0	CB
plum	DD	A0	DD
powderblue	B0	E0	E6
purple	80	00	80
red	FF	00	00
rosybrown	BC	8F	8F
royalblue	41	69	E1
saddlebrown	8B	45	13
salmon	FA	80	72
sandybrown	F4	A4	60
seagreen	2E	8B	57
seashell	FF	F5	EE
sienna	A0	52	2D
silver	C0	C0	C0
skyblue	87	CE	EB
slateblue	6A	5A	CD
slategray	70	80	90
snow	FF	FA	FA
springgreen	00	FF	7F
steelblue	46	82	B4

App
F

continues

Table F.3 Continued

Color/String Literal	Red	Green	Blue
tan	D2	B4	8C
teal	00	80	80
thistle	D8	BF	D8
tomato	FF	63	47
turquoise	40	E0	D0
violet	EE	82	EE
wheat	F5	DE	B3
white	FF	FF	FF
whitesmoke	F5	F5	F5
yellow	FF	FF	00
yellowgreen	9A	CD	32

Cookie

Syntax 1 *result = document*.Cookie

Syntax 2 *document*.Cookie = *string*

Type Read-Only Property

Synopsis Gets or sets the cookie of *document*.

Description Cookies are pieces of information that can be associated with a Web page (the *document*). Setting a cookie overrides any cookie that was previously associated with the Web page.

Confirm

Syntax *result = window*.Confirm*(string)*

Type Method; applies to Window objects

Synopsis Displays a message box with OK and Cancel buttons.

Description If *window* isn't specified, the current Window object is used.

The Confirm function returns True of the OK button is clicked; it returns False otherwise.

Example

```
<!-- This document shows how to use the
 Confirm method.
-->
<HTML>
```

```
<HEAD>
<TITLE>VBScript Example Page</TITLE>
</HEAD>
<BODY>
<H1>VBScript Example Page</H1>
<SCRIPT language="VBScript">
<!--
If Confirm("Click OK to take a survey.") Then
document.open
document.write "Here is the survey<P>"
Else
document.write "Thanks, anyway.<P>"
End If
document.close
-->
</SCRIPT>
</BODY>
</HTML>
```

Figure F.3 shows the message box displayed by the example HTML page.

FIG. F.3

A confirmation message box—basically, an Alert message box with two extra buttons.

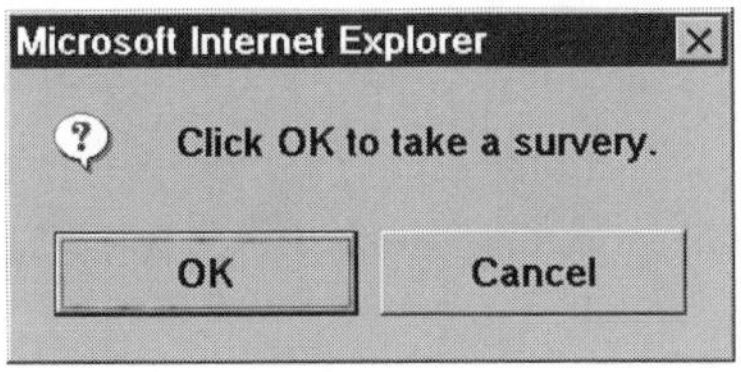

Constants

Type Definition

Description VBScript has five built-in constants, as shown in Table F.4. Notice that the descriptions of True and False don't mention an actual value. Their value is irrelevant—just the fact that they are opposites is important.

Table F.4 VBScript's Constants

Constant	Description
Empty	Indicates that a variable hasn't been initialized
False	The opposite of True
Nothing	Indicates that a reference doesn't refer to anything
Null	Indicates that a variable has no valid data
True	The opposite of False

Conversion Functions

Type   Definition

Description   VBScript offers quite a few intrinsic functions designed to convert from one data type to another, from one base to another, or simply from one format to another. Table F.5 lists the conversion functions available in VBScript.

Table F.5   VBScript Conversion Functions

Function	Page Number	Description
Abs	805	Returns the absolute value of a number
Asc	810	Returns the ANSI code of the first character in a string
AscB	811	Returns the first byte in a string
AscW	811	Returns the first Unicode character (32 bits) in a string
CBool	813	Converts a value into a Boolean subtype
CByte	813	Converts a value into a Byte subtype
CDate	814	Converts a value into a Date subtype
CDbl	814	Converts a value into a Double subtype
Chr	814	Returns the character associated with an ASCII code
ChrB	815	Returns the byte associated with a character code
ChrW	815	Returns the Unicode character associated with a character code
CInt	815	Converts a value into an Integer subtype
CLng	816	Converts a value into a Long subtype
CSng	825	Converts a value into a Single subtype
CStr	825	Converts a value into a String subtype
DateSerial	828	Returns a string representing the year, month, and day parameters
DateValue	829	Returns a Date value representing its parameter
Fix	843	Returns the integer portion of a number
Hex	849	Converts the value of a string into hexadecimal
Int	854	Returns the integer half of a number
Oct	872	Converts the value of a string into hexadecimal

Function	Page Number	Description
Sgn	891	Returns 1, –1, or 0, depending on the sign of the parameter
TimeSerial	897	Returns a Date variable representing the hour, minute, and second parameters
TimeValue	897	Returns a Date value representing its parameter

Cos

Syntax Cos(*angle*)

Type Intrinsic Math Function

Synopsis Returns the cosine of *angle*.

Description The cosine is the ratio of the length of a right angle's side adjacent to the angle divided by the length of the hypotenuse. The returned value is in the range –1 to 1.

See Also Abs, Atn, Exp, Log, Math Functions, Randomize, Rnd, Sin, Sqr, Tan

CSng

Syntax CSng(*expression*)

Type Intrinsic Conversion Function

Synopsis Converts *expression* into a Single subtype.

Description You use CSng when you need to force single-precision math. If *expression* lies outside the acceptable range for the Single subtype, an error occurs.

See Also CBool, CByte, CDate, CDbl, CInt, CLng, Conversion Functions, CStr

CStr

Syntax CStr(expression)

Type Intrinsic Conversion Function

Synopsis Converts *expression* into a String subtype.

Description The CStr function converts *expression* into a string in a manner that depends on the data type of *expression*. Table F.6 shows how the conversion is performed.

Table F.6 Return Values from CStr

Data Type	Return Format of Expression
Boolean	True or False
Date	The date expressed by using the short-date format of your system
Null	A runtime error occurs *continued*

App
F

Table F.6   Continued

Data Type	Return Format of Expression
Empty	A zero-length string (" ")
Error	A string with the word Error followed by the error number
Numeric	A string with the number

See Also   CBool, CByte, CDate, CDbl, CInt, CLng, Conversion Functions, CSng

Date

Syntax   Date

Type   Intrinsic Date/Time Function

Synopsis   Returns the current system date.

Example   Alert Date

Figure F.4 shows the message box displayed by the Alert Date statement.

FIG. F.4

The output from the Date function is displayed this way.

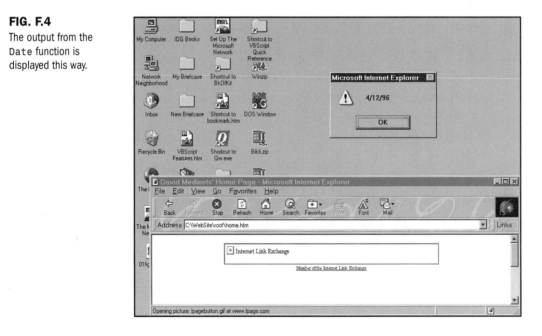

See Also   DateSerial, DateValue, Date/Time Functions, Day, Hour, Minute, Month, Now, Second, Time, TimeSerial, TimeValue, Weekday, Year

Date Variables

Type   Definition

Description   Date variables can range from January 1, 100, to December 31, 9999. Internally, the number 1 represents the date 1/1/100. Each whole number represents a day, and the decimal number represents the time. Negative numbers count back from December 30, 1899, and positive numbers count forward from that date. Decimal values of .0 represent midnight, and .5 represents noon.

You create literal dates by delimiting the date with the # character, as shown in the "Example" section.

Example

```
dtmFirstDay = CDate(1.234) ' equals 12/31/1899 5:36:58AM
dtmFirstDay = CDate(1) ' equals 12/31/1899
dblFirstday = CDbl(dtmFirstDay) ' equals 1
dtmBirthday = #09-20-96# ' equals 9/20/1996
```

Date/Time Functions

Type   Definition

Description   VBScript offers many intrinsic functions that work with date and time values. Table F.7 lists the date/time functions available in VBScript.

Table F.7   VBScript Date/Time Functions

Function	Page Number	Description
Date	826	Returns the current system date
DateSerial	828	Returns a string representing the year, month, and day parameters
DateValue	829	Returns a Date value representing its parameter
Day	829	Returns the day of the month of its parameter
Hour	851	Returns the hour of the day of its parameter
Minute	865	Returns the minute value of its parameter
Month	866	Returns the month value of its parameter
Now	871	Returns the current date and time as a Date value
Second	889	Returns the seconds value of its parameter
Time	897	Returns the current system time as a Date value
TimeSerial	897	Returns a Date value representing its parameters
TimeValue	897	Returns a Date value representing its parameter
Weekday	906	Returns the day of the week of its parameter
Year	909	Returns the year of its parameter

App

F

DateSerial

Syntax DateSerial(*year, month, day*)

Type Intrinsic Conversion and Date/Time Function

Synopsis Returns a string representing the year, month, and day parameters.

Description The *year* parameter can range from 100 to 9999 (the values of 0 to 99 are interpreted as the years 1900 to 1999). The *month* parameter can range from 1 to 12. And *day* can range from 1 to 31. You can pass expressions instead of literals to perform some basic date arithmetic. The example shows how to subtract two from a given month. Parameters too large to fit into the normal range carry over into the next larger unit. A *day* parameter of 34, for example, increments the *month* parameter. If one of the parameters falls outside the range –3,768 to 32,767, or if the date specified by the three arguments falls outside the acceptable range of dates, an error occurs.

Example

```
intMonth = 6
Alert DateSerial(1996, intMonth - 2, 12)
```

Figure F.5 shows the message box displayed by this statement.

FIG. F.5
The output from the
DateSerial function
is displayed this way.

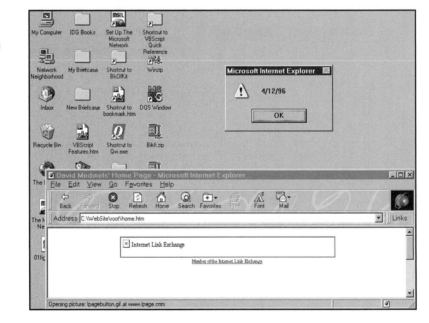

See Also Date, DateValue, Date/Time Functions, Day, Hour, Minute, Month, Now, Second, Time, TimeSerial, TimeValue, Weekday, Year

DateValue

Syntax DateValue(*date*)

Type Intrinsic Date/Time Function

Synopsis Returns a Date value representing *date*.

Description The *date* parameter is a literal string or a variable that holds a date string. However, *date* also can be any expression that represents a Date value. Time information in *date* is ignored, but incorrect time causes an error. DateValue can recognize the abbreviated forms of each month name (Jan, Feb, and so on). The current year of your computer's system date is used if *date* doesn't specify a year.

Example Alert DateValue("April 28, 1995")

Figure F.6 shows the message box displayed by this statement.

FIG. F.6

The output from the DateValue function is displayed this way.

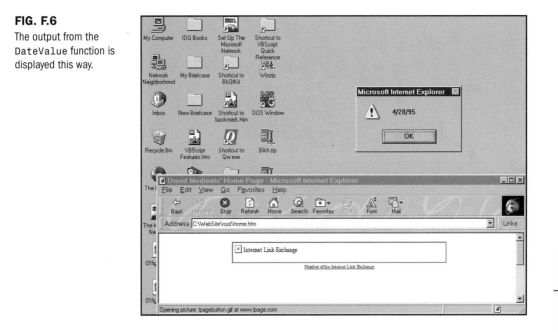

See Also Date, DateSerial, Date/Time Functions, Day, Hour, Minute, Month, Now, Second, Time, TimeSerial, TimeValue, Weekday, Year

Day

Syntax Day(*date*)

Type Intrinsic Date/Time Function

Synopsis Returns the day of the month of *date*, which can range from 1 to 31.

Description If *date* contains Null, Null is returned.

See Also Date, Date/Time Functions, DateSerial, DateValue, Hour, Minute, Month, Now, Second, Time, TimeSerial, TimeValue, Weekday, Year

DefaultChecked

Syntax 1 `element.DefaultChecked`

Syntax 2 `element.DefaultChecked = status`

Type Property

Synopsis Gets or sets the default checked state of `element`.

Description If you're testing the default checked state, 1 is returned if `element` is checked by default; otherwise, 0 is returned. If you're setting the default checked state, `status` can be either 1 or 0.

DefaultStatus

Syntax 1 `window.DefaultStatus`

Syntax 2 `window.DefaultStatus = string`

Type Property; applies to a `Window` object

Synopsis Gets or sets the default status text for the lower left portion of the status bar.

Example

```
' set the default status text.
self.defaultStatus = "Ready for Input"

' assign the default status text to a variable
strDefaultText = self.defaultStatus
```

DefaultValue

Syntax 1 `element.DefaultValue`

Syntax 2 `element.DefaultValue = string`

Type Property

Synopsis Gets or sets the default value of `element`.

Description

Syntax 1 `Err.Description`

Syntax 2 `Err.Description = stringExpression`

Type Property

Synopsis Gets or sets the description of an error.

Description The `Description` property holds a brief description of the error that the `Err` object represents. If `Err.Number` represents a runtime error and the `Description` property isn't explicitly set, the default error description is used.

Example

```
Err.Description = "No more items to process."
Err.Number = 2000
```

Dim

Syntax Dim varname[([subscripts])][, varname[([subscripts])]]...

Type Keyword

Synopsis Declares script-level or procedure-level variables.

Description The *varname* parameter indicates the name of the variable being declared. The *subscripts* parameter, if used, indicates the dimensions of the associated *varname* parameter. An array variable can have up to 60 dimensions. For example, Dim aryTemp(10, 15) creates an array of 11×16 elements. You need to specify only the upper bounds of each dimension; the lower bound is always zero. You can create dynamic arrays by using empty parentheses and the ReDim keyword. An error occurs if a variable is redimensioned.

All variables are initialized when declared with Dim. Strings are initialized to a zero-length string (" "), and number variables are initialized to zero.

You can create local variables by using Dim inside Sub or Function procedures. Otherwise, all procedures can access all variables—in other words, variables have a script-level scope by default.

Most programmers place all Dim statements at the beginning of a script or procedure where they're easy to find.

Example

```
Dim a(10,10,10) ' a is an array with three dimensions.
Dim b(), c() ' b and c are dynamic arrays.
```

See Also Array Variables, Erase, IsArray, LBound, ReDim, UBound

Division (/)

Syntax result = operand1 / operand2

Type Arithmetic Operator

Synopsis Divides *operand1* by *operand2*.

Description If either operand has the Null value, *result* is Null. Operands that have the Empty value are equivalent to zero. And, of course, division by zero results in a runtime error.

See Also On Error, Operators

Do

Syntax 1

```
Do While condition
[statements]
Loop
```

App

F

Syntax 2

```
Do Until condition
[statements]
Loop
```

Syntax 3

```
Do
[statements]
Loop While condition
```

Syntax 4

```
Do
[statements]
Loop Until condition
```

Type Keyword

Synopsis Repeatedly executes a statement block while a condition is true or until a condition becomes true.

Description The only difference between Do While...Loop and Do Until...Loop is how the conditional expression is tested. The While loop continues until the condition is false; the Until loop continues until the condition is true. You decide which one to use based on your own program logic.

Each Do...Loop statement has two forms. The first form tests the conditional expression before executing the statement block; the second checks the conditional statement after the statement block. Again, the choice depends on your program logic. The second form, however, implies that the statement block is executed only at least once—a handy feature to remember when you're reading and testing information from a data file.

You can use the Exit Do keyword to exit from the loop early. You can also nest one Do loop inside another.

Example

```
<SCRIPT LANGUAGE="VBScript">
<!--
 intTemp = 0
 Do While intTemp < 5
 Alert intTemp
 intTemp = intTemp + 1
 Loop

 intTemp = 0
 Do Until intTemp > 5
 Alert intTemp
 intTemp = intTemp + 1
 Loop
```

```
intTemp = 0
Do
Alert intTemp
intTemp = intTemp + 1
Loop Until intTemp > 5

intTemp = 0
Do
Alert intTemp
intTemp = intTemp + 1
Loop While intTemp < 5
-->
</SCRIPT>
```

See Also   Exit Do

Document (Object)

Type   Object

Synopsis   Represents the `Document` object associated with *window*.

Description   `Document` objects are directly analogous to HTML pages. You use the `Document` object to access hypertext links and form elements of the HTML page.

If the page has objects created with the `<OBJECT>` tag, you can refer directly to them by name instead of indirectly by using the `Document` object.

If *window* isn't specified, the `Document` object of the current window is returned.

Some of a document's properties can be set only in non-event statements. In other words, the properties can be set only when the HTML document is parsed. You can use an `OnLoad` event handler to set document properties.

Table F.8 lists the methods usable with the `Document` object; Table F.9 lists the properties usable with the `Document` object.

Table F.8   Methods of *Document* Objects

Method	Page Number	Description
Clear	815	Closes the document and updates the document's display
Close	817	Updates the document's display
Open	877	Opens a document for output
Write	908	Writes a string into a document
WriteLn	909	Writes a string into a document with a newline character at its end

App

F

Table F.9 Properties of *Document* Objects

Property	Page Number	Description
aLinkColor	806	Gets or sets the color of active links
Anchors	807	An array of a document's anchors
BgColor	812	Gets or sets a document's background color
Cookie	822	Gets or sets a document's cookie
FgColor	843	Gets or sets a document's foreground color
Forms	846	An array of a document's forms
LastModified	857	The last modified date of a document
LinkColor	861	Gets or sets the color of hyperlinks
Links	861	An array of a document's hyperlinks
Location	863	Gets the document's Location object
Referrer	887	Gets the URL of the referring document
Title	898	Gets the document's title
vLinkColor	905	Gets or sets the color of visited links

Document (Property)

Syntax   *window*.Document

Type   Property

Synopsis   Returns the Document object associated with *window*.

Description   For more information about Document objects, see the "Document (Object)" entry.

Double Precision Numbers

Type   Definition

Description   Double-precision numbers can have more than 300 digits; these numbers can become very large. Double-precision numbers are stored in variables of type Double (see the "Variables" entry).

Example

```
3.1415297
31415927e-7
.31415297E1
```

Element

Type   Object

Synopsis   Represents a control or object on an HTML document.

Description   Information about form elements is accessed through the `Elements` property of a `Form` object. See the "Elements" entry for more information.

Table F.10 lists the HTML element types and the events, methods, and properties that you can use with them. ActiveX controls can also be considered form elements, but there are too many of them to describe here. Refer to the documentation that came with the ActiveX controls for more information.

Table F.10   Element Types

Type	Events	Methods	Properties
Button	OnClick	Click, Reset, Submit	Form, Name, Value
Checkbox	OnClick	Click	Checked, DefaultChecked, Form, Name, Value
Hidden			Name, Value
Password		Blur, Focus, Select	DefaultValue, Form, Name, Value
Radio	OnClick	Click, Focus	Checked, Form, Name, Value
Select	OnBlur, OnChange, OnFocus	Blur, Focus	Length, Name, Options, SelectedIndex
Text	OnBlur, OnChange, OnFocus, OnSelect	Blur, Focus, Select	DefaultValue, Form, Name, Value
Textarea	OnBlur, OnChange, OnFocus, OnSelect	Blur, Focus, Select	DefaultValue, Form, Name, Value

Tables F.11, F.12, and F.13 list the events, methods, and properties of the `Element` object.

Table F.11   Events of an *Element* Object

Event	Page Number	Description
OnBlur	873	Happens when the element loses the focus
OnChange	873	Happens when the element changes
OnClick	873	Happens when the element is clicked
OnFocus	874	Happens when the element gets the focus

Table F.11   Continued

Event	Page Number	Description
OnSelect	875	Happens when the contents of the element are selected

Table F.12   Methods of an *Element* Object

Method	Page Number	Description
Blur	812	Clears the focus from an element
Click	816	Fires the OnClick event
Focus	843	Sets the focus to an element
Select	890	Selects the contents of the element

Table F.13   Properties of an *Element* Object

Property	Page Number	Description
Checked	814	Gets or sets the check box's checked state
DefaultChecked	830	Gets or sets the check box's default checked state
DefaultValue	830	Gets or sets the element's default value
Form	844	Gets the Form object containing the element
Length	858	Gets the number of options in a selected element
Name	868	Gets or sets the element's name
Options	882	Gets the <OPTIONS> tag for a selected element
SelectedIndex	890	Gets the index for the selected option
Value	900	Gets or sets the element's value

Elements

Syntax   *form.*Elements[*index*]

Type   Property

Synopsis   An array of objects and controls associated with *form*.

Description   If the form elements are named, you can access them directly by name. Otherwise, use *index* to specify which element in the array you want.

Example

```
' Find out how many elements the form called
' myForm has.
intNumElements = Document.myForm.Elements.Length

' Assign the name of the third element to strName
strName = Document.Forms[2].name
```

Empty

Syntax `Empty`

Type Constant

Synopsis Indicates that a variable hasn't been initialized.

Example `numRecords = Empty`

See Also IsEmpty, IsNull, Null

Encoding

Syntax 1 `form.Encoding`

Syntax 2 `form.Encoding = string`

Type Property

Synopsis Gets or sets the encoding for a form.

Description The encoding of a form is its MIME type—for example, text/html.

> **N O T E** In Internet Explorer 3.0, the `Encoding` property has no effect on the operation of the form. ▪

End Function

Type Keyword

Synopsis Ends a function definition.

See Also Function, Procedure

END SUB

Type Keyword

Synopsis Ends a subroutine definition.

See Also Sub, Procedure

Equality (=)

Syntax `operand1 = operand2`

Type Comparison Operator

Synopsis Returns `True` if *operand1* is equal to *operand2*.

App
F

Description   If either operand has the `Null` value, *result* is `Null`. Operands with the `Empty` value are equivalent to zero.

The equality operator is frequently used in conditional expressions for `If`, `Do`, and `For` statements.

Example

```
' In this If statement, the equality operator
' is used in the conditional expression.
if intNumPages = 15 Then
 Alert "Ok"
End If

' In the third assignment statement below, the
' equality operator is used to give a value of
' False to intTest.
intA = 10
intB = 5
intTest = (intA = intB) ' intTest equals False.
```

See Also   Operators

Eqv

Syntax   *result* = *operand1* Eqv *operand2*

Type   Operator

Synopsis   Returns `True` when both operands are logically equivalent.

Description   Both operands need to equal `True` or both operands must be `False` for `True` to be returned.

If the operands are numeric, a bitwise comparison of identically placed bits is performed.

See Also   Operators

Erase

Syntax   Erase *array*

Type   Intrinsic Array Function

Synopsis   Reinitializes fixed-size arrays and frees memory associated with dynamic arrays.

Description   Each element of a fixed-size array is set to zero if numeric, a zero-length string if a string, or the special `Nothing` value if an object reference. If you need to reuse an erased dynamic array, use `ReDim` to redeclare the array's dimensions.

See Also   Array Variables, Dim, IsArray, LBound, ReDim, UBound

Err

Syntax 1   Err.*property*

Syntax 2   Err.*method*

Type   Object

Synopsis   Holds information about runtime errors.

Description   The generator of an error (the VBScript engine, OLE objects, or the VBScript script) is responsible for setting the properties of the Err object. The Raise method generates a runtime error, and the Clear method clears a runtime error.

The Clear method is executed after every On Error Resume Next, Exit Sub, or Exit Function statement.

The Err object is available to all procedures; it has script-level scope.

Tables F.14 and F.15 list the methods and properties of the Err object.

Table F.14   Methods of an *Err* Object

Methods	Page Number	Description
Clear	815	Clears property settings for an Err object
Raise	886	Generates a runtime error

Table F.15   Properties of an *Err* Object

Property	Page Number	Description
Description	830	Gets or sets the description of an error
Number	871	Gets or sets a numeric value specifying an error
Source	892	Gets or sets the name of the object or application that originally generated the error

Event Handling

Type   Definition

Description   *Event handlers* are special procedures that give VBScript much of its power. By using them, you can look for specific user behavior in relation to the HTML page, such as clicking a form button or moving the mouse pointer over an anchor.

When an event occurs, the browser looks first in the tag for VBScript statements to handle the event, and then for a procedure named after the form element associated with the event. If a button named myButton is clicked, for example, VBScript looks for a procedure named myButton_OnClick.

When event handlers are embedded in HTML tags, they're typically used in forms, but some are also used in anchors and links tags. Virtually anything a user can do to interact with a page is covered with the event handlers, from moving the mouse to leaving the current page.

App

F

The three ways of creating event handlers are shown in the "Example" sections.

Example 1

```
<!--
 The event handler in this example is placed inside
 the HEAD section of the HTML page. This is a good
 idea of other procedures might call it. Or you want
 to add comments to your scripts.
-->
<HTML><HEAD>
<TITLE>My Test Page</TITLE>
<SCRIPT LANGUAGE="VBScript">
<!--
 Sub maleGender_OnClick
 MsgBox "Thanks for making a selection."
 End Sub
-->
</SCRIPT></HEAD>
<BODY><H1>My Test Page></H1>
<FORM>
<INPUT NAME="maleGender" TYPE="button" VALUE="Male">
</FORM></BODY></HTML>
```

Example 2

```
<!--
 In this example, the event handler is placed inside
 the form element definition surrounded by single
 quotes. Placing an event handler inside the form
 element should only be done if the hander is very
 small. Otherwise, your HTML page becomes cluttered.
-->
<INPUT NAME="maleGender" TYPE="button" VALUE="Male"
 OnClick='MsgBox "Thanks for making a selection."'
 LANGUAGE="VBScript">
```

Example 3

```
<!--
 This example defines the VBScript statements that
 get executed when a specific event happens for a
 specific control. The syntax used in this example
 can be used with any named form element or any
 elements defined by the OBJECT tag. Notice that
 the Sub keyword is not needed.
-->
<SCRIPT LANGUAGE="VBScript" EVENT="OnClick" FOR="maleGender">
<!--
 MsgBox "Thanks for making a selection."
-->
</SCRIPT>*
```

Events

Type   Definition

Description   The <A>, <BODY>, <FORM>, <INPUT>, and <OBJECT> HTML tags all have events associated with them. You can place VBScript statements directly inside the tags, or you can create an *event handler* procedure. Both methods of responding to events are covered later in the "Event Handling" entry.

Table F.16 lists the different events that VBScript responds to.

Table F.16   VBScript Events

Event	Page Number	Description
OnBlur	873	Happens when a control or object loses focus
OnChange	873	Happens when a control or object has changed
OnClick	873	Happens when a control, object, or hyperlink is clicked
OnFocus	874	Happens when a control or object gets the focus
OnLoad	874	Happens when a document is loaded
OnMouseMove	874	Happens when the mouse pointer moves while over a link
OnMouseOver	875	Happens when the mouse pointer moves over a link
OnSelect	875	Happens when the contents of a control or object are selected
OnSubmit	876	Happens just before the form's information is sent to the server
OnUnload	876	Happens when a document is unloaded

Exit

Syntax

```
Exit
Exit Do
Exit For
Exit Function
Exit Sub
```

Type   Keyword

Synopsis   Exits from a block of statements or ends the script.

Description   Exit statements usually are used to alter the flow of program logic in special situations. If, for example, the program is inside a loop and the user chooses to cancel the current operation, the Exit Do statement can be used to end the loop.

You can use the Exit Do statement to stop all four types of Do...Loop statements.

App

F

You must use each type of Exit statement in the appropriate context. You can't use an Exit For statement, for example, to exit a Do loop.

When an Exit statement is encountered, control is transferred to the statement immediately following the end of the statement block.

Exit Do and Exit For statements are usually combined with an If statement to conditionally exit a statement block. A For loop that counts from 10 to 1,000, for example, might need to be terminated if the user presses the Esc key.

Example

```
<SCRIPT LANGUAGE="VBScript">
<!--
' Exit Do
number = 0
Do While number < 100
Print number
If alert = True Then Exit Do
number = number + 1
Loop

' Exit For
For index = 1 to 10
Print index
If alert = True Then Exit For
Next

-->
</SCRIPT>
```

See Also   Do...Loops, For...Next Loops, Function, Sub

Exp

Syntax   Exp(number)

Type   Intrinsic Math Function

Synopsis   Returns e (the base of natural logarithms) raised to a power.

Description   If number is greater than roughly 709.782, an error occurs. The constant e is approximately 2.718. The Exp function is sometimes called the *antilogarithm* because it complements the Log function.

See Also   Abs, Atn, Cos, Log, Math Functions, Randomize, Rnd, Sin, Sqr, Tan

Exponentiation (^)

Syntax   result = operand1 ^ operand2

Type   Arithmetic Operator

Synopsis   Raises operand1 to the power of operand2.

Description   If either operand has the Null value, result is Null. Operands with the Empty value are equivalent to zero.

See Also Operators

FgColor

Syntax 1 `document.FgColor = rbgValue`

Syntax 2 `document.FgColor = string`

Type Property

Synopsis Gets or sets the foreground color of *document*.

Description You can set the color by specifying an RGB value in hexadecimal or by specifying a color name. The "Color Names" entry lists all the color names you can use.

You can set this property only while the document is being parsed. An OnLoad event handler procedure is a good place to set document properties.

Example

```
' Set the foreground color to gold.
Document.FgColor = &HFFD700
```

See Also BgColor

Fix

Syntax `Fix(number)`

Type Intrinsic Conversion and Math Function

Synopsis Returns the integer portion of *number*.

Description If *number* is negative, Fix returns the first negative number greater than or equal to *number*. Fix(*number*) is the same as Sgn(*number*) * Int(Abs(*number*)).

Example `a = Fix(-3.37) ' a equals -3.`

See Also CInt, Conversion Functions, Int, Math Functions

Focus

Syntax `element.Focus`

Type Method

Synopsis Sets the focus to *element*.

Description This method causes the OnFocus event.

For

Syntax

```
For loopVariable = start to end [STEP step]
[statements]
Next
```

Type Keyword

Synopsis   Repeatedly executes *statements* for a specific number of times.

Description   You use For...Next loops to execute a code block a specific number of times. You specify a loop variable for each For...Next statement. The loop variable is initialized to the starting value before the code block is executed. After the execution of the code block, the STEP value (*step*) is added to *loopVariable*. If no step is specified, the *loopVariable* is incremented by 1.

When For loops are nested, each loop needs to have a unique variable name. See the "Example" section for a demonstration of nested For loops.

Example

```
' Count forward from one to five.
For index = 1 to 5
 Alert index
Next

' Count backward from five to one.
For index = 5 to 1 Step -1
 Alert index
Next

' Use nested for loop to find row, column pairs.
For row = 0 to 2
 For col = 0 to 2
 Alert "[" & row & "," & col & "]"
 Next
Next
```

See Also   Do...Loop, Exit

Form

Syntax 1   Form.*property*

Syntax 2   Form.*method*

Type   Object

Synopsis   Represents an HTML form.

Description   Most HTML form elements have a Form property that references the form containing the element. If you need to find out which method of data transfer the form that contains the btnYield button uses, use btnYield.Form.Method.

You can access each element of a form through the form array that's part of the Document object. You can access the forms by name or by array index. See the "Example" section to see how to access the forms.

N O T E   Accessing forms by form name leads to self-documenting and more robust scripts. Forms are named by using the NAME attribute of the <FORM> HTML tag. By using the form name in a script, you gain the ability to rearrange the HTML forms (move one on top of another or to the end of the document, perhaps) without needing to recalculate the form's index. ▪

If the script tag is defined inside the form tag, you don't need to specify the document part of the object specification.

Tables F.17, F.18, and F.19 list the events, methods, and properties of the Form object.

Table F.17 Events of a *Form* Object

Event	Page Number	Description
OnSubmit	876	Happens when just before the form data is sent to the server

Table F.18 Methods of a *Form* Object

Method	Page Number	Description
Submit	896	Sends the form data to the server

Table F.19 Properties of a *Form* Object

Property	Page Number	Description
Action	805	Gets or sets the address that does the form's action
Elements	836	An array of Form objects and controls
Encoding	837	Gets or sets the encoding for the form
Method	864	Specifies how data is sent to the server (either GET or POST)
Target	896	Sets the name of the window where the form should be displayed

Example

```
<!-- This document shows that the document and
form names do not need to be specified if
the script is defined inside the form.
-->
<HTML>
<HEAD>
<TITLE>VBScript Example Page</TITLE>
</HEAD>
<BODY>
<H1>VBScript Example Page</H1>
<FORM NAME="myForm">
<INPUT NAME=btnLaugh TYPE=button VALUE="Want a laugh?">
<script language="VBScript" for="btnLaugh" event="OnClick">
btnLaugh.value="HA-HA!"
```

App

F

```
</script>
</FORM>
</BODY>
</HTML>
```

Forms

Syntax   `document.Forms[index]`

Type   Property

Synopsis   An array of `document`'s forms.

Description   See the "Form" entry for more information.

Forward

Syntax   `history.Forward(number)`

Type   Method

Synopsis   Moves forward in the history list—exactly as if the browser's forward button is clicked.

Example

```
' Move forward five times.
History.Forward(5)
```

Frames

Syntax   `window.Frames`

Type   Property; applies to `Window` objects

Synopsis   Returns an array of frames contained in `window`.

Example   `strURL = Parent.Frames[0].Location.Href`

CAUTION

Although the Microsoft documentation uses the preceding example, it generated an error message when I tried it. This problem may be resolved by the time you read this book.

Function

Syntax

```
Function name [(arglist)]
[statements]
[name = expression]
End Function
```

Type   Keyword

Synopsis   Creates a user-defined function called *name*.

Description   Function statements are used to create user-defined functions. Functions vary from subroutines because they return a value. Simply assign the return value to a variable with the same name as the function.

You should declare all functions toward the beginning of your script in the HEAD section of your HTML page. This way, you can ensure that the functions are available for use by later VBScript statements.

arglist is an optional list of arguments or parameters that the function can use. Functions always return a value, and you specify the value to return by assigning it to a variable named identically to *name*. If you want the function to assign values to the arguments, use the ByVal keyword inside the parameter list.

Example

```
' Define a function with one parameter
Function squareIt(intTemp)
 squareIt = intTemp * intTemp
End Function

' Define a function that can modify its
' parameter. This function determines if
' a field's value is in the correct range
' and if it is, adds the value to an ongoing
' total.
Function IsInValidRange(intField, intMin, intMax, intTotal)
 validate = False
 If intField >= intMin And intField <= intMax Then
 validate = True
 intTotal = intTotal + intField
 End If
End Function
```

See Also   Procedure, Sub

Go

Syntax   *history*.Go(*number*)

Type   Method

Synopsis   Connects to the URL at position *number* in the history list.

Example

```
' Connect to the first URL in the
' history list.
history.go(1)
```

Greater Than (>)

Syntax   *operand1* > *operand2*

Type   Comparison Operator

Synopsis   Returns True if *operand1* is greater than *operand2*.

App

F

Description   If either operand has the Null value, *result* is Null. Operands with an Empty value are equivalent to zero.

The greater-than operator is frequently used in conditional expressions for If, Do, and For statements.

Example

```
' In this If statement, the greater than operator
' is used in the conditional expression.
if intNumPages > 15 Then
 Alert "Ok"
End If

' In the third assignment statement below, the
' greater than operator is used to give a value of
' True to intTest.
intA = 10
intB = 5
intTest = (intA > intB)
```

See Also   Operators

Greater Than or Equal To (>=)

Syntax   *operand1* >= *operand2*

Type   Comparison Operator

Synopsis   Returns True if *operand1* is greater than or equal to *operand2*.

Description   If either operand has the Null value, *result* is Null. Operands with an Empty value are equivalent to zero.

The greater-than-or-equal-to operator is frequently used in conditional expressions for If, Do, and For statements.

Example

```
' In this If statement, the >= operator
' is used in the conditional expression.
if intNumPages >= 15 Then
 Alert "Ok"
End If

' In the third assignment statement below, the
' >= operator is used to give a value of
' True to intTest.
intA = 10
intB = 5
intTest = (intA >= intB)
```

See Also   Operators

Hash

Syntax 1   `link.Hash`

Syntax 2   `location.Hash`

Syntax 3   `location.Hash = string`

Type   Property

Synopsis   Gets the hash part of `link` or `location`. Sets the hash part of `location`.

Description   The hash part, or intra-Web page anchor, of an URL starts with a hash mark. In `http://www.planet.net/trains.htm#Amtrak`, for example, `#Amtrak` is the intra-Web page anchor of the URL. If the URL has no intra-Web page anchor, `Null` is returned.

Hex

Syntax   `Hex(number)`

Type   Intrinsic Conversion and Math Function

Synopsis   Returns a string that represents the value of *number* converted into hexadecimal.

Description   Only integer values can be converted. If *number* isn't an integer, it's rounded up to the nearest whole number.

See Also   Conversion Functions, Math Functions

Hierarchies

Type   Definition

Description   In a hierarchy, some relationship exists between all objects. Internet Explorer objects, for example, have a structure that reflects the construction of an HTML page. The `Window` object is the parent of all other Internet Explorer objects. The `Location`, `History`, and `Document` objects are all subordinate to the `Window` object.

Some objects are contained inside other objects. The form called `myForm` is an object, for example, and it's also the property of a `Document` object. Also, the `Document` object is a property of the `Window` object. Therefore, the form's full specification is `Window.Document.myForm`.

History (Object)

Type   Object

Synopsis   Represents the URLs visited by a window.

Description   The `History` object allows access to the browser's history list. You use the object's method to select which URL in the history list you need to connect with.

Tables F.20 and F.21 list the methods and properties of the `History` object.

App

F

Table F.20   Methods of a *History* Object

Object	Page Number	Description
Back	811	Like clicking the browser's Back button
Forward	846	Like clicking the browser's Forward button
Go	847	Connects to a specified entry in the history list

Table F.21   Properties of a *History* Object

Object	Page Number	Description
Length	858	The number of entries in the list

History (Property)

Syntax   *window*.History

Type   Property

Synopsis   Returns the History object of *window*.

Description   If *window* isn't specified, the History object of the current window is returned.

Host

Syntax 1   *link*.Host

Syntax 2   *location*.Host

Syntax 3   *location*.Host = *host*

Type   Property

Synopsis   Gets the host for *link* or *location*. Sets the host for *location*.

Description   The *host* parameter is a string of the following form: "*hostname*:*port*". The empty string ("") is returned for the file: protocol.

Hostname

Syntax 1   *link*.Hostname

Syntax 2   *location*.Hostname

Syntax 3   *location*.Hostname = *hostname*

Type   Property

Synopsis   Gets the host name for *link* or *location*. In the third syntax, sets the host name for *location*.

Description   The *hostname* parameter can specify either a server name or IP address. The empty string (`""`) is returned for the `file:` protocol.

Hour

Syntax   `Hour(time)`

Type   Intrinsic Time/Date Function

Synopsis   Returns the hour of the day (from 0 to 23) in *time*.

See Also   Date, Date/Time Functions, DateSerial, DateValue, Day, Month, Now, Second, Time, TimeSerial, TimeValue, Weekday, Year

Href

Syntax 1   `link.Href`

Syntax 2   `location.Href`

Syntax 3   `location.Href = url`

Type   Property

Synopsis   Gets the URL for `link` or `location`. In the third syntax, sets the URL for `location`.

If

Syntax 1

```
If condition Then statement
```

Syntax 2

```
If condition Then
[statements]
End If
```

Syntax 3

```
If condition Then
[statements]
    Else
    [statements]
End If
```

Type   Keyword

Synopsis   Optionally executes statements based on `condition`.

Description   The `Else` syntax is optional; use it only when statements need to be executed if `condition` is false.

Example

```
If maritalStatus = "Married" Then
 MsgBox "Congratulations!"
 moreQuestions = True
Else
 MsgBox "Good Luck!"
End If**
```

Imp

Syntax *result = operand1 Imp operand2*

Type Operator

Synopsis Performs a logical implication on two operands.

Description You can find the result of the logical implication by using Table F.22, unless the operands are numeric. If the operands are numeric, a bitwise comparison of identically placed bits is performed as shown in Table F.23.

Table F.22 The Results of the *Imp* Operator

operand1	operand2	result
True	True	True
True	False	False
True	Null	Null
False	True	True
False	False	True
False	Null	True
Null	True	True
Null	False	Null
Null	Null	Null

Table F.23 The Results of the *Imp* Operator for Numeric Operands

Bit in operand1	Bit in operand2	result
0	0	1
0	1	1
1	0	0
1	1	1

See Also Operators

Inequality (<>)

Syntax *operand1 <> operand2*

Type Comparison Operator

Synopsis   Returns True if *operand1* doesn't equal *operand2*.

Description   If either operand has the Null value, *result* is Null. Operands with an Empty value are equivalent to zero.

The inequality operator is used frequently in conditional expressions for If, Do, and For statements.

Example

```
' In this If statement, the inequality operator
' is used in the conditional expression.
if intNumPages <> 15 Then
 Alert "Ok"
End If

' In the third assignment statement below, the
' inequality operator is used to give a value of
' True to intTest.
intA = 10
intB = 5
intTest = (intA <> intB)
```

See Also   Operators

InputBox

Syntax   InputBox(*prompt* [, *title*][, *default*][, *xpos*][, *ypos*][, *helpfile, context*])

Type   Intrinsic Function

Synopsis   Displays a prompt in a dialog box; waits for the user to enter text or click a button.

Description   The *prompt* parameter is displayed in the dialog box for the user to read. The *title* parameter is displayed in the title bar of the dialog box. The *default* parameter is displayed in the text box where the user enters his input. The *xpos* and *ypos* parameters specify, in twips, the horizontal and vertical distance of the dialog box from the top-left edge of the screen. If *xpos* is omitted, the dialog box is horizontally centered. If *ypos* is omitted, the dialog box is placed about one-third of the way down the screen. The *helpfile* parameter is the name of a help file that provides context-sensitive help, and *context* is the ID number of the topic that should be displayed when the user presses the F1 key.

InputBox returns the contents of the text box if the user presses Enter or clicks OK. A zero-length string ("") is returned if the Cancel button is clicked.

Example

```
name = InputBox "Please enter your name",
 "Name Entry Phase", "John Doe"
```

InStr

Syntax   InStr([*start,*] *string1, string2* [, *compare*])

Type   Intrinsic String Function

Synopsis Returns the location of *string2* in *string1*.

Description By using the *start* parameter, you can start the search at a position other than the beginning of *string1*. The *compare* parameter controls the type of search that's performed. Normally, a binary comparison is performed. If you use a *compare* value of 1, however, a textual, case-insensitive comparison is performed. If *compare* is Null, an error occurs. The *start* parameter must be specified if the *compare* parameter is specified.

Example `Alert InStr(10, "This is a fine test", "test")`

See Also Asc, AscB, AscW, Chr, ChrB, ChrW, InStrB, Len, LenB, Left, LeftB, LCase, LTrim, Mid, MidB, Right, RightB, Space, StrComp, String, String Functions, Trim, UCase

InStrB

Syntax `InStrB([start, ] string1, string2 [, compare])`

Type Intrinsic String Function

Synopsis Returns the byte position of *string2* in *string1*.

Description InStrB is used for binary data contained in strings.

See Also Asc, AscB, AscW, Chr, ChrB, ChrW, InStr, Len, LenB, Left, LeftB, LCase, LTrim, Mid, MidB, Right, RightB, Space, StrComp, String, String Functions, Trim, UCase

Int

Syntax `Int(number)`

Type Intrinsic Conversion and Math Function

Synopsis Returns the integer half of *number*.

Description If *number* is negative, the first negative number less than or equal to *number* is returned.

Example

```
intA = Int(10.34) ' intA equals 10
intB = Int(-4.4) ' intB equal -5
```

See Also CInt, Conversion Functions, Fix, Math Functions

Integer

Type Definition

Description Integers are whole numbers such as 1, 16, and 456 and can range from –32,768 to 32,767. They can be expressed in decimal (base 10), hexadecimal (base 16), or octal (base 8) form.

Hexadecimal numbers include 0 through 9 and *a* through *f*. In VBScript, you represent these numbers by preceding the number with &H. Octal numbers include only 0 through 7 and are preceded by &O. Decimal 23 is represented in hexadecimal by &H17, for example, and in octal by &O27.

See Also   Hex, Oct, Variables

Integer Division (\)

Syntax   `result = operand1 \ operand2`

Type   Arithmetic Operator

Synopsis   Divides one number by another and rounds the result to the nearest whole number.

Description   If either operand has the `Null` value, `result` is `Null`. Operands with an `Empty` value are equivalent to zero. And, of course, division by zero results in a runtime error.

See Also   On Error, Operators

Is

Syntax   `result = object1 Is object2`

Type   Operator

Synopsis   Returns `True` if `object1` and `object2` refer to the same object; otherwise, `False` is returned.

Description   The `Is` operator compares two object reference variables. When assigning object references to variables, you must use the `Set` keyword as shown in the "Example" section.

Example

```
Set objA = objCar
Set objB = objCar
intTemp = objA Is objB   ' intTemp equals True.
```

See Also   Operators

IsArray

Syntax   `IsArray(varname)`

Type   Intrinsic Array and Variant Testing Function

Synopsis   Returns `True` if `varname` is an array variable; otherwise, `False` is returned.

See Also   Array Variables, Array Functions, Dim, Erase, IsDate, IsEmpty, IsNull, IsNumeric, IsObject, LBound, ReDim, UBound, VarType

IsDate

Syntax   `IsDate(expression)`

Type   Intrinsic Date/Time and Variant Testing Function

Synopsis   Returns `True` if `expression` represents a date; otherwise, `False` is returned.

Description   In Microsoft Windows, the range of valid dates is January 1, 100 A.D., through December 31, 9999 A.D.; the ranges vary among operating systems.

See Also   Date/Time Functions, IsArray, IsEmpty, IsNull, IsNumeric, IsObject, VarType

App

F

IsEmpty

Syntax   IsEmpty(*expression*)

Type   Intrinsic Variant Testing Function

Synopsis   Returns True if *expression* represents an uninitialized variable or has the Empty value; otherwise, False is returned.

Description   If *expression* contains more than one variable, IsEmpty always returns False.

See Also   Empty, IsArray, IsDate, IsNull, IsNumeric, IsObject, VarType

IsNull

Syntax   IsNull(*expression*)

Type   Intrinsic Variant Testing Function

Synopsis   Returns True if *expression* contains no valid data or has the Null value; otherwise, False is returned.

Description   If *expression* contains more than one variable, any Null value causes IsNull to return True.

Example

```
If IsNull(numRecords) Then
 Alert "No records were available!"
End If
```

See Also   IsArray, IsDate, IsEmpty, IsNumeric, IsObject, Null, VarType

IsNumeric

Syntax   IsNumeric(*expression*)

Type   Intrinsic Variant Testing Function

Synopsis   Returns True if *expression* contains a number; otherwise, False is returned.

Description   If *expression* contains a date, IsNumeric returns False.

Example

```
If IsNumeric(Document.myForm.myText.Value) Then
    MsgBox "The value is numeric"
Else
    MsgBox "Please enter a number!"
End If
```

See Also   IsArray, IsDate, IsEmpty, IsNull, IsObject, VarType

IsObject

Syntax   IsObject(*expression*)

Type   Intrinsic Variant Testing Function

Synopsis   Returns `True` if *expression* references an object; otherwise, `False` is returned.

See Also   IsArray, IsDate, IsEmpty, IsNull, IsNumeric, VarType

LastModified

Syntax   `document.LastModified`

Type   Read-Only Property

Synopsis   Returns a string containing the date that *document* was last modified.

LBound

Syntax   `LBound(arrayname [, dimension])`

Type   Intrinsic Array Function

Synopsis   Returns the smallest available subscript for *dimension*.

Description   The *dimension* parameter (which defaults to 1) controls which dimension of the array is examined when the `LBound` function is called. The default lower bound for any dimension is always zero.

Use the `LBound` function with the `UBound` function to determine an array's size. If the `LBound` function returns 10 and the `UBound` function returns 34, the array has 24 elements. The *dimension* parameter controls which dimension of the array is examined when the `UBound` function is called.

See Also   Array Variables, Dim, Erase, IsArray, ReDim, UBound

LCase

Syntax   `LCase(string)`

Type   Intrinsic String Function

Synopsis   Returns a copy of *string* with all characters converted to lowercase.

See Also   Asc, AscB, AscW, Chr, ChrB, ChrW, InStr, InStrB, LeftB, Len, LenB, LTrim, Mid, MidB, Right, RightB, Space, StrComp, String, String Functions, Trim, UCase

Left

Syntax   `Left(string, length)`

Type   Intrinsic String Function

Synopsis   Returns a copy of the first *length* characters of *string*.

Description   If *length* is greater than *string*'s length, the entire string is returned.

Example

```
' removes the last character from strA
strB = Left(strA, Len(strA) - 1)
```

See Also   Asc, AscB, AscW, Chr, ChrB, ChrW, InStr, InStrB, LCase, LeftB, Len, LenB, LTrim, Mid, MidB, Right, RightB, Space, StrComp, String, String Functions, Trim, UCase

App

F

LeftB

Syntax   LeftB(*string, length*)

Type   Intrinsic String Function

Synopsis   Returns a copy of the first *length* bytes of *string*.

Description   You should use LeftB with binary data. If *length* is greater than *string*'s length, the entire string is returned.

Example

```
' removes the last byte from strA
strB = Left(strA, Len(strA) - 1)
```

See Also   Asc, AscB, AscW, Chr, ChrB, ChrW, InStr, InStrB, LCase, Left, Len, LenB, LTrim, Mid, MidB, Right, RightB, Space, StrComp, String, String Functions, Trim, UCase

Len

Syntax   Len(*string* ¦ *varname*)

Type   Intrinsic String Function

Synopsis   Returns the number of characters in *string* or the number of bytes it takes to store the value of *varname*.

Description   If *string* or *varname* is Null, Null is returned.

Example

```
strA = "12345"
intB = Len(strA) ' intB equals 5
```

See Also   Asc, AscB, AscW, Chr, ChrB, ChrW, InStr, InStrB, LCase, Left, LeftB, LenB, LTrim, Mid, MidB, Right, RightB, Space, StrComp, String, String Functions, Trim, UCase

LenB

Syntax   LenB(*expression*)

Type   Intrinsic String Function

Synopsis   Returns the length of *expression* in bytes.

Description   You should use LenB with binary data.

See Also   Asc, AscB, AscW, Chr, ChrB, ChrW, InStr, InStrB, LCase, Left, LeftB, Len, LTrim, Mid, MidB, Right, RightB, Space, StrComp, String, String Functions, Trim, UCase

Length

Syntax 1   *element*.Length

Syntax 2   *history*.Length

Type   Property

Synopsis   Gets the number of options in a select *element* or gets the number of entries in the browser's history list.

N O T E   The Length property of History objects always returns zero in Internet Explorer version 3.0. ▪

Less Than (<)

Syntax   *operand1* < *operand2*

Type   Comparison Operator

Synopsis   Returns True if *operand1* is less than *operand2*.

Description   If either operand has the Null value, *result* is Null. Operands with an Empty value are equivalent to zero.

The less-than operator is frequently used in conditional expressions for If, Do, and For statements.

Example

```
' In this If statement, the less than operator
' is used in the conditional expression.
if intNumPages < 15 Then
 Alert "Ok"
End If
' In the third assignment statement below, the
' less than operator is used to give a value of
' False to intTest.
intA = 10
intB = 5
intTest = (intA < intB)
```

See Also   Operators

Less Than or Equal To (<=)

Syntax   *operand1* < *operand2*

Type   Comparison Operator

Synopsis   Returns True if *operand1* is less than or equal to *operand2*.

Description   If either operand has the Null value, *result* is Null. Operands with an Empty value are equivalent to zero.

The less-than-or-equal-to operator is frequently used in conditional expressions for If, Do, and For statements.

Example

```
' In this If statement, the <= operator
' is used in the conditional expression.
if intNumPages <= 15 Then
```

App
F

```
  Alert "Ok"
End If

' In the third assignment statement below, the
' <= operator is used to give a value of
' False to intTest.
intA = 10
intB = 5
intTest = (intA <= intB)
```

See Also   Operators

Link

Syntax   Link.*property*

Type   Object

Synopsis   Represents a hyperlink.

Description   Link objects are accessed by using the Links property of a Document object. See the "Links" entry for additional information.

Tables F.24 and F.25 list the events and properties of the Link Object.

Table F.24   Events of a *Link* Object

Event	Page	Description
OnClick	873	Happens when a hyperlink is clicked
OnMouseMove	874	Happens when the mouse pointer moves and is over a hyperlink
OnMouseOver	875	Happens when the mouse pointer moves over a hyperlink

Table F.25   Properties of a *Link* Object

Property	Page	Description
Hash	849	Gets or sets the hash part of the URL
Host	850	Gets or sets the host and port part of the URL
Hostname	850	Gets or sets the host name part of the URL
Href	851	Gets or sets the whole URL
Pathname	883	Gets or sets the path name part of the URL
Port	884	Gets or sets the port part of the URL
Protocol	885	Gets or sets the protocol part of the URL
Search	889	Gets or sets the search part of the URL
Target	896	Gets the target of the hyperlink

See Also   Links

LinkColor

Syntax 1   *document*.LinkColor = *rgbValue*

Syntax 2   *document*.LinkColor = *string*

Type   Property

Synopsis   Gets or sets the hyperlink color of *document*.

Description   You can set the color by specifying an RGB value in hexadecimal or by specifying a color name. The "Color Names" entry lists all the color names you can use.

You can set this property only while the document is being parsed. An OnLoad event handler procedure is a good place to set document properties.

Links

Syntax   *document*.Links[*index*]

Type   Read-Only Property

Synopsis   Returns an array of links, or you can specify an index to retrieve a single link.

Description   You can find out how many links *document* has by using the sample code in the "Example" section. Figure F.7 shows the results of the example HTML document. Notice that the number of links in the document changes as the document is parsed.

FIG. F.7
The number of links in a document depends a great deal on when the links are counted.

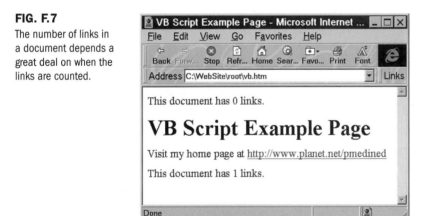

App

F

Example

```
<!-- This document shows how to determine
 the number of links in a document.
-->
<HTML>
 <HEAD>
 <TITLE>VBScript Example Page</TITLE>
```

```
<SCRIPT language="VBScript">
<!--
Sub dispLinks
intNumLinks = Document.Anchors.Length
Document.Open
Document.Write "This document has " &
intNumLinks &
" links.<P>"
Document.Clear
End Sub

dispLinks
-->
</SCRIPT>
</HEAD>
<BODY LANGUAGE="VBScript">
<H1>VBScript Example Page</H1>
    Visit my home page at
<A HREF="http://www.planet.net/pmedined">
http://www.planet.net/pmedined
</A>
<P>
<SCRIPT language="VBScript">
<!--
dispLinks
-->
</SCRIPT>
</BODY>
</HTML>
```

Literal Values

Type   Definition

Description   A literal is a value that's represented "as is" in your source code. VBScript uses several types of literals: Boolean, date, floating point (both single and double precision), integer, and string. Table F.26 shows an example of each data type. Also, each data type has its own entry in this book.

Table F.26   VBScript Literal Values

Data Type	Value	Page
Boolean	True or False	812
Date	"01/23/1996" "Jan 23, 1996"	826
Double Precision	34.67	834
Integer	45	854
Single Precision	12.34	892
String	"Hello, World"	893

Location (Object)

Syntax   Location.*property*

Type   Object

Synopsis   Represents the URL of a document or window.

Description   The Location object doesn't have any events or methods. Table F.27 lists the Location object's properties.

Table F.27   Properties of a *Location* Object

Property	Page	Description
Hash	849	Gets or sets the hash part of the URL
Host	850	Gets or sets the host and port parts of the URL
Hostname	850	Gets or sets the host name part of the URL
Href	851	Gets or sets the whole URL
Pathname	883	Gets or sets the path name part of the URL
Port	884	Gets or sets the port part of the URL
Protocol	885	Gets or sets the protocol part of the URL
Search	889	Gets or sets the search part of the URL

Location (Property)

Syntax 1   *document*.Location

Syntax 2   *window*.Location

Type   Read-Only Property

Synopsis   Returns the Location object for *document* or for *window*.

Description   If *window* isn't specified, the Location object of the current window is returned.

If you need the Location object for a document, you must specify the Document object (most of the time, you use *document*.Location). See the "Location (Object)" entry for more information.

Log

Syntax   Log(*number*)

Type   Intrinsic Math Function

Synopsis   Returns the natural logarithm of number.

Description   The natural logarithm is the logarithm to the base e. The constant e is approximately 2.718.

See Also   Abs, Atn, Cos, Exp, Math Functions, Randomize, Rnd, Sin, Sqr, Tan

App
F

Long Variables

Type   Definition

Synopsis   Long variables are whole numbers that can range from –2,147,483,648 to 2,147,483,647.

Example   `lngTemp = 1222333`

LTrim

Syntax   `LTrim(string)`

Type   Intrinsic Math Function

Synopsis   Returns a copy of *string* without leading spaces.

See Also   Asc, AscB, AscW, Chr, ChrB, ChrW, InStr, InStrB, LeftB, Len, LenB, Mid, MidB, Right, RightB, Space, StrComp, String, String Functions, Trim, UCase

Math Functions

Type   Definition

Description   VBScript has relatively few math functions; they're listed in Table F.28.

Table F.28   VBScript Math Functions

Function	Page Number	Description
Abs	805	Returns the absolute value of a number
Atn	811	Returns the arctangent of a number
Cos	825	Returns the cosine of an angle
Exp	842	Returns *e* raised to a power
Log	863	Returns the natural logarithm of a number
Randomize	886	Initializes the random-number generator
Rnd	888	Returns a random number
Sin	892	Returns the sine of an angle
Sqr	892	Returns the square root of a number
Tan	896	Returns the tangent of an angle

Method

Syntax 1   `form.Method`

Syntax 2   `form.Method = string`

Type   Property

Synopsis   Gets or sets the method for sending form information to the server.

Description You can send form information to the server by using either the GET or POST method.

Methods

Type Definition

Description A method is a function assigned to an object. For example, document.myForm. Submit() executes the Submit method and sends the information from the myForm form to the server.

See Also Procedures

Mid

Syntax Mid(*string, start* [, *length*])

Type Intrinsic String Function

Synopsis Returns a copy of the part of *string* beginning at *start* for *length* characters.

Description If *string* contains Null, Null is returned. If *start* is greater than the length of *string*, a zero-length string is returned. If no *length* parameter is specified, all characters from *start* to the end of the string are returned.

See Also Asc, AscB, AscW, Chr, ChrB, ChrW, InStr, InStrB, LeftB, Len, LenB, LTrim, MidB, Right, RightB, Space, StrComp, String, String Functions, Trim, UCase

MidB

Syntax MidB(*string, start* [, *length*])

Type Intrinsic String Function

Synopsis Returns a copy of the part of *string* beginning at *start* for *length* bytes.

Description You should use MidB for binary information.

See Also Asc, AscB, AscW, Chr, ChrB, ChrW, InStr, InStrB, LeftB, Len, LenB, LTrim, Mid, Right, RightB, Space, StrComp, String, String Functions, Trim, UCase

Minute

Syntax Minute(*time*)

Type Intrinsic Date/Time Function

Synopsis Returns the minute value in *time*, which can range from 0 to 59, inclusive.

See Also Date, Date/Time Functions, DateSerial, DateValue, Day, Month, Now, Second, Time, TimeSerial, TimeValue, Weekday, Year

Mod (Modulus)

Syntax *result = operand1* Mod *operand2*

Type Operator

Synopsis   Returns the remainder of *operand1* divided by *operand2*.

Description   The modulus operator is a special form of division that returns only the remainder of the operation. If either operand has the Null value, *result* is Null. Operands with an Empty value are equivalent to zero.

Example

```
i = 8 Mod 2 ' returns 0
i = 8 Mod 3 ' returns 2
```

See Also   Operators

Modulus (Mod)

Syntax   *result = operand1* Mod *operand2*

Type   Operator

Synopsis   Returns the remainder of *operand1* divided by *operand2*.

Description   The modulus operator is a special form of division that returns only the remainder of the operation. If either operand has the Null value, *result* is Null. Operands with an Empty value are equivalent to zero.

Example

```
i = 8 Mod 2 ' returns 0
i = 8 Mod 3 ' returns 2
```

See Also   Operators

Month

Syntax   Month(date)

Type   Intrinsic Date/Time Function

Synopsis   Returns the month value in *date,* which can range from 1 to 12, inclusive.

See Also   Date, Date/Time Functions, DateSerial, DateValue, Day, Minute, Now, Second, Time, TimeSerial, TimeValue, Weekday, Year

MouseOver

Type   Event

Synopsis   Happens when the user moves the mouse pointer over an object or control.

MsgBox

Syntax   MsgBox(*string* [, *buttons*][, *title*][, *helpfile, context*])

Type   Intrinsic Function

Synopsis   Displays a message in a dialog box and waits for the user to click a button. Returns a value related to the button that was clicked according to Table F.29.

Table F.29 Return Values from *MsgBox*

Value	Description
1	OK button was clicked
2	Cancel button was clicked or Esc key was pressed
3	Abort button was clicked
4	Retry button was clicked
5	Ignore button was clicked
6	Yes button was clicked
7	No button was clicked

Description

The *string* parameter is displayed inside the dialog box when it appears. You can display about 1,024 characters, depending on the font you use. You also can create multiline prompts by adding a carriage return character (Chr(13)) into *string* where you want the lines to end.

The *buttons* parameter controls which buttons are displayed in the dialog box. It also controls which icon is displayed, the modality, and which button is the default. The default value for *buttons* is zero, which displays the OK button. Use Table F.30 determine the value of *buttons* that you need.

Table F.30 The *buttons* Parameter of *MsgBox*

Value	Description
Values Affecting the Number and Type of Buttons	
0	Displays the OK button
1	Displays the OK and Cancel buttons
2	Displays the Abort, Retry, and Ignore buttons
3	Displays the Yes, No, and Cancel buttons
4	Displays the Yes and No buttons
5	Displays the Retry and Cancel buttons
Values Affecting the Icon Style	
16	Displays the Critical Message icon
32	Displays the Warning Query icon
48	Displays the Warning Message icon
64	Displays the Information Message icon

App
F

Table F.30 Continued	
Value	Description
Values That Set the Default Button	
0	Makes the first button the default
256	Makes the second button the default
512	Makes the third button the default
768	Makes the fourth button the default
Values That Set the Modality	
0	Makes the dialog box application modal; the user must respond before work can continue in the current application.
4096	Makes the dialog box system modal; the user must respond before work can continue in any applications. Use this option with care.

Add together one number from each subsection of Table F.30 to arrive at the correct value for *buttons*.

The *helpfile* and *context* parameters work together to define what happens if the user presses F1 or clicks the question-mark button while the dialog box is active.

Multiplication (*)

Syntax   *result = operand1 * operand2*

Type   Arithmetic Operator

Synopsis   Multiplies one number by another.

Description   If either operand has the Null value, *result* is Null. Operands with an Empty value are equivalent to zero.

See Also   Operators

name

Syntax 1   *anchor*.name

Syntax 2   *element*.name

Syntax 3   *element*.name = *string*

Syntax 4   *window*.name

Type   Read-Only Property

Synopsis   Gets the name of *anchor*, *element*, or *window*. In the third syntax, sets the name of *element*.

Description   If *window* has no name, `Null` is returned. If *window* isn't specified, the name of the current window is returned.

Example

```
' Assign the current window name to strWindowName.
strWindowName = name
```

Navigate

Syntax   *window*.Navigate(*url*)

Type   Method; applies to `Window` objects

Synopsis   Connects the current window to a new URL.

Description   If *window* isn't specified, the current window is used.

Example

```
' switch the current window to the Microsoft Home Page
Navigate("http://www.microsoft.com")
```

Navigator (Object)

Type   Object

Synopsis   Represents the browser.

Description   By using the `Navigator` object, you can access information about the browser.

Table F.31 lists the properties of the `Navigator` object.

Table F.31   Properties of a *Navigator* Object

Object	Page Number	Description
AppCodeName	808	The code name of the browser
AppName	809	The name of the browser
AppVersion	809	The version of the browser
UserAgent	899	The user agent name of the browser

App
F

Navigator (Property)

Syntax   *window*.Navigator

Type   Property

Synopsis   Returns the `Navigator` object associated with *window*.

Description   See the "Navigator (Object)" entry for more information.

Negation (–)

Syntax   `- operand`

Type   Arithmetic Operator

Synopsis   Negates the value of *operand*.

Example

```
intA = 10 ' intA equals positive 10.
intB = -10 ' intB equals negative 10.
```

See Also   Operators

Not

Syntax   `result = Not operand`

Type   Operator

Synopsis   Returns the logical opposite of *operand*.

Description   The `Not` operator returns `True` if *operand* is `False`, and `False` if *operand* is `True`. If *operand* is a variable, `Not` returns a copy of the variable with each bit inverted. If *operand* is `Null`, `Null` is returned.

See Also   Operators

Not Equal (<>)

Syntax   `operand1 <> operand2`

Type   Comparison Operator

Synopsis   Returns `True` if *operand1* doesn't equal *operand2*.

Description   If either operand has the `Null` value, *result* is `Null`. Operands with an `Empty` value are equivalent to zero.

The inequality operator is frequently used in conditional expressions for `If`, `Do`, and `For` statements.

Example

```
' In this If statement, the inequality operator
' is used in the conditional expression.
if intNumPages <> 15 Then
 Alert "Ok"
End If

' In the third assignment statement below, the
' inequality operator is used to give a value of
' True to intTest.
intA = 10
intB = 5
intTest = (intA <> intB)
```

See Also   Operators

Now

Syntax   Now

Type   Intrinsic Date/Time Function

Synopsis   Returns the current date and time.

See Also   Date, Date/Time Functions, DateSerial, DateValue, Day, Minute, Month, Second, Time, TimeSerial, TimeValue, Weekday, Year

Null

Syntax   Null

Type   Constant

Synopsis   Indicates that a variable has no valid data.

Description   Typically, Null is assigned to variables to indicate that they have no valid data. For instance, you might assign Null to a variable named numRecords to indicate that a data file can't be opened.

Null isn't the same as Empty, which indicates that a variable hasn't yet been initialized. It's also not the same as a zero-length string, which is sometimes referred to as a *null string*.

You can't directly test to see whether a variable has a Null value, because any expression containing Null is itself Null. Therefore, you must use the IsNull function to test for the Null value.

Example   numRecords = Null

See Also   Empty, IsNull

Number

Syntax 1   Err.Number

Syntax 2   Err.Number = *errornumber*

Type   Property

Synopsis   Gets or sets a numeric value specifying an error.

Description   You set Err.Number when returning a user-defined error. Add your error number to the variable vbObjectError when returning ActiveX errors. Normally, you create a list of pseudo-constants that hold error values to avoid reusing numbers.

Example

```
' Raise an error.
' Notice that I use my initials as a prefix
' for the pseudo-constants. This should avoid
' naming conflicts with another programmer's
' scripts.
dmErrNoFile = 1000
dmErrNoRecords = 1001
Err.Raise Number:= vbObjectError + dmErrNoFile, Source:= "myClass"
```

App
F

Objects

Type   Definition

Description   An object has properties that are either variables or references to other objects. Functions associated with objects are called the object's *methods*. You access the properties and methods of an object with the following simple notation:

```
objectName.propertyName
objectName.methodName
```

Not all names are not case-sensitive. Therefore, `OnClick` is the same as `onClick` or even `ONCLICK`.

Table F.32 lists the predefined objects in VBScript and the pages where you can find them.

Table F.32   Predefined Objects Associated with HTML

Object	Page Number	Description
Anchor	807	Represents a hyperlink in a document
Document	833	Represents the Document object associated with a window
Element	834	Represents a control or an object on an HTML document
Form	844	Represents an HTML form
History	849	Represents the URLs visited by a window
Link	860	Represents a hyperlink
Location	863	Represents the URL of a document or window
Navigator	869	Represents the browser
Window	907	Represents a window in the browser

Object Variables

Type   Definition

Description   Object variables are really pointers (or references) to a block of memory that holds an ActiveX object.

See Also   Objects

Oct

Syntax   Oct(*number*)

Type   Intrinsic Conversion and Math Function

Synopsis   Returns a string representing the octal value of *number*.

Description   If *number* is Null, Null is returned. If *number* is Empty, zero is returned. If *number* isn't an integer, it's rounded to the nearest whole number.

See Also   Conversion Functions, Math Functions

OnBlur

Syntax   *element*.OnBlur

Type   Event

Synopsis   Happens when *element* loses the focus.

See Also   Events, Event Handling, OnChange, OnClick, OnFocus, OnLoad, OnMouseMove, OnMouseOver, OnSelect, OnSubmit, OnUnload

OnChange

Syntax   *element*.OnChange

Type   Event

Synopsis   Happens when *element* has changed.

See Also   Events, Event Handling, OnBlur, OnClick, OnFocus, OnLoad, OnMouseMove, OnMouseOver, OnSelect, OnSubmit, OnUnload

OnClick

Syntax 1   *element*.OnClick

Syntax 2   *link*.OnClick

Type   Event

Synopsis   Happens when the user clicks an element or a hyperlink.

See Also   Events, Event Handling, OnBlur, OnChange, OnFocus, OnLoad, OnMouseMove, OnMouseOver, OnSelect, OnSubmit, OnUnload

On Error

Syntax   On Error Resume Next

Type   Keyword

Synopsis   Enables or disables an error-handling routine.

Description   If an On Error statement isn't used, all runtime errors are fatal.

The On Error Resume Next statement essentially causes runtime errors to be ignored. You can still examine the Err object, however, to see whether an error has occurred. You should check the Err object after each procedure call that has a high probability of generating a runtime error. Each procedure that you write needs its own On Error Resume Next statement so that it can trap errors local to that procedure.

See Also   Err

App
F

OnFocus

Syntax *element.*OnFocus

Type Event

Synopsis Happens when *element* gets the focus.

See Also Events, Event Handling, OnBlur, OnChange, OnClick, OnLoad, OnMouseMove, OnMouseOver, OnSelect, OnSubmit, OnUnload

OnLoad

Syntax OnLoad = *eventHandler*

Type Event

Synopsis Happens after all the HTML for a document is parsed and processed.

Description An OnLoad event handler function is a good place to put initialization statements. Because the OnLoad event handler is defined inside the HTML <BODY> tag, you can have only one function per HTML document.

Example

```
<!-- This document shows how to use the
 OnLoad event.
-->
<HTML>
 <HEAD>
 <TITLE>VBScript Example Page</TITLE>
 <SCRIPT language="VBScript">
 <!--
 Sub loadHandler
 Alert "The document has loaded!"
 End Sub
 -->
 </SCRIPT>
 </HEAD>
 <BODY LANGUAGE="VBScript" OnLoad="loadHandler">
 <H1>VBScript Example Page</H1>
 </BODY>
</HTML>
```

See Also Events, Event Handling, OnBlur, OnChange, OnClick, OnFocus, OnMouseMove, OnMouseOver, OnSelect, OnSubmit, OnUnload

OnMouseMove

Syntax link.OnMouseMove(*shift, button, x, y*)

Type Event

Synopsis Happens when the mouse pointer moves while over a hyperlink.

Description The parameters are automatically passed to your event handler routine by the browser. The *shift* parameter holds the status of the Shift key. The *button* indicates which mouse button is pressed, if any. The *x* and *y* parameters indicate the position of the mouse pointer in pixels.

The Microsoft documentation indicates that the *shift* and *button* parameters are now set to zero and therefore aren't accurate.

Example

```
' The following script handles the OnMouseMove
' event for a single hyperlink named lnkMicrosoftHome.

<SCRIPT LANGUAGE="VBScript" FOR="lnkMicrosoftHome"
 EVENT="OnMouseMove(shift, button, x, y)">
 <!--
 ' add the event handler statements here.
 -->
</SCRIPT>
```

See Also   Events, Event Handling, OnBlur, OnChange, OnClick, OnFocus, OnLoad, OnMouseOver, OnSelect, OnSubmit, OnUnload

OnMouseOver

Syntax   *link*.OnMouseOver

Type   Event

Synopsis   Happens when the mouse pointer moves over a hyperlink.

Description   You can attach a script to this event by using the HTML <SCRIPT> tag as shown in the "Example" section for the OnMouseMove event. Or you can place VBScript statements directly in an <A> tag by using OnMouseOver as an attribute.

Example

```
' The following script handles the OnMouseOver
' event for a single hyperlink named lnkMicrosoftHome.

<SCRIPT LANGUAGE="VBScript" FOR="lnkMicrosoftHome"
 EVENT="OnMouseOver">
 <!--
 ' add the event handler statements here.
 -->
</SCRIPT>
```

See Also   Events, Event Handling, OnBlur, OnChange, OnClick, OnFocus, OnLoad, OnMouseMove, OnSelect, OnSubmit, OnUnload

OnSelect

Syntax   *element*.OnSelect

Type   Event

Synopsis   Happens when the contents of *element* are selected.

See Also   Events, Event Handling, OnBlur, OnChange, OnClick, OnFocus, OnLoad, OnMouseMove, OnMouseOver, OnSubmit, OnUnload

App
F

OnSubmit

Syntax   *form.*OnUnload = *eventHandler*

Type   Event

Synopsis   Happens just before the form's information is sent to the server.

Description   You can use this event to perform information validation and prevent the information from being sent if it's not valid. A validation function must return False to prevent submitting the form.

Example

```
' The Return keyword must be used in order for VBScript
' to pay attention to the return value of a validation
' function. If the Return keyword is not used, the return
' value is ignored.
document.myForm.OnSubmit = "return IsValid()"
```

See Also   Events, Event Handling, OnBlur, OnChange, OnClick, OnFocus, OnLoad, OnMouseMove, OnMouseOver, OnSelect, OnUnload

OnUnload

Syntax   OnUnload = *eventHandler*

Type   Event

Synopsis   Happens after the document is unloaded.

Description   You can see the OnUnload event handler in action by loading the HTML document shown in the "Example" section and then clicking the browser's Refresh button.

Example

```
<!-- This document shows how to use the
 OnUnload event.
-->
<HTML>
 <HEAD>
 <TITLE>VBScript Example Page</TITLE>
 <SCRIPT language="VBScript">
 <!--
 Sub unloadHandler
 Alert "The document has loaded!"
 End Sub
 -->
 </SCRIPT>
 </HEAD>
 <BODY LANGUAGE="VBScript" OnUnload="unloadHandler">
 <H1>VBScript Example Page</H1>
 </BODY>
</HTML>
```

See Also   Events, Event Handling, OnBlur, OnChange, OnClick, OnFocus, OnLoad, OnMouseMove, OnMouseOver, OnSelect, OnSubmit

open

Syntax 1   *document*.open

Syntax 2   *newWindow* = Window.open(*url, target, options*)

Type   Method

Synopsis   Opens *document* for output or creates a new browser window.

Document Object Description   The open method opens *document* for output. Then Write or WriteLn methods are used to append HTML-based text to the document. After all text is written, the close or clear method is used to update the browser's window.

Window Object Description   When the new window is successfully created, the Window object associated with the new window is returned.

> **CAUTION**
>
> Although the Microsoft documentation indicates that using Window is optional, when it's not specified, a syntax error is created.

The *url* parameter can be either an absolute or a relative URL.

If *target* names an existing window, that window is reused. The *target* parameter is directly analogous to the TARGET attribute in HTML.

You can turn the following options on or off by using yes or no in a comma-delimited list: toolbar, location, directories, status, menubar, scrollbars, and resizeable. You can specify the height and width of the new window in pixels. Also, you can set the location of the top-left corner of the window by setting the Top and Left options.

> **CAUTION**
>
> This method seems to have some problems. Figure F.8 shows the results of the example HTML. Notice that although the parameters to the Open method indicate that the window shouldn't be resizeable, it is. Also, even though the Open method works, I received this error message:
>
> Microsoft VBScript runtime error [Line: 12] Object doesn't support this property or method.
>
> Please test thoroughly when using this method.

App
F

Example

```
<!-- This document shows how to use the
 open method.
-->
<HTML>
 <HEAD>
 <TITLE>VBScript Example Page</TITLE>
```

```
</HEAD>
<BODY>
<H1>VBScript Example Page</H1>
<SCRIPT language="VBScript">
<!--
newWin = window.open("C:/WebSite\root\index.htm",
"", "toolbar=no, menubar=no, resizeable=no")
-->
</SCRIPT>
</BODY>
</HTML>
```

Figure F.8 shows the window that's created by this example.

FIG. F.8

Although the parameters
indicate this window
isn't resizable, it is.

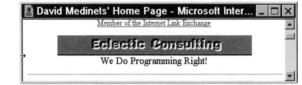

Opener

Syntax

window.Opener

Type   Read-Only Property; applies to a `Window` object

Synopsis   Returns the `Window` object that represents the window that opened the current window.

Operators

Type   Definition

Description   Operators are instructions you give to the computer so that it can perform some task or operation. All operators cause actions to be performed on *operands*. An operand can be anything on which you perform an operation. In practical terms, any particular operand is a literal, a variable, or an expression. VBScript operators can be divided into two basic classes: *binary* and *unary*. Binary operators need two operands; unary operators need a single operand.

I like to think about operators in the same way I would give instructions to the driver of a car. I might say "turn left" or "turn right." These commands can be considered directional operators in the same way that + and − mathematical operators say "add this" or "subtract this." If I yell "stop" while the car is moving, on the other hand, this command should supersede the other commands. Therefore, "stop" has precedence over "turn left" and "turn right."

The subtraction operator, for example, is a binary operator:

5 - 2

Of course, simply subtracting two numbers together doesn't mean much if you don't store the value somewhere. Variables play a role here. You can assign values to variables by using the assignment operator:

```
int_Num = 5 - 2
```

The minus sign can also act as a unary operator when placed in front of a number. For example,

```
int_Num = -34
```

Table F.33 lists all VBScript operators. Some of them may be familiar to you from high school math class; for others, you might need a description. For operators with their own entries in this book, a page number is indicted in the third column.

Table F.33   VBScript's Operators

Operator	Name	Page	Description
Arithmetic Operators			
+	Addition	800	Adds two operands together
/	Division	800	Divides one number by another
^	Exponentiation	801	Raises one number to the power of another
\	Integer division	802	Divides one number by another and rounds the result to the nearest whole number
Mod	Modulus	866	Returns the remainder of a division operation
*	Multiplication	804	Multiplies one number by another
–	Negation	804	Negates a number
–	Subtraction	804	Subtracts one number from another
Comparison Operators			
=	Equality	800	Returns True if one number equals another
>	Greater than	801	Returns True if one number is greater than another
>=	Greater than or equal to	801	Returns True if one number is greater than or equal to another.
<>	Inequality	802	Returns True if two numbers aren't equal

App
F

continues

Table F.33 Continued

Operator	Name	Page	Description
Comparison Operators			
<	Less than	803	Returns True if one number is greater than another
<=	Less than or equal to	803	Returns True if one number is less than or equal to another
Is	Object	855	Returns True if two object equivalence references refer to the same object
Logical Operators			
And	Conjunction	808	Returns True if its two operands are true
Eqv	Equivalence	838	Returns True if its two operands are logically equivalent
Imp	Implication	852	Performs a logical implication on two operands
Not	Negation	870	Returns the logical opposite of an operand
Or	Disjunction	882	Returns True if either of its operands is True
Xor	Exclusion	909	Returns True if only one of its operands is True
String Concatenation Operator			
&	Concatenation	804	Appends one string to another

Operator Precedence

Type Definition

Description Precedence is important in every computer language, and VBScript is no exception. *Order of precedence* indicates which operator should be evaluated first. You can use parentheses, however, to explicitly change the order of evaluation. Expressions inside parentheses are always evaluated before expressions outside the parentheses. Otherwise, regular operator precedence is always used.

Table F.34 lists the operators in order of precedence. When operators have equal precedence, they're evaluated left to right as they appear in the expression.

Table F.34   VBScript's Order of Operator Precedence

Operator	Description
Arithmetic Operators	
^	Exponentiation
−	Unary negation
*	Multiplication
/	Division
\	Integer division
Mod	Modulus
+	Addition
−	Subtraction
&	String concatenation
Comparison Operators	
All comparison operators have the same level of precedence.	
Logical Operators	
Not	Negation
And	Conjunction
Or	Disjunction
Xor	Exclusion
Eqv	Equivalence
Imp	Implication

Option Explicit

Syntax   Option Explicit

Type   Keyword

Synopsis   Ensures that all variables are explicitly declared.

Description   When you place the Option Explicit statement at the top of your script, an error is generated by any variable that isn't explicitly defined. The error is generated when the Web browser reads the HTML document file. Requiring every variable to be explicitly declared means that you can't misspell variables without generating an error message—a great bug prevention feature.

App

F

Example

```
<HTML>
<HEAD>
<SCRIPT>
<!--
 Option Explicit ' must be the first line
 ' in the script.

 Dim lngTemp
-->
</SCRIPT>
</HEAD>
</HTML>
```

See Also   Dim

Options

Syntax   *element*.Options

Type   Read-Only Property

Synopsis   Gets the <OPTIONS> tag for *element*.

Description   The *element* specified must be a Select element. An object is returned with the properties shown in Table F.35.

Table F.35   Properties for *Options*

Property	Description
DefaultSelected	Gets the currently selected attribute
Index	Gets the index of an option
Length	Gets the number of options in the selected object
Name	Gets the name of the selected object
Selected	Programmatically selects an option
SelectedIndex	Gets the index of the selected option
Text	Gets the text to be displayed
Value	Gets the value attribute

Or

Syntax   *result = operand1* Or *operand2*

Type   Operator

Synopsis   Returns True if either operand is True.

Description   If either operand is Null, Null is returned. If the operands are numeric, a bitwise comparison of identically positioned bits is performed.

See Also   Operators

Parent

Syntax   *window*.Parent

Type   Read-Only Property; applies to a Window object

Synopsis   Returns a reference to the parent Window object.

Description   The parent of the current window is the containing frame. If no containing frame exists, the current Window object is returned. Therefore, you can tell whether the current document is inside a frame by comparing the current Window object with the parent object. If they are the same, no frame is present.

Example

```
<!-- This document shows how to determine if
 the current document is inside a frame.
-->
<HTML>
 <HEAD>
 <TITLE>VBScript Example Page</TITLE>
 <script language="VBScript">
 <!--
 Function IsFrame
 IsFrame = NOT(window Is window.parent)
 End Function
 -->
 </script>
 </HEAD>
 <BODY>
 <H1>VBScript Example Page</H1>
 <SCRIPT language="VBScript">
 <!--
 Document.Open
 If IsFrame = True Then
 Document.Write "Frames"
 Else
 Document.Write "No Frames"
 End If
 Document.Close
 -->
 </SCRIPT>
 </BODY>
</HTML>
```

Pathname

Syntax 1   *link*.Pathname

Syntax 2   *location*.Pathname

Syntax 3   *location*.Pathname = *path*

App
F

884 Appendix F Visual Basic Script Quick Reference

Type Property

Synopsis Gets the path for *link* or *location*. In the third syntax, sets the path for *location*.

Description The path part of an URL is between the host part and the search or hash parts.

Port

Syntax 1 *link*.Port

Syntax 2 *location*.Port

Syntax 3 *location*.Port = *portnumber*

Type Property

Synopsis Gets the port for *link* or *location*. Sets the port for *location*.

Description The empty string ("") is returned for the file: protocol.

Procedures

Type Definition

Description A *procedure* is a user-defined or built-in method that performs a task. It can also return a value. Procedures are universal and don't need to be associated with an object to run, whereas methods are integrated with objects.

As a general rule, placing procedure definitions within the <HEAD> tags of a document is best. This practice ensures that any functions are loaded and ready before users have a chance to interact with the rest of the page.

All procedures can accept information in the form of *arguments* or *parameters*. If you have a procedure that calculates the floor space of a room, for example, you need to tell the procedure the length and width of the room. You place parameters inside parentheses immediately after the name of the procedure being called, as in the following:

calcSquareFootage(*width*, *length*)

The parentheses aren't required unless you also use the Call keyword.

If a procedure needs to change a variable used by another procedure or the calling procedure, the variable needs to have script-level scope. (See "Scope.")

Prompt

Syntax *result* = *window*.Prompt(*prompt* [, *default*])

Type Method; applies to Window objects

Synopsis Requests input from the user.

Description The Prompt method returns the string that the user enters. You use the *prompt* parameter to display a message, usually a question that indicates what kind of input is needed. You use the *default* parameter to provide a default answer.

The Microsoft documentation indicates that both *prompt* and *default* parameters are optional. As you can see in Figure F.9, the default string "undefined" is used if you don't specify these parameters.

FIG. F.9
A prompt box with no parameters specified.

Example

```
<!-- This document shows how to use the
  Confirm method.
-->
<HTML>
 <HEAD>
 <TITLE>VBScript Example Page</TITLE>
 </HEAD>
 <BODY>
 <H1>VBScript Example Page</H1>
 <SCRIPT language="VBScript">
 <!--
 result = Prompt()
 -->
 </SCRIPT>
 </BODY>
</HTML>
```

Properties

Type Definition

Description Properties are used to describe an object or its current state. A property is defined by assigning it a value. The value can be assigned by the browser, by the program, or as the user interacts with the page.

Protocol

Syntax 1 *link*.Protocol

Syntax 2 *location*.Protocol

Syntax 3 *location*.Protocol = *protocol*

Type Property

Synopsis Gets the protocol for *link* or *location*. In the third syntax, sets the protocol for *location*.

Description The *protocol* parameter is a string that represents the protocol you need to use. For example, you use ftp: for the file transfer protocol.

App
F

Raise

Syntax   Err.Raise(*number*, [*source*, [*description*, [*helpfile*, *contextID*]]])

Type   Method

Synopsis   Generates a runtime error.

Description   The *number* parameter indicates the nature of the runtime error and can range from 0 to 65,535.

The optional *source* parameter is the name of the error generator. If an Automation object generates an error, *source* should have the form myProject.myClass. The default value is the programmatic ID of the current VBScript project.

The optional *description* parameter describes the error. It defaults to the internal string associated with Err.Number or a generic error message.

You use the optional *helpfile* and *contextID* parameters to specify a topic inside a help file that can be used for context-sensitive help.

Randomize

Syntax   Randomize [*number*]

Type   Intrinsic Math Function

Synopsis   Initializes the random-number generator.

Description   To generate "true" random numbers, the random-number generator needs to be reseeded with a different number each time your script starts. If the *number* parameter isn't specified, a number based on the current date and time is used.

See Also   Abs, Atn, Cos, Exp, Log, Math Functions, Rnd, Sin, Sqr, Tan

ReDim

Syntax   ReDim [*Preserve*] *varname*(*subscripts*) [, *varname*(*subscripts*)] ...

Type   Keyword

Synopsis   Declares or modifies the bounds for dynamic arrays.

Description   You can use a ReDim statement to allocate or reallocate space to dynamic arrays. You also can modify the dimensions of an array an unlimited number of times. To create dynamic arrays, you use the Dim statement and empty parentheses.

By using the Preserve option, you can change an array's dimension and keep its existing data. You're limited, however, to changing only the last array dimension. If you reduce the size of the array, you lose the data in the freed-up element. Increasing the size of the array results in elements that are either zero (numeric), have a zero-length string (string), or have the Nothing value (object).

Example

```
Dim a() ' declare a dynamic array
ReDim a(10, 10) ' allocate memory for a 10x10 array
ReDim Preserve a(10, 15) ' make array larger, but keep the contents.
```

See Also   Array Variables, Dim, Erase, IsArray, LBound, UBound

Referrer

Syntax   *document*.Referrer

Type   Read-Only Property

Synopsis   Returns the URL of the referring document.

Description   The *referring document* is the document containing the hyperlink that the user clicks to get to *document*. If no referring document exists, Null is returned.

Rem

Syntax 1   Rem *comment*

Syntax 2   ' *comment*

Type   Keyword

Synopsis   Enables you to add comments to your scripts.

Description   Comments are important because they help you understand the intent behind the simple mechanics of a program. You can use either the Rem keyword or a single quotation mark to create comments. Most programmers, however, use the single quotation mark so they can easily add comments to the end of a line of code.

Example

```
REM This is a comment.
' This is another comment.
intA = intB ^ 4 ' yet another comment
```

Right

Syntax   *Right(string, length)*

Type   Intrinsic String Function

Synopsis   Returns a copy of length characters taken from the end of string.

See Also   Asc, AscB, AscW, Chr, ChrB, ChrW, InStr, InStrB, LeftB, Len, LenB, LTrim, Mid, MidB, RightB, Space, StrComp, String, String Functions, Trim, UCase

RightB

Syntax   RightB(*string, length*)

Type   Intrinsic String Function

Synopsis   Returns a copy of *length* bytes taken from the end of *string*.

App

F

Description   You use RightB for binary data.

See Also   Asc, AscB, AscW, Chr, ChrB, ChrW, InStr, InStrB, LeftB, Len, LenB, LTrim, Mid, MidB, Right, Space, StrComp, String, String Functions, Trim, UCase

Rnd

Syntax   Rnd[(*number*)]

Type   Intrinsic Math Function

Synopsis   Returns a random number that's greater than or equal to zero but less than 1.

Description   The random numbers are generated by using an algorithm that produces a sequence of numbers. If *number* isn't specified or is greater than zero, the next number in the random number sequence is returned. If *number* is less than zero, the same number is returned every time. If number is zero, the previous random number is returned again.

To generate random numbers in a certain range, use the following formula:

```
Int((upperbound - lowerbound + 1) * Rnd + lowerbound)
```

Example

```
' Simulate a six-sided die--the range is 1 to 6.
intResult = Int((6 - 1 + 1) * Rnd + 1)

' Simulate two six-sided dice--the range is 2 to 12.
intResult = Int((12 - 2 + 1) * Rnd + 2)
```

See Also   Abs, Atn, Cos, Exp, Log, Math Functions, Randomize, Sin, Sqr, Tan

RTrim

Syntax   RTrim(*string*)

Type   Intrinsic String Function

Synopsis   Returns a copy of *string* with no trailing spaces.

See Also   Asc, AscB, AscW, Chr, ChrB, ChrW, InStr, InStrB, LeftB, Len, LenB, LTrim, Mid, MidB, Right, RightB, Space, StrComp, String, String Functions, Trim, UCase

Scope

Type   Definition

Description   When variables are declared inside a procedure, only statements inside that procedure can use them. This limitation is referred to as the *scope* of the variable. *Local scope* means that a variable is declared inside a procedure. *Script-level scope* means that a variable is declared outside all procedures and therefore can be accessed by all procedures.

<SCRIPT>

Syntax

```
<SCRIPT [EVENT=event] [FOR=object] [LANGUAGE=lang]>
...
</SCRIPT>
```

Type   HTML Tag

Synopsis   Contains script statements inside an HTML document.

Description   The <SCRIPT> tag encloses VBScript statements so that the browser knows they're executable. If you use the EVENT attribute, it specifies the type of event that the script statements handle. You use the FOR attribute with EVENT to specify which object or control the script should be associated with.

You can enclose one or more VBScript commands in a <SCRIPT> tag. The advent of several scripting languages has made it necessary for you to identify for the browser which language is being used. For VBScript, the syntax is as follows:

```
<SCRIPT LANGUAGE="VBScript">
<!--
 [statements]
-->
</SCRIPT>
```

Note the use of the HTML comment tags, <!-- and -->. If the page containing the script is used on a browser that isn't compatible with the scripting languages, the script statements are normally displayed as any other text on the page, adding clutter and trash to the screen. If you use the comment tags, an incompatible browser ignores the script portion of the document.

See Also   Events, Event Handling

Search

Syntax 1   *link*.Search

Syntax 2   *location*.Search

Syntax 3   *location*.Search = *string*

Type   Property

Synopsis   Gets the search part of *link* or *location*. In the third syntax, sets the search part of *location*.

Description   The search part of an URL starts with a question mark. In http://www.planet. net/search.pl?trains, for example, ?trains is the search part of the URL. If the URL has no search part, Null is returned.

Second

Syntax   Second(*time*)

Type   Intrinsic Date/Time Function

Synopsis   Returns the seconds value from *time,* which can range from 0 to 59, inclusive.

See Also   Date, Date/Time Functions, DateSerial, DateValue, Day, Minute, Month, Now, Time, TimeSerial, TimeValue, Weekday, Year

Select

Syntax   `element.Select`

Type   Method

Synopsis   Selects the contents of `element`.

Select Case

Syntax

```
Select Case testexpression
[Case expression
[statements]]
...
[Case Else expression
[statements]]
End Select
```

Type   Keyword

Synopsis   Selectively executes a statement block when the `expression` associated with the statement block equals the `testexpression`. If no matches are found, the statement block in the `Else` clause is executed.

Description   If `testexpression` matches more than one expression, only the statement block associated with the first matching `expression` is executed. You can use string values in both the `testexpression` and `expression` parts of the `Select Case` statement.

The `Else` clause is frequently used to catch unexpected values. If you're processing payroll records by month, for example, you can use the `Else` clause to catch values that aren't in the range of 1 to 12.

SelectedIndex

Syntax   `element.SelectedIndex`

Type   Read-Only Property

Synopsis   Gets the index for the selected options.

Description   If you have multiple selected options, the index of the first option selected is returned.

Self

Syntax   `window.Self`

Type   Read-Only Property; applies to a `Window` object

Synopsis   Returns an object reference to `window`.

Description   If `window` isn't specified, the current `Window` object is returned.

Set

Syntax   Set *objectvar* = { *objectexpression* ¦ *Nothing*}

Type   Keyword

Synopsis   Assigns a value to an object variable.

Description   You must use the Set keyword when assigning objects to variables or properties. You can free memory associated with *objectvar* by assigning the special value Nothing to it.

Generally speaking, the values that you assign are object references, not copies of the object. Therefore, more than one variable can reference the same object. You also can use the Is operator to determine whether two variables point to the same object.

Example

```
Set index = 0
Set myForm = Document.ValidForm
```

See Also   Is

SetTimeout

Syntax   *timerID* = *window*.SetTimeout(*expression, msec, language*)

Type   Method; applies to Window objects

Synopsis   Executes a procedure after a specified amount of time elapses and returns a timer object.

Description   The *expression* parameter must evaluate to a procedure name or an object's method. The procedure or method is executed after *msec* milliseconds (1 second = 1,000 milliseconds). This method is an excellent way to create dialog box timeouts. In the example, the Quit button is clicked after five seconds.

Example   clickTimer = setTimeout ("quitButton.OnClick", 5000)

See Also   ClearTimeout

Sgn

Syntax   Sgn(*number*)

Type   Intrinsic Conversion or Math Function

Synopsis   Returns 1 if *number* is greater than zero, –1 if *number* is less than zero, and zero if *number* is zero.

Example   intResult = Sgn(-10) ' intResult equals –1

See Also   Conversion Functions, Math Functions

App

F

Sin

Syntax   Sin(*angle*)

Type   Intrinsic Math Function

Synopsis   Returns the sine of *angle*.

Description   The Sin function takes an angle and returns the ratio of two sides of a right triangle. The ratio is the length of the side opposite the angle divided by the length of the hypotenuse. The result lies in the range –1 to 1. To convert degrees to radians, multiply degrees by $\pi/180$. To convert radians to degrees, multiply radians by $180/\pi$.

See Also   Abs, Atn, Cos, Exp, Log, Math Functions, Randomize, Rnd, Sqr, Tan

Single-Precision Variables

Type   Definition

Description   Single-precision variables can have about 45 digits of precision—not even half the size of double-precision, regardless of the name. Because single-precision numbers can fit inside 32 bits, however, and double-precision numbers need 64 bits, extensive calculations perform faster when you use single-precision.

See Also   Variables

Source

Syntax 1   Err.Source

Syntax 2   Err.Source = *stringexpression*

Type   Property

Synopsis   Gets or sets the name of the object or application that originally generated the error.

Description   Source is usually the class name or programmatic ID of the object that caused the error.

Space

Syntax   Space(*number*)

Type   Intrinsic String Function

Synopsis   Returns a string with *number* spaces.

See Also   Asc, AscB, AscW, Chr, ChrB, ChrW, InStr, InStrB, LeftB, Len, LenB, LTrim, Mid, MidB, Right, RTrim, StrComp, String, String Functions, Trim, UCase

Sqr

Syntax   Sqr(*number*)

Type   Intrinsic Math Function

Synopsis   Returns the square root of *number*.

See Also   Abs, Atn, Cos, Exp, Log, Math Functions, Randomize, Rnd, Sin, Tan

Status

Syntax 1   *window*.Status

Syntax 2   *window*.Status = *string*

Type   Property; applies to a `Window` object

Synopsis   Returns or sets the status text for the lower left portion of the status bar.

Example

```
' set the default status text.
self.Status = "Ready for Input"

' assign the default status text to a variable
strText = self.Status
```

StrComp

Syntax   StrComp(*string1, string2* [, *compare*])

Type   Intrinsic String Function

Synopsis   Returns –1 if *string1* is less than *string2*, 0 if they're equal, 1 if *string1* is greater than *string2*, and `Null` if either *string1* or *string2* is `Null`.

See Also   Asc, AscB, AscW, Chr, ChrB, ChrW, InStr, InStrB, LeftB, Len, LenB, LTrim, Mid, MidB, Right, RTrim, Space, String, String Functions, Trim, UCase

String

Syntax   String(*number, character*)

Type   Intrinsic String Function

Synopsis   Returns a string that contains *character* repeated *number* times.

Description   If *character* is `Null`, the `Null` value is returned. If the value of *character* is greater than 255, it's turned into a valid character code by using the modulus operator (*character* Mod 256).

See Also   Asc, AscB, AscW, Chr, ChrB, ChrW, InStr, InStrB, LeftB, Len, LenB, LTrim, Mid, MidB, Right, RTrim, Space, StrComp, String Functions, Trim, UCase

String Functions

Type   Definition

Description   Table F.36 lists VBScript's string functions.

App
F

Table F.36   VBScript String Functions

Function	Page Number	Description
Asc	810	Returns the ANSI code of the first character in a string
AscB	811	Returns the first byte in a string
AscW	811	Returns the first Unicode character (32 bits) in a string
Chr	814	Returns the character associated with a character code
ChrB	815	Returns the byte associated with a character code
ChrW	815	Returns the Unicode character associated with a character code
InStr	853	Returns the location of one string in another
InStrB	854	Returns the byte position of one string in another
LCase	857	Returns a copy of a string with all characters converted to lowercase
Left	857	Returns a copy of the beginning of a string
LeftB	858	Returns a copy of the beginning of a string
Len	858	Returns the number of bytes it takes to store a variable's value
LenB	858	Returns the number of bytes it takes to store an expression's value
LTrim	864	Returns a copy of a string without leading spaces
Mid	865	Returns a copy of part of a string
MidB	865	Returns a copy of part of a string
Right	887	Returns a copy of the end of a string
RightB	887	Returns a copy of the end of a string
RTrim	888	Returns a copy of a string with no trailing spaces
Space	892	Returns a string of a specified number of spaces
StrComp	893	Compares two strings
String	893	Returns a string of a specified character repeated a specified number of times
Trim	898	Returns a copy of a string with no leading or trailing spaces

Function	Page Number	Description
UCase	899	Returns a copy of a string with all characters converted into uppercase

String Concatenation (&)

Syntax   `result = string1 & string2`

Type   String Concatenation Operator

Synopsis   Appends *string2* to *string1*.

Description   Although you also can use the + operator to concatenate two character strings, you should use the & operator for concatenation instead. The & operator eliminates ambiguity and provides self-documenting code.

See Also   Operators

String Variables

Type   Definition

Description   Strings are defined by a number of characters (up to 2 billion) within double quotation marks.

Example   `strTemp = "The Doctor said, \"You're Fine,\" to me."`

See Also   Variables

Sub

Syntax

```
Sub name [(arglist)]
[statements]
End Sub
```

Type   Keyword

Synopsis   Declares a user-defined subroutine called *name*.

Description   You use Sub statements to create user-defined subroutines. Subroutines differ from functions because they don't return any value.

You should declare all subroutines toward the beginning of your script in the HEAD section of your HTML page. This way, you can ensure that the subroutines are available for use by later VBScript statements.

arglist is an optional list of arguments or parameters that the subroutine can use. If you want the subroutine to assign values to the arguments, use the ByVal keyword inside the parameter list.

N O T E   Subroutines don't return values. It seems logical, therefore, that they shouldn't modify parameters either. If you need to return a value or modify a parameter, try creating a user-defined function instead. ▨

App

F

Example

```
' Define a subroutine with one parameter.
Sub displayIt(strMsg)
 Alert "Error: " & strMsg
End Sub
```

See Also   Call, Exit, Function, Scope

Submit

Syntax   *form*.Submit

Type   Method

Synopsis   Sends form information to the server.

See Also   OnSubmit

Subtraction (−)

Syntax   *result = operand1 - operand2*

Type   Arithmetic Operator

Synopsis   Subtracts *operand2* from *operand1*.

Description   If one of the operands contains the Null value, *result* is Null. If one of the operands contains the Empty value, it's treated as though it were zero.

See Also   Operators

Tan

Syntax   Tan(*angle*)

Type   Intrinsic Math Function

Synopsis   Returns the tangent of *angle*.

Description   Tan takes an angle and returns the ratio of two sides of a right triangle. The ratio
is the length of the side opposite the angle divided by the length of the side adjacent to the
angle.

See Also   Abs, Atn, Cos, Exp, Log, Math Functions, Randomize, Rnd, Sin, Sqr

Target

Syntax 1   *form*.Target

Syntax 2   *form*.Target = *string*

Syntax 3   *link*.Target

Type   Property

Form Synopsis   Gets or sets the name of the window in which to display form results.

N O T E   In Internet Explorer 3.0, the `Target` property has no effect on the operation of the form. ■

Link Synopsis   Gets the name of the window—the `TARGET` attribute of the HTML `<A>` tag— in which to display the URL.

Time

Syntax   `Time`

Type   Intrinsic Date/Time Function

Synopsis   **Returns the current system time**.

See Also   Date, Date/Time Functions, DateSerial, DateValue, Day, Minute, Month, Now, Second, TimeSerial, TimeValue, Weekday, Year

TimeSerial

Syntax   `TimeSerial(hour, minute, second)`

Type   Intrinsic Conversion and Date/Time Function

Synopsis   Returns a Date variable that represents `hour`, `minute`, and `second`.

Description   The `hour` parameter can range from 0 (midnight) to 23 (11:00 p.m.). The `minute` and `second` parameters can range from 0 to 59. You can pass expressions instead of literals to perform some basic date arithmetic. Parameters that are too large to fit into the normal range carry over into the next larger unit. A `minute` parameter of 70, for example, increments the `hour` parameter. If one of the parameters falls outside the range –32,768 to 32,767, or if the date specified by the three arguments falls outside the acceptable range of times, an error occurs.

See Also   Date, Date/Time Functions, DateSerial, DateValue, Day, Minute, Month, Now, Second, Time, TimeValue, Weekday, Year

TimeValue

Syntax   `TimeValue(time)`

Type   Intrinsic Conversion and Date/Time Function

Synopsis   Returns a Date value representing `time`.

Description   The `time` parameter can range from 0:00:00 (midnight) to 23:59:59 (11:59:59 p.m.). If `time` is `Null`, `Null` is returned. The `DateValue` function understands both 12-hour and 24-hour clocks. If `time` contains date information, it's ignored. If `time` includes invalid date information, however, an error occurs.

See Also   Date, Date/Time Functions, DateSerial, DateValue, Day, Minute, Month, Now, Second, Time, TimeSerial, Weekday, Year

App

F

Title

Syntax   *document*.Title

Type   Read-Only Property

Synopsis   Returns a string with the title of *document*.

Top

Syntax   *window*.Top

Type   Read-Only Property; applies to a Window object

Synopsis   Returns a Window object that represents the topmost window.

Trim

Syntax   Trim(*string*)

Type   Intrinsic String Function

Synopsis   Returns a copy of *string* with no leading or trailing spaces.

See Also   Asc, AscB, AscW, Chr, ChrB, ChrW, InStr, InStrB, LeftB, Len, LenB, LTrim, Mid, MidB, Right, RTrim, Space, StrComp, String, String Functions, UCase

Type Conversion

Type   Definition

Description   A variable's type depends on the kind of information it contains (see the "Literal Values" entry). VBScript is *loosely typed*, meaning that you don't need to declare what kind of variables you're using. The data type is automatically assigned depending on the value assigned to the variable.

VBScript automatically changes the data type of the variable depending on the operation taking place. The best example of automatic data type conversion involves the string concatenation operator. The following statements illustrate type conversion:

```
' example 1
var oneString = "1";
var oneInt = 1
var oneConcatenate = oneString + oneInt ' results in "11"
var oneAddition = oneInt + oneString ' results in 2
```

In the first addition statement here, the first operand is a string. VBScript assumes that the operation is to join two strings. When VBScript encounters an integer as the second operand, it converts the value of the variable into a string to meet its own expectations.

In the "Conversion Functions" entry, you can find a list of functions that can convert from one data type to another.

See Also   Conversion Functions, Variable Testing

UBound

Syntax   UBound(*arrayname* [, *dimension*])

Type   Intrinsic Array Function

Synopsis   Returns the largest subscript for dimension of an *arrayname*.

Description   The *dimension* parameter (which defaults to 1) controls which dimension of the array is examined when the UBound function is called.

You can use LBound with UBound to find out an array's size. If the LBound function returns 10 and the UBound function returns 34, the array has 24 elements.

Example

```
Dim C(50, 10) ' declare an array
d1 = UBound(C, 1) ' d1 equals 49
d2 = UBound(C, 2) ' d2 equals 9
```

See Also   Array Variables, Dim, Erase, IsArray, LBound, ReDim

UCase

Syntax   UCase(*string*)

Type   Intrinsic String Function

Synopsis   Returns a copy of *string* with all characters converted into uppercase.

Description   If *string* is Null, Null is returned.

See Also   Asc, AscB, AscW, Chr, ChrB, ChrW, InStr, InStrB, LCase, LeftB, Len, LenB, LTrim, Mid, MidB, Right, RTrim, Space, StrComp, String, String Functions, Trim

Unary Negation (–)

Type   Operator

Description   When you place the unary negation operator in front of an expression, the negative value of the expression is used. The unary negation operation and the subtraction operation both use the - character.

Example

```
intA = 234 ' intA equals 234.
intB = -intA ' intB equals -234.
```

See Also   Operators

App

F

UserAgent

Syntax   *navigator*.UserAgent

Type   Read-Only Property

Synopsis   The name of the current application user agent.

Description This property returns `Mozilla/2.0 (compatible; MSIE 3.0A; Windows 95)` when you're using Microsoft Internet Explorer version 3.0 (4.70.1158).

Example

```
' Display the application version
Alert Navigator.UserAgent
```

Value

Syntax 1 `element.Value`

Syntax 2 `element.Value = string`

Type Property

Synopsis Gets or sets the value of `element`.

Variable Naming

Type Guideline

Description Because VBScript is so loosely typed, it's critical that you remember what type of data is stored in each variable. One way of remembering is to create your own variable-naming guidelines. Table F.37 lists some prefixes you can use to help get you started on your own guidelines.

Table F.37   Suggested Variable-Naming Guidelines

Prefix	Data Type
ani	Animated button control
ary	Array
bln	Boolean
btn	Button control
byt	Byte
cbo	Combo box control
chk	Check box control
cht	Chart control
cmd	Command button
cst	Constant (actually, a pseudo-constant)
dlg	Dialog box control
dbl	Double-precision
dtm	Date/time
err	Error

Prefix	Data Type
`fra`	Frame object
`hsb`	Horizontal scroll bar control
`img`	Image control
`int`	Integer
`lbl`	Label control
`lin`	Line control
`lnk`	Hyperlink
`lst`	List control
`lng`	Long integer
`obj`	Object
`pnl`	Panel control
`sld`	Slider control
`sng`	Single-precision
`spn`	Spin button control
`str`	String
`txt`	Text control
`vsb`	Vertical scroll bar control

Variables

Type Definition

Description The `Variant` data type holds any form of information. The other variable types mentioned in this book—such as `Date`, `Integer`, and `Double`—are subtypes of the `Variant` data type. All VBScript functions return `Variant` data types.

If a variable holds a number and is used in a numeric context, it behaves like a number. If the variable is used in a string content, VBScript silently converts the number into a string. Uninitialized variables have the `Empty` value.

Some property names are reserved words, which means that you can't use them for your own variable names. To avoid having to remember which property names are reserved and which aren't, I suggest some prefixes that you can use to distinguish your variable names earlier in the "Variable Naming" section.

Table F.38 lists the 12 subtypes that automatically come into play, depending on the context in VBScript.

App

F

Table F.38   VBScript's Variant Subtypes

Subtype	Description
Empty	An uninitialized variable
Null	A variable containing no valid data
Boolean	Can be either True or False
Byte	Is in the range 0 to 255
Integer	Is in the range –32,768 to 32,767
Long	Is in the range –2,147,483,648 to 2,147,483,647
Single	A single-precision floating-point number that can be more than 35 digits long
Double	A double-precision floating-point number that can be more than 300 digits long
Date	Contains a date/time between 01/01/0100 and 12/31/9999
String	Contains a sequence of characters that can be up to about 2 billion characters long
Object	Contains an object
Error	Contains an error number

See Also   Boolean Variables, Empty, Null

Variant

Type   Definition

Description   Variant is the single data type that VBScript supports. Each Variant variable can contain any type of data. In fact, 12 data subtypes are available (they're described in the "Variables" entry). VBScript normally does an excellent job of automatically converting between the subtypes—matching the subtype to the task at hand. If you run into a problem, use one of the data type conversion functions listed in the "See Also" section.

One of the few times you might have trouble with the Variant data type is when you're using the + sign. You can use the + sign to add two numbers together and to concatenate two strings. VBScript decides between adding and concatenating by checking the subtype of the first operand. If the first operand is numeric, the second operand is converted into a number and added to the first. Otherwise, string concatenation is performed. If you're not careful, you might not get the results you expect.

> **TIP**   Always use the & operator for string concatenation to ensure consistent results.

See Also   Variables

Variant Testing Functions

Type   Definition

Description   VBScript provides several functions that let you determine what type of data is in a Variant variable (see Table F.39).

Table F.39 VBScript's Variant Testing Functions		
Function	**Page Number**	**Description**
IsArray	855	Returns True if its parameter is an array
IsDate	855	Returns True if its parameter is a date
IsEmpty	856	Returns True if its parameter has an Empty value
IsNull	856	Returns True if its parameter has a Null value
IsNumeric	856	Returns True if its parameter is numeric
IsObject	856	Returns True if its parameter is an object reference
VarType	903	Returns a value representing the data subtype of its parameter

VarType

Syntax   VarType(*varname*)

Type   Intrinsic Function

Synopsis   Returns a value representing the data subtype of *varname*.

Description   The VarType function never returns the array subtype value by itself. It's always added to some other value to indicate an array of a particular type. The value for Variant is returned only when it has been added to the value for Array to indicate that the argument to the VarType function is an array. The value returned for an array of integers, for example, is calculated as 8192 + 2, or 8194. If an object has a default property, VarType(*object*) returns the type of its default property.

Table F.40 lists the values returned by VarType function.

App

F

Table F.40 Return Values for the *VarType* Function		
Value	**Page**	**Description**
0	837	Empty (uninitialized)
1	871	Null (no valid data)
2	854	Integer
3		Long integer

continues

Table F.40 Continued

Value	Page	Description
4	892	Single-precision floating-point number
5	834	Double-precision floating-point number
6		Currency (not supported by VBScript)
7	826	Date
8	893	String
9		Automation object
10	838	ERR
11	812	Boolean
12	902	Variant (used only with Variant arrays)
13		Non-Automation object
17	813	Byte
8192	809	Array

Example

```
' create some pseudo-constants.
cstLong = 3
cstArray = 8192

lngTemp = CLng(324)
If VarType(lngTemp) = cstLong Then
 Alert "It's a long variable"
Else
 Alert "It's not long."
End If

' put the subtype of an array element into
' the intElementType variable. If the variable
' is not an array, then make the element type
' equal to Null.
If VarType(anyVar) And cstArray Then
 intElementType = VarType(anyVar) - cstArray
Else
 intElementType = Null
End If
```

See Also   IsArray, IsDate, IsEmpty, IsNull, IsNumeric, IsObject, Variables

VBScript Statements

Type   Definition

Description   The statements used to control program flow in VBScript are similar to Visual Basic, as you can see in Table F.41. A statement can span several lines, if needed, or you can place several statements on the same line, provided that you separate them with a colon.

Table F.41   VB Statement Types

Statement	Page Number	Description
Call	813	Runs a Sub or Function procedure
Dim	831	Declares script-level or procedure-level variables
Do	831	Repeatedly executes a statement block while a condition is true or until a condition becomes true
End Function	837	Ends a function definition
End Sub	837	Ends a subroutine definition
Exit	841	Exits a block of statements or ends the script
For	843	Repeatedly executes a statement block for a specific number of times
Function	846	Creates a user-defined function
If	851	Optionally executes statements based on a conditional expression
Option Explicit	881	Ensures that all variables are explicitly declared
ReDim	886	Declares or modifies the bounds for dynamic arrays
Set	891	Assigns a value to an object variable
Sub	895	Creates a user-defined subroutine
While	906	Not recommended; use Do instead

App

F

vLinkColor

Syntax 1   *document*.vLinkColor = *rgbValue*

Syntax 2   *document*.vLinkColor = *string*

Type   Property

Synopsis   Gets or sets the visited link color of *document*.

Description You can set the color by specifying an RGB value in hexadecimal or by specifying a color name. The "Color Names" entry lists all the color names you can use.

You can set this property only while the document is being parsed. An OnLoad event handler procedure is a good place to set document properties.

Weekday

Syntax `Weekday(date, [firstdayofweek])`

Type Intrinsic Date/Time Function

Synopsis Returns the day of the week (from 1 for Sunday to 7 for Saturday) on which *date* falls.

Description You can change the beginning day of the week by providing a *firstdayofweek* parameter by using the values in Table F.42.

Table F.42 Values for the *firstdayofweek* Parameter

Value	Description
0	Use NLS API setting
1	Sunday (the default value)
2	Monday
3	Tuesday
4	Wednesday
5	Thursday
6	Friday
7	Saturday

See Also Date, Date/Time Functions, DateSerial, DateValue, Day, Minute, Month, Now, Second, Time, TimeSerial, TimeValue, Year

While

Type Keyword

Synopsis The While statement, although supported, is no longer recommended. Use a Do...Loop statement instead.

See Also Do

White Space

Type Definition

Description *White space* refers to spaces, tabs, and carriage-return characters—in short, any character you can use to create white space on a piece of paper.

Window

Type Object

Synopsis Represents a window in the browser.

Description You can use `Window` to refer to the object associated with the current window. Using the `Window` object name, however, usually isn't necessary because your code is probably inside the window's scope. `Window` objects are at the top of the object hierarchy. They are directly analogous to browser windows.

Table F.43 lists the subobjects making up the `Window` object.

Table F.43   Objects Contained Inside a *Window* Object

Object	Page Number	Description
Document	833	Represents the document in the current window
Frames	846	Each element in this array represents one of the frames of the browser
History	849	Represents the history list of the browser
Location	863	Represents the URL of the current document
Navigator	869	Represents the browser application
Script	888	Represents all the scripts in the current window

Tables F.44, F.45, and F.46 list the events, methods and properties of the Window object.

Table F.44   Events of *Window* Objects

Event	Page Number	Description
OnLoad	874	Happens when a document is loaded
OnUnload	876	Happens when a document is unloaded

Table F.45   Methods of *Window* Objects

Method	Page Number	Description
Alert	805	Displays an alert message box
ClearTimeout	816	Clears a specified timer that was created by `SetTimeout`
Close	817	Closes a browser window
Confirm	822	Displays a message box with OK and Cancel buttons

App

F

continues

Table F.45   Continued

Method	Page Number	Description
Navigate	869	Opens a new URL in the window
Open	877	Creates a new browser window
Prompt	884	Prompts users for input with a dialog box
SetTimeout	891	Calls a specified function after a specified amount of time

Table F.46   Properties of *Window* Objects

Property	Page Number	Description
DefaultStatus	830	Gets or sets the default status text for the lower-left portion of the status bar
Document	833	Gets the Document object associated with a window
Frames	846	Gets an array of frames contained in a window
History	849	Gets the History object of a window
Location	863	Gets the Location object for a window
Name	868	Gets the name of a window
Navigator	869	Gets the Navigator object associated with a window
Opener	878	Gets the Window object that represents the window that opened the current window
Parent	883	Gets a reference to the parent Window object
Self	890	Gets an object reference to a window
Status	893	Gets or sets the status text for the lower left portion of the status bar
Top	898	Gets a Window object that represents the topmost window

Write

Syntax   document.Write(string)

Type   Method

Synopsis   Places *string* into *document*.

Description   The Write method appends *string* to *document*. Remember that *string* must have HTML tags if you need formatted output.

WriteLn

Syntax   `document.WriteLn(string)`

Type   Method

Synopsis   Places `string` into `document` and adds a new-line character.

Description   The `WriteLn` method appends `string` to `document`. Remember that `string` must have HTML tags if you need formatted output. Also remember that the new-line character doesn't show up in the browser's window unless you use the `<PRE>` HTML tag.

Xor

Syntax   `result = operand1 Xor operand2`

Type   Operator

Synopsis   Returns `True` if only one operand is `True`.

Description   If either operand is `Null`, `Null` is returned. If the operands are numeric, a bitwise comparison of identically positioned bits is performed.

See Also   Operators

Year

Syntax   `Year(date)`

Type   Intrinsic Date/Time Function

Synopsis   Returns the year part of `date`.

See Also   Date, Date/Time Functions, DateSerial, DateValue, Day, Minute, Month, Now, Second, Time, TimeSerial, TimeValue, Weekday

App
F

What's on the CD?

The CD included with this book contains the source pages and reference materials that have been referred to throughout the book. Some of you will simply open the files and projects from the CD and look at them as you read the book. And some of you will build the sample projects from scratch, following the instructions in each chapter, but will open these files on the CD so that you can copy large blocks of text without having to type.

As well, we have gathered together a number of electronic books on topics of interest to many Visual C++ programmers. These books are referred to throughout the book. You can read these books straight from the CD in a Web browser, for an in-depth explanation of topics that are introduced only in the printed book. Some of these electronic books are no longer available in a paper form; others are on the shelves of your bookstore right now. They combine to form a powerful reference set for today's Visual C++ programmer.

The CD contains several subdirectories located off the root directory. The directories you'll find on the CD will be as follows, with application, code, or chapter-specific subdirectories listed in Table F.1.

Table F.1 Directory Structure on the CD	
\BOOKS	Online books, each in their own subdirectory
\CODE	The source code from the book. Each chapter that contains sample files, source code, and so on will be contained in a subdirectory named for the chapter it references.

Using the Electronic Books

The electronic books on the CD are available to you as HTML documents that can be read from any World Wide Web browser that you may have currently installed on your machine (such as Internet Explorer or Netscape Navigator). The exception is *C++ By Example*, included as an Adobe PDF file. If you do not have the Adobe reader for these files, one is included on the CD in the \BOOKS\EXAMPLE directory.

The following books are included in electronic form:

- *ActiveX Programming with Visual C++*, by Jerry Anderson
- *Special Edition Using ISAPI*, by Stephen Genusa
- *Special Edition Using HTML*, Second Edition, by Tom Savola (among others)
- *C++ By Example*, by Scott Ladd
- *Special Edition Using MFC*, by Clayton Walnum

ActiveX Programming with Visual C++

This just-released book covers a wide variety of ActiveX programming concepts and applications. It explains how to build ActiveX Controls with MFC and with ATL and extends many of the concepts discussed in the ActiveX chapters of this book. You'll find it in \BOOKS\ACTIVEX.

Special Edition Using ISAPI

If you were curious about the power of server-side programming you glimpsed in Chapter 18, "Sockets, MAPI, and the Internet," then you will really enjoy reading *Using ISAPI*. It explores extensions and filters that will bring your Web server under your control. You'll find it in \BOOKS\ISAPI.

Special Edition Using HTML, Second Edition

Several of the programming examples in this book involve Web pages. If you've been meaning to learn how to use HTML to make Web pages of your own, here's your chance. *Using HTML* teaches you the basics of Hypertext Markup Language so that you can publish on the World Wide Web or a corporate intranet. You'll find it in \BOOKS\HTML.

C++ By Example

If you need a refresher on the syntax of C++, you need look no further. *C++ By Example* covers all the keywords of C++ and explains how it differs from C. There is even a little coverage of object-oriented programming. You'll find it in \BOOKS\EXAMPLE.

Special Edition Using MFC

Just released, *Using MFC* delves into the Microsoft Foundation Classes in greater detail than is possible in a book that covers all of Visual C++. You also learn to build your own classes based on MFC classes. You'll find it in \BOOKS\MFC.

Reading an Electronic Book as an HTML Document

To read any electronic book supplied as an HTML document, you need to start your Web browser and open the document file TOC.HTML located in the appropriate subdirectory of the CD. Alternatively, you can browse the CD directory by using File Manager and double-clicking TOC.HTML.

After you've opened the TOC.HTML page, you can access all of the book's contents by clicking the highlighted chapter number or topic name. The electronic book works like any other Web page; when you click a hot link, a new page is opened or the browser will take you to the new location in the document. As you read through the electronic book, you will notice other high-lighted words or phrases. Clicking these cross-references will also take you to a new location within the electronic book. You can always use your browser's forward or backward buttons to return to your original location.

Finding Sample Code

This book contains code examples that include listing headers (for example, see Listing 10.1.). These are sample documents presented for planning purposes and are indicated by the On the CD icon. For example, consider the following listing reference:

App
G

```
Listing 17.10—ShowStringDoc.cpp  CShowStringDoc::OnNewDocument()
```

This listing indicates that this particular code snippet (or example) is included electronically on the CD. To find it, browse to the \CODE subdirectory on the CD and from there to the Chap17 subdirectory. Select the file name that matches the one referenced in the listing header. In this example, you'd open the ShowStringDoc.cpp file. If you prefer, you can look for a project file and open the entire project in Visual C++, then use the file names in the listing headers as a guide to the file that you should switch to within Visual C++. ●

Index

Complete and Return this Card for a *FREE* Computer Book Catalog

Thank you for purchasing this book! You have purchased a superior computer book written expressly for your needs. To continue to provide the kind of up-to-date, pertinent coverage you've come to expect from us, we need to hear from you. Please take a minute to complete and return this self-addressed, postage-paid form. In return, we'll send you a free catalog of all our computer books on topics ranging from word processing to programming and the internet.

Mrs. ☐   Ms. ☐   Dr. ☐

(first) ☐☐☐☐☐☐☐☐☐☐☐☐   (M.I.) ☐   (last) ☐☐☐☐☐☐☐☐☐☐☐☐☐☐☐

ss ☐☐☐☐☐☐☐☐☐☐☐☐☐☐☐☐☐☐☐☐☐☐☐☐☐☐☐☐☐☐☐☐

☐☐☐☐☐☐☐☐☐☐☐☐☐☐☐☐☐☐☐☐☐☐☐☐☐☐☐☐☐☐☐

State ☐☐   Zip ☐☐☐☐☐ ☐☐☐☐

☐☐☐ ☐☐☐ ☐☐☐☐   Fax ☐☐☐ ☐☐☐ ☐☐☐☐

any Name ☐☐☐☐☐☐☐☐☐☐☐☐☐☐☐☐☐☐☐☐☐☐☐☐☐

address ☐☐☐☐☐☐☐☐☐☐☐☐☐☐☐☐☐☐☐☐☐☐☐☐☐

---

ase check at least (3) influencing factors for rchasing this book.

or back cover information on book .... ☐
al approach to the content .... ☐
leteness of content .... ☐
r's reputation .... ☐
her's reputation .... ☐
cover design or layout .... ☐
or table of contents of book .... ☐
of book .... ☐
al effects, graphics, illustrations .... ☐
(Please specify): _____

w did you first learn about this book?

n Macmillan Computer Publishing catalog .... ☐
nmended by store personnel .... ☐
he book on bookshelf at store .... ☐
nmended by a friend .... ☐
ved advertisement in the mail .... ☐
n advertisement in: _____ ☐
book review in: _____ ☐
(Please specify): _____ ☐

w many computer books have you rchased in the last six months?

book only .... ☐   3 to 5 books .... ☐
ks .... ☐   More than 5 .... ☐

4. Where did you purchase this book?

Bookstore .... ☐
Computer Store .... ☐
Consumer Electronics Store .... ☐
Department Store .... ☐
Office Club .... ☐
Warehouse Club .... ☐
Mail Order .... ☐
Direct from Publisher .... ☐
Internet site .... ☐
Other (Please specify): _____ ☐

5. How long have you been using a computer?

☐ Less than 6 months   ☐ 6 months to a year
☐ 1 to 3 years   ☐ More than 3 years

6. What is your level of experience with personal computers and with the subject of this book?

	With PCs	With subject of book
New	☐	☐
Casual	☐	☐
Accomplished	☐	☐
Expert	☐	☐

Source Code ISBN: 0-7897-1145-1

7. Which of the following best describes your job title?

Administrative Assistant .... ☐
Coordinator .... ☐
Manager/Supervisor .... ☐
Director .... ☐
Vice President .... ☐
President/CEO/COO .... ☐
Lawyer/Doctor/Medical Professional .... ☐
Teacher/Educator/Trainer .... ☐
Engineer/Technician .... ☐
Consultant .... ☐
Not employed/Student/Retired .... ☐
Other (Please specify): _____ ☐

8. Which of the following best describes the area of the company your job title falls under?

Accounting .... ☐
Engineering .... ☐
Manufacturing .... ☐
Operations .... ☐
Marketing .... ☐
Sales .... ☐
Other (Please specify): _____ ☐

9. What is your age?

Under 20 ....
21-29 ....
30-39 ....
40-49 ....
50-59 ....
60-over ....

10. Are you:

Male ....
Female ....

11. Which computer publications do you read regularly? (Please list)

_____
_____
_____
_____
_____
_____
_____
_____
_____
_____
_____

Comments: _____
_____
_____

Fold here and scotch-tape

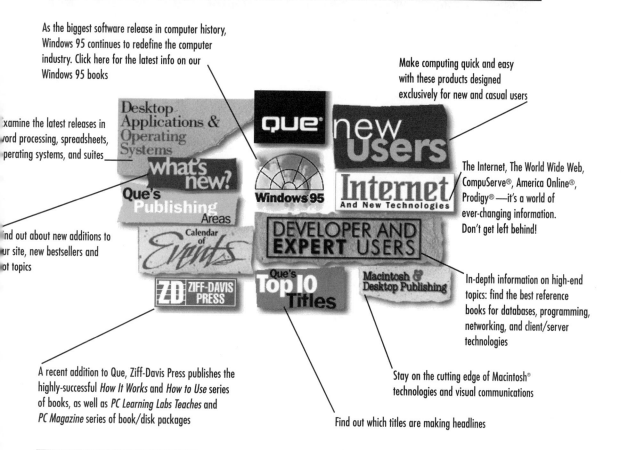

Licensing Agreement

By opening this package, you are agreeing to be bound by the following: